BIRDS of
WESTERN
CANADA

BIRDS of
WESTERN
CANADA

EDITOR

DAVID M. BIRD, Ph.D.

Emeritus Professor of Wildlife Biology

McGill University

DK | Penguin Random House

DORLING KINDERSLEY

FIRST EDITION

Senior Art Editors
Caroline Hill, Ina Stradins

Senior Editors
Angeles Gavira Guerrero,
Ankush Saikia

Canadian Editor
Barbara Campbell

Project Editor
Nathan Joyce

Project Designer
Mahua Sharma

Designers
Sonia Barbate, Helen McTeer

Editors
Jamie Ambrose, Lori Baird, Tamlyn
Calitz, Marcus Hardy, Patrick
Newman, Siobhan O'Connor,
Garima Sharma, David Summers,
Miezan van Zyl, Rebecca Warren

Design Assistant
Becky Tennant

Editorial Assistants
Elizabeth Munsey, Jaime Tenreiro

Creative Technical Support
John Goldsmid

DTP Coordinator
Balwant Singh

Senior DTP Designer
Harish Aggarwal

DTP Designers
Dheeraj Arora, Tarun Sharma

Production Editor
Maria Elia

Production Controller
Rita Sinha

Jacket Designer
Mark Cavanagh

Illustrators
John Cox, Andrew Mackay

Picture Editor
Neil Fletcher

Picture Researchers
Laura Barwick, Will Jones

Managing Art Editor
Phil Ormerod

Managing Editors
Glenda Fernandes, Sarah Larter

Publishing Manager
Liz Wheeler

Art Directors
Bryn Walls, Shefali Upadhyay

Publishers
Jonathan Metcalf, Aparna Sharma

THIS EDITION

Project Art Editor
Rupanki Arora Kaushik

Project Editor
Priyanjali Narain

Editor
Aashirwad Jain

Managing Art Editor
Sudakshina Basu

Senior Managing Editor
Rohan Sinha

DTP Designer
Bimlesh Tiwary

Senior DTP Designer
Harish Aggarwal

Production Editor
Vishal Bhatia

Preproduction Manager
Balwant Singh

Senior Production Controller
Meskerem Berhane

Jacket Designer
Gayatri Menon

Senior Jackets Coordinator
Priyanka Sharma Saddi

**Jacket Design
Development Manager**
Sophia MTT

Design Head (DK Delhi)
Malavika Talukder

Editorial Head (DK Delhi)
Glenda R Fernandes

Managing Art Editor
Michael Duffy

Managing Editor
Angeles Gavira Guerrero

Art Director
Karen Self

Design Director
Phil Ormerod

Associate Publishing Director
Liz Wheeler

Publishing Director
Jonathan Metcalf

This Canadian Edition, 2023
First Canadian Edition, 2013
Published in the United States and Canada by DK Publishing
1745 Broadway, 20th Floor, New York, NY 10019

Copyright © 2013, 2019, 2023 Dorling Kindersley Limited
DK, a Division of Penguin Random House LLC
23 24 25 26 27 10 9 8 7 6 5 4 3 2 1
001—331867—Apr/2023

Includes content previously published in *AMNH Birds
of North America* and *Birds of Canada*.

A catalog record for this book is available from the
Library of Congress.
ISBN 978-0-74407-072-9

DK books are available at special discounts when purchased
in bulk for corporate sales, sales promotions, premiums,
fund-raising, or educational use. For details, please contact
specialmarkets@dk.com

Printed in China

For the curious
www.dk.com

MIX
Paper | Supporting
responsible forestry
FSC™ C018179

This book was made with Forest
Stewardship Council™ certified
paper - one small step in DK's
commitment to a sustainable future.
**For more information go to
www.dk.com/our-green-pledge**

CONTRIBUTORS

David M. Bird
Nicholas L. Block
Peter Capainolo
Matthew Cormons
Malcolm Coulter
Joseph DiCostanzo
Shawneen Finnegan
Neil Fletcher
Ted Floyd
Jeff Groth
Paul Hess
Brian Hiller
Rob Hume
Thomas Brodie Johnson

Kevin T. Karlson
Stephen Kress
William Moskoff
Bill Pranty
Michael L. P. Retter
Noah Strycker
Paul Sweet
Rodger Titman
Elissa Wolfson

Map Editor Paul Lehman
Project Coordinator
Joseph DiCostanzo

CONTENTS

DK Bird sounds app
The songs and calls of more than 180 species of birds in this book are featured on the new DK AMNH Bird Sounds app. Bird calls are usually short and simple, and are used to pass on information, such as an alarm call that warns of a predator or a contact call that helps birds stay in touch with each other. Songs are longer and made up of a complex set of notes, and are used by males to defend a territory or attract a mate. A bird may have several sounds in its repertoire, but each type is usually constant and unique to a species. As bird sounds carry a long way, you will often hear a bird before you can see it, and this app will help you to identify it.

To download the app, go to:
www.dk.com/bird-sounds-na

🔊 The birds featured on the app have this symbol next to their common name in this book.

PREFACE

SUMMER SINGER
Male Indigo Buntings sing
from the highest available
perch all summer long.

Publishing an all-inclusive, up-to-date reference book on the bird species that are found in any delineated geographical entity, such as a country like Canada, is a constantly evolving chore. With never-ending new data on morphology and behavior coupled with rapidly changing molecular technology and innovative Citizen Science programs like eBird, taxonomists are incessantly making alterations to the official list of the birds of the world. But that's not the whole story. Changing weather patterns are causing more and more bird species to shift their breeding and wintering ranges further north, and extreme weather events like hurricanes and tropical storms are blowing more and more birds across entire continents and oceans, leading to newly established populations in regions where they did not exist before. So, if birders and ornithologists want to have the latest and correct information at their fingertips, that means putting new editions of reference books and field guides on their library shelves every few years or so. And that is exactly what we have done with these 3rd editions of *Birds of Eastern Canada* and *Birds of Western Canada*.

These two handy regional guides offer, for almost all Canadian bird species, profiles with detailed information, including beautiful photographs and precise distribution maps; readable accounts of notable characteristics; data on identification, behavior, habitat, voice, nest construction, breeding season, and food; diagrams of flight patterns; statistics of size, wingspan, weight, clutch size, number of broods per year, and lifespan; and geographical information about breeding, wintering, and migration. While the use of scientific jargon has been minimized, a glossary identifies concepts that benefit from an explanation. The user-friendly format should permit readers to enjoy either studying one species account at a time or browsing to make cross comparisons.

As before, the Eastern and Western ranges are split along the 100th Meridian, or around Winnipeg, an invisible barrier located in a transitional zone between habitats that represents Eastern versus Western landscape types or biomes. While almost all of the bird species residing in Canada are included, a handful of birds that spend most of their time in a Canadian range far out to sea, for example, were left out of these volumes.

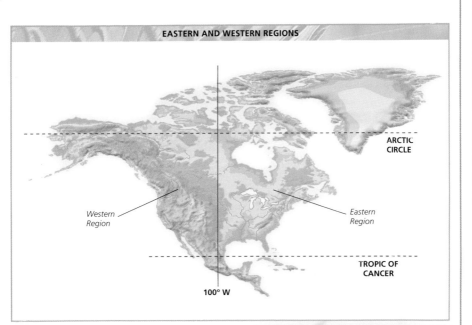

EASTERN AND WESTERN REGIONS

ARCTIC CIRCLE

Western Region

Eastern Region

TROPIC OF CANCER

100° W

During my tenure as a professor of ornithology for over 35 years, I have come to realize the real value of a concise reference work that can be conveniently carried around. I hope that these books will be useful to all persons interested in birds, whether young or older, enthusiastic birder or novice. If you are going birding, don't leave home without it!

David M. Bird
Emeritus Professor of Wildlife Biology
McGill University

TRAVELING BIRD
The Bohemian Waxwing is named for its nomadic lifestyle in the winter, as it travels around looking for fruit to eat.

HOW THIS BOOK WORKS

This guide covers just over 400 western Canadian bird species. The species are organized into two sections: the first profiles common Canadian species found in the west, with each given full-page treatment; the second covers rarer birds in quarter-page entries.

▽ COMMON SPECIES
The main section of the book features the 389 most commonly seen bird species in the western Canada region. Each entry is clear and detailed, following the same easy-to-access structure.

▽ INTRODUCTION
The species are organized conventionally by order, family, and genus. Related birds appear together, preceded by a group introduction. The book follows the most up-to-date avian classification system, based on the latest scientific research.

GROUP NAME
The common name of the group each species belongs to is at the top of each page.

COMMON NAME

IN FLIGHT
Illustrations show the bird in flight, from above and/or below —differences of season, age, or sex are not always visible.

DESCRIPTION
Conveys the main features and essential character of the species.

VOICE
A description of the species' calls and songs, given phonetically where possible.

NESTING
The type of nest and its usual location; the number of eggs in a clutch; the number of broods in a year; the breeding season.

FEEDING
How, where, and what the species feeds on.

SIMILAR SPECIES
Similar-looking species are identified and key differences pointed out.

LENGTH, WINGSPAN, AND WEIGHT
Length is tip of tail to tip of bill; measurements are averages or ranges.

SOCIAL
The social unit the species is usually found in.

LIFESPAN
The average or maximum life expectancy.

STATUS
The conservation status of the species; the symbol (p) means the data available can only suggest a provisional status. The term "Localized" suggests that the species may be widespread but restricted to smaller areas of suitable habitat and climatic conditions.

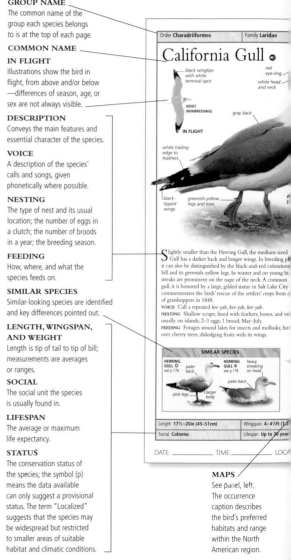

| Order **Charadriiformes** | Family **Laridae** |

California Gull

black wingtips with white terminal spot

red eye-ring

white head and neck

ADULT (NONBREEDING)

IN FLIGHT

gray back

white trailing edge to feathers

black-tipped wings

greenish-yellow legs and toes

Slightly smaller than the Herring Gull, the medium-sized Gull has a darker back and longer wings. In breeding pl it can also be distinguished by the black-and-red coloration bill and its greenish-yellow legs. In winter and on young bi streaks are prominent on the nape of the neck. A common gull, it is honored by a large, gilded statue in Salt Lake City commemorates the birds' rescue of the settlers' crops from a of grasshoppers in 1848.
VOICE Call a repeated *kee-yah, kee-yah, kee-yah.*
NESTING Shallow scrape, lined with feathers, bones, and vet usually on islands; 2–3 eggs; 1 brood; May–July.
FEEDING Forages around lakes for insects and mollusks; ho over cherry trees, dislodging fruits with its wings.

SIMILAR SPECIES		
HERRING GULL ♀ see p.176	paler back	HERRING GULL ♀ see p.176 — heavy streaking on head
	pink legs — larger body	paler back

| Length 17½–20in (45–51cm) | Wingspan 4–4½ft (1⅔ |
| Social **Colonies** | Lifespan Up to 30 year |

DATE: _____ TIME: _____ LOCA

MAPS
See panel, left. The occurrence caption describes the bird's preferred habitats and range within the North American region.

MAPS

In this book, North America is the region from the southern tip of Florida and the US–Mexico border to the Canadian High Arctic. Each profile includes a map showing the range of the species, with colors reflecting seasonal movements.

KEY
- Resident all year
- Summer distribution
- Winter distribution
- Seen on migration

CLASSIFICATION
The top band of each entry provides the scientific order, family, and species names (see glossary, pp. 446–449 for full definitions of these terms).

◁ **RARE SPECIES**
Twenty-two less common birds are presented on pp. 440–445. Arranged in the same group order used in the main section, these entries consist of one clear photograph of the species accompanied by a description of the bird.

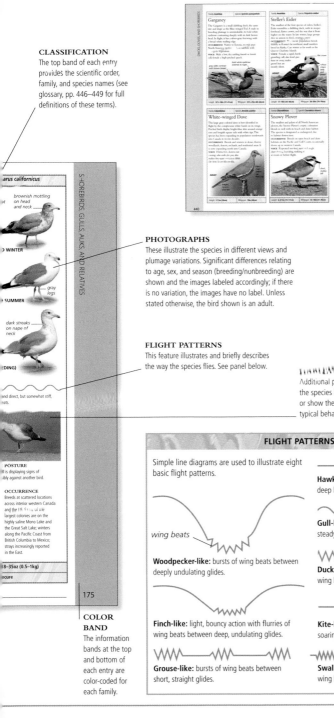

PHOTOGRAPHS
These illustrate the species in different views and plumage variations. Significant differences relating to age, sex, and season (breeding/nonbreeding) are shown and the images labeled accordingly; if there is no variation, the images have no label. Unless stated otherwise, the bird shown is an adult.

SYMBOLS

♂	Male	✹	Spring
♀	Female	✲	Summer
☾	Juvenile	☘	Autumn
◑	Immature	❄	Winter

FLIGHT PATTERNS
This feature illustrates and briefly describes the way the species flies. See panel below.

HABITAT/BEHAVIOR
Additional photographs reveal the species in its typical habitat or show the bird exhibiting typical behavior.

COLOR BAND
The information bands at the top and bottom of each entry are color-coded for each family.

FLIGHT PATTERNS

Simple line diagrams are used to illustrate eight basic flight patterns.

wing beats

Woodpecker-like: bursts of wing beats between deeply undulating glides.

Finch-like: light, bouncy action with flurries of wing beats between deep, undulating glides.

Grouse-like: bursts of wing beats between short, straight glides.

Hawk-like: straight, with several quick, deep beats between short, flat glides.

Gull-like: continually flapping, with slow, steady wing beats.

Duck-like: continually flapping, with fast wing beats.

Kite-like: deep, slow wing beats between soaring glides.

Swallow-like: swooping, with bursts of wing beats between glides.

EVOLUTION

ORNITHOLOGISTS AGREE THAT birds evolved from dinosaurs about 150 million years ago, but there is still debate about the dinosaur group from which they descended. Around 10,000 species of birds exist today, living in many different kinds of habitats across the world, from desert to Arctic tundra.

MISSING LINK?
Archaeopteryx, shown here as a 145-million-year-old fossil, had dinosaur-like teeth, but birdlike feathers.

SPECIATION

What are species and how do they evolve? Species are biological entities. When two species of a genus overlap they rarely interbreed and produce hybrids. The North American Flicker has an eastern (yellow-shafted) and a western (red-shafted) form; after the discovery that these two forms interbreed in the Great Plains, the flickers are now considered one species. In other cases, a previously single species, such as the Blue Grouse, has been divided into the Dusky Grouse and the Sooty Grouse. Such examples illustrate how species evolve, first by geographic separation, followed in time by overlap. This process can take millions of years.

BIRD GENEALOGY

The diagram below is called a phylogeny. It shows how selected groups of birds are related to each other. The timescale at the top of the diagram is derived from both fossil and DNA evidence, which allows ornithologists to estimate when different lineages of birds diverged. The names of groups shown in bold are those residing permanently in Canada.

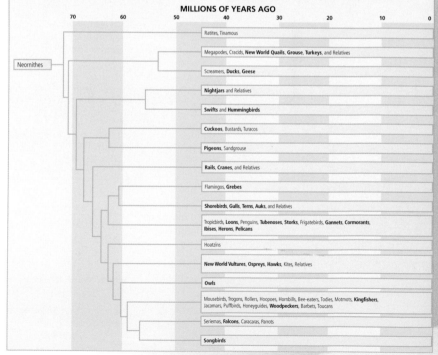

MILLIONS OF YEARS AGO

| 70 | 60 | 50 | 40 | 30 | 20 | 10 | 0 |

Neornithes

Ratites, Tinamous

Megapodes, Cracids, **New World Quails**, **Grouse**, **Turkeys**, and Relatives

Screamers, **Ducks**, **Geese**

Nightjars and Relatives

Swifts and **Hummingbirds**

Cuckoos, Bustards, Turacos

Pigeons, Sandgrouse

Rails, **Cranes**, and Relatives

Flamingos, **Grebes**

Shorebirds, **Gulls**, **Terns**, **Auks**, and Relatives

Tropicbirds, **Loons**, Penguins, **Tubenoses**, **Storks**, Frigatebirds, **Gannets**, **Cormorants**, **Ibises**, **Herons**, **Pelicans**

Hoatzins

New World Vultures, **Ospreys**, **Hawks**, Kites, Relatives

Owls

Mousebirds, Trogons, Rollers, Hoopoes, Hornbills, Bee-eaters, Todies, Motmots, **Kingfishers**, Jacamars, Puffbirds, Honeyguides, **Woodpeckers**, Barbets, Toucans

Seriemas, **Falcons**, Caracaras, Parrots

Songbirds

BLENDING IN

This magnificent species is diurnal, unlike most other owls, which are nocturnal. The Snowy Owl breeds in the Arctic tundra and if the ground is covered with snow, it blends in perfectly.

CONVERGENCE

The evolutionary process during which birds of two distantly related groups develop similarities is called convergence. Carrion-eating birds of prey are one example. Old World vultures belong to the hawk family (Accipitridae), while New World vultures are more closely related to storks. However, both groups are characterized by hooked bills, bare heads, and weak toes.

PARALLEL EVOLUTION

The African longclaws (family Motacillidae) and North American meadowlarks (family Icteridae) show convergence in plumage color and pattern.

CAPE LONGCLAW

WESTERN MEADOWLARK

EXTINCTION

During the last 150 years, North America has lost the Passenger Pigeon, the Great Auk, the Carolina Parakeet, the Labrador Duck, the Eskimo Curlew, and the Ivory-billed Woodpecker. Humans hunted them out of existence and/or destroyed their habitat. Some species that seemed doomed have had a reprieve. Thanks to captive breeding and release programs, birdwatchers can still see Whooping Cranes and California Condors in the wild today.

OVERHUNTING

The Passenger Pigeon was eradicated partly as a result of relentless hunting.

CLASSIFYING BIRDS

All past and present animal life is named and categorized into groups. Classifications reflect the genealogical relationships among groups, based on traits, such as color, bones, or DNA. Birds make up the class "Aves," which includes "orders." Each "order" is made up of one or more "families." "Genus" is a subdivision of "family," which contains one or more "species." A "species" is a unique group of similar organisms that interbreed and produce fertile offspring. Some species have distinct populations, which are known as "subspecies."

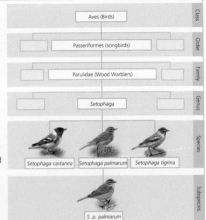

Class — Aves (Birds)

Order — Passeriformes (songbirds)

Family — Parulidae (Wood Warblers)

Genus — Setophaga

Species — Setophaga castanea | Setophaga palmarum | Setophaga tigrina

Subspecies — S. p. palmarum

ANATOMY AND FLIGHT

IN SPITE OF THEIR EXTERNAL DIVERSITY, birds are remarkably similar internally. To allow flight, birds require a skeleton that is both rigid and light. Rigidity is achieved by the fusion of some bones, especially the lower vertebrae, while lightness is maintained by having hollow limb bones. These are connected to air sacs, which, in turn, are connected to the bird's lungs.

SKELETON
Avian skeletal features include the furcula (wishbone), the keeled sternum (breastbone), and the fused tail vertebrae.

Labels on skeleton image: "hand", "forearm", neck vertebrae, bill, furcula, fused tail vertebrae, keeled sternum

FLIGHT ADAPTATIONS

For birds to be able to fly, they need light and rigid bones, a lightweight skull, and hollow wing and leg bones. In addition, pouch-like air sacs are connected to hollow bones, which reduce a bird's weight. The air sacs also function as a cooling system, which birds need because they have a high metabolic rate. The breast muscles, which are crucial for flight, are attached to the keeled sternum (breastbone).

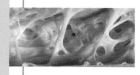

BIRD BONE STRUCTURE
Most bird bones, except those of penguins and other flightless birds, are hollow, which reduces their weight. A honeycomb of internal struts makes the bones remarkably strong.

Labels: secondaries, tail feathers, uppertail coverts, rump, tertials

LEGS, FEET, AND TOES

When you look at a bird's leg, you do not see their thigh, which is inside the body cavity, but just the leg from the knee down. When we talk about a bird's feet, we really mean its toes. The shin is a fused tibia and fibula. This fused bone plus the heel are collectively known as the "tarsometatarsus."

enables grip on ground

WALKING
Ground-foraging birds usually have a long hind claw.

enables strong grip on branches

CLIMBING
Most climbers have two toes forward and two backward

webbing provides thrust in water

SWIMMING
Water-loving birds have webbing between their toes.

used to grasp prey

HUNTING
Birds of prey have very sharp claws or talons.

UNDERPARTS
Underwing coverts have a regular pattern of overlapping rows. Short feathers cover the head, breast, belly, and flanks. In most birds, the toes are unfeathered.

Labels: primaries, axillaries, breast, bill, undertail coverts, belly, toes

FEATHERS

All birds, by definition, have feathers. These remarkable structures, which are modified scales, serve two main functions: insulation and flight. Special muscles allow birds to raise their feathers or to flatten them against the body. In cold weather, fluffed-out feathers keep an insulating layer of air between the skin and the outside. This insulating capacity is why humans often find wearing loose-fitting "down" jackets so effective against the cold. The first feathers that chicks have after hatching are down feathers. The rigidity of the flight feathers helps to create a supporting surface that birds use to generate thrust and lift.

primary coverts

secondary coverts

coverts

neck

nape

crown

chin

throat

mantle

scapulars

alula (bastard wing)

TYPES OF FEATHERS

Birds have three main kinds of feathers; down, contour, and flight feathers. The rigid axis seen in feathers is called the "rachis."

DOWN FEATHER **CONTOUR FEATHER** **FLIGHT FEATHER**

WING FUNCTIONS

Flapping, soaring, gliding, and hovering are among the ways birds can use their wings. They also exhibit colors or patterns as part of territorial and courtship displays. Some waterbirds, such as herons, attract fish by creating shade with their open wings. An important aspect of wings is their relationship to a bird's weight. The ratio of a bird's wing area to weight is called wing loading, but this may also be affected by wing shape. An eagle has a large wing area to weight ratio, which means it has lower wing loading, while a swallow has a small wing area to weight ratio, and therefore high wing loading. This means that the slow, soaring eagle is capable of much more energy-efficient flight than the fast, agile swallow.

UPPERPARTS

The wing feathers from the "hand" of the bird are the primaries and those on the "forearm" are the secondaries. Each set has its accompanying row of coverts—contour feathers that overlap the flight feathers. The tertials are adjacent to the secondaries.

LONG AND BROAD
The broad, long, rectangular wings of an eagle allow it to soar. The outstretched alulae (bastard wings) give it extra lift.

POINTED
Broad at their base and tapering toward a point, and bent at the wrist, a swallow's wings enable fast flight and sharp turns.

SHORT AND ROUND
Short, broad, and rounded wings enable warblers to move between perches and to migrate long distances.

WING AERODYNAMICS

The supporting surface of a bird's wing enables it to take off and stay aloft. Propulsion and lift are linked in birds—they use their wings for both—unlike in airplanes in which these two functions are separate. Large and heavy birds, like swans, flap their wings energetically to create propulsion, and need a long, watery runway before they can fly off. The Golden Eagle can take off from a cliff with little or no wing flapping, but the Turkey Vulture hops up from carrion, then flaps vigorously, and finally uses the air flowing across its wings to soar. This diagram shows how airflow affects lift.

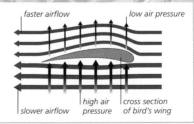

faster airflow *low air pressure*

slower airflow *high air pressure* *cross section of bird's wing*

MIGRATION

Until recently, the mechanics, or the "how" of migration was poorly understood. Today, however, ornithologists know that birds use a variety of cues including visual and magnetic, whether they migrate by day or by night. Birds do not leave northern breeding areas because of the winter cold, but because day length gets shorter and food scarcer.

NIGHT MIGRANTS
During migration, ornithologists can point a telescope on the moon and count the birds that cross its surface.

REFUELING
Red Knots make a stop on their long journey to eat horseshoe crab eggs.

INSTINCTIVE MOVE

Even though many birds use visual cues and landmarks during their migration, for example birds of prey flying along the Appalachians, "instinctive" behavior must control much of how and where they move. Instinct is a loose term that is hard to define, but ornithologists generally understand it as a genetically programmed activity. They assume that natural selection has molded a behavior as complex as migration by acting on birds' DNA; this hypothesis is reasonable but hard to prove. Nevertheless, it would seem to be the only explanation why many juvenile shorebirds leave their breeding grounds after their parents and yet still find their way to their final destination.

NAVIGATION

One of the most puzzling aspects of migration is understanding how birds make their way from their breeding grounds to their destination. Ornithologists have devised experiments to determine how the different components of a navigation system work. For example, if visual landmarks are hidden by fog, a faint sun can give birds a directional clue; if heavy clouds hide the sun, then the birds' magnetic compass may be used to ascertain their direction. Night migrants use star constellations.

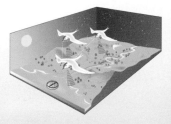

FINDING THE WAY
Birds coordinate information their brains receive from the sun, moon, stars, landmarks, and magnetite, or iron oxide, and use it as a compass.

OVERLAND FLIERS
Sandhill Cranes migrate over hills and mountains from their northern breeding grounds to the marshes of the Platte River and as far south as Texas and Mexico.

GLOBETROTTERS

Some bird species in Canada are year-round residents, although a few individuals of these species move away from where they hatched at some time in the year. However, a large number of Canadian species are migratory. A few species breed in Labrador, but winter in the Gulf of the Caribbean. Others breed in the Canadian Arctic Archipelago, fly over land and the Pacific Ocean, and spend the winter at sea off the coast of Peru. Many songbirds fly from Canada's boreal forests to Mexico and northern South America. The most amazing globetrotters, such as the Red Knot, fly all the way to Tierra del Fuego, making only a few stops along the way after their short breeding season in the Arctic tundra. The return journeys of some of these travelers are not over the same route—instead, their entire trip is elliptical in shape.

EPIC JOURNEY
The Arctic Tern is an amazing long-distance migrant, breeding in northern regions and wintering in the pack ice of Antarctica after flying a round-trip distance of about 25,000 miles (40,000km).

KEY
➤ *Trans-Pacific route*
➤ *Coastal Pacific route*
➤ *Arctic to Pacific route*
➤ *Trans-Gulf route*
➤ *Atlantic to Caribbean route*
➤ *Argentina to Arctic route*
➤ *Arctic-Atlantic Neotropical route*

NEOTROPICAL MIGRANT
Many wood warblers, such as this Blackpoll Warbler, breed in boreal forests before migrating to their wintering grounds in the Caribbean, or Central or South America.

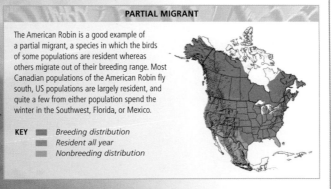

MIGRATION ROUTES
The map above shows the range of migration routes that some North American species take to and from their breeding grounds.

V-FORMATION
Geese and other large waterbirds fly in a V-formation to allow following birds to gain lift from those in front, thereby saving energy. The lead bird is regularly replaced.

PARTIAL MIGRANT

The American Robin is a good example of a partial migrant, a species in which the birds of some populations are resident whereas others migrate out of their breeding range. Most Canadian populations of the American Robin fly south, US populations are largely resident, and quite a few from either population spend the winter in the Southwest, Florida, or Mexico.

KEY ▦ *Breeding distribution*
▦ *Resident all year*
▦ *Nonbreeding distribution*

COURTSHIP AND MATING

W HETHER MONOGAMOUS OR NOT, males and females need to mate for their species to perpetuate itself. With most species, the male plays the dominant role of advertising a territory to potential mates using vocal or visual displays. Females then select a male and if the two respond positively to each other, a period of courtship follows, ending in mating. The next step is nest-building, egg-laying, and rearing the young.

DANCING CRANES
During courtship, Sandhill Cranes perform spectacular dances, the two birds of a pair leaping into the air with wings opened and legs splayed.

DISPLAYS

Mutual attraction between the sexes starts with some sort of display, usually performed by the male. These displays can take a number of forms, from flashing dazzling breeding plumage, conducting elaborate dancing rituals, and performing complex songs to offering food or nesting material, or actually building a nest. Some birds, such as grebes, have fascinatingly intricate ceremonies, in which both male and female simultaneously perform the same movements.

POLYGAMY
This Winter Wren collects nesting material for one of the several nests he will build.

LADIES' CHOICE
On a lek (communal display area), male sage-grouse inflate chest sacs and make a variety of sounds while females flock around them and select a mate.

COURTSHIP FEEDING

In some species, males offer food to their mate to maintain the pair bond. The male Common Tern routinely brings small fish to a mate in a nesting colony, spreading his wings and tail until she accepts the fish.

MAINTAINING RELATIONS
A male Northern Cardinal offers food to the female, which is a way of reinforcing their pair bond.

BREEDING

After mating, a nest is made, often by the female, where she lays from one to a dozen eggs. Not all birds make nests. Nightjars, for example, lay their eggs directly on the ground. In many species, incubation doesn't start until the female has laid all the eggs. Incubation, more often done by the female, varies from 12 days to about 45 days. Songbirds ranging from the temperate zone to the Arctic show a range in clutch size, with more eggs produced in the North than in the South. The breeding process can fail at any stage, for example a predator can eat the eggs or the chicks. Some birds will nest again, but others give up breeding for the season.

MATING

Mating is usually brief and typically takes place on a perch or on the ground, but a few species like swifts and swallows can mate in the air. This male Black Tern balances himself by opening his wings.

MUTUAL PREENING

Many species of albatross, like these Black-footed Albatrosses from the Pacific, preen each other—one bird softly nibbles the feathers on the other's head.

NOISY COURTSHIP

The Rednecked Grebe's courtship rituals are highly vocal.

MONOGAMOUS BONDS

Some birds, such as Snow Geese, mostly remain paired for life after establishing bond.

SINGLE FATHER

A male Red-necked Phalarope incubates eggs in the Arctic tundra. Phalaropes are well known for their reversal of breeding roles. The female, who is the larger and more colorful of the two sexes, aggressively competes for males, and after mating with several of them, plays no role in nest-building, incubating, or caring for chicks, but tends to her territory instead. Although the chicks can feed by themselves immediately after hatching, they remain with a male before growing feathers and living on their own.

NESTS AND EGGS

Most bird species build their own nest, which is a necessary container for their eggs. Exceptions include cowbirds, which lay their eggs in other species' nests. Nest-building is often done by the female alone, but in some species the male may help or even build it himself. Eggs are incubated either by females alone, or by males or females, depending on the species. Eggshells are thick enough to sustain the weight of incubating parents, yet thin enough for a chick to break its way out. Eggs, consisting of 60 percent water, contain a fatty yolk as well as sugars and proteins for nourishment of the embryo.

NEST TYPES

In addition to the four types shown below, nests range from a simple scrape in the ground with a few added pebbles to an elaborate woven basket-like structure. Plant matter forms basic nest material. This includes twigs, grass stems, bark, lichens, mosses, plant down, and rootlets. Some birds add mud to their nest for strength. Others incorporate animal hair or feathers to improve its softness and insulation. Female eider ducks pluck down feathers from their belly. Some birds include bits of plastic or threads in their nests. Many birds make their nest or lay their eggs deep inside the empty burrows of other animals. Burrowing Owls nest in prairie dog burrows, where they coexist with the rodents.

UNTIDY NEST
Huge stick nests, built on top of dead trees, are the hallmark of Ospreys. They also use a wide variety of artificial structures, including nesting platforms built for them by humans.

EGG CUP
A clutch of blue robin eggs in a cup lined with grass stems. Robins build their nests either in shrubs or trees, and sometimes on artificial structures like porch lights.

NATURAL CAVITY
This Northern Saw-whet Owl is nesting at the bottom of a tree cavity that was probably excavated by a woodpecker.

NEST BOX
Cavity-nesting bluebirds have been affected by habitat loss. They compete with other birds for nest sites, which may include human-made structures.

COMPLEX WEAVE
New World orioles weave intricate nests from dried grass stems and other plant material. They hang them from the tip of branches, often high up in trees.

EGG SHAPES

There are six basic egg shapes among birds, as illustrated to the right. The most common egg shapes are longitudinal and elliptical. Murres lay pear-shaped eggs. Formerly believed to prevent eggs from rolling off ledges, recent studies suggest that the pointed shape facilitates more efficient incubation. Spherical eggs with irregular red blotches are characteristic of birds of prey. Pigeons and doves lay white oval eggs, usually two per clutch. The eggs of many songbirds, including sparrows and buntings, are conical and have a variety of dark markings on a pale background.

COLOR AND SHAPE
Birds' eggs vary widely in terms of shape, colors, and markings. The American Robin's egg on the left is a beautiful blue.

PEAR-SHAPED   **LONGITUDINAL**   **ELLIPTICAL**

OVAL   **CONICAL**

SPHERICAL

NEAT ARRANGEMENT
Many shorebirds, such as plovers and sandpipers, lay four conical eggs with the narrow ends pointed in toward each other.

HATCHING CONDITION

After a period of incubation, which varies from species to species, chicks pierce the eggshell, some of them using an egg tooth, a special bill feature that falls off after hatching. After a long and exhausting struggle, the chick eventually tumbles out of the shell fragments. The transition from the watery medium inside the egg to the air outside is a tremendous physiological switch. Once free of their shell, the hatchlings recover from the exertion and either beg food from their parents or feed on their own.

FOOD DELIVERY
Tern chicks, although able to move around, cannot catch the fish they need to survive and must rely on their parents to provide food until they can fly.

PARENTAL CARE
Birds of prey, such as these Snowy Owl owlets, need their parents to care for them longer than some other bird species. They do not leave the nest until their feathers are sufficiently developed for their first flight.

BROOD PARASITISM

Neither cowbirds in the New World nor cuckoos in the Old World make a nest. Choosing from over 200 potential species, female cowbirds deposit up to 40 eggs in the nests of several species. If the foster parents accept the foreign egg, they feed the chick of the parasite until it fledges. In the picture below, a tiny wood warbler feeds its adopted chick, a huge cowbird hatchling that has overgrown the nest.

FAST FEEDER
Coots and rails hatch with a complete covering of down, and they can feed themselves immediately after birth.

IDENTIFICATION

S OME SPECIES ARE EASY TO IDENTIFY, but in many cases, species identification is tricky. In Canada, a notoriously difficult group to identify is the wood warblers, especially in the fall, when most species have similar greenish and/or yellowish plumage. Gulls and shorebirds are also challenging.

GEOGRAPHIC RANGE

Each bird species in Canada lives in a particular area that is called its geographic range. Some species have a restricted range. For example, the Whooping Crane breeds only in Wood Buffalo National Park in Alberta and the Northwest Territories. Other species, such as the Red-tailed Hawk, range from coast to coast and from northern Canada to Mexico. Species with a broad range usually breed in varied types of vegetation, while species with narrow ranges often have a specialized habitat. For example, rocky islands for the Horned Puffin.

BLUEBIRD VARIATIONS
Species of the genus *Sialia*, such as the all-blue Mountain Bluebird (above) and the Eastern Bluebird (left), are easy to identify.

bright-blue wings

white belly

chestnut flanks

SIZE AND WEIGHT

From hummingbird to Tundra Swan and from extra-light to heavy, such is the range of sizes and weights found among the bird species of Canada. Size can be measured in several ways, for example, the length of a bird from bill-tip to tail-tip, its wingspan, or even its weight. Size can also be estimated for a given bird in relationship with another that is familiar. For example, the less familiar Swainson's Thrush can be compared with the well-known American Robin.

SIZE MATTERS
Smaller shorebirds, with shorter legs and bills, forage in shallow water, but larger ones have longer legs and bills and can feed in deeper water.

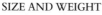

SEMIPALMATED PLOVER   LESSER YELLOWLEGS   HUDSONIAN GODWIT   LONG-BILLED CURLEW

GENERAL SHAPE

Just as birds come in all sizes, their body shapes also vary, but size and shape are not necessarily correlated. In the dense reed beds in which it lives, the streaked American Bittern's long and thin body blends in with reeds. The round-bodied Sedge Wren hops in shrubby vegetation or near the ground where slimness is not an advantage. In dense forest canopy, the slender and long-tailed Black-billed Cuckoo can maneuver easily. Mourning Doves inhabit rather open habitats and their plumpness is irrelevant when it comes to their living space.

tall, narrow body

BLACK-BILLED CUCKOO

long tail

slender shape

small head

short tail

AMERICAN BITTERN

tiny tail

round body

thickset body

MOURNING DOVE   SEDGE WREN

BILL SHAPE

These images show a range of bill shapes and sizes relative to the bird's head size. In general, bill form, including length or thickness, corresponds to the kinds of food a birds consumes. With its pointed bill, the Mountain Chickadee picks tiny insects from crevices in tree barks. At another extreme, dowitchers probe mud with their long thin bills, feeling for worms. The Avocet swishes its long, recurved bill back and forth in briny water in search of shrimp.

WING SHAPE

Birds' wing shapes are correlated with their flight style. The long, round-tipped wings of the Red-tailed Hawk are perfect for soaring, while the tiny wings of hummingbirds are exactly what is needed to hover in front of flowers and then to back away after a meal of nectar. When flushed, quails flutter with their round wings briefly and drop down.

TAIL SHAPE

It is not clear why some songbirds, like the American Goldfinch, have a notched tail while other similar-sized birds do not. Tail shapes vary as much as wing shapes, but are not so easily linked to a function. Irrespective of shape, tails are needed for balance. In some birds, tail shape, color, and pattern are used in courtship displays or in defensive displays when threatened.

COLORS AND MARKINGS

Melanin and carotenoid pigments largely determine color. Gray and brown birds have melanin (under hormonal influence), yellow and red ones have carotenoid (derived from food). House Finches are reddish because they eat a carotenoid-rich diet. Diversity in color and markings also results from scattering of white light by feathers (producing blue colors) and optical interference (iridescence) due to the structural properties of some feathers.

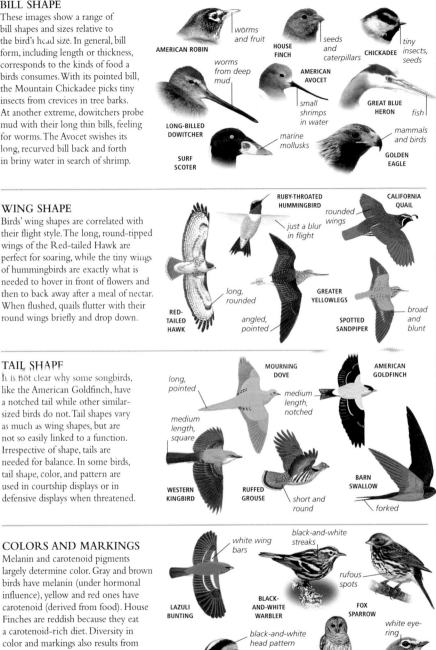

BILL SHAPE:
- AMERICAN ROBIN — worms and fruit
- HOUSE FINCH — seeds and caterpillars
- CHICKADEE — tiny insects, seeds
- LONG-BILLED DOWITCHER — worms from deep mud
- AMERICAN AVOCET — small shrimps in water
- GREAT BLUE HERON — fish
- SURF SCOTER — marine mollusks
- GOLDEN EAGLE — mammals and birds

WING SHAPE:
- RED-TAILED HAWK — long, rounded
- RUBY-THROATED HUMMINGBIRD — just a blur in flight
- CALIFORNIA QUAIL — rounded wings
- GREATER YELLOWLEGS — angled, pointed
- SPOTTED SANDPIPER — broad and blunt

TAIL SHAPE:
- WESTERN KINGBIRD — medium length, square
- MOURNING DOVE — long, pointed
- AMERICAN GOLDFINCH — medium length, notched
- RUFFED GROUSE — short and round
- BARN SWALLOW — forked

COLORS AND MARKINGS:
- LAZULI BUNTING — white wing bars
- BLACK-AND-WHITE WARBLER — black-and-white streaks
- FOX SPARROW — rufous spots
- WHITE-CROWNED SPARROW — black-and-white head pattern
- BARRED OWL — streaking on belly
- BLUE-HEADED VIREO — white eye-ring

SPECIES GUIDE

DUCKS, GEESE, AND SWANS

RECENT GENETIC studies indicate that waterfowl are most closely related to members of the order Galliformes. Most species of waterfowl molt all their flight feathers at once after breeding, making them flightless for several weeks until they grow new ones.

GEESE

Ornithologists group most geese and swans together into the subfamily Anserinae. Geese are generally intermediate between swans and ducks in body size and neck length. They are more terrestrial than either swans or ducks, often seen grazing on dry land. Like swans, geese often pair for life. They are also highly social, and most species are migratory, flying south for the winter in large flocks.

SWANS

Swans are essentially large, long-necked geese. Their heavier weight makes them ungainly on land, and they tend to be more aquatic than their smaller relatives. On water,

however, they are extremely graceful. When feeding, a swan stretches its long neck to reach water plants at the bottom, submerging up to half its body as it does so. The Trumpeter Swan is North America's largest native waterfowl, growing up to 5ft (1.5m) long and weighing up to 25lb (12kg).

DUCKS

Classified into several subfamilies, ducks are more varied than swans or geese, with many more species. They are loosely grouped by their feeding habits. Dabblers, or puddle ducks, such as the Mallard, teals, and wigeons, eat plants and invertebrates. They feed by upending on the surface of shallow water. By contrast, diving ducks, a group that includes scaups, scoters, eiders, mergansers, and the Ruddy Duck, dive deep underwater for their food.

INSTANT TAKEOFF
Puddle ducks like the Mallard can shoot out of the water and into the air.

GAGGLING GEESE
Gregarious Snow Geese form large, noisy flocks during migration and on winter feeding grounds.

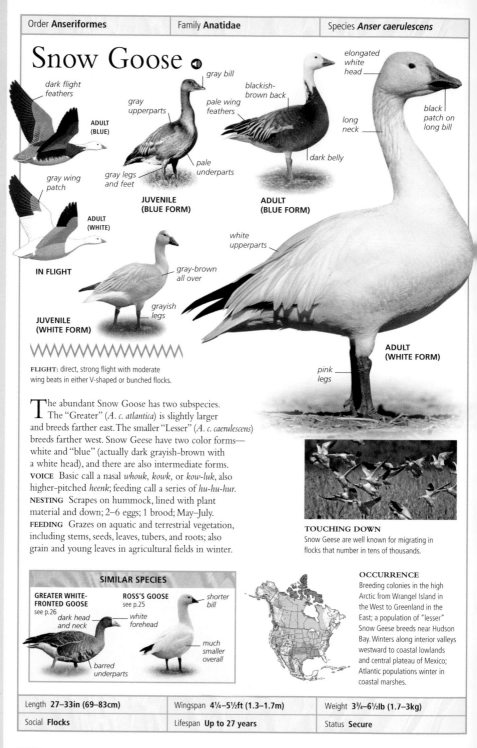

| Order **Anseriformes** | Family **Anatidae** | Species *Anser caerulescens* |

Snow Goose 🔊

dark flight
feathers

gray bill

blackish-
brown back

elongated
white
head

**ADULT
(BLUE)**

gray
upperparts

pale wing
feathers

black
patch on
long bill

long
neck

dark belly

gray wing
patch

gray legs
and feet

pale
underparts

**JUVENILE
(BLUE FORM)**

**ADULT
(BLUE FORM)**

**ADULT
(WHITE)**

white
upperparts

IN FLIGHT

gray-brown
all over

grayish
legs

**JUVENILE
(WHITE FORM)**

**ADULT
(WHITE FORM)**

pink
legs

FLIGHT: direct, strong flight with moderate
wing beats in either V-shaped or bunched flocks.

The abundant Snow Goose has two subspecies.
The "Greater" (*A. c. atlantica*) is slightly larger
and breeds farther east. The smaller "Lesser" (*A. c. caerulescens*)
breeds farther west. Snow Geese have two color forms—
white and "blue" (actually dark grayish-brown with
a white head), and there are also intermediate forms.
VOICE Basic call a nasal *whouk, kowk,* or *kow-luk,* also
higher-pitched *heenk;* feeding call a series of *hu-hu-hur.*
NESTING Scrapes on hummock, lined with plant
material and down; 2–6 eggs; 1 brood; May–July.
FEEDING Grazes on aquatic and terrestrial vegetation,
including stems, seeds, leaves, tubers, and roots; also
grain and young leaves in agricultural fields in winter.

TOUCHING DOWN
Snow Geese are well known for migrating in
flocks that number in tens of thousands.

SIMILAR SPECIES

**GREATER WHITE-
FRONTED GOOSE**
see p.26

ROSS'S GOOSE
see p.25

shorter
bill

dark head
and neck

white
forehead

much
smaller
overall

barred
underparts

OCCURRENCE
Breeding colonies in the high
Arctic from Wrangel Island in
the West to Greenland in the
East; a population of "lesser"
Snow Geese breeds near Hudson
Bay. Winters along interior valleys
westward to coastal lowlands
and central plateau of Mexico;
Atlantic populations winter in
coastal marshes.

| Length 27–33in (69–83cm) | Wingspan 4¼–5½ft (1.3–1.7m) | Weight 3¾–6½lb (1.7–3kg) |
| Social **Flocks** | Lifespan Up to 27 years | Status **Secure** |

DATE: _____ TIME: _____ LOCATION: _____

| Order **Anseriformes** | Family **Anatidae** | Species *Anser rossii* |

Ross's Goose

ADULT (WHITE)
black wingtips

IN FLIGHT

light-gray crown

dusky line through eye

gray wash on upperparts

JUVENILE (WHITE FORM)

round head

short, triangular bill

short, deeply furrowed neck

clean white upperparts

mostly dark-brown upperparts

white rump and tail

ADULT (BLUE FORM)

ADULT (WHITE FORM)

reddish-pink legs

FLIGHT: strong and direct, with rapid wing beats.

This diminutive white goose is not much bigger than a Mallard, and half the weight of a Snow Goose; like its larger relative, it also has a rare "blue" form. About 95 percent of Ross's Geese once nested at a single sanctuary in Arctic Canada, and breeding pairs have spread eastwards along the Hudson Bay and to several island locations. Hunting reduced the population to just 6,000 in the early 1950s, but since then the numbers have increased to around 2 million individuals.
VOICE Call a *keek keek keeek*, higher-pitched than Snow Goose; also a harsh, low *kork* or *kowk*; quiet when feeding.
NESTING Plant materials placed on ground, usually in colonies with Lesser Snow Geese; 3–5 eggs; 1 brood; June–August.
FEEDING Grazes on grasses, sedges, and small grains.

TRAVELING IN FAMILIES
Family groups migrate thousands of miles together, usually from northern Canada to central California.

SIMILAR SPECIES

SNOW GOOSE white form; see p.24
larger bill
longer neck
pink legs

SNOW GOOSE blue form; see p.24
longer neck
black patch on bill

OCCURRENCE
Breeding grounds are amidst tundra in a number of scattered, high Arctic locations. Main wintering areas in California. On the wintering grounds, it feeds in agricultural fields, and also grasslands. Roosts overnight in several types of wetlands.

| Length 22½–25in (57–64cm) | Wingspan 3¼ft (1.1m) | Weight 1¾–4½lb (0.85–2kg) |
| Social **Flocks** | Lifespan **Up to 21 years** | Status **Localized** |

DATE: _____ TIME:_____ LOCATION:_____

25

Order **Anseriformes**	Family **Anatidae**	Species *Anser albifrons*

Greater White-fronted Goose

gray wing feathers

ADULT

white rump band

IN FLIGHT

white tip to tail

pink bill with white base

brownish-gray head

white flank streak

darker chocolate-brown upperparts

dull yellowish-orange bill

brown underparts with black bands

larger body

longer legs, bill, and neck

bright-orange legs

MALE
A. a. frontalis (TUNDRA)

no belly barring

A. a gambeli (TULE)

JUVENILE

The Greater White-fronted Goose is the most widespread goose in the Northern Hemisphere. It is easily distinguished by its black-barred belly and the patch of white at the base of its bill. There are five subspecies, two of which are most commonly seen in North America. The "Tundra" (*A. a. frontalis*) makes up the largest population, breeding across northwestern Canada and western Alaska. The "Tule" (*A. a. gambeli*), while the largest in stature, occurs in the fewest numbers, and is restricted in range to northwest Canada.

VOICE Laugh-like *klow-yo* or *klew-yo-yo*; very musical in a flock.
NESTING Bowl-shaped nest made of plant material, lined with down, constructed near water; 3–7 eggs; 1 brood; May–August.
FEEDING Eats sedges, grasses, berries, and plants on both land and water in summer; feeds on grasses, seeds, and grains in winter.

FLIGHT: strong, direct flight; flies alone, in multiple lines, or in a V-formation.

FLIGHT FORMATIONS
This heavy-bodied, powerful flier can often be seen in tightly packed flocks.

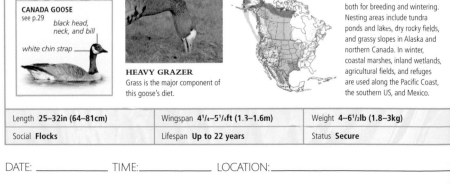

SIMILAR SPECIES

CANADA GOOSE
see p.29
black head, neck, and bill

white chin strap

HEAVY GRAZER
Grass is the major component of this goose's diet.

OCCURRENCE
Different habitats are utilized, both for breeding and wintering. Nesting areas include tundra ponds and lakes, dry rocky fields, and grassy slopes in Alaska and northern Canada. In winter, coastal marshes, inland wetlands, agricultural fields, and refuges are used along the Pacific Coast, the southern US, and Mexico.

Length **25–32in (64–81cm)**	Wingspan **4¼–5¼ft (1.3–1.6m)**	Weight **4–6½lb (1.8–3kg)**
Social **Flocks**	Lifespan **Up to 22 years**	Status **Secure**

DATE: _____ TIME: _____ LOCATION: _____

Order **Anseriformes**	Family **Anatidae**	Species ***Branta bernicla***

Brant 🔊

pale bars across wings

ADULT (WESTERN)

ADULT (EASTERN)

broad white necklace crosses throat

dark gray-brown upperparts

white rump

black neck and head

IN FLIGHT

grayish-white flank patch

black chest

bold white rump

small white "necklace" not crossing throat

barred flanks with pale belly

black neck stops abruptly at breast

bold barred flanks

very dark belly

**ADULT
B. b. nigricans
(WESTERN)**

B. b. hrota (EASTERN)

A small-billed, dark, stocky sea goose, the Brant winters on both the East and West Coasts of North America. There are two subspecies in North America—the pale-bellied "Atlantic" Brant (*B. b. hrota*), found in the east, and the darker "Black" Brant (*B. b. nigricans*), found in the west; an intermediate gray-bellied form, not yet named, breeds in the Canadian archipelago and winters in Boundary Bay, British Columbia. Unlike other North American geese, the Brant feeds mainly on eelgrass in winter.

VOICE Nasal *cruk*, harsh-sounding in tone; rolling series of *cut cut cut cronk*, with an upward inflection at the end.

NESTING Scrape lined with grass, plant matter, and down on islands or gravel spits; 3–5 eggs; 1 brood; May–July.

FEEDING Eats grass and sedges when nesting; eelgrass in winter; also green algae, salt marsh plants, and mollusks.

FLIGHT: rapid and strong; low, irregular flight formations.

GRASSY MEAL
In winter, Brants forage almost exclusively on eelgrass between the high and low tide marks.

SIMILAR SPECIES

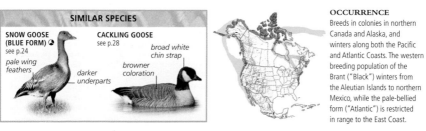

SNOW GOOSE (BLUE FORM) ♀
see p.24

pale wing feathers

darker underparts

CACKLING GOOSE
see p.28

broad white chin strap

browner coloration

OCCURRENCE
Breeds in colonies in northern Canada and Alaska, and winters along both the Pacific and Atlantic Coasts. The western breeding population of the Brant ("Black") winters from the Aleutian Islands to northern Mexico, while the pale-bellied form ("Atlantic") is restricted in range to the East Coast.

Length **22–26in (56–66cm)**	Wingspan **3¹/₂–4ft (1.1–1.2m)**	Weight **2¹/₂–4lb (1–1.8kg)**
Social **Flocks**	Lifespan **Up to 25 years**	Status **Secure**

DATE: _____ TIME: _____ LOCATION: _____

| Order **Anseriformes** | Family **Anatidae** | Species *Branta hutchinsii* |

Cackling Goose

plain, grayish-brown wings

ADULT

small, black head

white, U-shaped patch on rump **IN FLIGHT**

black tail

ADULT B. h. hutchinsii

broad white neck ring

black line separates white chin strap

darker breast

ADULT B. h. leucopareia

dark-brown breast

ADULT B. h. minima

small, stubby bill

white chin strap

no black under chin

pale breast

The Cackling Goose has recently been split from the Canada Goose; it can be distinguished from the latter by its short, stubby bill, steep forehead, and short neck. There are four subspecies of Cackling Goose, which vary in breast color—ranging from dark on *B. h. minima* and fairly dark on *B. h. leucopareia* to pale on *B. h. hutchinsii*. The Cackling Goose is much smaller than all subspecies of Canada Goose, except the "Lesser" Canada Goose, which has a longer neck and a less sloped forehead.
VOICE Male call a honk or bark; females have higher pitched *hrink;* also high-pitched yelps.
NESTING Scrape lined with available plant matter and down; 2–8 eggs; 1 brood; May–August.
FEEDING Consumes plants in summer; in winter, grazes on grass in livestock and dairy pastures; also in agricultural fields.

FLIGHT: strong with rapid wing beats; flies in bunched V-formations.

LITTLE GEESE
Cackling Geese are tiny when seen together with the larger Canada Goose.

SIMILAR SPECIES

CANADA GOOSE see p.29
more sloped forehead
larger overall (except one subspecies)

BRANT see p.27
all-black head
thin white neck ring

OCCURRENCE
At the northernmost fringe of the Canada Goose's range, in the tundra, it breeds on rocky tundra slopes from the Aleutians East to Baffin Island and Hudson Bay. Winters from British Columbia to California, also central US, Texas, and New Mexico in pastures and agricultural fields.

| Length **21½–30in (55–75cm)** | Wingspan **4¼–5ft (1.3–1.5m)** | Weight **2–6½lb (0.9–3kg)** |
| Social **Flocks** | Lifespan **Unknown** | Status **Secure** |

DATE: _____ TIME: _____ LOCATION: _____

Order **Anseriformes**	Family **Anatidae**	Species *Branta canadensis*

Canada Goose 🔊

plain, grayish brown wings with darker flight feathers

grayish-brown upperparts and sides

black head

very long neck

broad white chin strap

paler upper breast

ADULT

IN FLIGHT

white, U-shaped patch on rump

white undertail feathers

ADULT

smaller white chin strap

dark-brown overall

ADULT

ADULT

The Canada Goose is the most common, widespread, and familiar goose in North America. Given its col and range, it is not surprising that the Canada Goose has much geographic variation, and 12 subspecies have been recognized. With the exception of the Cackling Goose, from which it has recently been separated, it is difficult to confuse it—with its distinctive white chin strap, black head and neck, and grayish-brown body—with any other species of goose. It is a monogamous species, and once pairs are formed, most stay together for life.

VOICE Males mostly honk or bark; females have high pitched *hrink*.
NESTING Scrape lined with available plant matter and down, near water; 2–12 eggs; 1–2 broods; May–August.
FEEDING Grazes on grasses, sedges, leaves, seeds, agricultural crops, and berries; also insects.

FLIGHT: strong and direct with fairly slow, deep wing beats; often flies in V-formation.

TRICK OF THE LIGHT
A low sun can play tricks—these birds are actually pale grayish underneath.

SIMILAR SPECIES

GREATER WHITE-FRONTED GOOSE see p.26

white on base of pink bill

CACKLING GOOSE see p.28

steep forehead

smaller overall

bright-orange legs

OCCURRENCE
Variety of inland breeding habitats near water, including grassy urban areas, marshes, prairie, parkland, coastal temperate forest, northern coniferous forest, and the Arctic tundra. Winters in agricultural fields, mudflats, saltwater marshes, lakes, and rivers.

Length 2¼–3½ft (0.7–1.1m)	Wingspan 4¼–5½ft (1.3–1.7m)	Weight 6½–9¾lb (3–4.4kg)
Social **Flocks**	Lifespan **Up to 25 years**	Status **Secure**

DATE: _____ TIME: _____ LOCATION: _____

Order **Anseriformes**	Family **Anatidae**	Species **Cygnus olor**

Mute Swan

ADULT

extended neck

IN FLIGHT

long, pointed tail extends past toes

blotchy brown body

JUVENILE

black-based dusky bill

white overall

often arches wings over back

large, heavy body

small knob on bill

FEMALE

swollen knob during breeding

MALE

conspicuous black knob at base of orange bill

long, S-shaped neck

ADULT

One of the heaviest birds in North America, the Mute Swan was introduced from Europe due to its graceful appearance on water, if not on land, and easy domestication. However, this is an extremely territorial and aggressive bird. When threatened, it points its bill downward, arches its wings, hisses, and then attacks. Displacement of native waterfowl species and overgrazing by this species have led to efforts to reduce its numbers in North America.

VOICE Not mute; hisses, grunts, snorts, and snores; during courtship, trumpets, although more quietly than other swans.

NESTING Platform nest of plant materials, built on ground near water; 4–8 eggs; 1–2 broods; March–October.

FEEDING Dabbles, dips, and upends, mainly for underwater plants, but occasionally for small creatures too.

FLIGHT: strong, steady wing beats; creating a distinctive whirring and throbbing sound.

FORMATION FLYING
Groups of Mute Swans will sometimes fly in a line, and at other times, as here, they will arrange themselves in a V-formation.

SIMILAR SPECIES

TRUMPETER SWAN ◐
see p.31

larger head

gray plumage

TUNDRA SWAN ◐
much smaller;
see p.32

pink at base of bill

straighter black bill

straighter neck

OCCURRENCE
Bulk of population is found along the Atlantic Coast from Maine to North Carolina; smaller populations around the Great Lakes and southern British Columbia. Breeds and lives year-round on sluggish rivers, ponds, or lakes, preferring still water with emergent vegetation.

Length **4–5ft (1.2–1.5m)**	Wingspan **6¹/₂–7¹/₂ft (2–2.3m)**	Weight **12–32lb (5.5–14.5kg)**
Social **Pairs/Family groups**	Lifespan **Up to 21 years**	Status **Localized**

DATE: _____ TIME:_____ LOCATION:_____

Trumpeter Swan

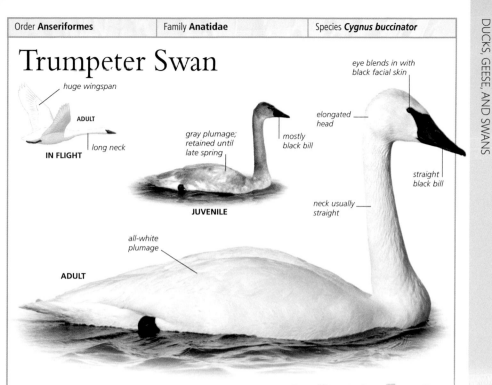

huge wingspan

ADULT

IN FLIGHT

long neck

gray plumage; retained until late spring

mostly black bill

JUVENILE

eye blends in with black facial skin

elongated head

straight black bill

neck usually straight

all-white plumage

ADULT

North America's quintessential swan and heaviest waterfowl, the Trumpeter Swan is a magnificent sight to behold. This species has made a remarkable comeback after numbers were severely reduced by hunting in the 1600–1800s; by the mid-1930s, fewer than a hundred were known to exist. Active reintroduction efforts were made in the upper Midwest and Ontario to reestablish the species to its former breeding range. The Trumpeter Swan's characteristic far-reaching call is usually the best way to identify it.

VOICE Call nasal, resonant *oh-OH* reminiscent of French horn.
NESTING Large mound made of plant matter on raised areas near or in freshwater; 3–6 eggs; 1 brood; April–September.
FEEDING Eats algae and aquatic plants, including moss, at or below the surface; feeds on grain in pastures and fields.

FLIGHT: slow, heavy, ponderous wing beats; "runs" on water's surface when taking off.

RUSTY STAINING
Trumpeter Swans often have rufous-stained heads and necks due to probing in iron-rich mud.

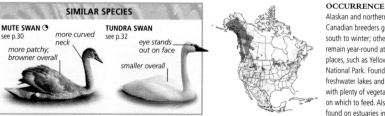

SIMILAR SPECIES

MUTE SWAN ♂
see p.30

more curved neck

more patchy; browner overall

TUNDRA SWAN
see p.32

eye stands out on face

smaller overall

OCCURRENCE
Alaskan and northern Canadian breeders go south to winter; others remain year-round at local places, such as Yellowstone National Park. Found on freshwater lakes and marshes with plenty of vegetation on which to feed. Also found on estuaries in winter.

| Length **4¼–5ft (1.3–1.5m)** | Wingspan **6½ft (2m)** | Weight **17–28lb (7.5–12.5kg)** |
| Social **Flocks** | Lifespan **Up to 24 years** | Status **Secure** |

DATE: _____ TIME: _____ LOCATION: _____

Order **Anseriformes** | Family **Anatidae** | Species ***Cygnus columbianus***

Tundra Swan

ADULT

small head and bill

dark legs | **IN FLIGHT** | fairly thick neck

dull grayish body

eye stands out from face at close range

yellow facial skin next to eye

dirty pink bill

JUVENILE

large yellow bill patch

BEWICK'S SWAN

all-white plumage

ADULT

Nesting in the Arctic tundra, this well-named species is North America's most widespread and smallest swan. Two populations exist, with one wintering in the West, and the other along the East Coast. The Tundra Swan can be confused with the Trumpeter Swan, but their different calls immediately distinguish the two species. When they are silent, weight and bill structure are the best way to tell them apart. In Eurasia, this species is known as Bewick's Swan and possesses a larger yellow patch at the base of its bill.

VOICE Clear, high-pitched yodeling *whoo-hooo* calls mixed with garbles, yelping, and barking sounds.

NESTING Mound-shaped nest made of plant matter near water; 3–6 eggs; 1 brood; May–September.

FEEDING Eats aquatic vegetation, insects, and mollusks; also grain.

FLIGHT: flight pattern like that of other swans but with slightly faster wing beats.

LARGE WINTER FLOCKS
Its size, white plumage, and flocking habits make the Tundra Swan a conspicuous species.

OCCURRENCE
Nests around lakes and pools in northern tundra from the Aleutians to the Yukon, and east to northwest Quebec. Winters in southern British Columbia, western US, and the mid-Atlantic states, mostly New Jersey to South Carolina. Winter habitat includes shallow coastal bays, ponds, and lakes.

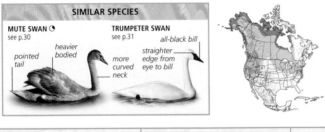

SIMILAR SPECIES

MUTE SWAN ♂
see p.30

pointed tail

heavier bodied

TRUMPETER SWAN
see p.31

more curved neck

straighter edge from eye to bill

all-black bill

Length **4–5ft (1.2–1.5m)**	Wingspan **6¼–7¼ft (1.9–2.2m)**	Weight **12–18lb (5.5–8kg)**
Social **Flocks**	Lifespan **Up to 21 years**	Status **Secure**

DATE: _____ TIME: _____ LOCATION: _____

| Order **Anseriformes** | Family **Anatidae** | Species *Aix sponsa* |

Wood Duck 🔊

blue wing patch

long wings

MALE

head held high

IN FLIGHT

bold, tear-shaped eye-ring

smaller crest

white-edged feathers

brownish breast

FEMALE

burgundy flanks

long, dark tail

MALE

subdued facial pattern

brown eye

grayish bill

JUVENILE

red eye

complex white facial markings

helmet-like head profile

black tip of bill

white-flecked maroon breast appears black at a distance

white vertical breast stripe

The male Wood Duck is perhaps the most striking of all North American ducks. With its gaudy plumage, red eye and bill, and its long sleek crest that gives its head a helmet-shaped profile, the male is unmistakable. It is related to the Mandarin Duck of Asia. The Wood Duck is very dependent on mature swampy forestland, and is typically found in marshes, shallow lakes, ponds, and park settings that are surrounded by trees. Although it adapts to human activity, it is quite shy. When swimming, the Wood Duck can be seen jerking its head front to back. Of all waterfowl, this is the only species that regularly raises two broods each season.

VOICE Male gives a wheezy upslurred whistle *zweeet*; female's call a double-note, rising *oh-eek oh-eek*.

NESTING Nests in natural tree cavities or nest boxes in close proximity to water; 10–13 eggs; 2 broods; April–August.

FEEDING Forages for seeds, tree fruit, and small acorns; also spiders, insects, and crustaceans.

FLIGHT: rapid flight with deep wing beats; flies with head up; leaps straight off the water.

PLAIN BELLY
Wings raised, a male reveals one of the only plain areas of its plumage—its pale belly and undertail.

SIMILAR SPECIES

BUFFLEHEAD ♀
see p.55

white on cheek

shorter neck

shorter tail

HOODED MERGANSER ♀
narrower wings;
see p.58

long tan crest

no eye-ring

OCCURRENCE
Usually found throughout the year, along rivers, streams, and creeks, in swamps, and marshy areas. Has a preference for permanent bodies of water. If good aquatic feeding areas are unavailable, the Wood Duck feeds in open areas, including agricultural fields.

| Length **18½–21½in (47–54cm)** | Wingspan **26–29in (66–73cm)** | Weight **16–30oz (450–850g)** |
| Social **Small flocks** | Lifespan **Up to 18 years** | Status **Secure** |

DATE: _____ TIME: _____ LOCATION: _____

| Order **Anseriformes** | Family **Anatidae** | Species ***Spatula discors*** |

Blue-winged Teal 🔊

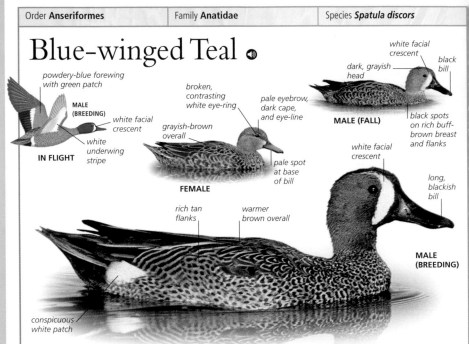

powdery-blue forewing with green patch

MALE (BREEDING)

white facial crescent

white underwing stripe

IN FLIGHT

broken, contrasting white eye-ring

grayish-brown overall

pale eyebrow, dark cape, and eye-line

pale spot at base of bill

FEMALE

white facial crescent

dark, grayish head

black bill

MALE (FALL)

black spots on rich buff-brown breast and flanks

white facial crescent

long, blackish bill

rich tan flanks

warmer brown overall

MALE (BREEDING)

conspicuous white patch

This small dabbling duck is a common and widespread North American breeding species. With a bold white crescent between bill and eye on its otherwise slate-gray head and neck, the male Blue-winged Teal is quite distinctive. The Blue-winged and Cinnamon Teals, along with the Northern Shoveler, constitute the three "blue-winged" ducks; this is a conspicuous feature when the birds are flying. The Cinnamon and the Blue-winged Teals are almost identical genetically and interbreed to form hybrids. The Blue-winged Teal winters mostly south of the US and migrates north in spring.
VOICE Male a high-pitched, raspy *peew* or low-pitched *paay* during courtship; female a loud single *quack*.
NESTING Bowl-shaped depression lined with grasses, close to water's edge, in meadows; 6–14 eggs; 1 brood; April–September.
FEEDING Eats seeds of a variety of plants; feeds heavily on insect larvae, crustaceans, and snails, when breeding.

FLIGHT: fast, twisting flight; flies in compact, small groups.

OUTSTRETCHED WING
Wing stretch behavior shows the white feathers between the blue forewing and green rearwing.

SIMILAR SPECIES

CINNAMON TEAL ♀
see p.35
plain face
warmer brown

GREEN-WINGED TEAL ♀
see p.42
different wing pattern
smaller, more compact body
smaller bill
streaked rump

OCCURRENCE
Nests across North America, with highest numbers in the prairie and parkland regions of the midcontinent. Prefers shallow ponds or marshes during nesting; freshwater to brackish water and (less so) saltwater marshes during migration. In winter, prefers saline environments, including mangroves.

| Length **14½–16in (37–41cm)** | Wingspan **23½–25in (60–64cm)** | Weight **11–18oz (300–500g)** |
| Social **Flocks** | Lifespan **Up to 17 years** | Status **Secure** |

DATE: _____ TIME: _____ LOCATION: _____

Order **Anseriformes**	Family **Anatidae**	Species *Spatula cyanoptera*

Cinnamon Teal

powdery-blue forewing

MALE

IN FLIGHT

white underwing stripe

solid cinnamon color

conspicuous orange to red eye

warm brown upperparts with rust tinge

plain face pattern

shoveler-like bill

FEMALE

dull-yellow legs

long, spoon-shaped black bill

MALE

True to its name, the male Cinnamon Teal is unmistakable in its overall rusty-brown color and blazing red eyes. A fairly small duck, the Cinnamon Teal is the only North American dabbling duck species that does not breed in the Great Plains and prairies of the mid-continent. Most of its population winters in the coastal marshes and interior wetlands of Mexico. The Cinnamon Teal is common in southwestern Canada and western US, and even seen in tiny roadside pools. Closely related to both the Northern Shoveler and Blue-winged Teal, the Cinnamon Teal's wing pattern is indistinguishable from that of the latter.
VOICE Male a snuffled *chuk chuk chuk*; female a loud single *quack* and soft *gack gack gack ga*.
NESTING Shallow depression lined with grass near water; 4–16 eggs; 1 brood; March–September.
FEEDING Feeds on seeds of many plant species; adds aquatic insects, crustaceans, and snails when breeding; omnivorous.

FLIGHT: rapid wing beats; very agile, making sharp turns.

FLOCKING TOGETHER
The cinnamon-colored males and tan females are often found in flocks.

SIMILAR SPECIES

BLUE-WINGED TEAL ♀
see p.34
darker cap and eye-line
colder brown-gray overall

NORTHERN SHOVELER ♀
see p.36
longer, thinner wings
white on flanks and upper breast
longer, paler bill

OCCURRENCE
Found in freshwater and brackish habitats of various sizes, such as marshes, reservoirs, flooded fields, ponds, ditches, and stock ponds. In the southern part of its wintering range, can also be found in tidal estuaries, salt marshes, and mangrove forests. Widespread in Central and South America.

Length **14–17in (36–43cm)**	Wingspan **22in (56cm)**	Weight **10–17oz (275–475g)**
Social **Winter flocks**	Lifespan **Up to 12 years**	Status **Secure**

DATE: _____ TIME: _____ LOCATION: _____

| Order **Anseriformes** | Family **Anatidae** | Species *Spatula clypeata* |

Northern Shoveler 🔊

IN FLIGHT

grayish-blue wing patch

whitish tail

FEMALE

long bill

pale-blue wing patch

MALE

heavy fronted

dark-green head

brown overall

dark, narrow eye-line

dusky olive-gray to orange bill

FEMALE

pale-edged, brown flank feathers

yellow eye

large, dark, spatula-shaped bill

MALE

white breast

black-and-white rump

chestnut belly and flanks

The Northern Shoveler is a common, medium-sized, dabbling duck found in North America and Eurasia. It is monogamous—pairs remain together longer than any other dabbler species. Its distinctive long bill is highly specialized; it is wider at the tip and contains thin, comb-like structures (called "lamellae") along the sides, used to filter food items from the water. Shovelers often form tight feeding groups, swimming close together as they sieve the water for prey.

VOICE Male call a nasal, muffled *thuk thuk…thuk thuk*; also a loud, nasal *paaaay*; female call a variety of quacks, singly or in a series of 4–5 descending notes.

NESTING Scrape lined with plant matter and down, in short plants, near water; 6–19 eggs; 1 brood; May–August.

FEEDING Forages for seeds; filters small crustaceans and mollusks out of the water.

FLIGHT: strong direct flight; male's wings make a rattling noise when taking off.

UPSIDE DOWN FEEDER
This male upends to feed below the water's surface, revealing his orange legs.

FILTER FEEDING
Their bills open, these ducks sieve small invertebrates from the water.

SIMILAR SPECIES

MALLARD ♀
larger; see p.40

darker blue wing patch

slimmer bill

CINNAMON TEAL ♀
see p.35

plainer plumage

plainer face

longer tail

OCCURRENCE
Widespread across North America, south of the tundra. Breeds in a variety of wetlands, in edges of shallow pools with nearby tall and short grasslands. Occurs in freshwater and saltmarshes, ponds, and other shallow bodies of water in winter; does not feed on land.

| Length **17½–20in (44–51cm)** | Wingspan **27–33in (69–84cm)** | Weight **14–29oz (400–825g)** |
| Social **Flocks** | Lifespan **Up to 18 years** | Status **Secure** |

DATE: _____ TIME: _____ LOCATION: _____

Order **Anseriformes**	Family **Anatidae**	Species ***Mareca strepera***

Gadwall 🔊

conspicuous white patch

mostly white underwings

MALE (WINTER)

white belly   **IN FLIGHT**

silvery-gray area

rusty sides

MALE (ECLIPSE)

brown, scalloped back

dark eyestripe

white wing patch

FEMALE

dark grayish overall

black uppertail

brown, rounded head

black bill

MALE (WINTER)

orange-yellow legs

finely patterned gray flanks and breast

Although the Gadwall's appearance is somewhat somber, many birders consider this duck one of North America's most elegant species because of the subtlety of its plumage. Despite being common and widespread, Gadwalls are often overlooked because of their retiring behavior and relatively quiet vocalizations. This dabbling duck is slightly smaller and more delicate than the Mallard, yet female Gadwalls are often mistaken for female Mallards. Gadwalls associate with other species, especially in winter.

VOICE Low, raspy *meep* or *reb* given in quick succession; female *quack* similar to that of female Mallard, but higher-pitched and more nasal; high-pitched *peep*, or *pe-peep*; both sexes give *tickety-tickety-tickety* chatter while feeding.

NESTING Bowl nest made of plant material in a scrape; 8–12 eggs; 1 brood; April–August.

FEEDING Dabbles on the surface or below for seeds, aquatic vegetation, and invertebrates, including mollusks and insects.

FLIGHT: direct flight with fast wing beats, leaps straight off the water.

BROOD ON THE MOVE
Females lead their ducklings from their nest to a brood-rearing habitat that provides cover and ample food for the ducklings to forage.

SIMILAR SPECIES

MALLARD ♀
see p.40

darker eye-line

whitish tail

MOTTLED DUCK ♀

thicker, longer bill

buffier face

olive to yellow bill

OCCURRENCE
From the western Prairie Pothole Country of Canada and the northern US, the Gadwall's range has expanded as it has adapted to artificial bodies of water, such as reservoirs and ponds. In winter, mostly found on lakes, marshes, and along rivers.

Length **18–22½in (46–57cm)**	Wingspan **33in (84cm)**	Weight **18–45oz (500–1,250g)**
Social **Winter flocks**	Lifespan **Up to 19 years**	Status **Secure**

DATE: _____ TIME: _____ LOCATION: _____

| Order **Anseriformes** | Family **Anatidae** | Species *Mareca americana* |

American Wigeon

MALE (BREEDING)

white underwing patch

IN FLIGHT

long, pointed tail

gray head contrasts with pinkish-brown breast and flanks

rufous-edged wing feathers

dark smudge around eye

gray head

FEMALE

narrow black line along bill

warm-brown breast and flanks

green band from eye to nape

cream forehead and crown

MALE (BREEDING)

black rump

pinkish-brown flanks

black-tipped bill

Often found in mixed flocks with other ducks, the American Wigeon is a common and widespread, medium-sized dabbling duck. This bird is an opportunist that loiters around other diving ducks and coots, feeding on the vegetation they dislodge. It is more social during migration and in the nonbreeding season than when breeding.

VOICE Slow and fast whistles; male's most common call a slow, high-pitched, wheezy, three-syllable *whew-whew-whew*, with middle note loudest; also, a faster *whee* whistle.

NESTING Depression lined with plant material and down, usually in tall grass away from water; 5–10 eggs; 1 brood; May–August.

FEEDING Grazes on grass, clover, algae and in agricultural fields; feeds on many seeds, insects, mollusks, and crustaceans during the breeding season.

FLIGHT: rapid, fairly deep wing beats; leaps almost vertically off the water.

COMING IN FOR A LANDING
This male's cream-colored forehead is clearly visible, as is the sharp contrast between the white belly, and the pinkish breast and flanks.

FLAPPING WINGS
This bird has a white patch on its underwing, while the Eurasian Wigeon has a gray patch.

SIMILAR SPECIES

EURASIAN WIGEON ♂
see p.39

bright-chestnut head

pinkish breast

EURASIAN WIGEON ♀
see p.39

warm-brownish head

pale throat

OCCURRENCE
As the northernmost breeder of the dabbling ducks, this species occurs from Alaska to the Maritimes. Prefers pothole and grassland habitats; found almost anywhere near water in winter. Winters south to northern South America and the Caribbean, in freshwater and coastal bay habitats.

| Length **17½–23in (45–58cm)** | Wingspan **33in (84cm)** | Weight **1⅛–3lb (0.5–1.3kg)** |
| Social **Flocks** | Lifespan **Up to 21 years** | Status **Secure** |

DATE: _____ TIME: _____ LOCATION: _____

| Order **Anseriformes** | Family **Anatidae** | Species *Mareca penelope* |

Eurasian Wigeon

MALE

smaller head than American Wigeon

IN FLIGHT

overall warm-brownish head, sometimes rusty on nape

primary tips close to tail tips

bright-chestnut head with buffy forehead

overall paler gray

FEMALE

pale, unmarked throat

pinkish breast

MALE (BREEDING)

The adult male Eurasian Wigeon is distinctive with its bright-chestnut head and broad creamy-yellow forehead. Its bold white forewing, with a green patch bordered in black, is conspicuous in flight. Females are plain brown with a short, pale bill. Eurasian Wigeons are often found among flocks of their closest relatives, the American Wigeons, and hybrids between the two species are not uncommon. In recent decades, the number of Eurasian Wigeons recorded has increased, particularly in the Pacific Northwest.

VOICE Males a two-note piping whistle, *whee-oooo* and a lower *wip-weu*; females a throaty growl.

NESTING Shallow depression lined with grass and down on the ground, usually near water; 8–9 eggs; up to 2 broods; April–August.

FEEDING Forages for leaves, stems, roots, and seeds by dabbling at surface of water or submerging the head and neck in the water; eats some insects in summer.

FLIGHT: continually flapping, with fast wingbeats.

PARTY OF FOUR
A party of Eurasian Wigeon drakes show off their typical chestnut heads with buffy foreheads.

SIMILAR SPECIES

AMERICAN WIGEON ♂ see p.38 — green band from eye to nape; pale-gray sides

AMERICAN WIGEON ♀ see p.38 — gray-brown head; grayish upper back

OCCURRENCE
Widespread and common in Eurasia near ponds, lakes, and marshes, and open fields nearby. Breeds at northern latitudes and winters on both the Atlantic and Pacific Coasts, with small numbers found inland. Regular winter visitor to North America, especially on the West Coast, from Canada to California.

| Length **16½–20½in (42–52cm)** | Wingspan **31.5in (80cm)** | Weight **17½–33½oz (500–950g)** |
| Social **Flocks** | Lifespan **Up to 34 years** | Status **Secure** |

| Order **Anseriformes** | Family **Anatidae** | Species *Anas platyrhynchos* |

Mallard 🔊

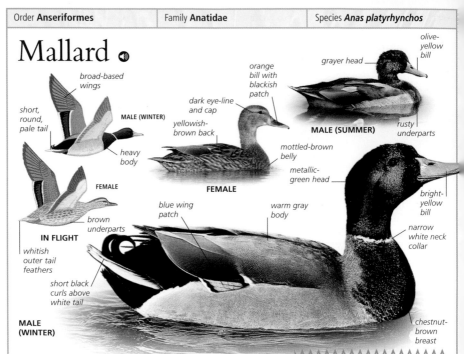

broad-based wings

short, round, pale tail

MALE (WINTER)

heavy body

FEMALE

IN FLIGHT

brown underparts

whitish outer tail feathers

short black curls above white tail

MALE (WINTER)

orange bill with blackish patch

dark eye-line and cap

yellowish-brown back

FEMALE

mottled-brown belly

metallic-green head

blue wing patch

warm gray body

grayer head

olive-yellow bill

MALE (SUMMER)

rusty underparts

bright-yellow bill

narrow white neck collar

chestnut-brown breast

The Mallard is perhaps the most familiar of all ducks, and occurs in the wild all across the Northern Hemisphere. It is the ancestor of most domestic ducks, and hybrids between the wild and domestic forms are frequently seen in city lakes and ponds, often with patches of white on the breast. Mating is generally a violent affair, but outside the breeding season the wild species is strongly migratory and gregarious, sometimes forming large flocks that may join with other species.
VOICE Male's call a quiet raspy *raab*; during courtship a high-pitched whistle; female call a *quack* or repeated in series.
NESTING Scrape lined with plant matter, usually near water, often on floating vegetation; 6–15 eggs; 1 brood; February–September.
FEEDING Feeds omnivorously on insects, crustaceans, mollusks, and earthworms when breeding; otherwise largely vegetarian; takes seeds, acorns, agricultural crops, aquatic vegetation, and bread.

FLIGHT: fast, shallow, and regular; often flies in groups.

STICKING TOGETHER
The mother leads her ducklings to water soon after they hatch. She looks after them until they can fend for themselves.

SIMILAR SPECIES

GADWALL ♀
see p.37
slimmer body

steeper forehead

white wing patch

orange strip on bill

AMERICAN BLACK DUCK ♀
dark tail

darker brown overall

dark-olive bill

OCCURRENCE
Occurs throughout the region, choosing shallow water in natural wetlands, such as marshes, prairie potholes, ponds, and ditches; can also be found in artificial habitats, such as city parks and reservoirs, preferring more open habitats in winter.

| Length **19½–26in (50–65cm)** | Wingspan **32–37in (82–95cm)** | Weight **1⅞–3lb (0.9–1.4kg)** |
| Social **Flocks** | Lifespan **Up to 29 years** | Status **Secure** |

DATE: _____ TIME:_____ LOCATION:_____

| Order **Anseriformes** | Family **Anatidae** | Species *Anas acuta* |

Northern Pintail

green wing patch with buff bar

MALE (WINTER)

white trailing edge of wing

FEMALE

outstretched head and neck

IN FLIGHT

whitish belly

pointed tail; shorter than male

dull-grayish body

gray bill

MALE (SUMMER)

blackish bill

plain buff face with dark eye

mottled gray-brown body

FEMALE

pale chocolate-brown head

long neck

long, pointed black tail

gray back and flanks

black bill with gray sides

MALE (WINTER)

black undertail with white flank patch

white neck and breast

An elegant, long-necked dabbler, the Northern Pintail has extremely distinctive marking and a very long tail—in fact, the longest tail to be found on any freshwater duck. One of the earliest breeders in the year, these ducks begin nesting soon after the ice thaws. Northern Pintails were once one of the most abundant prairie breeding ducks. However, in recent decades, drought, combined with the reduction of habitat on both their wintering and breeding grounds, have resulted in a significant decline in their population.

VOICE Male call a high-pitched rolling *prrreep prrreep;* lower-pitched wheezy *wheeeee*, which gets louder then drops off; female call a quiet, harsh *quack* or *kuk* singularly or as short series; also a loud *gaak*, often repeated.

NESTING Scrape lined with plant materials and down, usually in short grass, brush, or even in the open; 3–12 eggs; 1 brood; April–August.

FEEDING Feeds on grains, rice, seeds, aquatic weeds, insect larvae, crustaceans, and snails.

FLIGHT: fast, direct flight; can be very acrobatic in the air

FEEDING TIME
Even when tipping up to feed, these pintails can be identified by their long, black, pointed tails.

SIMILAR SPECIES

GADWALL ♀
see p.37

orange-sided bill

shorter tail

white wing patch

AMERICAN WIGEON ♀
see p.38

shorter tail

darker gray head

chestnut breast and flanks

OCCURRENCE
Widely distributed in North America; breeding in open country in shallow wetlands or meadows in mountainous forest regions. Found in tidal wetlands and saltwater habitats during migration and in winter; dry harvested and flooded agricultural fields in autumn and winter.

| Length **20–30in (51–76cm)** | Wingspan **35in (89cm)** | Weight **18–44oz (500–1250g)** |
| Social **Flocks** | Lifespan **Up to 21 years** | Status **Declining** |

DATE: _____ TIME: _____ LOCATION: _____

| Order **Anseriformes** | Family **Anatidae** | Species *Anas crecca* |

Green-winged Teal 🔊

MALE
green-and-black patch on hindwing

short neck

IN FLIGHT | *gray flanks*

rufous head

dark-green ear patch

horizontal white line on sides

lacks white vertical bar

small, narrow, black bill

A. c. crecca (EURASIAN)

black-spotted breast

darker face

steeper forehead

white vertical bar

FEMALE

finely detailed pattern

shoulder feathers with narrow, pale edges

weaker face pattern

yellowish-buff undertail feathers

MALE

JUVENILE

The Green-winged Teal, the smallest North American dabbling duck, is slightly smaller than the Blue-winged and Cinnamon Teals, and lacks their blue wing patch. Its population is increasing, apparently because it breeds in more pristine habitats, and farther north, than the prairie ducks. The species has three subspecies, *A. c. crecca* (Eurasia), *A. c. carolinensis* (North America), and *A. c. nimia* (Aleutian Islands). *Carolinensis* males have a conspicuous vertical white bar, whereas Eurasian *crecca* males do not.

VOICE Male call a high-pitched, slightly rolling *crick crick*, similar to crickets; female call a quiet *quack*.

NESTING Shallow scrape on ground lined with nearby vegetation, often placed in dense vegetation near water; 6–9 eggs; 1 brood; April–September.

FEEDING Eats seeds, aquatic insects, crustaceans, and mollusks year-round; also feeds in grain fields in winter.

FLIGHT: fast flight; often flying in twisting, tight groups reminiscent of shorebird flocks.

SINGLE PARENT
The female duck is deserted by her partner during incubation, so she must provide all parental care.

SIMILAR SPECIES

BLUE-WINGED TEAL ♀
larger overall; see p.34
whitish spot at base of bill
different wing pattern

CINNAMON TEAL ♀
larger overall; see p.35
longer bill
rich brown overall
yellowish legs

OCCURRENCE
Breeds north of the tree line in Alaska and Canada—around ponds in forest and deciduous woodlands. Prefers shallow wetlands with vegetation. In winter and migration, inland marshes, sloughs, agricultural fields, and coastal marshes. Winters south of the Caribbean and in southern Mexico.

| Length **12–15½in (31–39cm)** | Wingspan **20½–23in (52–59cm)** | Weight **7–16oz (200–450g)** |
| Social **Flocks** | Lifespan **Up to 20 years** | Status **Secure** |

DATE: _____ TIME: _____ LOCATION: _____

Order **Anseriformes**	Family **Anatidae**	Species *Aythya valisineria*

Canvasback

light-gray forewing

black rump and tail

MALE

belly appears white

long neck held horizontally in flight

IN FLIGHT

dark with mottled-gray patches

distinct white eye-ring

dingy brown underparts

JUVENILE

dingy brownish-gray upperparts and sides

extended teardrop

FEMALE

brown breast

rich chestnut head and neck

white to pale-gray back and flanks

black at both ends

high, peaked black crown

bright-red eye

black breast

MALE

A large, elegant, long-billed diving duck, the Canvasback is a bird of Prairie Pothole Country. Its specialized diet of aquatic plants has resulted in a smaller population than other ducks. With legs set far to the rear, it is an accomplished swimmer and diver, and is rarely seen on land. Weather conditions and brood parasitism by Redheads determine how successful the Canvasback's nesting is from year to year.
VOICE Mostly silent except during courtship when males make soft *cooing* noises; females emit a grating *krrrrr krrrrrr krrrrr*; females give loud quack when taking off; during winter, both sexes make soft wheezing series of *rrrr rrrr rrrr* sounds.
NESTING Platform over water built of woven vegetation; occasionally on shore; 8–11 eggs; 1 brood; April–September.
FEEDING Mainly eats aquatic tubers, buds, root stalks, and shoots, particularly those of wild celery; also eats snails when preferred plants are unavailable.

FLIGHT: direct in a flight, one of the fastest ducks; forms V-shaped flocks.

DEEP WATER
Canvasbacks prefer deeper-bodied waters that support the aquatic vegetation they eat.

SIMILAR SPECIES

REDHEAD ♂
see p.44

shorter gray, black-tipped bill

yellow eye

LESSER SCAUP ♂
see p.47

darker gray on back

smaller overall

yellow eye

OCCURRENCE
Found in potholes, marshes, and ponds in prairie parkland, tundra; northerly forests preferred where their favorite foods grow. Winters in large numbers in large bays and lakes, and deltas, with smaller numbers scattered across North America and Mexico.

Length **19–22in (48–56cm)**	Wingspan **31–35in (79–89cm)**	Weight **1¾–3½lb (0.8–1.6kg)**
Social **Flocks**	Lifespan **Up to 22 years**	Status **Secure**

DATE: _____ TIME: _____ LOCATION: _____

Order **Anseriformes**	Family **Anatidae**	Species **Aythya americana**

Redhead

MALE

dark-gray forewing

brick-red head

black breast

IN FLIGHT

dark crown

tawny brown overall

gray bill with black tip

FEMALE

yellow eye

MALE (ECLIPSE)

white band

brick-red upper neck and head

yellow eye

medium-gray mantle and sides

black rump

long blue bill with black tip

black lower neck

MALE

The Redhead, a medium-sized diving duck belonging to the Pochard group, is native only to North America. Only when seen up close is it apparent that the male's seemingly gray upperparts and flanks are actually white, with dense, black, wavy markings. The Redhead often feeds at night and forages mostly around dusk and dawn, drifting during the day. It parasitizes other duck nests more than any other duck species, particularly those of the Canvasback and even other Redheads.
VOICE Male courtship call a wheezy rising then falling *whee ough*, also *meow*; female call a low, raspy *kurr kurr kurr*.
NESTING Weaves solid nest over water in dense vegetation, such as cattails, lined with down; 7–14 eggs; 1 brood; May–September.
FEEDING Omnivorous; feeds on aquatic plants, seeds, tubers, algae, insects, spiders, fish eggs, snails, and insect larvae; diet is variable depending on location.

FLIGHT: direct flight; runs on water prior to takeoff.

MALE DISPLAY
This male is performing a spectacular courtship display called a head throw, while remaining otherwise completely still on the water.

EASY IDENTIFICATION
The long blue bill with a whitish band and black tip is clearly visible in males.

OCCURRENCE
Breeds in shallow wetlands across the Great Basin and Prairie Pothole Region, very densely in certain marsh habitats. The bulk of the population winters in coastal lagoons along the Atlantic Coast and the Gulf of Mexico.

SIMILAR SPECIES

CANVASBACK ♀
see p.43

wedge-shaped black bill

grayish back

RING-NECKED DUCK ♀
see p.45

peaked head shape

dark-brown back

Length **17–21in (43–53cm)**	Wingspan **30–31in (75–79cm)**	Weight **1⅜–3¼lbs (0.6–1.5kg)**
Social **Flocks**	Lifespan **Up to 21 years**	Status **Secure**

DATE: _____ TIME: _____ LOCATION: _____

| Order **Anseriformes** | Family **Anatidae** | Species **Aythya collaris** |

Ring-necked Duck 🔊

dark forewing

MALE

IN FLIGHT

bold white underwing

dark-brown back

bold white eye-ring

white band on bill

FEMALE

yellow eye

tall, peaked head

gray bill with white band at base and white and black tip

thin chestnut ring

black neck and breast

rounded gray sides

MALE

A resident of freshwater ponds and lakes, the Ring-necked Duck is a fairly common medium-sized diving duck. A more descriptive and suitable name might have been Ring-billed Duck as the bold white band on the bill tip is easy to see, whereas the thin chestnut ring around the neck can be very difficult to observe. The tall, pointed head is quite distinctive, peaking at the rear of the crown. When it sits on the water, this bird typically holds its head high.

VOICE Male normally silent; female makes low *kerp kerp* call.
NESTING Floating nest built in dense aquatic vegetation, often in marshes; 6–14 eggs; 1 brood; May–August.
FEEDING Feeds in water at all times, either by diving, tipping up, or dabbling for aquatic plant tubers and seeds; also eats aquatic invertebrates, such as clams and snails.

FLIGHT: strong flier with deep, rapid wing beats; flight somewhat erratic

UNIQUE BILL
A white outline around the base of the bill and the white band on the bill are unique markings.

FLAPPING WINGS
Bold white wing linings are apparent when the Ring-necked Duck flaps its wings.

SIMILAR SPECIES

LESSER SCAUP ♂
see p.47

wavy-patterned gray mantle

rounded head

TUFTED DUCK ♂

crested tufts

white sides

OCCURRENCE
Breeds across Canada, south of the Arctic zone, in shallow freshwater marshes and bogs; sporadically in the western US. Winters in freshwater and brackish habitats, such as swamps, lakes, estuaries, reservoirs, and flooded fields. Migrants are found in the Midwest near stands of wild rice.

| Length **15–18in (38–46cm)** | Wingspan **24–25in (62–63cm)** | Weight **1⅛–2lbs (500–900g)** |
| Social **Flocks** | Lifespan **Up to 20 years** | Status **Secure** |

DATE: _____ TIME:_____ LOCATION:_____

| Order **Anseriformes** | Family **Anatidae** | Species *Aythya marila* |

Greater Scaup

gray forewing

broad white wing stripe

MALE (NONBREEDING)

IN FLIGHT

little or no white around bill

medium to dark brown overall

gray-brown sides **JUVENILE**

bold white patches at base of bill

FEMALE (NONBREEDING)

smooth, round, black head with purple-green gloss

blue-gray bill, wider at tip

reduced white around bill

gray-frosted shoulder feathers and sides

wavy-patterned gray back

FEMALE (BREEDING)

dark brown overall

blackish-brown head

gray-and-brown back

MALE (BREEDING)

almost all-white sides

MALE (ECLIPSE)

A great swimmer and diver, the Greater Scaup is the only diving duck (genus *Aythya*) that breeds both in North America and Eurasia. Due to its more restricted coastal breeding and wintering habitat preference, it is far less numerous in North America than its close relative, the Lesser Scaup. The Greater Scaup forms large, often sexually segregated, flocks outside the breeding season. If both scaup species are present together, they will also segregate within the flocks according to species. Correct identification is difficult.
VOICE During courtship, male call a soft, fast, wheezy *week week wheew*; female gives a series of growled monotone *arrrr* notes.
NESTING Simple depression lined with grasses and down, nest sites need to have dense cover of vegetation from previous year; 6–10 eggs; 1 brood; May–September.
FEEDING Dives for aquatic plants, seeds, insects, crustaceans, snails, shrimp, and bivalves.

FLIGHT: strong, fast, and agile; flocks shift and twist during prolonged flight.

FOND OF FLOCKING
Male Greater Scaups, with distinct black-and-white markings, flock together on the water.

SIMILAR SPECIES

CANVASBACK ♂
see p.43

chestnut-brown head

black tail

LESSER SCAUP ♂
see p.47

slimmer, pointed head

grayer flanks

OCCURRENCE
Majority breed in western coastal Alaska on tundra wetlands; also in lower densities in northwest and eastern Canada. Almost all birds winter offshore, along the Atlantic and Pacific Coasts, or on the Great Lakes due to increased food availability. Small groups are found inland and midcontinent, on unfrozen water bodies.

| Length **15–22in (38–56cm)** | Wingspan **28–31in (72–79cm)** | Weight **1¼–3lb (0.6–1.4kg)** |
| Social **Flocks** | Lifespan **Up to 22 years** | Status **Declining** |

DATE: _____ TIME:_____ LOCATION:_____

| Order **Anseriformes** | Family **Anatidae** | Species *Aythya affinis* |

Lesser Scaup 🔊

MALE
whitish underwings
black head
whitish belly
IN FLIGHT

pale-brown flanks
brown rear end
MALE (1ST WINTER)

rich brown head and neck
brown back
white patch around base of gray bill
brown flank feathers with gray fringes
FEMALE
purple-green gloss on head

narrow head with bump at the rear
narrow, thin blue-gray bill

dark, wavy pattern on upperparts
black rear end
MALE
pale flanks
black breast and neck

The Lesser Scaup, far more numerous than its somewhat larger relative (their size and weight ranges overlap) is also the most abundant diving duck in North America. The two species are very similar in appearance and are best identified by shape. Identification must be done cautiously as head shape changes with position. For example, the crown feathers are flattened just before diving in both species; thus, scaups are best identified when they are not moving.
VOICE Males mostly silent except during courtship when they make a wheezy *wheeow wheeow wheeow* sound; females give repetitive series of grating *garrrf garrrf garrrf* notes.
NESTING Nest built in tall vegetation or under shrubs, sometimes far from water, also on islands and mats of floating vegetation; 8–11 eggs; 1 brood; May–September.
FEEDING Feeds mainly on leeches, crustaceans, mollusks, aquatic insects, and aquatic plants and seeds.

FLIGHT: rapid, direct flight, can jump off water more easily than other diving ducks.

PREENING SCAUP
Ducks are meticulous preeners, and the Lesser Scaup is no exception.

SIMILAR SPECIES

RING-NECKED DUCK ♀
see p.45
prominent white eye-ring
solid dark back

GREATER SCAUP ♀
see p.46
more tawny-brown upperparts
more white around bill

OCCURRENCE
Breeds inland from Alaska to eastern Canada in open northern forests and forest tundra, most farther north. Winters in the Caribbean, the southern US, and south to northern South America. Majority winter along coasts; others winter inland on lakes and reservoirs.

| Length **15½–17½in (39–45cm)** | Wingspan **27–31in (68–78cm)** | Weight **1–2¾lb (0.45–1.2kg)** |
| Social **Flocks** | Lifespan **Up to 18 years** | Status **Secure** |

DATE: _____ TIME:_____ LOCATION:_____

Order **Anseriformes**	Family **Anatidae**	Species *Somateria spectabilis*

King Eider

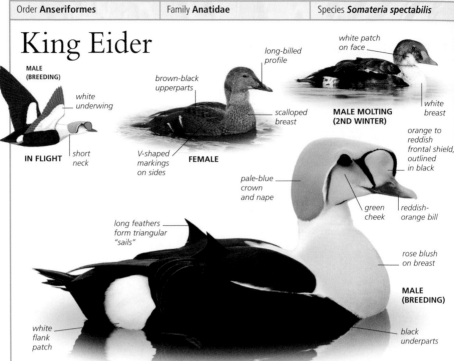

MALE (BREEDING)

white underwing

IN FLIGHT

short neck

long-billed profile

brown-black upperparts

scalloped breast

V-shaped markings on sides

FEMALE

white patch on face

MALE MOLTING (2ND WINTER)

white breast

orange to reddish frontal shield, outlined in black

pale-blue crown and nape

long feathers form triangular "sails"

green cheek

reddish-orange bill

rose blush on breast

MALE (BREEDING)

white flank patch

black underparts

The scientific name of the King Eider, *spectabilis*, means "worth seeing," and its gaudy marking and coloring around the head and bill make it hard to mistake. Females resemble the somewhat larger and paler Common Eider. The female King Eider has a more rounded head, more compact body, and a longer bill than the male. King Eiders may dive down to 180ft (55m) when foraging.
VOICE Courting males give a repeated series of low, rolled dove-like *arrrrooooo* calls, each rising, then falling, followed by softer *cooos*; females give grunts and croaks.
NESTING Slight depression in tundra, lined with nearby vegetation and down; 4–7 eggs; 1 brood; June–September.
FEEDING Dives for mollusks; other food items include crustaceans, starfish, and when breeding, insects and plants.

FLIGHT: direct and rapid flight; migrates in long lines, abreast in a broad front, or in clusters.

GROUP FLIGHT
Migratory King Eiders move in large groups to their northern breeding habitats.

SIMILAR SPECIES

COMMON EIDER ♀
larger overall; see p.49

longer, more wedge-shaped bill

flatter head

BLACK SCOTER ♀
smaller overall; see p.53

pale cheek and dark cap

longer, cocked tail

OCCURRENCE
Nests along coasts and farther inland than Spectacled or Steller's Eiders in the high Arctic, on a variety of habitats; around low marshes, lakes, and islands; prefers well-drained areas. During winter, found mostly along the southern edge of the ice pack, in coastal waters up to 66ft (20m) deep.

Length **18½–25in (47–64cm)**	Wingspan **37in (94cm)**	Weight **2¾–4¾lb (1.2–2.1kg)**
Social **Flocks**	Lifespan **Up to 15 years**	Status **Secure**

DATE: _____ TIME: _____ LOCATION: _____

| Order **Anseriformes** | Family **Anatidae** | Species *Somateria mollissima* |

Common Eider

black cap

dark brown overall

MALE (SUMMER)

FEMALE

brown overall

olive-green wash on nape

greenish-olive bill

white flecking

MALE (WINTER)

IN FLIGHT

whitish underwing

MALE (2ND WINTER)

black rump and tail

white breast with rose tinge

long, sloping forehead

mottled black-and-brown upperparts

MALE (WINTER)

FEMALE

The largest duck in North America, the Common Eider, is also the most numerous, widespread, and variable of the eiders. Four of its seven subspecies occur in North America, and vary in the markings and color of their heads and bills. Male Common Eiders also have considerable seasonal plumage changes, and do not acquire their adult plumage until the third year.

VOICE Repeated hoarse, grating notes *korr-korr-korr;* male's owl-like *ah-WOO-ooo;* female's low, guttural notes *krrrr-krrrr-krrrr.*

NESTING Depression on ground lined with down and plant matter, often near water; 2–7 eggs; 1 brood; June–September.

FEEDING Forages in open water and areas of shallow water; dives in synchronized flocks for mollusks and crustaceans, but consumes its larger prey above the surface.

FLIGHT: strong flight with relatively slow wing beats; flies in undulating lines, low over the water.

BROODING FEMALE
Females line their nests with down plucked from their bellies, and cover the eggs with their bodies.

SIMILAR SPECIES

KING EIDER ♀
smaller overall; see p.48

thicker neck

flatter crown

shorter, more concave bill

SURF SCOTER ♀
see p.51

dark brown overall

shorter, wedge-shaped bill

OCCURRENCE
Arctic breeder on coastal islands, peninsulas, seldom along freshwater lakes and deltas near coast. One population is sedentary in the Hudson Bay and James Bay regions. Other populations winter in the Bering Sea, Hudson Bay, north British Columbia, Gulf of St. Lawrence, and along the Atlantic Coast.

| Length **19½–28in (50–71cm)** | Wingspan **31–42in (80–108cm)** | Weight **2¾–5¾lb (1.2–2.6kg)** |
| Social **Flocks/Colonies** | Lifespan **Up to 21 years** | Status **Secure** |

DATE: _____ TIME: _____ LOCATION: _____

Harlequin Duck

MALE

dark wings above and below

IN FLIGHT

pointed tail

short neck

dark sooty-brown overall

broad face with whitish patches

FEMALE

scaly, pale-brown lower breast and belly

white bands down either side of back

slate-blue with bright rusty sides

two white bands perpendicular to breast and neck

rust crown stripes

two white facial spots

very round head

steep forehead

small, dark bill

white crescent

MALE

This small, hardy duck is a superbly skillful swimmer, diving to forage on the bottom of turbulent streams for its favorite insect prey. Despite the male's unmistakable plumage at close range, it looks very dark from a distance. With head and long tail held high, it can be found among crashing waves, alongside larger and bigger-billed Surf and White-winged Scoters, which feed in the same habitat.

VOICE Male a high-pitched squeak earning it the nickname "sea mouse"; female's call a raspy *ekekekekekek*.

NESTING Nests near water, under vegetation or base of tree; also tree cavities; 3–9 eggs; 1 brood; April–September.

FEEDING Dives for insects and their larvae, and fish roe when breeding; in winter, eats mollusks, crustaceans, crabs, snails, fish roe, and barnacles.

FLIGHT: rapid and regular wing beats; usually flies low over water, in pairs or small groups.

MALE GROUPS
After the breeding season, many males may gather and forage together.

PAIR IN FLIGHT
Note the crisp white markings on the slate-blue male in flight.

OCCURRENCE
Breeds near rushing coastal, mountain, or subalpine streams. During winter, found in small groups or mixed in with other sea ducks close to the shore, particularly along shallow rocky shorelines, jetties, rocky beaches, and headlands.

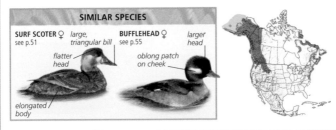

SIMILAR SPECIES	
SURF SCOTER ♀ see p.51	large, triangular bill	**BUFFLEHEAD** ♀ see p.55	larger head

flatter head

oblong patch on cheek

elongated body

Length **13–21½in (33–54cm)**	Wingspan **22–26in (56–66cm)**	Weight **18–26oz (500–750g)**
Social **Small flocks**	Lifespan **Unknown**	Status **Special Concern**

DATE: _____ TIME: _____ LOCATION: _____

Order **Anseriformes**	Family **Anatidae**	Species *Melanitta perspicillata*

Surf Scoter

MALE
— black wings overall

— compact body

IN FLIGHT

whitish facial patches —

dark-brown overall —

all-dark bill —

FEMALE

black forehead

small white patch on nape —

MALE (2ND WINTER)

white eye —

velvety black feathers —

white nape —

long tail feathers —

white forehead

large black spot on bill

swollen orange bill with white base

MALE

Surf Scoters, one of three species of scoters living in North America, migrate up and down both coasts, often with the other species. They take their name from the way they dive for mollusks on the mudflats, in shallow coastal waters, through heavy surf. Groups often dive and resurface in unison. Black and Surf Scoters can be difficult to tell apart as both have all-black wings. The underside of the Surf Scoter's wings are uniformly black, whereas the Black Scoter's have gray flight feathers, which contrast with the black underwing feathers.

VOICE Normally silent; courting male's variety of calls includes liquid gurgled *puk-puk*, bubbled whistles, and low croaks; female call a harsh *crahh*, reminiscent of a crow.

NESTING Ground nest lined with down and vegetation on brushy tundra, often under low branches of a conifer tree; 5–10 eggs; 1 brood; May–September.

FEEDING Dives for mollusks and other aquatic invertebrates.

FLIGHT Flight with beats, flies in bunched-up groups; male's wings hum or whistle in flight.

DISTINGUISHING FEATURES
The white forehead and bright orange bill, in addition to its red-orange legs and feet, identify male Surf Scoters.

SIMILAR SPECIES

GREATER SCAUP ♀
see p.46

no white patches on cheek

thinner bill

WHITE-WINGED SCOTER ♀
see p.52

long sloping forehead

longer bill

OCCURRENCE
Nests on lake islands in forested regions of interior Alaska and northern Canada. Nonbreeders in summer and adults in winter are strictly coastal, with numbers decreasing from north to south along the Pacific Coast. In the East, most overwinter in the mid-Atlantic Coast region.

Length **19–23½in (48–60cm)**	Wingspan **30in (77cm)**	Weight **1¾–2¾lb (0.8–1.2kg)**
Social **Flocks/Pairs**	Lifespan **Up to 10 years**	Status **Declining**

DATE: _____ TIME: _____ LOCATION: _____

| Order **Anseriformes** | Family **Anatidae** | Species **Melanitta deglandi** |

White-winged Scoter

white wing patch

ADULT

long, sloping head

blackish bill

two distinct pale patches on face

JUVENILE FEMALE

appears all-black in flight

IN FLIGHT

dark brown overall

feathers extend onto the bill

upturned, white "comma" around white eye

black knob at base of bill

FEMALE

all black with brownish sides

pinkish-red to yellow-orange bill

MALE

The White-winged Scoter is the largest of the three scoters. When visible, the white wing patch makes identification easy. Females are quite similar to juvenile male and female Surf Scoters and can be identified by head shape, extent of bill feathering, and shape of white areas on the face. When diving, this scoter leaps forward and up, arching its neck, and opens its wings when entering the water. Underwater, White-winged Scoters open their wings to propel and stabilize themselves.

VOICE Mostly silent; courting males emit a whistling note; female call a growly *karr*.

NESTING Depression lined with twigs and down in dense thickets, often far from water; 8–9 eggs; 1 brood; June–September.

FEEDING Dives for mollusks and crustaceans; sometimes eats fish and aquatic plants.

FLIGHT: direct with rapid wing beats; flies low over the water in small groups.

WHITE FLASH IN FLIGHT
Scoters often migrate or feed in mixed flocks. The white wing patches are striking in flight.

SIMILAR SPECIES

SURF SCOTER ♂
see p.51

white forehead

white nape

BLACK SCOTER ♂
see p.53

black overall

yellow-orange knob

OCCURRENCE
Majority breed in dense colonies in interior Alaska and western Canada on large freshwater or brackish lakes or ponds, sometimes on saltwater lakes. Winters along both coasts, large bays, inlets, and estuaries. Rarely winters inland, except on the Great Lakes.

| Length **19–23in (48–58cm)** | Wingspan **31in (80cm)** | Weight **2¾–4¾lb (0.9–1.9kg)** |
| Social **Flocks/Colonies** | Lifespan **Up to 18 years** | Status **Vulnerable** |

DATE: _____ TIME: _____ LOCATION: _____

Order **Anseriformes**	Family **Anatidae**	Species *Melanitta americana*

Black Scoter

pale silvery-gray flight feathers

black lining on underwings

ADULT

IN FLIGHT

dark cap

pale brownish-gray cheeks

black bill with small yellow patch

smaller bill

dark-brown overall

FEMALE

dark-brown eye

entirely black, heavily built body

conspicuous yellow-orange knob on black bill

MALE

Black Scoters, the most vocal of the scoters, are medium-sized sea ducks that winter along both coasts of North America. Riding high on the water they form dense flocks, often segregated by gender. While swimming, the Black Scoter sometimes flaps its wings and while doing so drops its neck low down, unlike the other two scoters. This scoter breeds in two widely separated sub-Arctic breeding areas and is one of the least studied ducks in North America. The Black Scoter was once thought to be a subspecies of the Common Scoter, but recent studies have split the American birds from their Eurasian relatives.

VOICE Male call a high-whistled *peeew*; female a low raspy *kraaa*.
NESTING Depression lined with grass and down, often in tall grass on tundra; 5–10 eggs; 1 brood; May–September.
FEEDING Dives in saltwater for mollusks, crustaceans, and plant matter; feeds on aquatic insects and freshwater mussels.

FLIGHT: strong wing beats, male's wings make whistling sound during takeoff.

YELLOW BILL
Male Black Scoters are distinctive with their black plumage and yellow bill-knob.

SIMILAR SPECIES

SURF SCOTER ♀
see p.51

flatter crown

two whitish patches

WHITE-WINGED SCOTER ♀
see p.52

larger bill

more sloping head

longer bill

OCCURRENCE
Breeding habitat is somewhat varied, but is generally close to fairly shallow, small lakes. Winters along both coasts. Populations wintering farther north prefer water over cobbles, gravel, or offshore ledges, whereas in southern locations, sandier habitats are chosen.

Length **17–21in (43–53cm)**	Wingspan **31–35in (79–90cm)**	Weight **1¾–2¾lb (0.8–1.2kg)**
Social **Flocks**	Lifespan **At least 8 years**	Status **Declining**

DATE: _____ TIME: _____ LOCATION: _____

| Order **Anseriformes** | Family **Anatidae** | Species *Clangula hyemalis* |

Long-tailed Duck

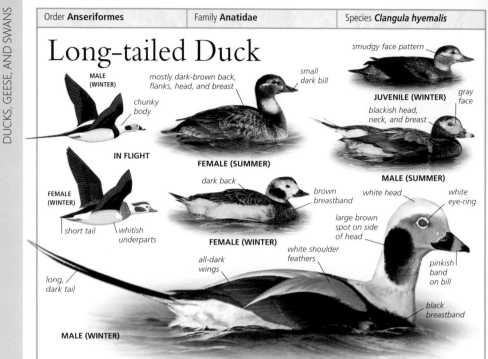

MALE (WINTER)

chunky body

IN FLIGHT

mostly dark-brown back, flanks, head, and breast

small dark bill

FEMALE (SUMMER)

smudgy face pattern

JUVENILE (WINTER)

gray face

blackish head, neck, and breast

dark back

brown breastband

white head

MALE (SUMMER)

white eye-ring

large brown spot on side of head

FEMALE (WINTER)

white shoulder feathers

pinkish band on bill

black breastband

FEMALE (WINTER)

short tail

whitish underparts

all-dark wings

long, dark tail

MALE (WINTER)

The Long-tailed Duck is a small, pudgy sea duck with a wide range of plumages depending on the season and the sex of the bird. The male has two extremely long tail feathers, which are often held up in the air like a pennant. The male's loud calls are quite musical, and, when heard from a flock, have a chorus-like quality, hence the name *Clangula*, which is Latin for "loud." This species can dive for a prolonged period of time, and can reach depths of 200ft (60m), making it one of the deepest diving ducks. Its three-part molt is more complex than that of other ducks.

VOICE Male call a *ang-ang-eeeooo* with yodelling quality; female barking *urk* or *uk* alarm call.

NESTING Shallow depression in ground lined with plant matter; 6–9 eggs; 1 brood; May–September.

FEEDING Dives to bottom of freshwater or saltwater habitats for mollusks, crustaceans, insects, fish, and roe.

FLIGHT: flies low over the water, somewhat erratically, with fast, fluttering wing beats.

UNMISTAKABLE MALE
In winter, dark wings, a white body with black breast-band, and a long tail make this male unmistakable.

SIMILAR SPECIES

BUFFLEHEAD ♀
see p.55

white wing patch

white cheek patch

BLACK GUILLEMOT ✿

pale rump

white wing patches

OCCURRENCE
Breeds in Arctic and sub-Arctic, nesting in small groups on islands and peninsulas on lakes, less commonly on tundra and freshwater ponds on islands. Winters mostly along rocky coasts and headlands, protected bays, or on large freshwater lakes.

| Length **14–23in (35–58cm)** | Wingspan **28in (72cm)** | Weight **18–39oz (500–1,100g)** |
| Social **Flocks** | Lifespan **Up to 22 years** | Status **Declining** |

DATE: _____ TIME:_____ LOCATION:_____

Bufflehead 🔊

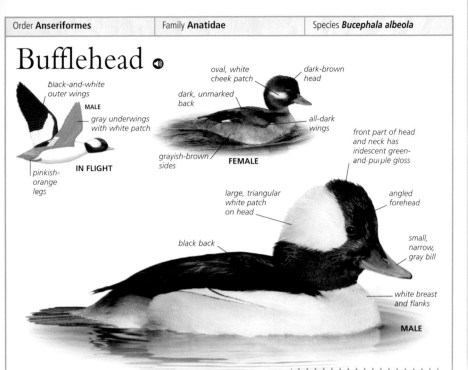

black-and-white outer wings

MALE

gray underwings with white patch

IN FLIGHT

pinkish-orange legs

oval, white cheek patch

dark, unmarked back

grayish-brown sides

FEMALE

dark-brown head

all-dark wings

front part of head and neck has iridescent green- and purple gloss

large, triangular white patch on head

black back

angled forehead

small, narrow, gray bill

white breast and flanks

MALE

The smallest diving duck in North America, the Bufflehead is a close relative of the Common and Barrow's Goldeneyes. Males make a bold statement with their striking head pattern. In flight, males resemble the larger Common Goldeneye, yet the large white area on their head makes them easy to distinguish. The Common Goldeneye's wings create a whirring sound in flight whereas the Bufflehead's do not. The northern limit of the Bufflehead's breeding range corresponds to that of the Northern Flicker, as the ducks usually nest in abandoned flicker cavities.
VOICE Male a low growl or squeal; chattering during breeding; female mostly silent except during courtship or calling to nestlings.
NESTING Cavity-nester, no nesting material added, near water; 7–9 eggs; 1 brood; April–September.
FEEDING Dives for aquatic invertebrates: usually insects in freshwater, mollusks and crustaceans in saltwater; also eats seeds.

FLIGHT: very rapid wing beats, no flight sound, unlike Goldeneyes.

IMMEDIATE TAKEOFF
Unlike other diving ducks, the small, compact Bufflehead can take off almost vertically.

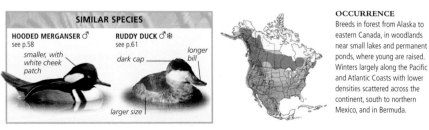

SIMILAR SPECIES

HOODED MERGANSER ♂
see p.58

smaller, with white cheek patch

RUDDY DUCK ♂ ✳
see p.61

dark cap

longer bill

larger size

OCCURRENCE
Breeds in forest from Alaska to eastern Canada, in woodlands near small lakes and permanent ponds, where young are raised. Winters largely along the Pacific and Atlantic Coasts with lower densities scattered across the continent, south to northern Mexico, and in Bermuda.

| Length **12½–15½in (32–39cm)** | Wingspan **21½–24in (54–61cm)** | Weight **10–18oz (275–500g)** |
| Social **Flocks** | Lifespan **Up to 15 years** | Status **Secure** |

DATE: _____ TIME: _____ LOCATION: _____

| Order **Anseriformes** | Family **Anatidae** | Species ***Bucephala clangula*** |

Common Goldeneye

white wing patch with two bars

FEMALE

white collar

mostly white inner wing

MALE (WINTER)

IN FLIGHT

dusky underwing

white patches on flanks and wings

warm brown head

bright-yellow eye

MALE (1ST WINTER)

FEMALE

large, round white spot

iridescent green head

extensive white shoulder feathers

MALE (WINTER)

Common Goldeneyes closely resemble Barrow's Goldeneyes. Found in North America and Eurasia, this is a medium-sized, compact, diving duck. It is aggressive and very competitive with members of its own species, as well as other cavity-nesting ducks. It regularly lays eggs in the nests of other species—a behavior that is almost parasitic. Before diving, the Common Goldeneye flattens its feathers in preparation for underwater foraging. The female's head shape changes according to her posture.

VOICE Courting males make a faint *peent* call; females a harsh *gack* or repeated *cuk* calls.

NESTING Cavity-nester in holes made by other birds, including Pileated Woodpeckers, in broken branches or hollow trees; also commonly uses nest boxes; 4–13 eggs; 1 brood; April–September.

FEEDING Dives during breeding season for insects; in winter, mollusks and crustaceans; sometimes eats fish and plant matter.

FLIGHT: rapid with fast wing beats; male's wings make a tinkling sound in flight.

MALE TAKING OFF
Quite a long takeoff, involving energetic running on the water, leaves a trail of spray.

SIMILAR SPECIES

BUFFLEHEAD ♀
see p.55

smaller overall

white oval patch behind eye

BARROW'S GOLDENEYE ♂
see p.57

smaller bill

large crescent on face

OCCURRENCE
Breeds along wetlands, lakes, and rivers with clear water in northern forests, where large trees provide appropriate nest cavities. Winters across continent, with highest densities located from north New England to the mid-Atlantic on coastal bays and in the West from coastal southeast Alaska to British Columbia.

| Length **15½–20in (40–51cm)** | Wingspan **30–33in (77–83cm)** | Weight **19–44oz (550–1,300g)** |
| Social **Flocks** | Lifespan **Up to 15 years** | Status **Secure** |

DATE: _____ TIME:_____ LOCATION:_____

Barrow's Goldeneye

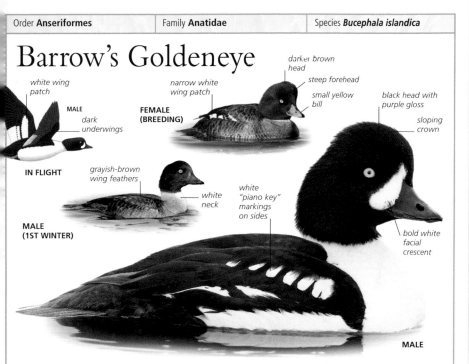

darker brown head

steep forehead

small yellow bill

black head with purple gloss

sloping crown

white wing patch

narrow white wing patch

MALE

dark underwings

FEMALE (BREEDING)

IN FLIGHT

grayish-brown wing feathers

white neck

white "piano key" markings on sides

MALE (1ST WINTER)

bold white facial crescent

MALE

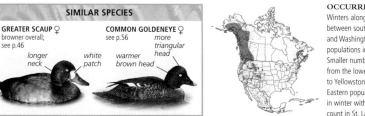

Barrow's Goldeneye is a slightly larger, darker version of the Common Goldeneye. Although the female can be identified by its different head structure and bill color, the bill color varies seasonally and geographically. Eastern Barrow's have blacker bills with less yellow, and western populations have entirely yellow bills, which darken in summer. During the breeding season, the majority of Barrow's Goldeneyes are found in mountainous regions of northwest North America.

VOICE Males normally silent; courting males grunt *ka-KAA*; females *cuc* call, slightly higher pitched than Common Goldeneye.

NESTING Tree cavity in holes formed by Pileated Woodpeckers, often broken limbs or hollow trees; also uses nest boxes; 6–12 eggs; 1 brood; April–September.

FEEDING Dives in summer for insects, some fish, and roe; in winter, mainly mollusks and crustaceans; some plant matter.

rapid flight with fast, deep wing beats; flies near water surface on short flights.

COURTING DISPLAY
A male thrusts his head back and gives a guttural call. His feet then kick back, driving him forward.

SIMILAR SPECIES

GREATER SCAUP ♀
browner overall;
see p.46

longer neck

white patch

COMMON GOLDENEYE ♀
see p.56

more triangular head

warmer brown head

OCCURRENCE
Winters along the Pacific Coast between southeast Alaska and Washington, with small populations in eastern Canada. Smaller numbers found inland from the lower Colorado River to Yellowstone National Park. Eastern population is localized in winter with the highest count in St. Lawrence estuary.

| Length **17–19in (43–48cm)** | Wingspan **28–30in (71–76cm)** | Weight **17–46oz (475–1,300g)** |
| Social **Flocks** | Lifespan **Up to 18 years** | Status **Special Concern** |

DATE: _____ TIME: _____ LOCATION: _____

| Order **Anseriformes** | Family **Anatidae** | Species *Lophodytes cucullatus* |

Hooded Merganser

IN FLIGHT
- triangular wings
- black-and-white inner wing patch
- long tail

MALE (BREEDING)

FEMALE
- reddish-tinged crest (folded)
- brownish-buff eye
- yellow-based thin black bill
- brownish-gray flanks

MALE (ECLIPSE)
- small gray-brown crest (raised)
- striking yellow eye

MALE (BREEDING)
- longish tail, often raised
- crested black-and-white head (crest not raised)
- black back
- yellow eye
- thin, black, serrated bill
- white breast
- warm-brown flanks
- bold vertical bars

This dapper, miniature fish-eater is the smallest of the three mergansers. Both male and female Hooded Mergansers have crests that they can raise or flatten. When the male raises his crest, the thin, horizontal, white stripe turns into a gorgeous white fan, surrounded by black. Although easily identified when swimming, the Hooded Merganser and the Wood Duck can be confused when seen in flight since they both are fairly small, with bushy heads and long tails.

VOICE Normally silent; during courtship, males produce a low, growly, descending *pah-hwaaaaa*, reminiscent of a frog; females give a soft *rrrep*.

NESTING Cavity-nester; nest lined with down feathers in a tree or box close to or over water; 6–15 eggs; 1 brood; February–June.

FEEDING Dives for fish, aquatic insects, and crayfish, preferably in clear and shallow fresh waters, but also in brackish waters.

FLIGHT: low, fast, and direct; shallow wing beats; quiet whirring noise produced by wings.

FANHEAD SPECTACULAR
The male's magnificent black-and-white fan of a crest is like a beacon in the late afternoon light.

SIMILAR SPECIES

WOOD DUCK ♀
see p.33
- bold white eye-ring
- blue wing patch

RED-BREASTED MERGANSER ♀
see p.60
- steel gray-and-white plumage
- rustier head with ragged crest

OCCURRENCE
Prefers forested small ponds, marshes, or slow-moving streams during the breeding season. During winter, occurs in shallow water in both fresh- and saltwater bays, estuaries, rivers, streams, ponds, freshwater marshes, and flooded sloughs.

| Length **15½–19½in (40–49cm)** | Wingspan **23½–26in (60–66cm)** | Weight **16–31oz (450–875g)** |
| Social **Small flocks** | Lifespan **At least 11 years** | Status **Secure** |

DATE: _____ TIME: _____ LOCATION: _____

| Order **Anseriformes** | Family **Anatidae** | Species **Mergus merganser** |

Common Merganser

dark outer wing

gray-and-white inner wing

reddish-brown head

FEMALE

silver-gray upperparts

bright rusty-brown head

black-tipped red bill

FEMALE

small white spot above eye

short, ragged crest

JUVENILE

thin black bar

gray rump and tail

MALE (NONBREEDING)

black head

IN FLIGHT

all-white or tinged-pink underparts

iridescent blackish-green head

long nape feathers

black center

black eye

reddish-orange hooked bill

serrated sides on bill

white breast and underparts

MALE (BREEDING)

The largest of the three merganser species in North America, the Common Merganser is called a Goosander in the UK. This large fish-eater is common and widespread, particularly in the northern portion of its range. It is often found in big flocks on lakes or smaller groups along rivers. It spends most of its time on the water, using its serrated bill to catch fish underwater.
VOICE Mostly silent, except when alarmed or during courtship; females give a low-pitched harsh *karr* or *gruk*, the latter also given in series; during courtship, males emit a high-pitched, bell-like note and other twangy notes; alarm call a hoarse *grrr* or *wak*.
NESTING Cavity-nester sometimes high in trees; uses nest boxes, nests on ground; 6–17 eggs; 1 brood; April–September.
FEEDING Eats mostly fish (especially fond of trout and salmon, but also carp and catfish), aquatic invertebrates, frogs, small mammals, birds, and plants.

FLIGHT: fast with shallow wing beats; often flying low over the water.

FEEDING ON THE MOVE
This female Common Merganser is trying to swallow, headfirst, a rather large fish.

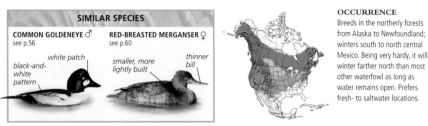

SIMILAR SPECIES

COMMON GOLDENEYE ♂
see p.56

white patch

black-and-white pattern

RED-BREASTED MERGANSER ♀
see p.60

smaller, more lightly built

thinner bill

OCCURRENCE
Breeds in the northerly forests from Alaska to Newfoundland; winters south to north central Mexico. Being very hardy, it will winter farther north than most other waterfowl as long as water remains open. Prefers fresh- to saltwater locations.

| Length **21½–28in (54–71cm)** | Wingspan **34in (86cm)** | Weight **1¾–4¾lb (0.8–2.1kg)** |
| Social **Flocks** | Lifespan **Up to 13 years** | Status **Secure** |

DATE: _____ TIME: _____ LOCATION: _____

| Order **Anseriformes** | Family **Anatidae** | Species **_Mergus serrator_** |

Red-breasted Merganser

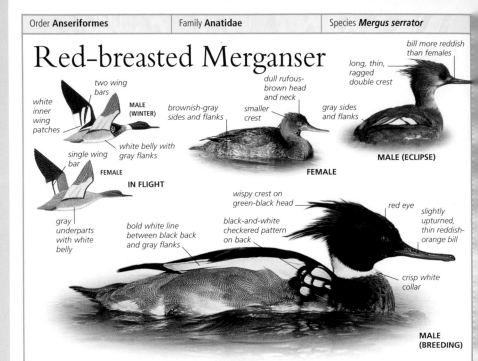

two wing bars

white inner wing patches

MALE (WINTER)

brownish-gray sides and flanks

dull rufous-brown head and neck

smaller crest

gray sides and flanks

bill more reddish than females

long, thin, ragged double crest

MALE (ECLIPSE)

FEMALE

single wing bar

white belly with gray flanks

FEMALE

IN FLIGHT

gray underparts with white belly

bold white line between black back and gray flanks

black-and-white checkered pattern on back

wispy crest on green-black head

red eye

slightly upturned, thin reddish-orange bill

crisp white collar

MALE (BREEDING)

The Red-breasted Merganser, like the other saw-billed mergansers, is an elegant fish-eating duck. Both sexes are easily recognized by their long, sparse, somewhat ragged-looking double crest. Red-breasted Mergansers are smaller than Common Mergansers, but much larger than the Hooded. The Red-breasted Merganser, unlike the other two mergansers, nests on the ground, in loose colonies, often among gulls and terns, and is protected by its neighbors.
VOICE During courtship males make a raucous _yeow-yeow_ call; females emit a raspy _krrr-krrr_.
NESTING Shallow depression on ground lined with down and plant material, near water; 5–11 eggs; 1 brood; May–July.
FEEDING Dives for small fish, such as herring and minnows; also salmon eggs; at times flocks coordinate and drive fish together.

FLIGHT: fast flying duck with very rapid, regular, and shallow flapping.

KEEPING CLOSE
Red-breasted Mergansers are gregarious at all times of year, often feeding in loose flocks.

SIMILAR SPECIES

HOODED MERGANSER ♀
see p.58

darker back

fuller cinnamon-tinged crest

smaller overall

COMMON MERGANSER ♀
see p.59

smaller bill

rusty-red head full crest

larger and more robust

white breast and chin

OCCURRENCE
Most northerly range of all the mergansers, nests across the Arctic and sub-Arctic regions, tundra and northerly forests, along coasts, inland lakes, river banks, marsh edges, and coastal islands. Winters farther south than other mergansers, mostly in protected bays, estuaries, or on the Great Lakes.

| Length **20–25in (51–64cm)** | Wingspan **26–29in (66–74cm)** | Weight **1¾–2¾lb (0.8–1.3kg)** |
| Social **Flocks/Colonies** | Lifespan **Up to 9 years** | Status **Secure** |

DATE: _____ TIME:_____ LOCATION:_____

| Order **Anseriformes** | Family **Anatidae** | Species *Oxyura jamaicensis* |

Ruddy Duck 🔊

broad, short wings with whitish wing linings

dull, gray-brown, two-tone body

duller head

blackish bill

pale belly

MALE (BREEDING)
IN FLIGHT

MALE (NONBREEDING)

arched dark line on cheek

dark bill

brownish upperparts

paler flanks

FEMALE

black cap and nape

large head

bright-blue bill, slightly knobby at base

large white cheek patches

rich cinnamon body and neck

long tail, often erect

MALE (BREEDING)

Small and stiff-tailed, the Ruddy Duck is comical in both its appearance and behavior. Both sexes often hold their tail in a cocked position, especially when sleeping. During courtship displays, the male points its long tail skyward while rapidly thumping its electric-blue bill against its chest, ending the performance with an odd, bubbling sound. In another display, males make a popping sound by slapping their feet on the water's surface. Large feet, on legs set far back on its body, make the Ruddy Duck an excellent swimmer and diver; however, on land it is perhaps one of the most awkward of diving ducks. Females are known to push themselves along instead of walking.

VOICE Females give a nasal *raanh* and high-pitched *eeek*; males are vocally silent, but make popping noises with feet.

NESTING Platform, bowl-shaped nest built over water in thick emergent vegetation, rarely on land; 6–10 eggs; 1 brood; May–September.

FEEDING Dives for aquatic insects, larvae, crustaceans, and other invertebrates, particularly when breeding; during winter, also eats plants.

FLIGHT: rapid and direct, with fast wing beats; not very agile in flight, which seems labored.

HEAVY HEAD
A female "sitting" on the water streamlines her body ready to dive, making her look large-headed.

SIMILAR SPECIES

MASKED DUCK ♂

black tip to bill

black face

ruddy-colored back with black streaks

OCCURRENCE
Breeds in the Prairie Pothole Region in wetland habitats; marshes, ponds, reservoirs, and other open shallow water with emergent vegetation and open areas. Majority winter on freshwater habitats from ponds to large lakes; smaller numbers found on brackish coastal marshes, bays, and estuaries.

Length **14–17in (35–43cm)**	Wingspan **22–24in (56–62cm)**	Weight **11–30oz (300–850g)**
Social **Flocks**	Lifespan **Up to 13 years**	Status **Secure**

DATE: _____ TIME: _____ LOCATION: _____

Families **Odontophoridae, Phasianidae**

QUAILS, GROUSE, TURKEYS, AND RELATIVES

THIS DIVERSE AND ADAPTABLE group of birds thrives in habitats ranging from hot desert to frozen tundra. They spend most of the time on the ground, springing loudly into the air when alarmed.

NEW WORLD QUAILS
Among the most terrestrial of all galliforms, quails are also renowned for their great sociability, often forming large family groups, or "coveys," of up to 100 birds. The five species found in western North America each live in a specific habitat or at a particular elevation, although the California Quail is becoming more common in parks and suburban areas.

GROUSE
The most diverse and widespread birds in the order Galliformes in North America, the 12 different species of grouse can be divided into three groups based on their preferred habitats. Forest grouse include the

Ruffed Grouse in the East, the Spruce Grouse in the North,

GRASSLAND GROUSE
The aptly named Sharp-tailed Grouse is locally common in the western prairies, strutting in search of grasshoppers.

and the Sooty Grouse and Dusky Grouse in the West. Prairie grouse, including the Sharp-tailed Grouse, are found throughout the middle of the continent. All three tundra and mountaintop grouse or ptarmigans are found in the extreme North and the Rockies. Grouse often possess patterns that match their surroundings, providing camouflage from enemies both animal and human.

DRESSED TO THRILL
With its striking plumage, the Ring-necked Pheasant is an impressive sight when flushed out of its cover.

PHEASANTS AND PARTRIDGES
These Eurasian birds were introduced into North America in the 19th and 20th centuries to provide additional targets for recreational hunters. While some introductions failed, species such as the colorful Ring-necked Pheasant adapted well in the new environment and now thrive in established populations.

SNOW BIRD
The Rock Ptarmigan's white winter plumage camouflages it against the snow, helping to hide it from predators.

| Order **Galliformes** | Family **Odontophoridae** | Species *Callipepla californica* |

California Quail 🔊

IN FLIGHT

bluish-gray overall

MALE (GRAY FORM)

duller, grayish-brown face

FEMALE (GRAY FORM)

darker gray breast

comb-like feathers on forehead

fine white dots on back of neck

curled crest

white "necklace"

bluish-gray breast

belly has scale-like appearance

solid, dark grayish-brown chest

FEMALE (BROWN FORM)

MALE (GRAY FORM)

streaked undertail feathers

FLIGHT: loud, whirring takeoff and short bursts of rapid wing beats.

The most widespread of the western North American quails, the California Quail thrives in a wide variety of habitats. In many parts of their range, these dapper birds are becoming increasingly common in parks and suburban habitats. This adaptability, and their popularity among hunters, has led to the California Quail being introduced throughout Mexico, the western US, and southern British Columbia, as well as Hawaii, New Zealand, Australia, Chile, and other areas outside North America.

VOICE Separated covey call three-syllable *chi-CA-go*; males use extended *cow* followed by *way way*, also low *kurrr*.

NESTING Shallow depression lined with grasses and hidden by vegetation; 10–12 eggs; 1 brood; May–August.

FEEDING Feeds primarily on green leaves and other plant matter; takes insects when available.

BIRDS OF A FEATHER
These gregarious quails are regularly found in flocks of up to 50 individuals.

SIMILAR SPECIES

MOUNTAIN QUAIL
long, straight plumes
"zebra stripes" on underparts

GAMBEL'S QUAIL
no scaling on belly

OCCURRENCE
Native range at mid- to low elevations along the mountain ranges and valleys from Baja California northward to central Oregon; introduced into southern British Columbia. Prefers mixture of patchy oak scrub combined with agriculture and fallow fields. A permanent resident.

| Length **9–11in (24–28cm)** | Wingspan **12–14in (30–35cm)** | Weight **6–7oz (175–200g)** |
| Social **Flocks** | Lifespan **Up to 6 years** | Status **Secure (p)** |

DATE: _____ TIME: _____ LOCATION: _____

Order **Galliformes**	Family **Phasianidae**	Species *Alectoris chukar*

Chukar

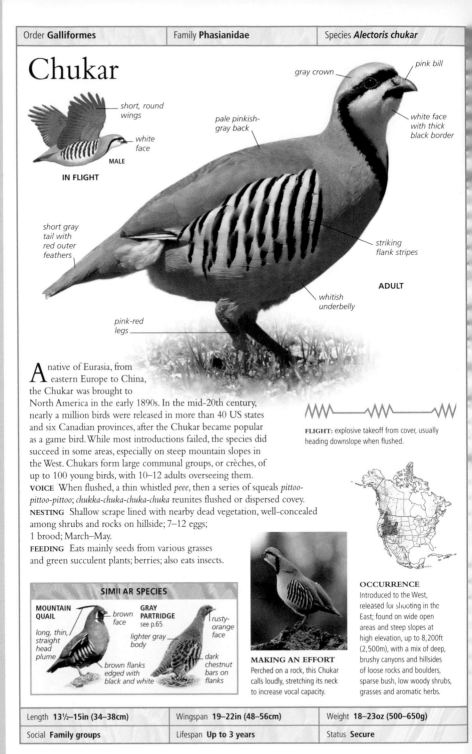

IN FLIGHT

short, round wings

white face

MALE

gray crown

pink bill

pale pinkish-gray back

white face with thick black border

short gray tail with red outer feathers

striking flank stripes

ADULT

whitish underbelly

pink-red legs

A native of Eurasia, from eastern Europe to China, the Chukar was brought to North America in the early 1890s. In the mid-20th century, nearly a million birds were released in more than 40 US states and six Canadian provinces, after the Chukar became popular as a game bird. While most introductions failed, the species did succeed in some areas, especially on steep mountain slopes in the West. Chukars form large communal groups, or crèches, of up to 100 young birds, with 10–12 adults overseeing them.

VOICE When flushed, a thin whistled *peee*, then a series of squeals *pittoo-pittoo-pittoo*; *chukka-chuka-chuka-chuka* reunites flushed or dispersed covey.

NESTING Shallow scrape lined with nearby dead vegetation, well-concealed among shrubs and rocks on hillside; 7–12 eggs; 1 brood; March–May.

FEEDING Eats mainly seeds from various grasses and green succulent plants; berries; also eats insects.

FLIGHT: explosive takeoff from cover, usually heading downslope when flushed.

SIMILAR SPECIES

MOUNTAIN QUAIL

long, thin, straight head plume

brown face

brown flanks edged with black and white

GRAY PARTRIDGE
see p.65

lighter gray body

rusty-orange face

dark chestnut bars on flanks

MAKING AN EFFORT
Perched on a rock, this Chukar calls loudly, stretching its neck to increase vocal capacity.

OCCURRENCE
Introduced to the West, released for shooting in the East; found on wide open areas and steep slopes at high elevation, up to 8,200ft (2,500m), with a mix of deep, brushy canyons and hillsides of loose rocks and boulders, sparse bush, low woody shrubs, grasses and aromatic herbs.

Length **13½–15in (34–38cm)**	Wingspan **19–22in (48–56cm)**	Weight **18–23oz (500–650g)**
Social **Family groups**	Lifespan **Up to 3 years**	Status **Secure**

DATE: _____ TIME: _____ LOCATION: _____

| Order **Galliformes** | Family **Phasianidae** | Species **Perdix perdix** |

Gray Partridge

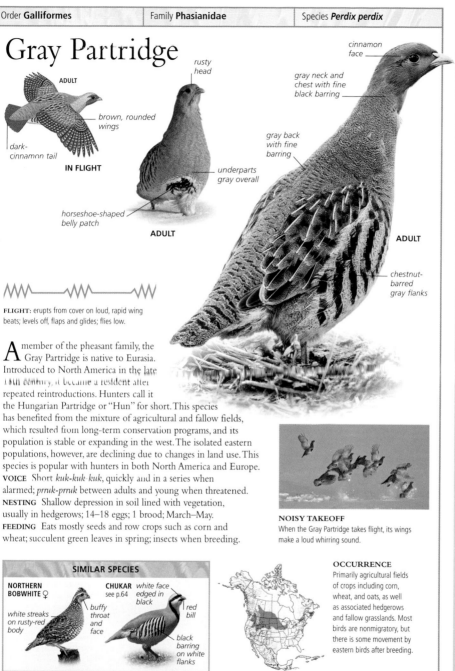

cinnamon face

gray neck and chest with fine black barring

rusty head

ADULT

brown, rounded wings

dark-cinnamon tail

IN FLIGHT

gray back with fine barring

underparts gray overall

horseshoe-shaped belly patch

ADULT

ADULT

chestnut-barred gray flanks

FLIGHT: erupts from cover on loud, rapid wing beats; levels off, flaps and glides; flies low.

A member of the pheasant family, the Gray Partridge is native to Eurasia. Introduced to North America in the late 18th century, it became a resident after repeated reintroductions. Hunters call it the Hungarian Partridge or "Hun" for short. This species has benefited from the mixture of agricultural and fallow fields, which resulted from long-term conservation programs, and its population is stable or expanding in the west. The isolated eastern populations, however, are declining due to changes in land use. This species is popular with hunters in both North America and Europe.

VOICE Short *kuk-kuk-kuk*, quickly and in a series when alarmed; *prruk-prruk* between adults and young when threatened.

NESTING Shallow depression in soil lined with vegetation, usually in hedgerows; 14–18 eggs; 1 brood; March–May.

FEEDING Eats mostly seeds and row crops such as corn and wheat; succulent green leaves in spring; insects when breeding.

NOISY TAKEOFF
When the Gray Partridge takes flight, its wings make a loud whirring sound.

SIMILAR SPECIES

NORTHERN BOBWHITE ♀

white streaks on rusty-red body

CHUKAR see p.64

white face edged in black

red bill

buffy throat and face

black barring on white flanks

OCCURRENCE
Primarily agricultural fields of crops including corn, wheat, and oats, as well as associated hedgerows and fallow grasslands. Most birds are nonmigratory, but there is some movement by eastern birds after breeding.

| Length **11–13in (28–33cm)** | Wingspan **17–20in (43–51cm)** | Weight **12–18oz (350–500g)** |
| Social **Family groups** | Lifespan **Up to 4 years** | Status **Declining** |

DATE: _____ TIME: _____ LOCATION: _____

| Order **Galliformes** | Family **Phasianidae** | Species *Phasianus colchicus* |

Ring-necked Pheasant 🔊

MALE
long tail
short, round wings
pale rump

FEMALE
pointed tail
IN FLIGHT

pale-brown body
green-black head
orange-copper flanks
MALE (DARK FORM)

bold black markings
red face wattles
FEMALE

iridescent "ear" tufts
white neck ring
iridescent bronze sheen

long, pointed tail

FLIGHT: bursts vertically from cover on loud, rapid wing beats; levels off, flaps, then glides.

barred underparts

MALE

A native of Asia, the variable-looking Ring-necked Pheasant was originally introduced in North America for recreational hunting purposes, and is now widely distributed across North America. Birds released after being bred in captivity are used to supplement natural reproduction for hunting purposes. In the wild, several females may lay eggs in the same nest—a phenomenon called "egg-dumping." There is a less common dark form, which can be distinguished principally because it lacks the distinctive white band around the neck.

VOICE Male emits a loud, raucous, explosive double note, *Karrk-KORK*, followed by loud wing-flapping; both sexes cackle when flushed.

NESTING Shallow bowl composed of grasses, usually on ground in tall grass or among low shrubs; 7–15 eggs; 1 brood; March–June.

FEEDING Feeds on corn and other grain, seeds, fruit, row crops, grass, leaves, and shoots; eats insects when available.

SIMILAR SPECIES

GREATER SAGE-GROUSE
larger; see p.68
long, dark tail
pale breast
dark belly

SHARP-TAILED GROUSE
slightly smaller; see p.75
shorter tail
darker brown overall

FLUSHED OUT
The Ring-necked Pheasant is a powerful flier when alarmed or flushed out of its cover.

OCCURRENCE
Widespread across southern Canada and the US; prefers mixture of active agricultural crops (especially corn fields), fallow fields, and hedgerows; also cattail marshes and wooded river bottoms. The Ring-necked Pheasant is native to Asia from the Caucasus to China.

| Length **19½–28in (50–70cm)** | Wingspan **30–34in (76–86cm)** | Weight **1¼–6½lb (0.5–3kg)** |
| Social **Solitary/Flocks** | Lifespan **Up to 4 years** | Status **Secure** |

DATE: _____ TIME: _____ LOCATION: _____

| Order **Galliformes** | Family **Phasianidae** | Species *Bonasa umbellus* |

Ruffed Grouse 🔊

ADULT (RUFOUS FORM)

IN FLIGHT

brown-barred underparts

rusty tail with black band

heavy white spotting on brown upperparts

dark patch on neck

raised crest

ADULT (RUFOUS FORM)

feathered legs

spotted-gray upperparts

gray-barred underparts

ADULT (GRAY FORM)

The Ruffed Grouse is perhaps the most widespread galliform in North America. There are two color forms, rufous and gray. Both allow the birds to remain camouflaged and undetected on the forest floor, until they eventually burst into the air in an explosion of whirring wings. The male is well known for his extraordinary wing beating or "drumming" display, which he performs year-round, but most frequently in the spring.

VOICE Hissing notes, and soft *purrt, purrt, purrt* when alarmed, by both sexes; male's "drumming" display when heard from distance resembles beating fists on one's chest, *thump…thump…thump…thump… thump…thuthuthuth.*
NESTING Shallow, leaf-lined bowl set against a tree trunk, rock or fallen log in forest; 6–14 eggs; 1 brood; March–June.
FEEDING Forages on ground for leaves, buds, and fruit; occasionally insects.

FLIGHT: an explosive takeoff, usually at close range, glides for a short distance before landing.

OCCURRENCE
Found in young, mixed habitat forests throughout northern US and Canada. Southern edge of range extends along higher elevations of the Appalachians and middle levels of the Rocky Mountains, if suitable habitat is available.

SIMILAR SPECIES

SPRUCE GROUSE ♀
smaller overall;
see p.69

rusty-orange tip

shorter tail

DUSKY GROUSE
see p.73

larger and darker overall

heavier barring on chest

less barring

WARM RED
The rufous form of the Ruffed Grouse is more common in hotter parts of the continent.

| Length **17–20in (43–51cm)** | Wingspan **20–23in (51–58cm)** | Weight **20–22oz (575–625g)** |
| Social **Solitary/Small flocks** | Lifespan **Up to 10 years** | Status **Secure** |

DATE: _____ TIME: _____ LOCATION: _____

Order **Galliformes**	Family **Phasianidae**	Species ***Centrocercus urophasianus***

Greater Sage-Grouse

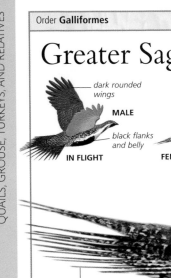

— dark rounded wings

MALE

— black flanks and belly

IN FLIGHT

smaller and drabber overall

FEMALE

black belly

dark head with dull yellowish eye combs

sparse nape plume

white neck and breast

mottled black, brown, and white back

spiky, pointed tail fanned in display

MALE

FLIGHT: fast, strong; rapid initial wing beats at takeoff, followed by a glide-and-flap sequence.

The Greater Sage-Grouse is by far the largest native North American grouse. Each spring, the males gather on communal sites, known as leks, where they compete for females with spectacular courtship displays. As many as 40 males may gather at a lek for these events. Once widespread, Greater Sage-Grouse populations have declined, as human encroachment on sagebrush habitats has increased.

VOICE Clucks repeatedly when flushed; male makes odd popping sounds with throat sacs when displaying.

NESTING Depression scraped into soil next to protective cover of grass or sagebrush branches; 6–10 eggs; 1 brood; March–May.

FEEDING Eats mainly sagebrush leaves; also eats insects, fruit, flowers, and succulent green plants when available.

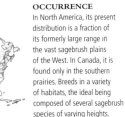

IMPRESSIVE SHOW
The male's courtship display is remarkable—he inflates his air sacs, fans his tail and struts around.

SIMILAR SPECIES

GUNNISON SAGE-GROUSE
thicker plume

RING-NECKED PHEASANT ♀
see p.66

smaller overall

pale-brown belly

OCCURRENCE
In North America, its present distribution is a fraction of its formerly large range in the vast sagebrush plains of the West. In Canada, it is found only in the southern prairies. Breeds in a variety of habitats, the ideal being composed of several sagebrush species of varying heights.

Length **19½–30in (50–76cm)**	Wingspan **32–39in (81–99cm)**	Weight **2½–6½lb (1–3kg)**
Social **Flocks**	Lifespan **Up to 6 years**	Status **Vulnerable**

DATE: _____ TIME:_____ LOCATION:_____

| Order **Galliformes** | Family **Phasianidae** | Species ***Canachites canadensis*** |

Spruce Grouse

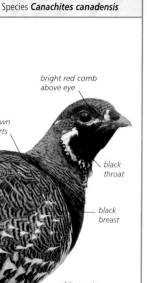

MALE (FRANKLIN'S)

ADULT

paler overall

FEMALE (TAIGA)

bright red comb above eye

mottled gray-brown upperparts

heavy barring on underparts

IN FLIGHT

white spots on black tail

black throat

black breast

gray upperparts

heavily barred underparts

white spots on underparts

MALE
C. c. canadensis
(TAIGA)

FEMALE
C. c. franklinii
(FRANKLIN'S)

mostly blackish tail with rufous tip

Perhaps because of the remoteness of their habitat and lack of human contact, Spruce Grouse are not afraid of humans. This lack of wariness when approached has earned them the name "fool hens." Their specialized diet of pine needles causes the intestinal tract to expand in order to accommodate a larger volume of food to compensate for its low nutritional value. There are two groups of Spruce Grouse, the Taiga and the Franklin's, both of which have red and gray forms.

VOICE Mostly silent; males clap their wings during courtship display; females often utter a long cackle at dawn and dusk.
NESTING Lined with moss, leaves, feathers; often at base of tree; naturally low area in forest floor; 4–6 eggs; 1 brood; May–July.
FEEDING Feeds mostly on pine but also spruce needles; will eat insects, leaves, fruit, and seeds when available.

FLIGHT: generally avoids flying; when disturbed, bursts into flight on whirring wings.

RUFOUS BAND
The male "Taiga" form displays the thin rufous band on the tip of his tail.

SIMILAR SPECIES

RUFFED GROUSE
see p.67
lighter overall
wide black band on tail tip
longer tail

DUSKY GROUSE
see p.73
much larger
longer charcoal-gray tail
grayer overall

OCCURRENCE
Present year-round in forests dominated by conifers, including Jack pine, lodgepole pine, red spruce, black spruce, balsam fir, subalpine fir, hemlock, and cedar. Found from western Alaska to the Atlantic Coast.

| Length **14–17in (36–43cm)** | Wingspan **21–23in (53–58cm)** | Weight **16oz (450g)** |
| Social **Solitary** | Lifespan **Up to 10 years** | Status **Secure** |

DATE: _____ TIME: _____ LOCATION: _____

| Order **Galliformes** | Family **Phasianidae** | Species *Lagopus lagopus* |

Willow Ptarmigan

reddish-brown body

black tail

white between eye and black bill

ADULT (WINTER)

all-white body

black bill

red comb

black bill

rich reddish-brown body

IN FLIGHT

MALE (SUMMER)

lacks red comb

ADULT (WINTER)

yellow-brown body

dark scaly bars

white belly

FEMALE (SUMMER)

MALE (SUMMER)

feathered feet

FLIGHT: strong, rapid wing beats before gliding; prefers to walk.

The most common of the three ptarmigan species, the Willow Ptarmigan also undertakes the longest migration of the group. The Willow Ptarmigan is an unusual Galliform species, as male and female remain bonded throughout the chick-rearing process, in which the male is an active participant. The Red Grouse of British moors is a subspecies (*L. l. scoticus*) of the Willow Ptarmigan, but it is classified as a separate species by some.

VOICE Variety of purrs, clucks, hissing, meowing noises; *Kow-Kow-Kow* call given before flushing, possibly alerting others.

NESTING Shallow bowl scraped in soil, lined with plant matter, protected by overhead cover; 8–10 eggs; 1 brood; March–May.

FEEDING Mostly eats buds, stems, and seeds, but also flowers, insects, and leaves when available.

PERFECT BLEND-IN
Its reddish-brown upperparts camouflage this summer ptarmigan in the shrubby areas it inhabits.

SIMILAR SPECIES

WHITE-TAILED PTARMIGAN ☼
see p.72

browner plumage

ROCK PTARMIGAN ☼
see p.71

grayer plumage

smaller overall

white belly

OCCURRENCE
Prefers tundra in the Arctic, sub-Arctic, and subalpine regions. Thrives in willow thickets along low moist river corridors; also in the low woodlands of the sub-Arctic tundra.

| Length **14–17½in (35–44cm)** | Wingspan **22–24in (56–61cm)** | Weight **15–28oz (425–800g)** |
| Social **Winter flocks** | Lifespan **Up to 9 years** | Status **Secure** |

DATE: _____ TIME:_____ LOCATION:_____

Order **Galliformes**	Family **Phasianidae**	Species *Lagopus muta*

Rock Ptarmigan

mostly gray upperparts

black tail

MALE (WINTER)

all-white wings

gray wing patch

IN FLIGHT

MALE (SUMMER)

black line between eye and bill

MALE (WINTER)

brown-and-black barring

white wings

small bill

small, round head

red comb

mottled belly

FEMALE (SUMMER)

"salt-and-pepper" barring on gray upperparts

small, delicate bill

white plumage

FEMALE (WINTER)

white belly

MALE (SUMMER)

feathered feet

FLIGHT: bursts into flight with rapid wing beats, followed by gliding and shallow flapping.

The Rock Ptarmigan is the most northerly of the three ptarmigan species found in North America. Although some birds make a short migration to more southern wintering grounds, many remain on their breeding grounds year-round. This species is well known for its distinctive seasonal variation in plumage, which helps to camouflage it against its surroundings. The Rock Ptarmigan is the official bird of Nunavut Territory.

VOICE Quiet; male call a raspy *krrrh*, also growls and clucks.
NESTING Small scrape or natural depression, lined with plant matter, often away from cover; 8–10 eggs; 1 brood; April–June.
FEEDING Feeds on buds, seeds, flowers, and leaves, especially birch and willow; eats insects in summer.

IN BETWEEN PLUMAGE
Various transitional plumage patterns can be seen on the Rock Ptarmigan in spring and fall.

SIMILAR SPECIES		
WHITE-TAILED PTARMIGAN ✸ all-white tail in winter; see p.72	**WILLOW PTARMIGAN** ✸ see p.70	
smaller overall	larger overall	
	lighter brown upperparts	

OCCURRENCE
Prefers dry, rocky tundra and shrubby ridge tops; will use edges of open meadows and dense evergreen stands along fairly high-elevation rivers and streams during winter. Occurs throughout the Northern Hemisphere in the Arctic tundra from Iceland to Kamchatka in far east Russia.

Length **12½–15½in (32–40cm)**	Wingspan **19½–23½in (50–60cm)**	Weight **16–23oz (450–650g)**
Social **Winter flocks**	Lifespan **Up to 8 years**	Status **Secure**

DATE: _____ TIME: _____ LOCATION: _____

| Order **Galliformes** | Family **Phasianidae** | Species *Lagopus leucura* |

White-tailed Ptarmigan

all-white overall

ADULT (WINTER)

IN FLIGHT

red naked skin over eye

lichen-like coloration and patterning

FEMALE (SUMMER)

small black bill

ADULT (WINTER)

varied breeding plumage is turning white with molting feathers

MALE (LATE SUMMER)

The smallest and most southerly of the three North American ptarmigans, the White-tailed Ptarmigan's native range is still largely intact. In the winter, its almost completely white plumage—unique among the Galliform species—blends it in perfectly to its icy mountainous home. Its plumage is one of several adaptations to the inhospitable environment it inhabits. The feathers on its feet increase the surface area in contact with the ground, and so help to prevent the bird from sinking into the snow.

VOICE Males emit various cackling clucks, *cuk-cuk-cuuuk* during display; females cluck, purr, and growl softly.

NESTING Scrape in ground lined with plants and feathers; 4–8 eggs; 1 brood; May–June.

FEEDING Feeds heavily on willows, eating mostly leaves, buds, and twigs; insects when nesting.

FLIGHT: rarely flies unless pursued; flush on explosive wing beats, then flap-and-glide sequence.

WHITE ON WHITE
Immobile on white snow, the male blends in superbly with the wintry surroundings.

SIMILAR SPECIES

ROCK PTARMIGAN ☼
see p.71
grayer summer plumage

larger overall

WILLOW PTARMIGAN ☼
see p.70
reddish-brown summer plumage

larger overall

red comb

white under-parts

OCCURRENCE
Has a more restricted distribution than Rock and Willow Ptarmigans, occurring from Alaska and the Yukon south to Idaho and Montana; small isolated populations exist in Colorado and New Hampshire. Associated with willow stands above tree-line; also meadows and evergreen stand mixtures.

| Length **12in (30–31cm)** | Wingspan **20–22in (51–56cm)** | Weight **12–16oz (350–450g)** |
| Social **Large flocks** | Lifespan **Up to 15 years** | Status **Secure** |

DATE: _____ TIME: _____ LOCATION: _____

| Order **Galliformes** | Family **Phasianidae** | Species *Dendragapus obscurus* |

Dusky Grouse

MALE

pale
underwing

IN FLIGHT

broad,
rounded
black tail

red wattle
over eye

bare red
or purple
air sacs

barred
crown
and neck

short, plain
brown wings

mottled-
brown back

small bill

gray belly

FEMALE

**MALE
(DISPLAY)**

gray
underparts

white
scales
on flanks

Once considered a Blue Grouse subspecies, the Dusky Grouse was later reclassified as a species in its own right, separate from the Sooty Grouse. Male Dusky Grouse can be identified by their courtship displays, which are primarily ground-based and quieter than those of the Sooty Grouse, and by their reddish-purple air sacs. The Dusky Grouse also has a plainer tail, lacking the grayer tip of the Sooty, and its chicks are more gray than brown.
VOICE A series of five soft hoots; also a hiss, growl, and cluck; females emit a whinnying cry.
NESTING Shallow scrape, usually lined with dead grass, leaves, or other plants, located under shrubs, against rocks or logs; 7–10 eggs; 1 brood; March–May.
FEEDING Feeds on leaves, flowers, fruit, also some insects; evergreen needles, buds, and cones in season.

FLIGHT: loud, short-distance flight with rapid wing beats before gliding to the ground.

FREEZING FOR SAFETY
This female Dusky Grouse stands still as a statue, relying on camouflage, not flight, for protection.

SIMILAR SPECIES

SPRUCE GROUSE ♀
see p.69

more
reddish
brown

smaller

shorter
tail

SOOTY GROUSE
see p.74

darker
overall

yellow
air sacs

OCCURRENCE
Found in the northern, central Rocky Mountains in Canada and the US in high or mid-altitude open forests and shrublands. Typically uses older, denser, mixed, or evergreen forests at higher elevations in winter, more open-country, lighter forests at lower elevations in summer.

| Length **16–20in (41–51cm)** | Wingspan **25–28in (64–71cm)** | Weight **2½–2¾lb (1.1–1.3kg)** |
| Social **Solitary/Winter flocks** | Lifespan **Up to 14 years** | Status **Localized** |

DATE: _____ TIME: _____ LOCATION: _____

Order **Galliformes**	Family **Phasianidae**	Species *Dendragapus fuliginosus*

Sooty Grouse

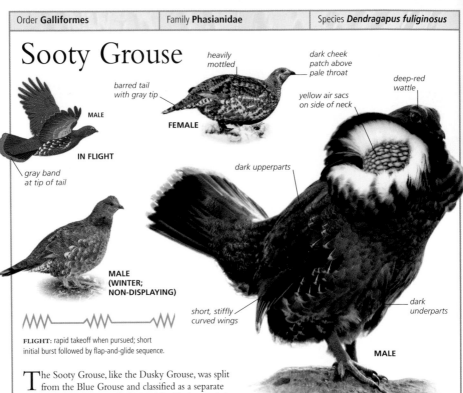

heavily mottled

barred tail with gray tip

MALE

IN FLIGHT

gray band at tip of tail

FEMALE

dark cheek patch above pale throat

yellow air sacs on side of neck

deep-red wattle

dark upperparts

MALE (WINTER; NON-DISPLAYING)

short, stiffly curved wings

dark underparts

MALE

FLIGHT: rapid takeoff when pursued; short initial burst followed by flap-and-glide sequence.

The Sooty Grouse, like the Dusky Grouse, was split from the Blue Grouse and classified as a separate species. Although primarily distinguished by its restriction to coastal mountain ranges, plumage and behavioral displays help differentiate the male Sooty Grouse from the Dusky Grouse. During courtship displays, which are most often performed in trees, the male Sooty Grouse shows rough yellow air sacs. Females and chicks have a browner overall appearance to their plumage than those of the Dusky Grouse.

VOICE Loud, six-syllable hooting; also growl, hiss, cluck, *purrr*.
NESTING Shallow depression lined with dead vegetation, usually under small pine trees; 5–8 eggs; 1 brood; March–May.
FEEDING Feeds primarily on evergreen needles, especially Douglas fir; will take leaves, grasses, fruit, and insects when seasonally available.

CAUTIOUS PEEK
Female Sooty Grouse disturbed on the ground peer up through grasses to check for danger.

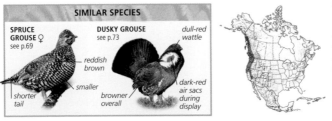

SIMILAR SPECIES

SPRUCE GROUSE ♀ see p.69

reddish brown

shorter tail

smaller

DUSKY GROUSE see p.73

browner overall

dull-red wattle

dark-red air sacs during display

OCCURRENCE
Found west of the Rocky Mountains in Canada and the US, from sea level to the timberline. Breeds at lower elevations in open areas with grassland, forest clearings, and shrubs, and moves up into thicker evergreen forests at higher elevations in winter.

Length **16–20in (41–51cm)**	Wingspan **25–28in (64–71cm)**	Weight **2½–2¾lb (1.1–1.3kg)**
Social **Solitary/Winter flocks**	Lifespan **Up to 14 years**	Status **Secure**

DATE: _____ TIME: _____ LOCATION: _____

| Order **Galliformes** | Family **Phasianidae** | Species *Tympanuchus phasianellus* |

Sharp-tailed Grouse

ADULT

mottled wings

tan eyebrow

long central tail feather

naked pink skin

heavily mottled brown, white, and black upperparts

IN FLIGHT

pale, wedge-shaped tail with protruding central feathers

white tail with two long, mottled center feathers

MALE

brown wings with white dots

white underside with dark-brown arrowheads along flanks

FLIGHT: flushes from hiding on rapid wing beats to flight speed, then onto glide-flap-glide sequence.

The most widespread species of its genus, the Sharp-tailed Grouse is able to adapt to the greatest variety of habitats. It is not migratory, but undertakes seasonal movements between grassland summer habitats and woodland winter habitats. Elements of this grouse's spectacular courtship display have been incorporated into the culture and dance of Native American people, including foot stomping and tail feather rattling. The Sharp-tailed Grouse is the provincial bird of Saskatchewan.

VOICE Male calls a variety of unusual clucks, cooing, barks, and gobbles during courtship; females cluck with different intonations.
NESTING Shallow depression lined with plant matter close at hand as well as some feathers from the female, usually near overhead cover; 10–12 eggs; 1 brood; March–May.
FEEDING Forages primarily for seeds, leaves, buds, and fruit; also takes insects and flowers when available.

PRAIRIE DANCER
The courtship dance of the Sharp-tailed Grouse heralds the arrival of spring to the grasslands.

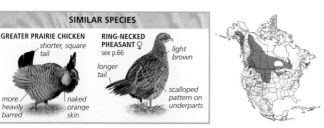

SIMILAR SPECIES		
GREATER PRAIRIE CHICKEN	**RING-NECKED PHEASANT ♀** see p.66	

shorter, square tail

longer tail

light brown

scalloped pattern on underparts

more heavily barred

naked orange skin

OCCURRENCE
Has a northern and western distribution in North America, from Alaska (isolated population) southward across Canada to northern prairie states. Prefers a mixture of fallow and active agricultural fields combined with brushy forest edges and woodlots along river beds.

Length **15–19in (38–48cm)**	Wingspan **23–26in (58–66cm)**	Weight **26–34oz (750–950g)**
Social **Flocks**	Lifespan **Up to 7 years**	Status **Declining (p)**

DATE: _____ TIME: _____ LOCATION: _____

| Order **Galliformes** | Family **Phasianidae** | Species *Meleagris gallopavo* |

Wild Turkey 🔊

MALE (EAST)

IN FLIGHT

tail fanned in display

humped back

no feathers on head

long legs

JUVENILE

rusty tail with black band

black-and-white barred wings

unfeathered blue-and-red head

large red wattles

hair-like "beard" on breast

dark overall

iridescent bronze-and-purplish body

FEMALE

dark body with bronze iridescence

MALE (WEST)

O nce proposed by Benjamin Franklin as the national emblem of the US, the Wild Turkey—the largest galliform in North America—was eliminated from most of its original range by the early 1900s due to over-hunting and habitat destruction. Since then, habitat restoration and the subsequent reintroduction of Wild Turkeys has been very successful.

VOICE Well-known gobble, given by males especially during courtship; female makes various yelps, clucks, and purrs, based on mood and threat level.

NESTING Scrape on ground lined with grass; placed against or under protective cover; 10–15 eggs; 1 brood; March–June.

FEEDING Omnivorous, it scratches in leaf litter on forest floor for acorns and other food, mostly vegetation; also takes plants and insects from agricultural fields.

FLIGHT: after running, leaps into the air with loud, rapid wing beats, then glides.

COLLECTIVE DISPLAY
Once the population expands into new areas, numerous males will be seen displaying together.

SIMILAR SPECIES

GREATER SAGE-GROUSE see p.68

dark head

pointed tail

white breast

TURKEY VULTURE see p.211

small, red head

dark overall

OCCURRENCE
Found in mixed mature woodlands and fields with agricultural crops; also in various grasslands, close to swamps, but adaptable and increasingly common in suburban and urban habitats. Quite widespread, but patchily distributed across the US and southern Canada.

Length 2¾–4ft (0.9–1.2m)	Wingspan 4–5ft (1.2–1.5m)	Weight 10–24lb (4.5–11kg)
Social **Flocks**	Lifespan **Up to 9 years**	Status **Secure**

DATE: _____ TIME:_____ LOCATION:_____

GREBES

GREBES RESEMBLE LOONS and share many of their aquatic habits, but anatomical and molecular features show that they are actually unrelated; and they are placed in a different order: the Podicipediformes. Grebe bodies are streamlined, offering little resistance when diving and swimming. Underwater, their primary means of propulsion is the sideways motion of their lobed toes. The legs are placed far back on the body, which greatly aids the bird when swimming above or below the surface. Grebes have short tails, and their trailing legs and toes serve as rudders when they fly. The position of the legs makes it impossible, however, for grebes to stand upright for long or to easily walk on land. Thus, even when breeding, they are tied to water; and their nests are usually partially floating platforms, built on beds of water plants. Grebes' toes have broad lobes that splay when the bird thrusts forward through the water with its feet. They dive to catch fish with a short, forward-arching spring. Unusual among birds, they swallow feathers, supposedly to trap fish bones and protect their stomachs, then periodically disgorge them. Like loons, grebes can control their buoyancy by exhaling air and compressing their plumage so that they sink quietly below the surface. They are strong fliers, as well as migratory.

PIED BILL
The black-and-white bill pattern clearly distinguishes this bird as the Pied-billed Grebe.

A FINE DISPLAY
This Horned Grebe reveals the colorful plumes on its head, as part of its elaborate courtship display.

SIDE BY SIDE
This pair of Western Grebes is displaying their elaborate courtship behavior.

| Order **Podicipediformes** | Family **Podicipedidae** | Species **Podilymbus podiceps** |

Pied-billed Grebe 🔊

outstretched neck

ADULT (BREEDING)

lighter flight feathers

IN FLIGHT

yellowish bill

whitish throat

ADULT (NONBREEDING)

brown eye

whitish hooked bill with a black ring

brownish-gray body

reddish-brown neck and breast

black throat patch

ADULT (BREEDING)

white undertail

The widest ranging of the North American grebes, the Pied-billed Grebe is tolerant of highly populated areas and is often seen breeding on lakes and ponds across North America. It is a powerful swimmer and can remain submerged for 16–30 seconds when it dives. In contrast to some of the elaborate displays from other grebe species, its courtship ritual is more vocal than visual, and a pair usually duet-call in the mating season. Migration, conducted at night, is delayed until its breeding area ices up and food becomes scarce. The Pied-billed Grebe is capable of sustained flights of over 2,000 miles (3,200km).

VOICE Various grunts and wails; in spring, call a cuckoo-like repeated gobble *kup-kup-Kaow-Kaow-kaow*, gradually speeding up.

NESTING Floating nest of partially decayed plants and clipped leaves, attached to emergent vegetation in marshes and quiet waters; 4–7 eggs; 2 broods; April–October.

FEEDING Dives to catch a variety of crustaceans, fish, amphibians, insects, and other invertebrates; also picks prey from emergent vegetation, or catches them mid-air.

FLIGHT: strong, direct flight with rapid wing beats, but rarely seen.

BACK OFF
When alarmed, a Pied-billed Grebe will flap its wings in a defensive display.

SIMILAR SPECIES

LEAST GREBE ☼

smaller bill

yellow eye

darker body

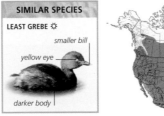

OCCURRENCE
Breeds on a variety of water bodies, including coastal brackish ponds, seasonal ponds, marshes, and even sewage ponds. Winters in the breeding area if food and open water are available, otherwise chooses still waters resembling its breeding habitat.

Length **12–15in (31–38cm)**	Wingspan **18–24in (46–62cm)**	Weight **13–17oz (375–475g)**
Social **Family groups**	Lifespan **At least 3 years**	Status **Vulnerable**

DATE: _____ TIME: _____ LOCATION: _____

Horned Grebe

IN FLIGHT

neck and head in line with body

ADULT (SUMMER)

white cheek

flattish top of head

white sides to neck

ADULT (WINTER)

gold streak from eye to nape

black crown

red eye

ADULT (SPRING MOLT)

short, dark bill with whitish tip

black throat

rufous neck

ADULT (SUMMER)

The timing of the Horned Grebe's migration depends largely on the weather – this grebe frequently does not leave until its breeding grounds get iced over, nor does it arrive before the ice melts. Its breeding behavior is well documented since it is approachable on nesting grounds and has an elaborate breeding ritual. This grebe's so-called "horns" are, in fact, yellowish feather patches located behind its eyes, which it can raise at will.

VOICE At least 10 calls, but descending *aaanrrh* call most common in winter, ends in trill; muted conversational calls when birds are in groups.

NESTING Floating, soggy nest, hidden in vegetation, in small ponds and lake inlets; 3–9 eggs; 1 brood; May–July.

FEEDING Dives in open water or forages among plants, mainly for small crustaceans and insects, but also leeches, mollusks, amphibians, fish, and some vegetation.

FLIGHT: strong, rapid wing beats; runs on water to become airborne; rarely takes off from land.

HITCHING A RIDE
In common with other grebes, Horned Grebe chicks often ride on the back of a swimming parent.

SIMILAR SPECIES

RED-NECKED GREBE ❊
see p.80

brownish cap

darker eye

EARED GREBE ❊
see p.81

upturned bill

dark cheek

OCCURRENCE
Breeds in small freshwater, even slightly brackish, ponds and marshes, including artificial ponds. Prefers areas with open water and patches of sedges, cattails, and other wetland vegetation in any ecosystem. Winters on saltwater close to shore; also on large bodies of freshwater.

Length **12–15in (30–38cm)**	Wingspan **18–24in (46–62cm)**	Weight **11–20oz (300–575g)**
Social **Pairs/Loose flocks/Colonies**	Lifespan **Up to 5 years**	Status **Special Concern**

DATE: _____ TIME: _____ LOCATION: _____

| Order **Podicipediformes** | Family **Podicipedidae** | Species **Podiceps grisegena** |

Red-necked Grebe

head and neck
in line with body

white-edged
inner wing

**ADULT
(BREEDING)**

IN FLIGHT

pale reddish-
brown crescent
near ear

brownish
cap

ADULT (NONBREEDING)

broad stripes on
cheek and ear

mostly
yellowish bill

JUVENILE

broad head
with crest
at rear

black cap

brown
eye

grayish-white
cheeks and
throat

chestnut-brown
neck and chest

gray flanks

**ADULT
(BREEDING)**

The Red-necked Grebe is smaller than Western and Clark's Grebes, but larger than the other North American grebes. It migrates over short to medium distances and spends the winter along both coasts, where large flocks may be seen during the day. It runs along the water's surface to become airborne, although it rarely flies. This grebe doesn't come ashore often; it stands erect, but walks awkwardly, and prefers to sink to its breast and shuffle along.
VOICE Nasal, gull-like call on breeding grounds, evolves into bray, ends with whinny; also honks, rattles, hisses, purrs, and ticks.
NESTING Compact, buoyant mound of decayed and fresh vegetation in sheltered, shallow marshes and lakes, or artificial wetlands; 4–5 eggs; 1 brood; May–July.
FEEDING An opportunistic hunter—eats fish, crustaceans, aquatic insects, worms, mollusks, salamanders, and tadpoles.

FLIGHT: fast, direct, wing beats, with head and outstretched neck mostly level with line of body.

COURTSHIP DISPLAY
This courting pair face each other, with outstretched necks and raised chests.

SIMILAR SPECIES

RED-THROATED LOON ✳
see p.186

white spots
on back

white
neck

no yellow
on bill

HORNED GREBE ✳
see p.79

reddish eye
paler neck

OCCURRENCE
Breeds from northern prairies and forests, almost to the tree line in the northwest; limited to suitable interior bodies of water, such as large marshes and small lakes. Winters primarily in estuaries, inlets, bays, and offshore shallows along the Atlantic and Pacific Coasts; can also be found on the Great Lakes.

| Length **16¹/₂–22in (42–56cm)** | Wingspan **24–35in (61–88cm)** | Weight **1³/₄–3¹/₂lb (0.8–1,6kg)** |
| Social **Pairs/Loose flocks** | Lifespan **Up to 6 years** | Status **Vulnerable** |

DATE: _____ TIME:_____ LOCATION:_____

| Order **Podicipediformes** | Family **Podicipedidae** | Species *Podiceps nigricollis* |

Eared Grebe

- darker flanks
- browner plumage
- white patch on wing
- **ADULT (SUMMER)**
- outstretched neck
- dusky white flanks
- **IN FLIGHT**
- dusky cheek
- upturned bill
- grayish neck
- **JUVENILE**
- large, wispy gold patch behind red eye
- dark back
- black neck
- **ADULT (WINTER)**
- **ADULT (SUMMER)**
- black crest
- red eye
- thin, upturned bill
- rufous breast and sides

The most abundant grebe in North America, the Eared Grebe is quite remarkable in terms of physiology. After breeding, it undergoes a complex and drastic reorganization of body-fat stores along with changes in muscle, heart, and digestive organ mass to prepare for fall migration. All of this increases the bird's energy reserves and body mass, but renders it flightless. It may have the longest periods of flightlessness of any flying bird—up to 10 months.

VOICE Various trills during courtship, including squeaky, rising *poo-eep*; sharp chirp when alarmed; usually silent at other times.
NESTING Sodden nest of decayed bottom plants anchored in thinly spaced reeds or submerged vegetation in shallow water of marshes, ponds, and lakes; 1 brood; 1–8 eggs; May–July.
FEEDING Forages underwater for small crustaceans and aquatic insects; also small fish and mollusks; consumes worms in winter.

FLIGHT: flies with neck outstretched, held at a low angle; rarely flies except during migration.

SALTY WATER
The Eared Grebe prefers salty water at all times except when breeding.

SIMILAR SPECIES

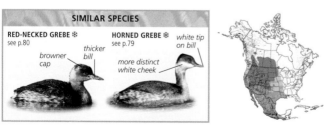

RED-NECKED GREBE ✳
see p.80
- browner cap
- thicker bill

HORNED GREBE ✳
see p.79
- white tip on bill
- more distinct white cheek

OCCURRENCE
Breeds in marshes, shallow lakes, and ponds in the four western provinces. After breeding, many birds seek highly saline, slow-to-freeze waters, such as Mono Lake, where their favorite foods thrive—brine shrimp and alkali flies. Winters in coastal bays of the Pacific Coast and is a vagrant on the Atlantic Coast.

| Length **12–14in (30–35cm)** | Wingspan **22¹⁄₂–24in (57–62cm)** | Weight **7–26oz (200–725g)** |
| Social **Flocks** | Lifespan **Up to 12 years** | Status **Secure** |

DATE: _____ TIME: _____ LOCATION: _____

Order **Podicipediformes**	Family **Podicipedidae**	Species *Aechmophorus occidentalis*

Western Grebe

ADULT

black nape stripe

whitish band on dark wing

IN FLIGHT

dark patch around eyes

light-gray back

light white-gray neck

JUVENILE

black nape stripe

dark-gray back

black crown extends below eye

distinctive red eye

long, slender, slightly upturned greenish-yellow bill

ADULT

brilliant white throat, breast, and belly

Western and Clark's Grebes are strictly North American species. They share much of their breeding habitat and elaborate mating rituals, and were, until 1985, classified as different color forms of a single species. Interbreeding is uncommon, perhaps because of slight differences in calls, bill colors, and facial patterns. Although hybrids are rare, they appear to be fertile, and produce chicks of their own. Female Western Grebes are smaller than males and have smaller, thinner, slightly upturned bills. The Western Grebe dives more frequently than Clark's, and remains submerged for about 30 seconds.

VOICE Nine calls, each with a specific purpose, such as alarm, begging, and mating calls; advertising call is a harsh, rolling two-noted *krrrikk krrreek*.

NESTING Floating pile of available plants, attached to thick growth of submerged vegetation; occasionally constructed on land; 2–3 eggs; 1 brood; May–July.

FEEDING Mainly catches a wide variety of freshwater or saltwater fish; also crustaceans, worms, occasionally insects.

FLIGHT: fast and direct with rapid wing beats; neck extended with feet stretched out behind.

SELF-DEFENSE
The posture of this Western Grebe shows that it is ready to defend itself when threatened.

OCCURRENCE
Western North America, breeds from southern Canada to Mexico, in freshwater lakes and marshes with open water and emergent vegetation; rarely on tidewater marshes; also artificial marshes and habitats. Winters along the Pacific Coast, in bays and estuaries in the southwest US and Mexico.

SIMILAR SPECIES

CLARK'S GREBE
see p.83

bright orange-yellow bill

white between crown and eye

HIGHLY SOCIAL
Western Grebes, much like Clark's Grebes, are highly gregarious in all seasons.

Length **21½–30in (55–75cm)**	Wingspan **30–39in (76–100cm)**	Weight **1¾–4lb (0.8–1.8kg)**
Social **Flocks**	Lifespan **At least 15 years**	Status **Special Concern**

DATE: _____ TIME: _____ LOCATION: _____

Clark's Grebe

outstretched neck

ADULT

white throat, breast, and belly

distinct white band on wings

IN FLIGHT

black crown, slightly crested

red eye

white space between black crown and eye

bright orange-yellow bill

very thin, black nape stripe

long, thin, swan-like neck

moderately dark, gray back

whitish flanks

ADULT

Clark's and Western Grebes are closely related and very difficult to distinguish. They rarely fly except when migrating at night. Both species seldom come to land, where their movement is awkward because their legs and toes are located so far back, although they have been reported to run upright rapidly. Their flight muscles suffer wastage after their arrival on the breeding grounds, which also inhibits their ability to travel, but during the incubation period adults may feed several miles from the colony by following continuous water trails.

VOICE Variety of different calls, including a harsh, reedy, grating, two-syllable, single, rising *kree-eekt* advertising call.

NESTING Floating pile of available plants, attached to thick growth of submerged vegetation; occasionally constructed on land; 2–3 eggs; 1 brood; May–July.

FEEDING Mainly catches saltwater or freshwater fish; also crustaceans.

FLIGHT: swift and direct with quick wing beats; neck extended with feet trailing.

HOW TO SWALLOW?
It is not unusual for grebes to catch large fish; they crush the head first before swallowing.

FORAGING IN DEEP WATER
Clark's Grebe has a distinctive white, S-shaped neck and black crown.

SIMILAR SPECIES

WESTERN GREBE ♂
see p.82

black crown extends below eye

WESTERN GREBE ♀
see p.82

lighter nape

dull greenish-yellow bill

lighter upperparts

OCCURRENCE
Breeds in freshwater lakes and marshes with open water bordered by emergent vegetation; rarely tidewater marshes; has been nesting in artificial Lake Havasu marshes since 1960s. Winters along the Pacific Coast, and in bays and estuaries in the southwest US and Mexico.

Length **21½–30in (55–75cm)**	Wingspan **32in (82cm)**	Weight **1½–3¾lb (0.7–1.7kg)**
Social **Flocks**	Lifespan **At least 15 years**	Status **Declining**

DATE: _____ TIME: _____ LOCATION: _____

PIGEONS AND DOVES

THE LARGER SPECIES WITHIN the family Columbidae are known as pigeons, and the smaller ones as doves, although there is no actual scientific basis for the distinction. They are all fairly heavy, plump birds with relatively small heads and short necks. They also possess slender bills with their nostrils positioned in a fleshy mound at the base.

NATIVE PIGEON
A western native species, the Band-tailed Pigeon is declining through much of its range.

Among other things, members of this family have strong wing muscles, making them powerful and agile fliers. When alarmed, they burst into flight with their wings emitting a distinctive clapping or swishing sound. Pigeons and doves produce a nutritious "crop-milk," which they secrete to feed their young. Despite human activity having severely affected members of this family in the past (the leading cause of the Passenger Pigeon's extinction in the 19th century is thought to be overhunting), the introduced Rock Pigeon has adapted and proliferated worldwide, as has the recently introduced Eurasian Collared-Dove, albeit on a smaller scale. Among the species native to North America, only the elegant Mourning Dove is as widespread as the various species of introduced birds.

DOVE IN THE SUN
The Mourning Dove sunbathes each side of its body in turns, its wings and tail outspread.

Order **Columbiformes**	Family **Columbidae**	Species *Columba livia*

Rock Pigeon 🔊

black wing bars

white underwings

white rump

ADULT

IN FLIGHT

iridescence on neck

gray back

short bill

no wing bars

variably colored body

two black wing bars

ADULT (FERAL)

ADULT (ANCESTRAL FORM)

dark-tipped tail

The Rock Pigeon was introduced to the Atlantic Coast of North America by 17th century colonists. Now feral, this species is found all over the continent, especially around farms, cities, and towns. This medium-sized pigeon comes in a wide variety of plumage colors and patterns, including bluish gray, checkered, rusty red, and nearly all-white. Its wings usually have two dark bars on them—unique among North American pigeons. The variability of the Rock Pigeon influenced Charles Darwin as he developed his theory of natural selection.
VOICE Soft, gurgling *coo, roo-c'too-coo,* for courtship and threat.
NESTING Twig nest on flat, sheltered surface, such as caves, rocky outcrops, and buildings; 2 eggs; several broods; year-round.
FEEDING Eats seeds, fruit, and rarely insects; human foods such as popcorn, bread, peanuts; various farm crops in rural areas.

FLIGHT: strong, direct; can reach speeds up to around 60mph (95kph).

CITY PIGEONS
Most Rock Pigeons in North America descend from domesticated forms and exhibit many colors.

SIMILAR SPECIES

WHITE-CROWNED PIGEON
mangroves

white crown

dark gray overall

BAND-TAILED PIGEON
western; see p.86

yellow bill with dark tip

white band on nape

OCCURRENCE
Across southern Canada and North America; nests in human structures of all sorts; resident. Original habitat in the Old World was (and still is) sea cliffs and inland canyons; found wild in some places, such as dry regions of North Africa, but feral in much of the world.

Length **11–14in (28–36cm)**	Wingspan **20–26in (51–67cm)**	Weight **9–14oz (250–400g)**
Social **Solitary/Flocks**	Lifespan **Up to 6 years**	Status **Secure**

| Order **Columbiformes** | Family **Columbidae** | Species ***Patagioenas fasciata*** |

Band-tailed Pigeon

IN FLIGHT

wide tail band

dark-gray outer wings

pale tail tip

light-gray inner wings

ADULT

dark-tipped yellow bill

white band on nape

iridescence on hind neck

ADULT

blue-gray upperparts

uniform blue-gray underparts

yellow legs and toes

gray tail

FLIGHT: direct, strong flight with powerful, regular wing beats.

The Band-tailed Pigeon is similar to the Rock Pigeon in its size, posture, body movements, and breeding and feeding behavior. However, in North America the Band-tailed Pigeon's distribution is limited to the dry, mountainous forests of four southwestern states, and the wet coastal forests of the West Coast, from the southeastern tip of Alaska down to South America. The distinguishing features of the Band-tailed Pigeon are its yellow bill and legs, a white band just above the iridescent green patch on the back of its neck, and its eponymous banded tail.

VOICE Often silent, but emits series of two-noted, low-frequency *whooos* punctuated with a pause.

NESTING Flat, saucer-shaped, rather flimsy platform of twigs, needles, and moss in a variety of trees; 1 egg; 1 brood; April–October.

FEEDING Forages on the ground for grain, seeds, fruit, acorns, and pine nuts; hangs upside down by its toes from the branches of shrubs and trees to eat dangling nuts and flowers that are otherwise out of reach.

LARGE PIGEON
This is North America's largest pigeon, bigger than the Rock Pigeon by some 10 percent.

UNIFORMITY
Unlike flocks of Rock Pigeons, Band-tailed Pigeon flocks have very uniform plumage.

OCCURRENCE
Breeds and winters in temperate coniferous rain forest along the Pacific Coast, and in mountain coniferous and mixed-species forests in the interior. Lives in urban and rural areas where there are evergreen trees and access to grains, fruit, and feeders. Some populations are resident, others migratory.

SIMILAR SPECIES

ROCK PIGEON
see p.85

two wing bars

dark bill

| Length **13–16in (33–41cm)** | Wingspan **26in (66cm)** | Weight **12–13oz (350–375g)** |
| Social **Flocks** | Lifespan **Up to 18 years** | Status **Special Concern** |

DATE: _____ TIME: _____ LOCATION: _____

Eurasian Collared-Dove

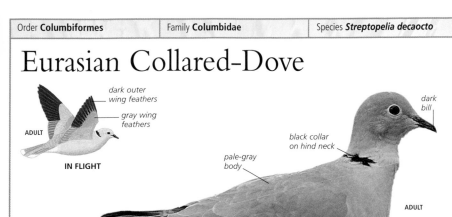

dark outer wing feathers

gray wing feathers

ADULT

IN FLIGHT

dark bill

black collar on hind neck

pale-gray body

ADULT

square tail

gray undertail wing feathers

A stocky bird, the Eurasian Collared-Dove is easily recognized by the black collar on the back of its neck and its square tail. First released at New Providence, Bahamas in the mid-1970s, this species is spreading rapidly across the continental mainland. This is thanks to multiple local releases, the planting of trees in urban and suburban habitats, the popularity of bird feeders making food readily available, and the bird's extraordinarily high reproductive rate. This species soon becomes very trusting and tolerant of humans, regularly nesting and feeding in urban areas. One consequence of this is that it often falls prey to domestic cats, but this has little effect on the expanding population. Based on sightings from locations all over North America—and on the evidence from Europe, throughout which it has spread since only the 1940s—it is highly likely that the Eurasian Collared-Dove will soon become a common species in North America.

VOICE Repeated four-note *coo-hoo-HOO-cook* that is quick and low pitched; also harsh, nasal *krreeew* in flight.

NESTING Platform of twigs, stems, and grasses in trees or on buildings; 2 eggs; multiple broods; March–November.

FEEDING Eats seed and grain, plant stems and leaves, berries, and some invertebrates; feeds on the ground for seed, but also visits elevated feeders.

FLIGHT: strong, stiff flight reminiscent of hawks; occasional swoops and dives.

COLLARED COLONIZER
The Eurasian Collared-Dove has spread throughout Europe in just a few decades, and now looks set to do the same in North America.

SIMILAR SPECIES

MOURNING DOVE
see p.88

black dot on face

black spots on wings

pointed tail

OCCURRENCE
Can be seen almost anywhere in North America south of the northern forest zone, but occurs mainly in suburban and urban areas (though not large cities) and agricultural areas with seeds and grain for food and deciduous trees for nesting and roosting. May roost in artificial structures, such as barns.

Length **11½–12in (29–30cm)**	Wingspan **14in (35cm)**	Weight **5–6oz (150–175g)**
Social **Large flocks**	Lifespan **Up to 13 years**	Status **Localized**

DATE: _____ TIME: _____ LOCATION: _____

| Order **Columbiformes** | Family **Columbidae** | Species ***Zenaida macroura*** |

Mourning Dove 🔊

mostly uniform gray wings

pointed tail

ADULT

IN FLIGHT

small "pin-head"

faint mottling on neck and underparts

JUVENILE

blue eye-ring

thin, dark bill

dark spots on wings

plump gray body

long, pointed tail

ADULT

pink legs and toes

One of the most familiar, abundant, and widespread North American birds, the Mourning Dove is a long, plump, medium-sized dove with an undersized head. It has a gray body with a pale, rosy breast and black spots on folded wings. While coveted by hunters—as many as 70 million are shot annually—the Mourning Dove is also well known to those who live on farms and in suburbia. Found all across North America, the species is divided into two subspecies—the larger, grayish-brown *Z. m. carolinensis*, east of the Mississippi River, and the smaller, paler *Z. m. marginella* in the west.

VOICE Mellow, owl-like call: *hoO-Oo-oo, hoo-hoo-hoo.*
NESTING Flat, flimsy twig platform, mostly in trees, sometimes on the ground; 2 eggs; 2 broods; February–October.
FEEDING Forages mainly for seeds on the ground; obtains food quickly and digests it later at roost.

FLIGHT: swift, direct flight, with fairly quick wing beats; twists and turns sometimes.

FAMILIAR SIGHT
The Mourning Dove is North America's most widespread member of this family.

OCCURRENCE
Breeds in a wide variety of habitats but shuns extensive forests; human-altered vegetation favored for feeding, including farmland and suburbia. Winters in small to medium sheltered woodland while feeding in grain fields; winters in southern Mexico and Central America.

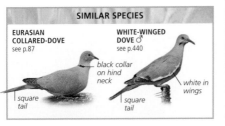

SIMILAR SPECIES

EURASIAN COLLARED-DOVE
see p.87

black collar on hind neck

square tail

WHITE-WINGED DOVE ♂
see p.440

white in wings

square tail

Length **9–13½in (23–34cm)**	Wingspan **14½–17½in (37–45cm)**	Weight **3–6oz (85–175g)**
Social **Pairs/Winter flocks**	Lifespan **Up to 19 years**	Status **Secure**

DATE: _____ TIME: _____ LOCATION: _____

CUCKOOS

THE FAMILY CUCULIDAE INCLUDES typical cuckoos, anis, and roadrunners. Cuckoos favor forested areas, anis prefer more open bush country, and roadrunners are found in dry, bushy semi-desert or desert regions. Cuckoos are notorious for laying eggs in other birds' nests, but the two species found in Canada seldom do so. The Black-billed Cuckoo is found across southern Canada, while the Yellow-billed Cuckoo is found only in the East. Generally shy and reclusive, they are more often heard than seen. Both species usually build a nest and raise their own offspring. In flight, cuckoos are often mistaken for small birds of prey. They are mainly insectivorous, specializing in caterpillars from the ground or gleaned from foliage; the Black-billed Cuckoo especially relishes tent caterpillars and gypsy moth larvae. However, the numbers of both species vary from year to year in a given locale in response to prey abundance. Besides their slender bodies and long tails, cuckoos have zygodactyl feet, with the two inner toes pointing forward and the two outer toes pointing

STRONG STOMACH
The Black-billed Cuckoo can safely eat caterpillars that are poisonous to other birds.

backward. Cuckoos in North America are vulnerable to pollutants, and the Yellow-billed Cuckoo is declining rapidly to the point of arousing serious concerns over its future. Their close relatives on the continent are the Greater Roadrunner, and two species of Ani. Anis have a more varied diet. They are sociable, blackish, heavy-billed birds, found only in Florida and along the Gulf Coast in the US but are more widespread in Central America. Roadrunners are ground-feeders, rarely flying but able to run fast in pursuit of prey, which ranges from insects through small lizards to snakes (famously including rattlesnakes) and small rodents.

NIGHT SINGER
During the breeding season, the Black-billed Cuckoo will often call throughout the night.

| Order **Cuculiformes** | Family **Cuculidae** | Species *Coccyzus erythropthalmus* |

Black-billed Cuckoo

bare red skin around eye

IN FLIGHT

long tail

ADULT

small white spots on tips of tail feathers

long wings

grayish-brown back

long, black, decurved bill

ADULT

pale grayish-white underparts

grayish feet

long tail

Although common, the Black-billed Cuckoo is usually difficult to spot because of its secretive nature and dense, leafy habitat. This species feeds mainly on spiny caterpillars, but the spines of these insects can become lodged in the cuckoo's stomach, obstructing digestion, so the bird periodically empties its stomach to clear any such blockage. The decline of this species is probably an indirect result of the chemical control of caterpillar outbreaks in forests throughout their range. During the breeding season, the birds call throughout the night, which leads some to believe erroneously that the cuckoo is nocturnal.

VOICE Series of 2–5 repeatedly whistled notes, *coo-coo-coo-coo*, with short breaks between series.

NESTING Shallow cup of sticks lined with moss, leaves, grass, and feathers; 2–4 eggs; 1 brood; May–July.

FEEDING Almost exclusively eats caterpillars, especially tent caterpillars and gypsy moths.

FLIGHT: flight is swift, direct, and graceful, with long, smooth wing beats.

SEARCHING FOR FOOD
These cuckoos spend a lot of their time in trees as they search for their favorite hairy caterpillars.

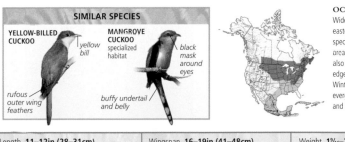

SIMILAR SPECIES

YELLOW-BILLED CUCKOO
yellow bill
rufous outer wing feathers

MANGROVE CUCKOO
specialized habitat
black mask around eyes
buffy undertail and belly

OCCURRENCE
Widespread northern and eastern North American species, lives in thickly wooded areas close to water, but can also be found in brushy forest edges and evergreen woods. Winters in South America in evergreen woodlands, scrub, and humid forests.

| Length **11–12in (28–31cm)** | Wingspan **16–19in (41–48cm)** | Weight **1⁹⁄₁₆–2oz (45–55g)** |
| Social **Solitary** | Lifespan **Up to 5 years** | Status **Declining** |

DATE: _____ TIME: _____ LOCATION: _____

NIGHTJARS

THE NIGHTJARS ARE ACTIVE mostly around dusk and dawn, and so are not well known to many people, although their remarkable songs and calls may be more familiar. Common Nighthawks are easily seen and may even be spotted over suburban areas, but most nightjars are elusive species. Some inhabit scrub and bushy slopes and plains, while others are found in woodlands. They are medium-sized birds with pointed wings and long tails. They have tiny legs and minute bills but very wide mouths: they catch flying insects such as moths in the air, directly into the open gape. Their mouths are surrounded by bristles that help guide insects in when the birds are foraging. Nightjars are generally similar in coloration and pattern, having a mottled mixture of various browns, grays, and blacks that provides impeccable camouflage when they remain hidden during daylight hours. This ability to hide in plain sight is useful during the nesting season when all nightjars lay their patterned eggs directly on the ground, without any nest material.

The nature of the camouflage pattern of their feathers makes it difficult to distinguish between species when they rest in trees or on the ground. The most reliable means of telling

NIGHT HUNTER
The nocturnal Common Poorwill hunts from the ground, looking up to spot its flying insect prey.

species apart is their voice. If seen, the placement and nature of white markings, combined with the style of flight are the best means of identification. Most members of the family migrate and move southward as insects become dormant in the North. Nightjars are also known as "Goatsuckers," because it was believed in ancient Greece that these birds sucked blood from goats.

SITTING PRETTY
Unusually for birds, members of the nightjar family, such as this Common Nighthawk, often perch lengthwise on branches.

| Order **Caprimulgiformes** | Family **Caprimulgidae** | Species **Chordeiles minor** |

Common Nighthawk 🔊

MALE

pointed wings

white bars on outer wing feathers

narrow wings

long wings

IN FLIGHT

white throat

white wing patch

MALE

very small bill

large, dark eye

delicate gray-black pattern overall

barring on gray underparts

FEMALE

FLIGHT: erratic flight with deep wing beats interrupted by banking glides.

Common Nighthawks are easy to spot as they swoop over parking lots, city streets, and athletics fields during the warm summer months. They are more active at dawn and dusk than at night, pursuing insect prey up to 250ft (76m) in the air. The species once took the name Booming Nighthawk, a reference to the remarkable flight display of the male birds, during which they dive rapidly toward the ground, causing their feathers to vibrate and produce a characteristic "booming" sound.

VOICE Nasal *peeent*; also soft clucking noises from both sexes.

NESTING Nests on ground on rocks, wood, leaves, or sand, also on gravel-covered rooftops in urban areas; 2 eggs; 1 brood; May–July.

FEEDING Catches airborne insects, especially moths, mayflies, and beetles, also ants; predominantly active at dusk and dawn.

A RARE SIGHT
Common Nighthawks are seen in flight more often than other caprimulgids, and it is a rare treat to see one resting on a perch.

SIMILAR SPECIES

LESSER NIGHTHAWK
more buffy barring on underside of wings

COMMON PAURAQUE
longer, rounded tail with white patches

browner plumage

larger overall

OCCURRENCE
Wide variety of open habitats such as cleared forests, fields, grassland, beaches, and sand dunes; also common in urban areas, including cities. The most common and widespread North American nighthawk, this species also occurs in Central and South America.

| Length **9–10in (23–26cm)** | Wingspan **22–24in (56–61cm)** | Weight **2⅞oz (80g)** |
| Social **Solitary/Flocks** | Lifespan **Up to 9 years** | Status **Threatened** |

DATE: _____ TIME:_____ LOCATION:_____

Common Poorwill

short, rounded wings with tawny underparts

ADULT

short tail

IN FLIGHT

large black eye

very small bill

delicately mottled brownish-gray to pale-gray plumage

broad white throat band

ADULT

grayish underparts, mottled dark-gray and black

white-tipped outer tail feathers

tiny dark legs and feet

This nocturnal bird is the smallest North American nightjar, with much shorter wings than its relatives, and a stubbier tail, but a comparatively large head. In 1946, scientists discovered that it was able to go into a state of torpor, similar to mammalian hibernation. During "hibernation," its body temperature is about 64°F (18°C) instead of the usual 106°F (41°C), and it may remain in this state for several weeks during cold weather when food is unavailable. This may account for its colloquial name, "sleeping one," among the Hopi of the Southwest. Males and females are similar in appearance, but the male has whitish corners to its tail, while the female's are more buffy.

VOICE Call low *purr-WHEEOO* or *pooor-WEELLUP*, whistled at night when perched in the open.

NESTING Eggs laid on the ground among rocks, sometimes under shrubs; 2 eggs; 2 broods; May–August.

FEEDING Jumps up from the ground and flies briefly to capture night-flying insects, such as moths and beetles.

FLIGHT: brief, erratic; with slow and deep wing beats

GRAVEL ROADS
The Common Poorwill uses gravel roads as a convenient place from which to jump at flying insects.

SIMILAR SPECIES

CHUCK-WILL'S-WIDOW

browner upperparts

larger overall

EASTERN WHIP-POOR-WILL
see p.94

larger bill

large white patches on tail

OCCURRENCE
Breeds from southwestern Canada and the western US southward into Mexico, in arid habitats with much bare ground and sparse vegetation, such as grasses, shrubs, and cacti. Winters in northern Mexico.

Length **7½–8½in (19–21cm)**	Wingspan **15½–19in (40–48cm)**	Weight **1¼–2oz (35–55g)**
Social **Solitary**	Lifespan **Up to 3 years**	Status **Secure**

DATE: _____ TIME: _____ LOCATION: _____

| Order **Caprimulgiformes** | Family **Caprimulgidae** | Species ***Antrostomus vociferus*** |

Eastern Whip-poor-will 🔊

rounded wings

MALE

IN FLIGHT

buffy throat stripe

buffy corners to tail

FEMALE

black-and-gray bands across back

tawny patch on cheeks

huge eye

flat, wide bill with long bristles

whitish throat stripe

MALE

cinnamon barring on dark wings

white corners to tail

As with many of the nightjars, the Eastern Whip-poor-will is heard more often than seen. Its camouflage makes it extremely difficult to spot on the forest floor, and it usually flies away only when an intruder is very close—sometimes within a few feet. This species apparently has an unusual breeding pattern—while the male feeds the first brood until fledging, the female lays eggs for a second brood. Both eggs from one brood may hatch simultaneously during full moon, when there is most light at night, allowing the parents more time to forage for their young.

VOICE Loud, incessant, three-syllable whistle *WHIP-perrr-WIIL*.
NESTING Lays eggs on leaf litter on forest floor, often near overhead plant cover; 2 eggs; 2 broods; April–July.
FEEDING Flies upward quickly from perch to capture passing moths and other insects, such as mosquitoes.

FLIGHT: slow, erratic flight, with alternating bouts of flapping and gliding.

WAITING IN AMBUSH
Like other nightjars, this species waits in ambush for its prey from a perch on the forest floor.

SIMILAR SPECIES

COMMON POORWILL
see p.93

smaller, grayer overall

square tail

CHUCK-WILL'S WIDOW

cinnamon-brown chin

larger overall

OCCURRENCE
Mixed mature forests with open understory, especially oak and pine forests on dry upland sites. Breeds from southeastern US up to southern Canada.

| Length **9–10in (23–26cm)** | Wingspan **17–20in (43–51cm)** | Weight **1⁹⁄₁₆–2¹⁄₄oz (45–65g)** |
| Social **Solitary** | Lifespan **Up to 15 years** | Status **Threatened** |

DATE: _____ TIME:_____ LOCATION:_____

Family **Apodidae**

SWIFTS

SWIFTS SPEND VIRTUALLY ALL their daylight hours, and many night hours as well, plying the skies. The most aerial birds in North America—if not the world—swifts eat, drink, court, mate, and even sleep on the wing. Unsurprisingly, swifts also are some of the fastest and most acrobatic flyers of the bird world. Several species have been clocked at over 100mph (160kmh). They feed on insects caught in zooming, zigzagging and dashing pursuits. The family name, based on the Greek *apous*, which means "without feet," originates from the ancient belief that swifts had no feet and lived their entire lives in the air.

ACROBATIC FLOCKS
White-throated Swifts are usually seen in groups of a handful to hundreds of birds.

Family **Trochilidae**

HUMMINGBIRDS

FOUND ONLY IN THE AMERICAS, hummingbirds are sometimes referred to as the crown jewels of the bird world. The first sight of a glittering hummingbird can be a life-changing experience. The amount of iridescence in their plumages varies from almost none to seemingly every feather. Most North American male hummingbirds have a colorful throat patch called a gorget, but most females lack this gorgeous attribute. Because iridescent colors are structural and not pigment-based, a gorget can often appear blackish until seen at the correct angle towards the light. Hummingbirds are the only birds that can fly backwards, an adaptation that allows them to move easily between flowers. Flying sideways, up, down, and hovering are also within hummingbirds' abilities, and all are achieved by their unique figure-eight, rapid wing strokes and reduced wing bone structure. Their long, thin bills allow them access to nectar in tubular flowers.

AGGRESSIVE MALES
This male Ruby-throated Hummingbird defends his territory from a perch.

NECTAR FEEDERS
All North American hummingbirds, such as this Black-chinned, consume nectar from wildflowers and sugar water from feeders. They also eat insects and spiders for protein.

| Order **Apodiformes** | Family **Apodidae** | Species ***Cypseloides niger*** |

Black Swift

IN FLIGHT

pale underwings

slightly notched tail

black body

ADULT

grayish-black head

black eye

blackish upperparts

black patch in front of eye

black tail lacks "spines"

dark plumage with glossy sheen

ADULT

very long, sickle-shaped wings

The largest of the North American swifts, the Black Swift is also the most enigmatic. It forages at high altitudes and nests on sea cliffs or behind waterfalls in mountainous terrains, and therefore, can be difficult to observe. On cold and cloudy days, when their aerial insect prey occurs closer to the ground, Black Swifts also forage lower, and are easier to see. Like other swifts, the Black Swift often forms large feeding flocks, particularly in areas where swarms of winged ants occur.

VOICE Generally silent, but gives twittering chips, sometimes in fast series, during interactions with other swifts; sharp *cheep* when approaching nest.

NESTING Shallow cup of moss and mud on ledge or in rocky niche, often behind waterfalls; 1 egg; 1 brood; June–September.

FEEDING Catches airborne flies, beetles, bees, spiders, and other arthropods on the wing.

FLIGHT: shallow, rapid wing beats; often soars; acrobatic, looping flight when feeding.

TOTAL COMMITMENT
The female incubates her egg for up to a month, then both parents feed the nestling for seven weeks.

SIMILAR SPECIES

VAUX'S SWIFT
see p.98

paler rump

smaller overall

PURPLE MARTIN ♂
see p.306

purplish-blue upperparts

longer, more notched tail

OCCURRENCE
Breeds from British Columbia in Canada, south to Mexico, Costa Rica, and the West Indies. Found in mountains from May or June to early October, feeding high over any habitat near nesting sites. Occasionally seen elsewhere during migration, often in flocks. Wintering areas still largely unknown.

| Length **7in (18cm)** | Wingspan **18in (46cm)** | Weight **1⁷⁄₁₆–2oz (40–55g)** |
| Social **Flocks** | Lifespan **Up to 16 years** | Status **Endangered** |

DATE: _____ TIME: _____ LOCATION: _____

Order **Apodiformes**	Family **Apodidae**	Species *Chaetura pelagica*

Chimney Swift

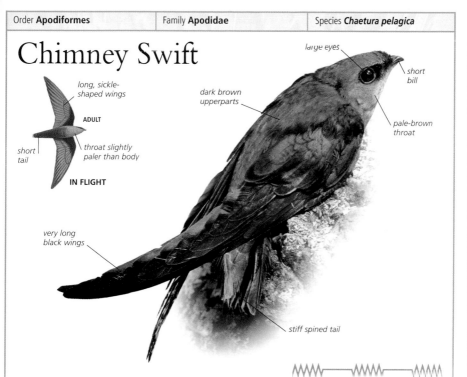

large eyes

short bill

dark brown upperparts

pale-brown throat

long, sickle-shaped wings

ADULT

short tail

throat slightly paler than body

IN FLIGHT

very long black wings

stiff spined tail

Nimble and limber tailed, the Chimney Swift is a familiar summer sight and sound, racing through the skies east of the Rockies, its rolling twitters often heard. This bird does almost everything on the wing—feeding, drinking, and even bathing and copulating. This species has adapted to nest in human structures, including chimneys, although it once nested in tree holes. It remains a common bird, although local populations have declined; and it has expanded its range west and south.

VOICE High, rapid chips and twittering, notes from individuals in a flock run together into a rapid, descending chatter.

NESTING Shallow cup of twigs and saliva attached to inside of chimney or other artificial structure, rarely hollow tree; 4–5 eggs; 1 brood; April–August.

FEEDING Pursues a large variety of small aerial insects.

FLIGHT: fast, acrobatic, and erratic; very rapid, vibrating wing beats; soars with tail fanned.

HIGH FLYER
Swifts feed at heights on sunny days, and only feed near the ground when it is cold and cloudy.

SIMILAR SPECIES

BLACK SWIFT
see p.96
broader wings
larger overall

VAUX'S SWIFT
see p.98
paler rump
shorter wings and tail
paler throat

OCCURRENCE
Widespread in eastern North America, over many habitats: urban and suburban areas, small towns; in sparsely populated areas, nests in hollow trees and caves; regular in summer in southern California, present late March to early November. Winters in Amazonian South America.

Length **5in (13cm)**	Wingspan **14in (36cm)**	Weight **⅝–1¹⁄₁₆oz (17–30g)**
Social **Flocks**	Lifespan **Up to 15 years**	Status **Threatened**

DATE: _____ TIME: _____ LOCATION: _____

| Order **Apodiformes** | Family **Apodidae** | Species ***Chaetura vauxi*** |

Vaux's Swift

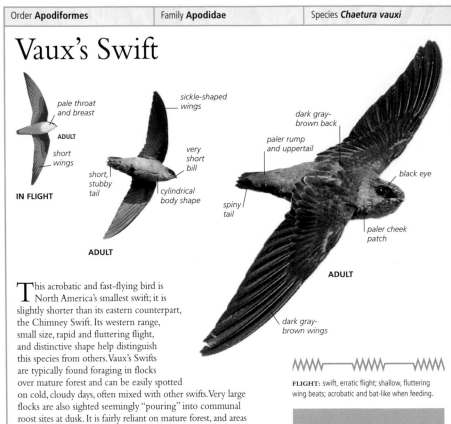

pale throat and breast

ADULT

short wings

IN FLIGHT

sickle-shaped wings

very short bill

short, stubby tail

cylindrical body shape

ADULT

dark gray-brown back

paler rump and uppertail

black eye

spiny tail

paler cheek patch

ADULT

dark gray-brown wings

This acrobatic and fast-flying bird is North America's smallest swift; it is slightly shorter than its eastern counterpart, the Chimney Swift. Its western range, small size, rapid and fluttering flight, and distinctive shape help distinguish this species from others. Vaux's Swifts are typically found foraging in flocks over mature forest and can be easily spotted on cold, cloudy days, often mixed with other swifts. Very large flocks are also sighted seemingly "pouring" into communal roost sites at dusk. It is fairly reliant on mature forest, and areas where this habitat has diminished have seen a corresponding decline in populations of Vaux's Swift. They may wander more widely in search of food in poor weather, even over towns.

VOICE High, insect-like chips and twittering in flight, often ending in buzzy trill.

NESTING Shallow cup of twigs, needles, and saliva attached to inside of hollow tree, rarely on chimneys; 4–6 eggs; 1 brood; June–September.

FEEDING Catches a wide variety of flying insects on the wing, including flies, moths, bees, beetles, and many others.

FLIGHT: swift, erratic flight; shallow, fluttering wing beats; acrobatic and bat-like when feeding.

AERIAL ACROBAT
Vaux's Swifts rarely land, spending all day hawking insects and even mating in flight.

| SIMILAR SPECIES | | OCCURRENCE |

BLACK SWIFT
see p.96
larger overall
blackish body
longer notched tail

CHIMNEY SWIFT
see p.97
longer tail and wings

OCCURRENCE
Occurs in North America from southeastern Alaska to California, where it breeds primarily in coniferous forests, nesting in large, hollow trunks; forages widely in many habitats. Resident population in Mexico; North American migrants move to Central America.

| Length **4¾in (12cm)** | Wingspan **12in (30cm)** | Weight **½–⅞oz (15–25g)** |
| Social **Migrant flocks** | Lifespan **Up to 7 years** | Status **Declining** |

DATE: _____ TIME: _____ LOCATION: _____

| Order **Apodiformes** | Family **Apodidae** | Species *Aeronautes saxatalis* |

White-throated Swift 🔊

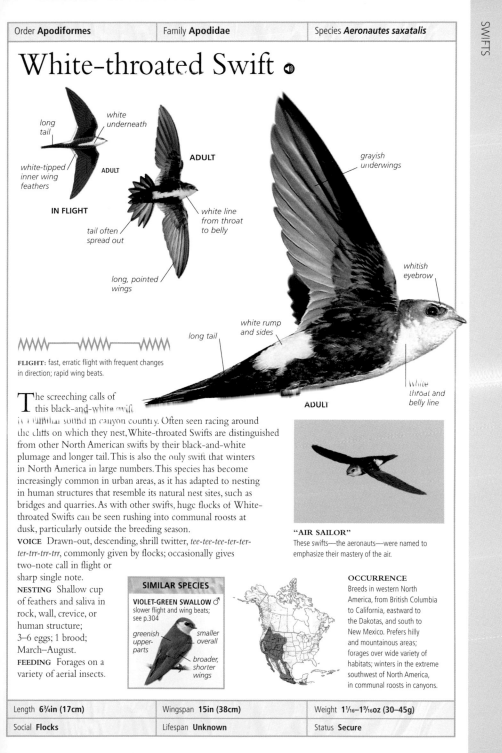

long tail

white underneath

ADULT

white-tipped inner wing feathers

ADULT

IN FLIGHT

grayish underwings

tail often spread out

white line from throat to belly

long, pointed wings

whitish eyebrow

long tail

white rump and sides

white throat and belly line

ADULT

FLIGHT: fast, erratic flight with frequent changes in direction; rapid wing beats.

The screeching calls of this black-and-white swift is a familiar sound in canyon country. Often seen racing around the cliffs on which they nest, White-throated Swifts are distinguished from other North American swifts by their black-and-white plumage and longer tail. This is also the only swift that winters in North America in large numbers. This species has become increasingly common in urban areas, as it has adapted to nesting in human structures that resemble its natural nest sites, such as bridges and quarries. As with other swifts, huge flocks of White-throated Swifts can be seen rushing into communal roosts at dusk, particularly outside the breeding season.

VOICE Drawn-out, descending, shrill twitter, *tee-tee-tee-ter-ter-ter-trr-trr-trr*, commonly given by flocks; occasionally gives two-note call in flight or sharp single note.

NESTING Shallow cup of feathers and saliva in rock, wall, crevice, or human structure; 3–6 eggs; 1 brood; March–August.

FEEDING Forages on a variety of aerial insects.

"AIR SAILOR"
These swifts—the aeronauts—were named to emphasize their mastery of the air.

SIMILAR SPECIES

VIOLET-GREEN SWALLOW ♂
slower flight and wing beats; see p.304

greenish upperparts

smaller overall

broader, shorter wings

OCCURRENCE
Breeds in western North America, from British Columbia to California, eastward to the Dakotas, and south to New Mexico. Prefers hilly and mountainous areas; forages over wide variety of habitats; winters in the extreme southwest of North America, in communal roosts in canyons.

| Length **6¾in (17cm)** | Wingspan **15in (38cm)** | Weight **1¹⁄₁₆–1⁹⁄₁₆oz (30–45g)** |
| Social **Flocks** | Lifespan **Unknown** | Status **Secure** |

| Order **Apodiformes** | Family **Trochilidae** | Species *Archilochus colubris* |

Ruby-throated Hummingbird 🔊

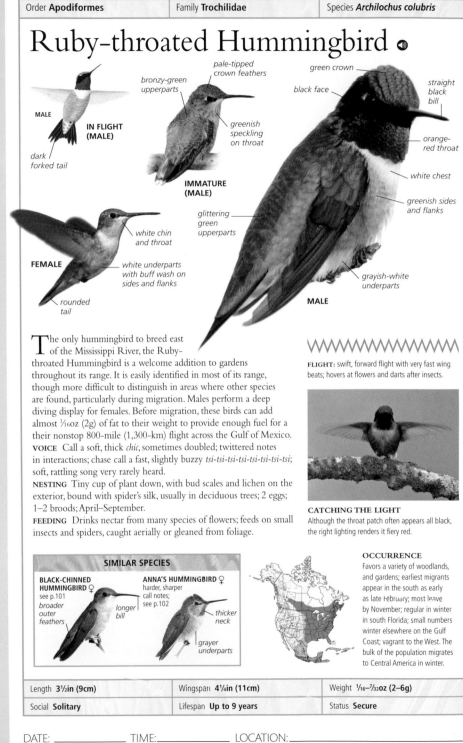

MALE

IN FLIGHT (MALE)

dark forked tail

pale-tipped crown feathers

bronzy-green upperparts

green crown

black face

straight black bill

greenish speckling on throat

orange-red throat

white chest

IMMATURE (MALE)

greenish sides and flanks

glittering green upperparts

white chin and throat

FEMALE

white underparts with buff wash on sides and flanks

rounded tail

grayish-white underparts

MALE

The only hummingbird to breed east of the Mississippi River, the Ruby-throated Hummingbird is a welcome addition to gardens throughout its range. It is easily identified in most of its range, though more difficult to distinguish in areas where other species are found, particularly during migration. Males perform a deep diving display for females. Before migration, these birds can add almost 1/16oz (2g) of fat to their weight to provide enough fuel for a their nonstop 800-mile (1,300-km) flight across the Gulf of Mexico.
VOICE Call a soft, thick *chic*, sometimes doubled; twittered notes in interactions; chase call a fast, slightly buzzy *tsi-tsi-tsi-tsi-tsi-tsi-tsi-tsi*; soft, rattling song very rarely heard.
NESTING Tiny cup of plant down, with bud scales and lichen on the exterior, bound with spider's silk, usually in deciduous trees; 2 eggs; 1–2 broods; April–September.
FEEDING Drinks nectar from many species of flowers; feeds on small insects and spiders, caught aerially or gleaned from foliage.

FLIGHT: swift, forward flight with very fast wing beats; hovers at flowers and darts after insects.

CATCHING THE LIGHT
Although the throat patch often appears all black, the right lighting renders it fiery red.

SIMILAR SPECIES

BLACK-CHINNED HUMMINGBIRD ♀
see p.101
broader outer feathers

longer bill

ANNA'S HUMMINGBIRD ♀
harder, sharper call notes;
see p.102
thicker neck

grayer underparts

OCCURRENCE
Favors a variety of woodlands, and gardens; earliest migrants appear in the south as early as late February; most leave by November; regular in winter in south Florida; small numbers winter elsewhere on the Gulf Coast; vagrant to the West. The bulk of the population migrates to Central America in winter.

| Length **3½in (9cm)** | Wingspan **4¼in (11cm)** | Weight **1/16–7/32oz (2–6g)** |
| Social **Solitary** | Lifespan **Up to 9 years** | Status **Secure** |

DATE: _____ TIME: _____ LOCATION: _____

| Order **Apodiformes** | Family **Trochilidae** | Species *Archilochus alexandri* |

Black-chinned Hummingbird

violet iridescence on lower part of throat

MALE

IN FLIGHT

notched tail

IMMATURE (MALE)

lighter gray-green crown

purple-and-black throat feathers

greenish upperparts

white tips to tail feathers

whitish underparts

FEMALE

dusky flanks

slightly decurved black bill

black or deep-purple throat

white collar below throat

dusky-green sides and flanks

MALE

notched greenish tail with darker outer feathers

The Black-chinned Hummingbird is found in southern British Columbia and is widespread across the western US, mainly due to its adaptability. It readily accepts offerings of sugar water from bird feeders. During courtship, the males perform a distinctive dive display comprising several broad arcs in addition to a short, back-and-forth shuttle display. The latter is accompanied by a droning noise produced by the bird's wings.
VOICE Call a soft, thick *chic*; fast, buzzy *tsi-tsi-tsi-tsi-tsi-tsi-tsi-tsi* is used to chase off other birds; song soft, warbling, very rarely heard.
NESTING Tiny cup of plant down, with leaves or lichen on the exterior, bound with spider's silk; usually built in a deciduous tree; 2 eggs; 1–2 broods; April–August.
FEEDING Drinks nectar from flowers; eats small insects and spiders, caught aerially or gleaned from foliage.

\/\/\/\/\/\/\/\/\/\/\/\/\/\/\/\

FLIGHT: rapid with very fast wing beats; hovers at flowers and darts after insects.

TAIL WAGGER
Black-chinned Hummingbirds regularly wag their tails from side to side while feeding.

SIMILAR SPECIES

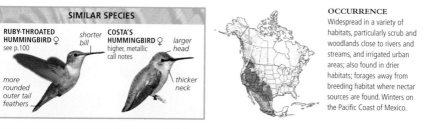

RUBY-THROATED HUMMINGBIRD ♀
see p.100

shorter bill

COSTA'S HUMMINGBIRD ♀
higher, metallic call notes

larger head

thicker neck

more rounded outer tail feathers

OCCURRENCE
Widespread in a variety of habitats, particularly scrub and woodlands close to rivers and streams, and irrigated urban areas; also found in drier habitats; forages away from breeding habitat where nectar sources are found. Winters on the Pacific Coast of Mexico.

| Length **3½in (9cm)** | Wingspan **4¾in (12cm)** | Weight **¹⁄₁₆–³⁄₁₆oz (2–5g)** |
| Social **Solitary** | Lifespan **Up to 8 years** | Status **Secure** |

DATE: _____ TIME: _____ LOCATION: _____

| Order **Apodiformes** | Family **Trochilidae** | Species **Calypte anna** |

Anna's Hummingbird 🔊

MALE

pale throat

IN FLIGHT

square tail

iridescent green upperparts

green crown and nape

rose-red head, sides of neck, and throat

short, straight black bill

green upperparts

reddish spots or flecks on throat

pale-gray underparts

FEMALE

rounded green tail

slightly notched, dark-green tail

mottled rosy crown

grayish underparts

MALE

greenish sides and flanks

IMMATURE (MALE)

The most common garden hummingbird along the Pacific Coast from British Columbia to northern Baja California, the iridescent rose-red helmet of a male Anna's Hummingbird is spectacular and distinctive. The females are rather drab by comparison. This adaptable hummingbird has expanded its range dramatically in the last century because of the availability of garden flowers and feeders. It previously bred only in areas of dense evergreen shrubs along the coast of southern California. The males perform an impressive diving display to court females.
VOICE Call a hard, sharp *tsit*, often doubled or given in series when perched; fast, buzzy chatter used to chase off other birds; song variable series of thin, high, buzzing, warbled notes.
NESTING Tiny cup of mostly plant down, with lichen on the exterior, bound with spider's silk, built in trees or shrubs; 2 eggs; 2 broods; December–July.
FEEDING Drinks nectar from flowers and feeders; eats small insects and spiders, caught aerially or gleaned from foliage.

FLIGHT: rapid flight with very fast wing beats; hovers at flowers and darts after insects.

VARIABLE THROAT
Mature female Anna's Hummingbirds often show small iridescent patches on their throats.

SIMILAR SPECIES

BLACK-CHINNED HUMMINGBIRD ♀
see p.101

thinner neck

whiter underparts

COSTA'S HUMMINGBIRD ♀

smaller overall

paler, cleaner underparts

OCCURRENCE
Primary breeding habitat is coastal dense shrubs and open woodland; also utilizes human areas. Habitat during migration and in winter largely dependent on available nectar sources; range expands northward and eastward during this time. Some birds winter in northwest Mexico; vagrant in the East.

| Length **4in (10cm)** | Wingspan **5in (13cm)** | Weight $^3/_{32}$–$^7/_{32}$oz (3–6g) |
| Social **Solitary** | Lifespan **Up to 8 years** | Status **Secure** |

DATE: _____ TIME:_____ LOCATION:_____

| Order **Apodiformes** | Family **Trochilidae** | Species *Selasphorus rufus* |

Rufous Hummingbird 🔊

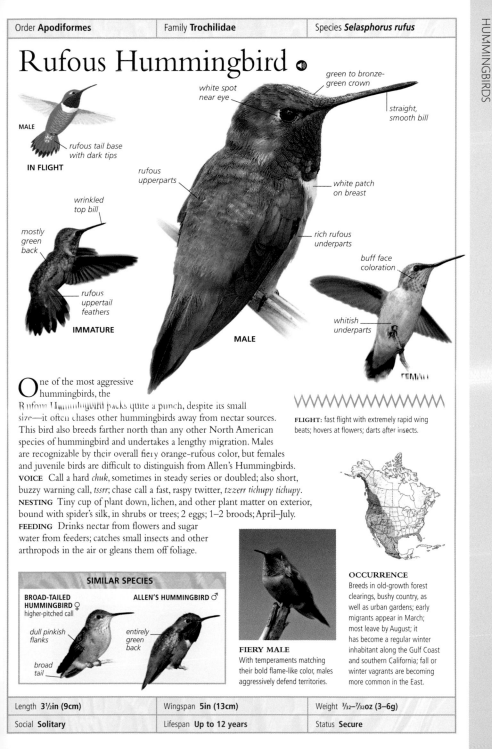

MALE
IN FLIGHT

green to bronze-green crown

white spot near eye

straight, smooth bill

rufous tail base with dark tips

rufous upperparts

white patch on breast

wrinkled top bill

mostly green back

rich rufous underparts

buff face coloration

rufous uppertail feathers

IMMATURE

whitish underparts

MALE

FEMALE

One of the most aggressive hummingbirds, the Rufous Hummingbird packs quite a punch, despite its small size—it often chases other hummingbirds away from nectar sources. This bird also breeds farther north than any other North American species of hummingbird and undertakes a lengthy migration. Males are recognizable by their overall fiery orange–rufous color, but females and juvenile birds are difficult to distinguish from Allen's Hummingbirds.
VOICE Call a hard *chuk*, sometimes in steady series or doubled; also short, buzzy warning call, *tssrr*; chase call a fast, raspy twitter, *tzzerr tichupy tichupy*.
NESTING Tiny cup of plant down, lichen, and other plant matter on exterior, bound with spider's silk, in shrubs or trees; 2 eggs; 1–2 broods; April–July.
FEEDING Drinks nectar from flowers and sugar water from feeders; catches small insects and other arthropods in the air or gleans them off foliage.

FLIGHT: fast flight with extremely rapid wing beats; hovers at flowers; darts after insects.

SIMILAR SPECIES

BROAD-TAILED HUMMINGBIRD ♀
higher-pitched call

dull pinkish flanks

broad tail

ALLEN'S HUMMINGBIRD ♂

entirely green back

FIERY MALE
With temperaments matching their bold flame-like color, males aggressively defend territories.

OCCURRENCE
Breeds in old-growth forest clearings, bushy country, as well as urban gardens; early migrants appear in March; most leave by August; it has become a regular winter inhabitant along the Gulf Coast and southern California; fall or winter vagrants are becoming more common in the East.

| Length **3½in (9cm)** | Wingspan **5in (13cm)** | Weight **³⁄₃₂–⁷⁄₃₂oz (3–6g)** |
| Social **Solitary** | Lifespan **Up to 12 years** | Status **Secure** |

| Order **Apodiformes** | Family **Trochilidae** | Species *Selasphorus calliope* |

Calliope Hummingbird

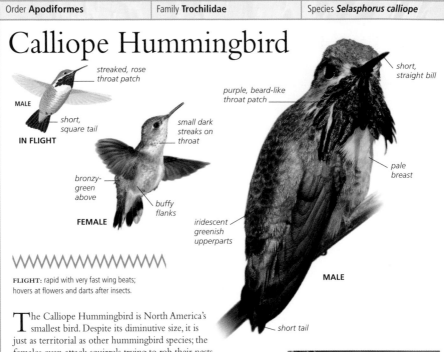

streaked, rose throat patch

MALE

IN FLIGHT

short, square tail

small dark streaks on throat

bronzy-green above

buffy flanks

FEMALE

purple, beard-like throat patch

short, straight bill

pale breast

iridescent greenish upperparts

MALE

short tail

FLIGHT: rapid with very fast wing beats; hovers at flowers and darts after insects.

The Calliope Hummingbird is North America's smallest bird. Despite its diminutive size, it is just as territorial as other hummingbird species; the females even attack squirrels trying to rob their nests. The streaky, purplish throat patch of the males is unique, but the plainer females can be confused with other hummingbird species when their small size is not evident in a direct comparison. The male courtship display includes a number of J-shaped dives, which are accompanied by a high *tzzt-zing* at the bottom, in addition to a buzzing hover display in front of a female.

VOICE Relatively silent for a hummingbird; call a soft, high *chip*, sometimes doubled or repeated; series of high buzzes and chips used to chase off other birds.

NESTING Tiny cup of plant material and lichen, bound with spider's silk and lined with plant down, usually under an overhanging conifer branch; 2 eggs; 1 brood; May–August.

FEEDING Catches insects aerially and from foliage, spiders; drinks nectar from flowers and feeders.

ATTRACTED TO SAP
The Calliope Hummingbird commonly feeds on sap and the insects attracted to it.

MOUNTAIN GEM
Like other hummingbirds, this mountain dweller hovers to take nectar from flowers.

OCCURRENCE
Present in western mountains primarily March–September; breeds mostly in coniferous mountainous forests, meadows, and thickets; spring migrants found in a variety of lower elevation habitats; fall migrants are found at higher elevations; very rare in winter along the Gulf Coast.

SIMILAR SPECIES

BROAD-TAILED HUMMINGBIRD ♀
sharper call note

larger overall

longer, more graduated tail

RUFOUS HUMMINGBIRD ♀
harder call note; see p.103

more rufous flanks

longer, more graduated tail

| Length **3¼in (8cm)** | Wingspan **4¼in (10.5cm)** | Weight **¹⁄₁₆–⁵⁄₃₂oz (2–4g)** |
| Social **Solitary** | Lifespan **Up to 12 years** | Status **Secure** |

DATE: _____ TIME: _____ LOCATION: _____

RAILS, CRANES, AND RELATIVES

THESE BIRDS OF THE MARSHES AND
WETLANDS include many distinctive
groups. The Rallidae, or rail family, is a
diverse group of small- to medium-sized
marsh birds, represented in Canada by
two long-billed rails, two short-billed
rails, two gallinules (only found in
Eastern Canada), and a coot. The cranes,
or Gruidae, include very large to huge
birds, superficially similar to storks and
the largest of the herons and egrets.
However, genetic and anatomical
differences place cranes in a different
order from storks, and herons and egrets.

RAILS AND COOTS

Rails are mostly secretive, solitary, and inconspicuous
in dense marsh vegetation, whereas coots are
seen on open water. Rails are all somewhat
chicken-like birds with stubby tails and short,
rounded wings. They look round-bodied from
the side but very slender from front to back—the
origin of the saying "as thin as a rail." The species
in the genus *Rallus* have excellent camouflage,
and are noted for their long legs, toes, and bills.
They are more often heard than seen. The two
short-billed rails are similar, but with shorter
necks and stout, stubby bills. Both groups walk
through wet marsh vegetation, though they can
swim well. The American Coot has broad lobes
along the sides of its toes,
making it a more proficient
swimmer and diver in
deeper water.
  None has a particularly
specialized diet; they eat
insects, small crabs, slugs,
snails, and plant matter.
Breeding pairs of rails
keep in close contact
in dense vegetation by
calling out loudly.

THIN AS A RAIL
This marsh-dwelling Virginia
Rail's narrow body enables it
to slip easily through reed beds.

CRANES

The two North American species of cranes have long
necks, small heads, and short bills. The long plumes
on their inner wing feathers form a bustle, cloaking
the tail on a standing crane, thereby giving them a
different profile than any heron. Cranes fly with their
necks straight out, rather than in the tight S-curve that
is regularly seen in similar-sized herons. Cranes are
long-distance migrants. The Whooping Crane, one
of the world's rarest birds, is the tallest bird in North
America, standing nearly 5ft (1.5m) high.

CRANE RALLY
Large numbers of Sandhill
Cranes gather on feeding
grounds in winter; groups
arrive in V-formation.

| Order **Gruiformes** | Family **Rallidae** | Species ***Coturnicops noveboracensis*** |

Yellow Rail

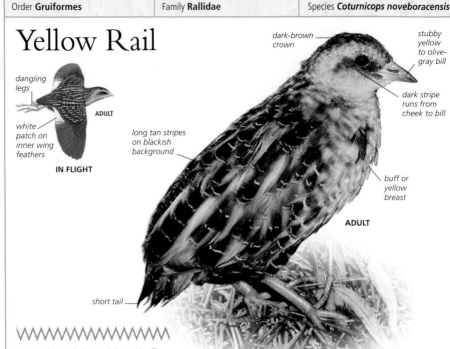

dark-brown crown

stubby yellow to olive-gray bill

dangling legs

ADULT

white patch on inner wing feathers

IN FLIGHT

dark stripe runs from cheek to bill

long tan stripes on blackish background

buff or yellow breast

ADULT

short tail

FLIGHT: low, weak, short, and direct with stiff wing beats; dangling legs.

Although widespread, the diminutive, secretive, nocturnal Yellow Rail is extremely difficult to observe in its dense, damp, grassy habitat. It is detected mainly by its voice. The Yellow Rail, whose Latin name *noveboracensis* means "of New York," has a small head, almost no neck, a stubby bill, a plump, almost tail-less body, and short legs. The bill of the male turns yellow in the breeding season; for the rest of the year, it is olive-gray like the female's. Although the Yellow Rail tends to dart for cover when disturbed, when it does fly, it reveals a distinctive white patch on its inner wing.

VOICE Two clicking calls followed by three more given by males, usually at night, reminiscent of two pebbles being struck together; also descending cackles, quiet croaking, and soft clucking.

NESTING Small cup of grasses and sedges, on the ground or in a plant tuft above water, concealed by overhanging vegetation; 8–10 eggs; 1 brood; May–June.

FEEDING Plucks seeds, aquatic insects, various small crustaceans, and mollusks (primarily small freshwater snails) from vegetation or ground; forages on the marsh surface or in shallow water, hidden by grass.

CURIOUS LISTENER
Imitating the Yellow Rail's "tick" calls by banging stones together can be an effective way to lure it out into the open.

OCCURRENCE
Breeds in brackish and freshwater marshes and wet sedge meadows in Canada and the north-central US; there is an isolated breeding population in Oregon. Winters predominantly in coastal marshes along the Eastern Seaboard.

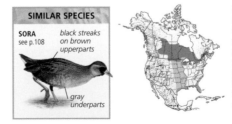

SIMILAR SPECIES

SORA
see p.108

black streaks on brown upperparts

gray underparts

| Length **7¼in (18.5cm)** | Wingspan **11in (28cm)** | Weight **1³/₄oz (50g)** |
| Social **Pairs** | Lifespan **Unknown** | Status **Special Concern** |

DATE: _____ TIME: _____ LOCATION: _____

| Order **Gruiformes** | Family **Rallidae** | Species *Rallus limicola* |

Virginia Rail

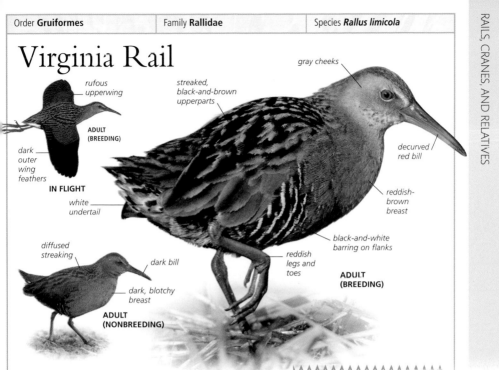

gray cheeks

rufous upperwing

streaked, black-and-brown upperparts

ADULT (BREEDING)

dark outer wing feathers

IN FLIGHT

white undertail

decurved red bill

reddish-brown breast

black-and-white barring on flanks

reddish legs and toes

ADULT (BREEDING)

diffused streaking

dark bill

dark, blotchy breast

ADULT (NONBREEDING)

A smaller version of the King Rail, this freshwater marsh dweller is similar to its other relatives, more often heard than seen. Distributed in a wide range, the Virginia Rail spends most of its time in thick, reedy vegetation, which it pushes aside using its "rail thin" body and flexible vertebrae. Although it spends most of its life walking, it can swim and even dive to escape danger. The Virginia Rail is a partial migrant that leaves its northern breeding grounds in winter.
VOICE Series of pig-like grunting oinks that start loud and sharp, becoming steadily softer; also emits a series of double notes *ka-dik ka-dik*.
NESTING Substantial cup of plant material, concealed by bent-over stems; 5–12 eggs; 1–2 broods; April–July.
FEEDING Actively stalks prey or may wait and dive into water; primarily eats snails, insects, and spiders, but may also eat seeds.

FLIGHT: weak and struggling with outstretched neck and legs trailing behind.

HARD TO SPOT
The secretive Virginia Rail is difficult to spot in its reedy habitat.

OCCURRENCE
Breeds in freshwater habitats across North America, though, it's found throughout the year along the West Coast of the US. In winter, moves to saltwater and freshwater marshes in the southern US, including Florida, and in northern and central Mexico.

SIMILAR SPECIES

CLAPPER RAIL

weak flank barring

orange face

dark undertail

KING RAIL   less gray face

larger overall

yellow-orange bill

| Length **9¹/₂in (24cm)** | Wingspan **13in (33cm)** | Weight **3oz (85g)** |
| Social **Pairs** | Lifespan **Unknown** | Status **Secure** |

DATE: _____ TIME: _____ LOCATION: _____

Order **Gruiformes**	Family **Rallidae**	Species **Porzana carolina**

Sora

white markings on back

ADULT (BREEDING)

IN FLIGHT

long, trailing legs

reduced black on face

ADULT (NONBREEDING)

white barring on flanks

short tail

no black mask

buffy breast

JUVENILE

brown cheek patch

yellow bill

black mask

gray breast

yellowish-green legs

ADULT (BREEDING)

Despite being the most widely distributed rail in North America, the Sora is rarely seen. It breeds in freshwater marshes and migrates hundreds of miles south in winter, despite its weak and hesitant flight. Although it has long, skinny toes, it swims well, with a characteristic head-bobbing action. The Sora can be spotted walking at the edge of emergent vegetation—its yellow bill and black mask distinguish it from other rails.

VOICE Call a long, high, and loud, descending, horse-like whinny *ko-wee-hee-hee-hee-hee*; has an upslurred whistle.

NESTING Loosely woven basket of marsh vegetation suspended above water or positioned in clumps of vegetation on the water's surface; 8–11 eggs; 1 brood; May–June.

FEEDING Rakes vegetation with feet or pulls with bill in search of seeds of wetland plants, insects, spiders, and snails.

FLIGHT: appears weak, yet strenuous; wing beats hurried and constant.

CHICKEN-LIKE WALK
A rare sight, the Sora walks chicken-like through a marsh, its body in a low crouch.

SIMILAR SPECIES

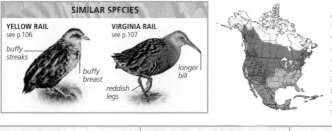

YELLOW RAIL
see p.106

buffy streaks

buffy breast

VIRGINIA RAIL
see p.107

longer bill

reddish legs

OCCURRENCE
Breeds in freshwater marshes with emergent vegetation across most of temperate North America; rarely in salt marshes along the Atlantic Coast. Winters in freshwater, saltwater, and brackish marshes with spartina grass from the southern US to northern South America.

Length **8¹/₂in (22cm)**	Wingspan **14in (36cm)**	Weight **2⁵/₈oz (75g)**
Social **Solitary**	Lifespan **Unknown**	Status **Secure**

DATE: _____ TIME: _____ LOCATION: _____

Order **Gruiformes**	Family **Rallidae**	Species *Fulica americana*

American Coot 🔊

ADULT (BREEDING)

black head

red eye

dark-gray body

white bill

white-edged feathers

IN FLIGHT

black ring on bill

dull, grayish plumage

long greenish-yellow legs

JUVENILE

ADULT (BREEDING)

lobed toes

This duck-like species of rail is the most abundant and widely distributed of North American rails. Its lobed toes make it well adapted to swimming and diving, but they are somewhat of an impediment on land. Its flight is clumsy; it becomes airborne with difficulty, running along the water's surface before taking off. American Coots form large flocks on open water in winter, often associating with ducks—an unusual trait for a member of the rail family.

VOICE Various raucous clucks, grunts, and croaks and an explosive *keek*.

NESTING Bulky cup of plant material placed in aquatic vegetation on or near water; 5–15 eggs; 1–2 broods; April–July.

FEEDING Forages on or under shallow water and feeds on land; primarily herbivorous, but also eats snails, insects, spiders, tadpoles, fish, and even carrion.

FLIGHT: low and labored; runs for quite a long distance to take off.

SWIMMING AWAY
The red-headed, baldish-looking American Coot chicks leave the nest a day after hatching.

SIMILAR SPECIES

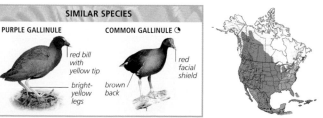

PURPLE GALLINULE

red bill with yellow tip

bright-yellow legs

COMMON GALLINULE ☾

red facial shield

brown back

OCCURRENCE
Breeds in open water habitats west of the Appalachians and in Florida. Moves from the northern parts of its range in winter to the southeastern US, where open water persists; also migrates to western and southern Mexico.

Length **15¹/₂in (40cm)**	Wingspan **24in (61cm)**	Weight **16oz (450g)**
Social **Flocks**	Lifespan **Up to 22 years**	Status **Secure**

| Order **Gruiformes** | Family **Gruidae** | Species ***Antigone canadensis*** |

Sandhill Crane 🔊

black wingtips

head held straight

ADULT

trailing legs · **IN FLIGHT**

brownish head

body with pale-brown smudges

JUVENILE

red crown

long black bill

pale cheek

long neck

ADULT

rusty body

shaggy feathers

long black legs

"IRON-STAINED" PLUMAGE

FLIGHT: alternates slow, steady flapping with periods of gliding; flocks in single-file.

These large, slender, and long-necked birds are famous for their elaborate courtship dances, far-carrying vocalizations, and remarkable migrations. Their bodies are sometimes stained with a rusty color, supposedly because they probe into mud which contains iron; when a bird preens, this is transferred from the bill to its plumage. Sandhill Cranes are broadly grouped into "Lesser" and "Greater" populations that differ in the geographical location of their breeding grounds and migration routes.

VOICE Call loud, wooden, hollow bugling, audible at great distances; noisy in flight and courtship.

NESTING Mound of sticks and grasses placed on ground; 1 egg; 1 brood; April–September.

FEEDING Eats shoots, grain; also aquatic mollusks, and insects.

MEMORABLE IMAGE
Its long neck, large wings, and distinctive red crown make it difficult to mistake.

SIMILAR SPECIES

GREAT BLUE HERON ◐ see p.203
dark crown
paler legs

WHOOPING CRANE see p.111
red on face
all-white plumage
larger overall

OCCURRENCE
Breeds in muskeg (peat bogs), tundra, and forest clearings across northwestern North America, east to Quebec and the Great Lakes; large wintering and migratory flocks, often densely packed, roost in or near marshes. Winters south to northern Mexico.

| Length 2³/₄–4ft (0.8–1.2m) | Wingspan 6–7¹/₂ft (1.8–2.3m) | Weight 7³/₄–11lb (3.5–5kg) |
| Social **Flocks** | Lifespan **Up to 40 years** | Status **Secure** |

DATE: _____ TIME: _____ LOCATION: _____

Order **Gruiformes**	Family **Gruidae**	Species ***Grus americana***

Whooping Crane

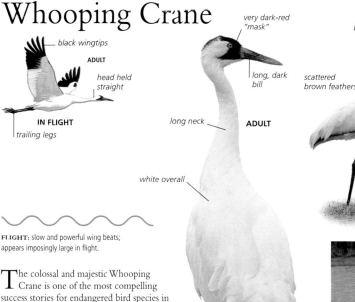

black wingtips

ADULT

head held straight

IN FLIGHT

trailing legs

very dark-red "mask"

long, dark bill

long neck

ADULT

white overall

brownish head

scattered brown feathers

JUVENILE

gray-black legs

~~~~~

FLIGHT: slow and powerful wing beats; appears imposingly large in flight.

The colossal and majestic Whooping Crane is one of the most compelling success stories for endangered bird species in Canada. Thanks to an ambitious campaign of habitat protection, captive breeding and release, and public education, the species has rebounded from just a few hundred birds in the mid-20th century to hundreds of individuals in the early 21st century. However, it still remains endangered, because it reproduces slowly in a restricted range, and additional intervention measures are required to help this fragile species continue its recovery.
VOICE Piercing and trumpeting, *kerloo!* and *kerleeyew*, audible from afar; bugling calls during courtship dances.
NESTING Mound of vegetation placed on ground; 2 eggs; 1 brood; April–August.
FEEDING Gleans animal and plant matter, such as frogs, mollusks, berries, and seeds, from the ground.

STATELY PROGRESS
Whooping Cranes move slowly and steadily through the shallows searching for prey.

OCCURRENCE
Breeds in marshy country with scattered ponds and prairies in a very small region of Canada; birds migrate along a narrow route to winter in coastal estuaries in Texas; on migration, uses both agricultural fields and marshland. Small numbers of migrants found with large numbers of Sandhill Cranes.

PREPARING TO LAND
The Whooping Crane brakes by opening its outer wing feathers to let air flow through.

SIMILAR SPECIES		
WHITE IBIS	**SANDHILL CRANE** see p.110	
less black in outer wings	smaller overall	
decurved bill		grayer overall

Length **4–4¹⁄₂ft (1.2–1.4m)**	Wingspan **7¹⁄₄ft (2.2m)**	Weight **15–18lb (7–8kg)**
Social **Solitary/Pairs**	Lifespan **Up to 30 years**	Status **Endangered**

DATE: _____ TIME: _____ LOCATION: _____

SHOREBIRDS, GULLS, AUKS, AND RELATIVES

THE DIVERSE SHOREBIRD, gull, and auk families together form the order Charadriiformes. They are small- to medium-sized, mostly migratory birds, associated with aquatic habitats. Over 100 species are found in North America.

TYPICAL GULL
Most large gulls, such as this Western Gull, have white heads and underparts with long, dark-tipped wings and a bright, sturdy bill.

SHOREBIRDS

The various species popularly known as shorebirds belong to several different families. In Canada, there are the oystercatchers (Haematopodidae), the avocets and stilts (Recurvirostridae), the plovers (Charadriidae), and the sandpipers and the phalaropes (Scolopacidae). They have long legs, in proportion to their bodies, and a variety of bills—ranging from short to long, thin, thick, straight, decurved, and recurved.

GULLS

The over 20 species of Canadian gulls in the subfamily Larinae all share a similar stout body shape, sturdy bills, and webbed toes. Nearly all are scavengers. Closely associated with coastal areas, few gulls venture far out to sea. Some species are seen around fishing ports and harbors, or inland, especially in urban areas, landfills, and farm fields.

TERNS

Terns are specialized, long-billed predators that dive for fish. More slender and elegant than gulls, nearly all are immediately recognizable when breeding, due to their black caps and long, pointed bills.

AUKS

Denizens of the northern oceans, these birds come to land only to breed. Most nest in colonies on sheer cliffs overlooking the ocean, but puffins excavate burrows in the ground, and some murrelets nest away from predators high up in treetops far inland.

COLOR-CHANGE BILL
The bright colors of a breeding Tufted Puffin's bill fade to more muted tones in winter, after the breeding season.

ON THE MOVE
Dunlins and other sandpipers gather in large, highly coordinated flocks on migration.

| Order **Charadriiformes** | Family **Recurvirostridae** | Species *Himantopus mexicanus* |

Black-necked Stilt

ADULT

long, angular black wings

white spot above the eye

long, slender neck

IN FLIGHT

scaly appearance

JUVENILE

less contrasting head pattern than adult

shorter, stubbier bill

white spot above red eye

black mask encircles eye

black upperparts

long, needle-like black bill

slender, tapered body

white underparts

MALE

long bright-pink legs

brownish wash to back

duller legs than male

FEMALE

This tall, slender, elegant, and black-and-white shorebird is a familiar sight at ponds and lagoons in the western and southern US and in the southern Canadian prairies. Even among the shorebirds, it is remarkably long-legged, at times almost grotesquely so: in flight, it often crosses its trailing feet as if for extra control and support. Breeding takes place in small colonies, with several pairs sharing the same site. In winter, these tall birds are often seen in small flocks of about 25 individuals. These small groups feed quietly in sheltered areas, but they aggressively drive visitors away with their raucous calls, dog-like yips, and noisy communal protests. The increased use of pesticides and loss of wetland habitat could cause a decline in their numbers in the future.

VOICE Flight and alarm call a loud, continuous poodle-like *yip-yip-yip*, given in a long series when alarmed.

NESTING Simple scrape lined with grass in soft soil; 4 eggs; 1 brood; April–May.

FEEDING Walks slowly in shallow water, picking food off surface; diet includes tadpoles, shrimps, snails, flies, worms, clams, small fish, and frogs.

FLIGHT: direct, but somewhat awkward due to long, trailing legs; deep wing beats.

FRIENDLY BUNCH
Black-necked Stilts are gregarious by nature, and they often roost together in shallow water.

OCCURRENCE
Breeds around marshes, shallow grassy ponds, lake margins, and artificial waterbodies, such as reservoirs; uses similar habitats during migration and winter, as well as shallow lagoons, flooded fields, and mangrove swamps. Southern birds only migrate locally.

| Length **14–15½in (35–39cm)** | Wingspan **29–32in (73–81cm)** | Weight **4–8oz (125–225g)** |
| Social **Small flocks** | Lifespan **Up to 19 years** | Status **Secure** |

| Order **Charadriiformes** | Family **Recurvirostridae** | Species *Recurvirostra americana* |

American Avocet

striking black-and-white pattern

ADULT (BREEDING)

IN FLIGHT

white eye-ring

dark eye

cinnamon-colored head

long, thin, recurved bill

bold shoulder feathers

cinnamon-colored neck

white underparts

no cinnamon color on head and neck

FEMALE

white plumage

long, bluish legs

less recurved bill

MALE

long, bluish legs

ADULT (NONBREEDING)

FLIGHT: fast, direct, and graceful; very long legs extend beyond tail.

With its long, thin, and upturned bill, this graceful, long-legged shorebird is unmistakable when foraging. When it takes off, its striking plumage pattern is clearly visible. It is the only one of the four avocet species in the world that changes plumage when breeding. Breeding birds have a cinnamon head and neck, and bold patterns on their black-and-white wings and upperparts. The American Avocet forms large flocks during migration and in winter.

VOICE Flight call a variable melodic *kleet*, loud and repetitive, given when alarmed and by foraging birds.

NESTING Simple scrape in shallow depression; 4 eggs; 1 brood; May–June.

FEEDING Uses specialized bill to probe, scythe, or jab a variety of aquatic invertebrates, small fish, and seeds; walks steadily in belly-deep water to chase its prey.

FORAGING FLOCK
These birds walk through shallow water in flocks, searching mainly for insects and crustaceans.

TRICKY BALANCE
During mating, the male supports himself with raised wings as the female extends her neck.

OCCURRENCE
Breeds in temporary wetlands, in dry to arid regions. During migration and in winter, found in shallow water habitats, including ponds, reservoirs, fresh- and saltwater marshes, tidal mudflats, and lagoons. Each year, flock of 10,000 birds winters at Bolivar Flats, Texas. Regular East Coast visitor.

| Length **17–18½in (43–47cm)** | Wingspan **29–32in (74–81cm)** | Weight **10–12oz (275–350g)** |
| Social **Large flocks** | Lifespan **Up to 9 years** | Status **Secure** |

DATE: _____ TIME: _____ LOCATION: _____

| Order **Charadriiformes** | Family **Haematopodidae** | Species *Haematopus bachmani* |

Black Oystercatcher 🔊

IN FLIGHT

ADULT

long orange-red bill

broad, powerful wings

dark-brown to black body

bright-yellow eye

orange-red eye-ring

ADULT

thick pink legs

dull-orange eye-ring

dark eye

dark tip of bill

JUVENILE

This large, striking oystercatcher shares the typical round-bodied, hunch-backed, and squat-necked shape of other oystercatchers as well as their typical thick legs and bill. But it is instantly obvious because of its all-dark plumage, making the pale eyes and colorful bill all the more conspicuous. It is restricted to rocky coasts, where it feeds in pairs or family groups, using well-defined territories in summer. In winter, the birds gather in larger flocks, sometimes in hundreds, where mussels are abundant. These are noisy, demonstrative birds, and always entertaining to watch.

VOICE Flight call a loud, whistled *wheeu*, with emphasis on first part of call; alarm call sharper *wheep*; courtship and posturing calls a series of whistles based on flight call, accelerating into descending piping calls.

NESTING Simple scrape just above high-tide line, often lined with broken shells and pebbles; 1–3 eggs; 1 brood; May–June.

FEEDING Feeds on slightly submerged shellfish beds; diet includes mollusks, particularly mussels and limpets; also eats a variety of crustaceans, such as crabs and barnacles; rarely consumes oysters.

FLIGHT: strong, powerful flight with shallow wing beats.

MUSSEL LOVER
The Black Oystercatcher can often be spotted walking noisily along mussel beds at low tide.

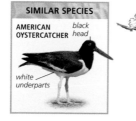

SIMILAR SPECIES

AMERICAN OYSTERCATCHER

black head

white underparts

OCCURRENCE
Feeds in the area between the high- and low-tide marks on rocky shores of western North America, from Alaska southward to Baja California. Breeds just above high-tide line on rocky headlands or sand, shell, and gravel beaches. In winter, also found on rocky jetties in southern part of range.

Length **16½–18½in (42–47cm)**	Wingspan **30–34in (77–86cm)**	Weight **18–25oz (500–700g)**
Social **Pairs/Flocks**	Lifespan **10–15 years**	Status **Secure**

DATE: _____ TIME:_____ LOCATION:_____

| Order **Charadriiformes** | Family **Charadriidae** | Species *Pluvialis squatarola* |

Black-bellied Plover 🔊

white rump

white-edged, dark-centered feathers

checkered upperparts

diffused streaks to upper breast

whitish crown

white rump

black outer wing feathers

MALE (BREEDING)

white wing stripe

markedly streaked breast

whitish underparts

ADULT (NONBREEDING)

black cheeks

JUVENILE

ADULT (NONBREEDING)

checkered black-and-white upperparts

checkered black-and-white upperparts

darker crown

black underwing patch

IN FLIGHT

black belly

duller plumage than male

MALE (BREEDING)

FEMALE (MOLTING TO BREEDING PLUMAGE)

FLIGHT: straight and fast; powerful wing beats.

The Black-bellied Plover is the largest and most common of the three North American *Pluvialis* plovers. Its preference for open feeding habitats, its bulky structure, and very upright stance make it a fairly conspicuous species. The Black-bellied Plover's black underwing patches, visible in flight, are present in both its breeding and nonbreeding plumages and distinguish it from the other *Pluvialis* plovers.

VOICE Typical call a three-syllabled, clear, plaintive, whistled *whEE-er-eee*, with middle note lower; flight song of male during breeding softer, with accent on second syllable.

NESTING Shallow depression lined with mosses and lichens in moist to dry lowland tundra; 1–5 eggs; 1 brood; May–July.

FEEDING Forages mainly along coasts in typical plover style: run, pause, and pluck; eats insects, worms, bivalves, and crustaceans.

CASUAL WADING
The Black-bellied Plover wades in shallow water but does most of its foraging in mudflats.

SIMILAR SPECIES

AMERICAN GOLDEN-PLOVER ✻
see p.117

dark cap

MOUNTAIN PLOVER ✻

sandy-brown upperparts

dingy brownish upperparts

white underparts

OCCURRENCE
Breeds in high-Arctic habitats from western Russia across the Bering Sea to Alaska, and east to Baffin Island; winters primarily in coastal areas from southern Canada and the US, south to southern South America. Found inland during migration. Migrates south all the way to South America.

| Length **10½–12in (27–30cm)** | Wingspan **29–32in (73–81cm)** | Weight **5–9oz (150–250g)** |
| Social **Flocks** | Lifespan **Up to 12 years** | Status **Secure** |

DATE: _____ TIME: _____ LOCATION: _____

Order **Charadriiformes**	Family **Charadriidae**	Species *Pluvialis dominica*

American Golden-Plover

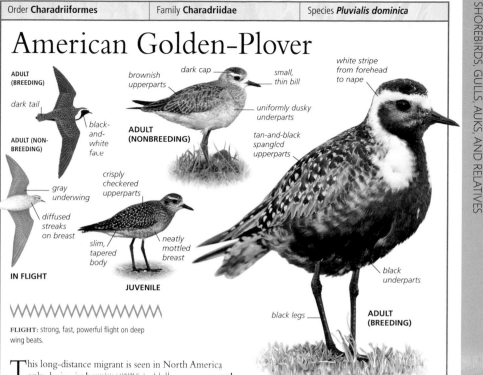

ADULT (BREEDING)

dark tail

black-and-white face

ADULT (NON-BREEDING)

gray underwing

diffused streaks on breast

IN FLIGHT

brownish upperparts

dark cap

crisply checkered upperparts

slim, tapered body

neatly mottled breast

JUVENILE

small, thin bill

uniformly dusky underparts

ADULT (NONBREEDING)

tan-and-black spangled upperparts

white stripe from forehead to nape

black underparts

black legs

ADULT (BREEDING)

WWWWWWWWWW

FLIGHT: strong, fast, powerful flight on deep wing beats.

This long-distance migrant is seen in North America only during its lengthy spring and fall journeys to and from its high-Arctic breeding grounds and wintering locations in southern South America. An elegant, slender, yet large plover, it prefers inland grassy habitats and plowed fields to coastal mudflats. The American Golden-Plover's annual migration route includes a feeding stop at Labrador, then a 1,550–1,860-mile (2,500–3,000km) flight over the Atlantic Ocean to South America.

VOICE Flight call a whistled two-note *queE-dle*, or *klee-u*, with second note shorter and lower pitched, male flight song a strong, melodious whistled *kid-eek*, or *kid-EEp*.

NESTING Shallow depression lined with lichens in dry, open tundra; 4 eggs; 1 brood; May–July.

FEEDING Forages in run, pause, and pluck sequence on insects, mollusks, crustaceans, and worms; also berries and seeds.

DISTRACTION TECHNIQUE
This breeding American Golden-Plover is feigning an injury to its wing to draw predators away from its chicks or eggs in its nest.

OCCURRENCE
Breeds in Arctic tundra habitats. During migration, it occurs in prairies, tilled farmlands, golf courses, pastures, airports; also mudflats, shorelines, and beaches. In spring, seen in Texas and the Great Plains; in fall, uncommon in northeast Maritimes and New England; scarce along the Pacific Coast.

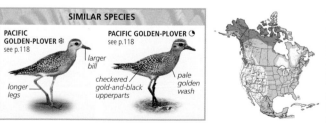

SIMILAR SPECIES

PACIFIC GOLDEN-PLOVER ❊
see p.118

longer legs

larger bill

PACIFIC GOLDEN-PLOVER ☽
see p.118

checkered gold-and-black upperparts

pale golden wash

Length **9½–11in (24–28cm)**	Wingspan **23–28in (59–72cm)**	Weight **4–7oz (125–200g)**
Social **Solitary/Small flocks**	Lifespan **At least 8 years**	Status **Secure**

DATE: _____ TIME: _____ LOCATION: _____

| Order **Charadriiformes** | Family **Charadriidae** | Species *Pluvialis fulva* |

Pacific Golden-Plover

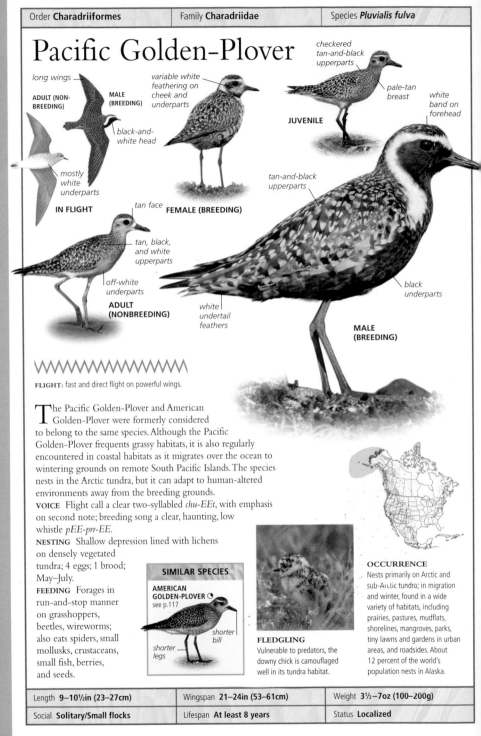

long wings

ADULT (NON-BREEDING)

MALE (BREEDING)

variable white feathering on cheek and underparts

black-and-white head

mostly white underparts

IN FLIGHT

tan face

FEMALE (BREEDING)

tan, black, and white upperparts

off-white underparts

ADULT (NONBREEDING)

checkered tan-and-black upperparts

JUVENILE

pale-tan breast

white band on forehead

tan-and-black upperparts

white undertail feathers

black underparts

MALE (BREEDING)

VVVVVVVVVV

FLIGHT: fast and direct flight on powerful wings.

The Pacific Golden-Plover and American Golden-Plover were formerly considered to belong to the same species. Although the Pacific Golden-Plover frequents grassy habitats, it is also regularly encountered in coastal habitats as it migrates over the ocean to wintering grounds on remote South Pacific Islands. The species nests in the Arctic tundra, but it can adapt to human-altered environments away from the breeding grounds.

VOICE Flight call a clear two-syllabled *chu-EEt*, with emphasis on second note; breeding song a clear, haunting, low whistle *pEE-prr-EE*.

NESTING Shallow depression lined with lichens on densely vegetated tundra; 4 eggs; 1 brood; May–July.

FEEDING Forages in run-and-stop manner on grasshoppers, beetles, wireworms; also eats spiders, small mollusks, crustaceans, small fish, berries, and seeds.

SIMILAR SPECIES

AMERICAN GOLDEN-PLOVER ☾
see p.117

shorter bill

shorter legs

FLEDGLING
Vulnerable to predators, the downy chick is camouflaged well in its tundra habitat.

OCCURRENCE
Nests primarily on Arctic and sub-Arctic tundra; in migration and winter, found in a wide variety of habitats, including prairies, pastures, mudflats, shorelines, mangroves, parks, tiny lawns and gardens in urban areas, and roadsides. About 12 percent of the world's population nests in Alaska.

| Length **9–10½in (23–27cm)** | Wingspan **21–24in (53–61cm)** | Weight **3½–7oz (100–200g)** |
| Social **Solitary/Small flocks** | Lifespan **At least 8 years** | Status **Localized** |

DATE: _____ TIME: _____ LOCATION: _____

Killdeer 🔊

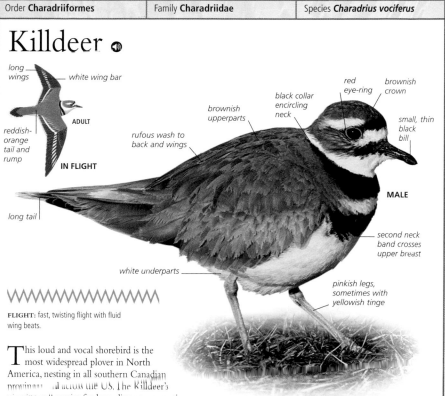

long wings
white wing bar
ADULT
reddish-orange tail and rump
IN FLIGHT
long tail

brownish upperparts
rufous wash to back and wings
black collar encircling neck
red eye-ring
brownish crown
small, thin black bill
MALE
second neck band crosses upper breast
white underparts
pinkish legs, sometimes with yellowish tinge

FLIGHT: fast, twisting flight with fluid wing beats.

This loud and vocal shorebird is the most widespread plover in North America, nesting in all southern Canadian provinces and across the US. The Killdeer's piercing call carries for long distances, sometimes causing other birds to fly away in fear of imminent danger. These birds often nest near human habitation, allowing a close observation of their vigilant parental nature with young chicks.

VOICE Flight call a rising, drawn out *deeee*; alarm call a loud, penetrating *dee-ee*, given repetitively; agitated birds also give series of *dee* notes, followed by a rising trill.

NESTING Scrape on ground, sometimes in slight depression; 4 eggs; 1 brood (north), 2–3 broods (south); March–July.

FEEDING Forages in typical plover style: run, pause, and pick; eats a variety of invertebrates, such as worms, snails, grasshoppers, and beetles; also small vertebrates and seeds.

CLEVER MANEUVER
The Killdeer lures intruders away from its nest with a "broken wing" display.

SIMILAR SPECIES

SEMIPALMATED PLOVER ❋
see p.100
orange-yellow legs
smaller overall
single dark neckband

WILSON'S PLOVER
see p.384
single black collar
pinkish legs
short tail

OCCURRENCE
Widespread across Canada and the US, the Killdeer occurs in a wide variety of habitats. These include shorelines, mudflats, lake and river edges, sparsely grassy fields and pastures, golf courses, roadsides, parking lots, flat rooftops, driveways, and other terrestrial habitats.

| Length **9–10in (23–26cm)** | Wingspan **23–25in (58–63cm)** | Weight **2¼–3⅛ oz (65–90g)** |
| Social **Small flocks** | Lifespan **Up to 10 years** | Status **Declining** |

DATE: _____ TIME: _____ LOCATION: _____

| Order **Charadriiformes** | Family **Charadriidae** | Species *Charadrius semipalmatus* |

Semipalmated Plover 🔊

IN FLIGHT
- pointed wings
- black tail band

ADULT (BREEDING)
- scalloped feather edges
- pale base of bill
- brownish breastband

JUVENILE

- white eyestripe
- brownish crown
- brownish upperparts
- diffused brownish collar

ADULT (NONBREEDING)

ADULT (BREEDING)
- yellow eye-ring
- black forecrown
- black bill with orange base
- black breastband
- orange legs
- white underparts
- yellowish legs

Similar in appearance to the Common Ringed Plover in Eurasia, the Semipalmated Plover is a small bird with a tapered shape. They are a familiar sight in a wide variety of habitats during migration and in winter, they gather in loose flocks. A casual walk down a sandy beach between fall and spring might awaken up to 100 Semipalmated Plovers, sleeping in slight depressions in the sand, though, flocks of up to 1,000 birds may also be encountered.

VOICE Flight call a whistled abrupt *chu-WEEp*, with soft emphasis on second syllable; courtship display song is quick version of flight call followed by rough *r-r-r-r-r-r*, ending with a slurred, descending *yelp*.

NESTING Simple scrape on bare or slightly vegetated ground in Arctic tundra; 3–4 eggs; 1 brood; May–June.

FEEDING Forages in typical plover style: run, pause, and pluck; eats aquatic mollusks, crustaceans, flies, beetles, and spiders.

FLIGHT: straight, fast; with fluttering wing beats.

BY SIGHT AND TOUCH
Semipalmated Plovers locate prey by sight or through the sensitive soles of their feet.

SIMILAR SPECIES

WILSON'S PLOVER
- heavier, dark bill
- pinkish legs

COMMON RINGED PLOVER
- wider breastband

OCCURRENCE
Breeding habitat is Arctic or sub-Arctic tundra with well-drained gravel, shale, or other sparsely vegetated ground. During migration, they inhabit mudflats, saltwater marshes, lake edges, tidal areas, and flooded fields. During winter, coastal or near coastal habitats are chosen.

| Length **6³⁄₄–7¹⁄₂in (17–19cm)** | Wingspan **17–20¹⁄₂in (43–52cm)** | Weight **1¹⁄₁₆–2¹⁄₂oz (30–70g)** |
| Social **Solitary/Flocks** | Lifespan **Up to 6 years** | Status **Secure** |

DATE: _____ TIME: _____ LOCATION: _____

Order **Charadriiformes**	Family **Charadriidae**	Species *Charadrius melodus*

Piping Plover

IN FLIGHT

prominent white
wing stripe

stubby bill

dusky
tail
band

**MALE
(BREEDING)**

less pronounced
black markings
than male

breastband
sometimes
incomplete

**FEMALE
(BREEDING)**

black
forecrown

pale-gray
upperparts

black-
tipped
orange
bill

dark
breastband

indistinct, partial
breastband

**ADULT
(NON-
BREEDING)**

mostly black
bill with slight
orange base

**MALE
(BREEDING)**

thin white collar
throughout year

orange legs

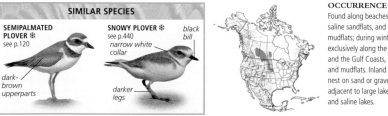

FLIGHT: fast, twisting flight; rapid wing beats.

Small and pale, the Piping Plover is at risk due
to eroding coastlines, human disturbance, and
predation by foxes, raccoons, and cats. With its pale-gray
back, it is well camouflaged along beaches or in dunes, but conservation
measures, such as fencing off nesting beaches and controlling predators,
are necessary to restore populations. Two subspecies of the Piping Plover
are recognized; one nests on the Atlantic Coast and the other inland.
VOICE Clear, whistled *peep* call in flight; quiet *peep-lo* during courtship
and contact; high-pitched *pipe-pipe-pipe* song.
NESTING Shallow scrape in sand, gravel, dunes, or salt flats; 4 eggs;
1 brood; April–May.
FEEDING Typical run-pause-pluck plover feeding style;
diet includes marine worms, insects, and mollusks.

VULNERABLE NESTS
The fragile nature of their preferred nesting sites
has led to this species becoming endangered.

SIMILAR SPECIES

**SEMIPALMATED
PLOVER** ❋
see p.120

dark-
brown
upperparts

SNOWY PLOVER ❋
see p.440

narrow white
collar

black
bill

darker
legs

OCCURRENCE
Found along beaches, in
saline sandflats, and adjacent
mudflats; during winter, found
exclusively along the Atlantic
and the Gulf Coasts, sandflats,
and mudflats. Inland subspecies
nest on sand or gravel beaches
adjacent to large lakes, rivers,
and saline lakes.

Length 6½–7in (17–18cm)	Wingspan 18–18½in (45–47cm)	Weight 1⅝–2⅜oz (45–65g)
Social **Small flocks**	Lifespan **Up to 11 years**	Status **Endangered**

DATE: _____ TIME:_____ LOCATION:_____

| Order **Charadriiformes** | Family **Scolopacidae** | Species *Bartramia longicauda* |

Upland Sandpiper

ADULT

long tail

long, narrow wings

IN FLIGHT

pale head

speckled breast

JUVENILE

large, dark eye

small, pigeon-like head

short, straight, mostly yellow bill

mostly brownish upperparts

buff feather fringes

long tail extends beyond wings

yellow legs

ADULT (BREEDING)

Unlike other sandpipers, this graceful bird spends most of its life away from water in grassy habitats. The Upland Sandpiper's coloration helps it camouflage itself in the grasslands, especially while nesting on the ground. It is well known for landing on fence posts and raising its wings while giving its tremulous, whistling call. The bird is currently listed as endangered in many of its breeding states/provinces due to the disappearance of its grassland habitat.

VOICE Flight call a low *qui-pi-pi-pi*; song consists of gurgling notes followed by long, descending "wolf whistle" *whoooleeeeee, wheeelooooo-ooooo*.

NESTING Simple depression in ground among grass clumps; 4 eggs; 1 brood; May.

FEEDING Feeds, with head-bobbing motion, on adult and larval insects, spiders, worms, centipedes; occasionally seeds.

FLIGHT: strong and swift; rapid, fluttering flight in breeding display.

DRY GROUND WADER
A true grassland species, the Upland Sandpiper is rarely found away from these habitats.

SIMILAR SPECIES

WHIMBREL
see p.123

long, decurved bill

dull bluish-gray legs

LONG-BILLED CURLEW ♂
see p.124

much larger overall

very long, decurved bill

OCCURRENCE
Breeds in native tallgrass or mixed-grass prairies. Airports make up a large portion of its breeding habitat in the northeast US. During migration and in winter, it prefers shortgrass habitats, such as grazed pastures, turf farms, and cultivated fields.

| Length **11–12½in (28–32cm)** | Wingspan **25–27in (64–68cm)** | Weight **4–7oz (150–200g)** |
| Social **Migrant flocks** | Lifespan **Up to 12 years** | Status **Declining** |

DATE: _____ TIME: _____ LOCATION: _____

| Order **Charadriiformes** | Family **Scolopacidae** | Species **Numenius phaeopus** |

Whimbrel

long, pointed wings

ADULT

all-dark rump

coarsely streaked face, neck, and breast

IN FLIGHT

striped crown

brownish patterned upperparts

large, heavy body

long, decurved, mostly black bill; orange base in winter

finely streaked neck, breast, and underparts

light-brown spotting to upper breast

brownish tail and rump

ADULT

long grayish legs

FLIGHT: steady and moderate wing beats; often glides.

This large, conspicuous shorebird is the most widespread of the curlew species, with four subspecies across North America and Eurasia. Its bold head stripes and clearly streaked face, neck, and breast make the species distinctive. The Whimbrel's fairly long, decurved bill allows it to probe into fiddler crab burrows, a favorite food item.

VOICE Characteristic call is a loud, staccato *pi-pi-pi-pi-pi*; flight song a series of haunting melodious whistles, followed by long trill.

NESTING Depression in hummock, mound, grass, sedge, or gravel; 4 eggs; 1 brood; May–August.

FEEDING Probes for crabs, in addition to worms, mollusks, and fish; also eats insects and berries.

LARGE MOUTHFUL
The Whimbrel often rinses muddy crabs in water before swallowing them whole.

UP CLOSE
A close look at the Whimbrel shows this bird's beautiful, fine patterning.

OCCURRENCE
Several populations breed in northern, sub-Arctic, and low-Arctic regions of North America; during migration and in winter, found mostly in coastal marshes, tidal creeks, flats, and mangroves; also at the inland Salton Sea, California. Winters along rocky coasts in South America.

SIMILAR SPECIES

BRISTLE-THIGHED CURLEW

pale rump

more spotted

longer, slightly curved bill

LONG-BILLED CURLEW
see p.124

larger overall

longer, decurved bill

| Length **15½–16½in (39–42cm)** | Wingspan **30–35in (76–89cm)** | Weight **11–18oz (300–500g)** |
| Social **Flocks** | Lifespan **Up to 19 years** | Status **Secure** |

DATE: _____ TIME: _____ LOCATION: _____

| Order **Charadriiformes** | Family **Scolopacidae** | Species ***Numenius americanus*** |

Long-billed Curlew

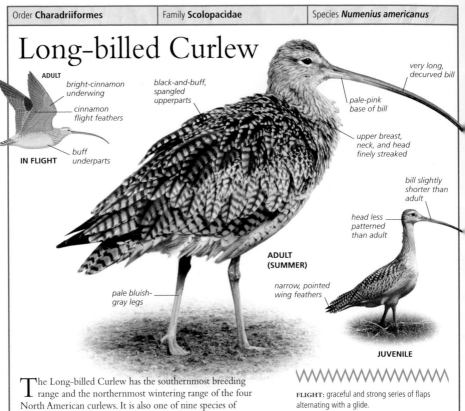

ADULT

bright-cinnamon underwing

cinnamon flight feathers

buff underparts

IN FLIGHT

black-and-buff, spangled upperparts

very long, decurved bill

pale-pink base of bill

upper breast, neck, and head finely streaked

bill slightly shorter than adult

head less patterned than adult

ADULT (SUMMER)

pale bluish-gray legs

narrow, pointed wing feathers

JUVENILE

T he Long-billed Curlew has the southernmost breeding range and the northernmost wintering range of the four North American curlews. It is also one of nine species of birds that are endemic to the grasslands of the Great Plains. Its large size and tame behavior on its wintering grounds in North America add to its mystique. The curvature of its bill is adapted to probe for food in soft mud and sand.

VOICE Flight call a two-note *cur-LUoo*, often accompanied by rapid *qui-pi-pi-pi-pi*; flight song consists of haunting whistles, trills *werr-EEEer*.

NESTING Shallow depression in sparsely vegetated prairie habitat; 4 eggs; 1 brood; April–May.

FEEDING Picks insects on the surface or probes in soft mud for insects, crustaceans, mollusks, and worms; also eats fish.

FLIGHT: graceful and strong series of flaps alternating with a glide.

APTLY NAMED
The Long-billed Curlew is the longest-billed shorebird in North America.

OCCURRENCE
Breeds in prairies, shortgrass and mixed-grass habitats of the Great Basin and the Great Plains. Winters in wet pastures, marshes, beaches, and tidal mudflats primarily of California, Texas, and Mexico, with some stragglers occurring in Florida. Generally not a "shorebird" found along shores.

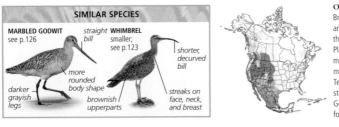

SIMILAR SPECIES

MARBLED GODWIT see p.126

straight bill

darker grayish legs

more rounded body shape

WHIMBREL smaller; see p.123

shorter, decurved bill

streaks on face, neck, and breast

brownish upperparts

| Length **20–26in (51–65cm)** | Wingspan **30–39in (75–100cm)** | Weight **16–28oz (450–800g)** |
| Social **Solitary/Winter flocks** | Lifespan **At least 8 years** | Status **Special Concern** |

DATE: _____ TIME: _____ LOCATION: _____

| Order **Charadriiformes** | Family **Scolopacidae** | Species *Limosa haemastica* |

Hudsonian Godwit

white wing stripe

white rump

IN FLIGHT

brownish-gray upperparts

ADULT (NONBREEDING)

pale eyebrow

off-white underparts

pale buffy feather fringes

JUVENILE

black-and-white upperparts

unpatterned brownish wing feathers

black tail

rich chestnut underparts with black barring

MALE (BREEDING)

long orange-based recurved bill

brownish streaked head and neck

white-feathered chestnut breast

FEMALE (BREEDING)

FLIGHT: swift and straight, with fast and powerful wing beats.

This large, graceful sandpiper, with a long and slightly recurved bill, undertakes a remarkable annual migration from its tundra breeding grounds in Alaska and Canada all the way to extreme southern South America—a distance probably close to 10,000 miles (16,000km) in one direction, with very few stopovers. There are perhaps 50,000–80,000 breeding pairs. Counts in Tierra del Fuego indicate a total of perhaps 30,000 to 40,000 birds wintering there, all found in two areas of tidal mudflats. Between the far North and the far South, North American stops are few, and only in the spring, along a mid-continental central route. Hudsonian Godwits spend six months wintering, two months breeding, and four flying between the two locations.

VOICE Flight call emphatic *peed-wid*; also high *peet* or *kwee*; display song *to-wida to-wida to-wida*, or *to-wit, to-wit, to-wit*.

NESTING Saucer-shaped depression on dry hummock or tussocks under cover; 4 eggs; 1 brood; May–July.

FEEDING Probes in mud for insects, insect grubs, worms, crustaceans, and mollusks; also eats plant tubers in fall.

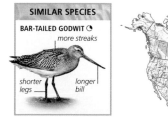

LONG-HAUL BIRD
Hudsonian Godwits only make a few stops on their long flights to and from South America.

SIMILAR SPECIES

BAR-TAILED GODWIT ☾
more streaks

shorter legs

longer bill

OCCURRENCE
Breeds in the high Arctic, in sedge meadows and bogs in scattered tundra; scarce along the Atlantic Coast in fall, near coastal freshwater reservoirs; but locally common in flooded rice fields, pastures, and reservoirs in spring. Winters in extreme southern Chile and Argentina.

| Length **14–16in (35–41cm)** | Wingspan **27–31in (68–78cm)** | Weight **7–12oz (200–350g)** |
| Social **Flocks** | Lifespan **Up to 29 years** | Status **Vulnerable** |

DATE: _____ TIME: _____ LOCATION: _____

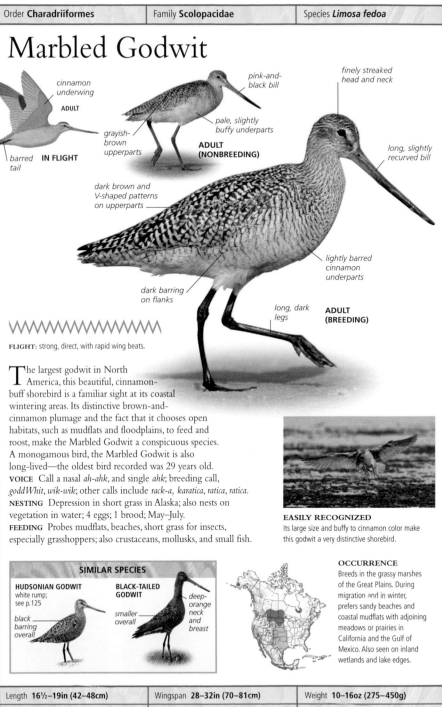

| Order **Charadriiformes** | Family **Scolopacidae** | Species *Limosa fedoa* |

Marbled Godwit

cinnamon underwing

ADULT

pink-and-black bill

finely streaked head and neck

barred tail   **IN FLIGHT**

grayish-brown upperparts

pale, slightly buffy underparts

ADULT (NONBREEDING)

long, slightly recurved bill

dark brown and V-shaped patterns on upperparts

dark barring on flanks

long, dark legs

ADULT (BREEDING)

lightly barred cinnamon underparts

FLIGHT: strong, direct, with rapid wing beats.

The largest godwit in North America, this beautiful, cinnamon-buff shorebird is a familiar sight at its coastal wintering areas. Its distinctive brown-and-cinnamon plumage and the fact that it chooses open habitats, such as mudflats and floodplains, to feed and roost, make the Marbled Godwit a conspicuous species. A monogamous bird, the Marbled Godwit is also long-lived—the oldest bird recorded was 29 years old.

VOICE Call a nasal *ah-ahk*, and single *ahk*; breeding call, *goddWhit, wik-wik*; other calls include *rack-a, karatica, ratica, ratica*.

NESTING Depression in short grass in Alaska; also nests on vegetation in water; 4 eggs; 1 brood; May–July.

FEEDING Probes mudflats, beaches, short grass for insects, especially grasshoppers; also crustaceans, mollusks, and small fish.

EASILY RECOGNIZED
Its large size and buffy to cinnamon color make this godwit a very distinctive shorebird.

SIMILAR SPECIES

HUDSONIAN GODWIT
white rump; see p.125

black barring overall

BLACK-TAILED GODWIT
smaller overall

deep-orange neck and breast

OCCURRENCE
Breeds in the grassy marshes of the Great Plains. During migration and in winter, prefers sandy beaches and coastal mudflats with adjoining meadows or prairies in California and the Gulf of Mexico. Also seen on inland wetlands and lake edges.

| Length **16½–19in (42–48cm)** | Wingspan **28–32in (70–81cm)** | Weight **10–16oz (275–450g)** |
| Social **Winter flocks** | Lifespan **Up to 29 years** | Status **Secure** |

DATE: _____ TIME:_____ LOCATION:_____

Ruddy Turnstone

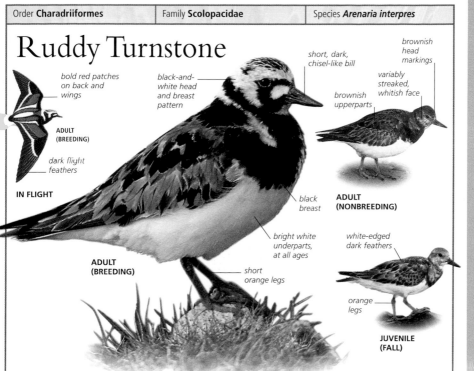

bold red patches on back and wings

ADULT (BREEDING)

dark flight feathers

IN FLIGHT

black-and-white head and breast pattern

short, dark, chisel-like bill

brownish head markings

brownish upperparts

variably streaked, whitish face

ADULT (NONBREEDING)

black breast

bright white underparts, at all ages

ADULT (BREEDING)

short orange legs

white-edged dark feathers

orange legs

JUVENILE (FALL)

This handsome, medium-sized, stocky sandpiper with a chisel-shaped bill is a common visitor along the shorelines of North and South America. On its high-Arctic breeding grounds, it is bold and aggressive and is able to drive off predators as large as the Glaucous Gull and the Parasitic Jaeger. The Ruddy Turnstone was given its name due to its reddish back color and because of its habit of flipping and overturning items like mollusk shells and pebbles, or digging in the sand and looking for small crustaceans and other marine invertebrates. Two subspecies live in Arctic North America: *A. i. interpres* in northeast Canada and *A. i. morinellas* elsewhere in Canada and Alaska.

VOICE Rapid chatter on breeding ground: *TIT-wooo TIT-woooRITititititit;* flight call a low, rapid *kut-a-kut.*

NESTING Simple scrape lined with lichens and grasses in dry, open areas; 4 eggs; 1 brood; June.

FEEDING Forages along shoreline for crustaceans, insects, including beetles, spiders; also eats plants.

FLIGHT: swift and strong flight, with quick wing beats.

WINTER GATHERINGS
Ruddy Turnstones often congregate in large winter flocks on rocky shorelines.

SIMILAR SPECIES

BLACK TURNSTONE see p.128

darker overall

no rust color in plumage

duller legs

OCCURRENCE
Breeds in high-Arctic: wide-open, barren, and grassy habitats and rocky coasts, usually near water. In winter, on sandy or gravel beaches and rocky shorelines, from northern California to South America, and from northern Massachusetts south along the Atlantic and Gulf Coasts.

Length **8–10½in (20–27cm)**	Wingspan **20–22½in (51–57cm)**	Weight **3½–7oz (100–200g)**
Social **Flocks**	Lifespan **Up to 7 years**	Status **Secure**

DATE: _____ TIME: _____ LOCATION: _____

| Order **Charadriiformes** | Family **Scolopacidae** | Species *Arenaria melanocephala* |

Black Turnstone

stocky, pointed wings

white patch on back

ADULT (NONBREEDING)

black tail band

IN FLIGHT

dark chocolate-brown head and breast

short, blackish, chisel-like bill

brownish upperparts, with scattered black feathers

black head and breast with white flecking

white patch

blackish back

pale edges to some feathers

white belly

ADULT (NONBREEDING)

yellowish legs

darker legs

ADULT (BREEDING)

The Black Turnstone is found along the entire North American Pacific coastline in winter, from Kodiak Island, Alaska, to the Gulf of California. Highly dependent on rocky shorelines, the cryptic plumage of this species blends in well, and it becomes almost invisible when it forages or roosts on dark, rocky surfaces. Although the Black Turnstone flips stones and beach litter in search of food, it uses its chisel-like bill to pry loose or crack tougher prey, particularly mussels and barnacles. On its breeding grounds, this species is a vocal and aggressive defender of the nesting community, even physically attacking predators, such as jaegars.

VOICE Flight call a *breerp*, often continued as rapid chattering; variety of trills, purrs, and a *tu-whit* call.

NESTING Hollow depression in tundra; 4 eggs; 1 brood; May–June.

FEEDING Eats invertebrates, such as mussels, barnacles, limpets, snails, and crabs, also seeds, small bird eggs, and carrion.

FLIGHT: swift and direct, with strong, shallow wing beats.

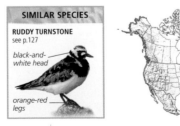

CRACKING IT
Black Turnstones use their chisel-shaped bills to break open barnacles on rocks.

SIMILAR SPECIES

RUDDY TURNSTONE
see p.127

black-and-white head

orange-red legs

OCCURRENCE
Breeds in tundra of western Alaska; also inland along rivers and lakes. It is strictly coastal during migration and winter, where it is found in the tidal zone of rocky shorelines—on sand and gravel beaches, mudflats, and rocky jetties of the West Coast, south to Baja, California.

| Length **8½–10½in (22–27cm)** | Wingspan **20–22½in (51–57cm)** | Weight **3⅛–6oz (90–175g)** |
| Social **Flocks** | Lifespan **At least 4 years** | Status **Secure** |

DATE: _____ TIME: _____ LOCATION: _____

Order **Charadriiformes**	Family **Scolopacidae**	Species *Calidris canutus*

Red Knot

grayish upperparts

white wing stripe

white eyebrow

JUVENILE

pale fringes to wing feathers

ADULT (WINTER)

IN FLIGHT

mostly pale-gray upperparts

gray spots on upper breast

yellowish-green legs

pale underparts

ADULT (WINTER)

boldly marked black, rust, and white upperparts

dark, straight, stocky bill

salmon-colored face and breast

white lower belly with dark V-shaped marks

short, dark legs

ADULT (SUMMER)

A substantial, plump sandpiper, the Red Knot is the largest North American shorebird in the genus *Calidris*. There are two North American subspecies—*C. c. rufa* and *C. c. roselaari*. Noted for its extraordinary long-distance migration, *C. c. rufa* flies about 9,300 miles (15,000km) between its high-Arctic breeding grounds and the wintering area in South America, especially in Tierra del Fuego, at the tip of South America. Recent declines have occurred in this population, attributed to overharvesting of horseshoe crab eggs—its critical food source. With the population of *C. c. rufa* having declined from over 100,000 birds in the mid-1980s to below 15,000 today, the Red Knot is now listed as endangered in New Jersey, and faces possible extinction.

VOICE Flight call a soft *kuEEt* or *kuup*; display song eerie *por-meeee por-meeee*, followed by *por-por por-por*.

NESTING Simple scrape in grassy or barren tundra, often lined; 4 eggs; 1 brood; June.

FEEDING Probes mud or sand for insects, plant material, small mollusks, crustaceans, especially small snails, worms, and other invertebrates.

FLIGHT: powerful, swift, direct flight with rapid wing beats.

STAGING AREAS
Red Knots form colossal flocks during migration and on their wintering grounds.

SIMILAR SPECIES

BLACK-BELLIED PLOVER
see p.116

large, dark eye

longer, dark legs

see p.116

OCCURRENCE
Breeds in flat, barren tundra in the high-Arctic islands and peninsulas. Mostly coastal during migration and winter, preferring sandbars, beaches, and tidal flats, where it congregates in huge flocks.

Length **9–10in (23–25cm)**	Wingspan **23–24in (58–61cm)**	Weight **3⅜–8oz (95–225g)**
Social **Large flocks**	Lifespan **Up to 19 years**	Status **Threatened**

DATE: _____ TIME: _____ LOCATION: _____

Order **Charadriiformes**	Family **Scolopacidae**	Species *Calidris virgata*

Surfbird

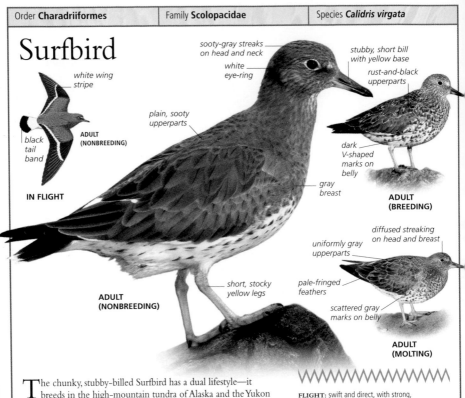

IN FLIGHT

white wing stripe

black tail band

sooty-gray streaks on head and neck

white eye-ring

plain, sooty upperparts

gray breast

ADULT (NONBREEDING)

short, stocky yellow legs

stubby, short bill with yellow base

rust-and-black upperparts

dark V-shaped marks on belly

ADULT (BREEDING)

diffused streaking on head and breast

uniformly gray upperparts

pale-fringed feathers

scattered gray marks on belly

ADULT (MOLTING)

The chunky, stubby-billed Surfbird has a dual lifestyle—it breeds in the high-mountain tundra of Alaska and the Yukon and then migrates to the rocky Pacific coasts of both North and South America. Some individuals migrate as far as southern Chile, a round trip of about 19,000 miles (30,500km) each year. This remarkable wintering range is among the largest of all North American shorebirds. The extent of the rust color on the upperparts of breeding Surfbirds is variable.

VOICE Flight call a soft *whiff-if-if;* feeding flocks soft, chattering *whiks;* display call *kree, kree…ki-drr ki-drr,* and *quoy quoy quoy.*

NESTING Shallow, lined depression on vegetated or bare ground; 4 eggs; 1 brood; May–June.

FEEDING Eats mainly insects, especially beetles; also aquatic mollusks and crustaceans, such as mussels and barnacles.

FLIGHT: swift and direct, with strong, powerful wing beats.

COASTAL PROXIMITY
Except when breeding, Surfbirds spend their lives along rocky intertidal shores.

SIMILAR SPECIES

PURPLE SANDPIPER ✳
see p.135

purplish-gray upperparts

longer bill

ROCK SANDPIPER
see p.134

darker feathers on back

longer, slightly decurved bill

short yellow-orange legs

OCCURRENCE
Breeds in low- to high-elevation steep, rocky slopes of ridges and mountains; the rest of the year, it spends exclusively on rocky Pacific coastlines, typically within 6½ft (2m) of the high-tide line (the narrowest range of all North American shorebirds).

Length **9½–10½in (24–27cm)**	Wingspan **25–27in (63–68cm)**	Weight **4–8oz (125–225g)**
Social **Small flocks**	Lifespan **Unknown**	Status **Secure**

DATE: _____ TIME: _____ LOCATION: _____

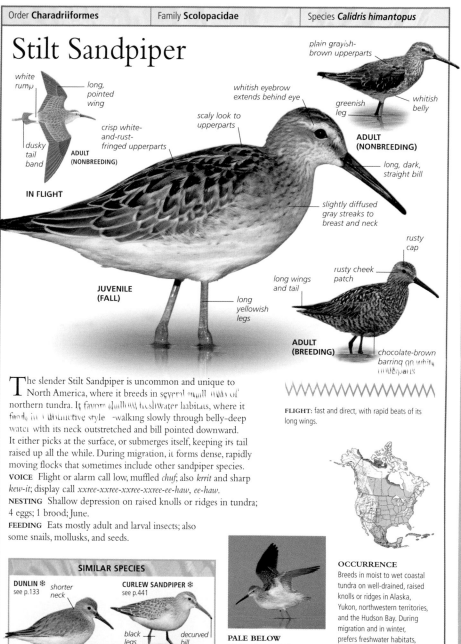

Stilt Sandpiper

plain grayish-brown upperparts

white rump

long, pointed wing

whitish eyebrow extends behind eye

scaly look to upperparts

greenish leg

whitish belly

dusky tail band

ADULT (NONBREEDING)

crisp white-and-rust-fringed upperparts

ADULT (NONBREEDING)

long, dark, straight bill

IN FLIGHT

slightly diffused gray streaks to breast and neck

rusty cap

rusty cheek patch

long wings and tail

JUVENILE (FALL)

long yellowish legs

ADULT (BREEDING)

chocolate-brown barring on white underparts

The slender Stilt Sandpiper is uncommon and unique to North America, where it breeds in several small areas of northern tundra. It favors shallow freshwater habitats, where it feeds in a distinctive style—walking slowly through belly-deep water with its neck outstretched and bill pointed downward. It either picks at the surface, or submerges itself, keeping its tail raised up all the while. During migration, it forms dense, rapidly moving flocks that sometimes include other sandpiper species.

VOICE Flight or alarm call low, muffled *chuf*; also *krrit* and sharp *kew-it*; display call *xxree-xxree-xxree-xxree-ee-haw, ee-haw*.

NESTING Shallow depression on raised knolls or ridges in tundra; 4 eggs; 1 brood; June.

FEEDING Eats mostly adult and larval insects; also some snails, mollusks, and seeds.

FLIGHT: fast and direct, with rapid beats of its long wings.

SIMILAR SPECIES

DUNLIN ❋ see p.133 — shorter neck — shorter black legs

CURLEW SANDPIPER ❋ see p.441 — black legs — decurved bill

PALE BELOW Wading through shallow water, this Stilt Sandpiper displays its whitish underparts.

OCCURRENCE
Breeds in moist to wet coastal tundra on well-drained, raised knolls or ridges in Alaska, Yukon, northwestern territories, and the Hudson Bay. During migration and in winter, prefers freshwater habitats, such as flooded fields, marsh pools, reservoirs, and sheltered lagoons to tidal mudflats.

| Length **8–9in (20–23cm)** | Wingspan **17–18½in (43–47cm)** | Weight **1¾–2⅛oz (50–60g)** |
| Social **Pairs/Flocks** | Lifespan **At least 3 years** | Status **Secure** |

DATE: _____ TIME: _____ LOCATION: _____

| Order **Charadriiformes** | Family **Scolopacidae** | Species *Calidris alba* |

Sanderling

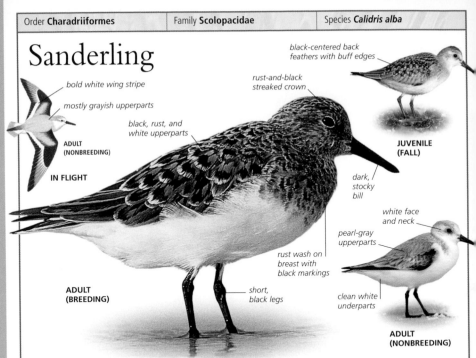

bold white wing stripe

mostly grayish upperparts

black, rust, and white upperparts

ADULT (NONBREEDING)

IN FLIGHT

rust-and-black streaked crown

black-centered back feathers with buff edges

JUVENILE (FALL)

dark, stocky bill

white face and neck

pearl-gray upperparts

rust wash on breast with black markings

clean white underparts

ADULT (BREEDING)

short, black legs

ADULT (NONBREEDING)

The Sanderling is among the best-known shorebirds in the world. It breeds in some of the most remote, high-Arctic habitats, from Greenland to Siberia, but occupies just about every temperate and tropical shoreline in the Americas when not breeding. Indeed, its wintering range spans both American coasts, from Canada to Argentina. Feeding in flocks, it is a common sight in winter on sandy beaches. In many places though, the bird is declining rapidly, with pollution of the sea and shore, and the disturbance caused by people using beaches for various recreational purposes being the main causes.

VOICE Flight call squeaky *pweet*, threat call *sew-sew-sew*; display song harsh, buzzy notes and chattering *cher-cher-cher*.

NESTING Small, shallow depression on dry, stony ground; 4 eggs; 1–3 broods; June–July.

FEEDING Probes along the surf-line in sand for insects, small crustaceans, small mollusks, and worms.

FLIGHT: rapid, free-form; birds in flocks twisting and turning as if they were one.

CHASING THE WAVES
The Sanderling scampers after retreating waves to pick up any small creatures stranded by the sea.

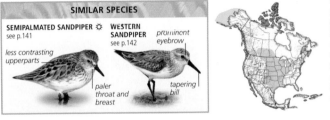

SIMILAR SPECIES

SEMIPALMATED SANDPIPER ☼
see p.141

less contrasting upperparts

WESTERN SANDPIPER
see p.142

prominent eyebrow

paler throat and breast

tapering bill

OCCURRENCE
Breeds in barren high-Arctic coastal tundra of northernmost Canada, including the islands, north to Ellesmere Island. During winter months and migration, found along all North American coastlines, but especially sandy beaches; inland migrants found along lake and river edges.

Length **7½–8in (19–20cm)**	Wingspan **16–18in (41–46cm)**	Weight **1⁷⁄₁₆–3½oz (40–100g)**
Social **Small flocks**	Lifespan **Up to 10 years**	Status **Declining**

DATE: _____ TIME:_____ LOCATION:_____

| Order **Charadriiformes** | Family **Scolopacidae** | Species *Calidris alpina* |

Dunlin

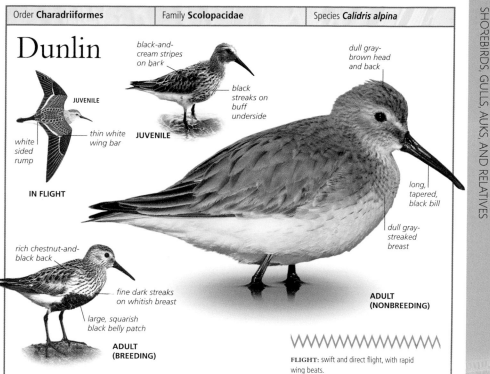

JUVENILE

black-and-cream stripes on back

black streaks on buff underside

JUVENILE

dull gray-brown head and back

white sided rump

thin white wing bar

IN FLIGHT

long, tapered, black bill

dull gray-streaked breast

ADULT (NONBREEDING)

rich chestnut-and-black back

fine dark streaks on whitish breast

large, squarish black belly patch

ADULT (BREEDING)

The Dunlin is one of the most abundant and widespread of North America's shorebirds, but of the ten nationally recognized subspecies, only two breed in Canada: *C. a. arcticola* and *C. a. hudsonia*. The Dunlin is unmistakable in its striking red-backed, black-bellied breeding plumage. In winter, it sports much drabber colors but more than makes up for this by gathering in spectacular flocks—of many thousands of birds—on its favorite coastal mudflats.

VOICE Call accented trill, *drurr-drurr*, that rises slightly, then descends; flight call *jeeezp*; song *wrraah-wrraah*.

NESTING Simple cup lined with grasses, leaves, and lichens in moist to wet tundra; 4 eggs; 1 brood; June–July.

FEEDING Probes for marine, freshwater, terrestrial invertebrates: clams, worms, insect larvae, crustaceans; also plants and small fish.

FLIGHT: swift and direct flight, with rapid wing beats.

OLD RED BACK
The Dunlin was once known as the Red-backed Sandpiper due to its distinct breeding plumage.

SIMILAR SPECIES

STILT SANDPIPER ❊
see p.131

CURLEW SANDPIPER ❊
see p.441

longer, thinner neck

yellowish-green legs

less streaking on chest

longer legs

OCCURRENCE
Breeds in Arctic and sub-Arctic moist, wet tundra, often near ponds, with drier islands for nest sites. In migration and winter, prefers coastal areas with extensive mudflats and sandy beaches; also feeds in flooded fields and seasonal inland wetlands.

Length **6¹/₂–8¹/₂in (16–22cm)**	Wingspan **12¹/₂–17¹/₂in (32–44cm)**	Weight **1⁹/₁₆–2¹/₄oz (45–65g)**
Social **Large flocks**	Lifespan **Up to 24 years**	Status **Declining**

DATE: _____ TIME: _____ LOCATION: _____

| Order **Charadriiformes** | Family **Scolopacidae** | Species *Calidris ptilocnemis* |

Rock Sandpiper

ADULT (NONBREEDING)

IN FLIGHT
- bold white wing stripe

greenish yellow on base of bill

dark-gray head, neck, and upper breast

slightly darker, uniform gray upperparts

variable gray streaks on breast

ADULT (NONBREEDING)

crisply fringed white, rust, and buff upperparts

white belly

JUVENILE

rounded head

rusty cap

medium-length, dark bill

gray-streaked nape

reddish-and-black feathers on upperparts

rust-and-black cheek patch

white throat

diffused black streaks on upper breast

**ADULT
C. p. couesi
(ALEUTIAN; BREEDING)**

variable black belly patch

FLIGHT: strong, swift, and direct flight, often low, with clipped wing beats.

dull, yellowish legs

**ADULT
C. p. ptilocnemis
(PRIBILOF; BREEDING)**

All three regularly occurring North American subspecies of this bird breed in the Bering Sea region. The Rock Sandpiper is the western, and closely related, counterpart of the Purple Sandpiper. The two species have the most northerly wintering range of any shorebird in North America. Only one subspecies, *C. p. tschuktschorum*, migrates to the Pacific Coast of North America.

VOICE Call short squeaking *chreet*, *cheet*, or *cheerrt*; song *di-jerr*, *di-jerr*, *di-jerr* and more melodic *quida-se-quida-we-quida*.

NESTING Simple scrape in coastal lowland and mountain tundra; 4 eggs; 1 brood; May–June.

FEEDING Probes for clams and snails in seaweed; in breeding season eats mainly land insects, especially beetles.

CLOSE ENCOUNTER
The Rock Sandpiper is not easily frightened, allowing it to be clearly identified.

SIMILAR SPECIES

SURFBIRD
see p.130

short, stout bill

spotted underparts

PURPLE SANDPIPER
see p.135

longer bill

dark-centered shoulder feathers

OCCURRENCE
Breeds in Arctic lowland coastal heath tundra or mountain tundra. On migration and in winter, can be found in a variety of habitats including rocky headlands, gravel beaches, mudflats, and sandflats, perhaps commonest along rocky shores south to southern California.

| Length **7¼–9½in (18.5–24cm)** | Wingspan **13–18½in (33–47cm)** | Weight **2½–4oz (70–125g)** |
| Social **Large flocks** | Lifespan **At least 7 years** | Status **Secure** |

DATE: _____ TIME: _____ LOCATION: _____

| Order **Charadriiformes** | Family **Scolopacidae** | Species *Calidris maritima* |

Purple Sandpiper

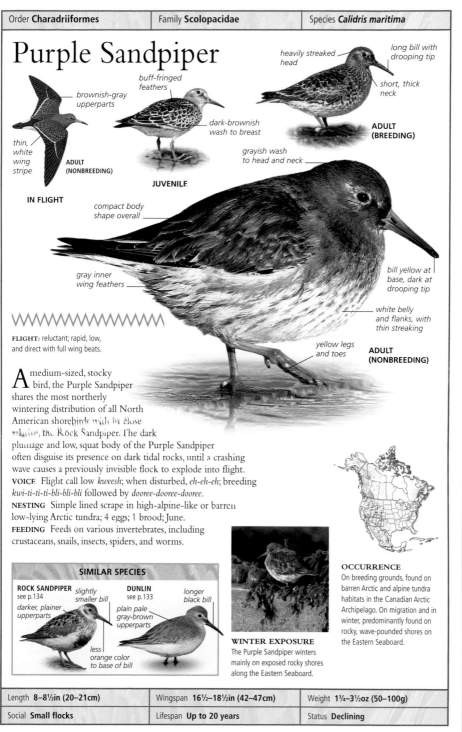

brownish-gray
upperparts

buff-fringed
feathers

heavily streaked
head

long bill with
drooping tip

short, thick
neck

**ADULT
(BREEDING)**

thin,
white
wing
stripe

**ADULT
(NONBREEDING)**

dark-brownish
wash to breast

JUVENILE

grayish wash
to head and neck

IN FLIGHT

compact body
shape overall

gray inner
wing feathers

bill yellow at
base, dark at
drooping tip

white belly
and flanks, with
thin streaking

FLIGHT: reluctant; rapid, low,
and direct with full wing beats.

yellow legs
and toes

**ADULT
(NONBREEDING)**

A medium-sized, stocky bird, the Purple Sandpiper shares the most northerly wintering distribution of all North American shorebirds with its close relative, the Rock Sandpiper. The dark plumage and low, squat body of the Purple Sandpiper often disguise its presence on dark tidal rocks, until a crashing wave causes a previously invisible flock to explode into flight.
VOICE Flight call low *kweesh*; when disturbed, *eh-eh-eh*; breeding *kwi-ti-ti-ti-bli-bli-bli* followed by *dooree-dooree-dooree*.
NESTING Simple lined scrape in high-alpine-like or barren low-lying Arctic tundra; 4 eggs; 1 brood; June.
FEEDING Feeds on various invertebrates, including crustaceans, snails, insects, spiders, and worms.

SIMILAR SPECIES

ROCK SANDPIPER
see p.134
*darker, plainer
upperparts*

slightly
smaller bill

DUNLIN
see p.133
*plain pale
gray-brown
upperparts*

longer
black bill

less
orange color
to base of bill

WINTER EXPOSURE
The Purple Sandpiper winters
mainly on exposed rocky shores
along the Eastern Seaboard.

OCCURRENCE
On breeding grounds, found on
barren Arctic and alpine tundra
habitats in the Canadian Arctic
Archipelago. On migration and in
winter, predominantly found on
rocky, wave-pounded shores on
the Eastern Seaboard.

| Length **8–8½in (20–21cm)** | Wingspan **16½–18½in (42–47cm)** | Weight **1¾–3½oz (50–100g)** |
| Social **Small flocks** | Lifespan **Up to 20 years** | Status **Declining** |

DATE: _____ TIME: _____ LOCATION: _____

| Order **Charadriiformes** | Family **Scolopacidae** | Species *Calidris bairdii* |

Baird's Sandpiper

long, pointed wings

finely streaked head

ADULT

blackish upperparts with silver-edged feathers

ADULT

dark patch between eye and bill

straight, fine-tipped dark bill

clean white underparts

indistinct, pale eye-line

streaked back

scalloped look to upperparts

IN FLIGHT

wings extend beyond tail

buff, finely streaked upper breast

JUVENILE

blackish legs

FLIGHT: strong and direct, with deep, quick wing beats.

Baird's Sandpiper is less well known than the other North American *Calidris* sandpipers. It was named in 1861, later than its relatives, by the famous North American ornithologist Elliott Coues, a former surgeon in the US Army, in honor of Spencer Fullerton Baird. Both men were founding members of the AOS (the American Ornithological Society). From its high-Arctic tundra habitat, Baird's Sandpiper moves across North America and the western US into South America, and all the way to Tierra del Fuego—a remarkable biannual journey of 6,000–9,000 miles (9,700–14,500km).

VOICE Flight call a low, dry *preep*; song on Arctic breeding ground: *brraay, brray, bray*, followed by *hee-aaw, hee-aaw, hee-aaw*.

NESTING Shallow depression in coastal or upland tundra; 4 eggs; 1 brood; June.

FEEDING Picks and probes for insects and larvae; also spiders and pond crustaceans.

FEEDING IN FLOCKS
Flocks of this sandpiper rush about in search of food in shallow water and muddy areas.

SIMILAR SPECIES

WHITE-RUMPED SANDPIPER
see p.138

prominent white eyebrow

slightly bulkier body

PECTORAL SANDPIPER
larger; see p.140

yellowish legs

streaked breast-band

OCCURRENCE
Breeds in tundra habitats of high-Arctic Alaska and Canada. During migration and winter, inland freshwater habitats: lake and river margins, wet pastures, rice fields; also tidal flats at coastal locations. In winter, common in the high Andes of South America, and sometimes all the way to Tierra del Fuego.

| Length **5¾–7¼in (14.5–18.5cm)** | Wingspan **16–18½in (41–47cm)** | Weight **1¹⁄₁₆–2oz (30–55g)** |
| Social **Flocks** | Lifespan **Unknown** | Status **Secure** |

DATE: _____ TIME: _____ LOCATION: _____

Order **Charadriiformes**	Family **Scolopacidae**	Species *Calidris minutilla*

Least Sandpiper

ADULT

buff to
rust fringed
inner wing

faint
tail
band

IN FLIGHT

uniform
brownish-gray
upperparts

JUVENILE

short tail
and wings

small, rounded head

dark patch
between eye
and bill

**ADULT
(BREEDING)**

short
yellowish
legs

pale, whitish
eyebrow

**ADULT
(NONBREEDING)**

white
chin and
belly

streaked brownish
breast and head

yellow to yellowish-
green legs

FLIGHT: level flight; fast and direct
on quick wing beats; in mixed flocks.

The little Least Sandpiper is often
overlooked because of its muted
plumage and preference for feeding
unobtrusively near vegetative cover. With its brown
or brownish-gray plumage, the Least Sandpiper virtually disappears
in the landscape when feeding crouched down on wet margins of
water bodies. The bird is often found in small to medium flocks,
members of which typically are nervous when foraging, and
frequently burst into flight, only to alight a short way off.
VOICE Its flight call, *kreeeep*, rises in pitch, often repeated
two-syllable *kree-ep*; display call trilled *b-reeee, b-reeee, b-reeee*.
NESTING Depression in open, sub-Arctic habitat near water;
4 eggs; 1 brood; May–June.
FEEDING Forages for variety of small terrestrial and aquatic
prey, especially sand fleas, mollusks, and flies.

FLOCK IN FLIGHT
The narrow pointed wings of the Least Sandpiper
allow it to fly fast and level.

SIMILAR SPECIES

SEMIPALMATED SANDPIPER ✿ see p.141	**PECTORAL SANDPIPER** see p.140
grayer overall	larger overall
whiter throat	heavier bill
larger overall	

OCCURRENCE
Breeds in wet low-Arctic areas
from Alaska and the Yukon to
Quebec and Newfoundland.
During migration and in winter,
uses muddy areas, such as lake
shores, riverbanks, flooded fields,
and tidal flats. Winters from
southern North America south
to Peru and Brazil.

Length **4¾in (12cm)**	Wingspan **13–14in (33–35cm)**	Weight **⁵⁄₁₆–1oz (9–27g)**
Social **Flocks**	Lifespan **Up to 16 years**	Status **Declining**

DATE: _____ TIME: _____ LOCATION: _____

| Order **Charadriiformes** | Family **Scolopacidae** | Species *Calidris fuscicollis* |

White-rumped Sandpiper

easily visible white rump

long, tapered wings

ADULT

IN FLIGHT

dark feathers with rust edges

1ST SUMMER

dark bill with curved tip

heavily streaked breast

grayish-brown upperparts

rust-colored cap and cheek

streaked head

fine streaks on breast

crisp, pale fringed feathers

ADULT

The White-rumped Sandpiper undertakes one of the longest migrations of any bird in the Western Hemisphere. From its high-Arctic breeding grounds in Alaska and Canada, it migrates in several long jumps to extreme southern South America—about 9,000–12,000 miles (14,500–19,300km), twice a year. Almost the entire population migrates through the central US and Canada in spring, with several stopovers, which are critical to the success of its journey. While associating with other shorebird species during migration and winter, it can be overlooked in the crowd. Its insect-like call and white rump aid identification.

VOICE Call a very high-pitched, insect-like *tzeet*; flight song an insect-like, high-pitched, rattling buzz, interspersed with grunts.

NESTING Shallow depression in usually wet but well-vegetated tundra; 4 eggs; 1 brood; June.

FEEDING Picks and probes for insects, spiders, earthworms, and marine worms; also some plant matter.

FLIGHT: fast, strong, and direct flight with deep wing beats.

WING POWER
Long, narrow wings enable this species to migrate to and from the Arctic and Tierra del Fuego.

SIMILAR SPECIES

SEMIPALMATED SANDPIPER
see p.141

slightly rufous crown

more distinct streaks on breast

BAIRD'S SANDPIPER
see p.136

no white rump

OCCURRENCE
Breeds in wet but well-vegetated tundra, usually near ponds, lakes, or streams. During migration and winter, grassy areas: flooded fields, grassy lake margins, rivers, ponds, grassy margins of tidal mudflats, and roadside ditches. On wintering grounds, often associates with Baird's Sandpiper.

| Length **6–6¾in (15–17cm)** | Wingspan **16–18in (41–46cm)** | Weight **⅞–1¾oz (25–50g)** |
| Social **Flocks** | Lifespan **Unknown** | Status **Secure** |

DATE: _____ TIME:_____ LOCATION:_____

Order **Charadriiformes**	Family **Scolopacidae**	Species *Calidris subruficollis*

Buff-breasted Sandpiper

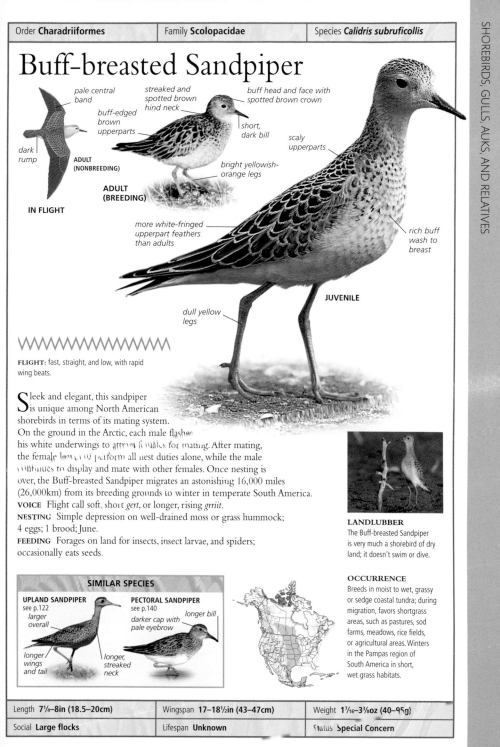

pale central band

streaked and spotted brown hind neck

buff head and face with spotted brown crown

buff-edged brown upperparts

short, dark bill

dark rump

ADULT (NONBREEDING)

scaly upperparts

bright yellowish-orange legs

ADULT (BREEDING)

IN FLIGHT

more white-fringed upperpart feathers than adults

rich buff wash to breast

JUVENILE

dull yellow legs

FLIGHT: fast, straight, and low, with rapid wing beats.

Sleek and elegant, this sandpiper is unique among North American shorebirds in terms of its mating system. On the ground in the Arctic, each male flashes his white underwings to attract females for mating. After mating, the female leaves to perform all nest duties alone, while the male continues to display and mate with other females. Once nesting is over, the Buff-breasted Sandpiper migrates an astonishing 16,000 miles (26,000km) from its breeding grounds to winter in temperate South America.

VOICE Flight call soft, short *gert*, or longer, rising *griit*.
NESTING Simple depression on well-drained moss or grass hummock; 4 eggs; 1 brood; June.
FEEDING Forages on land for insects, insect larvae, and spiders; occasionally eats seeds.

LANDLUBBER
The Buff-breasted Sandpiper is very much a shorebird of dry land; it doesn't swim or dive.

OCCURRENCE
Breeds in moist to wet, grassy or sedge coastal tundra; during migration, favors shortgrass areas, such as pastures, sod farms, meadows, rice fields, or agricultural areas. Winters in the Pampas region of South America in short, wet grass habitats.

SIMILAR SPECIES

UPLAND SANDPIPER
see p.122
larger overall
longer wings and tail

PECTORAL SANDPIPER
see p.140
darker cap with pale eyebrow
longer bill
longer, streaked neck

Length **7¼–8in (18.5–20cm)**	Wingspan **17–18½in (43–47cm)**	Weight **1⁷⁄₁₆–3⅜oz (40–95g)**
Social **Large flocks**	Lifespan **Unknown**	Status **Special Concern**

DATE: _____ TIME: _____ LOCATION: _____

Order **Charadriiformes**	Family **Scolopacidae**	Species *Calidris melanotos*

Pectoral Sandpiper

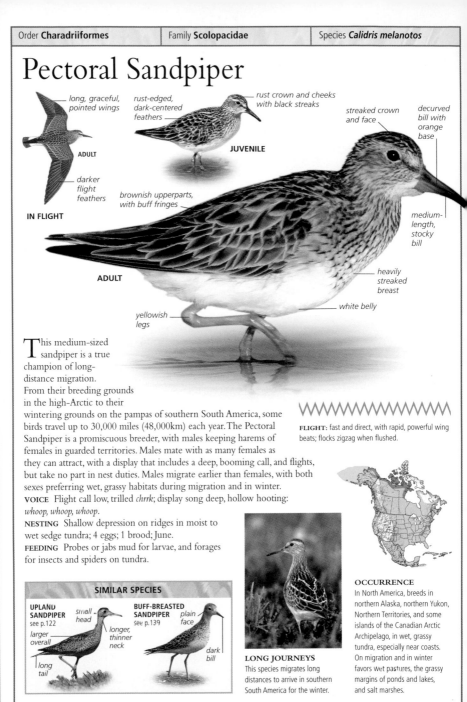

long, graceful, pointed wings

ADULT

darker flight feathers

IN FLIGHT

rust-edged, dark-centered feathers

JUVENILE

rust crown and cheeks with black streaks

brownish upperparts, with buff fringes

ADULT

yellowish legs

streaked crown and face

decurved bill with orange base

medium-length, stocky bill

heavily streaked breast

white belly

This medium-sized sandpiper is a true champion of long-distance migration. From their breeding grounds in the high-Arctic to their wintering grounds on the pampas of southern South America, some birds travel up to 30,000 miles (48,000km) each year. The Pectoral Sandpiper is a promiscuous breeder, with males keeping harems of females in guarded territories. Males mate with as many females as they can attract, with a display that includes a deep, booming call, and flights, but take no part in nest duties. Males migrate earlier than females, with both sexes preferring wet, grassy habitats during migration and in winter.

VOICE Flight call low, trilled *chrrk*; display song deep, hollow hooting: *whoop, whoop, whoop.*

NESTING Shallow depression on ridges in moist to wet sedge tundra; 4 eggs; 1 brood; June.

FEEDING Probes or jabs mud for larvae, and forages for insects and spiders on tundra.

FLIGHT: fast and direct, with rapid, powerful wing beats; flocks zigzag when flushed.

SIMILAR SPECIES

UPLAND SANDPIPER see p.122
small head
larger overall
long tail
longer, thinner neck

BUFF-BREASTED SANDPIPER see p.139
plain face
dark bill

LONG JOURNEYS
This species migrates long distances to arrive in southern South America for the winter.

OCCURRENCE
In North America, breeds in northern Alaska, northern Yukon, Northern Territories, and some islands of the Canadian Arctic Archipelago, in wet, grassy tundra, especially near coasts. On migration and in winter favors wet pastures, the grassy margins of ponds and lakes, and salt marshes.

Length 7½–9in (19–23cm)	Wingspan 16½–19½in (42–49cm)	Weight 1¾–4oz (50–125g)
Social **Migrant flocks**	Lifespan **Up to 4½ years**	Status **Secure**

DATE: _____ TIME: _____ LOCATION: _____

| Order **Charadriiformes** | Family **Scolopacidae** | Species *Calidris pusilla* |

Semipalmated Sandpiper

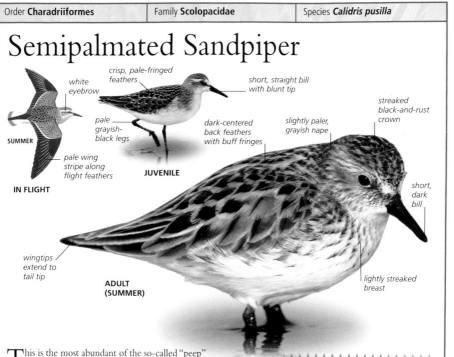

crisp, pale-fringed feathers

white eyebrow

short, straight bill with blunt tip

streaked black-and-rust crown

pale grayish-black legs

dark-centered back feathers with buff fringes

slightly paler, grayish nape

SUMMER

pale wing stripe along flight feathers

JUVENILE

IN FLIGHT

short, dark bill

wingtips extend to tail tip

ADULT (SUMMER)

lightly streaked breast

This is the most abundant of the so-called "peep" *Calidris* sandpipers, especially in the eastern US. Flocks of up to 300,000 birds gather on migration staging areas. As a species, though, it can be hard to identify due to plumage variation between juveniles and breeding adults, and a bill that varies markedly in size and shape from West to East. Semipalmated sandpipers may fly from their northeasterly breeding grounds nonstop to their South American wintering grounds in the fall.

VOICE Flight call *chrrk* or higher, sharper *chit*; display song monotonous, droning trill, often repeated for minutes at a time.

NESTING Shallow, lined scrape in shortgrass habitat; 4 eggs; 1 brood; May–June.

FEEDING Probes mud for aquatic and terrestrial invertebrates, such as mollusks, worms, and spiders.

FLIGHT: fast and direct on narrow, pointed, wings; flies in large flocks in winter.

SLEEPING TOGETHER
Semipalmated Sandpipers form large feeding or resting flocks on migration and in winter.

OCCURRENCE
Breeds in Arctic and sub-Arctic tundra habitats near water; in Alaska, on outer coastal plain. Migrants occur in shallow fresh- or saltwater and open muddy areas with little vegetation, such as intertidal flats or lake shores. Winters in Central and South America, south to Brazil and Peru.

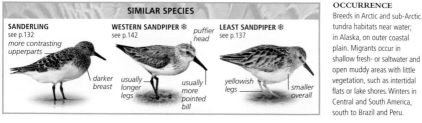

SIMILAR SPECIES

SANDERLING see p.132
more contrasting upperparts

darker breast

WESTERN SANDPIPER ✸ see p.142
puffier head

usually longer legs

usually more pointed bill

LEAST SANDPIPER ✸ see p.137

yellowish legs

smaller overall

Length **5¼–6in (13.5–15cm)**	Wingspan **13½–15in (34–38cm)**	Weight **½–1⁷⁄₁₆oz (14–40g)**
Social **Large flocks**	Lifespan **Up to 12 years**	Status **Secure**

Order **Charadriiformes**	Family **Scolopacidae**	Species *Calidris mauri*

Western Sandpiper

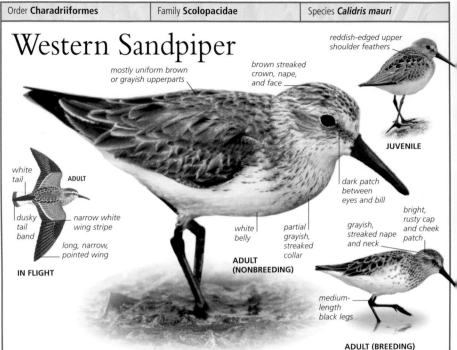

reddish-edged upper shoulder feathers

JUVENILE

mostly uniform brown or grayish upperparts

brown streaked crown, nape, and face

white tail

ADULT

dusky tail band

narrow white wing stripe

long, narrow, pointed wing

IN FLIGHT

dark patch between eyes and bill

white belly

partial grayish, streaked collar

ADULT (NONBREEDING)

grayish, streaked nape and neck

bright, rusty cap and cheek patch

medium-length black legs

ADULT (BREEDING)

Despite its restricted breeding range in western Alaska, the Western Sandpiper is one of the most common shorebirds in the Western Hemisphere. During its spring migration, spectacularly large flocks are seen at several Pacific Coast locations: at the mudflats of Roberts Bank in British Columbia, around two million Western Sandpipers stop on their way to their tundra breeding grounds to fatten up and refuel for the last hop northward. Many of these migrate over relatively short distances to winter along US coastlines, so the timing of their molt in fall is earlier than that of the similar Semipalmated Sandpiper, which migrates later in winter.

VOICE Flight call loud *chir-eep*; flushed birds make *sirp* call, or *chir-ir-ip*; song *tweer, tweer, tweer*, followed by descending trill.

NESTING Shallow depression on drained Arctic and sub-Arctic tundra; 4 eggs; 1 brood; May–June.

FEEDING Probes mud for insect larvae, crustaceans, and worms.

FLIGHT: direct, rapid flight on narrow, pointed wings; in large flocks.

FORAGING FOR FOOD
The Western Sandpiper feels for hidden prey with the touch-sensitive tip of its bill.

OCCURRENCE
Breeds in wet sedge, grassy habitats with well-drained microhabitats; in migration and in winter, prefers shallow freshwater or saltwater habitats with open muddy or sandy areas and little vegetation, such as intertidal mudflats and lake shores.

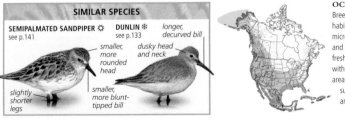

SIMILAR SPECIES

SEMIPALMATED SANDPIPER ☼
see p.141

smaller, more rounded head

slightly shorter legs

DUNLIN ❋
see p.133

longer, decurved bill

dusky head and neck

smaller, more blunt-tipped bill

Length **5½–6½in (14–16cm)**	Wingspan **14–15in (35–38cm)**	Weight **1¹⁄₁₆–1¼oz (19–35g)**
Social **Flocks**	Lifespan **Up to 9 years**	Status **Secure**

DATE: _____ TIME:_____ LOCATION:_____

| Order **Charadriiformes** | Family **Scolopacidae** | Species *Limnodromus griseus* |

Short-billed Dowitcher

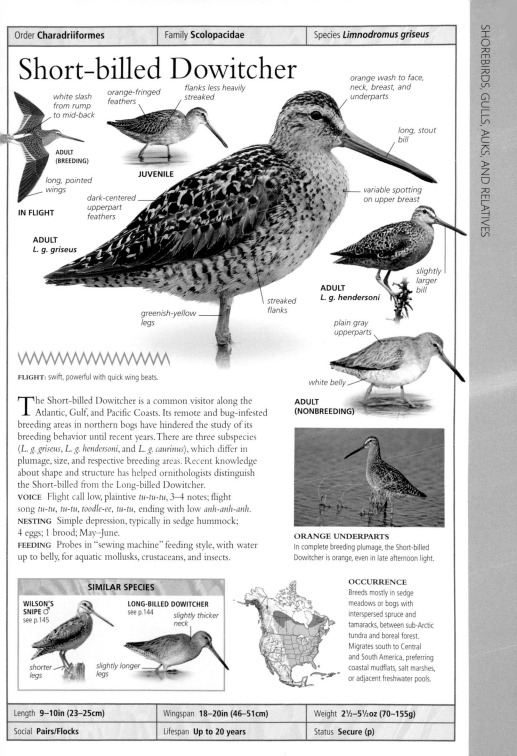

orange wash to face, neck, breast, and underparts

white slash from rump to mid-back

orange-fringed feathers

flanks less heavily streaked

long, stout bill

ADULT (BREEDING)

JUVENILE

long, pointed wings

variable spotting on upper breast

IN FLIGHT

dark-centered upperpart feathers

ADULT
L. g. griseus

slightly larger bill

ADULT
L. g. hendersoni

streaked flanks

greenish-yellow legs

plain gray upperparts

FLIGHT: swift, powerful with quick wing beats.

white belly

ADULT (NONBREEDING)

The Short-billed Dowitcher is a common visitor along the Atlantic, Gulf, and Pacific Coasts. Its remote and bug-infested breeding areas in northern bogs have hindered the study of its breeding behavior until recent years. There are three subspecies (*L. g. griseus*, *L. g. hendersoni*, and *L. g. caurinus*), which differ in plumage, size, and respective breeding areas. Recent knowledge about shape and structure has helped ornithologists distinguish the Short-billed from the Long-billed Dowitcher.

VOICE Flight call low, plaintive *tu-tu-tu*, 3–4 notes; flight song *tu-tu, tu-tu, toodle-ee, tu-tu*, ending with low *anh-anh-anh*.

NESTING Simple depression, typically in sedge hummock; 4 eggs; 1 brood; May–June.

FEEDING Probes in "sewing machine" feeding style, with water up to belly, for aquatic mollusks, crustaceans, and insects.

ORANGE UNDERPARTS
In complete breeding plumage, the Short-billed Dowitcher is orange, even in late afternoon light.

SIMILAR SPECIES

WILSON'S SNIPE ♂
see p.145

LONG-BILLED DOWITCHER
see p.144

slightly thicker neck

shorter legs

slightly longer legs

OCCURRENCE
Breeds mostly in sedge meadows or bogs with interspersed spruce and tamaracks, between sub-Arctic tundra and boreal forest. Migrates south to Central and South America, preferring coastal mudflats, salt marshes, or adjacent freshwater pools.

| Length **9–10in (23–25cm)** | Wingspan **18–20in (46–51cm)** | Weight **2½–5½oz (70–155g)** |
| Social **Pairs/Flocks** | Lifespan **Up to 20 years** | Status **Secure (p)** |

DATE: _____ TIME: _____ LOCATION: _____

Order **Charadriiformes**	Family **Scolopacidae**	Species *Limnodromus scolopaceus*

Long-billed Dowitcher

bands on tail

ADULT (BREEDING)

white rump patch

long, pointed wings

IN FLIGHT

dark upperparts with reddish markings

ADULT (BREEDING)

brick-red underparts

lightly streaked head

white belly

JUVENILE

black-centered feathers

short but distinct white eyebrow

long, stout bill

dark patch between eye and bill

mostly dusky-gray upperparts

variable dark barring on flanks

white belly

ADULT (NONBREEDING)

I t was not until 1950 that museum and field studies identified two separate species of dowitcher in North America. The Long-billed Dowitcher is usually slightly larger, longer-legged, and heavier in the chest and neck than the Short-billed Dowitcher. The breeding ranges of the two species are separate, but their migration and en route stopover areas overlap. The Long-billed Dowitcher is usually found in freshwater wetlands, and in the fall most of its population is found west of the Mississippi River.

VOICE Flight and alarm call sharp, whistled *keek*, given singly or in series when agitated; song buzzy *pipipipipipi-chi-drrr*.

NESTING Deep sedge or grass-lined depression in sedge or grass; 4 eggs; 1 brood; May–June.

FEEDING Probes wet ground with "sewing-machine" motion for spiders, snails, worms, insects, and seeds.

FLIGHT: swift, direct flier with fast, powerful wing beats.

TOUCHY FEELY
Sensitive touch receptors at the tip of the bird's bill enable it to feel in the mud for food.

OCCURRENCE
Breeds in wet, grassy meadows or coastal sedge tundra near freshwater pools. Migrates to Mexico and Central America, south to Panama, found in freshwater habitats, including ponds, flooded fields, lake shores, also sheltered lagoons, salt marsh pools, and tidal mudflats.

SIMILAR SPECIES

WILSON'S SNIPE
see p.145

pale, central crown stripe

SHORT-BILLED DOWITCHER
see p.143

slightly smaller overall

shorter legs

orangish underparts

Length **9½–10in (24–26cm)**	Wingspan **18–20½in (46–52cm)**	Weight **3–4oz (85–125g)**
Social **Pairs/Flocks**	Lifespan **Up to 7 years**	Status **Vulnerable**

DATE: _____ TIME: _____ LOCATION: _____

| Order **Charadriiformes** | Family **Scolopacidae** | Species ***Gallinago delicata*** |

Wilson's Snipe

high-set large, dark eye

streaked face

long, thick, tapered bill slightly drooping at tip

white vertical streaks

long, pointed, angled wings

long bill

ADULT

short tail

IN FLIGHT

mostly brown upperparts

brown spots on breast and neck

white underparts with barring on flanks

short russet tail

MALE

FLIGHT: extremely fast and zigzagging, rapid wing beats; erratic-looking changes of direction.

This secretive and well-camouflaged member of the sandpiper family has an unsettled taxonomic history, but is now classified individually. On its breeding grounds, the Wilson's Snipe produces rather eerie sounds during its aerial, mainly nocturnal, display flights. The birds fly up silently from the ground, and then, from about 330ft (100m) up, they descend quickly—their tail feathers spread, producing a unique loud and vibrating sound through modified feathers.

VOICE Alarm and overhead flight call raspy *kraitsch*; perched and low-flying breeding birds give repetitive, monotonous *kup-kup-kup-kup* in alarm or aggression; distinctive winnowing sound during territorial displays.

NESTING Elaborate woven nest lined with fine grass on ground, sedge, or moss; 4 eggs; 1 brood; May–June.

FEEDING Forages in mud or shallow water; probes deep into subsoil; diet includes mostly insect larvae, but also crustaceans, earthworms, and mollusks.

RUSSET TAIL
Wilson's Snipe's russet-colored tail is usually hard to see, but it is evident on this preening bird.

OCCURRENCE
Widespread from Alaska to Quebec and Labrador, south of the tundra zone; breeds in a variety of wetlands, including marshes, bogs, and open areas with rich soil. Winters farther south, where it prefers damp areas with vegetative cover, such as marshes, wet fields, and other bodies of water.

SIMILAR SPECIES

AMERICAN WOODCOCK

plump body

buffy-orange underparts

SHORT-BILLED DOWITCHER see p.143

smaller eye

orange tint to breast

LONG-BILLED DOWITCHER see p.144

no white streaks on back

longer legs

| Length **10–11in (25–28cm)** | Wingspan **17–19in (43–48cm)** | Weight **2⅞–5oz (80–150g)** |
| Social **Solitary** | Lifespan **Up to 10 years** | Status **Secure** |

DATE: _____ TIME:_____ LOCATION:_____

| Order **Charadriiformes** | Family **Scolopacidae** | Species **Actitis macularius** |

Spotted Sandpiper

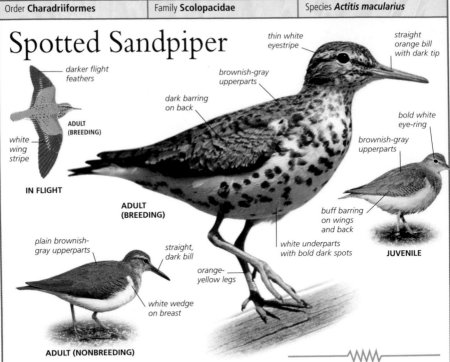

thin white eyestripe

straight orange bill with dark tip

brownish-gray upperparts

darker flight feathers

dark barring on back

ADULT (BREEDING)

white wing stripe

IN FLIGHT

bold white eye-ring

brownish-gray upperparts

buff barring on wings and back

ADULT (BREEDING)

white underparts with bold dark spots

JUVENILE

plain brownish-gray upperparts

straight, dark bill

orange-yellow legs

white wedge on breast

ADULT (NONBREEDING)

One of only two species of the genus *Actitis*, from the Latin meaning "a coastal inhabitant," this small, short-legged sandpiper is the most widespread shorebird in North America. It is characterized by its quick walking pace, as well as by its unique habit of constantly teetering and bobbing its tail and style of flying low over water. Spotted Sandpipers have an unusual mating behavior, in which the females take on an aggressive role—defending territories and mating with three or more males per season.

VOICE Call a clear, ringing note *tee-tee-tee-tee*; flight song a monotonous *cree-cree-cree*.

NESTING Nest cup shaded by or scrape built under herbaceous vegetation; 3 eggs; 1–3 broods; May–June.

FEEDING Eats many items, including adult and larval insects, mollusks, small crabs, and worms.

FLIGHT: mostly shallow, rapidly, stiffly fluttering wing beats, usually low above water.

BEHAVIORAL QUIRKS
This bird "teeters," uniquely raising and lowering its tail while walking along the water's edge.

SIMILAR SPECIES

SOLITARY SANDPIPER ☾
see p.147

more slender body

longer legs

streaked breast

COMMON SANDPIPER

longer tail

more grayish-green legs

OCCURRENCE
Breeds across North America in a wide variety of grassy, brushy, forested habitats near water, but not high-Arctic tundra. During migration and in winter, found in habitats near freshwater, including lake shores, rivers, streams, beaches, sewage ponds, ditches, seawalls, sometimes estuaries.

| Length **7¼–8in (18.5–20cm)** | Wingspan **15–16in (38–41cm)** | Weight **1⁹⁄₁₆–1¾oz (45–50g)** |
| Social **Small flocks** | Lifespan **Up to 12 years** | Status **Secure** |

DATE: _____ TIME: _____ LOCATION: _____

Order **Charadriiformes**	Family **Scolopacidae**	Species *Tringa solitaria*

Solitary Sandpiper

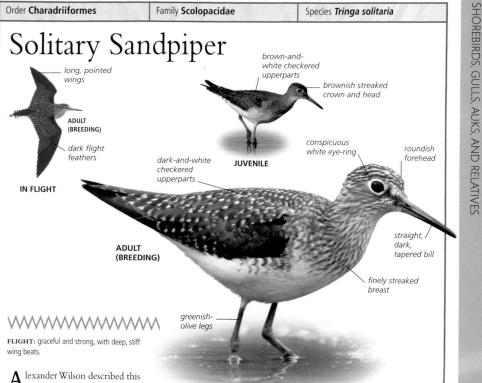

long, pointed wings

ADULT (BREEDING)

dark flight feathers

IN FLIGHT

brown-and-white checkered upperparts

brownish streaked crown and head

JUVENILE

dark-and-white checkered upperparts

conspicuous white eye-ring

roundish forehead

straight, dark, tapered bill

finely streaked breast

ADULT (BREEDING)

greenish-olive legs

WWWWWWWWW

FLIGHT: graceful and strong, with deep, stiff wing beats.

A lexander Wilson described this species in 1813, naming it, quite appropriately, "Solitary." This sandpiper seldom associates with other shorebirds as it moves nervously along margins of wetlands. When feeding, the Solitary Sandpiper constantly bobs its head like the Spotted Sandpiper. When disturbed, the Solitary Sandpiper often flies directly upward, and when landing, it keeps its wings upright briefly, flashing the white underneath, before carefully folding them to its body.

VOICE Flight and alarm call a high-pitched *weet-weet-weet* or *pit*; display song a *pit-pit-pit-pit*; *kik-kik-kik*.

NESTING Abandoned nests in trees (a unique behavior for a North American shorebird); 4 eggs; 1 brood; May–June.

FEEDING Eats insects, small crustaceans, snails, and small frogs.

LONE RANGER
This sandpiper is often solitary and is found in quiet, sheltered habitats and along river shores.

SIMILAR SPECIES		

LESSER YELLOWLEGS ☾
see p.149

slimmer body

yellow-orange legs

SPOTTED SANDPIPER
see p.146

bulkier body

shorter bill

shorter legs

OCCURRENCE
Breeds primarily in bogs in northern forests; in winter and during migration, occurs in sheltered pools or muddy areas near forests. Winters from Mexico down to South America, sometimes in tiny pools at high altitude in the Andes; also riverbanks, streams, rain pools, and ditches.

Length **7½–9in (19–23cm)**	Wingspan **22–23in (56–59cm)**	Weight **1¹⁄₁₆–2¼oz (30–65g)**
Social **Solitary/Small flocks**	Lifespan **Unknown**	Status **Secure**

DATE: _____ TIME: _____ LOCATION: _____

| Order **Charadriiformes** | Family **Scolopacidae** | Species *Tringa incana* |

Wandering Tattler

long, pointed wings

dark-gray flight feathers

fairly long, straight bill

ADULT (BREEDING)

IN FLIGHT

grayish upperparts

thin, pale feather edges

white stripe above eye

dark patch between eye and bill

barring on gray breast

1ST FALL

plain gray upperparts

straight, dark bill

yellow legs

fine dark barring on underparts

dull yellow-green legs

ADULT (BREEDING)

While "Wandering" refers to this species' widespread annual migration, "Tattler" highlights the loud nature of the calls and songs. It makes in its mountain breeding haunts in Alaska and northwestern Canada. There is still much to learn about this mostly-solitary species, including its remote wintering range, especially given its small world population numbers (10,000–25,000 birds). Seen singly or occasionally in small groups on the rocky Pacific Coast shoreline from late summer to spring, this enigmatic species is often overlooked.

VOICE Flight call a ringing, trilled *didididididi*; song a sharp, 3–4 note whistle *treea-treea-treea-tree*.

NESTING Depression on rocks in mountain tundra; 4 eggs; 1 brood; May–July.

FEEDING Picks worms, mollusks, and crustaceans from intertidal habitats; also eats insects, sand fleas, and fish.

FLIGHT: swift and direct, can also be buoyant, may dip, soar, nose-dive, and glide.

DISTINCTIVE WALKING
This bird may be seen walking with a teetering motion on rocky shores, away from breeding habitats.

SIMILAR SPECIES

WILLET ❀
see p.150

gray-black legs

heavier bill

GRAY-TAILED TATTLER ♂

broader eyebrow

overall paler plumage

OCCURRENCE
Breeds in shrubby mountainous western Arctic tundra, close to water bodies formed as a result of melting glaciers. During migration and winter, uses rocky coastlines, particularly in the area between the high- and low-tide marks; also reefs, jetties, and piers.

| Length **10½–12in (27–30cm)** | Wingspan **20–22in (51–56cm)** | Weight **3½–5oz (100–150g)** |
| Social **Solitary/Pairs** | Lifespan **Unknown** | Status **Secure** |

DATE: _____ TIME:_____ LOCATION:_____

| Order **Charadriiformes** | Family **Scolopacidae** | Species *Tringa flavipes* |

Lesser Yellowlegs 🔊

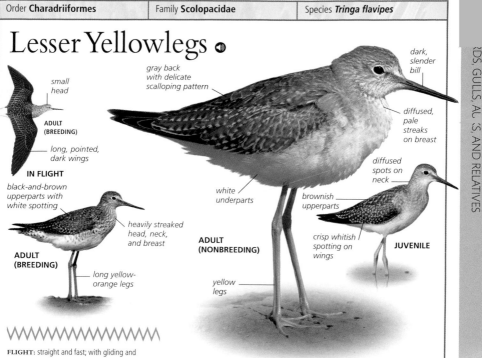

ADULT (BREEDING)
small head

gray back with delicate scalloping pattern

dark, slender bill

diffused, pale streaks on breast

long, pointed, dark wings

IN FLIGHT

black-and-brown upperparts with white spotting

ADULT (BREEDING)

heavily streaked head, neck, and breast

long yellow-orange legs

white underparts

ADULT (NONBREEDING)

yellow legs

brownish upperparts

diffused spots on neck

crisp whitish spotting on wings

JUVENILE

FLIGHT: straight and fast; with gliding and sideways banking; legs trail behind body.

With its smaller head, thinner bill, and smoother body shape, the Lesser Yellowlegs has a more elegant profile than the Greater Yellowlegs. It prefers smaller, freshwater, or brackish pools to open saltwater habitats, and it walks quickly and methodically while feeding. Although this species is a solitary feeder, it is often seen in small to large loose flocks during migration and winter.

VOICE Low, whistled *tu-tu* call; series of *tu* or *cuw* notes when agitated; display song a *pill-e-wee, pill-e-wee, pill-e-wee*.

NESTING Depression in ground or moss, lined with grass and leaves; 4 eggs; 1 brood; May–June.

FEEDING Eats a wide variety of aquatic and terrestrial insects, mollusks, and crustaceans, especially flies and beetles; also seeds.

BALANCING ACT
The Lesser Yellowlegs uses its long, raised wings for balance while feeding in soft mud.

SIMILAR SPECIES

GREATER YELLOWLEGS
see p.151

larger and heavier

SOLITARY SANDPIPER
see p.147

longer, thicker, recurved bill

shorter greenish-yellow legs

more defined breast streaks

OCCURRENCE
Breeds in northerly forest with clearings, and where forest meets tundra. In migration and in winter, uses a wide variety of shallow wetlands, including flooded pastures and agricultural fields, swamps, lake and river shores, tidal creeks, and brackish mudflats. Winters from Mexico to Argentina.

| Length **9–10in (23–25cm)** | Wingspan **23–25in (58–64cm)** | Weight **2–3⅜oz (55–95g)** |
| Social **Flocks** | Lifespan **Up to 5 years** | Status **Secure** |

DATE: _____ TIME: _____ LOCATION: _____

| Order **Charadriiformes** | Family **Scolopacidae** | Species ***Tringa semipalmata*** |

Willet 🔊

bold black-and-white wing pattern

ADULT (WESTERN WINTER)

IN FLIGHT

unpatterned pale underparts

crisp, thin buff fringes

grayish upperparts

JUVENILE
T. s. inornata **(WESTERN)**

white stripe above eye

dark patch between eye and bill

heavily streaked brownish head and neck

straight, thick bill with pinkish base

brownish upperparts with dense dark feathers

ADULT
T. s. semipalmata **(EASTERN BREEDING)**

grayish legs

bold dark barring on underside

plain gray upperparts

long, grayish, straight bill

pale underparts

ADULT
T. s. inornata **(WESTERN WINTER)**

FLIGHT: strong, fast, and direct on powerful wing beats.

The two distinct subspecies of the Willet, Eastern (*T. s. semipalmata*) and Western (*T. s. inornata*), differ in breeding habits, plumage coloration, vocalizations, and migratory habits. The Eastern Willet leaves North America from September to March, whereas the Western Willet winters along the southern North American shorelines south to South America.
VOICE Flight call a loud *kyah-yah*; alarm call a sharp, repeated *kleep*; song an urgent, rapid *pill-will-willet*.
NESTING Depression in vegetated dunes, wetlands, prairies, or salt marshes; 4 eggs; 1 brood; April–June.
FEEDING Picks, probes, or swishes for crustaceans, such as fiddler and mole crabs, aquatic insects, marine worms, small mollusks, and fish.

EXPOSED PERCH
Willets roost on exposed perches at breeding grounds.

OCCURRENCE
Eastern subspecies breeds in coastal saltwater habitats: salt marshes, barrier islands, beaches, and mangroves; winters in similar habitats. Western subspecies breeds near sparsely vegetated prairie wetlands or adjacent semiarid grasslands; winters in coastal regions.

SIMILAR SPECIES

GREATER YELLOWLEGS
see p.151
slightly recurved bill
longer neck
yellowish-orange legs

WANDERING TATTLER 🔊 1ST🔊
see p.148
stockier body
yellowish legs

| Length **12½–16½in (32–42cm)** | Wingspan **21½–28½in (54–72cm)** | Weight **7–12oz (200–350g)** |
| Social **Flocks** | Lifespan **Up to 10 years** | Status **Secure** |

DATE: _____ TIME: _____ LOCATION: _____

| Order **Charadriiformes** | Family **Scolopacidae** | Species *Tringa melanoleuca* |

Greater Yellowlegs 🔊

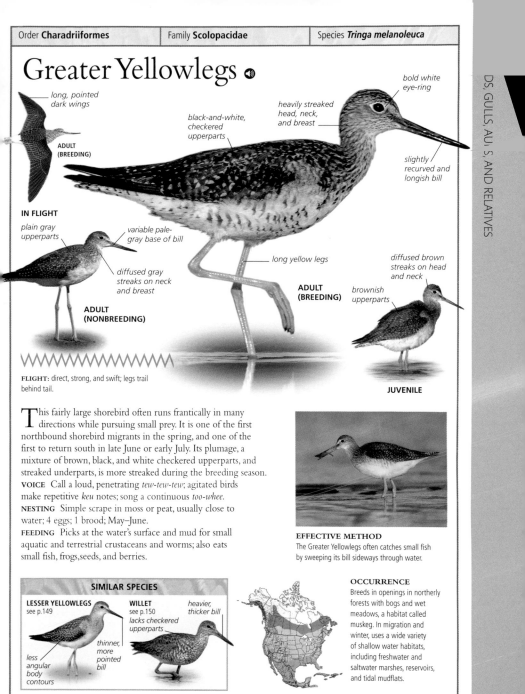

long, pointed
dark wings

**ADULT
(BREEDING)**

IN FLIGHT

plain gray
upperparts

variable pale-
gray base of bill

diffused gray
streaks on neck
and breast

**ADULT
(NONBREEDING)**

heavily streaked
head, neck,
and breast

black-and-white,
checkered
upperparts

bold white
eye-ring

slightly
recurved and
longish bill

long yellow legs

**ADULT
(BREEDING)**

diffused brown
streaks on head
and neck

brownish
upperparts

FLIGHT: direct, strong, and swift; legs trail
behind tail.

JUVENILE

DS, GULLS, AU, S, AND RELATIVES

This fairly large shorebird often runs frantically in many
directions while pursuing small prey. It is one of the first
northbound shorebird migrants in the spring, and one of the
first to return south in late June or early July. Its plumage, a
mixture of brown, black, and white checkered upperparts, and
streaked underparts, is more streaked during the breeding season.
VOICE Call a loud, penetrating *tew-tew-tew*; agitated birds
make repetitive *keu* notes; song a continuous *too-whee*.
NESTING Simple scrape in moss or peat, usually close to
water; 4 eggs; 1 brood; May–June.
FEEDING Picks at the water's surface and mud for small
aquatic and terrestrial crustaceans and worms; also eats
small fish, frogs, seeds, and berries.

EFFECTIVE METHOD
The Greater Yellowlegs often catches small fish
by sweeping its bill sideways through water.

OCCURRENCE
Breeds in openings in northerly
forests with bogs and wet
meadows, a habitat called
muskeg. In migration and
winter, uses a wide variety
of shallow water habitats,
including freshwater and
saltwater marshes, reservoirs,
and tidal mudflats.

SIMILAR SPECIES

LESSER YELLOWLEGS
see p.149

less
angular
body
contours

thinner,
more
pointed
bill

WILLET
see p.150

lacks checkered
upperparts

heavier,
thicker bill

| Length **11½–13in (29–33cm)** | Wingspan **28–29in (70–74cm)** | Weight **4–8oz (125–225g)** |
| Social **Solitary/Flocks** | Lifespan **Unknown** | Status **Secure** |

DATE: _____ TIME: _____ LOCATION: _____

| Order **Charadriiformes** | Family **Scolopacidae** | Species *Phalaropus tricolor* |

Wilson's Phalarope

reddish-brown markings on sides of back

plain gray upperparts

largely white face

white cheek

FEMALE (BREEDING)

yellowish legs

grayish-brown wings

white underparts

IN FLIGHT

MOLTING TO 1ST WINTER

gray and reddish-brown back

black stripe from bill to nape

plain gray-and-black upperparts

paler head markings

MALE

white eyebrow

fairly long, straight bill

rust neck and throat

FEMALE (BREEDING)

A truly American phalarope, Wilson's is the largest of the three phalarope species. Unlike its two relatives, it does not breed in the Arctic, but in the shallow wetlands of western North America, and winters mainly in continental habitats of Bolivia and Argentina instead of in the ocean. This species can be found employing the following feeding technique: spinning in shallow water to churn up adult and larval insects, or running in various directions on muddy wetland edges with its head held low to the ground while chasing and picking up insects. Wilson's phalaropes are quite tolerant of humans on their breeding grounds, but they become more wary immediately before migration because they are heavier and more sluggish.

VOICE Flight call a low, nasal *werpf*; also higher, repetitive *emf, emf, emf, emf*, or *luk, luk, luk*.

NESTING Simple scrape lined with grass; 4 eggs; 1 brood; May–June.

FEEDING Eats brine shrimp, various insects, and insect larvae.

FLIGHT: fast and direct with quick wing beats.

ODD ONE OUT
Unlike its two essentially oceanic cousins, Wilson's Phalarope is also found in freshwater habitats.

SIMILAR SPECIES

LESSER YELLOWLEGS
see p.149

darker, spotted back

streaked head and neck

RED-NECKED PHALAROPE
see p.153

black cheek patch

shorter bill

OCCURRENCE
Breeds in shallow, grassy wetlands of interior North America; during migration and winter, occurs in salty lakes and saline ponds as well as inland waterbodies. In winter, tens of thousands can be seen in the middle of Titicaca Lake in Bolivia.

Length 8½–9½in (22–24cm)	Wingspan 15½–17in (39–43cm)	Weight 1¼–3oz (35–85g)
Social **Large flocks**	Lifespan **Up to 10 years**	Status **Secure**

DATE: _____ TIME: _____ LOCATION: _____

Red-necked Phalarope

pointed wings

narrow white wing stripe

dark cap and cheek patch

black back with dull white lines

dark upperparts with buff stripes

dark-gray crown and face

JUVENILE

white throat

FEMALE (BREEDING)

IN FLIGHT

JUVENILE (WORN PLUMAGE)

dark upperparts with buff or rust feather edges

needle-like, dark bill

rust neck and upper breast

FEMALE (BREEDING)

white underparts with dusky, streaked flanks

This aquatic sandpiper spends much of its life in deep ocean waters feeding on tiny plankton; each year, after nine months at sea, it comes to nest in the Arctic. Its Latin name *lobatus* reflects the morphology of its feet, which are webbed (lobed). Both the Red-necked Phalarope and the Red Phalarope are oceanic birds that are found in large flocks or "rafts" far from shore. However, both species are occasionally found swimming inland in freshwater habitats. Like the other two phalaropes, the Red-necked has a fascinating and unusual reversal of typical sex roles. The female is more brightly colored and slightly larger than the male; she will also pursue the male, compete savagely for him, and will migrate shortly after laying her eggs, leaving him to care for them.

VOICE Flight call a hard, squeaky *pwit* or *kit*; on breeding grounds, vocalizations include variations of flight call notes.

NESTING Depression in wet sedge or grass; 3–4 eggs; 1–2 broods; May–June.

FEEDING Eats plankton; also insects, brine shrimp, and mollusks.

FLIGHT: fast and direct, with rapid wing beats.

SINGLE FATHER
Male phalaropes perform all nesting and rearing duties after the female lays the eggs.

SIMILAR SPECIES

WILSON'S PHALAROPE ♀
see p.152

paler face

larger overall

RED PHALAROPE ♀
see p.154

slightly thicker bill

larger head and thicker neck

OCCURRENCE
Breeds in wet tundra, on raised ridges, or hummocks, but during migration and in winter, occurs far out to sea and away from shores, although sometimes found in a number of freshwater habitats.

Length **7–7½in (18–19cm)**	Wingspan **12½–16in (32–41cm)**	Weight **1¹/₁₆–1⁹/₁₆oz (30–45g)**
Social **Flocks**	Lifespan **At least 10 years**	Status **Special Concern**

DATE: _____ TIME: _____ LOCATION: _____

| Order **Charadriiformes** | Family **Scolopacidae** | Species *Phalaropus fulicarius* |

Red Phalarope

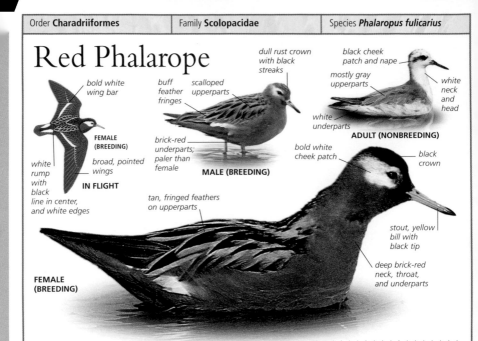

bold white wing bar

dull rust crown with black streaks

buff feather fringes

scalloped upperparts

black cheek patch and nape

mostly gray upperparts

white neck and head

white underparts

ADULT (NONBREEDING)

brick-red underparts; paler than female

MALE (BREEDING)

FEMALE (BREEDING)

white rump with black line in center, and white edges

broad, pointed wings

IN FLIGHT

bold white cheek patch

black crown

tan, fringed feathers on upperparts

stout, yellow bill with black tip

deep brick-red neck, throat, and underparts

FEMALE (BREEDING)

The Red Phalarope spends more than ten months each year over deep ocean waters. It also migrates across the ocean, which explains why few birds of this species are ever seen inland. Many Red Phalaropes winter in tropical waters, with concentrations in the Humboldt Current off Peru and Chile, and in the Benguela current off southwestern Africa. During migration over Alaskan waters, flocks of Red Phalaropes feed on crustaceans in the mud plumes that are created during foraging by gray and bowhead whales on the ocean floor.

VOICE Flight call a sharp *psip* or *pseet*, often in rapid succession; alarm call a drawn-out, two-syllabled *sweet*.

NESTING Depression on ridge or hummock in coastal sedge; 3–4 eggs; 1 brood; June.

FEEDING Plucks prey from sea; marine crustaceans, fish eggs, larval fish; adult or larval insects.

FLIGHT: direct with rapid wing beats, birds in flocks often synchronize.

DIFFERENT COLOR
In nonbreeding plumage, phalaropes are gray and white.

NO TIES
After mating and laying eggs, females leave the male and play no role in raising the young.

OCCURRENCE
Breeds in coastal Arctic tundra; during migration and in winter, occurs in deep ocean waters; small numbers are seen near the shore in coastal California in fall and winter. The Red Phalarope is rare inland.

SIMILAR SPECIES

WILSON'S PHALAROPE
more terrestrial; see p.152

RED-NECKED PHALAROPE
see p.153

no black mask

larger overall

smaller head

more slender body

| Length **8–8½in (20–22cm)** | Wingspan **16–17½in (41–44cm)** | Weight **1¼–2⅝oz (35–75g)** |
| Social **Large flocks** | Lifespan **At least 6 years** | Status **Secure** |

DATE: _____ TIME:_____ LOCATION:_____

Pomarine Jaeger

prominent white "flash" in feathers

ADULT (BREEDING; PALE FORM)

all-dark body

blackish cap

pale-based, thick bill

deep, barrel breast

JUVENILE (FALL; DARK FORM)

white wing flash

barred flanks

ADULT (NONBREEDING; PALE FORM)

dusky breastband

gray-brown back

cream cheeks

ADULT (DARK FORM)

dark overall

blunt tail spike

IN FLIGHT

twisted, spoon-like central tail feathers

dusky breast-band

ADULT (BREEDING; PALE FORM)

The intimidating Pomarine Jaeger uses its size and strength to overpower larger seabirds, such as gulls and shearwaters, in order to steal their food. Thought to be nomadic during the breeding season, it only nests opportunistically, when populations of lemmings are at their peak to provide food for its young. Although larger and more powerful than the Parasitic Jaeger, the Pomarine Jaeger is not as acrobatic in the air. It is readily driven away from breeding territories by the more dynamic Parasitic Jaeger. Interestingly, research suggests that the Pomarine Jaeger is actually more closely related to the large skuas—such as the Great and the South Polar Skuas—than to other jaegers.

VOICE Nasal *cow-cow-cow* and various sharp, low whistles.

NESTING Shallow, unlined depression on a rise or hummock in open tundra; 2 eggs; 1 brood; June–August.

FEEDING Hunts lemmings and other rodents; eats fish or scavenges refuse from fishing boats during nonbreeding season; often steals fish from other seabirds, such as gulls.

FLIGHT: powerful, deep, quick wing beats, with glides; rapid twists and turns in pursuit of prey.

SIMILAR SPECIES

PARASITIC JAEGER see p.156

white "necklace"

gray breastband

LONG-TAILED JAEGER ☼ see p.157

extremely long tail

pale breast

OBVIOUS FEATURE
The twisted, spoon-like central tail feathers are clearly visible when the Pomarine Jaeger flies.

OCCURRENCE
Breeds on open tundra in the Canadian Arctic. Migrates north in spring and south in fall, along coasts and also far offshore. Most often seen when brought close to land by gales. Storm-driven birds are very occasionally found inland. More commonly seen on the West Coast than the East Coast; winters far out at sea.

Length **17–20in (43–51cm)**	Wingspan **4ft (1.2m)**	Weight **23–26oz (650–750g)**
Social **Solitary**	Lifespan **Unknown**	Status **Secure**

Order **Charadriiformes**	Family **Stercorariidae**	Species *Stercorarius parasiticus*

Parasitic Jaeger

pale cheek patch

ADULT (DARK FORM)

white wing patch

barring on wings

mostly dark-brown overall

dark cap

pale cheek

IN FLIGHT

dark upperparts

dark upperparts

ADULT (PALE FORM)

ADULT (DARK FORM)

long, pointed, central feathers

ADULT (PALE FORM)

dark legs and toes

gray breastband

white wing patch

FLIGHT: swift wing beats interspersed with fast glides, interrupted by twisting and climbing.

A true avian pirate of the high seas, the Parasitic Jaeger routinely seeks food by chasing, bullying, and forcing other seabirds to drop or regurgitate fish or other food they have caught. Unlike most jaegers, the Parasitic Jaeger is adaptable in its feeding habits so that it can forage and raise its young under a wide range of environmental conditions. Breeding on the Arctic tundra, it migrates to offshore areas during the nonbreeding season.

VOICE Variety of terrier-like yelps and soft squeals, often during interactions with other jaegers or predators, usually around nesting territories.

NESTING Shallow, unlined depression on a rise or hummock in open tundra; 2 eggs; 1 brood; May–August.

FEEDING Steals fish and other aquatic prey from gulls and terns; catches small birds, eats eggs, or hunts small rodents on breeding grounds.

PARASITIC PIRATE
This Parasitic Jaeger is harrying a gull by pecking at it to make it disgorge its hard-won meal.

SIMILAR SPECIES

POMARINE JAEGER
see p.155

two long, central, twisted tail feathers

heavy, hooked bill

LONG-TAILED JAEGER
see p.157

black cap

longer, pointed tail

OCCURRENCE
Breeds on tundra in northern Canada and Alaska (breeds farther south than other jaegers); during migration and in winter, uses both nearshore and offshore waters; rarely found inland outside the breeding season.

Length **16–18½in (41–47cm)**	Wingspan **3ft 3in–3½ft (1–1.1m)**	Weight **13–18oz (375–500g)**
Social **Solitary/Small flocks**	Lifespan **Up to 18 years**	Status **Secure**

DATE: _____ TIME: _____ LOCATION: _____

Long-tailed Jaeger

gray-and-black
upperwing

**ADULT
(BREEDING)**

IN FLIGHT

thin
wings

slim, long
body

2ND SUMMER

dark
cap

yellowish-
cream
cheeks

dark grayish
back

grayish brown

**JUVENILE
(DARK
FORM)**

extremely long
tail streamers

**ADULT
(BREEDING)**

pale breast,
with no
breastband

FLIGHT: direct, swift glides with rapid wing beats;
more buoyant and light than other jaegers.

This elegant and striking species is a surprisingly fierce Arctic and marine predator. Though the Long-tailed Jaeger occasionally steals food from small gulls and terns, it is much less proficient at such piracy than its larger relatives, and usually hunts for its own food. Indeed, the Long-tailed Jaeger is so dependent on there being an abundance of lemmings in the Arctic that in years when lemming numbers dip low, the bird may not even attempt to nest. This is because there would not be enough lemmings with which to feed its chicks.

VOICE Calls include a chorus of *kreek*, a loud *kreer* warning call, whistles, and high-pitched, sharp clicks.

NESTING Shallow, unlined depression on a rise or hummock in open tundra; 2 eggs; 1 brood; May–August.

FEEDING Hunts lemmings on tundra breeding grounds; takes fish, beetles, and mayflies from the water's surface; occasionally steals small fish from terns.

DEFENSIVE MOVES
This species protects its territory with angry calls, aggressive swoops, and distraction displays.

SIMILAR SPECIES

POMARINE JAEGER
see p.155

long, twisted
feathers

PARASITIC JAEGER
see p.156

thin bill

hooked bill

shorter
tail

OCCURRENCE
Breeds on tundra in northern Canada and Alaska—generally the most northern breeding jaeger; on migration and in winter, uses mostly offshore waters; very rarely seen inland in winter.

Length **19–21in (48–53cm)**	Wingspan **3½ft (1.1m)**	Weight **10–11oz (275–300g)**
Social **Solitary/Flocks**	Lifespan **Up to 8 years**	Status **Secure**

DATE: _____ TIME: _____ LOCATION: _____

| Order **Charadriiformes** | Family **Alcidae** | Species *Uria aalge* |

Common Murre

black wing

ADULT (BREEDING)

white eye-ring

white line extending backwards from eye

dark-brown upperparts and breast

slender head and bill

black head

long, straight black bill

ADULT (WHITE BRIDLED FORM)

IN FLIGHT

curved black line droops behind eye

white underparts

white face and throat

black back

ADULT (NONBREEDING)

ADULT (BREEDING)

grayish legs and feet

WWWWWWWWWWW

FLIGHT: fairly quick with rapid wing beats; close to water's surface.

Abundant, penguin-like birds of the cooler northern oceans, Common Murres are often seen standing upright on cliffs. They are strong fliers and adept divers— to a depth of 500ft (150m). Their large nesting colonies, on rocky sea cliff ledges, are so densely packed that incubating adults may touch each other on both sides. Common Murre eggs are pointed at one end—perhaps to reduce the chance of the egg rolling off the ledge, but more likely to help maximize contact with the brood patch. The egg's unique markings could facilitate clutch recognition by the parents.
VOICE Low-pitched, descending call given from cliffs or water, reminiscent of trumpeting elephant.
NESTING Directly on bare rock near shore, on wide cliff ledge, or large crevice; 1 egg; 1 brood; May–July.
FEEDING Pursues small schooling fish, such as herring, sand lance, and haddock; also crustaceans, marine worms, and squid.

BREEDING COLONY
Crowded together, Common Murres are not territorial but will defend a personal space.

SIMILAR SPECIES

THICK-BILLED MURRE
see p.159

RAZORBILL ☼

thick, pale line between eye and bill

bill with white bar near tip

OCCURRENCE
Breeds close to rocky shorelines, nesting on coastal cliff ledges or flat rocks on top of sea stacks on both the East and West Coasts. Found farther offshore during nonbreeding season, spending extended periods on the open ocean and in large bays. Winters at sea.

| Length **17½in (44cm)** | Wingspan **26in (65cm)** | Weight **35oz (1kg)** |
| Social **Colonies** | Lifespan **At least 40 years** | Status **Localized** |

DATE: _____ TIME: _____ LOCATION: _____

Order **Charadriiformes**	Family **Alcidae**	Species **Uria lomvia**

Thick-billed Murre

brownish-black
sides of head

**ADULT
(BREEDING)**

white breast
and underparts

white line
along bill

short
black tail

IN FLIGHT

hunched
in flight

reduced or absent
white line on bill

all-blackish
upperparts

**ADULT
(BREEDING)**

more extensive
white on throat

**ADULT
(NONBREEDING)**

FLIGHT: near the water's surface with strong,
rapid wing beats.

Large and robust, the Thick-billed Murre is one
of the most abundant seabirds in the whole of the
Northern Hemisphere. Its dense, coastal cliff breeding
colonies can be made up of around a million birds each.
Chicks leave the colony when they are only about 25 percent
of the adult's weight. Their growth is completed at sea, while
being fed by the male parent alone. The Thick-billed Murre
can dive to a remarkable 600ft (180m) to catch fish and squid.
VOICE Roaring, groaning, insistent sounding *aoorrr*; lower-pitched
than the Common Murre.
NESTING Rocky coast or narrow sea cliff ledge in
dense colony; 1 egg; 1 brood; March–September.
FEEDING Cod, herring, capelin, and sand lance in
summer; also crustaceans, worms, and squid.

OCCURRENCE
Breeds on rocky shorelines,
using the same nest each
year. Winters at sea, spending
extended periods of time on
very cold, deep, and often
remote ocean waters and
pack ice edges or openings.

SIMILAR SPECIES		

COMMON MURRE
see p.158

longer,
thinner
bill

more
upright
posture

RAZORBILL

flat,
dark
bill

thick
neck

CLIFF HANGER
Thick-billed Murres breed in
dense colonies on steep cliffs,
often in very remote areas.

Length **18in (46cm)**	Wingspan **28in (70cm)**	Weight **34oz (975g)**
Social **Colonies**	Lifespan **At least 25 years**	Status **Secure**

DATE: _____ TIME:_____ LOCATION:_____

Order **Charadriiformes**	Family **Alcidae**	Species **Cepphus columba**

Pigeon Guillemot

oval snowy-white upperwing patch

dusky neck and face

dusky crown

black upperparts

ADULT

IN FLIGHT

JUVENILE

ADULT (BREEDING)

feet and legs trail in flight

stocky, round body

broad, rounded wings

dark bar across white wing patch

dark rump

bright red-orange legs and feet

The Pigeon Guillemot, a North Pacific seabird, is found along rocky shores in small colonies or isolated pairs. This auk nests in burrows or under rocks, often on small islands that provide protection from land-bound predators. The male excavates a burrow, or chooses an abandoned burrow or crevice, to build a nest. During the breeding season, the bird's striking red-orange legs and mouth lining are used in courtship displays to attract a mate.

VOICE Excited, squeaky whistles, and twitters; nesting birds give a weak whistle *peeeee*.

NESTING Shallow scrape in burrow or crevice; 2 eggs; 1 brood; May–August.

FEEDING Feeds near shore; dives to seabed, then uses bill to forage for small rock eels, sculpins, crabs, shrimp, marine worms, and mollusks; carries food for chicks in beak.

FLIGHT: flies close to the water's surface with very rapid, fluttering wing beats.

VULNERABLE TO PREDATORS
Predatory gulls can kill adult Pigeon Guillemots and sometimes eat their chicks and eggs.

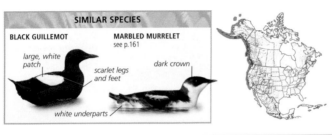

SIMILAR SPECIES

BLACK GUILLEMOT

large, white patch

scarlet legs and feet

MARBLED MURRELET
see p.161

dark crown

white underparts

OCCURRENCE
Breeds on rocky islands, coastlines, and cliffs where it is less accessible to predators. At sea, it generally remains close to rocky coasts, except in the Bering Sea, where it is found further out along the edges of the pack ice. In winter, some populations are forced south by sea ice.

Length **13½in (34cm)**	Wingspan **23in (58cm)**	Weight **18oz (500g)**
Social **Colonies**	Lifespan **Up to 14 years**	Status **Localized**

DATE: _____ TIME: _____ LOCATION: _____

Marbled Murrelet

dark face patch

white collar

ADULT (NONBREEDING)

dark-brown head

ADULT (NONBREEDING)

dark overall

ADULT (BREEDING)

white patches on side of rump

IN FLIGHT

dark tail

speckled upperparts

dark-brown back

dark-brown head

spotted chin, throat, and chest

ADULT (BREEDING)

mottled underparts

The breeding habits of the Marbled Murrelet, a bird of both sea and forest, remained a mystery until 1974, when the first nest was discovered high in a Douglas fir in a California park. Unlike most auks and their relatives, which have black and white breeding plumage, the Marbled Murrelet's breeding plumage is brown, to camouflage the bird on its nest in the branches of trees or, in places, on the ground. Ornithologists are eager to learn more about this secretive seabird, even as its numbers decline due to clear-cutting of old-growth coniferous forests where it nests, as well as entanglement of the bird in fishing gear and oil pollution out at sea where it feeds.

VOICE Flight call series of high-pitched, squealing, slightly descending *kleeer* notes.

NESTING In northern part of its range, on island mountainsides; in the south, on tree limbs in old-growth forests; 1 egg; 1 brood; April–September.

FEEDING Short dives to catch small fish and crustaceans in shallow, offshore waters, "flying" underwater; feeds at night, in pairs.

FLIGHT: straight, fast, and low over water, with extremely rapid wing beats.

RUNNING ON WATER
The Marbled Murrelet flaps its wings energetically and runs across the surface to become airborne.

OCCURRENCE
Relies on marine and forested habitats on Pacific coasts from Alaska to California, for both feeding and breeding. At sea, usually found near coast, in relatively shallow waters. In the breeding season, travels back and forth between the sea and inland breeding grounds.

SIMILAR SPECIES

ANCIENT MURRELET (NONBREEDING)
see p.162

pale tip

no white patches

Length **10in (26cm)**	Wingspan **16in (41cm)**	Weight **8oz (225g)**
Social **Pairs/Small groups**	Lifespan **Unknown**	Status **Threatened**

DATE: _____ TIME: _____ LOCATION: _____

Ancient Murrelet

ADULT (BREEDING)

white underwing

IN FLIGHT

white underparts with gray sides

lacks distinctive white plumes behind eyes

lacks black throat

ADULT (NONBREEDING)

uniform gray upperparts

distinctive white plumes behind eyes

black face and throat

pale bill tip

distinctive white collar on side of neck

ADULT (BREEDING)

Of the six murrelets that occur regularly in North America, this little species is the most numerous. Like its close relatives, Scripps's Murrelet and Craveri's Murrelet, the Ancient Murrelet usually raises two chicks, and takes them out to sea when they are just a few days old, usually under the cover of darkness. The Ancient Murrelet can also leap straight out of the sea and into flight. White eyebrow-like plumes on the head, combined with a shawl-like gray back, give the bird its supposedly "ancient" appearance.
VOICE Short, high-pitched trills and rattles given by nesting birds while perched in trees.
NESTING Burrow in soft soil, often among forest tree roots; 2 eggs; 1 brood; June-August.
FEEDING Dives for prey in groups, often at the same time, driving schools of small fish to the surface; Euphansiid shrimps, which are about 1in (2.5cm) long, are its primary diet.

FLIGHT: flies fast, low, and straight with rapid wing beats; capable of quick takeoff from water.

GROUP FEEDER
The Ancient Murrelet flies low over the water, in flocks, on the lookout for food.

OCCURRENCE
Lives in the North Pacific and the Bering Sea. Concentrates where food is abundant—most often in straits, sounds, and coastal waters—where it often feeds quite close to shore. Nests on coastal islands, mainly on the forest floor but also where there is proper cover and sufficient peaty soil to dig burrows.

SIMILAR SPECIES

SCRIPPS'S MURRELET

lacks white head plumes

gray back

white throat

MARBLED MURRELET (NONBREEDING)
see p.161

white patches on side

| Length **10in (26cm)** | Wingspan **17in (43cm)** | Weight **7oz (200g)** |
| Social **Colonies** | Lifespan **At least 4 years** | Status **Special Concern** |

DATE: _____ TIME: _____ LOCATION: _____

SHOREBIRDS, GULLS, AUKS,

| Order **Charadriiformes** | Family **Alcidae** | Species ***Ptychoramphus aleuticus*** |

Cassin's Auklet

rounded wingtips

ADULT (NONBREEDING)

dark underwing with pale stripe

IN FLIGHT

whitish belly

pale, gray underparts

white patch

ADULT (NONBREEDING)

sooty overall

pale eyes

thin white eyebrow

short, thick gray bill

pale patch at base of bill

ADULT (BREEDING)

This secretive little seabird usually nests in an underground burrow, which can take a breeding pair many weeks to scratch out. Parent birds fish by day, returning to the nest in the safety of darkness to avoid gulls and other predators. Nestlings encourage regurgitation by nibbling at a white spot at the base of the parent's lower mandible. Unique for a member of the alcidae, Cassin's Auklet has been known to raise more than one brood in a season.

VOICE Hoarse, rhythmic night calls in colonies; squeals and peeps when in burrow; silent at sea.

NESTING On offshore islands, in crevices or burrows; 1 egg; 1–2 broods; March–September.

FEEDING Dives and swims underwater using wings to pursue small crustaceans, fish, and squid.

FLIGHT: low over the surface of the sea, with rapid wing beats.

RUNNING ON WATER
After a long run and some energetic wing beating, Cassin's Auklet eventually takes off from the water.

SIMILAR SPECIES

MARBLED MURRELET (BREEDING)
see p.161

paler head

reddish-brown upperparts

KITTLITZ'S MURRELET (BREEDING)
lacks white stripe on underwing

mottled brown-and-white feathers

OCCURRENCE
Pacific distribution; breeds on cliffs, grassy plains, or slopes on coastal islands. During the nonbreeding season, northern birds found in deep waters beyond the continental shelf, where upwelling currents bring food from the depths. Southern birds remain near their colonies year-round.

Length **9in (23cm)**	Wingspan **15in (38cm)**	Weight **6oz (175g)**
Social **Colonies**	Lifespan **At least 6 years**	Status **Special Concern**

DATE: _____ TIME: _____ LOCATION: _____

SHOREBIRDS, GULLS, AUKS, Aͬ

Rhinoceros Auklet

dark wings

ADULT (NONBREEDING)

lacks facial plumes

smaller bill

ADULT (NONBREEDING)

horny structure at base of upper bill

white belly

IN FLIGHT

dark upperparts

thin white plumes curving backward

ADULT (BREEDING)

This robust bird is closely related to puffins, and is the only auk with a prominent "horn" on top of its bill; it is this structure that gives the bird its common name. The Rhinoceros Auklet forages closer to shore than its puffin relatives, and usually returns to its nesting colonies at night. This trusting seabird often allows boats to approach very close. It became locally extinct, but reestablished its population on California's Farallon Islands in the 1970s, when non-native rabbits that were competing for nesting burrows were removed. When fishing, it carries its catch in its beak, rather than in a throat pouch like other auks.

VOICE Adults give series of low, mooing calls, as well as short barks and groans.

NESTING Cup of moss or twigs on islands, under vegetation, in crevice or long, soil burrow; 1 egg; 1 brood; April–September.

FEEDING Forages underwater during breeding season, looks for small schooling fish for nestlings; also eats crustaceans; powerful diver and swimmer.

FLIGHT: swift, direct with quick wing beats; takeoff appears labored.

SUBMARINE-LIKE
Its body nearly submerged and its head looking behind, this Rhinoceros Auklet is ready to dive.

SIMILAR SPECIES

PARAKEET AUKLET ♂

paler breast

OCCURRENCE
Throughout temperate North Pacific waters, generally south of puffin habitat. Typically lives far out at sea, but may feed near shore where currents concentrate food; usually forages and returns to nesting colonies by night.

Length **15in (38cm)**	Wingspan **22in (56cm)**	Weight **16oz (450g)**
Social **Colonies**	Lifespan **Unknown**	Status **Localized**

DATE: _____ TIME:_____ LOCATION:_____

Horned Puffin

IN FLIGHT

dark wing

no fleshy "horn" above eye

brown base to bill

ADULT (NONBREEDING)

gray face

fleshy "horn" above eye

white face

black neck collar

large yellow bill with orange tip

dark upperparts

white underparts

ADULT (BREEDING)

bright-orange legs and toes

FLIGHT: swift and direct, with rapid wing beats; usually near the water's surface.

This hardy alcidae is similar to the Atlantic Puffin in appearance and behavior, but the Horned Puffin is larger and lives on the other side of North America, in the North Pacific and Bering Sea, where it nests on even more remote, rocky offshore islands than its Atlantic relative. Outside the breeding season, Horned Puffins spend month after month far out at sea, hundreds of miles from the nearest land. When the birds return to their breeding grounds, pairs often head straight for the same rock crevice they nested in the year before.

VOICE Low-pitched, rumbling growls in rhythmic phrases.

NESTING Deep rock crevices lined with grass and feathers; 1 egg; 1 brood; May–August.

FEEDING Dives for herring, sand lance, capelin, smelt, and other small fishes to feed to chicks; adults consume squid, crustaceans, and marine worms underwater.

SIMILAR SPECIES

TUFTED PUFFIN ♂
see p.166

stocky black body

orange bill

ATLANTIC PUFFIN ♂ ☼

no fleshy "horn" above eye

blue-gray on bill

BACK AND FORTH
Parent birds fly repeatedly to and from the nest to catch fish for their chicks.

OCCURRENCE
Breeds on rocky islands off the Alaskan and North Pacific Coasts (where crevices for nesting are plentiful); feeds close to these shores. Often found with Tufted Puffins, but generally farther north. Rarely wanders as far south as California in the nonbreeding season. Winters on ocean waters, far from land.

Length **15in (38cm)**	Wingspan **23in (59cm)**	Weight **23oz (650g)**
Social **Colonies**	Lifespan **At least 20 years**	Status **Localized**

DATE: _____ TIME: _____ LOCATION: _____

, AND RELATIVES

Tufted Puffin

ADULT (NONBREEDING)

lacks long golden head plumes

dark face

IN FLIGHT

no plumes

yellow bill

ADULT (POSTBREEDING)

large, rounded head

white face

long golden plumes on back of head and nape

orange bill

stocky, black body

rounded wings

dark underparts

ADULT (BREEDING)

orange legs and feet

WWWWWWWWWW

FLIGHT: just above the ocean with strong, rapid wing beats.

Tufted Puffins, found along the northern Pacific Coast, may be spotted hopping over rocky ledges, sitting alone on the sea, paddling along the surface before taking off, or flying only a couple of feet above the water. Like other puffin species, they partially open their wings underwater as they pursue prey, keeping their tail and feet spread to aid propulsion and steering. This bird's name arises from the curly golden plumes of feathers that adorn its head during the breeding season. It is the largest of the three puffin species. It can be distinguished from the Horned Puffin by its dark underparts, and from the Atlantic Puffin by its distribution.

VOICE Low, moaning growl given from burrow.

NESTING Chamber, lined with grass or feathers, at end of tunnels, under rocks, or in burrows; 1 egg; 1 brood; May–August.

FEEDING Dives deep to capture small fish, especially sand lance, juvenile pollock, and capelin; adults consume prey underwater, or take it ashore to feed their chicks.

TUFTED PAIR
These distinctive and popular birds breed in colonies and usually mate for life.

SIMILAR SPECIES

ATLANTIC PUFFIN ♂ ☼

gray face

red eye-ring

white breast

HORNED PUFFIN see p.165

lacks golden plumes

yellow bill with orange tip

white underparts

OCCURRENCE
Breeds on rocky islands, and coastal cliffs of the North Pacific, especially treeless, offshore islands with sea cliffs or grassy slopes; elevation may help them take flight. Found over unusually wide geographic and climatic range. Winters at sea, usually over deep waters of the central North Pacific.

Length **15in (38cm)**	Wingspan **25in (64cm)**	Weight **27oz (775g)**
Social **Colonies**	Lifespan **Up to 30 years**	Status **Localized**

DATE: _____ TIME: _____ LOCATION: _____

Black-legged Kittiwake

yell_
bill

white head

pale-gray
back feathers

pale outer
wing feathers

black "M"
pattern wings

pale-gray
upperparts

black
bill

black
tip to
tail

ADULT

IN FLIGHT

JUVENILE

black
wingtip

ADULT

black legs
and feet

dark neck
collar

dark wing bar

JUVENILE

A kittiwake nesting colony is an impressive sight, with, sometimes, thousands of birds lined up along steep cliff ledges overlooking the sea. The ledges are often so narrow that the birds' tails stick out over the edge. Kittiwakes have sharper claws than other gulls, probably to give them a better grip on their ledges. In the late 20th century, the Black-legged Kittiwake population expanded greatly in the Canadian Maritime Provinces, with numbers doubling in the Gulf of St. Lawrence.

VOICE Repeated, nasal *kit-ti-wake, kit-ti-wake* call; vocal near nesting cliffs; usually silent in winter.

NESTING Mound of mud and vegetation on narrow cliff ledge, 1–3 eggs; 1 brood; April–August.

FEEDING Snatches small marine fish and invertebrates from the surface, or dives just below the water's surface; feeds in flocks.

FLIGHT: very stiff-winged; rapid, shallow wing beats; overall more buoyant than most gulls

LIVING ON THE EDGE
Young and adult kittiwakes pack together tightly on their precariously narrow cliff ledges.

SIMILAR SPECIES

RING-BILLED GULL
see p.173

RED-LEGGED KITTIWAKE

darker
shoulder
feathers

heavier,
dark-marked
bill

red
legs

white spots
in outer
wing feathers

gray
underwings

OCCURRENCE
Rarely seen far from the ocean; common in summer around sea cliffs, with ledges suitable for nesting, and nearby offshore waters; winters at sea; most likely to be seen from land during and after storms; strays have appeared throughout the interior.

Length **15–16in (38–41cm)**	Wingspan **3ft 1in–4ft (0.95m–1.2m)**	Weight **11–18oz (300–500g)**
Social **Colonies**	Lifespan **Up to 26 years**	Status **Secure**

DATE: _____ TIME: _____ LOCATION: _____

SHOREBIRDS, GULL

Sabine's Gull

IN FLIGHT
white triangle on wing
black outer wing feathers
ADULT
JUVENILE
black band on tail

red eye-ring
gray hood
black border
yellow-tipped black bill
gray back
white underparts
black legs
ADULT (BREEDING)

barring on gray-brown back
black bill
JUVENILE

This strikingly patterned gull was discovered in Greenland by the English scientist, Edward Sabine, during John Ross's search for the Northwest Passage in 1818 (it was described in 1819). The distinctive wing pattern and notched tail make it unmistakable in all plumages—only juvenile kittiwakes are superficially similar. Previously thought to be related to the larger, but similarly patterned, Swallow-tailed Gull of the Galapagos, recent research indicates that Sabine's Gull is more closely related to the Ivory Gull. This species breeds in the Arctic and winters at sea, off the coasts of the Americas (south to Peru) and Africa (south to the Cape region).
VOICE Raucous, harsh *kyeer, kyeer, kyeer*, tern-like.
NESTING Shallow depression in marsh or tundra vegetation usually near water, lined with grass or unlined; 3–4 eggs; 1 brood; May–August.
FEEDING Catches aquatic insects from the water's surface while swimming, wading, or flying during breeding season; winter diet mainly includes crustaceans, small fish, and plankton.

FLIGHT: wing beats shallow and stiff; tern-like, buoyant.

STRIKING WING PATTERN
Juvenile Sabine's Gulls have a muted version of the distinctive triangular wing pattern seen in the adults.

SIMILAR SPECIES
BLACK-LEGGED KITTIWAKE ☾ see p.167
partial black collar
black wing bar

OCCURRENCE
In the summer, breeds near the Arctic Coast and on wet tundra in freshwater and brackish habitats, but also occurs near salt water. Winters far offshore in tropical and subtropical waters; widespread in the Pacific and Atlantic Oceans on migration.

Length **13–14in (33–36 cm)**	Wingspan **2ft 11in–3ft 3in (90–100cm)**	Weight **5–9oz (150–250g)**
Social **Colonies**	Lifespan **At least 8 years**	Status **Secure**

DATE: _____ TIME:_____ LOCATION:_____

| Order **Charadriiformes** | Family **Laridae** | Species *Chroicocephalus philadelphia* |

Bonaparte's Gull

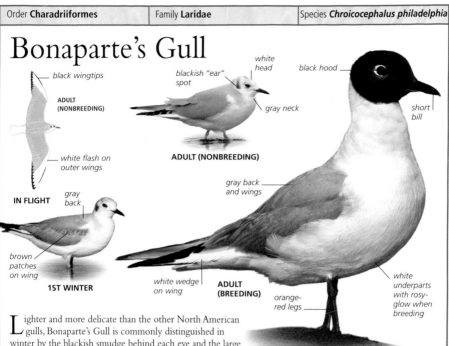

black wingtips

ADULT (NONBREEDING)

white flash on outer wings

IN FLIGHT

gray back

brown patches on wing

1ST WINTER

white head

blackish "ear" spot

gray neck

ADULT (NONBREEDING)

black hood

short bill

gray back and wings

white wedge on wing

ADULT (BREEDING)

orange-red legs

white underparts with rosy-glow when breeding

Lighter and more delicate than the other North American gulls, Bonaparte's Gull is commonly distinguished in winter by the blackish smudge behind each eye and the large white wing patch. It is one of North America's most common and widespread gulls. During migration and in winter, flocks of this species can number in the thousands. This species was named after the 19th-century French ornithologist Charles Lucien Bonaparte (nephew of Napoleon).

VOICE Harsh *keek, keek*; can be vocal in feeding flocks, *kew, kew, kew*.

NESTING Stick nest of twigs, branches, tree bark, lined with mosses or lichens; usually in conifers 5–20ft (1.5–6m) above ground; also in rushes over water; 1–4 eggs; 1 brood; May–July.

FEEDING Catches insects in flight on breeding grounds; picks crustaceans, mollusks, and small fish from water's surface; also plunge-dives.

FLIGHT: graceful, light, and agile; rapid wing beats; can be mistaken for a tern in flight.

TERN-LIKE GULL
Bonaparte's Gulls are very social and, flying in flocks, these pale, delicate birds look like terns.

WHITE UNDERWINGS
In all plumages, Bonaparte's Gull has white underwings, unlike other similar small gulls.

SIMILAR SPECIES

BLACK-HEADED GULL

dark outer wing feathers

larger overall

LITTLE GULL

smaller overall

uniform gray upperwing

red bill

OCCURRENCE
During breeding season, found in northern forest zone, in lakes, ponds, or bogs; on migration, may be found anywhere where there is water: ponds, lakes, sewage pools, or rivers. Winters on Great Lakes and along the coast; often found in large numbers at coastal inlets.

| Length **11–12in (28–30cm)** | Wingspan **35–40in (90–100cm)** | Weight **6–8oz (175–225g)** |
| Social **Flocks** | Lifespan **Up to 18 years** | Status **Secure** |

DATE: _____ TIME: _____ LOCATION: _____

| Order **Charadriiformes** | Family **Laridae** | Species *Leucophaeus pipixcan* |

Franklin's Gull

black wingtips bordered by white band

dark-gray wings

ADULT (WINTER)

IN FLIGHT

dark back of head

gray back

short, straight bill

ADULT (WINTER)

partial hood

1ST SUMMER

broken, white eye-ring

black head

red bill

pink blush underneath

white in outer wing feathers

ADULT (SUMMER)

FLIGHT: stiff and direct; relatively fast wing beats; agile flier.

Since its discovery, Franklin's Gull has carried a number of names: Prairie Dove, Rosy Dove, and Franklin's Rosy Gull—"Dove" alluding to its dainty appearance and "rosy" to the pink blush of its undersides. Its official name honors British Arctic explorer, John Franklin, on whose first expedition, the bird was discovered in 1823. Unlike other gulls, this species has two complete molts each year. As a result, its plumage usually looks fresh and it rarely has the scruffy look of some other gulls.

VOICE Nasal *weeh-a, weeh-a*; shrill *kuk kuk kuk kuk*; extremely vocal around breeding colonies.

NESTING Floating mass of bulrushes or other plants; material added as nest sinks; 2–4 eggs; 1 brood; April–July.

FEEDING Feeds mainly on earthworms and insects, and some seeds during breeding, picked while walking or flying; opportunistic feeder during migration and winter.

PROMINENT EYES
In all plumages, Franklin's Gull has much more prominent white eye-crescents than similar species.

SIMILAR SPECIES

LAUGHING GULL

longer, drooped bill

longer legs

LAUGHING GULL ☾ ❄

smaller eye-rings

longer legs

longer, drooped bill

OCCURRENCE
In summer, a bird of the high prairies; always nests over water. On migration often found in agricultural areas; large numbers frequent plowed fields or follows plows. Winters mainly along the Pacific Coast of South America.

| Length **12½–14in (32–36cm)** | Wingspan **2ft 9in–3ft 1in (85–95cm)** | Weight **8–11oz (225–325g)** |
| Social **Colonial** | Lifespan **At least 10 years** | Status **Declining** |

DATE: _____ TIME: _____ LOCATION: _____

| Order **Charadriiformes** | Family **Laridae** | Species *Larus heermanni* |

Heermann's Gull

ADULT (BREEDING)

1ST WINTER

white trailing edge feathers

all-dark wings

gray underparts

IN FLIGHT

dark-brown body

pale base to bill

chocolate-brown body

1ST WINTER

red eye-ring

white head

gray body

red bill with black tip

duller bill

mottled head

black legs

ADULT (BREEDING)

FLIGHT: flight strong, direct, and a bit heavy.

ADULT (NONBREEDING)

In North America during the breeding Heermann's Gull is the only gull with a dark-gray body and white head. These features, along with its bright-red bill, make this gull unmistakable. In nonbreeding plumage, the head is mottled and dark, and the bill is black-tipped. Juveniles are generally dark brown, with pale patches at the base of their bills. These gulls have black legs in all plumages, unlike any other North American gull, except the Black-legged Kittiwake.
VOICE Nasal *caw* or *cow-awk* call; not very vocal away from breeding grounds.
NESTING Depression lined with dead grass or twigs in sand, small rocks, or grass; usually nests with terns; 1–3 eggs; 1 brood; March–July.
FEEDING Feeds on fish, crustaceans, mollusks, squid, and lizards; in breeding colonies, takes eggs of terns and gulls; also scavenges.

WHITE EDGES
The white trailing edge of the wing and the white tip of the tail are obvious in flight.

OCCURRENCE
A truly western North American gull, it nests on islands off Baja California; over 90 percent of the world's population nests on Isla Raza; occasionally in California; after breeding, spreads north along the coast to British Columbia, uncommon north of Monterey; rare inland and accidental elsewhere.

SIMILAR SPECIES

POMARINE JAEGER (DARK FORM)
see p.155

dark bill

white flash in outer wing

PARASITIC JAEGER (DARK FORM)
see p.156

white flash in outer wing feathers

| Length **18–21in (46–53cm)** | Wingspan **4¼ft (1.3m)** | Weight **13–23oz (375–650g)** |
| Social **Colonies** | Lifespan **Up to 13 years** | Status **Secure** |

DATE: _____ TIME:_____ LOCATION:_____

Order **Charadriiformes**	Family **Laridae**	Species *Larus brachyrhynchus*

Short-billed Gull

1ST WINTER

barred rump

brownish-gray wings

IN FLIGHT

dark gray back

all-yellow bill

small, short bill, often with dusky ring

streaks on rounded head

ADULT (BREEDING)

prominent gray back

yellow legs

dusky mottling

white spot on wingtip

ADULT (BREEDING)

1ST SUMMER

dull pink legs and feet

small head

black tip to bill

brown belly

ADULT (NONBREEDING)

yellow to green legs

1ST WINTER

Formerly known as the Mew Gull, its small bill and rounded head give the aptly renamed Short-billed Gull a rather dove-like profile. It can be confused with the widespread Ring-billed Gull, which it resembles in all plumages. The smallest of the "white-headed gulls" in North America, the Short-billed Gull is highly variable in its choice of habitats and its reproductive and feeding behaviors.

VOICE Shrill mewing calls; higher pitched than other gulls.
NESTING Platform of mainly dry vegetation in trees or on ground; 1–5 eggs; 1 brood; May–August.
FEEDING Eats aquatic crustaceans and mollusks, insects, fish, bird eggs, chicks; scavenges trash and steals food from other birds.

FLIGHT: wing beats faster than larger, similar-looking gulls.

PLAIN YELLOW BILL
Although back color and bill size vary in different forms, all adult Short-billed Gulls have plain yellow bills.

SIMILAR SPECIES

RING-BILLED GULL
see p.173

paler back

dark mark on bill

smaller white spots in wingtips

RING-BILLED GULL ♀
see p.173

flatter head

paler back

larger bill

OCCURRENCE
Breeds in Alaska and northwest Canada south along the coast into British Columbia; winters along the Pacific Coast, south to Baja California and inland on major river systems. Casual to accidental across the continent to the Atlantic Coast.

Length **15–16in (38–41cm)**	Wingspan **3ft 3in–4ft (1–1.2m)**	Weight **13–18oz (375–500g)**
Social **Pairs/Colonies**	Lifespan **Up to 24 years**	Status **Secure**

DATE: _____ TIME: _____ LOCATION: _____

Order **Charadriiformes**	Family **Laridae**	Species *Larus delawarensis*

Ring-billed Gull 🔊

white wing spots

ADULT (BREEDING)

black-tipped pink bill

dark eye

mottled-gray back

white neck

1ST WINTER

heavily mottled back

mottled underparts

pink legs

JUVENILE

black band on yellow bill

fine streaks on head

IN FLIGHT

gray back

olive-yellow legs

ADULT (NONBREEDING)

pale-gray back

2ND WINTER

white markings on outer wing feathers

pale eye with red eye-ring

pale-gray back

ADULT (BREEDING)

white underparts

yellowish or [illegible]

FLIGHT: quick, deep wing beats; strong, direct flight, soaring on thermals.

One of the most common birds in North America, the medium-sized Ring-billed Gull is distinguished by the black band on its yellow bill. From the mid-19th to the early 20th century, population numbers crashed due to shooting and habitat loss. Protection allowed the species to make a spectacular comeback, and in the 1990s, there were an estimated 3–4 million birds. It can often be seen scavenging in parking lots at malls and following farmers' tractors.

VOICE Call a slightly nasal and whiny *kee-ow* or *meee-ow*; series of 4–6 *kyaw* notes, higher pitched than Herring Gull.

NESTING Shallow cup of plant matter on ground in open areas, usually near low vegetation; 1–5 eggs; 1 brood; April–August.

FEEDING Picks food while walking; also dips and plunges in water; eats small fish, insects, grain, small rodents; also scavenges.

BLACK WING MARKING
The sharply demarcated black wingtips are prominent from both above and below.

SIMILAR SPECIES

SHORT-BILLED GULL
see p.172

darker mantle

round head

small bill

SHORT-BILLED GULL ♀1ST❄
see p.172

less distinct streaks

round head

small bill

OCCURRENCE
Breeds in freshwater habitats in the interior of the continent. In winter, switches to mostly saltwater areas and along both the East and West Coasts; also along major river systems and reservoirs. Found year-round near the southern Great Lakes.

Length **17–21½in (43–54cm)**	Wingspan **4–5ft (1.2–1.5m)**	Weight **11–25oz (300–700g)**
Social **Colonies**	Lifespan **Up to 32 years**	Status **Secure**

DATE: _____ TIME: _____ LOCATION: _____

Order **Charadriiformes**	Family **Laridae**	Species *Larus occidentalis*

Western Gull

orange eye-ring

uniform brown back

white head

black wingtip with white edges

ADULT
L. o. wymani
(BREEDING)

large yellow beak with red spot

JUVENILE

dark-gray wings

slate-gray mantle

IN FLIGHT

brownish-gray mantle

broad white trailing edge feathers

1ST WINTER

dusky head

dark-gray mantle

ADULT
L. o. wymani
(BREEDING)

pinkish legs

paler gray back

ADULT
L. o. occidentalis

2ND WINTER

The Western Gull is the only dark-backed gull found regularly within its normal range and habitat. However, identification is complicated due to having two subspecies: the paler *occidentalis* in the north, and the darker *wymani* in the south. Western Gulls interbreed with Glaucous-winged Gulls, producing confusing hybrids. The total population of these gulls is small, and the small number of nesting colonies makes conservation a concern.

VOICE Shrill, repeated *heyaa…heyaa…heyaa* similar to the Herring Gull, but lower in pitch, harsher; very vocal at breeding sites.
NESTING Scrape filled with vegetation, usually next to bush or rock; 3–4 eggs; 1 brood; April–August.
FEEDING Eats crabs, squid, insects, fish, bird eggs, and chicks; also eats sea lion pups; scavenges.

FLIGHT: strong, slow with heavy wing beats; also, commonly soars.

DARK UNDERWINGS
The undersides of the outer wing feathers are much darker in this bird than in similar species.

SIMILAR SPECIES

YELLOW-FOOTED GULL

darker back

yellow legs

SLATY-BACKED GULL
see p.442

thinner bill

OCCURRENCE
Nests on offshore islands along the West Coast; all ages disperse north after the breeding season as far as British Columbia; nonbreeders and wintering birds occur along the coast and in major bays and estuaries southward to Baja California; very rare inland or far offshore.

Length **22–26in (56–66cm)**	Wingspan **4¼–4½ft (1.3–1.4m)**	Weight **1¾–2¾lb (0.8–1.2kg)**
Social **Colonies**	Lifespan **Up to 28 years**	Status **Vulnerable**

DATE: _____ TIME:_____ LOCATION:_____

| Order **Charadriiformes** | Family **Laridae** | Species *Larus californicus* |

California Gull 🔊

ADULT (NONBREEDING)

black wingtips with white terminal spot

IN FLIGHT

white trailing edge to feathers

black-tipped wings

greenish-yellow legs and toes

red eye-ring

white head and neck

gray back

black line and red spot on bill

brownish mottling on head and neck

2ND WINTER

gray legs

3RD SUMMER

white underparts

ADULT (BREEDING)

dark streaks on nape of neck

ADULT (NONBREEDING)

Slightly smaller than the Herring Gull, the medium-sized California Gull has a darker back and longer wings. In breeding plumage, it can also be distinguished by the black-and-red coloration on its bill and its greenish-yellow legs. In winter and on young birds, dark streaks are prominent on the nape of the neck. A common interior gull, it is honored by a large, gilded statue in Salt Lake City that commemorates the birds' rescue of the settlers' crops from a plague of grasshoppers in 1848.

VOICE Call a repeated *kee-yah, kee-yah, kee-yah*.

NESTING Shallow scrape, lined with feathers, bones, and vegetation, usually on islands; 2–3 eggs; 1 brood; May–July.

FEEDING Forages around lakes for insects and mollusks; hovers over cherry trees, dislodging fruits with its wings.

FLIGHT: strong and direct, but somewhat stiff, with deep wing beats.

AGGRESSIVE POSTURE
This California Gull is displaying signs of aggression—possibly against another bird.

OCCURRENCE
Breeds at scattered locations across interior western Canada and the US. Some of the largest colonies are on the highly saline Mono Lake and the Great Salt Lake; winters along the Pacific Coast from British Columbia to Mexico; strays increasingly reported in the East.

SIMILAR SPECIES

HERRING GULL ☼ see p.176 — paler back — pink legs — larger body

HERRING GULL ❄ see p.176 — heavy streaking on head — paler back

| Length **17½–20in (45–51cm)** | Wingspan **4–4½ft (1.2–1.4m)** | Weight **18–35oz (0.5–1kg)** |
| Social **Colonies** | Lifespan **Up to 30 years** | Status **Secure** |

DATE: _____ TIME: _____ LOCATION: _____

| Order **Charadriiformes** | Family **Laridae** | Species *Larus argentatus* |

Herring Gull 🔊

white spots near wingtips

ADULT (BREEDING)

light head

barred gray-brown overall

gray wings

2ND WINTER

mottled-brown back

barred brown body

1ST WINTER

white head and neck

large yellow bill with red spot

gray back

streaked head

ADULT (NONBREEDING)

black outer wing feathers

IN FLIGHT

white underparts

pink legs

ADULT (BREEDING)

streaked head and neck

ADULT (NONBREEDING)

The Herring Gull is the archetypal, large "white-headed" gull that nearly all other gulls are compared with. When people mention "seagulls" they usually refer to the Herring Gull. The term "seagull" is actually misleading because the Herring Gull, like most other gulls, does not commonly go far out to sea—it is a bird of near-shore waters, coasts, lakes, rivers, and inland waterways. Now very common, the Herring Gull was nearly wiped out in the late 19th and early 20th century by plumage hunters and egg collectors.

VOICE Typical call a high-pitched, shrill, repeated *heyaa…heyaa… heyaa…heyaa*; vocal throughout the year.

NESTING Shallow bowl on ground, lined with feathers, vegetation, detritus; 2–4 eggs; 1 brood; April–August.

FEEDING Eats fish, crustaceans, mollusks, worms; eggs and chicks of other seabirds; scavenges carrion, garbage; steals from other birds.

FLIGHT: steady, regular, slow wing beats; also commonly soars and glides.

MASTER SCAVENGER
A common sight near any water body, the Herring Gull is an expert scavenger of carrion and trash.

SIMILAR SPECIES

RING-BILLED GULL
see p.173
smaller overall
black ring on bill
yellow-green legs

CALIFORNIA GULL
see p.175
black-and-red spot on bill
greenish legs

OCCURRENCE
Found throughout North America along coasts and inland on lakes, rivers, and reservoirs; also frequents garbage dumps. Breeds in northeastern US and across Canada. Migrates southward across much of the continent to winter in coastal areas and along lakes and major rivers.

| Length **22–26in (56–66cm)** | Wingspan **4–5ft (1.2–1.5m)** | Weight **28–42oz (0.8–1.2kg)** |
| Social **Colonies** | Lifespan **At least 35 years** | Status **Secure** |

DATE: _____ TIME: _____ LOCATION: _____

| Order **Charadriiformes** | Family **Laridae** | Species *Larus glaucoides* |

Iceland Gull

gray wingtips

pale-brown plumage

ADULT (WINTER)

1ST WINTER

IN FLIGHT

wingtip white or marked with gray

short, pale-yellow bill with red spot

markedly streaked head

gray back

white belly

ADULT (WINTER)
L. g. kumlieni

pink legs

brown, barred plumage

blackish bill

head mostly white

pale, barred underparts

1ST WINTER

2ND WINTER

Iceland Gulls of the subspecies *kumlieni* (seen in all the images here) are the most familiar form of this species in North America. They breed in the Canadian Arctic and winter farther south. Young birds have a dark tail band and brown streaks on the wingtip, while adults vary from white wingtips to gray with white spots. A darker subspecies, *thayeri*, breeds on Arctic islands west of the *kumlieni*'s range, and has black-and-white wingtips like the Herring Gull and a darker eye. Thayer's Gull was considered to be a different species until 2017, when it was grouped with the Iceland Gull. The "Iceland" form of the gull, *L. g. glaucoides*, breeds in Greenland but is found farther eastward in winter, including in Iceland.

VOICE Call a *clew, clew, clew* or *kak-kak-kak*; vocal around breeding colonies; virtually silent on wintering grounds.

NESTING Loose nest of moss, vegetation, and feathers, usually on narrow rock ledge; 2–3 eggs; 1 brood; May–August.

FEEDING Grabs small fish from surface while in flight; also eats crustaceans, mollusks, carrion, and garbage.

FLIGHT: light and graceful; wings long in proportion to body.

WINGTIP COLOR VARIATION
Some adult Iceland Gulls found in North America have wingtips that are almost pure white.

SIMILAR SPECIES

GLAUCOUS GULL
see p.179

larger bill

much larger body

white wingtips

OCCURRENCE
Usually nests on ledges on vertical cliffs overlooking the sea; winters where it finds regions of open water in frozen seas and along coasts. A few wander to open water areas in the interior, such as the Niagara Falls, the Great Lakes and major rivers.

| Length **20½–23½in (52–60cm)** | Wingspan **4½–5ft (1.4–1.5m)** | Weight **21–39oz (0.6–1.1kg)** |
| Social **Colonies** | Lifespan **Up to 33 years** | Status **Secure** |

DATE: _____ TIME:_____ LOCATION:_____

SHOREBIRDS, GULLS, AUKS, AND RELATIVES

177

| Order **Charadriiformes** | Family **Laridae** | Species *Larus glaucescens* |

Glaucous-winged Gull

pale tan overall

1ST WINTER

string of white spots in outer feathers

uniform gray-brown plumage

gray mantle

pale base of dark bill

light-brown tail

1ST WINTER

2ND WINTER

white head

thick bill

IN FLIGHT

ADULT (BREEDING)

very faint to dark markings on head and neck

pale blue-gray wings

pale-gray mantle

pale blue-gray wings

ADULT (NONBREEDING)

ADULT (BREEDING)

pale-pink legs

white underparts

The Glaucous-winged Gull, the most common large gull on the North Pacific Coast, is found around towns and cities, even nesting on the roofs of shorefront buildings. This species commonly interbreeds with Western Gulls in the southern part of its range, and with Herring and Glaucous Gulls in the north, producing intermediate birds that are more difficult to identify.
VOICE Call a slow, deep *aah-aah-aah*; many types of calls heard around colonies; lower-pitched than Herring Gull.
NESTING Scrape surrounded by ring of torn up grass or other vegetation; forms colonies usually on small, low islands; 2–3 eggs; 1 brood; May–August.
FEEDING Snatches fish, aquatic mollusks, and crustaceans while walking, swimming, or diving; also scavenges carrion and trash.

FLIGHT: strong and graceful; shallow wing beats; also soars.

PALE WINGS
The Glaucous-winged Gull is named for its delicate, pale bluish-gray wings.

SIMILAR SPECIES

GLAUCOUS GULL ❋
see p.179

larger and paler body

white wingtips

ICELAND GULL
see p.177

smaller bill

rounder head

OCCURRENCE
Breeds along the coast of northwest Oregon northward to the Bering Sea coast of Alaska; winters within its breeding range and southward, to Gulf of California; primarily a coastal and offshore gull (farther offshore in winter); it is very rare inland and accidental to central North America.

Length **23–24in (58–62cm)**	Wingspan **4½–5ft (1.4–1.5m)**	Weight **2–2¾lb (0.9–1.3kg)**
Social **Colonies**	Lifespan **Up to 32 years**	Status **Secure**

DATE: _____ TIME:_____ LOCATION:_____

| Order **Charadriiformes** | Family **Laridae** | Species *Larus hyperboreus* |

Glaucous Gull

mottled pale-brown back

white head

yellow bill with distinct red spot

1ST WINTER

pale-brown underparts

ADULT (WINTER)

streaking on head

mottled-white plumage

pale-gray upperparts

1ST WINTER, FADED

IN FLIGHT

white wingtips

light-brownish plumage

1ST WINTER

white underparts

pink legs

ADULT (SUMMER)

FLIGHT: heavy, slow, and powerful; often glides and soars.

The Glaucous Gull is the largest of the "white-winged" gulls. Its bulk and pale shape is immediately apparent in a group of gulls as it appears like a large white spectre among its smaller, darker cousins. In the southern part of its US winter range, pale juveniles are encountered more frequently than adults. In the Arctic, successful pairs of Glaucous Gulls maintain the bonds with their mates for years, often returning to the same nest site year after year.

VOICE Similar to that of the Herring Gull, but slightly harsher and deeper; hoarse, nasal *ku-ku-ku*.

NESTING Shallow cup, lined with vegetation on ground, at edge of tundra pools, on cliffs and ledges and islands; 1–3 eggs; 1 brood; May–July.

FEEDING Eats fish, crustaceans, mollusks; also eggs and chicks of waterfowl, small seabirds, and small mammals.

NORTHERN VISITOR
This large gull is an uncommon visitor over most of North America during the winter months.

SIMILAR SPECIES

GLAUCOUS-WINGED GULL see p.178

dusky wingtips

ICELAND GULL see p.177

much smaller bill

much smaller overall

OCCURRENCE
Breeds along the high-Arctic coast, rarely inland; winters along the northern Atlantic and Pacific Coasts and the Great Lakes; frequently seen at the Niagara Falls. Strays, usually juveniles, can occur inland anywhere where concentrations of gulls are found, such as landfill sites and dumps.

| Length **26–30in (65–75cm)** | Wingspan **5–6ft (1.5–1.8m)** | Weight **2¾–6lb (1.2–2.7kg)** |
| Social **Colonies** | Lifespan **Up to 21 years** | Status **Secure** |

DATE: _____ TIME: _____ LOCATION: _____

179

| Order **Charadriiformes** | Family **Laridae** | Species *Hydroprogne caspia* |

Caspian Tern

streaked dark crown

dark markings on upperparts

JUVENILE

ADULT (BREEDING)

short tail

dark-tipped outer wing feathers

IN FLIGHT

ADULT (NONBREEDING)

slightly crested black cap

slightly crested black cap

light-gray back

thick red bill with dark tip

ADULT (BREEDING)

white underparts

black legs and feet

FLIGHT: strong, swift flier; heavy, powerful wing beats; the most gull-like of North American terns.

R ivalling some of the gulls in size, the Caspian Tern is the world's largest tern. Unlike other "black-capped" terns, it never has a completely white forehead, even in winter. In non-breeding plumage, the cap is very heavily streaked. The Caspian Tern is known for its predatory habits, stealing prey from other seabirds, as well as snatching eggs and eating the chicks of gulls and other terns. It is aggressive in defending its nesting territory, giving hoarse alarm calls, and rhythmically opening and closing its beak in a threatening display to intruders.

VOICE Hoarse, deep *kraaa, kraaa*; also barks at intruders; male's wings vibrate loudly in courtship flight.

NESTING Shallow scrape on ground; 2–3 eggs; 1 brood; May–August.

FEEDING Plunges into water to snatch fish, barnacles, and snails.

AGRESSIVE BIRDS
The Caspian Tern is one of the most aggressive terns, though actual physical contact is rare.

SIMILAR SPECIES

ELEGANT TERN

smaller overall

ROYAL TERN

thin orange-yellow bill

thinner orange bill

slender build

OCCURRENCE
Found in a variety of aquatic habitats, freshwater and marine; rare offshore; breeds on interior lakes, salt marshes, and on coastal barrier islands; winters on and near the coast. May be seen on marshes and wetlands during migration.

| Length **18½–21½in (47–54cm)** | Wingspan **4¼–5ft (1.3–1.5m)** | Weight **19–27oz (525–775g)** |
| Social **Colonies/Pairs** | Lifespan **Up to 30 years** | Status **Secure** |

DATE: _____ TIME: _____ LOCATION: _____

Order **Charadriiformes**	Family **Laridae**	Species *Chlidonias niger*

Black Tern

IN FLIGHT

dark-gray wings

dark-gray tail

ADULT (BREEDING)

ADULT (NONBREEDING)

whitish underparts

white forehead

black head

black bill

dark smudge on sides

gray upperparts

black breast

ADULT (BREEDING)

white rump

black legs and toes

FLIGHT: very agile, but somewhat erratic-looking, bouncy flight; strong, deep wing beats.

The Black Tern is a small, elegant, marsh-dwelling tern that undergoes a remarkable change in appearance from summer to winter—more so than any other regularly occurring North American tern. The Black Tern's breeding plumage can cause the bird to be confused with the closely related White-winged Tern, which is an accidental visitor to North America. The Black Tern's nonbreeding plumage is much paler than its breeding plumage—the head turns white with irregular black streaks, and the neck, breast, and belly become whitish gray.

VOICE Call nasal and harsh *krik*, *kip*, or *kik*; most vocal during breeding, but calls throughout the year.

NESTING Shallow cup on top of floating mass of vegetation, sometimes on top of muskrat lodges; usually 3 eggs; 1 brood; May–August.

FEEDING Picks prey off water's surface or vegetation; rarely plunge-dives; in summer, feeds mainly on insects, caught from the air or ground, also freshwater fish; in winter, eats mainly small sea fish.

FLOATING NEST
A floating nest is a dry place to lay eggs and raise chicks in a watery environment.

SIMILAR SPECIES

SOOTY TERN ☾

white spots on back

much larger overall

OCCURRENCE
Freshwater marshes in summer, but nonbreeding-plumaged birds—probably young—occasionally seen along the coast. During migration, can be found almost anywhere near water. Winters in the marine coastal waters of Central and South America.

Length **9–10in (23–26cm)**	Wingspan **25–35in (63–88cm)**	Weight **1¾–2½oz (50–70g)**
Social **Colonies**	Lifespan **Up to 9 years**	Status **Vulnerable**

DATE: _____ TIME: _____ LOCATION: _____

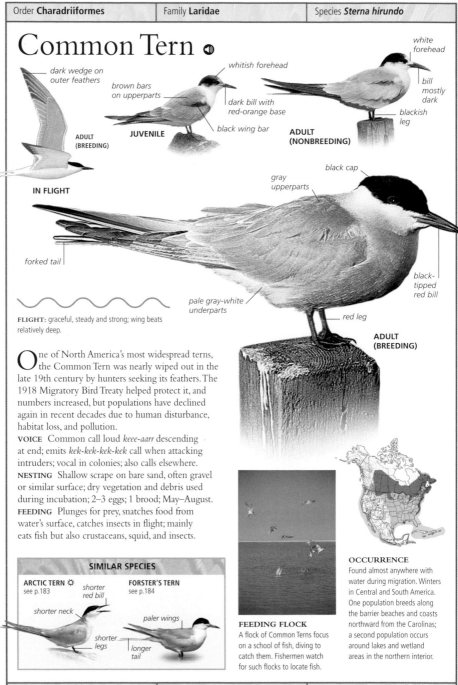

| Order **Charadriiformes** | Family **Laridae** | Species *Sterna hirundo* |

Common Tern 🔊

dark wedge on outer feathers

brown bars on upperparts

whitish forehead

dark bill with red-orange base

black wing bar

ADULT (BREEDING)

JUVENILE

white forehead

bill mostly dark

blackish leg

ADULT (NONBREEDING)

IN FLIGHT

black cap

gray upperparts

forked tail

pale gray-white underparts

black-tipped red bill

red leg

ADULT (BREEDING)

FLIGHT: graceful, steady and strong; wing beats relatively deep.

One of North America's most widespread terns, the Common Tern was nearly wiped out in the late 19th century by hunters seeking its feathers. The 1918 Migratory Bird Treaty helped protect it, and numbers increased, but populations have declined again in recent decades due to human disturbance, habitat loss, and pollution.

VOICE Common call loud *keee-aarr* descending at end; emits *kek-kek-kek-kek* call when attacking intruders; vocal in colonies; also calls elsewhere.

NESTING Shallow scrape on bare sand, often gravel or similar surface; dry vegetation and debris used during incubation; 2–3 eggs; 1 brood; May–August.

FEEDING Plunges for prey, snatches food from water's surface, catches insects in flight; mainly eats fish but also crustaceans, squid, and insects.

SIMILAR SPECIES

ARCTIC TERN ☼
see p.183

shorter red bill

shorter neck

shorter legs

FORSTER'S TERN
see p.184

paler wings

longer tail

FEEDING FLOCK
A flock of Common Terns focus on a school of fish, diving to catch them. Fishermen watch for such flocks to locate fish.

OCCURRENCE
Found almost anywhere with water during migration. Winters in Central and South America. One population breeds along the barrier beaches and coasts northward from the Carolinas; a second population occurs around lakes and wetland areas in the northern interior.

| Length **12–14in (31–35cm)** | Wingspan **30–31in (75–80cm)** | Weight **3⅜–5oz (95–150g)** |
| Social **Colonies** | Lifespan **Up to 26 years** | Status **Vulnerable** |

DATE: _____ TIME:_____ LOCATION:_____

Arctic Tern

ADULT (BREEDING)

barring on upperparts

white forehead

short, dark bill

dark tips to translucent outer wing feathers

long, forked tail

short red bill

IN FLIGHT

JUVENILE

black cap extends to nape

short, blood-red bill

short neck

white cheek

gray upperparts

ADULT (BREEDING)

long wings

pale-gray underparts

short red legs and feet

The majority of these remarkable birds breed in the Arctic, then migrate to the Antarctic seas for the Southern Hemisphere summer before returning north. On this round-trip, the Arctic Tern travels at least 25,000 miles (40,000km). Apart from during migration, it spends its life in areas of near-continuous daylight and rarely comes to land except to nest. It looks very similar to the Common Tern, but the Arctic Tern has a comparatively smaller bill, shorter legs, and a shorter neck.

VOICE Descending *keeyaar* call; nearly all calls similar to Common Tern's, but higher-pitched and harsher.

NESTING Shallow scrape on bare ground or low vegetation in open areas; 2 eggs; 1 brood; May–August.

FEEDING Mostly plunge-dives for small fish and crustaceans, including crabs and shrimps; will also take prey from surface, sometimes catches insects in flight.

FLIGHT: downstroke slower than upstroke; buoyant and elegant with regular wing beats.

FEEDING THE YOUNG
Both parents feed chicks—males bring more food than females, especially right after hatching.

TRANSLUCENT FEATHERS
The translucent outer wing feathers of the Arctic Tern are evident on these two flying birds.

SIMILAR SPECIES

COMMON TERN ☼
see p.182

longer neck

longer legs

FORSTER'S TERN
see p.184

longer bill

longer orange bill

longer legs

OCCURRENCE
Breeds in far north, mostly in open, unforested areas near water and along the coast; generally migrates far offshore. Spends more time away from land than other northern terns. Winters on edge of pack ice in Antarctica.

Length **11–15½in (28–39cm)**	Wingspan **26–30in (65–75cm)**	Weight **3⅛–4oz (90–125g)**
Social **Colonies**	Lifespan **Up to 34 years**	Status **Vulnerable**

DATE: _____ TIME: _____ LOCATION: _____

Order **Charadriiformes**	Family **Laridae**	Species *Sterna forsteri*

Forster's Tern

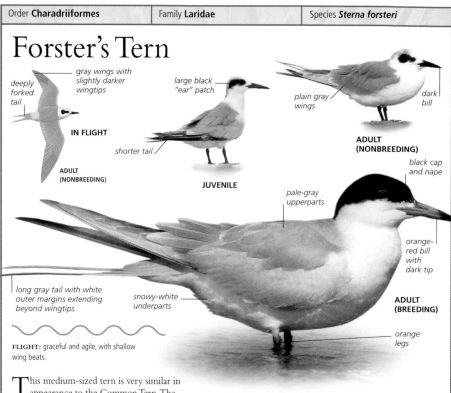

deeply forked tail

gray wings with slightly darker wingtips

IN FLIGHT

ADULT (NONBREEDING)

large black "ear" patch

shorter tail

JUVENILE

plain gray wings

dark bill

ADULT (NONBREEDING)

pale-gray upperparts

black cap and nape

orange-red bill with dark tip

long gray tail with white outer margins extending beyond wingtips

snowy-white underparts

ADULT (BREEDING)

orange legs

FLIGHT: graceful and agile, with shallow wing beats.

This medium-sized tern is very similar in appearance to the Common Tern. The features that differentiate it from the Common Tern are its lighter outer wing feathers and longer tail. Early naturalists could not tell the two species apart until 1834, when English botanist Thomas Nuttall made the distinction. He named this tern after Johann Reinhold Forster, a naturalist who accompanied the English explorer Captain Cook on his epic second voyage (1772–75).

VOICE Harsh, descending *kyerr*; more nasal than Common Tern.

NESTING Shallow scrape in mud or sand, but occasionally nests on top of muskrat lodge or on old grebe nest; sometimes constructs raft of floating vegetation; 2–3 eggs; 1 brood; May–August.

FEEDING Catches fish and crustaceans with shallow plunge-diving, often only head submerges; also catches insects in flight.

BLACK EARS
With its black "ear" patch, Forster's Tern is more distinctive in nonbreeding than breeding plumage.

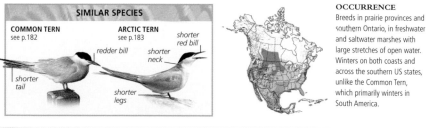

SIMILAR SPECIES

COMMON TERN see p.182

shorter tail

ARCTIC TERN see p.183

redder bill

shorter neck

shorter legs

shorter red bill

OCCURRENCE
Breeds in prairie provinces and southern Ontario, in freshwater and saltwater marshes with large stretches of open water. Winters on both coasts and across the southern US states, unlike the Common Tern, which primarily winters in South America.

Length **13–14in (33–36cm)**	Wingspan **29–32in (73–82cm)**	Weight **4–7oz (125–190g)**
Social **Colonies**	Lifespan **Up to 16 years**	Status **Secure**

DATE: _____ TIME:_____ LOCATION:_____

LOONS

ORLDWIDE THERE ARE only five species of loons, comprising a single genus (*Gavia*), a single family (the Gaviidae), and a single order (the Gaviiformes). The five species are limited to the Northern Hemisphere, where they are found in both northern North America and northern Eurasia. One feature of loons is that their legs are positioned so far to the rear of their body that they must shuffle on their bellies when they step out of the water onto land. Not surprisingly, therefore, loons are almost entirely aquatic birds. In summer, they are found on rivers, lakes, and ponds, where they nest close to the water's edge. After breeding, they occur along coasts,

often after flying hundreds of miles away from their freshwater breeding grounds. Excellent swimmers and divers, loons are unusual among birds in that their bones are less hollow than those of other groups. Consequently, they can expel air from their lungs and compress their body feathers until they slowly sink beneath the surface. They can remain submerged like this for several minutes. A loon's wings are relatively small in proportion to its body weight. This means that they have to run a long way across the surface of the water, flapping energetically, before they can get airborne. Once in the air, they keep on flapping and can fly at up to 60mph (95kmh).

PROVIDING FOR THE FUTURE
A Red-throated Loon gives a fish to its chick to gulp down headfirst and whole.

Families **Diomedeidae, Oceanitidae, Hydrobatidae, Procellariidae**

TUBENOSES

HE TUBENOSES ARE DIVIDED into several families, but all are characterized by the tubular nostrils for which the order is named. These nostrils help to get rid of excess salt, and may enhance their sense of smell.

ALBATROSSES

The long, narrow wings of albatrosses (family Diomedeidae) are perfectly suited for tackling the strong, constant winds that prevail on the southern oceans that form their main habitat. While these birds are expert gliders, they can also land on water to rest and acquire food, using wind to take off from water and land.

STORM-PETRELS

The smallest tubenoses in North American waters, the storm-petrels (families Oceanitidae and Hydrobatidae) are also the most agile fliers. They often patter or "dance" as they fly low to the surface of the ocean in search of small fish, squid, and crustaceans. Storm-petrels spend most of their lives flying over the open sea, only visiting land in the breeding season, when they form huge colonies.

SHEARWATERS AND PETRELS

Shearwaters and gadfly petrels (family Procellariidae) are smaller than albatrosses. Like their larger relatives, they are excellent gliders, but their lighter weight and proportionately shorter wings mean that they use more powered flight than albatrosses. They range over all the world's oceans. With its far more numerous islands, the Pacific Ocean is home to a greater variety of these seabirds than the Atlantic. During and after storms are the best times to look for these birds from land or boats, as this is when they drift away from the deep sea due to wind and waves.

FLAP AND GLIDE
Shearwaters alternate stiff-winged flapping with gliding just over the ocean's surface.

Order **Gaviiformes**	Family **Gaviidae**	Species *Gavia stellata*

Red-throated Loon

white, speckled back

white face

ADULT (NONBREEDING)

white underparts

ADULT (BREEDING)

humped back

head lower than body

ADULT (NONBREEDING)

IN FLIGHT

upturned bill

pale, dusky face

JUVENILE

upturned gray bill

gray face and neck

all-brown back

striped gray nape

tapering dark reddish-brown throat patch

ADULT (BREEDING)

E ven when seen from a distance, this elegant loon is almost unmistakable, with a pale, slim body, upward-tilted head, and a thin, upturned bill. Unlike other loons, the Red-throated Loon can leap straight into the air from both land and water, although most of the time it needs a "runway." The Red-throated Loon has an elaborate breeding ritual—side by side, a pair of birds races upright across the surface of water. Downy chicks climb onto the parents' back only when very young.

VOICE High gull-like or even cat-like wail and low goose-like growl; vocal on breeding grounds, otherwise silent.

NESTING Scrape, with mud and vegetation added during incubation, placed at water's edge in coastal and lake bays, shallow ponds, often at high altitudes; 2 eggs; 1 brood; April–July.

FEEDING Mainly eats fish; also spiders, crustaceans, and mollusks; flies long distances from shallow ponds when food is scarce.

FLIGHT: very direct; fast, with constant wing beats; head held lower than other loons.

TAKING OFF
While this bird is using the water's surface to take off, it can leap directly into flight from water or land.

SIMILAR SPECIES

YELLOW-BILLED LOON ❀
see p.189

massive, light-colored bill

larger overall

RED-NECKED GREBE ❀
see p.80

yellow in bill

darker back

smaller overall

OCCURRENCE
Lives in open areas within northern boreal forest, muskeg, and tundra; in Canadian Arctic Archipelago, sometimes in areas almost devoid of vegetation. Winters on the Great Lakes, and both coasts southward to Florida and northern Mexico.

Length **24–27in (61–69cm)**	Wingspan **3½ft (1.1m)**	Weight **3¼lb (1.5kg)**
Social **Solitary/Loose flocks**	Lifespan **Up to 23 years**	Status **Declining**

DATE: _____ TIME: _____ LOCATION: _____

| Order **Gaviiformes** | Family **Gaviidae** | Species *Gavia pacifica* |

Pacific Loon

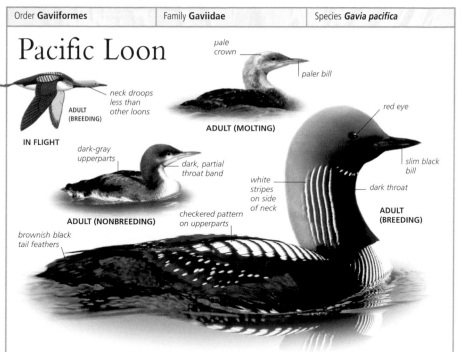

pale crown

paler bill

ADULT (MOLTING)

IN FLIGHT

ADULT (BREEDING)

neck droops less than other loons

red eye

slim black bill

dark throat

ADULT (BREEDING)

dark-gray upperparts

dark, partial throat band

white stripes on side of neck

ADULT (NONBREEDING)

checkered pattern on upperparts

brownish black tail feathers

Although the Pacific Loon's breeding range is about a third of that of the Common Loon, it is believed to be the most abundant loon species in North America. It shares its habitat in northern Alaska with the nearly identical, but slightly larger and darker Arctic Loon. It is a conspicuous migrant along the Pacific Coast in spring, but disappears to its remote breeding grounds in summer. The Pacific Loon is an expert diver and swimmer, capable of remaining underwater for sustained periods of time, usually in pursuit of fish. However, on its terrestrial nesting site, its chicks are vulnerable to a number of mammalian predators.
VOICE Deep, barking *kowk*; high-pitched wail, croaks, and growls when breeding; makes a yelping noise when diving.
NESTING Simple scrape in flat area close to water, vegetation and mud added during incubation; 1–2 eggs; 1 brood; June–July.
FEEDING Eats fish, aquatic insects, and mollusks in breeding lake or nearby waters; may dip or dive, depending on the depth.

FLIGHT: swift and direct with constant wing beats; humped back, but head in line with body.

LEVEL GROUND
As loons cannot take off from land, nest sites need to be on flat land close to the water.

SIMILAR SPECIES

ARCTIC LOON ☼

darker nape

bolder black-and-white stripes on neck

ARCTIC LOON ❋

heavier bill

brownish neck and head

OCCURRENCE
Breeds across Arctic and sub-Arctic North America, from Alaska and northern Canadian provinces to Hudson Bay and on some islands of the Canadian Arctic; in tundra lakes and muskeg. Winters on the Pacific Coast, with small numbers in the Great Lakes and along the Atlantic Coast from Quebec to Florida. Vagrant elsewhere.

| Length **23–29in (58–74cm)** | Wingspan **2¾–4¼ft (0.9–1.3m)** | Weight **2½–5½lb (1–2.5kg)** |
| Social **Flocks** | Lifespan **Up to 25 years** | Status **Secure** |

DATE: _____ TIME: _____ LOCATION: _____

Order **Gaviiformes**	Family **Gaviidae**	Species *Gavia immer*

Common Loon 🔊

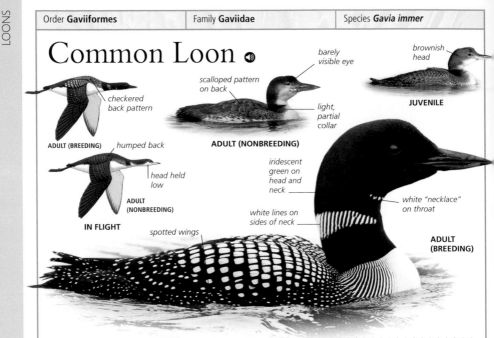

barely visible eye

scalloped pattern on back

checkered back pattern

ADULT (BREEDING)

humped back

head held low

ADULT (NONBREEDING)

IN FLIGHT

spotted wings

brownish head

JUVENILE

light, partial collar

ADULT (NONBREEDING)

iridescent green on head and neck

white lines on sides of neck

white "necklace" on throat

ADULT (BREEDING)

The Common Loon has the largest range of all loons in North America and is the only species to nest in a few of the northern states. It is slightly smaller than the Yellow-billed Loon but larger than the other three loons. It can remain underwater for well over 10 minutes, although it usually stays submerged for 40 seconds to 2 minutes while fishing, or a few more minutes if it is being pursued. Evidence shows that, occasionally, it interbreeds with its closest relative, the Yellow-billed Loon, in addition to the Arctic and Pacific Loons. The Common Loon is the provincial bird of Ontario.

VOICE Most recognized call a 3–10 note falsetto yodel, rising, then fading; other calls similar in quality.

NESTING Simple scrape in large mound of vegetation, a few feet from open water; 2 eggs; 1 brood; April–June.

FEEDING Feeds primarily on fish underwater; also eats crustaceans, mollusks, amphibians, leeches, insects, and aquatic plants.

FLIGHT: fast, direct, with constant wing beats; head and neck held just above belly.

COZY RIDE
Downy Common Loon chicks climb up the backs of male and female adults for a safe ride.

BATHING RITUAL
Common Loons often shake their wings after bathing.

OCCURRENCE
Breeds across North America—Canada and south to the northern US. Winters on large, ice-free lakes in Canada and the US, and along the Pacific and Atlantic Coasts, south to Baja California and Florida.

SIMILAR SPECIES

YELLOW-BILLED LOON
see p.189

large, whitish or yellow bill

larger, checkered back pattern

RED-NECKED GREBE ❄
see p.80

much smaller overall

yellowish bill

brownish-gray cheeks

Length **26–36in (66–91cm)**	Wingspan **4¼–5ft (1.3–1.5m)**	Weight **4½–18lb (2–8kg)**
Social **Family groups**	Lifespan **Up to 30 years**	Status **Vulnerable**

DATE: _____ TIME:_____ LOCATION:_____

Yellow-billed Loon

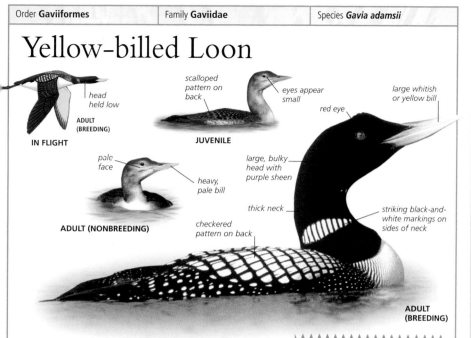

head held low

ADULT (BREEDING)

IN FLIGHT

scalloped pattern on back

eyes appear small

red eye

large whitish or yellow bill

JUVENILE

pale face

heavy, pale bill

ADULT (NONBREEDING)

checkered pattern on back

large, bulky head with purple sheen

thick neck

striking black-and-white markings on sides of neck

ADULT (BREEDING)

The largest of the loons, the Yellow-billed Loon has the most restricted range and smallest global population. About three-quarters of the estimated 16,000–30,000 birds live in North America, and unsustainable levels of harvesting have caused recent declines. It makes the most of the short nesting season, arriving at its breeding grounds already paired and immediately breeding, although extensive ice formation can prevent it from breeding in some years. Yellow-billed Loons have more rugged proportions than other loons; their feet, for example, extend further away from their bodies.

VOICE Tremulous call much like Common Loon's, but louder, harsher, and even more "mournful"; yodels, wails, and "laughs."
NESTING Depression in mass of mud and vegetation, on shores of tundra lakes and ponds, and on river islands at high altitudes; 1–2 eggs; 1 brood; June–July.
FEEDING Dives underwater to catch small fish; also eats crustaceans, worms, and some vegetation.

FLIGHT: rapid and direct; head and neck held lower than body.

BOLDLY PATTERNED
The adult Yellow-billed Loon is strikingly patterned, like a checkerboard.

SIMILAR SPECIES

COMMON LOON ❋
see p.188

dark crown and pale cheeks

RED-NECKED GREBE ❋
see p.80

heavy, dark bill

shorter bill, yellowish at base

smaller overall

OCCURRENCE
Breeds from extreme northern edge of Alaska to eastern Northwest Territories and Nunavut. Also breeds in northern Siberia. Winters along the Pacific Coast of Alaska and British Columbia, and has been sighted in a number of US states.

| Length **30–36in (77–92cm)** | Wingspan **4–5ft (1.2–1.5m)** | Weight **8¾–14lb (4–6.5kg)** |
| Social **Solitary/Pairs/Family groups** | Lifespan **Up to 30 years** | Status **Vulnerable** |

| Order **Procellariiformes** | Family **Diomedeidae** | Species *Phoebastria nigripes* |

Black-footed Albatross

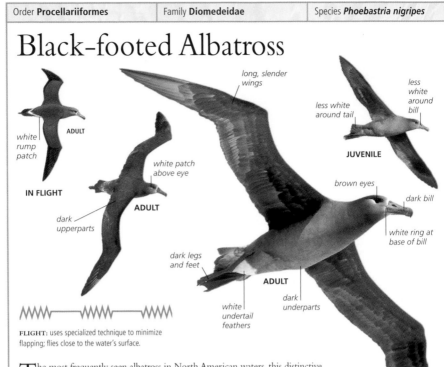

long, slender wings

white rump patch

ADULT

IN FLIGHT

white patch above eye

dark upperparts

ADULT

dark legs and feet

less white around tail

JUVENILE

less white around bill

brown eyes

dark bill

white ring at base of bill

white undertail feathers

dark underparts

ADULT

FLIGHT: uses specialized technique to minimize flapping; flies close to the water's surface.

The most frequently seen albatross in North American waters, this distinctive all-dark bird breeds mainly on the Hawaiian Islands, and regularly visits the Pacific Coast during the nonbreeding season. Unfortunately, a tendency to scavenge around fishing boats results in this and other species of albatross being drowned when they are accidentally hooked on long lines or tangled in drift nets—a major conservation concern for this particular species.

VOICE Generally silent outside the breeding season, but utters weak squeals while scavenging; variety of noises made during courtship.

NESTING Shallow depression in ground on higher reaches of sandy beaches; 1 egg; 1 brood; October–June.

FEEDING Dives for fish and squid, and picks floating masses of fish eggs from the ocean's surface with its bill.

TAKING OFF
Like other albatross species, the big-winged Black-footed Albatross takes off from the water by running across the surface, heading into the wind.

OCCURRENCE
Breeds on sandy beaches, almost exclusively on remote, uninhabited islands in Hawaii; during the nonbreeding season, the Black-footed Albatross disperses across the whole northern Pacific Ocean.

SIMILAR SPECIES

NORTHERN FULMAR (DARK FORM)
see p.193

broader, shorter wings

WESTERN GULL ⊙
see p.174

much shorter wings

black-tipped bill

yellow bill

pink legs and feet

| Length **25–29in (64–74cm)** | Wingspan **6¼–7¼ft (1.9–2.2m)** | Weight **6¼lb (2.8kg)** |
| Social **Solitary/Flocks** | Lifespan **Up to 28 years** | Status **Special Concern** |

DATE: _____ TIME: _____ LOCATION: _____

Order **Procellariiformes**	Family **Hydrobatidae**	Species **Hydrobates furcatus**

Fork-tailed Storm-Petrel

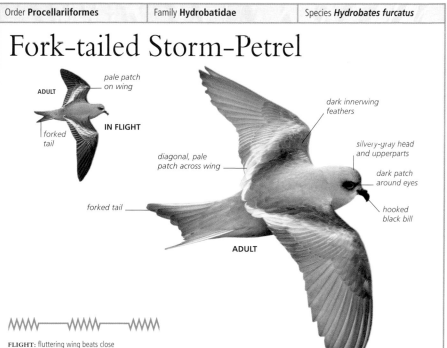

ADULT

pale patch on wing

IN FLIGHT

forked tail

dark innerwing feathers

silvery-gray head and upperparts

diagonal, pale patch across wing

dark patch around eyes

forked tail

hooked black bill

ADULT

FLIGHT: fluttering wing beats close to the ocean, alternating with long glides.

The Fork-tailed Storm-Petrel is one of the most distinctive of all storm-petrels in North American waters, with its ghostly silvery-gray plumage, and forked tail. It is the most northerly breeding storm-petrel in the North Pacific, nesting all the way north to the Aleutian Islands. It incubates its eggs at lower temperatures than other petrels do, and its chicks can be left alone between feedings for a longer time—apparently an adaptation to northern conditions. Its chicks can also lower their body temperature, thereby conserving energy.

VOICE Silent at sea; various purring sounds at colonies.
NESTING Underground burrow on offshore island; 1 egg; 1 brood; March–November.
FEEDING Plucks shrimps, squids, and small fish from the surface of the ocean.

AERIAL SURVEY
Flying low over the ocean, the Fork-tailed Storm-Petrel looks out for fish below.

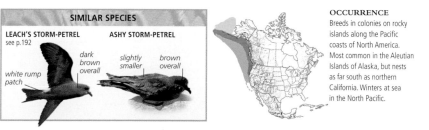

SIMILAR SPECIES

LEACH'S STORM-PETREL
see p.192

white rump patch

dark brown overall

ASHY STORM-PETREL

slightly smaller

brown overall

OCCURRENCE
Breeds in colonies on rocky islands along the Pacific coasts of North America. Most common in the Aleutian Islands of Alaska, but nests as far south as northern California. Winters at sea in the North Pacific.

Length **8in (20cm)**	Wingspan **18in (46cm)**	Weight **2oz (55g)**
Social **Colonies**	Lifespan **At least 14 years**	Status **Secure**

DATE: _____ TIME:_____ LOCATION:_____

Order **Procellariiformes**	Family **Hydrobatidae**	Species **Hydrobates leucorhus**

Leach's Storm-Petrel

long, angled wings

ADULT

white rump with thin, dark line down center

IN FLIGHT

ADULT

brown bar across blackish wings

dark, sooty-black underwings

dark smudge beside eye

forked tail

FLIGHT: buoyant, deep wing beats low over ocean's surface, interrupted by twists and turns.

dark, sooty-brown underparts

ADULT

Leach's Storm-Petrel is widespread in both the Atlantic and Pacific Oceans, unlike most other storm-petrels. It breeds in colonies on islands off the coasts, coming to land at night and feeding offshore during the day, often many miles from the colony. This wide-ranging storm-petrel has both geographical and individual variation; most populations show a white rump, but others have a dark rump that is the same color as the rest of the body. Leach's Storm-Petrel and the very similar, endangered, Townsend's Storm-Petrel (*H. socorroensis*) were thought to be a single species until they were split in 2016. The latter is identified only by its breeding location and smaller size.

VOICE At nesting sites, often from burrows, calls are long series of soft purring and chattering sounds.

NESTING Underground burrow on island free of predators such as rats; 1 egg; 1 brood; May–November.

FEEDING Gleans small crustaceans and small fish from the water's surface while in flight.

BALANCING ACT
Leach's Storm-Petrel will often balance itself with its wings while walking.

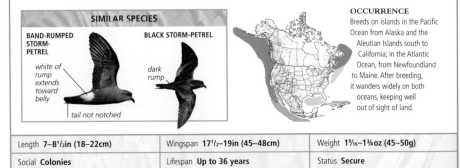

SIMILAR SPECIES

BAND-RUMPED STORM-PETREL

white of rump extends toward belly

tail not notched

BLACK STORM-PETREL

dark rump

OCCURRENCE
Breeds on islands in the Pacific Ocean from Alaska and the Aleutian Islands south to California; in the Atlantic Ocean, from Newfoundland to Maine. After breeding, it wanders widely on both oceans, keeping well out of sight of land.

Length 7–8½in (18–22cm)	Wingspan 17½–19in (45–48cm)	Weight 1⁹⁄₁₆–1¾oz (45–50g)
Social **Colonies**	Lifespan **Up to 36 years**	Status **Secure**

DATE: _____ TIME: _____ LOCATION: _____

| Order **Procellariiformes** | Family **Procellariidae** | Species *Fulmarus glacialis* |

Northern Fulmar

white patch on wing

ADULT (ATLANTIC FORM)

IN FLIGHT

paddle-like wings

gray back — white head

small, dark patch in front of eye

ADULT (ATLANTIC FORM)

short, rounded gray tail

ADULT (LIGHT PACIFIC FORM)

thick yellow bill

white underparts

FLIGHT: snappy wing beats and long glides near the surface of the ocean.

dark gray overall

ADULT (DARK PACIFIC FORM)

Possessing paddle-shaped wings and distinctive color patterns ranging from almost all-white to all-gray, the Northern Fulmar is among the most common seabirds in places like the Bering Sea. It breeds at high latitudes, then disperses south to offshore waters on both coasts of the continent. The Northern Fulmar can often be seen in large mixed flocks containing albatrosses, shearwaters, and petrels. Fulmars often follow boats, eager to pounce on the offal thrown overboard by fishermen.

VOICE Mostly silent at sea; occasionally utters cackles and grunts.
NESTING Scrape in rock or soil on edge of cliff; 1 egg; 1 brood; May–October.
FEEDING Picks fish and offal from the surface of the ocean; also dives underwater to catch fish.

FEEDING FRENZY
Large numbers of Northern Fulmars compete for the offal discarded by fishing trawlers.

SIMILAR SPECIES

SOOTY SHEARWATER
see p.194

more slender wings

dark bill

dark overall

GREAT SHEARWATER

more slender wings

dark cap

white collar

OCCURRENCE
Breeds on remote, high, coastal cliffs in Alaska and northern Canada; winters at sea in offshore Pacific and Atlantic waters, generally farther north than most other seabirds. Breeds in Europe, to Greenland, Svalbard; also parts of Russia.

| Length **17½–19½in (45–50cm)** | Wingspan **3¼–3½ft (1–1.1m)** | Weight **16–35oz (0.45–1kg)** |
| Social **Flocks** | Lifespan **Up to 50 years** | Status **Secure** |

DATE: _____ TIME: _____ LOCATION: _____

| Order **Procellariiformes** | Family **Procellariidae** | Species ***Ardenna grisea*** |

Sooty Shearwater

silvery-white patch along underwing

ADULT

ADULT

ADULT

all-dark underparts

IN FLIGHT

long, slender wings

all-dark upperparts

ADULT

sooty head

long, hooked bill

FLIGHT: rapid, stiff wing beats, interspersed with glides; arcs up highly in strong winds.

Sooty Shearwaters are extremely long-distance migrants, with both the Atlantic and Pacific populations undergoing lengthy circular migrations. Pacific birds, in particular, travel as far as 300 miles (480km) per day and an extraordinary 45,000 miles (72,500km) or more per year. Huge flocks of this species are often seen off the coast of California. It is fairly easy to identify off the East Coast of North America, as it is the only all-dark shearwater found there.
VOICE Silent at sea; occasionally gives varied, agitated vocalizations when feeding, very loud calls at breeding colonies.
NESTING In burrow or rocky crevice; 1 egg; 1 brood; October–May.
FEEDING Dives and picks at surface for small schooling fish and mollusks, such as squid.

HUGE FLOCKS
Sooty Shearwaters are often found in "rafts" numbering many thousands of birds.

TUBENOSE
Shearwaters are tubenoses, so-called for the salt-excreting tubes on their bills.

SIMILAR SPECIES

SHORT-TAILED SHEARWATER see p.443

dark upperparts

dark cap

shorter bill

pale throat

GREAT SHEARWATER
white tail band

white collar

OCCURRENCE
Sooty Shearwaters breed on islands in the Southern Ocean and nearby waters, some colonies numbering thousands of pairs. Postbreeding movements take them north into the Pacific and the Atlantic Oceans, on 8-shaped migrations.

| Length **18in (46cm)** | Wingspan **3ft 3in (1m)** | Weight **27oz (775g)** |
| Social **Flocks** | Lifespan **Unknown** | Status **Secure** |

DATE: _____ TIME: _____ LOCATION: _____

Pink-footed Shearwater

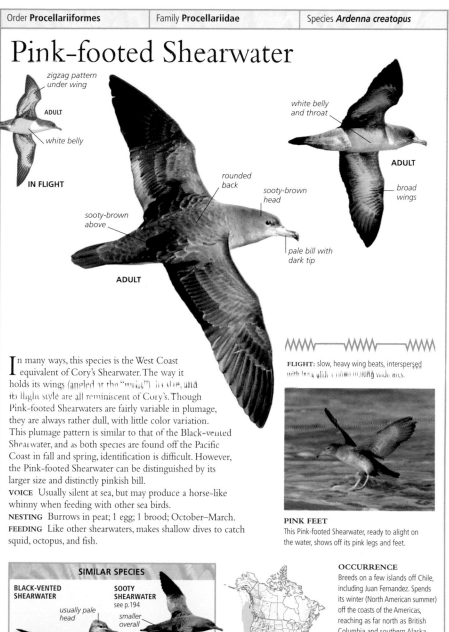

zigzag pattern under wing

ADULT

white belly

IN FLIGHT

white belly and throat

ADULT

rounded back

sooty-brown head

broad wings

sooty-brown above

pale bill with dark tip

ADULT

I n many ways, this species is the West Coast equivalent of Cory's Shearwater. The way it holds its wings (angled at the "wrist"), its size, and its flight style are all reminiscent of Cory's. Though Pink-footed Shearwaters are fairly variable in plumage, they are always rather dull, with little color variation. This plumage pattern is similar to that of the Black-vented Shearwater, and as both species are found off the Pacific Coast in fall and spring, identification is difficult. However, the Pink-footed Shearwater can be distinguished by its larger size and distinctly pinkish bill.

VOICE Usually silent at sea, but may produce a horse-like whinny when feeding with other sea birds.

NESTING Burrows in peat; 1 egg; 1 brood; October–March.

FEEDING Like other shearwaters, makes shallow dives to catch squid, octopus, and fish.

FLIGHT: slow, heavy wing beats, interspersed with long glides from making wide arcs.

PINK FEET
This Pink-footed Shearwater, ready to alight on the water, shows off its pink legs and feet.

SIMILAR SPECIES

BLACK-VENTED SHEARWATER

usually pale head

smaller overall

pale chest

SOOTY SHEARWATER
see p.194

smaller overall

sooty brown overall

OCCURRENCE
Breeds on a few islands off Chile, including Juan Fernandez. Spends its winter (North American summer) off the coasts of the Americas, reaching as far north as British Columbia and southern Alaska. Found closer to shore than other shearwaters. On Juan Fernandez, population reduced due to predation by introduced rats.

Length **19in (48cm)**	Wingspan **3½ft (1.1m)**	Weight **26oz (725g)**
Social **Flocks**	Lifespan **Unknown**	Status **Endangered**

DATE: _____ TIME: _____ LOCATION: _____

Family **Phalacrocoracidae**

CORMORANTS

U NTIL RECENTLY, CORMORANTS were grouped with pelicans under the order Pelicaniformes. Now they are part of the order Suliformes, which also includes gannets (found only in eastern Canada), frigatebirds, boobies, and anhingas.

With 36 species worldwide, cormorants are medium to large waterbirds—some are marine, others are freshwater. They have broad and long wings, rounded tails, short and strong legs, and hook-tipped bills that are often tilted upwards while swimming. In flight, the neck is extended but noticeably kinked. When hunting for fish, cormorants dive from the surface of the water, rolling smoothly under or with a noticeable forward leap; they then swim underwater with closed wings, using their webbed toes for propulsion. Cormorants are able to fill their hollow wing feathers with water for ballast, which they later drain with wings outspread while perched. Most cormorants are dark birds, apart from some distinctive facial patterns

CLOSE TO SHORE
The Pelagic Cormorant prefers to inhabit inshore coastal waters.

on areas of bare skin, which become more colorful in spring. Many of these birds nest on cliff ledges, while some prefer trees, and yet others are happy to use both cliffs and trees. There is one flightless cormorant species in the Galápagos.

DARK PLUMAGE
Grooming for this Double-crested Cormorant includes spreading its wings to dry them in the sun.

Order **Suliformes**	Family **Phalacrocoracidae**	Species *Urile penicillatus*

Brandt's Cormorant

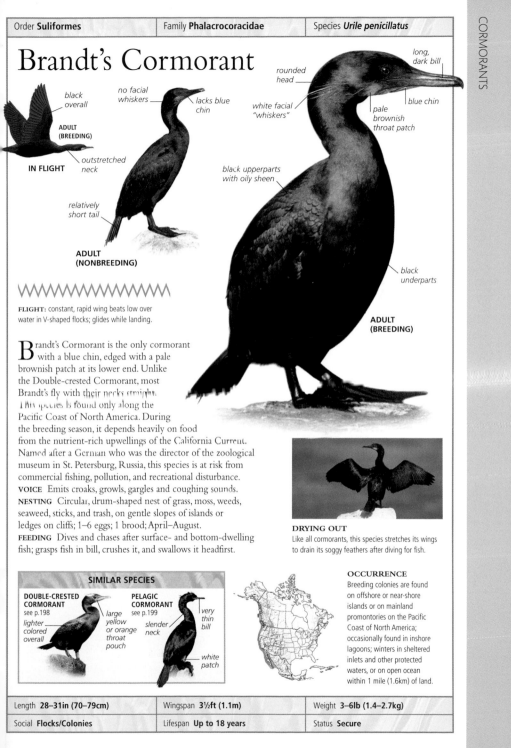

long, dark bill

rounded head

black overall

ADULT (BREEDING)

IN FLIGHT

no facial whiskers

lacks blue chin

white facial "whiskers"

blue chin

pale brownish throat patch

outstretched neck

black upperparts with oily sheen

relatively short tail

black underparts

ADULT (NONBREEDING)

ADULT (BREEDING)

FLIGHT: constant, rapid wing beats low over water in V-shaped flocks; glides while landing.

B randt's Cormorant is the only cormorant with a blue chin, edged with a pale brownish patch at its lower end. Unlike the Double-crested Cormorant, most Brandt's fly with their necks straight. This species is found only along the Pacific Coast of North America. During the breeding season, it depends heavily on food from the nutrient-rich upwellings of the California Current. Named after a German who was the director of the zoological museum in St. Petersburg, Russia, this species is at risk from commercial fishing, pollution, and recreational disturbance.

VOICE Emits croaks, growls, gargles and coughing sounds.

NESTING Circular, drum-shaped nest of grass, moss, weeds, seaweed, sticks, and trash, on gentle slopes of islands or ledges on cliffs; 1–6 eggs; 1 brood; April–August.

FEEDING Dives and chases after surface- and bottom-dwelling fish; grasps fish in bill, crushes it, and swallows it headfirst.

DRYING OUT
Like all cormorants, this species stretches its wings to drain its soggy feathers after diving for fish.

SIMILAR SPECIES

DOUBLE-CRESTED CORMORANT see p.198

lighter colored overall

large yellow or orange throat pouch

PELAGIC CORMORANT see p.199

slender neck

very thin bill

white patch

OCCURRENCE
Breeding colonies are found on offshore or near-shore islands or on mainland promontories on the Pacific Coast of North America; occasionally found in inshore lagoons; winters in sheltered inlets and other protected waters, or on open ocean within 1 mile (1.6km) of land.

Length **28–31in (70–79cm)**	Wingspan **3½ft (1.1m)**	Weight **3–6lb (1.4–2.7kg)**
Social **Flocks/Colonies**	Lifespan **Up to 18 years**	Status **Secure**

DATE: _____ TIME:_____ LOCATION:_____

Order **Suliformes**	Family **Phalacrocoracidae**	Species **Nannopterum auritum**

Double-crested Cormorant

ADULT (BREEDING)

long neck

no crest

pale neck and breast

browner plumage overall

ADULT (NONBREEDING)

black overall

white crest

bluish eye

orange facial skin

black underparts

blackish crest

JUVENILE

pale throat and chest

JUVENILE

IN FLIGHT

FLIGHT: regular wing beats, occasional glides; over water, flies close to the surface; often soars.

**ADULT
N. a. auritum
(NORTHEASTERN BREEDING)**

**ADULT
N. a. cincinatus
(WESTERN; BREEDING)**

This species is the most widespread of the North American cormorants. It often flies high over land in V-shaped flocks, but is mostly seen swimming in the water with its head and neck visible, or resting on trees and rocks, sometimes with its wings spread to drain and dry its feathers. While fishing, it dives from the surface of the water and chases fish underwater, using its webbed toes for propulsion.

VOICE Deep grunt-like calls while nesting, roosting, and fishing; *t-t-t-t* call before taking off and *urg-urg-urg* before landing; prolonged *arr-r-r-r-t-t* while mating, and *eh-hr* as threat.

NESTING Nests of twigs and sticks, seaweed, and trash, lined with grass; built on ground, cliffs, or in trees usually in colonies; 3-5 eggs; 1 brood; April–August.

FEEDING Pursues slow-moving or schooling fish; feeds on insects, crustaceans, amphibians, and, rarely, on voles and snakes.

DRYING OFF
Typical of cormorants, this species perches with wings spread to drain and dry its feathers.

SIMILAR SPECIES

BRANDT'S CORMORANT
see p.197

throat pouch paler and less visible

NEOTROPIC CORMORANT

shorter body

longer tail

OCCURRENCE
Breeds in a wide range of aquatic habitats, including ponds, artificial and natural lakes, slow-moving rivers, estuaries, lagoons, and seashores; winters on coastlines and sandbars in coastal inlets; roosts near catfish farms in some areas.

Length **28–35in (70–90cm)**	Wingspan **3½–4ft (1.1–1.2m)**	Weight **2¾–5½lb (1.2–2.5kg)**
Social **Flocks**	Lifespan **Up to 18 years**	Status **Secure**

DATE: _____ TIME:_____ LOCATION:_____

Order **Suliformes**	Family **Phalacrocoracidae**	Species *Urile pelagicus*

Pelagic Cormorant

tufts on crown and nape

red patch at base of bill

all-dark face

thin, pale bill

thin, dark bill with blunt or hooked end

IN FLIGHT

outstretched head and tail level in flight

small head

ADULT

brownish-bronze upperparts

blackish breast and belly

glossy purple tinge on neck

glossy green to greenish-bronze on upperparts

long, thin neck with white flecks

JUVENILE

iridescent greenish-black underparts

ADULT (BREEDING)

long blackish tail

white patch on flank

FLIGHT: rapid with regular, steady wing beats; glides before landing.

The Pelagic Cormorant is the smallest cormorant species in North America. Although a marine bird, its English (and scientific) name, *pelagic*, meaning "oceanic," is misleading because this bird mostly inhabits inshore waters. This bird is most visible at its roosting sites, where it spends much of its time drying and draining its feathers. The Pelagic Cormorant has not been well studied because it is more solitary than the other cormorant species in North America; however, like all cormorants, it is threatened by the disturbance of its nesting colonies, oil spills, entanglement in fishing nets, pollution, and illegal cull programs.
VOICE Female two-note call *igh-ugh*, similar to ticking grandfather clock; male call note *purring* or *arr-arr-arr*; both utter croaks, hisses, and low groans.
NESTING Saucer-shaped nest of grass, seaweed, sticks, feathers, and marine debris, cemented to cliff face with guano; 3–5 eggs; 1 brood; May–October.
FEEDING Dives from water's surface for any medium-sized fish, and also invertebrates, such as shrimps, worms, and hermit crabs.

SITTING LOW
Pelagic Cormorants sit low in the water with only their head, neck, and back visible.

SIMILAR SPECIES

BRANDT'S CORMORANT
see p.197

round head

thicker neck

shorter tail

larger overall

OCCURRENCE
Found in rocky habitats on outer coasts, shallow bays, inlets, estuaries, harbors, and lagoons; nesting colonies found on steep cliffs on forested and grassy islands, and on rocky promontories along the shoreline; also seen on built structures, such as wharf pilings, bridges, and harbor buoys.

Length **20–30in (51–76cm)**	Wingspan **3¼–4ft (1–1.2m)**	Weight **2¾–5¼lb (1.3–2.4kg)**
Social **Solitary/Pairs**	Lifespan **Up to 17 years**	Status **Secure**

DATE: _____ TIME: _____ LOCATION: _____

Families **Pelecanidae, Ardeidae, Threskiornithidae**

PELICANS, HERONS, IBISES, AND RELATIVES

THESE RELATED WATERBIRDS exploit a diversity of water and waterside habitats in different ways, from plunge-diving in the ocean to wading at the edge of mangroves and freshwater marshes, from scooping up fish to hunting with stealth and patience from overhanging branches.

PELICANS
Pelicans are large fish-eating birds, bulky but buoyant on water. Brown Pelicans, vagrants in Canada, dive headfirst to catch fish, while White Pelicans work together to herd fish into shallow bays, and scoop them up in their large, flexible bill pouches beneath their long bills.

HERONS, EGRETS, AND BITTERNS
The long toes of these waterside birds enable them to walk on wet mud and wade among reed stems. Some herons and egrets roost in trees. Their toes also aid their balance as they lean forward in search of fish and catch prey in their long, pointed bills. Herons and egrets have slender, feathered necks with a distinct kink that gives a lightning forward thrust when catching prey. Herons are known to use bait to catch fish. Most herons and egrets make bulky nests in treetop colonies, whereas bitterns nest on the ground in marshes. Unlike storks and cranes, they all fly with their heads withdrawn into their shoulders.

EYE-CATCHING IBIS
The White-faced Ibis has a distinctive white patch around its eye in the breeding season.

IBISES
Waterside or dry-land birds, ibises are long-legged and walk with great strides. They have long, decurved bills that are adapted to picking insects, worms, small mollusks, and crustaceans from wet mud. Ibises often fly in long lines or V-formations.

DANCING ON AIR
The Great Egret's courtship display often involves spreading its wings and leaping in a kind of aerial dance.

Order **Pelecaniformes**	Family **Pelecanidae**	Species *Pelecanus erythrorhynchos*

American White Pelican

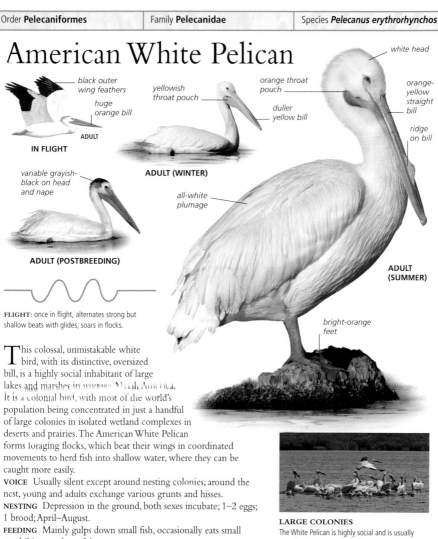

black outer wing feathers

huge orange bill

ADULT

IN FLIGHT

yellowish throat pouch

orange throat pouch

duller yellow bill

ADULT (WINTER)

white head

orange-yellow straight bill

ridge on bill

variable grayish-black on head and nape

all-white plumage

ADULT (POSTBREEDING)

ADULT (SUMMER)

bright-orange feet

FLIGHT: once in flight, alternates strong but shallow beats with glides; soars in flocks.

This colossal, unmistakable white bird, with its distinctive, oversized bill, is a highly social inhabitant of large lakes and marshes in western North America. It is a colonial bird, with most of the world's population being concentrated in just a handful of large colonies in isolated wetland complexes in deserts and prairies. The American White Pelican forms foraging flocks, which beat their wings in coordinated movements to herd fish into shallow water, where they can be caught more easily.

VOICE Usually silent except around nesting colonies; around the nest, young and adults exchange various grunts and hisses.

NESTING Depression in the ground, both sexes incubate; 1–2 eggs; 1 brood; April–August.

FEEDING Mainly gulps down small fish, occasionally eats small amphibians, and crayfish.

LARGE COLONIES
The White Pelican is highly social and is usually seen feeding or roosting in large groups.

SIMILAR SPECIES

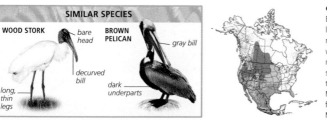

WOOD STORK

bare head

decurved bill

long, thin legs

BROWN PELICAN

gray bill

dark underparts

OCCURRENCE
Breeds on islands in freshwater lakes in south-central Canada, mountainous areas of the western US, and in coastal northeast Mexico; an early spring migrant, often returning to breeding grounds in early March. Winters in coastal regions from California and Texas to Mexico and Central America.

Length **4¼–5½ft (1.3–1.7m)**	Wingspan **7¾–9½ft (2.4–2.9m)**	Weight **12–20lb (5.5–9kg)**
Social **Colonies**	Lifespan **Up to 26 years**	Status **Vulnerable**

DATE: _____ TIME: _____ LOCATION: _____

American Bittern

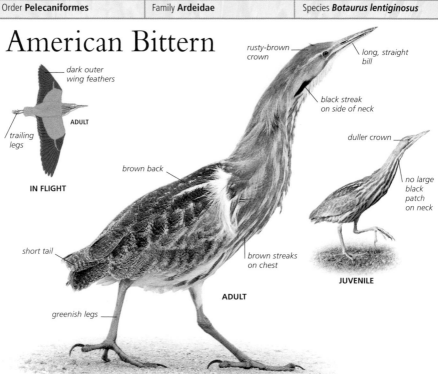

rusty-brown crown

long, straight bill

dark outer wing feathers

ADULT

trailing legs

black streak on side of neck

IN FLIGHT

duller crown

brown back

no large black patch on neck

short tail

brown streaks on chest

JUVENILE

greenish legs

ADULT

The American Bittern's camouflaged plumage and secretive behavior help it to blend into its thick reed habitat. It is heard much more often than it is seen; its call is unmistakable and has given rise to many evocative colloquial names, such as "thunder pumper."

VOICE Deep, resonant *pump-er-unk, pump-er-unk*; calls mainly at dawn, dusk, and night time, but also during the day in the early mating season.

NESTING Platform or mound constructed of available marsh vegetation, usually over shallow water; 2–7 eggs; 1 brood; April–August.

FEEDING Stands still or moves slowly, then strikes downward with bill to catch prey; eats fish, insects, crustaceans, snakes, amphibians, and small mammals.

FLIGHT: steady, deep, slightly stiff wing beats; usually flies relatively low and direct.

LOOK STRAIGHT
Even with the bill pointed straight upward, a bittern can still see in front of it.

OCCURRENCE
Breeds in heavily vegetated freshwater wetlands across the northern US and southern Canada; also occasionally in estuarine wetlands; winters in southern and coastal wetlands where temperatures stay above freezing; can appear in any wetland habitat during migration.

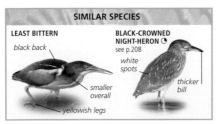

SIMILAR SPECIES

LEAST BITTERN
black back

smaller overall

yellowish legs

BLACK-CROWNED NIGHT-HERON ☾
see p.208
white spots

thicker bill

Length **23½–31in (60–80cm)**	Wingspan **3½–4¼ft (1.1–1.3m)**	Weight **13–20oz (375–575g)**
Social **Solitary**	Lifespan **At least 8 years**	Status **Declining**

DATE: _____ TIME: _____ LOCATION: _____

| Order **Pelecaniformes** | Family **Ardeidae** | Species *Ardea herodias* |

Great Blue Heron 🔊

dark wingtips

dark tail

brownish body

white face

dark bill

gray neck

ADULT

yellowish bill

crooked neck **JUVENILE**

blue-gray body

IN FLIGHT

lighter-colored neck, almost beige

light bill

large white bird

overall similar to Great Blue Heron

shaggy plumes

light legs

WURDEMANN'S HERON (WHITE-HEADED FORM)

MALE

dark legs

GREAT WHITE HERON (WHITE FORM)

〰〰〰〰〰

FLIGHT: deep-flapping, regular wing beats.

This is one of the world's largest herons, slightly smaller than Africa's Goliath Heron but of similar stature to the more closely related Gray Heron of Eurasia and Cocoi Heron of South America. It is a common inhabitant of a variety of North American waterbodies, from marshes to swamps, as well as along sea coasts. Its majestic flight is wonderful to behold, especially when it migrates or makes local movements between feeding and roosting sites.

VOICE Mostly silent; gives a loud, barking squawk or *crank* in breeding colonies or when disturbed.

NESTING Nest of twigs and branches; usually in colonies, but also singly; in trees, often over water, but also over ground; 2–4 eggs; 1–2 broods; February–August.

FEEDING Catches prey, sometimes spearing with quick jab of bill; primarily fish but also ducklings, frogs, muskrats, and even mice in fields.

LOFTY ABODE
Great Blue Herons nest in small colonies in trees, and often roost in them.

SIMILAR SPECIES

TRICOLORED HERON

dark bill

smaller overall

white underparts

LITTLE BLUE HERON
smaller overall; see p.444

greenish legs

darker overall

OCCURRENCE
Across southern Canada and the US in wetlands, such as marshes, lake edges, and along rivers and swamps; also in marine habitats, especially tidal grass flats. The Great White Heron is primarily found in marine habitats in southern Florida.

Length 2¾–4¼ft (0.9–1.3m)	Wingspan 5¼–6½ft (1.6–2m)	Weight 4¾–5½lb (2.1–2.5kg)
Social **Solitary/Flocks**	Lifespan **Up to 20 years**	Status **Secure**

DATE: _____ TIME: _____ LOCATION: _____

Order **Pelecaniformes**	Family **Ardeidae**	Species **Ardea alba**

Great Egret 🔊

SUMMER

IN FLIGHT

large size

white overall

all-white plumage

long, S-curved neck

long yellow bill

long black plumes

black legs and feet

lime-green patch between eye and bill

ADULT (NONBREEDING)

ADULT (BREEDING)

FLIGHT: flies with regular, deep wing beats.

This large white heron is found on every continent except Antarctica. When feeding, the Great Egret apparently prefers to forage alone rather than in flocks. It maintains space around itself, and will defend a territory of 10ft (3m) in diameter from other wading birds, especially Great Blue Herons. This territory "moves" with the bird as it feeds. In years of scarce food supplies, a chick may kill a sibling, permitting the survival of at least one bird.

VOICE Largely vocal during courtship and breeding; otherwise, *kraak* or *cuk-cuk-cuk* when disturbed or in a combative encounter.

NESTING Nest of twigs in trees, over land or water; 2–4 eggs; 1 brood; March–July.

FEEDING Catches prey with quick thrust of bill; feeds on aquatic prey, primarily fish, also crustaceans.

TREE PERCHES
Great Egrets nest in trees and regularly perch in them when not feeding.

SIMILAR SPECIES

LITTLE BLUE HERON ☾
see p.444

two-toned bill

smaller overall

yellow-green legs

SNOWY EGRET
black bill;
see p.205

smaller overall

yellow feet

OCCURRENCE
Breeds in trees over water or on islands; forages in freshwater and marine wetlands from marshes and ponds to rivers. Migratory over much of its North American range; more southerly populations resident. Range has expanded northward into Canada. Distance migrated depends on severity of winter.

Length **3¼ft (1m)**	Wingspan **6ft (1.8m)**	Weight **1¾–3¼lb (0.8–1.5kg)**
Social **Solitary**	Lifespan **Up to 25 years**	Status **Secure**

DATE: _____ TIME: _____ LOCATION: _____

Order **Pelecaniformes**	Family **Ardeidae**	Species *Egretta thula*

Snowy Egret

long, extended legs

ADULT

IN FLIGHT

red patch between eye and bill

paler patch of skin at base of bill

plumes on head

all-white plumage

greenish-yellow legs

JUVENILE

yellow patch between eye and bill

black bill

wispy breast plumes

ADULT (HIGH BREEDING)

orangish legs

ADULT (BREEDING)

black legs

yellow feet

FLIGHT: flies with deep wing beats; gliding descent before landing.

A New World species, the Snowy Egret is similar to an Old World species, the Little Egret. It is very adaptable in estuarine and freshwater habitats. When foraging, it uses a wide variety of behaviors, including wing-flicking, foot-stirring, and foot-probing to get its prey moving, making it easier to capture.
VOICE High-pitched *aargaarg* common. when flushed; low-pitched *arg* and *raah* aggressive calls; *aarg* call during attacks and pursuits.
NESTING Small sticks, branches, and rushes over water or on land; also on ground, in shrubs, mangroves, and other trees; 3–5 eggs; 1 brood; March–August.
FEEDING Feeds on aquatic prey, from invertebrates, such as insects, shrimp, and prawns, to small fish, amphibians, and snakes.

WIDESPREAD SPECIES
Snowy Egrets feed in a wide variety of wetland habitats, using different foraging techniques.

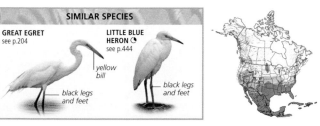

SIMILAR SPECIES

GREAT EGRET see p.204

LITTLE BLUE HERON ◐ see p.444

yellow bill

black legs and feet

black legs and feet

OCCURRENCE
Found in a wide variety of wetlands throughout North and South America: from mangroves in Florida to marshlands in New England and the western US. Highly adaptable and widely found. Sites of breeding colonies may change from year to year within a set range.

Length **24in (62cm)**	Wingspan **3½ft (1.1cm)**	Weight **12oz (350g)**
Social **Solitary**	Lifespan **Up to 22 years**	Status **Declining**

DATE: _____ TIME: _____ LOCATION: _____

| Order **Pelecaniformes** | Family **Ardeidae** | Species *Bubulcus ibis* |

Cattle Egret

rich buff crown

rich buff on back

all-white body

yellow bill

ADULT (BREEDING)

IN FLIGHT

yellow bill, reddish in spring

short neck

white body and wings

rich buff on breast in spring

ADULT (NONBREEDING)

looks all-white in flight at long range

dark legs and feet

ADULT (BREEDING)

ADULT (BREEDING)

yellow legs and feet

FLIGHT: flies with regular wing beats; neck crooked and legs extended.

Unlike most other herons, the Cattle Egret is a grassland species that rarely wades in water, and is often seen with livestock, feeding on the insects disturbed by their feet. It is thought to have originated in the savannas of Africa and is now found worldwide. It was first seen in Florida in 1941, but expanded rapidly and has now bred in over 40 US states and up into the southern provinces of Canada.
VOICE Generally silent; vocal at the nest: *rick-rack* common.
NESTING Nest of branches or plants placed in trees over ground; also in trees or shrubs over water; 2–5 eggs; 1 brood; March–October.
FEEDING Eats in groups; consumes insects, spiders as well as larger animals, such as frogs; insects stirred up in grasslands by cattle.

VOCAL BREEDERS
This bird almost never calls away from a breeding colony, but it is vocal near its nest.

SIMILAR SPECIES

GREAT EGRET
see p.204

long bill

much larger

black legs and toes

SNOWY EGRET
see p.205

black bill

yellow toes

OCCURRENCE
Since the 1940s, it has expanded to many habitats in much of North America, primarily in grasslands and prairies, but also wetland areas. In tropical regions, the Cattle Egrets flock around the cattle feeding in shallow wetlands.

| Length **20in (51cm)** | Wingspan **31in (78cm)** | Weight **13oz (375g)** |
| Social **Colonies** | Lifespan **Up to 17 years** | Status **Secure** |

DATE: _____ TIME:_____ LOCATION:_____

| Order **Pelecaniformes** | Family **Ardeidae** | Species ***Butorides virescens*** |

Green Heron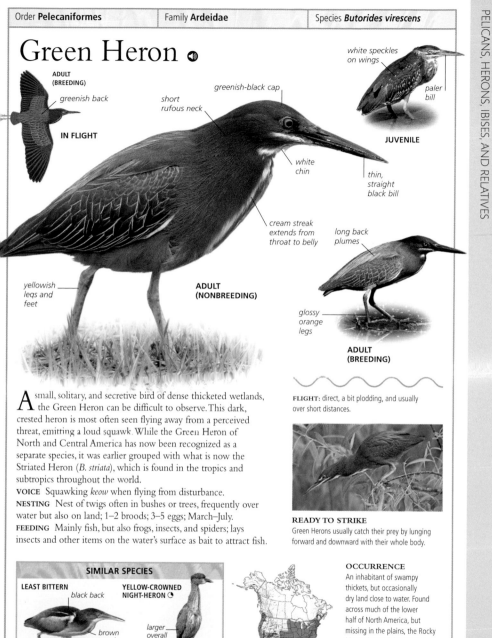

**ADULT
(BREEDING)**

greenish back

short
rufous neck

greenish-black cap

IN FLIGHT

white speckles
on wings

paler
bill

JUVENILE

white
chin

thin,
straight
black bill

cream streak
extends from
throat to belly

long back
plumes

yellowish
legs and
feet

**ADULT
(NONBREEDING)**

glossy
orange
legs

**ADULT
(BREEDING)**

A small, solitary, and secretive bird of dense thicketed wetlands, the Green Heron can be difficult to observe. This dark, crested heron is most often seen flying away from a perceived threat, emitting a loud squawk. While the Green Heron of North and Central America has now been recognized as a separate species, it was earlier grouped with what is now the Striated Heron (*B. striata*), which is found in the tropics and subtropics throughout the world.

VOICE Squawking *keow* when flying from disturbance.
NESTING Nest of twigs often in bushes or trees, frequently over water but also on land; 1–2 broods; 3–5 eggs; March–July.
FEEDING Mainly fish, but also frogs, insects, and spiders; lays insects and other items on the water's surface as bait to attract fish.

FLIGHT: direct, a bit plodding, and usually over short distances.

READY TO STRIKE
Green Herons usually catch their prey by lunging forward and downward with their whole body.

SIMILAR SPECIES

LEAST BITTERN

black back

brown
streaks
on chest

**YELLOW-CROWNED
NIGHT-HERON** ◑

larger
overall

OCCURRENCE
An inhabitant of swampy thickets, but occasionally dry land close to water. Found across much of the lower half of North America, but missing in the plains, the Rocky Mountains, and the western deserts that do not provide appropriate wetlands. Winters in coastal wetlands.

| Length **14½–15½in (37–39cm)** | Wingspan **25–27in (63–68cm)** | Weight **7–9oz (200–250g)** |
| Social **Solitary/Pairs/Small flocks** | Lifespan **Up to 10 years** | Status **Secure** |

DATE: _____ TIME: _____ LOCATION: _____

| Order **Pelecaniformes** | Family **Ardeidae** | Species *Nycticorax nycticorax* |

Black-crowned Night-Heron 🔊

gray wings

heavily speckled back and wings

long white head plumes

black back

white spots on brown back

pale lower bill

JUVENILE

ADULT **JUVENILE**

broad, rounded wings

black crown

IN FLIGHT

short, thick bill

short neck

yellow legs; red in spring

ADULT

FLIGHT: strong, steady flight; wing beats faster than larger herons and egrets; glides into landing.

The Black-crowned Night-Heron is chunky and squat. It is also one of the most common and widespread herons in North America and in the world. However, as its name suggests, it is mainly active at twilight and at night, and thus, is mostly seen roosting along a shoreline. Its distinctive barking call can be heard at night—even at the center of large cities.

VOICE Loud, distinctive *quark* or *wok*, often given in flight and around colonies.

NESTING Large stick nests built usually 20–40ft (6–12m) up in trees; 3–5 eggs; 1 brood; November–August.

FEEDING Feeds primarily on aquatic animals, such as fish, crustaceans, insects, and mollusks; also eggs and chicks of colonial birds, such as egrets, ibises, and terns.

LONG PLUMES
In breeding plumage, the plumes of the male of this species are longer than the female's.

SIMILAR SPECIES

YELLOW-CROWNED NIGHT-HERON *gray neck*

GREEN HERON *rufous neck* smaller overall; see p.207

black-and-white head

thinner bill

OCCURRENCE
Widespread; can be found wherever there are waterbodies, such as lakes, ponds, and streams; generally absent from higher elevations. Colonies often on islands or in marshes; colony sites may be used for decades. In winter, found in areas where water remains open.

| Length **23–26in (58–65cm)** | Wingspan **3¹/₂–4ft (1.1–1.2m)** | Weight **1¹/₂–2¹/₂lb (0.7–1kg)** |
| Social **Colonies** | Lifespan **Up to 21 years** | Status **Secure** |

DATE: _____ TIME: _____ LOCATION: _____

Order **Pelecaniformes**	Family **Threskiornithidae**	Species *Plegadis chihi*

White-faced Ibis

dark legs

greenish iridescent wings

dark face

ADULT (NONBREEDING)

dark bronze-green overall

bronze metallic gloss

white face

ADULT (BREEDING)

trailing legs

IN FLIGHT

dull, non-iridescent plumage

paler face and neck

ADULT (BREEDING)

dark-chestnut chest and neck

pink to red, naked skin between eye and long, decurved bill

reddish legs and feet

JUVENILE

The White-faced Ibis is not only the most widespread member of its family in North America but also the only ibis found commonly in its range. It prefers fresh marshes and irrigated land, and is quick to take advantage of any new habitat caused by heavy rains or flooding. Nesting sites may vary from year to year, depending on changes in water levels.

VOICE Generally silent; soft calls at the nest, including feeding calls, vocalizations after mating, and greeting calls to mates and chicks; outside breeding, a raucous *khah* or *krah*.

NESTING Flat or columnar nest lined with plant matter, such as cattail or bulrush, in low trees or shrubs over shallow water, or on ground on small islands; 2–5 eggs; 1 brood; May–July.

FEEDING Captures prey below soil by probing with bill; eats aquatic prey, such as crayfish, small fish, and frogs.

FLIGHT: strong and direct, with rapid wing beats, alternating with glides; soars on thermals.

LARGE FLOCKS
The White-faced Ibis is social, feeding and traveling in flocks, which can be large.

SIMILAR SPECIES

GLOSSY IBIS

BLACK-CROWNED NIGHT-HERON ◗ see p.208

less white on face

darker legs

white spots on brown back

thick, straight bill

OCCURRENCE
Found in freshwater wetlands, especially in flooded fields, marshes, and lake edges with cattails and bulrushes. These birds may disperse farther east after breeding, but are mostly restricted to the western part of the US and up into the southern prairies in Canada, and in Central and South America.

Length **23in (59cm)**	Wingspan **36in (92cm)**	Weight **22oz (625g)**
Social **Flocks/Colonies**	Lifespan **Up to 14 years**	Status **Secure**

DATE: _____ TIME:_____ LOCATION:_____

Family **Cathartidae**

NEW WORLD VULTURES

NEW WORLD VULTURES are not related to Old World vultures, although they look somewhat similar, having long, broad wings with "fingered" tips. Their heads and necks are more or less bare, which helps prevent meat and bacteria from collecting in their feathers when they feed on carcasses. Their bills are large and hooked to tear flesh, but their feet are unspecialized, with short claws, and are not used for capturing prey. All the birds in this group have exceptional eyesight and find their food by sight while soaring high over open ground. The Turkey Vulture, a common sight in many areas, also has a keen sense of smell, which it can use to find dead animals in dense woodland.

WEAK TOOL
In spite of its sharp beak, the Turkey Vulture cannot always break the skin of carcasses. Thus, it must wait for another predator to tear open the skin or for the carcass to rot and soften.

Families **Pandionidae, Accipitridae**

HAWKS, EAGLES, AND RELATIVES

THESE DIURNAL BIRDS OF PREY include several loosely related groups. All have hooked bills and large eyes, but their shapes and lifestyles are varied.

OSPREY
The sole member of the Pandionidae family, the Osprey catches fish in a headlong dive from a hover. Its feet have long, curved claws and toes equipped with sharp spicules to provide extra grip for slippery fish.

HAWKS AND EAGLES
The Accipitridae family covers a range of raptors with much variation in shape, size, and habitat. Graceful, long-winged harriers are medium-sized birds that feed in open spaces or over marshes. Huge, powerful eagles of mountains and open country have long, broad wings and feathered legs. "Sea-eagles," such as the Bald Eagle, have massive bills and long wings but somewhat short tails and bare legs. Sea-eagles feed on fish as well as birds,

mammals, and carrion. Bird-eating hawks (in the genus *Accipiter*) have rounded wings and slender tails, and long claws for catching prey with their feet. Soaring hawks (in the genus *Buteo*) are more like small eagles, with smaller but powerful bills and feet. Some are more widespread than eagles, and are found in a broader range of habitats.

DOUBLE SHOT
With lots of fish running in a tight school, this Osprey has the strength and skill to catch two with one dive.

| Order **Cathartiformes** | Family **Cathartidae** | Species *Cathartes aura* |

Turkey Vulture

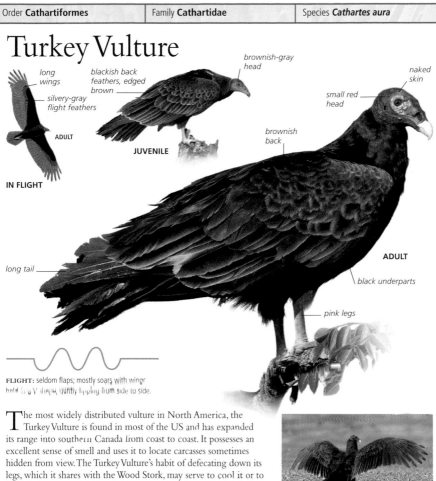

long wings

silvery-gray flight feathers

ADULT

IN FLIGHT

blackish back feathers, edged brown

JUVENILE

brownish-gray head

naked skin

small red head

brownish back

ADULT

black underparts

long tail

pink legs

FLIGHT: seldom flaps; mostly soars with wings held in a 'V' shape, gently tipping from side to side.

The most widely distributed vulture in North America, the Turkey Vulture is found in most of the US and has expanded its range into southern Canada from coast to coast. It possesses an excellent sense of smell and uses it to locate carcasses sometimes hidden from view. The Turkey Vulture's habit of defecating down its legs, which it shares with the Wood Stork, may serve to cool it or to kill bacteria with its ammonia content.

VOICE Silent, but will hiss at intruders; also grunts.

NESTING Dark recesses, such as under large rocks or stumps, on rocky ledges in caves, and crevices, in mammal burrows and hollow logs, and abandoned buildings; 1–3 eggs; 1 brood; March–August.

FEEDING Feeds on a wide range of wild and domestic carrion, mostly mammals, but also birds, reptiles, amphibians, and fish; occasionally takes live prey, such as nestlings or trapped birds.

SOAKING UP THE SUN
Turkey Vultures often spread their wings to sun themselves and increase their body temperature.

SIMILAR SPECIES

BLACK VULTURE

all-black body

shorter tail

OCCURRENCE
Generally forages and migrates over mixed farmland and forest but also beaches; prefers to nest in forested or partly forested hillsides; roosts in large trees, such as cottonwoods, on rocky outcrops, and on power line transmission towers; some winter in urban areas and near landfills. Also widespread in the Caribbean, and in Central and South America.

| Length **25–32in (64–81cm)** | Wingspan **5½–6ft (1.7–1.8m)** | Weight **4½lb (2kg)** |
| Social **Flocks** | Lifespan **At least 17 years** | Status **Secure** |

| Order **Accipitriformes** | Family **Pandionidae** | Species *Pandion haliaetus* |

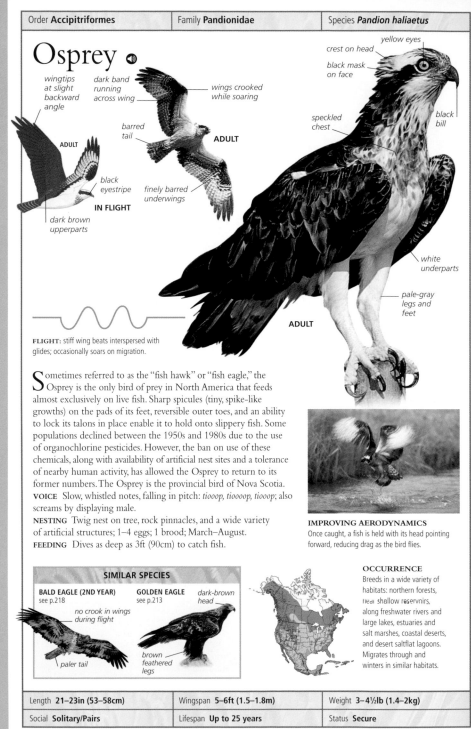

Osprey 🔊

wingtips at slight backward angle

dark band running across wing

wings crooked while soaring

barred tail

ADULT

ADULT

black eyestripe

finely barred underwings

IN FLIGHT

dark brown upperparts

yellow eyes

crest on head

black mask on face

speckled chest

black bill

white underparts

pale-gray legs and feet

ADULT

FLIGHT: stiff wing beats interspersed with glides; occasionally soars on migration.

Sometimes referred to as the "fish hawk" or "fish eagle," the Osprey is the only bird of prey in North America that feeds almost exclusively on live fish. Sharp spicules (tiny, spike-like growths) on the pads of its feet, reversible outer toes, and an ability to lock its talons in place enable it to hold onto slippery fish. Some populations declined between the 1950s and 1980s due to the use of organochlorine pesticides. However, the ban on use of these chemicals, along with availability of artificial nest sites and a tolerance of nearby human activity, has allowed the Osprey to return to its former numbers. The Osprey is the provincial bird of Nova Scotia.
VOICE Slow, whistled notes, falling in pitch: *tioop, tioooop, tiooop*; also screams by displaying male.
NESTING Twig nest on tree, rock pinnacles, and a wide variety of artificial structures; 1–4 eggs; 1 brood; March–August.
FEEDING Dives as deep as 3ft (90cm) to catch fish.

IMPROVING AERODYNAMICS
Once caught, a fish is held with its head pointing forward, reducing drag as the bird flies.

SIMILAR SPECIES

BALD EAGLE (2ND YEAR)
see p.218

no crook in wings during flight

paler tail

GOLDEN EAGLE
see p.213

dark-brown head

brown feathered legs

OCCURRENCE
Breeds in a wide variety of habitats: northern forests, near shallow reservoirs, along freshwater rivers and large lakes, estuaries and salt marshes, coastal deserts, and desert saltflat lagoons. Migrates through and winters in similar habitats.

| Length **21–23in (53–58cm)** | Wingspan **5–6ft (1.5–1.8m)** | Weight **3–4½lb (1.4–2kg)** |
| Social **Solitary/Pairs** | Lifespan **Up to 25 years** | Status **Secure** |

DATE: _____ TIME: _____ LOCATION: _____

Order **Accipitriformes**	Family **Accipitridae**	Species *Aquila chrysaetos*

Golden Eagle

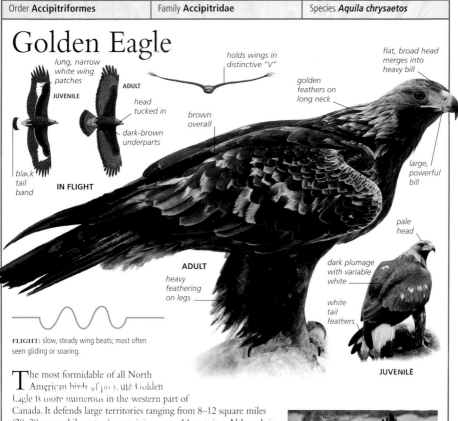

long, narrow white wing patches

JUVENILE

ADULT

holds wings in distinctive "V"

flat, broad head merges into heavy bill

golden feathers on long neck

head tucked in

brown overall

dark-brown underparts

black tail band

IN FLIGHT

large, powerful bill

ADULT

heavy feathering on legs

pale head

dark plumage with variable white

white tail feathers

JUVENILE

FLIGHT: slow, steady wing beats; most often seen gliding or soaring.

The most formidable of all North American birds of prey, the Golden Eagle is more numerous in the western part of Canada. It defends large territories ranging from 8–12 square miles (20–30 square kilometers), containing up to 14 nest sites. Although it appears sluggish, it is amazingly swift and agile, and employs a variety of hunting techniques to catch specific prey. Shot and poisoned by ranchers and trappers, it is unfortunately also faced with dwindling habitat and food sources due to human development.

VOICE High-pitched far-carrying yelps and deep liquid babbling notes.
NESTING Large pile of sticks and vegetation on cliffs, in trees, and on artificial structures; 1–3 eggs; 1 brood; April–August.
FEEDING Eats mammals, such as hares, rabbits, ground squirrels, prairie dogs, marmots, foxes, and coyotes; also large birds.

POWER AND STRENGTH
With its sharp talons and strong wings, legs, and feet, the Golden Eagle can take prey as large as a coyote.

SIMILAR SPECIES

BALD EAGLE ☾
see p.218

dark-brown overall

FERRUGINOUS HAWK ☾ **(DARK FORM)**
see p.223

large head and bill

no golden tinge

smaller overall

OCCURRENCE
In North America, occurs mostly in grasslands, wetlands, and rocky areas; breeds south to Mexico, in open and semi-open habitats from sea level to 12,000ft (3,500m) including tundra, shrublands, grasslands, coniferous forests, and farmland, areas close to streams or rivers; winters in open habitat.

Length **28–33in (70–84cm)**	Wingspan **6–7¼ft (1.8–2.2m)**	Weight **6½–13lb (3–6kg)**
Social **Solitary/Pairs**	Lifespan **Up to 39 years**	Status **Declining (p)**

DATE: _____ TIME: _____ LOCATION: _____

| Order **Accipitriformes** | Family **Accipitridae** | Species **Circus hudsonius** |

Northern Harrier

MALE
black wingtips
wings held in V-shape
white rump
IN FLIGHT

FEMALE
dark barring on silver-gray underwings
bluish-gray upperparts

dark bill with yellow skin near bluish base

bluish-gray head

reddish underparts

JUVENILE

gray uppertail with light undertail feathers

MALE

white ring around owl-like face

brown upperparts

white underparts with reddish-brown markings

FEMALE

F ound nearly all over North America, the Northern Harrier is most often seen flying buoyantly low in search of food. A white rump, V-shaped wings, and tilting flight make this species easily identifiable. The blue-gray males are strikingly different from the dark-brown females. The bird's most recognizable characteristic is its owl-like face, which contains stiff feathers to help channel in sounds from prey. Northern Harriers are highly migratory throughout their range.

VOICE Call given by both sexes in rapid succession at nest: *kek* becomes more high-pitched when intruders are spotted.

NESTING Platform of sticks on ground in open, wet field; 4–6 eggs; 1 brood; April–September.

FEEDING Mostly hunts rodents like mice and muskrats; also birds, frogs, reptiles; occasionally takes larger prey, such as rabbits.

FLIGHT: low and slow with lazy flaps, alternating with buoyant, brusquely tilting glides.

WATERY DWELLING
To avoid predators, Northern Harriers prefer to raise their young on wet sites in tall, dense vegetation.

SIMILAR SPECIES

MISSISSIPPI KITE
whitish head
dark eye patch
gray underparts

ROUGH-LEGGED HAWK
see p.222
broader wings
shorter tail

OCCURRENCE
Breeds in a variety of open wetlands: marshes, meadows, pastures, and fallow fields across most of North America; winters in open habitats like deserts, coastal sand dunes, cropland, grasslands, and marshy and riverside areas.

| Length **18–20in (46–51cm)** | Wingspan **3½–4ft (1.1–1.2m)** | Weight **11–26oz (300–750g)** |
| Social **Solitary/Pairs/Colonies** | Lifespan **Up to 16 years** | Status **Secure** |

DATE: _____ TIME: _____ LOCATION: _____

| Order **Accipitriformes** | Family **Accipitridae** | Species *Accipiter striatus* |

Sharp-shinned Hawk

grayish blue crown

reddish-yellow eye

rounded head

square-tipped tail

short, rounded wings

grayish-blue upperparts

head tucked in

JUVENILE

slightly browner upperparts than male

wide, dark, horizontal bars on gray tail

IN FLIGHT

yellow legs and toes

MALE

dark-brown upperparts

light yellowish eye

wide brown streaks on underparts

ADULT

reddish-brown bars on underparts

white, fluffy undertail feathers

FEMALE

JUVENILE FEMALE

This small and swift hawk is quite adept at capturing birds, occasionally even taking species larger than itself. The Sharp-shinned Hawk's short, rounded wings and long tail allow it to make abrupt turns and lightning-fast dashes in thick woods and dense, shrubby terrain. With needle-like talons, long, spindle-thin legs, and long toes, this hawk is well adapted to snatching birds in flight. The prey is plucked before being consumed or fed to the nestlings.

VOICE High-pitched, repeated *kiu kiu kiu* call; sometimes makes squealing sound when disturbed at nest.

NESTING Sturdy nest of sticks lined with twigs or pieces of bark; sometimes an old crow or squirrel nest; 3–4 eggs; 1 brood; March–June.

FEEDING Catches small birds, such as sparrows and wood warblers, on the wing, or takes them unaware while perched; often frequents feeders to catch songbirds.

FLIGHT: Rapid, direct, and strong; nimble enough to maneuver in dense forest; soars during migration.

HUNTING BIRDS
A Sharp-shinned Hawk pauses on the ground with a freshly captured sparrow in its talons.

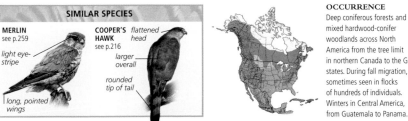

SIMILAR SPECIES		
MERLIN see p.259	**COOPER'S HAWK** see p.216	flattened head
light eye-stripe		larger overall
long, pointed wings		rounded tip of tail

OCCURRENCE
Deep coniferous forests and mixed hardwood-conifer woodlands across North America from the tree limit in northern Canada to the Gulf states. During fall migration, sometimes seen in flocks of hundreds of individuals. Winters in Central America, from Guatemala to Panama.

Length **11in (28 cm)**	Wingspan **23in (58cm)**	Weight **3½–6oz (100–175g)**
Social **Solitary/Flocks**	Lifespan **At least 10 years**	Status **Secure**

DATE: _____ TIME: _____ LOCATION: _____

| Order **Accipitriformes** | Family **Accipitridae** | Species *Accipiter cooperii* |

Cooper's Hawk 🔊

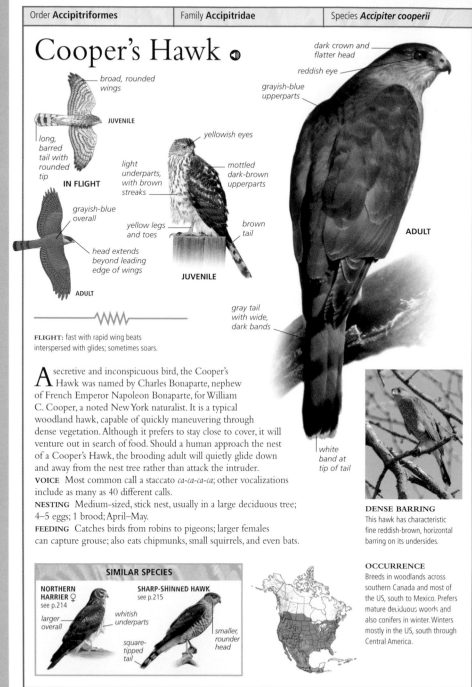

broad, rounded wings

JUVENILE

long, barred tail with rounded tip

IN FLIGHT

grayish-blue overall

head extends beyond leading edge of wings

ADULT

yellowish eyes

light underparts, with brown streaks

mottled dark-brown upperparts

yellow legs and toes

brown tail

JUVENILE

dark crown and flatter head

reddish eye

grayish-blue upperparts

ADULT

gray tail with wide, dark bands

white band at tip of tail

FLIGHT: fast with rapid wing beats interspersed with glides; sometimes soars.

A secretive and inconspicuous bird, the Cooper's Hawk was named by Charles Bonaparte, nephew of French Emperor Napoleon Bonaparte, for William C. Cooper, a noted New York naturalist. It is a typical woodland hawk, capable of quickly maneuvering through dense vegetation. Although it prefers to stay close to cover, it will venture out in search of food. Should a human approach the nest of a Cooper's Hawk, the brooding adult will quietly glide down and away from the nest tree rather than attack the intruder.

VOICE Most common call a staccato *ca-ca-ca-ca*; other vocalizations include as many as 40 different calls.

NESTING Medium-sized, stick nest, usually in a large deciduous tree; 4–5 eggs; 1 brood; April–May.

FEEDING Catches birds from robins to pigeons; larger females can capture grouse; also eats chipmunks, small squirrels, and even bats.

DENSE BARRING
This hawk has characteristic fine reddish-brown, horizontal barring on its undersides.

OCCURRENCE
Breeds in woodlands across southern Canada and most of the US, south to Mexico. Prefers mature deciduous woods and also conifers in winter. Winters mostly in the US, south through Central America.

SIMILAR SPECIES

NORTHERN HARRIER ♀
see p.214

larger overall

whitish underparts

square-tipped tail

SHARP-SHINNED HAWK
see p.215

smaller, rounder head

| Length **15½–17½in (40–45cm)** | Wingspan **28–34in (70–86cm)** | Weight **13–19oz (375–525g)** |
| Social **Solitary/Pairs** | Lifespan **At least 10 years** | Status **Secure** |

DATE: _____ TIME:_____ LOCATION:_____

Order **Accipitriformes**	Family **Accipitridae**	Species *Accipiter gentilis*

Northern Goshawk

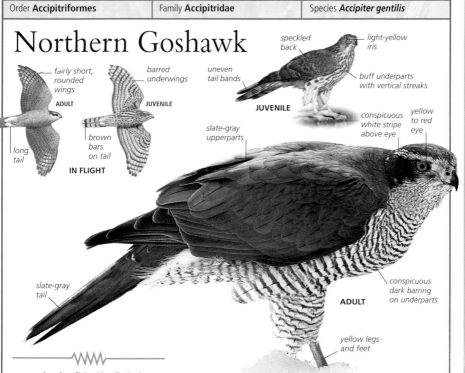

speckled back

light-yellow iris

fairly short, rounded wings

ADULT

barred underwings

JUVENILE

uneven tail bands

buff underparts with vertical streaks

JUVENILE

long tail

brown bars on tail

IN FLIGHT

slate-gray upperparts

conspicuous white stripe above eye

yellow to red eye

slate-gray tail

conspicuous dark barring on underparts

ADULT

yellow legs and feet

FLIGHT: fast, direct flight with swift wing beats and alternating glides; occasionally soars.

The powerful and agile Northern Goshawk is secretive by nature and not easily observed, even in regions where it is common. It has few natural enemies, but will defend its territories, nests, and young fiercely by repeatedly diving and screaming at intruders that get too close. Spring hikers and turkey-hunters occasionally discover Northern Goshawks by wandering into their territory and are driven off by the angry occupants.

VOICE Loud, high-pitched *gek-gek-gek* when agitated.

NESTING Large stick structures lined with bark and plant matter in the mid- to lower region of trees; 1–3 eggs; 1 brood; May–June.

FEEDING Sits and waits on perch before diving rapidly; preys on birds as large as grouse and pheasants; also mammals, including hares and squirrels.

OCCASIONAL SOARER
A juvenile Northern Goshawk takes advantage of a thermal, soaring during migration.

OCCURRENCE
Breeds in deep deciduous, coniferous, and mixed woodlands in northern North America, from the tundra–taiga border, south to California, northern Mexico, and Pennsylvania in the eastern US, absent from east-central US. Likes to nest in monoculture forests.

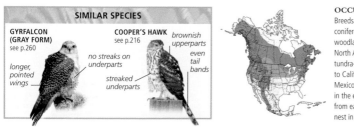

SIMILAR SPECIES

GYRFALCON (GRAY FORM)
see p.260

longer, pointed wings

COOPER'S HAWK
see p.216

no streaks on underparts

streaked underparts

brownish upperparts

even tail bands

Length **21in (53cm)**	Wingspan **3½ft (1.1m)**	Weight **2–3lb (0.9–1.4kg)**
Social **Solitary/Pairs**	Lifespan **Up to 20 years**	Status **Secure**

DATE: _____ TIME: _____ LOCATION: _____

| Order **Accipitriformes** | Family **Accipitridae** | Species *Haliaeetus leucocephalus* |

Bald Eagle 🔊

JUVENILE

dark head, jutting out

ADULT

white head

brown body

white tail

IN FLIGHT

dark-brown eyes

all-white head with yellow eyes

white belly and underwings mottled brown

2ND YEAR

dark brown overall

dark bill starting to turn yellow at base

1ST YEAR

yellow hooked bill

dark eyestripe on whitish face

4TH YEAR

dark chocolate-brown overall

long, wedge-shaped white tail

yellow legs and feet

ADULT

FLIGHT: slow, powerful wing beats; soars and glides on broad, wide wings held at a right angle.

The Bald Eagle, although an opportunist, prefers to scavenge on carrion and steal prey from other birds, including Ospreys. It was nearing extinction due to bounties and reproductive failure caused by DDT. Declared endangered in 1967, its populations have rebounded to high numbers, especially on the coasts. The Bald Eagle was selected, by an act of Congress in 1782, as the national emblem of the US.

VOICE Surprisingly high-pitched voice, 3–4 notes followed by a rapidly descending series.

NESTING Huge stick nest, usually in tallest tree; 1–3 eggs; 1 brood; March–September.

FEEDING Favors carrion, especially fish, also eats birds, mammals, reptiles; steals fish from Osprey.

SIMILAR SPECIES

FERRUGINOUS HAWK
dark head;
see p.223

whitish underparts

GOLDEN EAGLE ☾
white in-flight feathers;
see p.213

feathered legs

SUBSTANTIAL ABODE
Bald eagles make the largest stick nest of all raptors; it can weigh up to two tons.

OCCURRENCE
Widespread across Canada and much of the US. Breeds in forested areas near water; also shoreline areas ranging from undeveloped to relatively well-developed with marked human activity; winters along major river systems and in coastal areas and occasionally even in arid regions of the southwest US.

| Length **28–38in (71–96cm)** | Wingspan **6½ft (2m)** | Weight **6½–14lb (3–6.5kg)** |
| Social **Solitary/Pairs** | Lifespan **Up to 28 years** | Status **Secure** |

DATE: _____ TIME: _____ LOCATION: _____

Order **Accipitriformes**	Family **Accipitridae**	Species **Buteo platypterus**

Broad-winged Hawk

indistinct "mustache"

dark border on edges of wings

ADULT

one to two broad white bands visible on tail

ADULT

upperparts brown with white flecking

ADULT

JUVENILE

pale tan wings with dark tips

pale outer wing feathers

pale underparts, with conspicuous tear-shaped brown spots

short yellow feet

IN FLIGHT

finely barred, all-brown tail

JUVENILE

JUVENILE

Ohe of the most numerous of all North American birds of prey, the Broad-winged Hawk migrates in huge flocks or "kettles," with thousands of birds gliding on rising thermals. Some birds winter in Florida, but the majority travel about 70 miles (110km) a day to log more than 4,000 miles (6,500km) before ending up in Brazil, Bolivia, and even some of the Caribbean islands. Compared to its two cousins, the Red-shouldered and Red-tailed Hawks, the Broad-winged Hawk is slightly smaller, but stockier. Adults are easily identified by a broad white-and-black band on their tails. Broad-winged Hawks have two color forms, the light one being more common than the dark, sooty-brown one.

VOICE High-pitched *peeoweee* call, first note shorter and higher-pitched.
NESTING Platform of fresh twigs or dead sticks, often on old squirrel, hawk, or crow nest in tree; 2–3 eggs; 1 brood; April–August.
FEEDING Eats small mammals, toads, frogs, snakes, grouse chicks, insects, and spiders; crabs in winter.

FLIGHT: circles above forest canopy with wings and tail spread; short flights from branch to branch.

SIMILAR SPECIES

RED-SHOULDERED HAWK	**RED-TAILED HAWK** see p.221
larger overall	larger overall
thin white bands on tail	red patch on shoulder / more slender	dark band on belly

WATCHING FOR PREY
From an elevated perch, this hawk scans for vertebrate prey, such as rodents.

OCCURRENCE
Breeds across Canada (but not the Rockies) and in the eastern US (not west of the 100th meridian), in forested areas with deciduous, conifers, and mixed trees, with clearings and water nearby. Concentrations of migrants can be seen at bottlenecks, such as the Isthmus of Tehuantepec, Mexico and Panama.

Length **13–17in (33–43cm)**	Wingspan **32–39in (81–100cm)**	Weight **10–19oz (275–550g)**
Social **Flocks**	Lifespan **Up to 14 years**	Status **Secure**

DATE: _____ TIME: _____ LOCATION: _____

Order **Accipitriformes** | Family **Accipitridae** | Species ***Buteo swainsoni***

Swainson's Hawk

long, pointed wings

dark wingtips

ADULT (LIGHT FORM)

JUVENILE (LIGHT FORM)

dark chest

IN FLIGHT

whitish head

spotted underparts

JUVENILE (LIGHT FORM)

white face and chin

reddish breast and belly

slender shape overall

ADULT (INTERMEDIATE FORM)

dark-brown head and breast

pale reddish upper chest

spotted underparts

white underbelly

ADULT (DARK FORM)

longish tail

wingtips reach end of tail when perched

FLIGHT: soaring, buoyant flight with deep wing beats; will often hover and hang motionless.

ADULT (LIGHT FORM)

The Swainson's Hawk is perhaps most famous for its spectacular 6,000-mile (9,650km) fall migration from the Canadian prairies to the lower regions of South America, when thousands can be observed soaring in the air at any one time. While migrating, this hawk averages 125 miles (200km) a day. There are three color forms: light, dark, and an intermediate form between the two.
VOICE Alarm call a shrill, plaintive scream *kreeeee* given by both sexes; high-pitched *keeeoooo* fading at the end.
NESTING Bulky, flimsy pile of sticks or various debris, in solitary tree or on utility poles; 1–4 eggs; 1 brood; April–July.
FEEDING Eats ground squirrels, pocket gophers, mice, voles, bats, rabbits; also snakes, lizards, songbirds.

SIMILAR SPECIES

FERRUGINOUS HAWK DARK HEAD;
see p.223

feathered legs

all-white underparts

RED-TAILED HAWK
see p.221

bulkier overall

shorter, broader wings

red tail

ON THE LOOKOUT
This slim, elegant species usually prefers to dive for its prey from a perch.

OCCURRENCE
Breeds in scattered trees along streams; found in areas of open woodland, sparse shrubland, grasslands, and agricultural land; winters in native Argentinian grassland, and in harvested fields where grasshoppers are found abundantly.

| Length **19–22in (48–56cm)** | Wingspan **4½ft (1.4m)** | Weight **1½–3lb (0.7–1.4kg)** |
| Social **Solitary/Pairs/Flocks** | Lifespan **Up to 19 years** | Status **Declining (p)** |

DATE: _____ TIME: _____ LOCATION: _____

| Order **Accipitriformes** | Family **Accipitridae** | Species *Buteo jamaicensis* |

Red-tailed Hawk 🔊

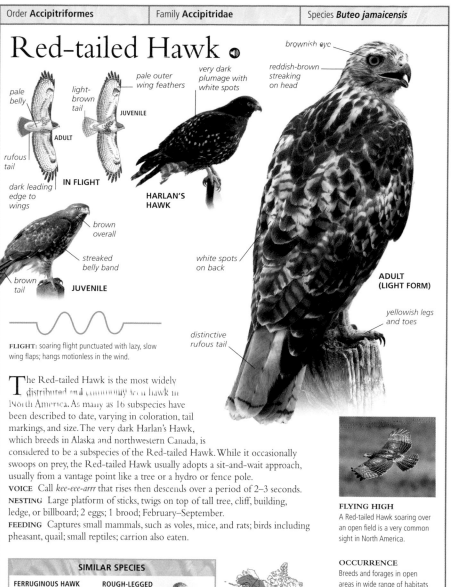

pale belly

pale outer wing feathers

light-brown tail

JUVENILE

very dark plumage with white spots

brownish eye

reddish-brown streaking on head

ADULT

rufous tail

IN FLIGHT

dark leading edge to wings

HARLAN'S HAWK

brown overall

streaked belly band

white spots on back

brown tail **JUVENILE**

distinctive rufous tail

ADULT (LIGHT FORM)

yellowish legs and toes

FLIGHT: soaring flight punctuated with lazy, slow wing flaps; hangs motionless in the wind.

The Red-tailed Hawk is the most widely distributed and commonly seen hawk in North America. As many as 16 subspecies have been described to date, varying in coloration, tail markings, and size. The very dark Harlan's Hawk, which breeds in Alaska and northwestern Canada, is considered to be a subspecies of the Red-tailed Hawk. While it occasionally swoops on prey, the Red-tailed Hawk usually adopts a sit-and-wait approach, usually from a vantage point like a tree or a hydro or fence pole.

VOICE Call *kee-eee-arrr* that rises then descends over a period of 2–3 seconds.

NESTING Large platform of sticks, twigs on top of tall tree, cliff, building, ledge, or billboard; 2 eggs; 1 brood; February–September.

FEEDING Captures small mammals, such as voles, mice, and rats; birds including pheasant, quail; small reptiles; carrion also eaten.

FLYING HIGH
A Red-tailed Hawk soaring over an open field is a very common sight in North America.

OCCURRENCE
Breeds and forages in open areas in wide range of habitats and altitudes: scrub desert, grasslands, agricultural fields and pastures, coniferous and deciduous woodlands, and tropical rainforest. Prefers areas with tall perch sites; can be found in suburban woodlots.

SIMILAR SPECIES		
FERRUGINOUS HAWK (LIGHT FORM) see p.223	**ROUGH-LEGGED HAWK (DARK FORM)** see p.222	

larger bill

larger overall

dark band on white tail

mostly white underparts

Length **18–26in (46–65cm)**	Wingspan **3½–4¼ft (1.1–1.3m)**	Weight **1½–3¼lb (0.7–1.5kg)**
Social **Solitary/Pairs**	Lifespan **Up to 21 years**	Status **Secure**

DATE: _____ TIME: _____ LOCATION: _____

Order **Accipitriformes**	Family **Accipitridae**	Species ***Buteo lagopus***

Rough-legged Hawk

FEMALE

black trailing edge

one line before tail tip

pale head

dark wingtips

bold black patch

dark wrist patches

ADULT

dark tail band

IN FLIGHT

short, broad head

MALE

JUVENILE

black belly

barred underparts

thin bands near tail tip

FLIGHT: strong wing beats; usually soars on thermals; frequently hovers in one spot.

white tail with faint black band at tip

plain gray, brown, or frosty feather edges

MALE

The Rough-legged Hawk is known for its extensive variation in plumage—some individuals are almost completely black, whereas others are much paler, very nearly cream or white. The year-to-year fluctuation in numbers of breeding pairs in a given region strongly suggests that this species is nomadic, moving about as a response to the availability of its rodent prey.

VOICE Wintering birds silent; breeding birds utter loud, cat-like mewing or thin whistles, slurred downward when alarmed.

NESTING Bulky mass of sticks, lined with grasses, sedges, feathers and fur from prey, constructed on cliff ledge; 2–6 eggs; 1 brood; April–August.

FEEDING Hovers in one spot over fields in search of prey; lemmings and voles in spring and summer; mice and shrews in winters; variety of birds, ground squirrels, and rabbits year-round.

ABUNDANT FOOD SUPPLY
When small mammals are abundant, these hawks produce large broods on cliff ledges in the tundra.

SIMILAR SPECIES

NORTHERN HARRIER ♀
see p.214

reddish underparts

FERRUGINOUS HAWK
see p.223

reddish upperparts

white underparts

longer wings

OCCURRENCE
Breeds in rough, open country with low crags and cliffs, in high sub-Arctic and Arctic regions; found on the edge of extensive forest or forest clearings, and in treeless tundra, uplands, and alpine habitats. Winters in open areas with fields, marshes, and rough grasslands.

Length **19–20in (48–51cm)**	Wingspan **4¼–4½ft (1.3–1.4m)**	Weight **1½–3lb (0.7–1.4kg)**
Social **Solitary**	Lifespan **Up to 18 years**	Status **Secure**

DATE: _____ TIME: _____ LOCATION: _____

| Order **Accipitriformes** | Family **Accipitridae** | Species ***Buteo regalis*** |

Ferruginous Hawk

ADULT (LIGHT FORM)

dark chocolate brown

brown-and-white contrast on wings

relatively long, pointed wings

white undertail

large bill

dark-brown overall

ADULT (DARK FORM)

ADULT (LIGHT FORM)

IN FLIGHT

JUVENILE (DARK FORM)

reddish tinge to tail

all-white underparts

ADULT (LIGHT FORM)

dark spots on belly

fully feathered legs

JUVENILE (LIGHT FORM)

This inhabitant of open country is the largest North American hawk. Its Latin name *regalis* means "kingly," and its English name refers to its rusty coloring. It is a versatile nester, building its stick nests on cliffs or nearly level ground, trees, and human-made structures like farm buildings. Regrettably, its preference for prairie dogs, which are declining because of habitat loss, shooting, and pesticide use, threatens Ferruginous Hawk populations.

VOICE Screaming *Kree-aa* or *kaah, kaah* during courtship; quieter, lower-pitched, longer alarm call.

NESTING Large stick nest of old sagebrush stems, sticks, and various debris, lined with bark strips; 2–4 eggs; 1 brood; March–August.

FEEDING Hunts mainly rabbits, hares, ground squirrels, and prairie dogs; rarely fledgling birds, amphibians, and reptiles.

FLIGHT: slow, deep wing beats alternating with lazy glides; soars high with thermals.

PERCHED HUNTER
The Ferruginous Hawk usually hunts from a perch, such as a rock or a branch.

OCCURRENCE
In western North America, breeds in low-elevation grasslands interrupted by cliffs or isolated trees for nesting; winters across the southwestern US and Mexico in open terrain ranging from grassland to desert.

SIMILAR SPECIES

RED-TAILED HAWK, (LIGHT FORM) see p.221

smaller bill

ROUGH-LEGGED HAWK see p.222

smaller bill

dark-rufous tail

smaller overall

white tail with dark band

| Length **22–27in (56–69cm)** | Wingspan **4¼–4½ft (1.3–1.4m)** | Weight **2½–4½lb (1–2kg)** |
| Social **Solitary/Pairs** | Lifespan **Up to 20 years** | Status **Secure** |

DATE: _____ TIME: _____ LOCATION: _____

OWLS

Partly because of their nocturnal habits and eerie cries, owls have fascinated humans throughout history. They are placed in the order Strigiformes, and two families are represented in North America: the Barn Owl belongs to the family Tytonidae, while the rest of the owl species belong to the Strigidae. Most owls are active primarily at night and have developed adaptations for living in low-light environments. Their large eyes are sensitive enough to see in the dark and face forward to maximize binocular vision. Since the eyes are fixed in their sockets, a flexible neck helps owls turn the head almost 270° toward a direction

OWL IN DAYLIGHT
The habits of the Barn Owl remain secretive because it is not often seen in daylight.

of interest. Ears are offset on each side of the head to help identify the source of a sound. Some species have "ear" tufts, which are used for camouflage and communication, not for hearing. Many owls have serrations on the forward edges of their flight feathers to cushion airflow, so their flight is silent while stalking prey. All North American owls are predatory to some degree, and they inhabit most areas of the continent. The western Burrowing Owl is unique in that it hunts during the day and nests underground.

BIG HORNS
The "ear" tufts of the Great Horned Owl and Long-eared Owl are among the tallest for owls.

SNOW SWOOP
The Great Gray Owl can hunt by sound alone, allowing it to locate and capture prey hidden even beneath a thick snow cover.

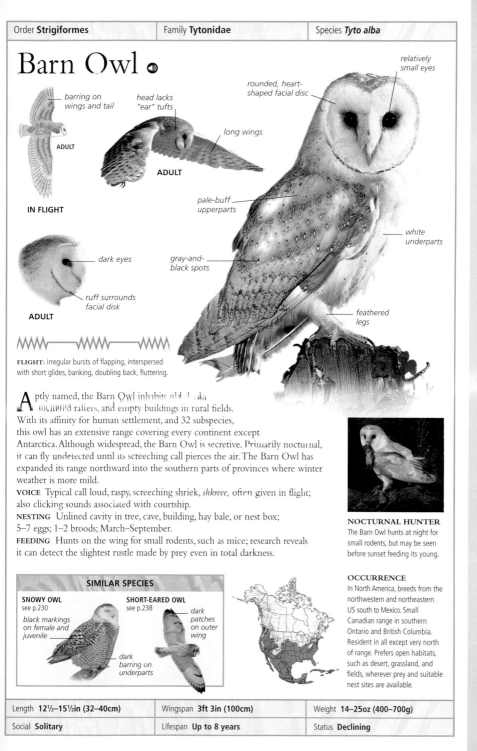

| Order **Strigiformes** | Family **Tytonidae** | Species **Tyto alba** |

Barn Owl 🔊

relatively small eyes

rounded, heart-shaped facial disc

barring on wings and tail

head lacks "ear" tufts

long wings

ADULT

ADULT

IN FLIGHT

pale-buff upperparts

white underparts

dark eyes

gray-and-black spots

ruff surrounds facial disk

feathered legs

ADULT

FLIGHT: irregular bursts of flapping, interspersed with short glides, banking, doubling back, fluttering.

Aptly named, the Barn Owl inhabits old barns, uncultured rafters, and empty buildings in rural fields. With its affinity for human settlement, and 32 subspecies, this owl has an extensive range covering every continent except Antarctica. Although widespread, the Barn Owl is secretive. Primarily nocturnal, it can fly undetected until its screeching call pierces the air. The Barn Owl has expanded its range northward into the southern parts of provinces where winter weather is more mild.

VOICE Typical call loud, raspy, screeching shriek, *shkreee,* often given in flight; also clicking sounds associated with courtship.

NESTING Unlined cavity in tree, cave, building, hay bale, or nest box; 5–7 eggs; 1–2 broods; March–September.

FEEDING Hunts on the wing for small rodents, such as mice; research reveals it can detect the slightest rustle made by prey even in total darkness.

NOCTURNAL HUNTER
The Barn Owl hunts at night for small rodents, but may be seen before sunset feeding its young.

OCCURRENCE
In North America, breeds from the northwestern and northeastern US south to Mexico. Small Canadian range in southern Ontario and British Columbia. Resident in all except very north of range. Prefers open habitats, such as desert, grassland, and fields, wherever prey and suitable nest sites are available.

SIMILAR SPECIES

SNOWY OWL see p.230
black markings on female and juvenile
dark barring on underparts

SHORT-EARED OWL see p.238
dark patches on outer wing

| Length 12½–15½in (32–40cm) | Wingspan 3ft 3in (100cm) | Weight 14–25oz (400–700g) |
| Social **Solitary** | Lifespan **Up to 8 years** | Status **Declining** |

DATE: _____ TIME: _____ LOCATION: _____

Order **Strigiformes**	Family **Strigidae**	Species *Psiloscops flammeolus*

Flammulated Owl

small "ear" tufts, often hidden

dark eyes

reddish-brown facial disc

long, rounded wings

ADULT

tawny underwings

short tail **IN FLIGHT**

grayish-brown body

tawny "shoulder" bar

dark streaks on underparts

smaller in size than gray form

ADULT (RED FORM)

ADULT (GRAY FORM)

FLIGHT: straight flight with steady wing beats; often hovers while foraging.

The tiny Flammulated Owl nests in dry, mountain pine forests from British Colombia south to Mexico. From most of its range, birds move south to Mexico and Central America in winter. Its dark, watery-looking eyes distinguish it from other species of small North American owls. Entirely nocturnal, it is heard more often than seen. A resting Flammulated Owl blends well with the color of pine bark: like some other owls, it has "red" and "gray" forms, both beautifully patterned for camouflage. This species breeds in loose groups, perhaps reflecting a patchiness in habitat quality.

VOICE Series of soft low-frequency toots, often difficult to locate, can continue for hours; barks and screams when disturbed at nest site.

NESTING Cavity in tree, woodpecker hole, nest box; 3–4 eggs; 1–2 broods; May–August.

FEEDING Hunts from stationary perch, from which it flies to capture insects—mostly moths, and beetles—from branches, foliage, or ground.

BLENDING IN
When this owl peeks out of a tree-hole, its plumage blends in remarkably well with the bark.

OCCURRENCE
Breeds in semiarid mountain forests, especially ponderosa and yellow pines, open wooded areas at middle elevations with scattered clearings, older trees, and groves of saplings. Winters in habitat similar to breeding season, primarily in southern Mexico, Guatemala, and El Salvador.

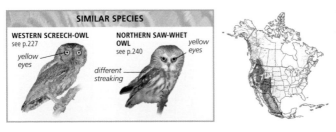

SIMILAR SPECIES

WESTERN SCREECH-OWL
see p.227
yellow eyes

NORTHERN SAW-WHET OWL
see p.240
yellow eyes
different streaking

Length **6–6¾in (15–17cm)**	Wingspan **16in (41cm)**	Weight **1⁹⁄₁₆–2¼oz (45–65g)**
Social **Solitary**	Lifespan **Up to 8 years**	Status **Secure**

DATE: _____ TIME:_____ LOCATION:_____

Order **Strigiformes**	Family **Strigidae**	Species **Megascops kennicottii**

Western Screech-Owl 🔊

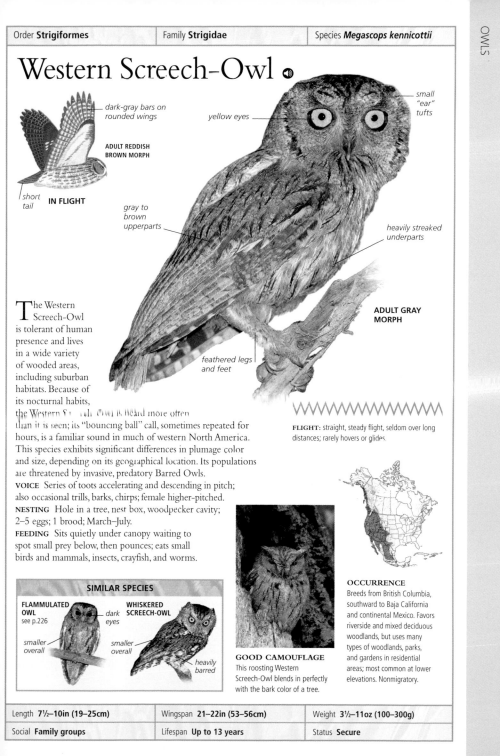

dark-gray bars on rounded wings

yellow eyes

small "ear" tufts

ADULT REDDISH BROWN MORPH

short tail **IN FLIGHT**

gray to brown upperparts

heavily streaked underparts

ADULT GRAY MORPH

feathered legs and feet

The Western Screech-Owl is tolerant of human presence and lives in a wide variety of wooded areas, including suburban habitats. Because of its nocturnal habits, the Western Screech-Owl is heard more often than it is seen; its "bouncing ball" call, sometimes repeated for hours, is a familiar sound in much of western North America. This species exhibits significant differences in plumage color and size, depending on its geographical location. Its populations are threatened by invasive, predatory Barred Owls.

VOICE Series of toots accelerating and descending in pitch; also occasional trills, barks, chirps; female higher-pitched.

NESTING Hole in a tree, nest box, woodpecker cavity; 2–5 eggs; 1 brood; March–July.

FEEDING Sits quietly under canopy waiting to spot small prey below, then pounces; eats small birds and mammals, insects, crayfish, and worms.

FLIGHT: straight, steady flight, seldom over long distances; rarely hovers or glides.

GOOD CAMOUFLAGE
This roosting Western Screech-Owl blends in perfectly with the bark color of a tree.

OCCURRENCE
Breeds from British Columbia, southward to Baja California and continental Mexico. Favors riverside and mixed deciduous woodlands, but uses many types of woodlands, parks, and gardens in residential areas; most common at lower elevations. Nonmigratory.

SIMILAR SPECIES

FLAMMULATED OWL see p.226
smaller overall

dark eyes

WHISKERED SCREECH-OWL
smaller overall

heavily barred

Length **7½–10in (19–25cm)**	Wingspan **21–22in (53–56cm)**	Weight **3½–11oz (100–300g)**
Social **Family groups**	Lifespan **Up to 13 years**	Status **Secure**

DATE: _____ TIME: _____ LOCATION: _____

| Order **Strigiformes** | Family **Strigidae** | Species **_Megascops asio_** |

Eastern Screech-Owl 🔊

"ear" tufts

yellow eyes

white spots on inner wing feathers

dark-gray bars on short, rounded wings

ADULT

streaked underparts

IN FLIGHT

short tail

ADULT (GRAY FORM)

feathered legs

FLIGHT: direct, purposeful flight; straight with steady wing beats, typically below tree cover.

This widespread little owl has adapted to suburban areas, and its distinctive call is a familiar sound across the eastern US and southern Canada at almost any time of the year. Although it is an entirely nocturnal species, it may be found roosting in a birdhouse or tree cavity during the day. With gray and red color morphs, this species shows considerable plumage variation. The relatively high mortality rate of Eastern Screech-Owls, especially juveniles, is caused in part by predation by Great Horned Owls and collisions with motor vehicles.

VOICE Most familiar call a descending whinny—often used in movie soundtracks; also an even trill; occasional barks and screeches; female higher-pitched than male.

NESTING No nest; lays eggs in cavity in tree, woodpecker hole, rotted snag, nest box; 2–6 eggs; 1 brood; March–August.

FEEDING Captures prey with toes; eats insects, earthworms, rodents, songbirds, crayfish, small fish, frogs, snakes, and lizards.

STANDING OUT
The striking red color morph of the Eastern Screech-Owl is less common than the gray.

SIMILAR SPECIES

BOREAL OWL see p.239

brown back

no "ear" tufts

NORTHERN SAW-WHET OWL see p.240

white spots

long, brown streaks

OCCURRENCE
In the US and southern Canada, breeds in a variety of different lowland wooded areas east of the Rockies. Also breeds south to northeast Mexico. Can be found in suburban and urban parks and gardens; usually avoids mountain forests.

| Length **6½–10in (16–25cm)** | Wingspan **19–24in (48–61cm)** | Weight **5–7oz (150–200g)** |
| Social **Solitary** | Lifespan **Up to 13 years** | Status **Secure** |

DATE: _____ TIME: _____ LOCATION: _____

Order **Strigiformes**	Family **Strigidae**	Species *Bubo virginianus*

Great Horned Owl 🔊

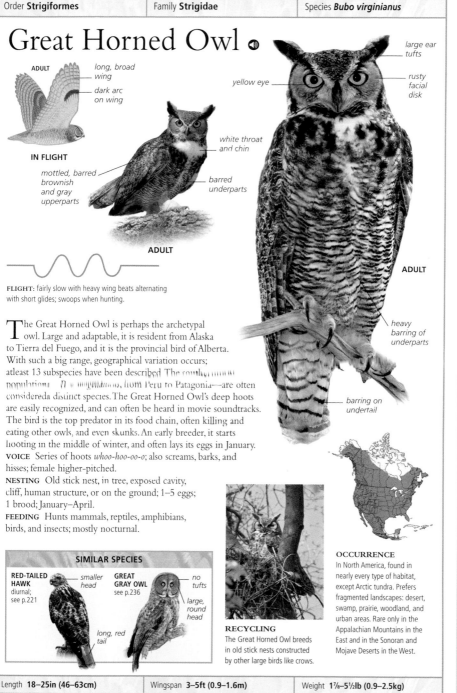

ADULT

long, broad wing

dark arc on wing

IN FLIGHT

large ear tufts

yellow eye

rusty facial disk

white throat and chin

mottled, barred brownish and gray upperparts

barred underparts

ADULT

ADULT

heavy barring of underparts

barring on undertail

FLIGHT: fairly slow with heavy wing beats alternating with short glides; swoops when hunting.

The Great Horned Owl is perhaps the archetypal owl. Large and adaptable, it is resident from Alaska to Tierra del Fuego, and it is the provincial bird of Alberta. With such a big range, geographical variation occurs; atleast 13 subspecies have been described. The southernmost populations—those populations from Peru to Patagonia—are often considereda distinct species. The Great Horned Owl's deep hoots are easily recognized, and can often be heard in movie soundtracks. The bird is the top predator in its food chain, often killing and eating other owls, and even skunks. An early breeder, it starts hooting in the middle of winter, and often lays its eggs in January.

VOICE Series of hoots *whoo-hoo-oo-o*; also screams, barks, and hisses; female higher-pitched.

NESTING Old stick nest, in tree, exposed cavity, cliff, human structure, or on the ground; 1–5 eggs; 1 brood; January–April.

FEEDING Hunts mammals, reptiles, amphibians, birds, and insects; mostly nocturnal.

SIMILAR SPECIES

RED-TAILED HAWK
diurnal; see p.221

smaller head

long, red tail

GREAT GRAY OWL
see p.236

no tufts

large, round head

RECYCLING
The Great Horned Owl breeds in old stick nests constructed by other large birds like crows.

OCCURRENCE
In North America, found in nearly every type of habitat, except Arctic tundra. Prefers fragmented landscapes: desert, swamp, prairie, woodland, and urban areas. Rare only in the Appalachian Mountains in the East and in the Sonoran and Mojave Deserts in the West.

Length **18–25in (46–63cm)**	Wingspan **3–5ft (0.9–1.6m)**	Weight **1⅞–5½lb (0.9–2.5kg)**
Social **Solitary**	Lifespan **Up to 28 years**	Status **Secure**

DATE: _____ TIME:_____ LOCATION:_____

Order **Strigiformes**	Family **Strigidae**	Species *Bubo scandiacus*

Snowy Owl

white face

large, round head

yellow eyes

flecked gray-brown

JUVENILE

IN FLIGHT

dusky barring

variably barred underparts

JUVENILE

variable barring on wings

nearly all-white breast

feathered legs

ADULT

FLIGHT: slow, steady flight with strong, deep wing beats; flaps interspersed with glides.

An icon of the far north and the provincial bird of Quebec, the Snowy Owl occasionally appears far to the south of its usual range, making an eye-catching addition to the local landscape. This is a bird of the open tundra, where it hunts from headlands or hummocks and nests on the ground. In such a harsh environment, the Snowy Owl largely depends on lemmings for prey. It is fiercely territorial, and will valiantly defend its young in the nest even against larger animals, such as the Arctic Fox.

VOICE Deep hoots, doubled or given in a short series, usually by male; also rattles, whistles, and hisses.

NESTING Scrape on a mound in short vegetation or dirt, with no lining; 3–12 eggs; 1 brood; May–September.

FEEDING Mostly hunts lemmings, but takes whatever other small mammals, birds, and occasionally fish, it can find.

SNOWY MALE
Some adult males display no barring at all and have entirely pure white plumage.

SIMILAR SPECIES

BARN OWL see p.225

black eyes

golden brown

SHORT-EARED OWL see p.238

mottled-brown markings

larger overall

OCCURRENCE
Breeds in the tundra of Eurasia and northern North America, north to Ellesmere Island; North American birds winter south to the Great Plains. In some years, many North American birds winter south of their normal range, including in dunes, marshes, and airfields, as far south as Florida and California.

Length **20–27in (51–68cm)**	Wingspan **4¼–5¼ft (1.3–1.6m)**	Weight **3½–6½lb (1.6–2.9kg)**
Social **Solitary**	Lifespan **Up to 9 years**	Status **Vulnerable**

DATE: _____ TIME: _____ LOCATION: _____

Order **Strigiformes**	Family **Strigidae**	Species *Surnia ulula*

Northern Hawk Owl

fine spotting on forehead and crown

yellowish eyes

black line around white face

brownish-black upperparts

heavy white marking

whitish facial discs

ADULT

long wings

patterned face

long tail **IN FLIGHT**

heavy barring below

hawk-like posture

ADULT

regularly barred underparts

ADULT

Whether swooping low through a bog or perching at the tip of a branch, the Northern Hawk Owl is as falcon-like as it is owl-like, being streamlined, a powerful flier, and an active daytime hunter. It is patchily distributed across the northern North American forests far from most human settlements, so is seldom seen—and is not well studied—on its breeding grounds. In winter, though, the bird is somewhat nomadic, and is occasionally seen south of its breeding range for a few days or weeks in southern Canada and the northern US.

VOICE Ascending, whistled, drawn-out trill; also chirps, screeches, and yelps.

NESTING Cavities, hollows, broken-off branches, old stick nests, nest boxes; 3–13 eggs; 1 brood; April–August.

FEEDING Swoops like a falcon from an elevated perch to pounce on prey; preys mainly on rodents in summer, and on grouse and ptarmigan in winter.

FLIGHT: powerful, deep wing beats; glides; highly maneuverable, occasionally soars.

KEEN-EYED OWL
The Northern Owl hunts mainly by sight, swooping on prey spotted from a high perch.

OCCURRENCE
Breeds across the forests of northern Canada, from Alaska to Quebec and Newfoundland, in sparse woodland or mixed conifer forest with swamps, bogs, burned areas, or storm damage. In winter, occasionally moves south to southern Canada, Great Lakes region, and New England.

SIMILAR SPECIES

MERLIN see p.259 — small head; smaller overall; buffy-orange underneath

GREAT HORNED OWL see p.229 — "ear" tufts; chunky shape; much larger overall

Length **14–17½in (36–44cm)**	Wingspan **31in (80cm)**	Weight **11–12oz (300–350g)**
Social **Family groups**	Lifespan **Up to 10 years**	Status **Secure**

DATE: _____ TIME: _____ LOCATION: _____

Order **Strigiformes**	Family **Strigidae**	Species *Glaucidium gnoma*

Northern Pygmy-Owl

rounded wings

brown to gray upperparts with white spots

ADULT

IN FLIGHT

long tail

ADULT

spotted crown

round head

yellow eye

yellowish bill

heavily streaked, whitish underparts

ADULT

FLIGHT: undulating, rapid series of flaps followed by glide with wings tucked.

long tail, with brown-and-white barring

In spite of its small size, the Northern Pygmy-Owl is a fierce hunter. It regularly preys on other birds, including relatively large ones, such as Northern Bobwhites. When hunting, it gradually moves closer to its prey by making short, zigzagging flights from tree to tree before pouncing. It is often active during the day, most frequently around dawn and dusk, and in winter it is frequently seen in gardens, pouncing on birds at feeders. The Northern Pygmy-Owl is one of two *Glaucidium* pygmy-owls in North America. Like the rare Ferruginous Pygmy-Owl (*G. brasilianum*), it has "false eyes"—a pair of black-feathered spots on the back of its head. These may act as a deterrent to potential attackers, especially when the owl is sleeping.

VOICE Hollow *poot*, *poot*, *poot* calls, 1–2 seconds apart, continuing in series for minutes or more; also excited trill.

NESTING Usually unlined cavity in tree; 2–7 eggs; 1 brood; April–July.

FEEDING Pounces from perch, pinning prey to the ground; eats, insects, reptiles, birds, and mammals.

DAYTIME HUNTER
Unlike most other species of owl, the Northern Pygmy-Owl is often active during the day.

OCCURRENCE
Breeds in western North American mountains from British Columbia to California, Arizona, and New Mexico, and from Mexico to Honduras; can be found in mixed spruce, fir, pine, hemlock, cedar, and oak woodlands; nests at higher elevations, and often winters lower down.

SIMILAR SPECIES

NORTHERN SAW-WHET OWL
see p.240

thick, brown streaks

short tail

FERRUGINOUS PYGMY-OWL

streaked crown

Length **6½–7in (16–18cm)**	Wingspan **15in (38cm)**	Weight **2⅛–2½oz (60–70g)**
Social **Family groups**	Lifespan **Unknown**	Status **Secure**

DATE: _____ TIME: _____ LOCATION: _____

| Order **Strigiformes** | Family **Strigidae** | Species *Athene cunicularia* |

Burrowing Owl

short, rounded wings

ADULT

IN FLIGHT

short tail

brown ear feathers

ADULT

white streaking on forehead and crown

chest spotted with white

short tail

yellow eyes

white contrasting with dark-brown band below

brown upperparts with white spotting

white spots

brown streaks on lower belly

ADULT

short tail

long, feathered legs

FLIGHT: buoyant, often undulating; close to ground; sometimes hovers while hunting.

The Burrowing Owl is unique among North American owls in nesting underground. Usually it uses the abandoned burrows of prairie dogs, ground squirrels, armadillos, badgers, and other mammals. Where such burrows are scarce, however—in built-up areas of Florida, notably—it excavates its own burrow, digging out the soil with its bill and scraping it away with its feet. Usually, it nests in loose colonies, too. Active by day or night, the Burrowing Owl hunts prey on foot or on the wing. Populations of the bird in southern areas of North America tend to stay there year-round, but those farther north move south to Mexico for the winter.
VOICE *Coo-cooo*, or *ha-haaa*, with accent on second syllable; nestlings imitate the rattling of a rattlesnake.
NESTING Cavity lined with grass, feathers, sometimes animal dung, at end of burrow; 8–10 eggs; 1 brood; March–August.
FEEDING Walks, hops, runs, hovers, or flies from perch to capture mainly insects, and occasionally small mammals, birds, reptiles, and amphibians.

ON THE ALERT
A Burrowing Owl keeps watch from the entrance of its burrow, which can be 10ft (3m) long.

SIMILAR SPECIES

SHORT-EARED OWL
see p.238
larger overall

streaked below

OCCURRENCE
Breeds in Florida, the western US, and southwestern Canada, in a wide range of open, well-drained habitats not prone to flooding, including pastures, plains, deserts, grasslands, and steppes, but also developed area, up to about 6,500ft (2,000m). Partial migrant.

| Length **7½–10in (19–25cm)** | Wingspan **21½in (55cm)** | Weight **5oz (150g)** |
| Social **Loose colonies** | Lifespan **Up to 9 years** | Status **Declining** |

DATE: _____ TIME:_____ LOCATION:_____

| Order **Strigiformes** | Family **Strigidae** | Species *Strix occidentalis* |

Spotted Owl

pale underwings

ADULT

IN FLIGHT

large, puffy head, without "ear" tufts

down feathers around head

dark eye

pale bill

rich, dark-brown upperparts with white spots

barred flanks

rusty belly

JUVENILE (SOUTHWEST US, CENTRAL MEXICO)

pale, oval bars on underparts

ADULT (NORTHWEST US, NORTHERN CALIFORNIA)

FLIGHT: short flights; quick flaps interspersed with short glides; heavier flaps when flying upward.

Threatened by competition from expanding Barred Owl populations, and especially habitat loss by clear-cutting of old-growth forests, the Spotted Owl has entered the political arena, and is a topic of hot debate between conservationists and forest managers. Spotted owls have traditionally been divided into three subspecies: *S. o. caurina*, the Northern Spotted Owl, from British Columbia to northern California; *S. o. occidentalis*, the California Spotted Owl in southern California; and *S. o. lucida*, the Mexican Spotted Owl in Arizona and Mexico. Recent studies suggest that these three are sufficiently distinct to warrant full species status. To complicate matters, Spotted and Barred Owls interbreed, producing hybrids.

VOICE Typical call of four notes, *whoo hoo-hoo hooo*, with emphasis on the last syllable; also whistles and barks.

NESTING No nest; lays eggs in broken-off snags, cavities, and platforms, occasionally cliffs; 1–4 eggs; 1 brood; March–July.

FEEDING Sits, waits and pounces on prey; eats small rodents.

FLUFFY FLEDGLINGS
Juveniles can be recognized by lingering down feathers, especially around the head.

SIMILAR SPECIES

GREAT HORNED OWL see p.229

tufts
yellow eyes

larger overall

BARRED OWL see p.235

streaked underparts

OCCURRENCE
In three geographically separated populations; lives in old-growth and mature stands of fir, hemlock, redwood, pine, cedar, oak, and mixed riverside woodlands. Occasionally seen elsewhere, but breeding only occurs in forested areas.

| Length **18–19in (46–48cm)** | Wingspan **3½ft (1.1m)** | Weight **17–28oz (475–800g)** |
| Social **Solitary** | Lifespan **Up to 17 years** | Status **Declining** |

DATE: _____ TIME: _____ LOCATION: _____

| Order **Strigiformes** | Family **Strigidae** | Species *Strix varia* |

Barred Owl

rounded wings

ADULT

IN FLIGHT

large, round head

dark eyes

conspicuously yellowish bill

brown upperparts

heavy white spotting

barring on breast

streaking on belly

barred tail

ADULT

ADULT

FLIGHT: glides silently among trees, interspersed with flaps; rarely hovers.

The Barred Owl is more adaptable and aggressive than its close relative, the Spotted Owl. Recent range expansions have brought the two species into closer contact. This has resulted in the Barred Owl displacing the Spotted Owl, as well as occasional interbreeding. The Barred Owl is mostly nocturnal, but may also call or hunt during the day. It often breeds in suburban habitats.

VOICE Series of hoots in rhythm: *who-cooks-for-you, who-cooks-for-you-all*; also pair duetting (at different pitches), cawing, cackling, and guttural sounds.

NESTING No nest; lays eggs in broken-off branches, cavities, old stick nests; 1–5 eggs; 1 brood; January–September.

FEEDING Perches quietly and waits to spot prey below, then pounces; eats small mammals, birds, amphibians, reptiles, insects, and spiders.

WOODED HABITATS
The Barred Owl is very much at home in deep woodlands, including coniferous forests.

OCCURRENCE
Widespread, though not evenly so, across North America from British Columbia across to the Maritimes and much of the eastern US. Found in a variety of wooded habitats—from cypress swamps in the south to conifer rainforest in the northwest—and in mixed hardwoods.

SIMILAR SPECIES		

GREAT HORNED OWL see p.229

"ear" tufts

SPOTTED OWL see p.234

yellow eyes

larger overall

horizontal barring on underparts

longer tail

pale, oval bars

Length **17–19½in (43–50cm)**	Wingspan **3½ft (1.1m)**	Weight **17–37oz (475–1,050g)**
Social **Solitary**	Lifespan **Up to 18 years**	Status **Secure**

DATE: _____ TIME: _____ LOCATION: _____

| Order **Strigiformes** | Family **Strigidae** | Species *Strix nebulosa* |

Great Gray Owl

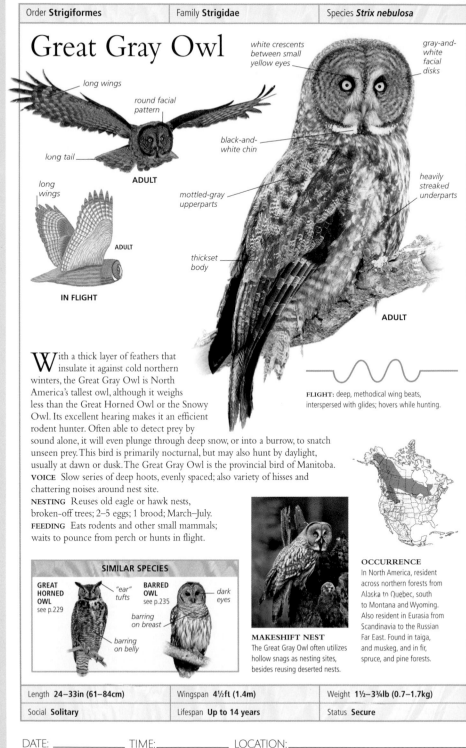

white crescents between small yellow eyes

gray-and-white facial disks

long wings

round facial pattern

black-and-white chin

long tail

ADULT

long wings

heavily streaked underparts

mottled-gray upperparts

ADULT

thickset body

IN FLIGHT

ADULT

With a thick layer of feathers that insulate it against cold northern winters, the Great Gray Owl is North America's tallest owl, although it weighs less than the Great Horned Owl or the Snowy Owl. Its excellent hearing makes it an efficient rodent hunter. Often able to detect prey by sound alone, it will even plunge through deep snow, or into a burrow, to snatch unseen prey. This bird is primarily nocturnal, but may also hunt by daylight, usually at dawn or dusk. The Great Gray Owl is the provincial bird of Manitoba.

FLIGHT: deep, methodical wing beats, interspersed with glides; hovers while hunting.

VOICE Slow series of deep hoots, evenly spaced; also variety of hisses and chattering noises around nest site.

NESTING Reuses old eagle or hawk nests, broken-off trees; 2–5 eggs; 1 brood; March–July.

FEEDING Eats rodents and other small mammals; waits to pounce from perch or hunts in flight.

SIMILAR SPECIES

GREAT HORNED OWL see p.229

"ear" tufts

BARRED OWL see p.235

dark eyes

barring on breast

barring on belly

MAKESHIFT NEST
The Great Gray Owl often utilizes hollow snags as nesting sites, besides reusing deserted nests.

OCCURRENCE
In North America, resident across northern forests from Alaska to Quebec, south to Montana and Wyoming. Also resident in Eurasia from Scandinavia to the Russian Far East. Found in taiga, and muskeg, and in fir, spruce, and pine forests.

| Length **24–33in (61–84cm)** | Wingspan **4½ft (1.4m)** | Weight **1½–3¾lb (0.7–1.7kg)** |
| Social **Solitary** | Lifespan **Up to 14 years** | Status **Secure** |

DATE: _____ TIME: _____ LOCATION: _____

Order **Strigiformes**	Family **Strigidae**	Species **Asio otus**

Long-eared Owl

tan patch on outer wing

rusty face disks

dark wrist patch

gray tips

IN FLIGHT

tall "ear" tufts

slender body

finely streaked underparts

ADULT

white eyebrows

dark eye-ring

yellow eye

black bill

mottled upper wings

ADULT

FLIGHT: quick, deep wing beats and long glides; often hovers while hunting.

Although widely distributed across North America, the Long-eared Owl is seldom seen, being secretive and nocturnal. By day, it roosts high up and out of sight in thick cover. Only at nightfall does it fly out to hunt on the wing over open areas, patrolling for small mammals. Its wing feathers, like those of many other owls, have sound-suppressing structures that allow it to fly almost silently, so it can hear the slightest rustle on the ground below.

VOICE Evenly spaced *hooo* notes, continuously repeated, about 3 seconds apart, typically 10–50 per series, sometimes more; barks when alarmed.

NESTING Old stick nests of ravens, crows, magpies, and hawks; 2–7 eggs; 1 brood; March–July.

FEEDING Preys mainly on mice and other small rodents, occasionally small birds.

OWL ON THE WING
In flight, this bird's "ear" tufts are flattened back and not visible, but the face and underwing markings are clearly revealed.

SIMILAR SPECIES

GREAT HORNED OWL see p.229

much larger overall

tufts farther apart

SHORT-EARED OWL see p.238

patterned buffy above

horizontal barring on underparts

pale below

larger overall

OCCURRENCE
Breeds in old nests, especially in dense stands of cottonwood, willow, juniper, and conifers by open areas suitable for hunting. Occasionally uses old nests in tree holes, cliffs, or on ground in dense vegetation; in winter, up to 100 birds in roosts. Northern birds move south for winter; some western birds resident.

Length **14–15½in (35–40cm)**	Wingspan **34–39in (86–98cm)**	Weight **8–15oz (225–425g)**
Social **Solitary/Winter flocks**	Lifespan **Up to 27 years**	Status **Secure**

DATE: _____ TIME: _____ LOCATION: _____

| Order **Strigiformes** | Family **Strigidae** | Species *Asio flammeus* |

Short-eared Owl

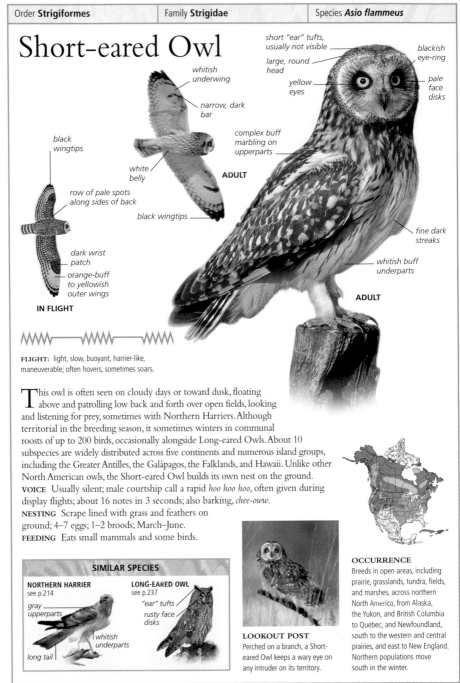

short "ear" tufts, usually not visible

large, round head

whitish underwing

yellow eyes

blackish eye-ring

pale face disks

narrow, dark bar

complex buff marbling on upperparts

ADULT

black wingtips

white belly

row of pale spots along sides of back

black wingtips

fine dark streaks

dark wrist patch

whitish buff underparts

orange-buff to yellowish outer wings

ADULT

IN FLIGHT

FLIGHT: light, slow, buoyant, harrier-like, maneuverable; often hovers, sometimes soars.

This owl is often seen on cloudy days or toward dusk, floating above and patrolling low back and forth over open fields, looking and listening for prey, sometimes with Northern Harriers. Although territorial in the breeding season, it sometimes winters in communal roosts of up to 200 birds, occasionally alongside Long-eared Owls. About 10 subspecies are widely distributed across five continents and numerous island groups, including the Greater Antilles, the Galápagos, the Falklands, and Hawaii. Unlike other North American owls, the Short-eared Owl builds its own nest on the ground.
VOICE Usually silent; male courtship call a rapid *hoo hoo hoo*, often given during display flights; about 16 notes in 3 seconds; also barking, *chee-oww*.
NESTING Scrape lined with grass and feathers on ground; 4–7 eggs; 1–2 broods; March–June.
FEEDING Eats small mammals and some birds.

SIMILAR SPECIES

NORTHERN HARRIER
see p.214

gray upperparts

whitish underparts

long tail

LONG-EARED OWL
see p.237

"ear" tufts

rusty face disks

LOOKOUT POST
Perched on a branch, a Short-eared Owl keeps a wary eye on any intruder on its territory.

OCCURRENCE
Breeds in open areas, including prairie, grasslands, tundra, fields, and marshes, across northern North America, from Alaska, the Yukon, and British Columbia to Quebec, and Newfoundland, south to the western and central prairies, and east to New England. Northern populations move south in the winter.

| Length **13½–16in (34–41cm)** | Wingspan **2¾–3½ft (0.9–1.1m)** | Weight **11–13oz (325–375g)** |
| Social **Solitary/Winter flocks** | Lifespan **Up to 13 years** | Status **Vulnerable** |

DATE: _____ TIME: _____ LOCATION: _____

Order **Strigiformes**	Family **Strigidae**	Species *Aegolius funereus*

Boreal Owl

usually flat-topped head, with fine white spots

yellow eyes

pale bill

ADULT

rounded wings

finely spotted crown

IN FLIGHT

black border around face

white-and-brown streaked underparts

ADULT

short tail

ADULT

FLIGHT: quick, strong wing beats; adept at maneuvering; glides down to attack prey.

The female Boreal Owl is much bigger than the male. Males will mate with two or three females in years when lemmings and other small rodents are abundant. The Boreal Owl roosts on an inconspicuous perch by day and hunts at night, detecting its prey by sound. In the US and Canada, it is elusive and rarely seen since it breeds at high elevations in isolated western mountain ranges. White spotting on the crown, a grayish bill, and a black facial disk distinguish the Boreal Owl from the Northern Saw-whet Owl.

VOICE Prolonged series of whistles, usually increasing in volume and intensity toward the end; also screeches and hisses; can be heard from afar.

NESTING Natural and woodpecker-built tree cavities, also nest boxes; 3–6 eggs; 1 brood; March–July.

FEEDING Mainly eats small mammals, occasionally birds and insects; pounces from elevated perch; sometimes stores prey.

WARM-UP ROUTINE
Boreal Owls are known to use body warmth to thaw frozen prey.

SIMILAR SPECIES

NORTHERN PYGMY-OWL
see p.232

black streaks on belly

longer tail

NORTHERN SAW-WHET OWL
see p.240

lacks dark frame to facial disk

dark bill

OCCURRENCE
Breeds in northern forests from Alaska to Newfoundland and Quebec, south into the Rockies to Colorado and New Mexico. Largely sedentary, but irregular movements take place south of the breeding range, southward to New England and New York.

Length 8½–11in (21–28cm)	Wingspan 21½–24in (54–62cm)	Weight 3⅜–8oz (90–225g)
Social **Solitary**	Lifespan **Up to 11 years**	Status **Secure**

DATE: _____ TIME: _____ LOCATION: _____

| Order **Strigiformes** | Family **Strigidae** | Species *Aegolius acadicus* |

Northern Saw-whet Owl

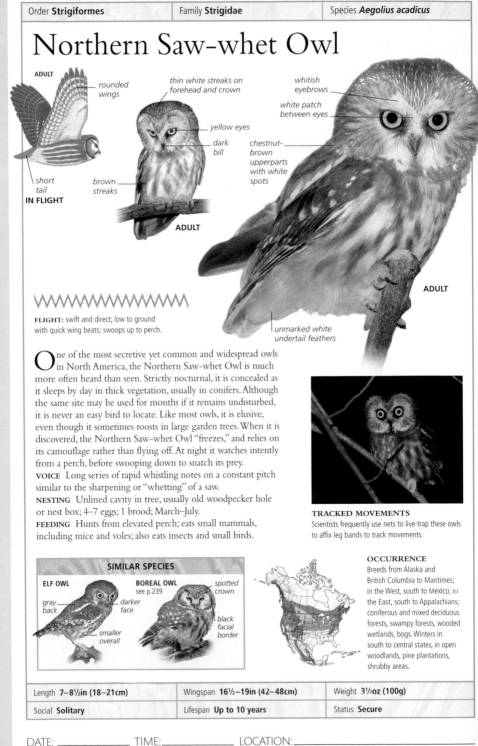

ADULT

rounded wings

thin white streaks on forehead and crown

whitish eyebrows

white patch between eyes

yellow eyes

dark bill

chestnut-brown upperparts with white spots

short tail

brown streaks

IN FLIGHT

ADULT

ADULT

FLIGHT: swift and direct; low to ground with quick wing beats; swoops up to perch.

unmarked white undertail feathers

One of the most secretive yet common and widespread owls in North America, the Northern Saw-whet Owl is much more often heard than seen. Strictly nocturnal, it is concealed as it sleeps by day in thick vegetation, usually in conifers. Although the same site may be used for months if it remains undisturbed, it is never an easy bird to locate. Like most owls, it is elusive, even though it sometimes roosts in large garden trees. When it is discovered, the Northern Saw-whet Owl "freezes," and relies on its camouflage rather than flying off. At night it watches intently from a perch, before swooping down to snatch its prey.

VOICE Long series of rapid whistling notes on a constant pitch similar to the sharpening or "whetting" of a saw.

NESTING Unlined cavity in tree, usually old woodpecker hole or nest box; 4–7 eggs; 1 brood; March–July.

FEEDING Hunts from elevated perch; eats small mammals, including mice and voles; also eats insects and small birds.

TRACKED MOVEMENTS
Scientists frequently use nets to live-trap these owls to affix leg bands to track movements.

SIMILAR SPECIES

ELF OWL
gray back
smaller overall

BOREAL OWL
see p.239
darker face
spotted crown
black facial border

OCCURRENCE
Breeds from Alaska and British Columbia to Maritimes; in the West, south to Mexico; in the East, south to Appalachians; coniferous and mixed deciduous forests, swampy forests, wooded wetlands, bogs. Winters in south to central states, in open woodlands, pine plantations, shrubby areas.

Length 7–8½in (18–21cm)	Wingspan 16½–19in (42–48cm)	Weight 3½oz (100g)
Social **Solitary**	Lifespan **Up to 10 years**	Status **Secure**

DATE: _____ TIME: _____ LOCATION: _____

KINGFISHERS

KINGFISHERS ARE PRIMARILY a tropical family that apparently originated in the Australasian region. There are approximately 90 species of kingfishers in the world, and most have large heads with long, pointed bills, short legs, stubby tails, and bright plumage. Three species are found in North America, but only one, the Belted Kingfisher, is widespread and found in Canada. Like most species of kingfishers, Belted Kingfishers are large-headed and large-billed but have comparatively short legs and toes. Although lacking the array of bright blues, greens, and reds associated with their tropical and European counterparts, Belted Kingfishers are striking birds, distinguished by shaggy head crests, breastbands, and white underparts. The females of the species are more brightly colored than the males, sporting chestnut-colored belly bands. While they also eat amphibians, reptiles, insects, and crustaceans,

Belted Kingfishers are primarily fish-eaters. They will frequent a favorite perch along a waterway for hunting, or hover if no perch is available, and plunge headfirst into the water to catch their prey. After catching a fish, they routinely stun their prey by beating it against a perch before turning the fish around so that it can be eaten head first. Mating pairs dig a burrow in a bank about 3–6ft (1–2m) long. The female lays 6–7 eggs; both adults share the task of incubating the eggs and feeding the young. Parents entice the young to leave the burrow by perching outside with a fish in their bill and calling to them. It usually takes a week for the fledglings to be able to capture live fish. Migration depends on the availability of open water—kingfishers will stay in an area year-round if they have access to fishing grounds.

FISH DINNER
A female, Belted Kingfisher, distinguished by her rust-colored belly band, uses its large bill to catch and hold slippery prey.

DULL MALE
Unlike many birds, the male Belted Kingfisher is not as colorful as the female.

Order **Coraciiformes**	Family **Alcedinidae**	Species ***Megaceryle alcyon***

Belted Kingfisher 🔊

MALE

large head

single blue breastband

barred tail

IN FLIGHT

bluish-gray head with shaggy crest

white collar

bluish-slate upperparts

white belly

MALE

prominent crest

long, thick, powerful bill

chestnut band across belly

chestnut flanks

FEMALE

double crest

white collar

single dark breastband

JUVENILE MALE

I ts stocky body, double-pointed crest, large head, and contrasting white collar distinguish the Belted Kingfisher from other species in its range. This kingfisher's loud and far-carrying, angry rattles are heard more often than the bird is seen. Interestingly, it is one of the few birds in North America in which the female is more colorful than the male. The Belted Kingfisher can be found in a large variety of aquatic habitats, both coastal and inland, vigorously defending its territory, all year round.

VOICE Harsh mechanical rattle given in flight or from a perch; sometimes emits screams or trill-like warble during breeding.

NESTING Unlined chamber in subterranean burrow 3–6ft (1–2m) deep, excavated in earthen bank usually over water, but sometimes in ditches, sand, or gravel pits; 6–7 eggs; 1 brood; March–July.

FEEDING Plunge-dives from branches or wires to catch a wide variety of fish near the surface, including sticklebacks and trout; also takes crustaceans, such as crayfish.

FLIGHT: strongly flaps its wings and then glides after two or three beats; frequently hovers.

SIMILAR SPECIES

RINGED KINGFISHER ♂

larger overall

chestnut belly

CATCH OF THE DAY
The female's chestnut belly band and flanks are clearly visible here as she perches with her catch.

OCCURRENCE
Breeds and winters around clear, open waters of streams, rivers, lakes, estuaries, and protected marine shorelines, where perches are available and prey is visible. Avoids water with emergent vegetation. Northern populations migrate south to Mexico, Central America, and the West Indies.

Length **11–14in (28–35cm)**	Wingspan **19–23in (48–58cm)**	Weight **5–6oz (150–175g)**
Social **Solitary**	Lifespan **At least 4 years**	Status **Secure**

DATE: _____ TIME: _____ LOCATION: _____

WOODPECKERS

WOODPECKERS ARE FOUND throughout North America except in the tundra. They are adapted to gripping upright tree trunks, using the tail as a support or prop. Most woodpeckers have two toes facing forward and two facing backward for an extra-strong grip on wooden surfaces. Unlike nuthatches, they do not perch upside-down but can cling to the underside of angled branches. They have striking plumage patterns with simple, bold colors. Many proclaim their territory by instrumental rather than vocal means, hammering the bill against a hard surface—even metal—to give a brief but rapid "drumroll." The bill is also used for chipping into bark and excavating deep nestholes in solid wood. Sapsuckers make rows or rings of small holes on tree trunks, allowing sap to ooze freely: they feed on the sap and also on the insects that are attracted to it. Some species of woodpeckers, especially flickers, feed on the ground, probing inside ant nests for larvae and catching them with their long, sticky tongues.

BALANCING ACT
The Yellow-bellied Sapsucker rests its stiff tail against a tree to maintain its balance.

RED ALERT
With its crimson head, the Red-headed Woodpecker is an instantly recognizable bird in North America.

COMMON BIRD
The Northern Flicker can be found across the entire North American continent.

| Order **Piciformes** | Family **Picidae** | Species ***Melanerpes lewis*** |

Lewis's Woodpecker

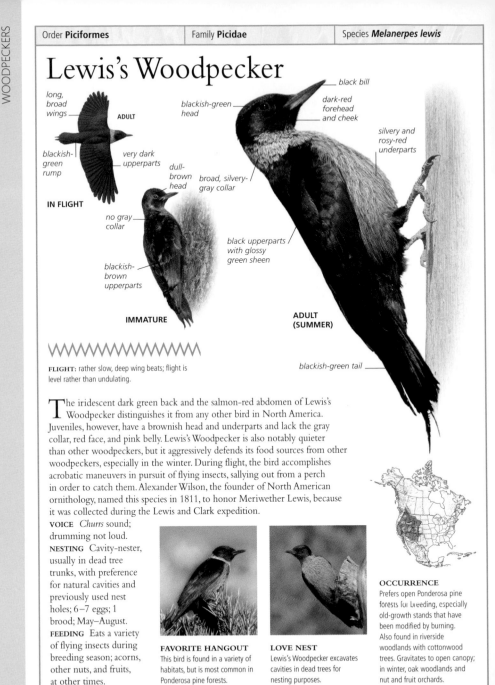

long, broad wings — **ADULT**

blackish-green head

black bill

dark-red forehead and cheek

silvery and rosy-red underparts

blackish-green rump

very dark upperparts

dull-brown head

broad, silvery-gray collar

IN FLIGHT

no gray collar

black upperparts with glossy green sheen

blackish-brown upperparts

IMMATURE

ADULT (SUMMER)

FLIGHT: rather slow, deep wing beats; flight is level rather than undulating.

blackish-green tail —

The iridescent dark green back and the salmon-red abdomen of Lewis's Woodpecker distinguishes it from any other bird in North America. Juveniles, however, have a brownish head and underparts and lack the gray collar, red face, and pink belly. Lewis's Woodpecker is also notably quieter than other woodpeckers, but it aggressively defends its food sources from other woodpeckers, especially in the winter. During flight, the bird accomplishes acrobatic maneuvers in pursuit of flying insects, sallying out from a perch in order to catch them. Alexander Wilson, the founder of North American ornithology, named this species in 1811, to honor Meriwether Lewis, because it was collected during the Lewis and Clark expedition.

VOICE *Churrs* sound; drumming not loud.

NESTING Cavity-nester, usually in dead tree trunks, with preference for natural cavities and previously used nest holes; 6–7 eggs; 1 brood; May–August.

FEEDING Eats a variety of flying insects during breeding season; acorns, other nuts, and fruits, at other times.

FAVORITE HANGOUT
This bird is found in a variety of habitats, but is most common in Ponderosa pine forests.

LOVE NEST
Lewis's Woodpecker excavates cavities in dead trees for nesting purposes.

OCCURRENCE
Prefers open Ponderosa pine forests for breeding, especially old-growth stands that have been modified by burning. Also found in riverside woodlands with cottonwood trees. Gravitates to open canopy; in winter, oak woodlands and nut and fruit orchards.

| Length **10–11in (25–28cm)** | Wingspan **19–20in (48–51cm)** | Weight **3¼–5oz (90–150g)** |
| Social **Solitary** | Lifespan **Unknown** | Status **Threatened** |

DATE: _____ TIME: _____ LOCATION: _____

Order **Piciformes**	Family **Picidae**	Species *Melanerpes erythrocephalus*

Red-headed Woodpecker

white rump

red head

ADULT

IN FLIGHT

bright-red hood

bluish-gray bill

upperparts black with bluish sheen

narrow black "necklace"

ADULT

brownish head

wing feathers white with black barring

IMMATURE

white wing feathers

The Red-headed Woodpecker is the only member of this family that has a completely red head, and is therefore easy to identify. Unlike most other woodpecker species, it forages for food—both insects and nuts—and stores it for eating at a later time. It is one of the most skilled flycatchers in the woodpecker family. Its numbers have declined, largely because of the destruction of its habitat, especially the removal of dead trees in urban and rural areas, and clearing and cutting of trees for firewood in rural areas. The Red-headed Woodpecker is a truly North American bird, not extending south of the Rio Grande.

VOICE Primary call an extremely harsh and loud *churr*, also produces breeding call and alarm; no song; active drummer.

NESTING Excavates cavity in dead wood; 3–5 eggs; 1–2 broods; May–August.

FEEDING Forages in flight, on ground, and in trees; feeds on a variety of insects, spiders, nuts, seeds, berries, and fruit; in rare cases, small mammals, such as mice.

WORK IN PROGRESS
The Red-headed Woodpecker excavates its breeding cavities in tree trunks and stumps.

FLIGHT: strong flapping; undulation not as marked as in other woodpecker species.

OCCURRENCE
Breeds in a variety of habitats, especially open deciduous woodlands, including riverine areas, orchards, municipal parks, agricultural areas, forest edges, and forests affected by fire. Uses the same habitats during the winter as in the breeding season.

Length **8½–9½in (22–24cm)**	Wingspan **16–18in (41–46cm)**	Weight **2–3oz (55–85g)**
Social **Solitary**	Lifespan **At least 10 years**	Status **Endangered**

Order **Piciformes**	Family **Picidae**	Species *Melanerpes carolinus*

Red-bellied Woodpecker 🔊

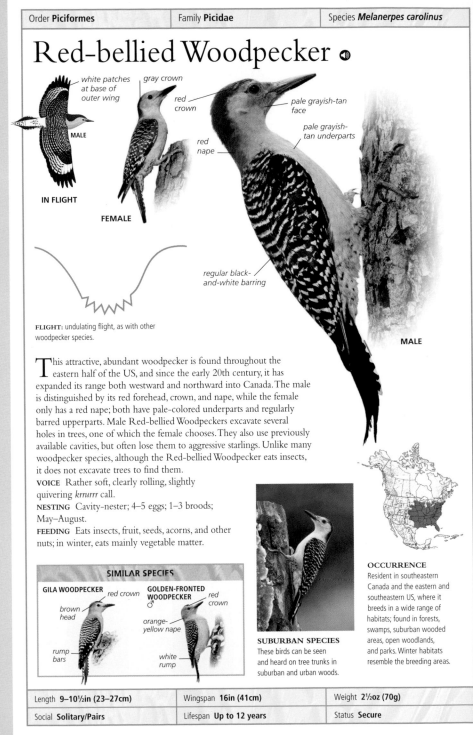

white patches at base of outer wing

gray crown

MALE

IN FLIGHT

red crown

red nape

FEMALE

pale grayish-tan face

pale grayish-tan underparts

regular black-and-white barring

MALE

FLIGHT: undulating flight, as with other woodpecker species.

This attractive, abundant woodpecker is found throughout the eastern half of the US, and since the early 20th century, it has expanded its range both westward and northward into Canada. The male is distinguished by its red forehead, crown, and nape, while the female only has a red nape; both have pale-colored underparts and regularly barred upperparts. Male Red-bellied Woodpeckers excavate several holes in trees, one of which the female chooses. They also use previously available cavities, but often lose them to aggressive starlings. Unlike many woodpecker species, although the Red-bellied Woodpecker eats insects, it does not excavate trees to find them.

VOICE Rather soft, clearly rolling, slightly quivering *krrurrr* call.

NESTING Cavity-nester; 4–5 eggs; 1–3 broods; May–August.

FEEDING Eats insects, fruit, seeds, acorns, and other nuts; in winter, eats mainly vegetable matter.

SIMILAR SPECIES

GILA WOODPECKER

red crown

brown head

rump bars

GOLDEN-FRONTED WOODPECKER ♂

red crown

orange-yellow nape

white rump

SUBURBAN SPECIES
These birds can be seen and heard on tree trunks in suburban and urban woods.

OCCURRENCE
Resident in southeastern Canada and the eastern and southeastern US, where it breeds in a wide range of habitats; found in forests, swamps, suburban wooded areas, open woodlands, and parks. Winter habitats resemble the breeding areas.

Length **9–10½in (23–27cm)**	Wingspan **16in (41cm)**	Weight **2½oz (70g)**
Social **Solitary/Pairs**	Lifespan **Up to 12 years**	Status **Secure**

DATE: _____ TIME: _____ LOCATION: _____

Order **Piciformes**	Family **Picidae**	Species *Sphyrapicus thyroideus*

Williamson's Sapsucker

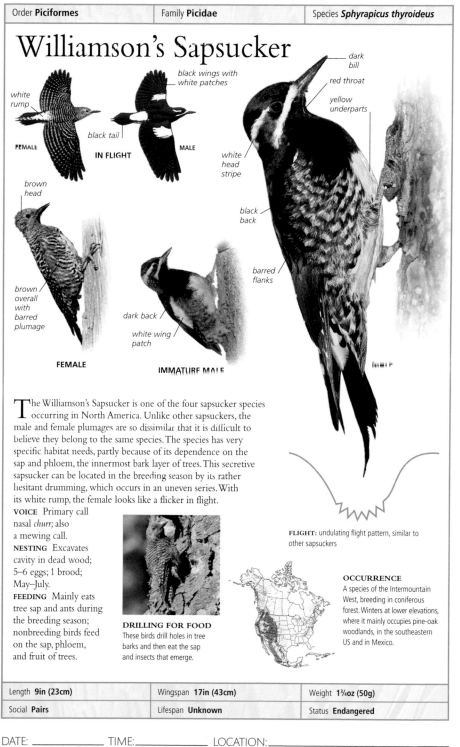

white rump

FEMALE

black wings with white patches

black tail

MALE

IN FLIGHT

brown head

brown overall with barred plumage

FEMALE

dark back

white wing patch

IMMATURE MALE

dark bill

red throat

yellow underparts

white head stripe

black back

barred flanks

MALE

The Williamson's Sapsucker is one of the four sapsucker species occurring in North America. Unlike other sapsuckers, the male and female plumages are so dissimilar that it is difficult to believe they belong to the same species. The species has very specific habitat needs, partly because of its dependence on the sap and phloem, the innermost bark layer of trees. This secretive sapsucker can be located in the breeding season by its rather hesitant drumming, which occurs in an uneven series. With its white rump, the female looks like a flicker in flight.

VOICE Primary call nasal *churr;* also a mewing call.

NESTING Excavates cavity in dead wood; 5–6 eggs; 1 brood; May–July.

FEEDING Mainly eats tree sap and ants during the breeding season; nonbreeding birds feed on the sap, phloem, and fruit of trees.

DRILLING FOR FOOD
These birds drill holes in tree barks and then eat the sap and insects that emerge.

FLIGHT: undulating flight pattern, similar to other sapsuckers

OCCURRENCE
A species of the Intermountain West, breeding in coniferous forest. Winters at lower elevations, where it mainly occupies pine-oak woodlands, in the southeastern US and in Mexico.

Length **9in (23cm)**	Wingspan **17in (43cm)**	Weight **1¾oz (50g)**
Social **Pairs**	Lifespan **Unknown**	Status **Endangered**

DATE: _____ TIME: _____ LOCATION: _____

| Order **Piciformes** | Family **Picidae** | Species *Sphyrapicus varius* |

Yellow-bellied Sapsucker 🔊

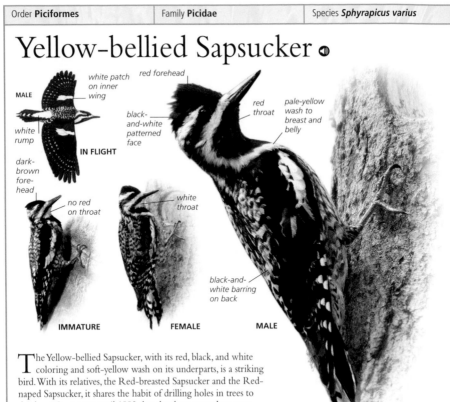

MALE

white patch on inner wing

red forehead

black-and-white patterned face

red throat

pale-yellow wash to breast and belly

white rump

IN FLIGHT

dark-brown fore-head

no red on throat

white throat

black-and-white barring on back

IMMATURE   **FEMALE**   **MALE**

The Yellow-bellied Sapsucker, with its red, black, and white coloring and soft-yellow wash on its underparts, is a striking bird. With its relatives, the Red-breasted Sapsucker and the Red-naped Sapsucker, it shares the habit of drilling holes in trees to drink sap. It was not until 1983 that the three sapsuckers were allocated to separate species. Sapsuckers are the only wholly migratory woodpeckers; female Yellow-bellied Sapsuckers move farther south than males.

VOICE Primary call a mewing *wheer-wheer-wheer*.

NESTING Cavities in dead trees; 5–6 eggs; 1 brood; May–June.

FEEDING Drinks sap; eats ants and other small insects; feeds on the inner bark of trees, also a variety of fruit.

FLIGHT: typical woodpecker, undulating flight pattern with intermittent flapping and gliding.

STRIKING SPECIES
The Yellow-bellied Sapsucker's white rump and black-and-white forked tail are clearly evident here.

SIMILAR SPECIES

WILLIAMSON'S SAPSUCKER ♀
see p.247

brown head

more extensive barring on back

RED-NAPED SAPSUCKER
see p.249

red patch on forehead

two rows of white bars on back

OCCURRENCE
Breeds in eastern Alaska, Canada, and south to the Appalachians. Prefers either deciduous forests or mixed deciduous-coniferous forests; prefers young forests. In winter, it is found in open wooded areas in southeastern states, Caribbean islands, and Central America.

Length **8–9in (20–23cm)**	Wingspan **16–18in (41–46cm)**	Weight **1¾oz (50g)**
Social **Solitary/Pairs**	Lifespan **Up to 7 years**	Status **Secure**

DATE: _____ TIME: _____ LOCATION: _____

Order **Piciformes**	Family **Picidae**	Species *Sphyrapicus nuchalis*

Red-naped Sapsucker

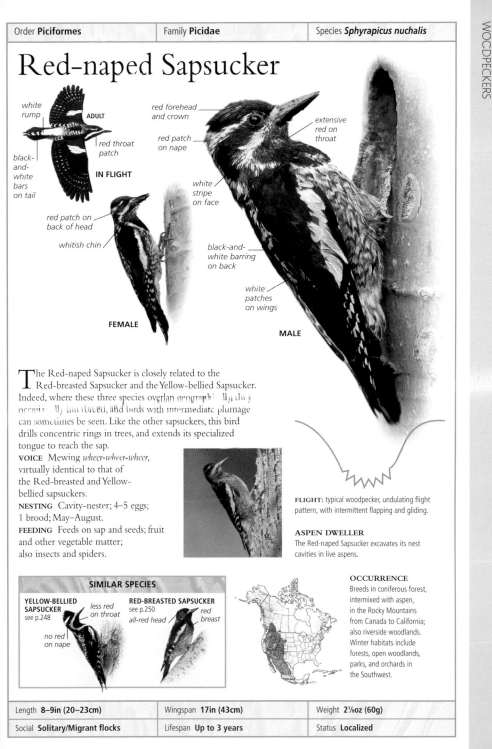

white rump

ADULT

red throat patch

black-and-white bars on tail

IN FLIGHT

red forehead and crown

red patch on nape

extensive red on throat

white stripe on face

red patch on back of head

whitish chin

black-and-white barring on back

white patches on wings

FEMALE

MALE

The Red-naped Sapsucker is closely related to the Red-breasted Sapsucker and the Yellow-bellied Sapsucker. Indeed, where these three species overlap geographically, they occur. If introduced, and birds with intermediate plumage can sometimes be seen. Like the other sapsuckers, this bird drills concentric rings in trees, and extends its specialized tongue to reach the sap.

VOICE Mewing *wheer-wheer-wheer*, virtually identical to that of the Red-breasted and Yellow-bellied sapsuckers.

NESTING Cavity-nester; 4–5 eggs; 1 brood; May–August.

FEEDING Feeds on sap and seeds; fruit and other vegetable matter; also insects and spiders.

FLIGHT: typical woodpecker, undulating flight pattern, with intermittent flapping and gliding.

ASPEN DWELLER
The Red-naped Sapsucker excavates its nest cavities in live aspens.

SIMILAR SPECIES	
YELLOW-BELLIED SAPSUCKER see p.248 — less red on throat, no red on nape	**RED-BREASTED SAPSUCKER** see p.250 — all-red head, red breast

OCCURRENCE
Breeds in coniferous forest, intermixed with aspen, in the Rocky Mountains from Canada to California; also riverside woodlands. Winter habitats include forests, open woodlands, parks, and orchards in the Southwest.

Length **8–9in (20–23cm)**	Wingspan **17in (43cm)**	Weight **2⅛oz (60g)**
Social **Solitary/Migrant flocks**	Lifespan **Up to 3 years**	Status **Localized**

DATE: _____ TIME: _____ LOCATION: _____

Order **Piciformes**	Family **Picidae**	Species *Sphyrapicus ruber*

Red-breasted Sapsucker

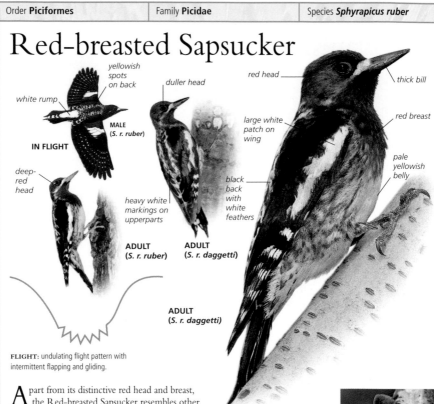

yellowish spots on back

white rump

**MALE
(S. r. ruber)**

IN FLIGHT

duller head

red head

thick bill

deep-red head

large white patch on wing

red breast

heavy white markings on upperparts

black back with white feathers

pale yellowish belly

**ADULT
(S. r. ruber)**

**ADULT
(S. r. daggetti)**

**ADULT
(S. r. daggetti)**

FLIGHT: undulating flight pattern with intermittent flapping and gliding.

A part from its distinctive red head and breast, the Red-breasted Sapsucker resembles other sapsuckers—so much so that the closely related Red-breasted, Red-naped, and Yellow-bellied Sapsuckers were once all considered to belong to the same species. Like its relatives, the Red-breasted Sapsucker drills holes in tree trunks to extract sap. Other birds, and mammals such as squirrels and bats, obtain food from these holes. The northern form, *S. r. ruber*, occurs from Alaska to Oregon, and has a back lightly marked with gold spots and a brightly coloredsss head. Its southern counterpart, *S. r. daggetti*, has a back more heavily marked with white.

VOICE Call reminiscent of a mewing cat; normally does not vocalize outside the breeding season.

NESTING Excavates cavity in deciduous trees, such as aspen and willow, but will also nest in conifers if deciduous trees are not available; 4–5 eggs; 1 brood; May–July.

FEEDING Mainly drills for sap from a number of plants; also eats the insects that have become trapped in the sap.

RED-HEADED DRILLER
Red-breasted Sapsuckers drill holes in trees to drink sap and eat the insects attracted to it.

SIMILAR SPECIES

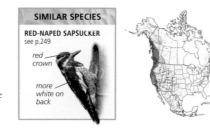

RED-NAPED SAPSUCKER
see p.249

red crown

more white on back

OCCURRENCE
Breeds in a wide range of habitats, including coniferous forests, but may also select deciduous forests and habitats along rivers. Prefers areas with dead trees. A partial migrant, it winters within its breeding range but also moves south, as far as northern Baja California.

Length **8–9in (20–23cm)**	Wingspan **15–16in (38–41cm)**	Weight **2oz (55g)**
Social **Solitary**	Lifespan **2–3 years**	Status **Localized**

DATE: _____ TIME: _____ LOCATION: _____

Order **Piciformes**	Family **Picidae**	Species **Picoides dorsalis**

American Three-toed Woodpecker

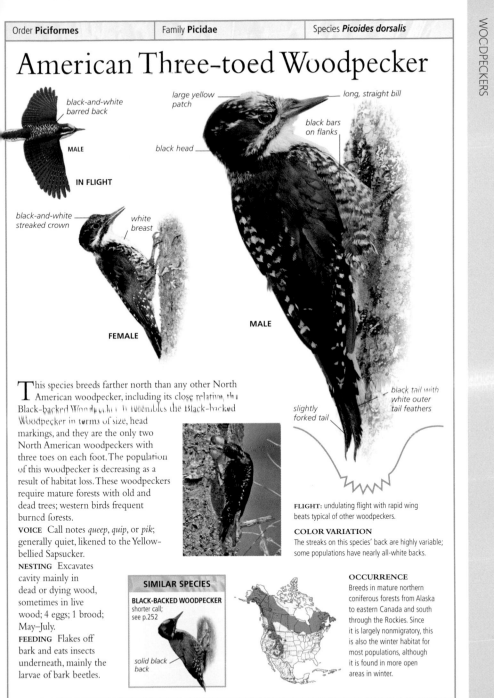

black-and-white
barred back

MALE

IN FLIGHT

large yellow
patch

black head

long, straight bill

black bars
on flanks

black-and-white
streaked crown

white
breast

FEMALE

MALE

black tail with
white outer
tail feathers

slightly
forked tail

This species breeds farther north than any other North American woodpecker, including its close relative, the Black-backed Woodpecker. It resembles the Black-backed Woodpecker in terms of size, head markings, and they are the only two North American woodpeckers with three toes on each foot. The population of this woodpecker is decreasing as a result of habitat loss. These woodpeckers require mature forests with old and dead trees; western birds frequent burned forests.

VOICE Call notes *queep*, *quip*, or *pik*; generally quiet, likened to the Yellow-bellied Sapsucker.

NESTING Excavates cavity mainly in dead or dying wood, sometimes in live wood; 4 eggs; 1 brood; May–July.

FEEDING Flakes off bark and eats insects underneath, mainly the larvae of bark beetles.

FLIGHT: undulating flight with rapid wing beats typical of other woodpeckers.

COLOR VARIATION
The streaks on this species' back are highly variable; some populations have nearly all-white backs.

SIMILAR SPECIES

BLACK-BACKED WOODPECKER
shorter call;
see p.252

solid black
back

OCCURRENCE
Breeds in mature northern coniferous forests from Alaska to eastern Canada and south through the Rockies. Since it is largely nonmigratory, this is also the winter habitat for most populations, although it is found in more open areas in winter.

Length **8–9in (20–23cm)**	Wingspan **15in (38cm)**	Weight **2¼–2½oz (65–70g)**
Social **Solitary/Pairs**	Lifespan **Unknown**	Status **Vulnerable**

DATE: _____ TIME: _____ LOCATION: _____

251

| Order **Piciformes** | Family **Picidae** | Species **Picoides arcticus** |

Black-backed Woodpecker

white spots on outer wings

long black bill

yellow cap on black head

white stripe on head

white underparts

black back

MALE

IN FLIGHT

black cap

black back and wings

MALE

FEMALE

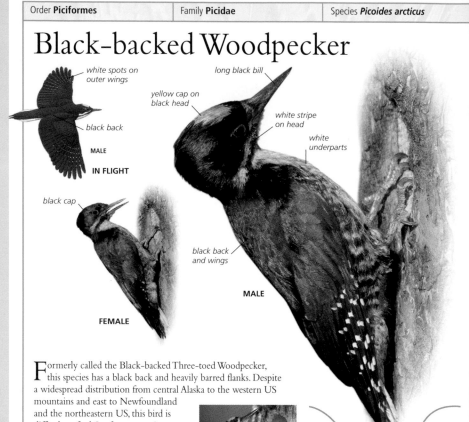

Formerly called the Black-backed Three-toed Woodpecker, this species has a black back and heavily barred flanks. Despite a widespread distribution from central Alaska to the western US mountains and east to Newfoundland and the northeastern US, this bird is difficult to find. It often occurs in areas with burned forest, eating wood-boring beetles that occur after outbreaks of fire. This diet is very restrictive, and the species is greatly affected by forestry programs, which prevent the spread of fire. Although it overlaps geographically with the American Three-toed Woodpecker, the two are rarely found together in the same locality.

VOICE Main call a single *pik*.

NESTING Cavity excavated in tree; 3–4 eggs; 1 brood; May–July.

FEEDING Eats beetles, especially larvae of wood-boring beetles, by flaking off bark.

FLIGHT: typical undulating flight of woodpeckers.

FREQUENT MOVING
This bird excavates a new nest cavity each year, rarely returning in subsequent years.

SIMILAR SPECIES

AMERICAN THREE-TOED WOODPECKER
see p.251

black-and-white barred upperparts

OCCURRENCE
Inhabitant of northerly and mountainous coniferous forests that require fire for renewal. Breeding occurs soon after sites are burned as new colonies are attracted to the habitat. Occasional irruptive movements into the Great Lakes region and the Maritimes in response to outbreaks of wood-boring beetles.

| Length **9–9½in (23–24cm)** | Wingspan **15–16in (38–41cm)** | Weight **2½oz (70g)** |
| Social **Pairs** | Lifespan **Up to 10 years** | Status **Secure** |

DATE: _____ TIME: _____ LOCATION: _____

Order **Piciformes**	Family **Picidae**	Species *Dryobates pubescens*

Downy Woodpecker 🔊

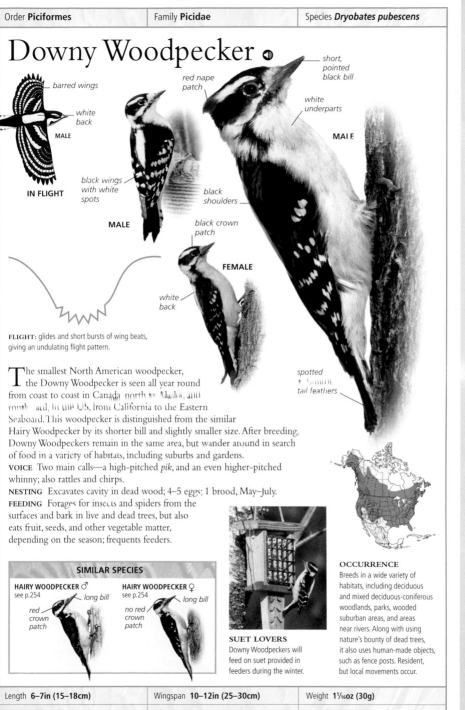

barred wings

white back

MALE

IN FLIGHT

red nape patch

black wings with white spots

MALE

black crown patch

FEMALE

white back

short, pointed black bill

white underparts

MALE

black shoulders

spotted tail feathers

FLIGHT: glides and short bursts of wing beats, giving an undulating flight pattern.

The smallest North American woodpecker, the Downy Woodpecker is seen all year round from coast to coast in Canada north to Alaska, and south and, in the US, from California to the Eastern Seaboard. This woodpecker is distinguished from the similar Hairy Woodpecker by its shorter bill and slightly smaller size. After breeding, Downy Woodpeckers remain in the same area, but wander around in search of food in a variety of habitats, including suburbs and gardens.

VOICE Two main calls—a high-pitched *pik*, and an even higher-pitched whinny; also rattles and chirps.

NESTING Excavates cavity in dead wood; 4–5 eggs; 1 brood, May–July.

FEEDING Forages for insects and spiders from the surfaces and bark in live and dead trees, but also eats fruit, seeds, and other vegetable matter, depending on the season; frequents feeders.

SIMILAR SPECIES

HAIRY WOODPECKER ♂
see p.254
long bill
red crown patch

HAIRY WOODPECKER ♀
see p.254
long bill
no red crown patch

SUET LOVERS
Downy Woodpeckers will feed on suet provided in feeders during the winter.

OCCURRENCE
Breeds in a wide variety of habitats, including deciduous and mixed deciduous-coniferous woodlands, parks, wooded suburban areas, and areas near rivers. Along with using nature's bounty of dead trees, it also uses human-made objects, such as fence posts. Resident, but local movements occur.

Length **6–7in (15–18cm)**	Wingspan **10–12in (25–30cm)**	Weight **1¹⁄₁₆oz (30g)**
Social **Solitary/Flocks**	Lifespan **Up to 11 years**	Status **Secure**

DATE: _____ TIME:_____ LOCATION:_____

| Order **Piciformes** | Family **Picidae** | Species *Dryobates villosus* |

Hairy Woodpecker 🔊

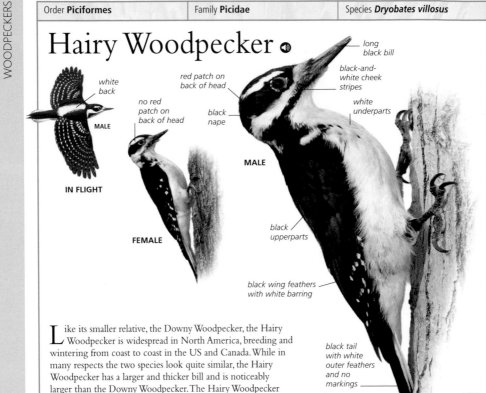

IN FLIGHT

white back

MALE

no red patch on back of head

red patch on back of head

black nape

FEMALE

MALE

long black bill

black-and-white cheek stripes

white underparts

black upperparts

black wing feathers with white barring

black tail with white outer feathers and no markings

Like its smaller relative, the Downy Woodpecker, the Hairy Woodpecker is widespread in North America, breeding and wintering from coast to coast in the US and Canada. While in many respects the two species look quite similar, the Hairy Woodpecker has a larger and thicker bill and is noticeably larger than the Downy Woodpecker. The Hairy Woodpecker is a bird of forests, where it uses live tree trunks for nesting and foraging.

VOICE Call a bold, grating, sharp *Peek,* similar to that of the Downy Woodpecker, but lower in pitch, and louder. Drumming a rather loud, even series of taps.

NESTING Excavates cavity in live trees; 4 eggs; 1 brood; May–July.

FEEDING Eats mainly insects and their larvae; also nuts and seeds; frequents bird feeders.

FLIGHT: undulating; short glides alternating with wing beats.

HOME SWEET HOME
The Hairy Woodpecker is generally found in forests and prefers mature woodland areas, using both deciduous and coniferous trees.

OCCURRENCE
Breeds primarily in forests, both deciduous and coniferous, but also in more open woodlands, swamps, suburban parks, and wooded areas. Resident in North America all year round, though in the far north of its range it may move south for the winter.

SIMILAR SPECIES

DOWNY WOODPECKER ♂
see p.253

shorter bill

white markings on outer wing feathers

DOWNY WOODPECKER ♀
see p.253

shorter bill

white markings on outer wing feathers

| Length **9–9½in (23–24cm)** | Wingspan **15–16in (38–41cm)** | Weight **2½oz (70g)** |
| Social **Solitary/Winter flocks** | Lifespan **At least 16 years** | Status **Secure** |

DATE: _____ TIME:_____ LOCATION:_____

Order **Piciformes**	Family **Picidae**	Species **Colaptes auratus**

Northern Flicker 🔊

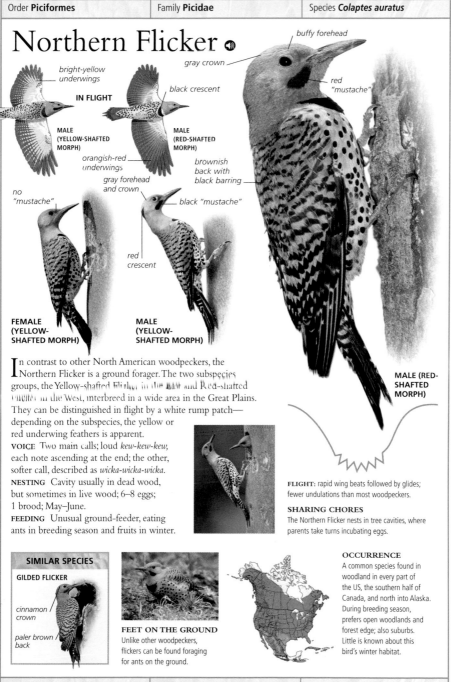

buffy forehead

gray crown

red "mustache"

bright-yellow underwings

IN FLIGHT

black crescent

MALE (YELLOW-SHAFTED MORPH)

MALE (RED-SHAFTED MORPH)

orangish-red underwings

gray forehead and crown

brownish back with black barring

no "mustache"

black "mustache"

red crescent

FEMALE (YELLOW-SHAFTED MORPH)

MALE (YELLOW-SHAFTED MORPH)

MALE (RED-SHAFTED MORPH)

In contrast to other North American woodpeckers, the Northern Flicker is a ground forager. The two subspecies groups, the Yellow-shafted Flicker in the east and Red-shafted Flicker in the West, interbreed in a wide area in the Great Plains. They can be distinguished in flight by a white rump patch—depending on the subspecies, the yellow or red underwing feathers is apparent.

VOICE Two main calls; loud *kew-kew-kew*, each note ascending at the end; the other, softer call, described as *wicka-wicka-wicka*.

NESTING Cavity usually in dead wood, but sometimes in live wood; 6–8 eggs; 1 brood; May–June.

FEEDING Unusual ground-feeder, eating ants in breeding season and fruits in winter.

FLIGHT: rapid wing beats followed by glides; fewer undulations than most woodpeckers.

SHARING CHORES
The Northern Flicker nests in tree cavities, where parents take turns incubating eggs.

OCCURRENCE
A common species found in woodland in every part of the US, the southern half of Canada, and north into Alaska. During breeding season, prefers open woodlands and forest edge; also suburbs. Little is known about this bird's winter habitat.

SIMILAR SPECIES

GILDED FLICKER

cinnamon crown

paler brown back

FEET ON THE GROUND
Unlike other woodpeckers, flickers can be found foraging for ants on the ground.

Length **12–13in (31–33cm)**	Wingspan **19–21in (48–53cm)**	Weight **4oz (125g)**
Social **Solitary**	Lifespan **9 years**	Status **Secure**

DATE: _____ TIME: _____ LOCATION: _____

| Order **Piciformes** | Family **Picidae** | Species ***Dryocopus pileatus*** |

Pileated Woodpecker 🔊

IN FLIGHT

large overall

MALE

large white patch

long tail

red crest

black forehead

black "mustache"

red crest

FEMALE

red forehead

red crest

large black bill

white chin

scarlet "mustache"

black back

white patch on wing

MALE

The largest woodpecker in North America, the Pileated Woodpecker is instantly recognizable by its spectacular large, tapering bright-red crest. A mated pair of Pileated Woodpeckers defends their breeding territory all year—even if one bird dies, the other does not desert the territory. Indeed, a pair may live in the same dead tree every year, but will hammer out a new nest cavity with their powerful bills each season. Their abandoned squarish nest cavities created by the Pileated Woodpecker are sometimes reused by other birds, and occasionally inhabited by mammals.

VOICE Two primary calls, both high-pitched and quite loud— *yuck-yuck-yuck*, and *yuka-yuka-yuka*.

NESTING Excavates cavity, usually in dead tree; 3–5 eggs; 1 brood; May–July.

FEEDING Bores deep into trees and peels off large strips of bark to extract carpenter ants and beetle larvae; also digs on ground and on fallen logs, and opportunistically eats fruit and nuts.

EASY PICKINGS
Pileated woodpeckers occasionally visit feeders to supplement their diet.

FLIGHT: slow, deep wing beats, with occasional undulation when wings briefly folded.

OCCURRENCE
Resident throughout eastern North America, across central Canada to the Pacific Northwest, in deciduous and coniferous forest and woodlands; also found in swampy areas. In some areas, chooses young forests with dead trees but in other places, old-growth conifers.

| Length **16–18in (41–46cm)** | Wingspan **26–30in (66–76cm)** | Weight **10oz (275g)** |
| Social **Pairs** | Lifespan **Up to 10 years** | Status **Secure** |

DATE: _____ TIME: _____ LOCATION: _____

FALCONS

Recently separated from other diurnal birds of prey, such as eagles and hawks, falcons and caracaras form a distinctive group of raptors. Caracaras are found in the New World but not in Canada, while falcons have a worldwide distribution, with a much larger number of species.

Falcons are known for their speed and agility inflight, but paradoxically, spend long periods perched on a rock ledge or tree branch. The larger, bird-hunting species, such as the Peregrine Falcon, draw attention to their presence by creating panic among other birds when they fly over, ready to chase prey as large as ducks and pigeons. Falcons include birds that catch and eat insects on the wing, those that hover in one place searching for small prey below, and yet others that are more dramatic aerial hunters. Falcons in dramatic pursuits, or in high-speed "stoops" from above, seize birds up to their own size. Large species, such as the Gyrfalcon, may kill prey bigger than themselves. Falcons are distinguished from bird-eating hawks belonging to the genus *Accipiter* by their dark eyes. They also have a notch, or tooth, on the upper mandible, possibly to help them to dispatch and dismember their prey. Unlike the Accipiters, they do not build nests, but many falcons use abandoned nests of other birds and some lay eggs on a bare ledge or in an unlined cavity.

ARCTIC GIANT
The Arctic-dwelling Gyrfalcon is the largest of the falcons.

PRECISION LANDING
A Peregrine Falcon swoops down to settle on the branch, thrusting out its feet to absorb the shock of landing.

| Order **Falconiformes** | Family **Falconidae** | Species *Falco sparverius* |

American Kestrel 🔊

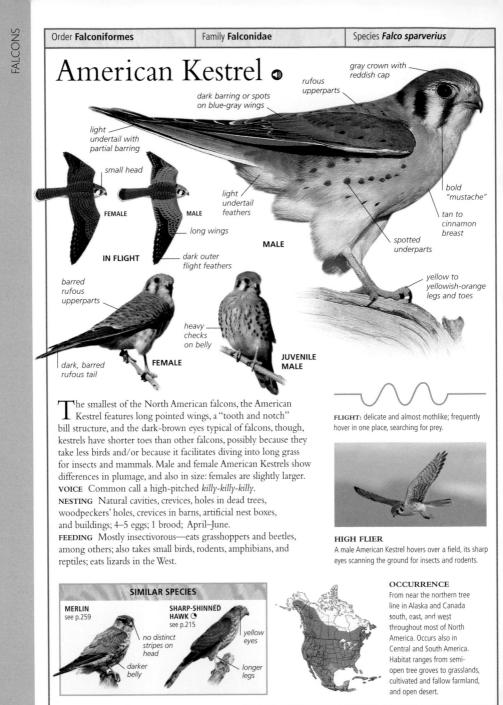

gray crown with reddish cap

rufous upperparts

dark barring or spots on blue-gray wings

light undertail with partial barring

small head

light undertail feathers

FEMALE   **MALE**

long wings

IN FLIGHT

dark outer flight feathers

barred rufous upperparts

bold "mustache"

tan to cinnamon breast

spotted underparts

MALE

heavy checks on belly

dark, barred rufous tail

FEMALE

JUVENILE MALE

yellow to yellowish-orange legs and toes

The smallest of the North American falcons, the American Kestrel features long pointed wings, a "tooth and notch" bill structure, and the dark-brown eyes typical of falcons, though, kestrels have shorter toes than other falcons, possibly because they take less birds and/or because it facilitates diving into long grass for insects and mammals. Male and female American Kestrels show differences in plumage, and also in size: females are slightly larger.
VOICE Common call a high-pitched *killy-killy-killy*.
NESTING Natural cavities, crevices, holes in dead trees, woodpeckers' holes, crevices in barns, artificial nest boxes, and buildings; 4–5 eggs; 1 brood; April–June.
FEEDING Mostly insectivorous—eats grasshoppers and beetles, among others; also takes small birds, rodents, amphibians, and reptiles; eats lizards in the West.

FLIGHT: delicate and almost mothlike; frequently hover in one place, searching for prey.

HIGH FLIER
A male American Kestrel hovers over a field, its sharp eyes scanning the ground for insects and rodents.

SIMILAR SPECIES

MERLIN
see p.259

SHARP-SHINNED HAWK 🕓
see p.215

no distinct stripes on head

darker belly

yellow eyes

longer legs

OCCURRENCE
From near the northern tree line in Alaska and Canada south, east, and west throughout most of North America. Occurs also in Central and South America. Habitat ranges from semi-open tree groves to grasslands, cultivated and fallow farmland, and open desert.

| Length **9in (23cm)** | Wingspan **22in (56cm)** | Weight **3½–4oz (100–125g)** |
| Social **Family groups** | Lifespan **10–15 years** | Status **Secure** |

DATE: _____ TIME: _____ LOCATION: _____

| Order **Falconiformes** | Family **Falconidae** | Species *Falco columbarius* |

Merlin

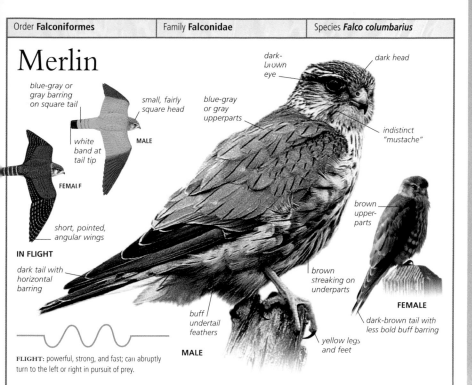

blue-gray or gray barring on square tail

small, fairly square head

MALE

white band at tail tip

FEMALE

short, pointed, angular wings

IN FLIGHT

dark tail with horizontal barring

dark-brown eye

dark head

blue-gray or gray upperparts

indistinct "mustache"

brown upper-parts

brown streaking on underparts

FEMALE

dark-brown tail with less bold buff barring

buff undertail feathers

MALE

yellow legs and feet

FLIGHT: powerful, strong, and fast; can abruptly turn to the left or right in pursuit of prey.

Merlins are small, fast-flying falcons that were formerly known as "pigeon hawks" because their shape and flight are similar to those strong fliers. Merlins can overtake and capture a wide variety of prey, but mostly small birds. They can turn on a dime and use their long, thin middle toes, typical of falcons, to pluck birds from the air after launching a direct attack. The smaller males are different in color. Both males and females show geographical color variations.

VOICE Male call a high-pitched *ki-ki-ki-ki*; female call a low-pitched *kek-ek-ek-ek-ek*.

NESTING Small scrapes on ground in open country, or abandoned nests of other species, such as crows, in forested areas and more recently in suburban green spaces; 4–6 eggs; 1 brood; April–June.

FEEDING Catches small birds in midair, and occasionally birds as large as doves; also feeds on small mammals, including bats.

ABOUT TO ROUSE
An adult female Merlin sits on a moss-covered rock, about to "rouse," or fluff out and shake her feathers.

SIMILAR SPECIES

AMERICAN KESTREL see p.258

cinnamon flanks

tan breast

SHARP-SHINNED HAWK see p.215

rounder wings

barred underparts

longer tail

OCCURRENCE
In North America, breeds throughout Alaska and Canada. Highly migratory; winters throughout the US south to northern South America. Merlins can be seen hunting along coastlines, over marshlands and open fields, and in desert areas.

| Length **10in (25cm)** | Wingspan **24in (61cm)** | Weight **5–7oz (150–200g)** |
| Social **Pairs/Family groups** | Lifespan **10–15 years** | Status **Secure** |

DATE: _____ TIME: _____ LOCATION: _____

| Order **Falconiformes** | Family **Falconidae** | Species *Falco rusticolus* |

Gyrfalcon

pointed tips

dark-brown to black all over

almost completely white

JUVENILE (GRAY MORPH)

ADULT (DARK MORPH)

darker wing linings

paler flight feathers

yellow bill

ADULT (WHITE MORPH)

IN FLIGHT

paler upperparts with brown barring

dark-brown iris

yellow patch of skin near bill

gray, barred upperparts

heavily streaked head

blue bill with dark tip

yellow toes and legs

ADULT (GRAY MORPH)

long, barred tail

lighter underparts with spots

ADULT (GRAY MORPH)

As an Arctic breeder, the Gyrfalcon is used to harsh environments. It is the largest of all the falcons and one of the most majestic species of bird in the world. For centuries, the Gyrfalcon has been sought by both the nobility and falconers for its power, beauty, and gentle nature; it is also the official bird of the Northwest Territories. It uses its speed to pursue prey in a "tail chase," sometimes striking its quarry on the ground, but also in flight. Three forms are known, ranging from almost pure-white to gray and blackish.
VOICE Loud, harsh *KYHa-KYHa-KYHa*.
NESTING Scrape on cliff or old Common Ravens' nests; 2–7 eggs; 1 brood; April–July.
FEEDING Feeds mostly on large birds, such as ptarmigan, pigeons, grouse; may also hunt mammals, such as Arctic hare.

FLIGHT: powerful and direct; continuous, rapid, stiff wing beats.

SNOWY PLUMAGE
A Gyrfalcon stands on an Arctic hillside. From a distance, it might be mistaken for a patch of snow.

SIMILAR SPECIES

PRAIRIE FALCON
light brown-spotted underparts
see p.262

PEREGRINE FALCON
see p.261

dark "hood" on head

light sandy-brown upperparts

smaller overall

light, barred underparts

OCCURRENCE
Breeds in Alaska and Arctic Canada. In winter, some birds move south as far as the northern US. A truly Arctic species, it is found in the most barren regions of the tundra, high mountains and foothills of the tundra, and Arctic and sub-Arctic evergreen forests and woodlands. Not common outside its breeding range.

| Length **22in (56cm)** | Wingspan **4ft (1.2m)** | Weight **2¾–4lb (1.2–1.8kg)** |
| Social **Solitary/Pairs** | Lifespan **Up to 30 years** | Status **Localized** |

DATE: _____ TIME: _____ LOCATION: _____

Order **Falconiformes**	Family **Falconidae**	Species *Falco peregrinus*

Peregrine Falcon 🔊

long, pointed wings

streaked brown underparts

short tail

IN FLIGHT

ADULT

brown upperparts

JUVENILE

dark spots on light-buff breast

light-yellow or bluish-gray legs and toes

barred underwings

barred undertail feathers

prominent dark "mustache"

ADULT

light underparts with horizontal barring

ADULT

dark "hood" on head

yellow eye-ring

dark "mustachial" stripe

bluish-gray upperparts

yellow toes and legs

FLIGHT: powerful and direct; faster, deeper wing beats during pursuit; also soars.

Peregrine Falcons are distributed worldwide and are long-distance ... "Peregrine" means "wanderer." It has been known to dive from great heights at speeds of up to 200mph (320kmh)—a technique known as "stooping." Like all true falcons, this species has a pointed "tooth" on its upper beak and a "notch" on the lower one, and it instinctively bites the neck of captured prey to kill it. From the 1950s to the 1980s, its breeding ability was reduced by the insecticide DDT, which resulted in thin eggshells that could easily be crushed by the parent. Peregrines were then bred in captivity, and later released into the wild. Their status is now secure.
VOICE Sharp *kak, kak, kak* when alarmed.
NESTING Shallow scrape on cliff or building (nest sites are used year after year); 2–5 eggs; 1 brood; March–June.
FEEDING Dives on birds from jays to ducks in flight; feeds on pigeons and migratory birds in cities, and occasionally mammals.

PARENTAL CARE
An adult Peregrine gently feeds a hatchling bits of meat; the remaining egg is not likely to hatch.

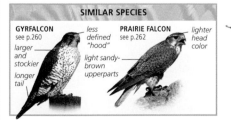

SIMILAR SPECIES

GYRFALCON see p.260
larger and stockier
longer tail

less defined "hood"

PRAIRIE FALCON see p.262
light sandy-brown upperparts

lighter head color

OCCURRENCE
A variety of habitats across northern North America, ranging from open valleys to cities with tall buildings. Peregrines prefer to inhabit cliffs along sea coasts, in addition to inland mountain ranges, but also occur in open country, such as scrubland and salt marshes.

Length **16in (41cm)**	Wingspan **3¼–3½ft (1–1.1m)**	Weight **22–35oz (620g–1kg)**
Social **Solitary/Pairs**	Lifespan **Up to 20 years**	Status **Secure**

DATE: _____ TIME: _____ LOCATION: _____

| Order **Falconiformes** | Family **Falconidae** | Species *Falco mexicanus* |

Prairie Falcon

long, pointed wings

ADULT

longish tail

distinctive, triangle-shaped patch on axillary feathers

IN FLIGHT

yellow eye-ring

light head and dark "mustache"

yellow patch of skin near bill

light sandy-brown upperparts with incomplete barring

white cheek

light underparts with brown spots

ADULT

yellow legs and toes

light undertail feathers

Prairie Falcons are light-colored, buoyant residents of the arid regions of North America. They blend in well with their surroundings (cliff faces and dry grass), where they are invisible to their prey. Prairie Falcons chase their prey close to the ground and do not often dive or "stoop" on prey from a great height. Ground squirrels are important prey items in some areas, and breeding is often linked with the ground squirrels' emergence. The sexes are very similar in coloration, though juveniles have a streaked rather than spotted breast. The underwing pattern with almost black feathers in the "wingpits" is distinctive; no other North American falcon shows this mark.
VOICE Repeated shrill *kik-kik-kik-kik-kik-kik*.
NESTING Slight, shallow scrapes, almost always located on high cliff ledges or bluffs; 3–6 eggs; 1 brood; March–July.
FEEDING Feeds on small- to medium-sized birds and small mammals, such as ground squirrels.

FLIGHT: fast flight; capable of soaring and diving; usually chases prey low above the ground.

STRIKING MUSTACHE
An inquisitive Prairie Falcon stares at the camera. The white cheek is obvious from this angle.

SIMILAR SPECIES

MERLIN
see p.259

smaller overall

heavily streaked underparts

PEREGRINE FALCON ☽
see p.261

darker head

streaked underparts

yellow or bluish-gray legs and toes

OCCURRENCE
Interior North America, from central British Columbia east to western North Dakota and south to southern California, and Mexico, Arizona, northern Texas. Found in open plains, prairies, and grasslands, dotted with buttes or cliffs. A partial migrant, it moves east of its breeding range in winter.

| Length **16in (41cm)** | Wingspan **3¼ft (1m)** | Weight **22–30oz (625–850g)** |
| Social **Solitary/Pairs** | Lifespan **Up to 20 years** | Status **Localized** |

DATE: _____ TIME: _____ LOCATION: _____

NEW WORLD FLYCATCHERS

Birds popularly known as "flycatchers" occur in many parts of the world; however, several different families of songbird have this name. With the exception of some Old World species that may stray into Alaska, the North American species are all members of a single family—the Tyrant Flycatchers (Tyrannidae). With about 400 species, this is the largest bird family in the New World. The North American species are uniform in appearance, with only a hint of the family's diversity found in Central and South America. Most are drab-colored olive-green or gray birds, sometimes with yellow on the underparts, but an

ERECT STANCE
A large-headed look and erect posture are typical of this Eastern Phoebe.

exception is the Scissor-tailed Flycatcher, seen on rare occasions in Canada. The members of the genus *Empidonax* include some of the most difficult birds to identify in North America; they are best distinguished by their songs. Typical flycatcher feeding behavior is to sit on a branch or exposed perch and sally forth to catch flying insects.

KEEPING WATCH
This Alder Flycatcher is on the alert to spot a potential meal.

Tyrannid flycatchers are found across North America, except in the Arctic regions. Most are found in wooded habitats, though the kingbirds (genus *Tyrannus*) prefer woodland edges and deserts. Nearly all flycatchers are long-distance migrants and spend the winter in Central and South America.

BIG MOUTHS
Young Dusky Flycatchers display the wide bills that help them to catch flying insects as adults.

| Order **Passeriformes** | Family **Tyrannidae** | Species *Myiarchus crinitus* |

Great Crested Flycatcher 🔊

ADULT

rusty edges
to outer wing
feathers

whitish
wing bars

IN FLIGHT

brown
crest

olive-brown
back

long,
thin
bill

gray breast
and face

ADULT

yellow
belly

brownish legs
and feet

long
tail

FLIGHT: fast and direct; can glide between perches; will also hover.

The Great Crested Flycatcher is locally common and geographically quite widespread in summer from Alberta and the Maritimes to Florida and Texas. However, it is often overlooked because it remains in the forest canopy, though it visits the ground for food and nest material. Its presence is usually given away by its loud, sharp, double-syllabled notes. It lines its nest with shed snakeskins like other *Myiarchus* flycatchers, possibly to reduce predation by flying squirrels.

VOICE Principal call is a loud, abrupt *purr-it* given by both sexes; male song is a repeated *whee-eep*, occasionally *wheeyer*.

NESTING In deep cavity, usually woodpecker hole, lined with leaves, bark, trash, and snakeskins; 4–6 eggs; 1 brood; May–July.

FEEDING Picks flying insects, moths, and caterpillars mainly from leaves and branches in the canopy; also small berries and fruit.

SIMILAR SPECIES

ASH-THROATED FLYCATCHER

silvery-
white
throat

paler
yellow
belly

BROWN-CRESTED FLYCATCHER

more
rufous
wings

heavier
bill

paler
yellow
belly

TRICOLORED SPECIES
Viewed from the front, the eastern Great Crested Flycatcher is tricolored.

OCCURRENCE
Widespread in eastern North America, from Alberta to the Maritimes in Canada, and, in the US, south to Texas and Florida. Migrates to Mexico, Central America, and northern South America. Breeds in deciduous and mixed woodlands with clearings.

| Length **7–8in (18–20cm)** | Wingspan **13in (33cm)** | Weight **⅞–1⁷⁄₁₆oz (25–40g)** |
| Social **Solitary** | Lifespan **Up to 13 years** | Status **Secure** |

DATE: _____ TIME: _____ LOCATION: _____

| Order **Passeriformes** | Family **Tyrannidae** | Species *Tyrannus verticalis* |

Western Kingbird 🔊

olive-gray back

strong, dark eye-line

small bill

ADULT

white chin

white-edged tail

dark wing with no wing bars

gray head

gray chest

IN FLIGHT

gray back

white edge to outer tail feathers

gray back

yellow belly

ADULT

notched tail

ADULT

A conspicuous summer breeder in the US and lower parts of the western provinces, the Western Kingbird occurs in open habitats in much of western North America. The white outer edges on its outer tail feathers distinguish it from other kingbirds. Its population has expanded eastward over the last 100 years. A large, loosely defined territory is defended against other kingbirds when breeding begins in spring; a smaller core area is defended as the season progresses.

VOICE Calls include *whit*, *pwee-t*, and chatter; song, regularly repeated sharp *kip* notes and high-pitched notes.

NESTING Open, bulky cup of grass, rootlets, and twigs in tree, shrub, or utility pole; 2–7 eggs; 1 brood; April–July.

FEEDING Feeds on insects and fruit.

FLIGHT: light, fast, direct, flapping flight; flies to catch insects; hovers to pick bugs on vegetation.

FENCE POST
A favorite place for the Western Kingbird to perch and look around is on fenceposts.

QUENCHING THIRST
An immature Western Kingbird drinks at the edge of a shallow pool of water.

SIMILAR SPECIES

TROPICAL KINGBIRD

heavier bill

olive-yellow chest

CASSIN'S KINGBIRD

paler wings

gray tip to tail

OCCURRENCE
Widespread in southwestern Canada and the western US, in open habitats, such as grasslands, prairie, desert shrub, pastures, and cropland, near elevated perches; particularly near water. Winters in similar habitats and in tropical forest and shrubbery from Mexico to Costa Rica.

| Length **8–9in (20–23cm)** | Wingspan **15–16in (38–41cm)** | Weight **1¼–1⁹⁄₁₆oz (35–45g)** |
| Social **Solitary** | Lifespan **Up to 6 years** | Status **Secure** |

DATE: _____ TIME:_____ LOCATION:_____

| Order **Passeriformes** | Family **Tyrannidae** | Species *Tyrannus tyrannus* |

Eastern Kingbird 🔊

ADULT

dark crown and cheeks, almost black

dark eyes

faint gray "necklace"

white throat and underparts

relatively short, thick bill

IN FLIGHT

white-tipped tail

white throat

slate-gray back

pale edges to wing feathers

ADULT

white belly

black legs and toes

ADULT

white undertail feathers

black tail with white tip

The Eastern Kingbird is a tame and widely distributed bird. It is a highly territorial species and is known for its aggressive behavior toward potential predators, particularly crows and hawks, which it pursues relentlessly. It is able to identify and remove the eggs of the Brown-headed Cowbird when they are laid in its nest. The Eastern Kingbird is generally monogamous and pairs will return to the same territory in subsequent years. This species winters in tropical South America, where it forages for fruit in the treetops of evergreen forests.

VOICE Principal call is a loud, metallic *chatter-zeer*; song is a rapid, electric *kdik-kdik-kdik-pika-pika-pika-kzeeeer*.

NESTING Open cup of twigs, roots, stems in hawthorn, elm, stump, fence, or post; 2–5 eggs; 1 brood; May–August.

FEEDING Catches flying insects from elevated perch or gleans insects from foliage; eats berries and fruit, except in spring.

FLIGHT: strong, direct, and very agile with vigorous, rapid wing beats; hovers and sails.

WHITE-TIPPED
The white-tipped tails of these two Eastern Kingbirds are conspicuous as they sit on a budding twig.

SIMILAR SPECIES

THICK-BILLED KINGBIRD
dark mask
thicker bill
yellowish belly

GRAY KINGBIRD
larger bill
gray crown and back
no white on tail

OCCURRENCE
Breeds across much of North America in a variety of open habitats, including urban areas, parks, golf courses, fields with scattered shrubs, beaver ponds, and along forest edges. Long-distance migrant; winters in South America, south to Argentina.

| Length **7–9in (18–23cm)** | Wingspan **13–15in (33–38cm)** | Weight **1¹⁄₁₆–2oz (30–55g)** |
| Social **Solitary/Pairs** | Lifespan **Up to 7 years** | Status **Secure** |

DATE: _____ TIME: _____ LOCATION: _____

| Order **Passeriformes** | Family **Tyrannidae** | Species **_Contopus cooperi_** |

Olive-sided Flycatcher 🔊

short tail

ADULT (SUMMER)

pointed wings

IN FLIGHT

large, dark head

lower base of bill often dull orange

brownish-gray back

dull-white throat

brownish-olive flanks

white belly

ADULT (SUMMER)

FLIGHT: fast and direct, with deep, rapid wing beats; turns sharply to chase prey.

The Olive-sided Flycatcher is identified by its distinctive song, relatively large size, and contrasting belly and flank colors, which make its underside appear like a vest with the buttons undone. Both the male and a breeding pair are known to defend their territory aggressively. This flycatcher undertakes a long journey from northern parts of North America to winter in Panama and the Andes.

VOICE Call an evenly spaced _pip-pip-pip_; song a loud 3-note whistle: _quick-THREE-BEERS_ or _whip-WEE-DEER_.

NESTING Open cup of twigs, rootlets, lichens; 2–5 eggs; 1 brood; May–August.

FEEDING Sits and waits for prey to fly past its perch before swooping after it; eats flying insects, such as bees, wasps, and flying ants.

BUILDING THE NEST
The female Olive-sided Flycatcher usually constructs the nest on her own.

EXPOSED PERCH
This species can often be found singing from an exposed twig emerging from the canopy.

OCCURRENCE
Breeds in mountainous, northern coniferous forests at edges or openings around ponds, bogs, and meadows where standing dead trees occur. Also found in post-fire forests with abundant stumps. Winters in forest edges with tall trees and stumps.

SIMILAR SPECIES

EASTERN PHOEBE
see p.277

lacks "vest"

WESTERN WOOD-PEWEE
see p.268

lacks "vest"

longer tail

| Length **7–8in (18–20cm)** | Wingspan **13in (33cm)** | Weight **1¹⁄₁₆–1¼oz (30–35g)** |
| Social **Solitary** | Lifespan **Up to 7 years** | Status **Declining** |

DATE: _____ TIME: _____ LOCATION: _____

| Order **Passeriformes** | Family **Tyrannidae** | Species **Contopus sordidulus** |

Western Wood-Pewee 🔊

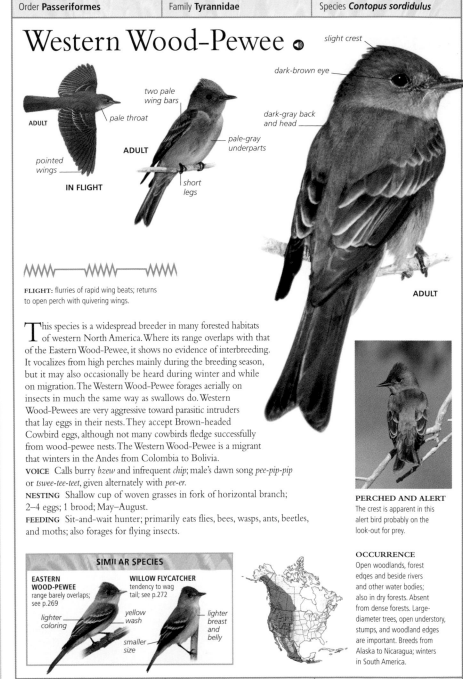

slight crest

dark-brown eye

dark-gray back and head

pale-gray underparts

ADULT

two pale wing bars

pale throat

ADULT

short legs

pointed wings

IN FLIGHT

ADULT

FLIGHT: flurries of rapid wing beats; returns to open perch with quivering wings.

This species is a widespread breeder in many forested habitats of western North America. Where its range overlaps with that of the Eastern Wood-Pewee, it shows no evidence of interbreeding. It vocalizes from high perches mainly during the breeding season, but it may also occasionally be heard during winter and while on migration. The Western Wood-Pewee forages aerially on insects in much the same way as swallows do. Western Wood-Pewees are very aggressive toward parasitic intruders that lay eggs in their nests. They accept Brown-headed Cowbird eggs, although not many cowbirds fledge successfully from wood-pewee nests. The Western Wood-Pewee is a migrant that winters in the Andes from Colombia to Bolivia.

VOICE Calls burry *bzew* and infrequent *chip*; male's dawn song *pee-pip-pip* or *tswee-tee-teet*, given alternately with *pee-er*.

NESTING Shallow cup of woven grasses in fork of horizontal branch; 2–4 eggs; 1 brood; May–August.

FEEDING Sit-and-wait hunter; primarily eats flies, bees, wasps, ants, beetles, and moths; also forages for flying insects.

PERCHED AND ALERT
The crest is apparent in this alert bird probably on the look-out for prey.

SIMILAR SPECIES

EASTERN WOOD-PEWEE
range barely overlaps; see p.269

lighter coloring

WILLOW FLYCATCHER
tendency to wag tail; see p.272

yellow wash

lighter breast and belly

smaller size

OCCURRENCE
Open woodlands, forest edges and beside rivers and other water bodies; also in dry forests. Absent from dense forests. Large-diameter trees, open understory, stumps, and woodland edges are important. Breeds from Alaska to Nicaragua; winters in South America.

| Length 6¼in (16cm) | Wingspan 10½in (27cm) | Weight ³⁄₈–½oz (11–14g) |
| Social **Solitary** | Lifespan **Up to 6 years** | Status **Declining** |

DATE: _____ TIME:_____ LOCATION:_____

| Order **Passeriformes** | Family **Tyrannidae** | Species **Contopus virens** |

Eastern Wood-Pewee 🔊

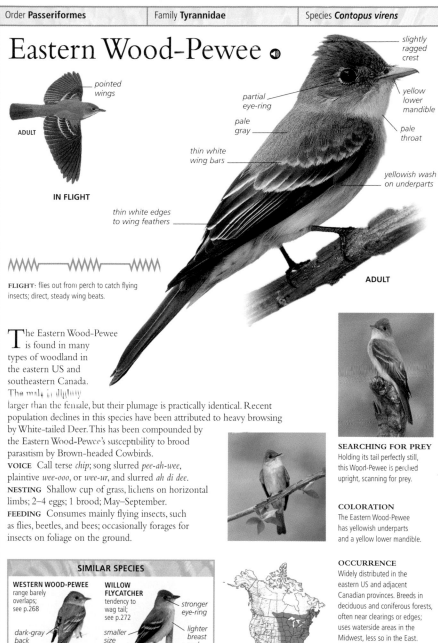

pointed wings

ADULT

IN FLIGHT

slightly ragged crest

partial eye-ring

pale gray

thin white wing bars

yellow lower mandible

pale throat

yellowish wash on underparts

thin white edges to wing feathers

ADULT

FLIGHT: flies out from perch to catch flying insects; direct, steady wing beats.

The Eastern Wood-Pewee is found in many types of woodland in the eastern US and southeastern Canada. The male is slightly larger than the female, but their plumage is practically identical. Recent population declines in this species have been attributed to heavy browsing by White-tailed Deer. This has been compounded by the Eastern Wood-Pewee's susceptibility to brood parasitism by Brown-headed Cowbirds.

VOICE Call terse *chip*; song slurred *pee-ah-wee*, plaintive *wee-ooo*, or *wee-ur*, and slurred *ah di dee*.

NESTING Shallow cup of grass, lichens on horizontal limbs; 2–4 eggs; 1 brood; May–September.

FEEDING Consumes mainly flying insects, such as flies, beetles, and bees; occasionally forages for insects on foliage on the ground.

SEARCHING FOR PREY
Holding its tail perfectly still, this Wood-Pewee is perched upright, scanning for prey.

COLORATION
The Eastern Wood-Pewee has yellowish underparts and a yellow lower mandible.

OCCURRENCE
Widely distributed in the eastern US and adjacent Canadian provinces. Breeds in deciduous and coniferous forests, often near clearings or edges; uses waterside areas in the Midwest, less so in the East. Late-arriving migrant. Winters in shrubby, second-growth forests of South America.

SIMILAR SPECIES

WESTERN WOOD-PEWEE
range barely overlaps; see p.268

dark-gray back

WILLOW FLYCATCHER
tendency to wag tail; see p.272

smaller size

stronger eye-ring

lighter breast and head

| Length **6in (15cm)** | Wingspan **9–10in (23–26cm)** | Weight **³⁄₈–¹¹⁄₁₆oz (10–19g)** |
| Social **Solitary** | Lifespan **Up to 7 years** | Status **Special Concern** |

DATE: _____ TIME: _____ LOCATION: _____

Order **Passeriformes**	Family **Tyrannidae**	Species *Empidonax flaviventris*

Yellow-bellied Flycatcher

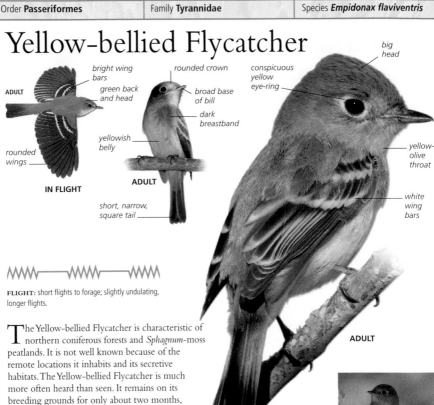

ADULT

bright wing bars

green back and head

rounded wings

IN FLIGHT

rounded crown

broad base of bill

dark breastband

yellowish belly

ADULT

short, narrow, square tail

conspicuous yellow eye-ring

big head

yellow-olive throat

white wing bars

ADULT

FLIGHT: short flights to forage; slightly undulating, longer flights.

The Yellow-bellied Flycatcher is characteristic of northern coniferous forests and *Sphagnum*-moss peatlands. It is not well known because of the remote locations it inhabits and its secretive habitats. The Yellow-bellied Flycatcher is much more often heard than seen. It remains on its breeding grounds for only about two months, then migrates through the eastern US to its winter quarters in southern Mexico and Central America to Panama, where it favors the shade of bird-friendly coffee plantations.

VOICE Call *chu-wee* and abrupt *brrrrt*; song abrupt *killink, che-lek,* or *che-bunk,* with variations.

NESTING Cup of moss, twigs, and needles on or near ground, often in a bog; 3–5 eggs; 1 brood; June–July.

FEEDING Catches insects in the air or gleans mosquitoes, midges, and flies from foliage; sometimes eats berries and seeds.

WELL HIDDEN
These birds, subtly patterned with pale yellow and green, have excellent camouflage in foliage.

OCCURRENCE
Breeds from Alaska to Quebec, Newfoundland, and the northeast US (New England) in boreal forests and bogs dominated by spruce trees. Winters in Mexico and Central America to Panama, in lowland forests, second-growth, and riverside habitats.

SIMILAR SPECIES

ACADIAN FLYCATCHER

larger bill

larger overall

longer, wider tail

LEAST FLYCATCHER
distinctive call; see p.273

lacks olive on breast

darker lower mandible

distinct, pale throat patch

Length **5½in (14cm)**	Wingspan **8in (20cm)**	Weight **9/32–½oz (8–15g)**
Social **Solitary**	Lifespan **At least 4 years**	Status **Secure**

DATE: _____ TIME:_____ LOCATION:_____

| Order **Passeriformes** | Family **Tyrannidae** | Species *Empidonax alnorum* |

Alder Flycatcher 🔊

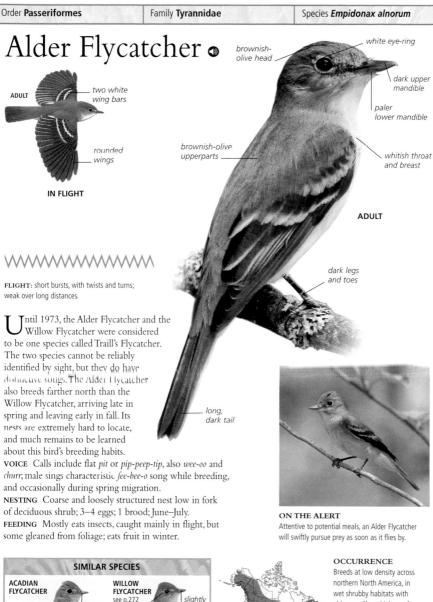

ADULT

two white wing bars

IN FLIGHT

rounded wings

brownish-olive head

white eye-ring

dark upper mandible

paler lower mandible

whitish throat and breast

brownish-olive upperparts

ADULT

dark legs and toes

FLIGHT: short bursts, with twists and turns; weak over long distances.

Until 1973, the Alder Flycatcher and the Willow Flycatcher were considered to be one species called Traill's Flycatcher. The two species cannot be reliably identified by sight, but they do have distinctive songs. The Alder Flycatcher also breeds farther north than the Willow Flycatcher, arriving late in spring and leaving early in fall. Its nests are extremely hard to locate, and much remains to be learned about this bird's breeding habits.

VOICE Calls include flat *pit* or *pip-peep-tip*, also *wee-oo* and *churr*; male sings characteristic *fee-bee-o* song while breeding, and occasionally during spring migration.

NESTING Coarse and loosely structured nest low in fork of deciduous shrub; 3–4 eggs; 1 brood; June–July.

FEEDING Mostly eats insects, caught mainly in flight, but some gleaned from foliage; eats fruit in winter.

long, dark tail

ON THE ALERT
Attentive to potential meals, an Alder Flycatcher will swiftly pursue prey as soon as it flies by.

SIMILAR SPECIES

ACADIAN FLYCATCHER

greener back

longer, deeper bill

WILLOW FLYCATCHER see p.272

fainter eye-ring

slightly longer bill

OCCURRENCE
Breeds at low density across northern North America, in wet shrubby habitats with alder or willow thickets, often close to streams. Winters at low elevations in South America, in tropical second-growth forest and forest edges.

| Length **5¾in (14.5cm)** | Wingspan **8½in (22cm)** | Weight **½oz (14g)** |
| Social **Solitary** | Lifespan **At least 3 years** | Status **Secure** |

| Order **Passeriformes** | Family **Tyrannidae** | Species **Empidonax traillii** |

Willow Flycatcher 🔊

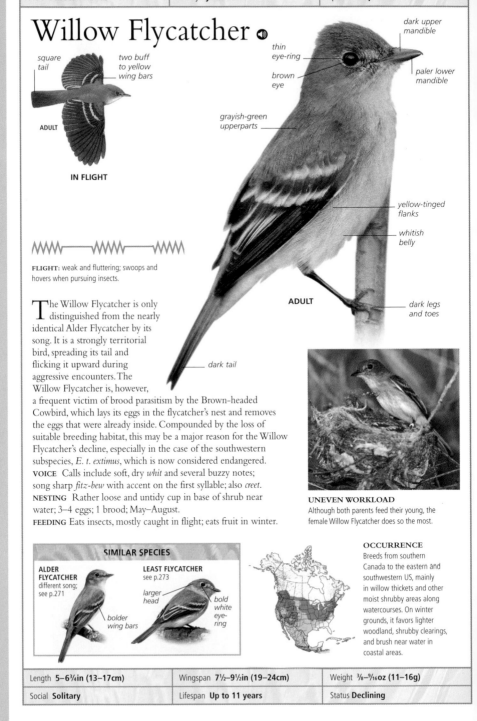

square tail

two buff to yellow wing bars

ADULT

IN FLIGHT

thin eye-ring

brown eye

dark upper mandible

paler lower mandible

grayish-green upperparts

yellow-tinged flanks

whitish belly

ADULT

dark legs and toes

dark tail

FLIGHT: weak and fluttering; swoops and hovers when pursuing insects.

The Willow Flycatcher is only distinguished from the nearly identical Alder Flycatcher by its song. It is a strongly territorial bird, spreading its tail and flicking it upward during aggressive encounters. The Willow Flycatcher is, however, a frequent victim of brood parasitism by the Brown-headed Cowbird, which lays its eggs in the flycatcher's nest and removes the eggs that were already inside. Compounded by the loss of suitable breeding habitat, this may be a major reason for the Willow Flycatcher's decline, especially in the case of the southwestern subspecies, *E. t. extimus*, which is now considered endangered.

VOICE Calls include soft, dry *whit* and several buzzy notes; song sharp *fitz-bew* with accent on the first syllable; also *creet*.

NESTING Rather loose and untidy cup in base of shrub near water; 3–4 eggs; 1 brood; May–August.

FEEDING Eats insects, mostly caught in flight; eats fruit in winter.

UNEVEN WORKLOAD
Although both parents feed their young, the female Willow Flycatcher does so the most.

SIMILAR SPECIES

ALDER FLYCATCHER
different song;
see p.271

bolder wing bars

LEAST FLYCATCHER
see p.273

larger head

bold white eye-ring

OCCURRENCE
Breeds from southern Canada to the eastern and southwestern US, mainly in willow thickets and other moist shrubby areas along watercourses. On winter grounds, it favors lighter woodland, shrubby clearings, and brush near water in coastal areas.

| Length 5–6¾in (13–17cm) | Wingspan 7½–9½in (19–24cm) | Weight ⅜–⁹⁄₁₆oz (11–16g) |
| Social **Solitary** | Lifespan **Up to 11 years** | Status **Declining** |

DATE: _____ TIME: _____ LOCATION: _____

| Order **Passeriformes** | Family **Tyrannidae** | Species *Empidonax minimus* |

Least Flycatcher 🔊

short, narrow tail

large head

ADULT

two wing bars

IN FLIGHT

short, broad-based bill

pale throat

buffy wing bars

IMMATURE

marked white eye-ring

greenish-brown back

short wings

ADULT

pale-yellow belly

FLIGHT: direct, short forays with rapid wing beats to catch prey; sometimes hovers briefly.

The smallest eastern member of the *Empidonax* genus is a solitary bird and is very aggressive toward intruders encroaching upon its breeding territory, including other species of own kind. This combative behavior reduces the likelihood of acting as unwitting host parents to eggs laid by the Brown-headed Cowbird. The Least Flycatcher is very active, and frequently flicks its wings and tail upward. It is common in the eastern US and across Canada in mixed and deciduous woodland, especially at the edges. It spends a short time—up to only two months—on its northern breeding grounds before migrating south. Adults molt in winter, while the young molt before and during fall migration.

VOICE Call soft, short *whit*; song frequent, persistent, characteristic *tchebeck*, sings during spring migration and breeding season.

NESTING Compact cup of tightly woven bark strips and plant fibers in fork of deciduous tree; 3–5 eggs; 1 brood; May–July.

FEEDING Feeds principally on insects, such as flies, midges, beetles, ants, butterflies, and larvae; occasionally eats berries and seeds.

YELLOW TINGE
The subtle yellow tinge to its underparts and white undertail feathers are evident here.

| SIMILAR SPECIES | | |

WILLOW FLYCATCHER
see p.272

larger body

longer bill

ALDER FLYCATCHER
see p.271

larger overall

wider tail

OCCURRENCE
Breeds in coniferous and mixed deciduous forests across North America, east of Rockies to the East Coast; occasionally in conifer groves or wooded wetlands, often near openings or edges. Winters in Central America in varied habitat from second-growth evergreen woodland to arid scrub.

| Length **5¼in (13.5cm)** | Wingspan **7¾in (19.5cm)** | Weight **⁹⁄₃₂–⁷⁄₁₆oz (8–13g)** |
| Social **Solitary** | Lifespan **Up to 6 years** | Status **Secure** |

DATE: _____ TIME:_____ LOCATION:_____

| Order **Passeriformes** | Family **Tyrannidae** | Species *Empidonax hammondii* |

Hammond's Flycatcher

notched tail

olive back

ADULT

IN FLIGHT

gray head

small, dark bill

tear-shaped spot behind eye

grayish-white throat and upper breast

olive breast and flanks

two white wing bars

olive breast and flanks

olive breast and flanks

ADULT

yellow tinge to lower belly

FLIGHT: short, direct flights to pursue prey; occasionally hovers.

A small gray bird of mature coniferous forests in western North America, the Hammond's Flycatcher is generally silent on its wintering grounds, but starts performing its distinctive song shortly after arriving on its breeding grounds. In the breeding season, males are competitive and aggressive, and are known to lock together in mid-air to resolve their territorial squabbles. Since this species is dependent on mature old-growth forest, logging is thought to be adversely affecting its numbers.

VOICE Calls *peek* or *wheep*; song of three elements—dry, brisk *se-put*, low, burry *tsurrt*, or *greep*, and drawn-out *chu-lup*.

NESTING Compact open cup of plant fibers and fine grass saddled on large branch; 3–4 eggs; 1 brood; May–August.

FEEDING Sit-and-wait predator; pursues flying insects from perch.

notched tail

DISTINCTIVE EYE-RING
Hammond's Flycatcher's white tear-shaped spot behind the eye is only visible in good lighting.

SIMILAR SPECIES

DUSKY FLYCATCHER
distinctive "whit" call; see p.275

mouse-gray overall

wider, longer bill

GRAY FLYCATCHER
wags tail

smaller body

paler overall

OCCURRENCE

Breeds in mature coniferous and mixed woodland from Alaska to California. Also found in the Rockies and the Great Basin. Inhabits mainly firs or conifers, but also occurs in aspen and other broadleaf mixed forests. Winters in oak-pine forests and dry shrubbery in Mexico and Central America.

| Length **5–6in (12.5–15cm)** | Wingspan **9in (22cm)** | Weight **$^{9}/_{32}$–$^{7}/_{16}$oz (8–12g)** |
| Social **Solitary** | Lifespan **Up to 7 years** | Status **Secure** |

DATE: _____ TIME:_____ LOCATION:_____

| Order **Passeriformes** | Family **Tyrannidae** | Species **Empidonax oberholseri** |

Dusky Flycatcher

inconspicuous eye-ring

dark-gray upperparts

grayish-olive above

ADULT

wing bars

faint white edge to tail

IN FLIGHT

rounded head

less defined markings than adult

wide wing bars

narrow tail

IMMATURE

notched or square tail

ADULT

long tail

FLIGHT: flies out or hovers for prey; also drops to the ground.

The Dusky Flycatcher waits on a perch to locate a flying insect, flies out to catch it, and then returns to consume it. The bird often wipes its bill on the perch while completing its meal. It lives in mountainous areas of the western US and Canada, where it is vulnerable to storms that can severely impact a local breeding population by flattening the trees. The Dusky Flycatcher prefers shrubby habitats, and can benefit from forestry practices that open up dense stands of conifers.

VOICE Call a soft *whit*, vocal in early morning; song a two-syllabled rising *prll-it*, rough, low-pitched *prrdrrt*, high, clear *pseet*.

NESTING Tight, open grass cup in upright fork of shrub or low tree; 3–5 eggs; 1 brood; May–August.

FEEDING Catches insects in flight; sometimes from bark, rarely from ground; also eats caterpillars, wasps, bees, moths, butterflies.

FEEDING TIME
This adult Dusky Flycatcher is feeding three hungry nestlings in an open-cupped nest.

SIMILAR SPECIES

HAMMOND'S FLYCATCHER
see p.274

eye-ring expands behind eye

longer wings

GRAY FLYCATCHER

shorter, thinner, darker bill

distinctive downward tail dip

OCCURRENCE
Breeds in North America from western Canada through the western US into Mexico, in open coniferous forest, mountain thickets, aspen groves, water-side thickets, open brush, and chaparral. Winters in the highlands of Mexico, south to Oaxaca, in oak scrub and pine-oak; also in open riverside woods and semi-arid scrub.

| Length **5–6in (13–15cm)** | Wingspan **8–9in (20–23cm)** | Weight **5/16–3/8oz (9–11g)** |
| Social **Solitary** | Lifespan **Up to 8 years** | Status **Secure** |

DATE: _____ TIME: _____ LOCATION: _____

| Order **Passeriformes** | Family **Tyrannidae** | Species *Empidonax difficilis* |

Pacific-slope Flycatcher

ADULT

yellow-washed throat

rounded wings

IN FLIGHT

slight crest

wide bill

tear-shaped eye-ring extending behind eye

olive back and head

yellow-orange lower mandible

brown-washed breast

ADULT

FLIGHT: sallies forth from a perch to hawk or glean insects.

The Pacific-slope Flycatcher is virtually identical to the Cordilleran Flycatcher—both were formerly considered to be one species called the Western Flycatcher. Differences in song led researchers to find genetic and behavioral differences between the two species. A population of Pacific-slope Flycatchers found on the Channel Islands off California may also be a distinct species, larger than the mainland forms. The Pacific-slope Flycatcher is a short-distance migrant that winters in Mexico. The female is active during nest-building and incubation, but the male provides food for nestlings.
VOICE Call *chrrip, seet, zeet*; song three squeaky, repeated syllables *ps-SEET, ptsick, seet*, or *TSEE-wee, pttuck, tseep*.
NESTING Open cup, often with shelter above, in fork of tree or shelf on bank or bridge; 2–4 eggs; 2 broods; April–July.
FEEDING Feeds on insects caught in air or gleaned from foliage: beetles, wasps, bees, flies, moths, caterpillars, spiders; rarely berries.

DISTINCT MARKINGS
The Pacific-slope Flycatcher has distinct buffy wing bars and a streaked breast and belly.

SIMILAR SPECIES

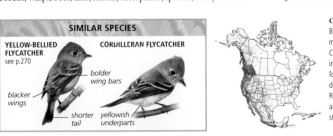

YELLOW-BELLIED FLYCATCHER see p.270

CORDILLERAN FLYCATCHER

bolder wing bars

blacker wings

shorter tail

yellowish underparts

OCCURRENCE
Breeds to the west of the mountains from northern British Columbia to southern California, in humid coastal coniferous forest, pine-oak forest, and dense second-growth forest. Resides in well-shaded woods, along stream bottoms and steep-walled ravines.

| Length **6–7in (15–17.5cm)** | Wingspan **8–9in (20–23cm)** | Weight **9/32–7/16 oz (8–12g)** |
| Social **Solitary** | Lifespan **Up to 6 years** | Status **Declining** |

DATE: _____ TIME:_____ LOCATION: _____

| Order **Passeriformes** | Family **Tyrannidae** | Species *Sayornis phoebe* |

Eastern Phoebe 🔊

ADULT

rounded wings with two faint wing bars

white throat

IN FLIGHT

round, dark-capped head

dark eye

ADULT (FALL)

yellowish tint on lower belly

olive tint to sides and breast

long, dark tail

ADULT (BREEDING)

The Eastern Phoebe is an early spring migrant that tends to nest under bridges, culverts, and on buildings, in addition to rocky outcroppings. Most people are familiar. Because of its *fee-bee* vocalization and constant tail wagging. By tying a thread on the leg of several Eastern Phoebes, ornithologist John James Audubon established that individuals return from the south to a previously used nest site. Although difficult to tell apart, males tend to be slightly larger and darker than females.
VOICE Common call a clear, weak *chip*; song an emphatic *fee-bee* or *fee-b-be-bee*.
NESTING Open cup of mud, moss, and leaves, almost exclusively on artificial structures; 3–5 eggs; 2 broods; April–July.
FEEDING Feeds mainly on flying insects; also consumes small fruit from fall through winter.

Direct flight with steady wing beats; hovers occasionally; approaches nest with a low swoop.

PALE EDGES
Perched on a twig, a male shows off the pale margins of his wing feathers.

LIGHTER FEMALE
They are difficult to distinguish, but the female is slightly lighter-colored overall than the male.

OCCURRENCE
Found in open woodland and along deciduous or mixed forest edges, in gardens and parks, near water. Breeds across Canada from the Northwest Territories south of the tundra belt and in the eastern half of the US. Winters in the southeast US and Mexico.

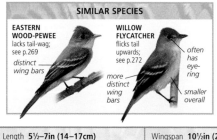

SIMILAR SPECIES

EASTERN WOOD-PEWEE lacks tail-wag; see p.269 / distinct wing bars

WILLOW FLYCATCHER flicks tail upwards; see p.272 / often has eye-ring / more distinct wing bars / smaller overall

| Length 5½–7in (14–17cm) | Wingspan 10½in (27cm) | Weight ¹¹⁄₁₆oz (20g) |
| Social **Solitary** | Lifespan **Up to 9 years** | Status **Secure** |

DATE: _____ TIME: _____ LOCATION: _____

| Order **Passeriformes** | Family **Tyrannidae** | Species ***Sayornis saya*** |

Say's Phoebe

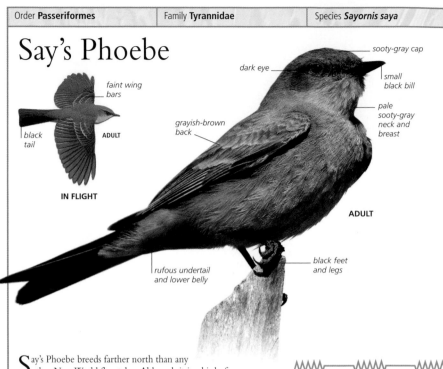

sooty-gray cap

dark eye

small black bill

pale sooty-gray neck and breast

faint wing bars

grayish-brown back

black tail

ADULT

IN FLIGHT

ADULT

rufous undertail and lower belly

black feet and legs

Say's Phoebe breeds farther north than any other New World flycatcher. Although it is a bird of open country, it is not particularly shy around people, and from early spring to late fall, it is a common sight on ranches and farms. Its contrasting dark cap is conspicuous even at a distance as it perches on bushes, boulders, or power lines, often wagging its tail. Shortly after a pair is formed on the breeding grounds, the male will hover in front of potential nest sites, in a manner similar to the Black Phoebe. The pair bond among Say's Phoebes is relatively weak, though, and does not last through the summer.

VOICE Call a *pee-ee* or *pee-ur*, also a whistled churr-eep, which may be integrated with a chatter; primary song a *pit-see-eur* and *pit-eet*.

NESTING Shallow cup of twigs, moss, or stems on ledge or in rocky crevice; 3–7 eggs; 1–2 broods; April–July.

FEEDING Catches insects in flight, such as beetles, wasps, grasshoppers, and crickets; also eats berries.

FLIGHT: direct, with regular wing beats; chases may be erratic; hovers while foraging.

PALE WING FEATHERS
Say's Phoebe's pale underwings are clearly visible from below as it hovers.

SIMILAR SPECIES

VERMILION FLYCATCHER ♀

pale eyebrow

white throat

faintly streaked breast

CASSIN'S KINGBIRD

gray-olive upperparts

yellow belly

OCCURRENCE
Breeds in dry, open, or semi-open country, such as desert canyons, sagebrush ranch, and agricultural areas; also breeds in tundra in Alaska; avoids watercourses. Birds in the southwestern US are resident year-round, but those breeding farther north fly south for the winter.

| Length **7in (17.5cm)** | Wingspan **13in (33cm)** | Weight **¹¹⁄₁₆oz (20g)** |
| Social **Solitary** | Lifespan **At least 4 years** | Status **Secure** |

DATE: _____ TIME:_____ LOCATION:_____

VIREOS

Vireos are a family of songbirds restricted to the New World, with 15 species occurring in Canada and the United States. The classification of vireos has long been problematic—traditionally they were associated with warblers, but recent molecular studies suggest that they are actually related to crow-like birds. Vireo plumage is drab, often predominantly greenish or grayish above and whitish below, augmented by eye-rings, "spectacles," eyestripes, and wing bars. Most vireos have a preference for broad-leaved habitats, where they move about deliberately, hopping and climbing as they slowly forage for their prey. Because they are mainly insect-eaters, most are mid- to long-distance migrants, retreating to warmer climes in winter, when insects are dormant. Vireos are most often detected by the male's loud and clear territorial song, which is repetitive and persistent.

SEPARATE SPECIES
The Blue-headed Vireo is one of three species, formerly known as just one species, the Solitary Vireo.

KEEN SONGSTER
The Red-eyed Vireo sings almost continuously, from dawn until dusk.

Family **Corvidae**

JAYS AND CROWS

Although jays and crows belong to a highly diverse family, the corvids, most members share some important characteristics. They are remarkably social, some species even breed cooperatively, but at the same time they can be quiet and stealthy. Always the opportunists, corvids use strong bills and toes to obtain a varied, omnivorous diet. Ornithologists have shown that ravens, magpies, jays, and crows are among the most intelligent birds. They exhibit self-awareness when looking into mirrors, can make tools, and successfully tackle difficult counting and problem-solving. As a rule, most corvid plumage comes in shades of blue, black, and/or white. The plumage of adult corvids does not vary by season. Corvidae are part of an ancient bird lineage (Corvoidea) that originated in Australasia. Crows and jays were among the birds most affected by the spread of West Nile virus in the early 2000s, but most populations seem to have recovered quickly.

BLACK AND BLUE
Many corvids (especially jays, such as this Steller's Jay) have plumage in shades of black, blue, and gray.

Order **Passeriformes**	Family **Laniidae**	Species *Lanius ludovicianus*

Loggerhead Shrike 🔊

ADULT

white flash in wings

white edges to tail

IN FLIGHT

gray crown

hooked bill

black mask

black wings

pale undertail feathers

IMMATURE

unstreaked gray underparts

ADULT

rounded tail

FLIGHT: fast with rapid wing beats, sometimes interspersed with glides; swoops from perches.

While formally regarded as a songbird, the Loggerhead Shrike, with its prominent black face mask, has a hooked bill and behaves like a small bird of prey. It sits atop posts or tall trees, swooping down to catch prey on the ground. It has the unusual habit of then impaling its prey on thorns, barbed wire, or sharp twigs, which is the reason for the nickname "butcher bird." Unfortunately, Loggerhead Shrike numbers are declining, possibly because of human alteration of its habitat and/or food resources.

VOICE Quiet warbles, trills, and harsh notes; song harsh notes singly or in series: *chaa chaa chaa*.

NESTING Open cup of vegetation, placed in thorny tree; 5 eggs; 1 brood; March–June.

FEEDING Kills large insects and small vertebrates—rodents, birds, reptiles—with its powerful bill.

GEARED FOR HUNTING
The Loggerhead Shrike perches upright on tall shrubs or small trees, where it scans for prey.

SIMILAR SPECIES

NORTHERN SHRIKE see p.281

smaller bill

NORTHERN MOCKINGBIRD see p.331

darker upperparts

lighter upperparts

longer tail

OCCURRENCE
Found in semi-open country with scattered perches, but its distribution is erratic, occurring in relatively high densities in certain areas, but absent from seemingly suitable habitat. Occurs in congested residential areas in some regions (south Florida), but generally favors fairly remote habitats.

Length **9in (23cm)**	Wingspan **12in (31cm)**	Weight **1¼–2⅛oz (35–60g)**
Social **Solitary**	Lifespan **Unknown**	Status **Declining**

DATE: _____ TIME: _____ LOCATION: _____

| Order **Passeriformes** | Family **Laniidae** | Species *Lanius borealis* |

Northern Shrike

ADULT

- conspicuous white wing bar
- pale-gray upperparts

IN FLIGHT

- strongly hooked bill
- delicately barred breast
- brownish underparts
- long tail

IMMATURE

- large head
- narrow black mask
- pale-gray upperparts
- black wings
- black tail with white inner tail feathers
- gray-white underparts

ADULT

FLIGHT: short flights between hunting perches; pounces on prey.

This northern relative of the familiar Loggerhead Shrike is an uncommon winter visitor to the northern US and southern Canada. In some winters, this species is widespread across the midlatitudes of North America; in other winters it is nearly absent. The Northern Shrike is paler, larger bodied, and larger billed than the Loggerhead Shrike, which enables it to attack and subdue larger prey than the Loggerhead. Mostly, this bold, eye-catching shrike looks like an obvious whitish "spot" on top of an isolated tree or bush, but at times it can be remarkably elusive, perching lower down among foliage.

VOICE Variety of short warbles, trills, and harsh notes; generally silent on wintering grounds.

NESTING Open, bulky cup in low tree or large shrub, lined with feathers and hair; 4–6 eggs; 1 brood; May–June.

FEEDING Swoops down on prey, such as rodents, small birds, and insects, which it impales on thorns or pointed branches.

BLACK-AND-WHITE DISPLAY
The Northern Shrike flashes its distinctive black-and-white markings while in flight.

SIMILAR SPECIES

LOGGERHEAD SHRIKE
see p.280
- shorter bill
- darker, smaller overall

NORTHERN MOCKINGBIRD
see p.331
- straight white-edged tail
- thin bill
- less black in wings

OCCURRENCE
Breeds in sub-Arctic coniferous forests, across Canada and Alaska. Winters in more southerly open country with sufficient perches. Avoids built-up and residential districts, but spends much time perching on fence posts and roadside signs.

| Length **10in (25cm)** | Wingspan **14in (35cm)** | Weight **1¾–2⅝oz (50–75g)** |
| Social **Solitary** | Lifespan **Unknown** | Status **Vulnerable** |

DATE: _____ TIME: _____ LOCATION: _____

| Order **Passeriformes** | Family **Vireonidae** | Species *Vireo huttoni* |

Hutton's Vireo

short, rounded wings

ADULT

IN FLIGHT

large, rounded head

pale patch

broken eye-ring

white wing bars

thick, slightly hooked bill

ADULT

blue-gray legs

This unobtrusive bird is understood at present to be a geographically variable species with about a dozen subspecies. These subspecies can be grouped into two populations. The first is a coastal population occurring from British Columbia to Baja California; the second is an interior population found from the Southwest and south to Central America. These two isolated populations, widely separated by desert, may actually represent different species. Very similar in appearance to the Ruby-crowned Kinglet, with which it flocks in winter, Hutton's Vireo is distinguishable by its larger size and thicker bill. Unlike other vireos, this bird is largely nonmigratory.

VOICE Varied calls include harsh mewing and nasal, raspy *spit*; male's song a repetition of a simple phrase, *tu-wee, tu-wee, tu-wee*.
NESTING Deep cup constructed from plant and animal fibers, lined with finer materials, often incorporating lichens, suspended from twigs by the rim; 3–5 eggs; 1–2 broods; February–May.
FEEDING Hops diligently from branch to branch searching for caterpillars, spiders, and flies; also eats berries; gleans from leaves usually while perched, but occasionally sallies or hovers.

FLIGHT: weak and bouncy with rapid wing beats.

FOLLOW THE SONG
This kinglet-sized vireo is easily overlooked and is often detected by its song.

SIMILAR SPECIES

PACIFIC-SLOPE FLYCATCHER
see p.276

unbroken eye-ring

long tail

wide, flat bill

RUBY-CROWNED KINGLET ♂
see p.311

thin bill

smaller overall

OCCURRENCE
Year-round resident in mixed evergreen forests; particularly common in live oak woods. Breeds in mixed oak-pine woodlands along the Pacific Coast from British Columbia southward to northern Baja California, and from southwest California and New Mexico to Mexico and Guatemala.

| Length **5in (13cm)** | Wingspan **8in (20cm)** | Weight **⅜oz (11g)** |
| Social **Solitary/Pairs** | Lifespan **Up to 13 years** | Status **Secure** |

DATE: _____ TIME: _____ LOCATION: _____

Yellow-throated Vireo 🔊

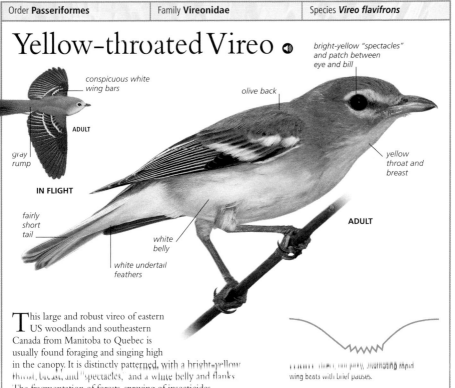

bright-yellow "spectacles" and patch between eye and bill

conspicuous white wing bars

olive back

ADULT

gray rump

IN FLIGHT

yellow throat and breast

fairly short tail

ADULT

white belly

white undertail feathers

This large and robust vireo of eastern US woodlands and southeastern Canada from Manitoba to Quebec is usually found foraging and singing high in the canopy. It is distinctly patterned, with a bright-yellow throat, breast, and "spectacles," and a white belly and flanks. The fragmentation of forests, spraying of insecticides, and cowbird parasitism have led to regional declines in Yellow-throated Vireo populations, but the bird's range, as a whole, has actually expanded.

VOICE Scolding, hoarse, rapid calls; male song a slow, repetitive, two- or three-note phrase, separated by long pauses.

NESTING Rounded cup of plant and animal fibers bound with spider webs, usually located toward the top of a large tree and hung by the rim; 3–5 eggs; 1 brood; April–July.

FEEDING Forages high in trees, picking insects from the branches; also eats fruit when available.

Fluttery flight, not jerky, alternating rapid wing beats with brief pauses.

CANOPY SINGER
The Yellow-throated Vireo sings from the very tops of tall trees.

HIGH FORAGER
This bird finds much of its food in the peeling bark of mature trees.

SIMILAR SPECIES

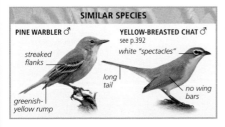

PINE WARBLER ♂

streaked flanks

greenish-yellow rump

YELLOW-BREASTED CHAT ♂
see p.392

white "spectacles"

long tail

no wing bars

OCCURRENCE
Breeds in extensive mature deciduous and mixed woodlands in the eastern half of the US, and extreme southern Canada. Winters mainly from southern Mexico to northern South America, primarily in wooded areas.

Length **5½in (14cm)**	Wingspan **9½in (24cm)**	Weight **⅝oz (18g)**
Social **Solitary/Pairs**	Lifespan **Up to 6 years**	Status **Secure**

DATE: _____ TIME: _____ LOCATION: _____

| Order **Passeriformes** | Family **Vireonidae** | Species **Vireo cassinii** |

Cassin's Vireo

two whitish
wing bars

ADULT

IN FLIGHT

ADULT

dark patch
between
eye and bill

slightly
hooked
bill

white
"spectacles"

gray head

greenish-gray
back

short tail

pale yellowish
flanks

whitish
belly

FLIGHT: short, direct movement with strong wing beats; can hover briefly.

Cassin's Vireo is similar to the closely related Plumbeous and Blue-headed Vireos in appearance and song. It is conspicuous and vocal throughout its breeding grounds in the far west of the US and north into southwest Canada. In winter, virtually the entire population migrates to Mexico. Cassin's Vireo was named in honor of John Cassin, who published the first comprehensive study of North American birds in 1865.
VOICE Call a harsh, scolding chatter; male's song a broken series of whistles, which ascend then descend; lower in tone than Blue-headed Vireo and higher than the Plumbeous.
NESTING Cup of fibers, lined with fine plant down; suspended from twigs; 2–5 eggs; 1–2 broods; April–July.
FEEDING Picks insects and spiders from leaves and twigs as it hops from branch to branch; occasionally sallies out or hovers.

TIRELESS SINGER
Cassin's Vireo is well known for its loud and incessant singing throughout the spring and into the summer.

SIMILAR SPECIES

PLUMBEOUS VIREO

broader gray
overall with
no green

white
wing
bars

**BLUE-HEADED
VIREO**
see p.285

blue-gray
head

brighter
overall

OCCURRENCE
Breeds in coniferous and mixed forests in the hills and mountains of British Columbia and Alberta, and in the US. In the Pacific Northwest through to southern California. Winters in western Mexico.

| Length 5½in (14cm) | Wingspan 9½in (24cm) | Weight ⁹⁄₁₆oz (16g) |
| Social **Solitary/Pairs** | Lifespan **Unknown** | Status **Secure** |

DATE: _____ TIME:_____ LOCATION:_____

Order **Passeriformes**	Family **Vireonidae**	Species *Vireo solitarius*

Blue-headed Vireo 🔊

blue-gray head

conspicuous white "spectacles"

two wing bars

looks "big-headed"

contrasting white throat

greenish back

ADULT

ADULT

IN FLIGHT

white belly

bright greenish flanks

relatively short tail

FLIGHT: slow, heavy, undulating flight with a series of deep wing beats followed by short pauses.

Closely related to the Cassin's Vireo and Plumbeous Vireo, the fairly common Blue-headed Vireo is the brightest and most colorful of the three. Its blue-gray, helmeted head, adorned with striking white "spectacles" around its dark eyes, also helps to distinguish it from other vireos in its range. This stocky and slow-moving bird is heard more often than it is seen in its forest breeding habitat. However, during migration it can be more conspicuous, and it is the first vireo to return in spring.

VOICE Call a harsh, scolding chatter; male's song a series of rich, sweet, high phrases of two to six notes slurred together.

NESTING Shallow, rounded cup loosely constructed of animal and plant fibers, lined with finer material and suspended from twigs by the rim; 3–5 eggs; 2 broods; May–July.

FEEDING Gleans insects from branches and leaves, usually high in shrubs and trees; often makes short sallies after prey.

SPECTACLED VIREO
Its rather thick head with conspicuous "spectacles" and gray color are distinctive field marks.

SIMILAR SPECIES

BLACK-CAPPED VIREO 🔊

smaller overall

CASSIN'S VIREO
see p.284

thin bill

duller overall

OCCURRENCE
Breeds in large tracts of undisturbed coniferous and mixed forests with a rich understory, largely across eastern North America. It winters in woodlands across the southeastern US from Virginia to Texas, as well as in Mexico and northern Central America to Costa Rica.

Length **5½in (14in)**	Wingspan **9½in (24cm)**	Weight **⁹⁄₁₆oz (16g)**
Social **Solitary/Pairs**	Lifespan **Up to 7 years**	Status **Secure**

DATE: _____ TIME: _____ LOCATION: _____

Order **Passeriformes**	Family **Vireonidae**	Species *Vireo philadelphicus*

Philadelphia Vireo

gray cap

slightly hooked black bill

ADULT

IN FLIGHT

white eyebrow

dark line through eye

greenish upperparts

yellow throat

yellowish underparts

ADULT

FLIGHT: fast, bouncy, undulating flight with strong wing beats.

Despite being widespread, the Philadelphia Vireo remains rather poorly studied. It shares its breeding habitat with the similar-looking, but larger and more numerous, Red-eyed Vireo, and, interestingly, it modifies its behavior to avoid competition. It is the most northerly breeding vireo, with its southernmost breeding range barely reaching the US. Its scientific and English names derive from the fact that the bird was first discovered near Philadelphia in the mid-19th century.

VOICE Song a series of two- and four-note phrases, remarkably similar to the song of the Red-eyed Vireo.

NESTING Rounded cup of plant fibers bound by spider webs, hanging between forked twigs that narrows at the rim; 3–5 eggs; 1–2 broods; June–August.

FEEDING Gleans caterpillars, bees, flies, and bugs from leaves; usually forages high in trees, moving with short hops and flights.

DISTINGUISHED APPEARANCE
The Philadelphia Vireo's gentle expression and pudgy appearance help separate it from its neighbor, the Red-eyed Vireo.

SIMILAR SPECIES

BELL'S VIREO

faint wing bar

longer tail

WARBLING VIREO
see p.287

plainer face

less yellow below

OCCURRENCE
Breeds in deciduous woodlands, mixed woodlands, and woodland edges, in a wide belt across Canada, reaching the Great Lakes and northern New England. The Philadelphia Vireo winters from Mexico to Panama and northern Colombia.

Length **5¼in (13.5cm)**	Wingspan **8in (20cm)**	Weight **⁷⁄₁₆oz (12g)**
Social **Solitary/Pairs**	Lifespan **Up to 8 years**	Status **Secure**

DATE: _____ TIME: _____ LOCATION: _____

| Order **Passeriformes** | Family **Vireonidae** | Species *Vireo gilvus* |

Warbling Vireo 🔊

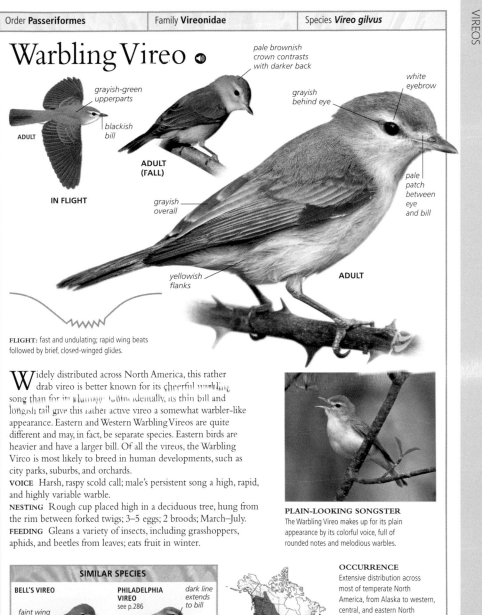

grayish-green upperparts

ADULT

IN FLIGHT

blackish bill

pale brownish crown contrasts with darker back

ADULT (FALL)

grayish behind eye

grayish overall

yellowish flanks

white eyebrow

pale patch between eye and bill

ADULT

FLIGHT: fast and undulating; rapid wing beats followed by brief, closed-winged glides.

Widely distributed across North America, this rather drab vireo is better known for its cheerful warbling song than for its plumage. Incidentally, its thin bill and longish tail give this rather active vireo a somewhat warbler-like appearance. Eastern and Western Warbling Vireos are quite different and may, in fact, be separate species. Eastern birds are heavier and have a larger bill. Of all the vireos, the Warbling Vireo is most likely to breed in human developments, such as city parks, suburbs, and orchards.

VOICE Harsh, raspy scold call; male's persistent song a high, rapid, and highly variable warble.

NESTING Rough cup placed high in a deciduous tree, hung from the rim between forked twigs; 3–5 eggs; 2 broods; March–July.

FEEDING Gleans a variety of insects, including grasshoppers, aphids, and beetles from leaves; eats fruit in winter.

PLAIN-LOOKING SONGSTER
The Warbling Vireo makes up for its plain appearance by its colorful voice, full of rounded notes and melodious warbles.

SIMILAR SPECIES

BELL'S VIREO

faint wing bar

longer tail

PHILADELPHIA VIREO
see p.286

no wing bar

dark line extends to bill

shorter bill

yellow on breast and throat

OCCURRENCE
Extensive distribution across most of temperate North America, from Alaska to western, central, and eastern North America. Breeds in deciduous and mixed forests, particularly near water. Winters in southern Mexico and Central America.

| Length **5½in (14cm)** | Wingspan **8½in (21cm)** | Weight **7⁄16oz (12g)** |
| Social **Solitary/Pairs** | Lifespan **Up to 13 years** | Status **Secure** |

DATE: _____ TIME: _____ LOCATION: _____

| Order **Passeriformes** | Family **Vireonidae** | Species *Vireo olivaceus* |

Red-eyed Vireo 🔊

generally olive above

head held at downward angle

ADULT

IN FLIGHT

bird appears long and slender

gray crown

white eyestripe with black upper border

heavy eye-line

long bill

deep-red eye

ADULT

whitish underparts

bluish legs and toes

Probably the most common songbird of northern and eastern North America, the Red-eyed Vireo is perhaps the quintessential North American vireo, although it is heard far more often than it is seen. It sings persistently and monotonously all day long and late into the season, long after other species have stopped singing. It generally stays high in the canopy of the deciduous and mixed woodlands where it breeds. The entire population migrates to central South America in winter. To reach their Amazonian winter habitats, Red-eyed Vireos migrate in fall (August–October) through Central America, Caribbean Islands, and northern South America to Educador, Peru, and Brazil.

VOICE Nasal mewing call; male song consists of slurred short, robin-like, three-note phrases.

NESTING Open cup nest hanging on horizontal fork of tree branch; built with plant fibers bound with spider's web; exterior is sometimes decorated with lichen; 3–5 eggs; 1 brood; May–July.

FEEDING Gleans insects from leaves, hopping methodically in the canopy and sub-canopy of deciduous trees; during fall and winter, primarily feeds on fruit.

FLIGHT: fast, strong, and undulating with the body angled upwards.

HOPPING BIRD
The Red-eyed Vireo's primary form of locomotion is hopping; at ground level and in trees.

OCCURRENCE
Breeds across North America from the Yukon and British Columbia east to the Canadian Maritimes, and from Washington to the eastern and southeastern US. Inhabits canopy of deciduous forests and pine hardwood forests.

SIMILAR SPECIES

BLACK-WHISKERED VIREO
duller green upperparts
faint black "mustache"

BROWN EYES
Immature Red-eyed Vireos have brown eyes, but those of the adult birds are red.

| Length **6in (15cm)** | Wingspan **10in (25cm)** | Weight **⅝oz (17g)** |
| Social **Solitary/Pairs** | Lifespan **Up to 10 years** | Status **Secure** |

DATE: _____ TIME: _____ LOCATION: _____

| Order **Passeriformes** | Family **Corvidae** | Species *Perisoreus canadensis* |

Canada Jay

ADULT

brownish back with white streaks

P. c. obscurus (NORTHWESTERN)

dark-gray upperparts

dark crown

white forehead

white collar

short bill

long tail with white corners

IN FLIGHT

gray overall, darker upperparts

whitish "mustache"

uniform medium- to dark-gray

IMMATURE

dark smoky-gray tail and wings

black legs and toes

P. c. canadensis (NORTHERN)

Fearless and cunning, the Canada Jay, also called the Whiskey Jack by some, is widely regarded by Canadians to be the country's national bird. As opportunistic foragers, these jays commonly perch on the hands and limbs of campers, hikers, and skiers, looking for handouts. This tough, non-migratory bird, capable of incubating its eggs at -30°C (-22°F), relies on cold fall and winter temperatures to preserve its food items, storing them under tree bark above the snow with sticky saliva. While numbers are stable across the country, a long-studied population in Algonquin Park has seen its breeding population halved in recent years, likely due to global warming causing its stored food to rot.

VOICE Mostly silent, but also produces variety of odd clucks and screeches; sometimes Blue Jay-like *jay!* and eerie warning whistles, including bisyllabic *whee-oo* or *ew*.

NESTING Bulky platform of sticks with cocoons on south side of coniferous tree; 2–5 eggs; 1 brood; February–May.

FEEDING Forages for insects and berries; also raids birds' nests.

FLIGHT: hollow-sounding wing beats followed by slow, seemingly awkward, rocking glides.

BUILT FOR COLD
The Canada Jay's short extremities and dense, fluffy plumage are perfect for long, harsh winters.

SIMILAR SPECIES

CLARK'S NUTCRACKER
see p.292
white wing patch
longer bill

NORTHERN MOCKINGBIRD
see p.331
no dark crown
longer tail
white wing patch

OCCURRENCE
Northerly forests, especially lichen-festooned areas with firs and spruces. Found in coniferous forests across northern North America from Alaska to Newfoundland, the Maritimes, and north New York and New England; south to the western mountains.

| Length **10–11½in (25–29cm)** | Wingspan **18in (46cm)** | Weight **2⅛–2⅞oz (60–80g)** |
| Social **Family groups** | Lifespan **Up to 10 years** | Status **Secure** |

DATE: _____ TIME: _____ LOCATION: _____

Order **Passeriformes**	Family **Corvidae**	Species *Cyanocitta stelleri*

Steller's Jay 🔊

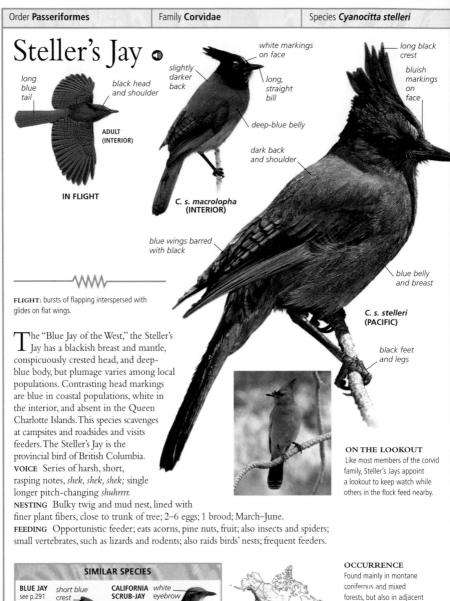

white markings on face

slightly darker back

long, straight bill

deep-blue belly

long black crest

bluish markings on face

long blue tail

black head and shoulder

ADULT (INTERIOR)

IN FLIGHT

dark back and shoulder

C. s. macrolopha (INTERIOR)

blue wings barred with black

blue belly and breast

C. s. stelleri (PACIFIC)

black feet and legs

FLIGHT: bursts of flapping interspersed with glides on flat wings.

The "Blue Jay of the West," the Steller's Jay has a blackish breast and mantle, conspicuously crested head, and deep-blue body, but plumage varies among local populations. Contrasting head markings are blue in coastal populations, white in the interior, and absent in the Queen Charlotte Islands. This species scavenges at campsites and roadsides and visits feeders. The Steller's Jay is the provincial bird of British Columbia.

VOICE Series of harsh, short, rasping notes, *shek, shek, shek;* single longer pitch-changing *shuhrrrr.*

NESTING Bulky twig and mud nest, lined with finer plant fibers, close to trunk of tree; 2–6 eggs; 1 brood; March–June.

FEEDING Opportunistic feeder; eats acorns, pine nuts, fruit; also insects and spiders; small vertebrates, such as lizards and rodents; also raids birds' nests; frequent feeders.

ON THE LOOKOUT
Like most members of the corvid family, Steller's Jays appoint a lookout to keep watch while others in the flock feed nearby.

SIMILAR SPECIES

BLUE JAY see p.291
short blue crest
grayish-white below

CALIFORNIA SCRUB-JAY see p.444
white eyebrow
whitish below

OCCURRENCE
Found mainly in montane coniferous and mixed forests, but also in adjacent broad-leafed habitats; occasionally, in winter, makes sudden migrations to lower elevations, east onto the Great Plains. Interbreeds locally with the Blue Jay where their ranges overlap the Rockies.

Length **11–12½in (28–32cm)**	Wingspan **19in (48cm)**	Weight **3½–5oz (100–150g)**
Social **Small flocks**	Lifespan **Up to 15 years**	Status **Secure**

DATE: _____ TIME:_____ LOCATION:_____

| Order **Passeriformes** | Family **Corvidae** | Species *Cyanocitta cristata* |

Blue Jay 🔊

long tail with white corners
white streak in blue wings
ADULT
white trailing edge feathers
blue wings and tail

IN FLIGHT

black bars on tail

black legs and feet

blue crest
black patch between eye and bill
black collar
plain blue mantle
long black bill
whitish throat

ADULT

grayish underparts

The Blue Jay is common in rural and suburban backyards across Canada and the eastern US. Beautiful as it is, the Blue Jay has a darker side. It often raids the nests of smaller birds for eggs and nestlings. Although usually thought of as a nonmigratory species, some Blue Jays undertake impressive migrations, with loose flocks sometimes numbering in the hundreds visible overhead in spring and fall. The Blue Jay is the provincial bird of Prince Edward Island.

VOICE Harsh, screaming *jay! jay!;* other common call an odd ethereal, chortling *queedle-ee-dee;* soft clucks when feeding. Known to mimic hawks.

NESTING Cup of strong twigs at variable height in trees or shrubs; 3–6 eggs; 1 brood; March–July.

FEEDING Eats insects, acorns, small vertebrates, such as lizards, rodents, bird eggs, birds, tree frogs; fruit and seeds.

FLIGHT: bursts of flapping followed by long glides on flat wings

UNIQUE FEATURES
The Blue Jay is unique among American jays, in having white patches on its wings and tail.

VERSATILE BIRD
Blue Jays are true omnivores, eating almost anything they can find. They are also excellent imitators of other bird calls.

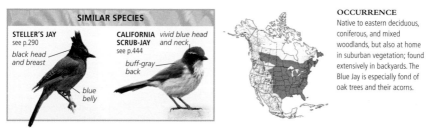

SIMILAR SPECIES

STELLER'S JAY see p.290 — black head and breast, blue belly

CALIFORNIA SCRUB-JAY see p.444 — vivid blue head and neck, buff-gray back

OCCURRENCE
Native to eastern deciduous, coniferous, and mixed woodlands, but also at home in suburban vegetation; found extensively in backyards. The Blue Jay is especially fond of oak trees and their acorns.

| Length **9½–12in (24–30cm)** | Wingspan **16in (41cm)** | Weight **2¼–3½oz (65–100g)** |
| Social **Small flocks** | Lifespan **Up to 7 years** | Status **Secure** |

DATE: ___ TIME: ___ LOCATION: ___

Order **Passeriformes**	Family **Corvidae**	Species ***Nucifraga columbiana***

Clark's Nutcracker 🔊

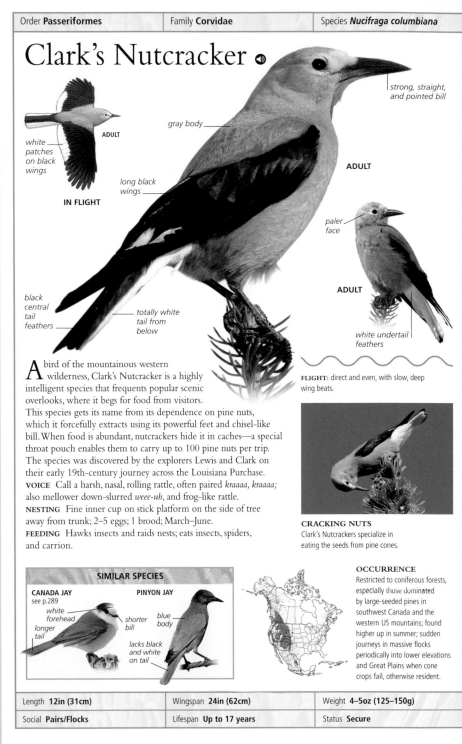

ADULT

white patches on black wings

gray body

IN FLIGHT

long black wings

ADULT

strong, straight, and pointed bill

paler face

ADULT

black central tail feathers

totally white tail from below

white undertail feathers

A bird of the mountainous western wilderness, Clark's Nutcracker is a highly intelligent species that frequents popular scenic overlooks, where it begs for food from visitors. This species gets its name from its dependence on pine nuts, which it forcefully extracts using its powerful feet and chisel-like bill. When food is abundant, nutcrackers hide it in caches—a special throat pouch enables them to carry up to 100 pine nuts per trip. The species was discovered by the explorers Lewis and Clark on their early 19th-century journey across the Louisiana Purchase.
VOICE Call a harsh, nasal, rolling rattle, often paired *kraaaa, kraaaa;* also mellower down-slurred *weee-uh,* and frog-like rattle.
NESTING Fine inner cup on stick platform on the side of tree away from trunk; 2–5 eggs; 1 brood; March–June.
FEEDING Hawks insects and raids nests; eats insects, spiders, and carrion.

FLIGHT: direct and even, with slow, deep wing beats.

CRACKING NUTS
Clark's Nutcrackers specialize in eating the seeds from pine cones.

SIMILAR SPECIES

CANADA JAY
see p.289

white forehead

longer tail

PINYON JAY

shorter bill

blue body

lacks black and white on tail

OCCURRENCE
Restricted to coniferous forests, especially those dominated by large-seeded pines in southwest Canada and the western US mountains; found higher up in summer; sudden journeys in massive flocks periodically into lower elevations and Great Plains when cone crops fail, otherwise resident.

Length **12in (31cm)**	Wingspan **24in (62cm)**	Weight **4–5oz (125–150g)**
Social **Pairs/Flocks**	Lifespan **Up to 17 years**	Status **Secure**

DATE: _____ TIME: _____ LOCATION: _____

| Order **Passeriformes** | Family **Corvidae** | Species *Pica hudsonia* |

Black-billed Magpie 🔊

large white patches on outer wings

ADULT

white shoulder feathers

IN FLIGHT

blue-green iridescence to wings and tail

black back and head

thick black bill

black breast

ADULT

white belly

long, dark tail

L oud, flashy and conspicuous, the Black-billed Magpie is abundant in the northwestern quarter of the continent, from Alaska to the interior of the US. It has adapted to suburbia, confidently strutting across front lawns in some places. Until recently, it was considered to be the same species as the Eurasian Magpie (*P. pica*), but even though they look nearly identical, scientific evidence points instead to a close relationship with the other North American magpie, the Yellow-billed Magpie. Its long tail enables it to make rapid changes in direction in flight. The male will also use his tail to perform a variety of displays while courting a female. Black-billed Magpies are rarely found in large flocks, but they form them sometimes in fall.

VOICE Common call a questioning, nasal *ehnk*; also raspy *shenk, shenk, shenk*, usually in series.

NESTING Large, domed, often made of thorny sticks; 5–8 eggs; 1 brood; March–June.

FEEDING Omnivorous; forages on ground, mainly for insects, worms, seeds and carrion; even picks ticks from mammals.

FLIGHT: direct, with slow, steady, and often shallow wing beats; occasional shallow glides.

IRIDESCENT SHEEN
In bright sunlight, beautiful iridescent blues, greens, golds, and purples appear on the wings and tail.

SIMILAR SPECIES

YELLOW-BILLED MAGPIE

yellow bill

yellow patch around eye

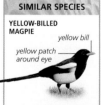

OCCURRENCE
Found in open habitats, foothills, and plains of the western US and Canada; nests in streamside vegetation; persecution has made it wary and restricted to wilderness in some areas, but in others it has adapted to suburbs of towns and cities.

| Length **17–19½in (43–50cm)** | Wingspan **25in (63cm)** | Weight **6–7oz (175–200g)** |
| Social **Small flocks** | Lifespan **Up to 15 years** | Status **Secure** |

DATE: _____ TIME: _____ LOCATION: _____

| Order **Passeriformes** | Family **Corvidae** | Species **Corvus brachyrhynchos** |

American Crow 🔊

black overall

black overall, with greenish sheen

long black bill

ADULT

IN FLIGHT

shorter bill

dull-black overall

ADULT

strong legs and feet

IMMATURE

~~~~~~~

FLIGHT: direct and level with slow, steady flapping; does not soar.

One of the most widespread and familiar of North American birds, the highly intelligent American Crow is common in almost all habitats—from wilderness to urban centers. Like most birds with large ranges, there is substantial geographical variation in this species. Birds are black across the whole continent, but size and bill shape vary from region to region. The birds of the coastal Pacific Northwest (*C. b. hesperis*), are on average smaller and have a lower-pitched voice; Floridian birds (*C. b. pascuus*) are more solitary and warier than most.

VOICE Call a loud, familiar *caw!*; immature birds' call higher-pitched.

NESTING Stick base with finer inner cup; 3–7 eggs; 1 brood; April–June.

FEEDING Feeds omnivorously on fruit, carrion, garbage, insects, spiders; raids nests.

LOOKING AROUND
Extremely inquisitive, American Crows are always on the look-out for food or something of interest.

SIMILAR SPECIES

COMMON RAVEN
see p.295

larger, decurved bill

much larger overall

shaggy throat feathers

OCCURRENCE
Often seen converging on favored roosting areas; most numerous in relatively open areas with widely spaced, large trees; has become abundant in some cities; a partial migrant, some populations are more migratory than others.

| Length **15½–19½in (39–49cm)** | Wingspan **3ft (1m)** | Weight **15 22oz (425–625g)** |
| Social **Social** | Lifespan **Up to 15 years** | Status **Secure** |

DATE: _____ TIME: _____ LOCATION: _____

Common Raven 🔊

long black wings

ADULT

flared outer wing feathers

large, protruding head

black upperparts with purplish gloss

thick, long bill with pronounced curvature

shaggy throat

dark-gray neck and underparts

IN FLIGHT

wedge-shaped tail

ADULT

long black legs and feet

The Common Raven is twice the size of the American Crow, a bird of indigenous legends, literature, and scientific wonder. Its Latin name, *Corvux corax*, means "crow of crows." Ravens are perhaps the most intelligent of all birds on the planet: they learn quickly, adapt to new circumstances with remarkable mental agility, and communicate with each other through an array of vocal and motional behaviors. The Common Raven is the official bird of the Yukon Territory.

VOICE Varied vocalizations, including hoarse, rolling *krruuk*, twangy peals, guttural clicks, and resonant *bonks*.

NESTING Platform of sticks with fine inner material on trees, cliffs, or artificial structure; 4–5 eggs; 1 brood; March–June.

FEEDING Feeds omnivorously on carrion, small crustaceans, fish, rodents, fruit, grain, and garbage; also raids nests and kill rabbits.

FLIGHT: slow, steady, and direct; can also be quite acrobatic; commonly soars.

SHARING INFORMATION
Ravens in flocks can communicate information about food sources.

SIMILAR SPECIES

AMERICAN CROW
lacks shaggy throat feathers;
see p.294

lacks wedge-shaped tail

CHIHUAHUAN RAVEN

smaller bill

much smaller overall

slightly smaller overall

OCCURRENCE
Found in almost every kind of habitat, including tundra, mountainous areas, northern forest, woodlands, prairies, arid regions, coasts, and around human settlements; has recently recolonized areas on southern edge of range, from which it was once expelled by humans.

| Length **23½–27in (60–69cm)** | Wingspan **4½ft (1.4m)** | Weight **2½–3¼lb (1–1.5kg)** |
| Social **Solitary/Pairs/Small flocks** | Lifespan **Up to 15 years** | Status **Secure** |

CHICKADEES

CHICKADEES MAY BE some of the most well-known and widespread birds in North America. Scientific studies have shown that more than one genus exists, despite the bird's plumage similarities.

Chickadees are readily identified by their smooth-looking dark caps and black bibs. The name "chickadee" is derived from the common calls of several species. Highly social outside the breeding season and generally tolerant of people, these energetic little birds form flocks in winter. Some species, such as the Black-capped Chickadee, can lower their body temperature to survive the cold, but others, like the similar-looking Carolina Chickadee (a vagrant species in Canada), have a high winter mortality rate. Most species eat a combination of insects and plant material.

TAME BIRDS
Black-capped Chickadees have distinctive black-and-white markings and are often very tame.

SWALLOWS

SWALLOWS ARE A COSMOPOLITAN family of birds with species found nearly everywhere, except in the polar regions and some of the largest deserts. However, during migration they fly over some of the world's harshest deserts, including the Sahara and the Atacama. Most species have relatively short, notched tails, but some have elongated outer tail feathers. Among these latter species, females appear to prefer males with the longest tails as mates. The Bank Swallow and the Barn Swallow, which are also found across Eurasia, are the most widespread. All North American swallows are migratory, and most of them winter in Central and South America, where they feed on flying insects that occur year-round. They are all superb fliers, and skilled at aerial pursuit and capture of flying insects. They are sometimes confused with swifts, which belong to a different family and order, and have a different style of flight. Swallows have relatively shorter, broader wings and less stiff wing beats.

SURFACE SKIMMER
This Tree Swallow flies low over fresh water to catch insects as they emerge into the air.

Order **Passeriformes**	Family **Paridae**	Species ***Poecile atricapillus***

Black-capped Chickadee 🔊

white on wings and tail

black-and-white head

grayish-brown upperparts

ADULT

IN FLIGHT

white edges on wing feathers

white edges on outer tail feathers

faded-buff flanks

bright-white cheeks

short black bill

black cap and bib

ADULT

The Black-capped Chickadee is the most widespread chickadee in North America, equally at home in the cold far north and in the warm Appalachian valleys. To cope with the harsh northern winters, this species can decrease its body temperature, entering a state of controlled hypothermia to conserve energy. Black-capped Chickadees grow new neurons in their hippocampus each fall to remember stored seed locations. There is some variation in appearance according to geographical location, with northern birds being slightly larger and possessing brighter white wing edgings than southern birds. Although it is a nonmigratory species, flocks occasionally travel south of their traditional range in large numbers in winter. The Black-capped Chickadee is the provincial bird of New Brunswick.

VOICE Raspy *tsick-a-dee-dee-dee* call; song loud, clear whistle *bee-bee* or *bee-bee-be*, first note higher in pitch.

NESTING Cavity in rotting tree stump, lined with hair, fur, feathers, plant fibers; 6–8 eggs; 1 brood; April–June.

FEEDING Forages for insects and their eggs, and spiders in trees and bushes; mainly seeds in winter; may take seeds from an outstretched hand.

FLIGHT: swift and undulating, with fast wing beats.

ROUGH-EDGED BIB
The Black-capped Chickadee has a smaller bib than the Chestnut-backed Chickadee.

SIMILAR SPECIES

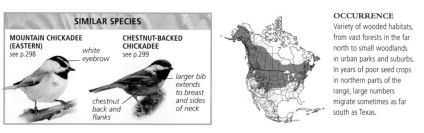

MOUNTAIN CHICKADEE (EASTERN) see p.298

white eyebrow

CHESTNUT-BACKED CHICKADEE see p.299

larger bib extends to breast and sides of neck

chestnut back and flanks

OCCURRENCE
Variety of wooded habitats, from vast forests in the far north to small woodlands in urban parks and suburbs. In years of poor seed crops in northern parts of the range, large numbers migrate sometimes as far south as Texas.

Length **5¼in (13.5cm)**	Wingspan **8½in (22cm)**	Weight **⅜oz (11g)**
Social **Mixed flocks**	Lifespan **Up to 12 years**	Status **Secure**

DATE: _____ TIME:_____ LOCATION:_____

Order **Passeriformes**	Family **Paridae**	Species *Poecile gambeli*

Mountain Chickadee 🔊

ADULT
(EASTERN)

black crown

short
black bill

white
eyebrow

white
cheeks

dull-gray
upperparts

ADULT
(THE ROCKIES)

black
bib

buff-tinged
flanks

IN FLIGHT

gray flanks

pale-gray
underparts

ADULT
(CALIFORNIA)

FLIGHT: bouncy, with fast wing beats; interrupted by brief glides.

The Mountain Chickadee is aptly named as it is found at elevations of up to 12,000ft (3,600m). Like other chickadees, it stores pine and spruce seeds for harsh mountain winters. Social groups defend their winter territories and food resources, migrating to lower elevations when seeds are scarce. Birds in the Rocky Mountains have a conspicuous white eyebrow and buff-tinged flanks; those in the California mountains have grayish flanks and a fainter eyebrow.

VOICE Call raspy *tsick-jee-jee-jee*; whistle song of descending notes *bee-bee-bay*.

NESTING Natural tree cavity or old woodpecker hole, lined with moss and fur; 7–9 eggs; 1–2 broods; May–June.

FEEDING Forages high in trees for insects and spiders; eats seeds and berries; stores seeds in fall in preparation for winter.

VARIABLE EYEBROW
The white eyebrow is evident, but it may become duller and worn in spring and summer plumage.

TYPICAL PERCH
The species spends much time perched in conifer trees, where it feeds.

OCCURRENCE
High elevations, preferring coniferous forests. May even be seen higher than the limit of tree growth. Some birds, especially the young, move down to foothills and valleys in winter and may visit feeders. Some also wander away from the mountains and out onto the Great Plains.

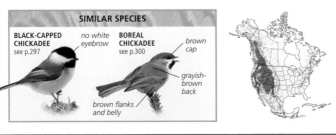

SIMILAR SPECIES

BLACK-CAPPED
CHICKADEE
see p.297

no white
eyebrow

BOREAL
CHICKADEE
see p.300

brown
cap

grayish-
brown
back

brown flanks
and belly

Length **5¼in (13.5cm)**	Wingspan **8½in (22cm)**	Weight **⅜oz (11g)**
Social **Winter flocks**	Lifespan **Up to 10 years**	Status **Secure**

DATE: _____ TIME:_____ LOCATION:_____

| Order **Passeriformes** | Family **Paridae** | Species *Poecile rufescens* |

Chestnut-backed Chickadee 🔊

chestnut back and rump

paler gray wings

dark-brown cap

narrow white cheeks

gray sides and flanks

ADULT

rich-chestnut back

P. r. barlowi

dark-gray wings

IN FLIGHT

white edges on outer wing feathers

black bib extends to sides of neck and breast

chestnut sides

ADULT

FLIGHT: bouncy, fast wing beats with brief glides

The Chestnut-backed is the smallest of all chickadees and possesses the shortest tail. Northern populations have the most brightly colored sides and flanks of all North American chickadees— rich-chestnut or rufous, matching the bright back and rump. Birds found southward into California (subspecies *barlowi*) have paler and less extensive rufous underparts. Farther south still, in California, the sides and flanks are dull olive brown or gray. The Chestnut-backed Chickadee may nest in loose colonies, unlike any other chickadee species.

VOICE A fast, high-pitched *sic-zee-zee, seet-seet-seet*, sharp *chek-chek*, crisp *twit-twit-twit*, and many variations; no whistled song.

NESTING Excavates hole, or uses natural cavity or old woodpecker hole; lined with moss, hair, fur; 5–8 eggs; 1 brood; April–June.

FEEDING Forages high in conifers for caterpillars and other insects; eats seeds and berries in winter.

A DASH OF WHITE
Bright white edges on the wing feathers are often a conspicuous field mark of this species.

SIMILAR SPECIES

BOREAL CHICKADEE
see p.300
grayish-brown back

gray cheeks

rich brown flanks and belly

CONIFER LOVER
These birds prefer to focus on insects that live in Douglas firs and other conifers.

OCCURRENCE
Year-round resident in humid coniferous forests of the Pacific Northwest; in drier mixed and deciduous woodlands, and even in urban and suburban habitats south of San Francisco, California. Northern coastal populations have one of the most specialized habitats of all chickadee species.

| Length **4¾in (12cm)** | Wingspan **7½in (19cm)** | Weight **⅜oz (10g)** |
| Social **Flocks** | Lifespan **Up to 9 years** | Status **Secure** |

DATE: _____ TIME: _____ LOCATION: _____

| Order **Passeriformes** | Family **Paridae** | Species *Poecile hudsonicus* |

Boreal Chickadee

brown cap

grayish-brown back

black bib

gray cheeks

ADULT

gray tail

IN FLIGHT

gray wings

rich-brown flanks and belly

ADULT

FLIGHT: bouncy, fast wing beats with brief glides.

The Boreal Chickadee was previously known by other names, including Hudsonian Chickadee, referring to its northern range, and the Brown-capped Chickadee, due to its appearance. In the past, this species made large, irregular journeys south of its usual range during winters of food shortage, but this pattern of invasions has not occurred in recent decades. Its back color is an interesting example of geographic variation—grayish in the West and brown in the central and eastern portions of its range.

VOICE Call a low-pitched, buzzy, lazy *tsee-day-day*; also a high-pitched trill, *dididididididi*; no whistled song.

NESTING Cavity lined with fur, hair, plant down; in natural, excavated, or old woodpecker hole; 4–9 eggs; 1 brood; May–June.

FEEDING Gleans insects, conifer seeds; hoards larvae and seeds in bark crevices in fall in preparation for winter.

IDENTIFICATION TIP
A grayish-brown back or flank helps distinguish a Boreal Chickadee from a Black-capped Chickadee.

SIMILAR SPECIES

CHESTNUT-BACKED CHICKADEE see p.299 — narrow white cheeks

chestnut sides

ACROBATIC FORAGER
This acrobatic feeder is able to cling on to conifer needles as it searches for insects and spiders.

OCCURRENCE
Found across the vast northern spruce-fir forests, from Alaska to Newfoundland, and from the treeline at the tundra south to the northeastern and northwestern states. The southern edge of the range appears to be retracting for unknown reasons.

| Length **5½in (14cm)** | Wingspan **8½in (21cm)** | Weight **⅜oz (10g)** |
| Social **Flocks** | Lifespan **Up to 5 years** | Status **Secure** |

DATE: _____ TIME:_____ LOCATION:_____

| Order **Passeriformes** | Family **Alaudidae** | Species *Eremophila alpestris* |

Horned Lark 🔊

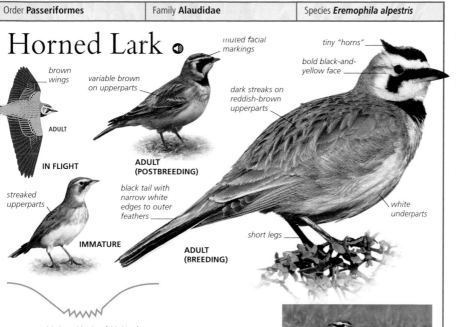

brown wings

muted facial markings

tiny "horns"

bold black-and-yellow face

variable brown on upperparts

dark streaks on reddish-brown upperparts

ADULT

IN FLIGHT

ADULT (POSTBREEDING)

streaked upperparts

black tail with narrow white edges to outer feathers

IMMATURE

short legs

white underparts

ADULT (BREEDING)

FLIGHT: undulating, with wings folded in after every few beats.

The Horned Lark is a bird of open country, especially places with extensive bare ground. The species is characteristic of arid, alpine, and Arctic regions; in these areas, it flourishes in the bleakest of habitats imaginable, from sun-scorched, arid lakes in the Great Basin to windswept tundra above the timberline. In some places, the only breeding bird species are the Horned Lark and the equally resilient Common Raven. In Europe and Asia, this species is known as the Shore Lark.

VOICE Flight call a sharp *sweet* or *soo-weet*; song, either in flight or from the ground, pleasant, musical tinkling series, followed by *sweet… swit… sweet… s'sweea'weea'witta'swit*.

NESTING In depression in bare ground, somewhat sheltered by grass or low shrubs, lined with plant matter; 2–5 eggs; 1–3 broods; March–July.

FEEDING Survives exclusively on seeds of grasses and sedges in winter; eats mostly insects in summer.

GROUND FORAGER
With its short legs bent under its body, an adult looks for insects and seeds.

VERY VOCAL
The Horned Lark is a highly vocal bird, singing from the air, the ground, or low shrubs.

OCCURRENCE
Breeds widely, in any sort of open, even barren habitat with extensive bare ground, especially shortgrass prairies and deserts. Winters wherever there are snow-free openings, including places along beaches and roads. Winters from southern Canada southward to Florida and Mexico.

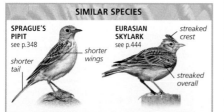

SIMILAR SPECIES

SPRAGUE'S PIPIT see p.348

shorter tail

shorter wings

EURASIAN SKYLARK see p.444

streaked crest

streaked overall

| Length **7in (18cm)** | Wingspan **12in (30cm)** | Weight **1¹/₁₆oz (30g)** |
| Social **Winter flocks** | Lifespan **Up to 8 years** | Status **Secure** |

DATE: _____ TIME: _____ LOCATION: _____

| Order **Passeriformes** | Family **Hirundinidae** | Species *Riparia riparia* |

Bank Swallow

ADULT

dark breastband

dark-brown head

dark-brown upperparts

whitish chin and throat

white belly

IN FLIGHT

brownish cheeks

forked tail

whitish underparts

ADULT

ADULT

wings dark underneath

The Bank Swallow, known in the UK as the Sand Martin, is the slimmest and smallest of North American swallows. As its scientific name *riparia* (meaning "riverbanks") and common name suggest, the Bank Swallow nests in the banks and bluffs of rivers, streams, and lakes. It also favors sand and gravel quarries in the East. It is widely distributed across North America, breeding from south of the tundra–taiga line down to the central US. The nesting colonies can range from as few as 10 pairs to as many as 2,000, which are quite noisy when all the birds are calling or coming in to feed the young.

VOICE Call a soft *brrrrr* or *breee* often issued in pairs; song a harsh twittering or continuous chatter.

NESTING Burrow in soft, sandy bank containing a flat platform of grass, feathers, and twigs; 2–6 eggs; 1 brood; April–August.

FEEDING Catches insects, such as flies, moths, dragonflies, and bees in flight, but occasionally skims aquatic insects or their larvae off the water or terrestrial insects from the ground.

FLIGHT: fast, frantic, butterfly-like flight with glides, twists, and turns; shallow, rapid wing beats.

WAITING FOR MOM
Hungry youngsters still expect to be fed, even when they're ready to fledge.

SIMILAR SPECIES

TREE SWALLOW ☾
larger; gray-brown upperparts with greenish tinge; see p.303

incomplete breastband

NORTHERN ROUGH-WINGED SWALLOW
larger overall; see p.305

uniformly colored upperparts

OCCURRENCE
Widespread in North America. Breeds in lowland habitats associated with rivers, streams, lakes, reservoirs, and coasts, as well as in sand and gravel quarries. Often prefers artificial sites; winters in grasslands, open farm habitat, and freshwater areas in South America.

| Length **4¾–5½in (12–14cm)** | Wingspan **10–11in (25–28cm)** | Weight **⅜–¹¹⁄₁₆oz (10–19g)** |
| Social **Colonies** | Lifespan **Up to 9 years** | Status **Threatened** |

DATE: _____ TIME:_____ LOCATION:_____

Order **Passeriformes**	Family **Hirundinidae**	Species *Tachycineta bicolor*

Tree Swallow 🔊

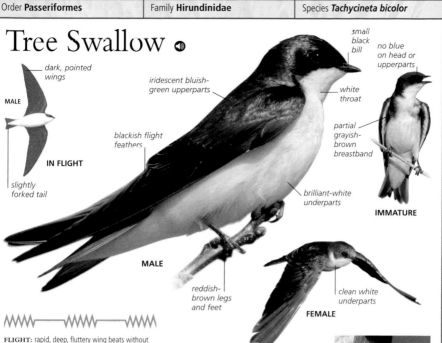

dark, pointed wings

MALE

IN FLIGHT

slightly forked tail

iridescent bluish-green upperparts

blackish flight feathers

small black bill

no blue on head or upperparts

white throat

partial grayish-brown breastband

IMMATURE

brilliant-white underparts

MALE

reddish-brown legs and feet

clean white underparts

FEMALE

FLIGHT: rapid, deep, fluttery wing beats without pause; quick turns and twists.

One of the most common North American swallows, the Tree Swallow is found from coast to coast in the upper half of the continent all the way up to Alaska. As its Latin name *bicolor* suggests, it has iridescent bluish-green upperparts and white underparts. Immature birds can be confused with the smaller Bank Swallow, which has a more complete breastband. The Tree Swallow lives in a variety of habitats, but its hole-nesting habit makes it completely dependent on abandoned woodpecker cavities in dead trees and on artificial "housing," such as nest boxes. The size of the population fluctuates according to the availability of the nesting sites.

VOICE Ranges from variable high, chirping notes to chatters and soft trills; also complex high and clear two-note whistle phrases.

NESTING Layer of fine plant matter in abandoned woodpecker hole or nest box, lined with feathers; 4–6 eggs; 1 brood; May–July.

FEEDING Swoops after flying insects from dawn to dusk; also takes bayberries.

KEEPING LOOKOUT
This species uses artificial nest boxes, which the males defend as soon as they arrive.

OCCURRENCE
Typically breeds close to water in open habitat, such as fields, marshes, lakes, and swamps, especially those with standing dead wood for cavity-nesting. Hundreds of thousands of birds winter in tall marsh vegetation.

SIMILAR SPECIES		
BANK SWALLOW paler brown rump; see p.302	**VIOLET-GREEN SWALLOW** white flank patch see p.304	

distinct dusky breastband

violet-green upperparts

white eye patch

Length **5–6in (13–15cm)**	Wingspan **12–14in (30–35cm)**	Weight **⅝–⅞oz (17–25g)**
Social **Large flocks**	Lifespan **Up to 11 years**	Status **Secure**

DATE: _____ TIME: _____ LOCATION: _____

| Order **Passeriformes** | Family **Hirundinidae** | Species *Tachycineta thalassina* |

Violet-green Swallow

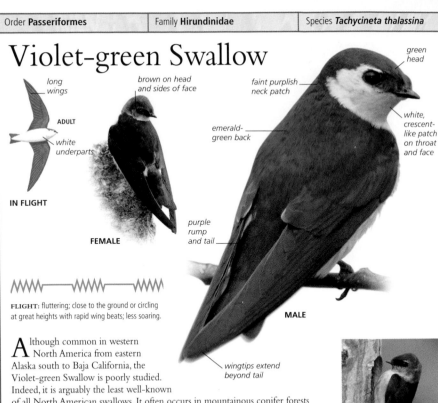

long wings

ADULT

white underparts

IN FLIGHT

brown on head and sides of face

FEMALE

faint purplish neck patch

emerald-green back

purple rump and tail

green head

white, crescent-like patch on throat and face

wingtips extend beyond tail

MALE

FLIGHT: fluttering; close to the ground or circling at great heights with rapid wing beats; less soaring.

Although common in western North America from eastern Alaska south to Baja California, the Violet-green Swallow is poorly studied. Indeed, it is arguably the least well-known of all North American swallows. It often occurs in mountainous conifer forests where it breeds in woodpecker holes in dead trees, or in cliff crevices, but it also uses birdhouses. A distinguishing feature of this swallow is the white patch that covers its throat and forms a line over its eyes. Its Latin name *thalassina* means "sea-green," while its common name refers to the same color, along with the violet of its rump. In its mountain habitat, the Violet-green Swallow can be encountered together with the White-throated Swift.

VOICE Primary call a twittering *chee-chee* of brief duration; alarm call a dry, brief *zwrack*.

NESTING Nest of grass, twigs, straw, and feathers in a natural or woodpecker cavity in a tree, also cliff or nesting box; 4–6 eggs; 2 broods; March–August.

FEEDING Catches flying insects, such as bees, wasps, moths, and flies; usually at higher levels than other species of swallows.

AT THE NEST HOLE
The female of this species can be distinguished from the male by her darker face.

OCCURRENCE
In the US and Canada, breeds in open deciduous, coniferous, and mixed woodlands, especially with ponderosa and Monterey pines and quaking aspen; also wooded canyons. Frequents waterways during migration; prefers higher elevations in general. Breeds south of the US, in Mexico.

SIMILAR SPECIES

WHITE-THROATED SWIFT
see p.99

white sides of rump

TREE SWALLOW ♂
see p.303
iridescent greenish blue upperparts

blackish-brown crown

| Length **5in (13cm)** | Wingspan **11in (28cm)** | Weight **½oz (14g)** |
| Social **Solitary/Colonies** | Lifespan **At least 6 years** | Status **Secure** |

DATE: _____ TIME:_____ LOCATION:_____

Northern Rough-winged Swallow 🔊

light crescent from cheek to crown

brown head

dark-brown overall

black eye

ADULT

IMMATURE

tan-buffy wing bars

pale-brown breast

dark face

pale underparts

pale, grayish-brown belly

IN FLIGHT

long brown wings

ADULT

square tail

G iven the name *serripennis*— "saw-feather—" by Audubon in 1888, and characterized by stiff barbs on the leading edges of its outer wing feathers, this species is otherwise somewhat drab in color and aspect. The Northern Rough-winged Swallow has a broad distribution in North America, being found across southern Canada and throughout the US. With no obvious discernible markings, this brown-backed, dusky-throated swallow can be spotted by hunting insects over water. In size and habit, the Northern Rough-winged Swallow shares many similarities with the Bank Swallow, including breeding habits and color, but the latter's notched tail and smaller size make it easy to tell them apart.

VOICE Steady repetition of short, rapid *brrrt* notes inflected upward; sometimes a buzzy *jee-jee-jee* or high-pitched *brzzzzzt*.

NESTING Loose cup of twigs and straw in a cavity or burrow in a bank, such as road cuts; 4–7 eggs; 1 brood; May–July.

FEEDING Captures flying insects, including flies, wasps, bees, damselflies, and beetles in the air; more likely to feed over water and at lower altitudes than other swallows.

Moderate wing beats, short to long glides, long, straight flight, ends in steep climb.

JUST A BROWN BIRD
This swallow is brownish above and pale grayish below, with a brown smudge on its neck.

SIMILAR SPECIES

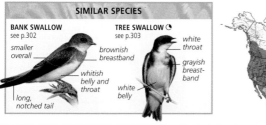

BANK SWALLOW
see p.302

smaller overall

whitish belly and throat

long, notched tail

brownish breastband

TREE SWALLOW ☾
see p.303

white throat

grayish breast-band

white belly

OCCURRENCE
In North America, widespread from coast to coast. Nests at a wide variety of altitudes, prefers exposed banks of clay, sand, or gravel, such as gorges, shale banks, and gravel pits. Forages along watercourses where aerial insects are plentiful. Breeds south to Costa Rica. Winters in Central America.

| Length **4¾–6in (12–15cm)** | Wingspan **11–12in (28–30cm)** | Weight **⅜–⅝oz (10–18g)** |
| Social **Solitary** | Lifespan **At least 5 years** | Status **Secure** |

DATE: _____ TIME: _____ LOCATION: _____

| Order **Passeriformes** | Family **Hirundinidae** | Species **Progne subis** |

Purple Martin

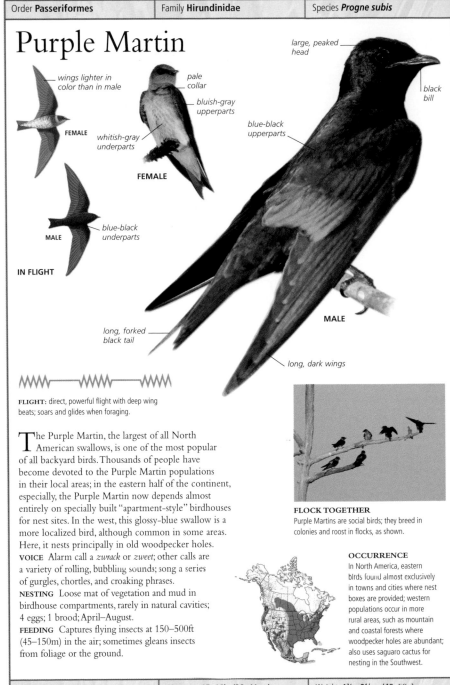

large, peaked head

black bill

wings lighter in color than in male

pale collar

FEMALE

bluish-gray upperparts

whitish-gray underparts

blue-black upperparts

FEMALE

blue-black underparts

MALE

IN FLIGHT

MALE

long, forked black tail

long, dark wings

FLIGHT: direct, powerful flight with deep wing beats; soars and glides when foraging.

The Purple Martin, the largest of all North American swallows, is one of the most popular of all backyard birds. Thousands of people have become devoted to the Purple Martin populations in their local areas; in the eastern half of the continent, especially, the Purple Martin now depends almost entirely on specially built "apartment-style" birdhouses for nest sites. In the west, this glossy-blue swallow is a more localized bird, although common in some areas. Here, it nests principally in old woodpecker holes.
VOICE Alarm call a *zwrack* or *zweet*; other calls are a variety of rolling, bubbling sounds; song a series of gurgles, chortles, and croaking phrases.
NESTING Loose mat of vegetation and mud in birdhouse compartments, rarely in natural cavities; 4 eggs; 1 brood; April–August.
FEEDING Captures flying insects at 150–500ft (45–150m) in the air; sometimes gleans insects from foliage or the ground.

FLOCK TOGETHER
Purple Martins are social birds; they breed in colonies and roost in flocks, as shown.

OCCURRENCE
In North America, eastern birds found almost exclusively in towns and cities where nest boxes are provided; western populations occur in more rural areas, such as mountain and coastal forests where woodpecker holes are abundant; also uses saguaro cactus for nesting in the Southwest.

| Length **7–8in (18–20cm)** | Wingspan **15–16in (38–41cm)** | Weight **1⁷⁄₁₆–2¹⁄₈oz (40–60g)** |
| Social **Large flocks/Colonies** | Lifespan **Up to 13 years** | Status **Secure** |

DATE: _____ TIME: _____ LOCATION: _____

| Order **Passeriformes** | Family **Hirundinidae** | Species *Hirundo rustica* |

Barn Swallow 🔊

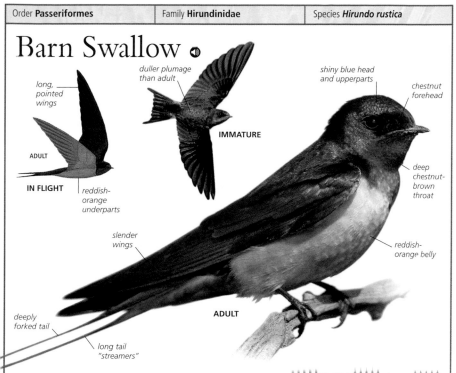

long, pointed wings

ADULT

IN FLIGHT

reddish-orange underparts

duller plumage than adult

IMMATURE

shiny blue head and upperparts

chestnut forehead

deep chestnut-brown throat

slender wings

reddish-orange belly

deeply forked tail

long tail "streamers"

ADULT

The most widely distributed and abundant swallow in the world, the Barn Swallow is found just about everywhere in North America south of the Arctic timberline. Originally a cave-nester before Europeans settlers came to the New World, the Barn Swallow readily adapted to nesting under the eaves of houses, under bridges, and inside buildings, such as barns. It is now rare to find this elegant swallow breeding in a natural site. Steely-blue upperparts, reddish underparts, and a deeply forked tail identify the Barn Swallow. North American breeders have deep, reddish-orange underparts, but birds from Eurasia are white-bellied.

VOICE High-pitched, squeaky *chee-chee* call; song a long series of chatty, pleasant *churrs*, squeaks, chitterings, and buzzes.

NESTING Deep cup of mud and grass-stems attached to vertical surfaces or on ledges; 4–6 eggs; 1–2 broods; May–September.

FEEDING Snatches flying insects, such as flies, mosquitoes, wasps, and beetles in the air at lower altitudes than other swallows; sometimes eats wild berries and seeds.

FLIGHT: bursts of straight flight; close to the ground; weaves left and right, with sharp turns.

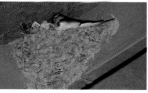

WELL PROTECTED
Whether in a barn or other structure, a Barn Swallow nest is protected from wind and rain.

SIMILAR SPECIES

TREE SWALLOW ♂
see p.303
lacks forked tail and dark breast band

white underparts

OCCURRENCE
Breeds across North America, except in the tundra zone; south as far as central Mexico. Found in most habitats, but prefers agricultural regions, towns, and highway overpasses; migrates over coastal marshes; winters near sugarcane fields, grain fields, and marshes.

| Length **6–7½in (15–19cm)** | Wingspan **11½–13in (29–33cm)** | Weight **⅝–¹¹⁄₁₆oz (17–20g)** |
| Social **Small colonies/flocks** | Lifespan **Up to 8 years** | Status **Threatened** |

DATE: _____ TIME: _____ LOCATION: _____

Order **Passeriformes**	Family **Hirundinidae**	Species *Petrochelidon pyrrhonota*

Cliff Swallow 🔊

long, roundish wings

brown-tinged black back

rusty cheek patch

mottled throat

IMMATURE

bluish-black back

ADULT

IN FLIGHT

rusty-brown cheeks

bluish-black cap

pale hind neck collar

whitish forehead

dark throat

ADULT

pale underparts

slight notch in squared tail

pale reddish rump

The Cliff Swallow is one of North America's most social land birds, sometimes nesting in colonies of over 3,500 pairs, especially in the western US. It is more locally distributed across the east. It can be distinguished from other North American swallows by its square tail and orange rump, but it resembles its close relative, the Cave Swallow, in color, pattern, and in affixing its mud nests to the sides of highway culverts, bridges, and buildings. The considerable increase in such structures has allowed the species to expand its range from the west to breed almost everywhere, except in dense forests and desert habitats.

VOICE Gives *purr* and *churr* calls when alarmed; song a low, squeaky, 6-second twitter given in flight and near nests.

NESTING Domed nests of mud pellets on cave walls, buildings, culverts, bridges, and dams; 3–5 eggs; 1–2 broods; April–August.

FEEDING Catches flying insects (often swarming varieties) while on the wing; sometimes forages on the ground; ingests grit to aid digestion.

FLIGHT: strong, fast wing beats; glides more often but less acrobatically than other swallows.

GATHERING MUD
The Cliff Swallow gathers wet mud from puddles, pond edges, and streamsides to build its nests.

SIMILAR SPECIES

CAVE SWALLOW brighter orange cheek

paler overall

INDIVIDUAL HOMES
In a Cliff Swallow colony, each nest has a single opening.

OCCURRENCE
Breeds almost anywhere in North America from Alaska to Mexico, except deserts, tundra, and unbroken forest; prefers concrete or cliff walls, culverts, buildings, and undersides of piers on which to affix mud nests; feeds over grasslands, marshes, lakes, and reservoirs. Migrates to South America.

Length **5in (13cm)**	Wingspan **11–12in (28–30cm)**	Weight **¹¹⁄₁₆–1¼oz (20–35g)**
Social **Colonies**	Lifespan **Up to 11 years**	Status **Secure**

DATE: _____ TIME:_____ LOCATION:_____

Order **Passeriformes**	Family **Aegithalidae**	Species *Psaltriparus minimus*

Bushtit

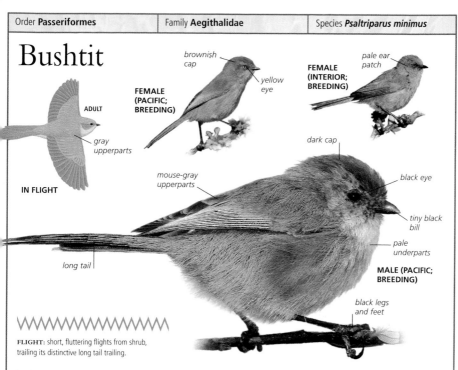

FEMALE (PACIFIC; BREEDING)
brownish cap
yellow eye

FEMALE (INTERIOR; BREEDING)
pale ear patch

ADULT
gray upperparts

IN FLIGHT

mouse-gray upperparts

long tail

dark cap

black eye

tiny black bill

pale underparts

MALE (PACIFIC; BREEDING)

black legs and feet

FLIGHT: short, fluttering flights from shrub, trailing its distinctive long tail trailing.

The Bushtit is most often found roaming the foothills and valleys of the western US in flocks that usually number just a handful, but occasionally total many hundreds. This little bird is constantly on the move, foraging busily in the foliage of shrubs and small trees. Even during the breeding season, when most other perching birds become territorial, the Bushtit retains something of its social nature—raising the young is often a communal affair, with both siblings and single adults helping in the rearing of a pair's chicks.

VOICE Basic call a 2–3-part soft lisp, *ps psss pit*, interspersed with hard spit and spick notes, like little sparks.

NESTING Enormous pendant structure of cobwebs and leaves, hung from branch; 4–10 eggs; 2 broods; April–July.

FEEDING Gleans spiders and insects from vegetation; acrobatic while feeding, often hangs upside-down; will visit suet feeders.

GANG FORAGING
Constantly aflutter, Bushtits flit noisily through the foliage in gangs searching for insects and spiders.

SIMILAR SPECIES

PYGMY NUTHATCH
see p.317
larger bill
black eyestripe
short tail

DARK-EYED JUNCO
see p. 376
dark-gray head
pale bill
white belly

OCCURRENCE
Away from the coast, common in open woodlands and areas of shrubs, mainly on hillsides in summer; some birds move down to low-elevation valleys in the fall. Coastal populations, commonly seen in cities and gardens as well as on hillsides, live in native and non-native plant communities.

Length **4½in (11.5cm)**	Wingspan **6in (15.5cm)**	Weight **³⁄₁₆–⁷⁄₃₂oz (4.5–6g)**
Social **Flocks**	Lifespan **Up to 8 years**	Status **Secure**

DATE: _____ TIME: _____ LOCATION: _____

NUTHATCHES

Common woodland birds, nuthatches are easily recognized by their distinctive shape and characteristic feeding techniques, and often located by loud squeaky calls. They are tree-dwellers, feeding around branches and nesting in small holes. Nuthatches are plump-bodied, short-tailed but large-headed birds, with strong, pointed bills and short legs, strong toes, and arched claws. Unlike woodpeckers and creepers, which mostly climb in an upward direction, they do not need to use the tail as a prop when exploring a tree's bark. These birds rely solely on their strong and secure grip to hop and shuffle in all directions, frequently hanging upside down. They feed on spiders and also probe for insects and their larvae in the cracks of tree bark. They also eat seeds and nuts, which they may wedge into a crevice and break open with noisy taps of the bill—hence, the name "nuthatch."

ACROBATIC POSE
Downward-facing nuthatches, such as this White-breasted Nuthatch, often lift their heads in a characteristic pose.

WRENS

With one exception, the Eurasian Wren, wrens are North American songbirds. They are sharp-billed birds with short- or medium-length tails that are frequently cocked upward. Wrens are intricately patterned, mostly with dark bars and streaks, and pale spots on buff-and-rusty backgrounds. Their family name, *Troglodytidae,* derives from a Greek word for "cave-dweller"—while they do not really inhabit caves, the description is apt as some North American species, such as the Winter Wren, forage deep inside thick cover of all kinds, from scrub to upturned tree roots and overgrown stumps, or in dense growth inside ditches. The aptly named Marsh Wrens are found in marshes and Sedge Wrens in sedge meadows. Wrens are often best located by their calls, which are fairly loud for such small birds. Some wren species sing precisely synchronized duets.

COCKED TAIL
As they sing, Winter Wrens often hold their tails upward, in a near-vertical position.

| Order **Passeriformes** | Family **Regulidae** | Species **Corthylio calendula** |

Ruby-crowned Kinglet

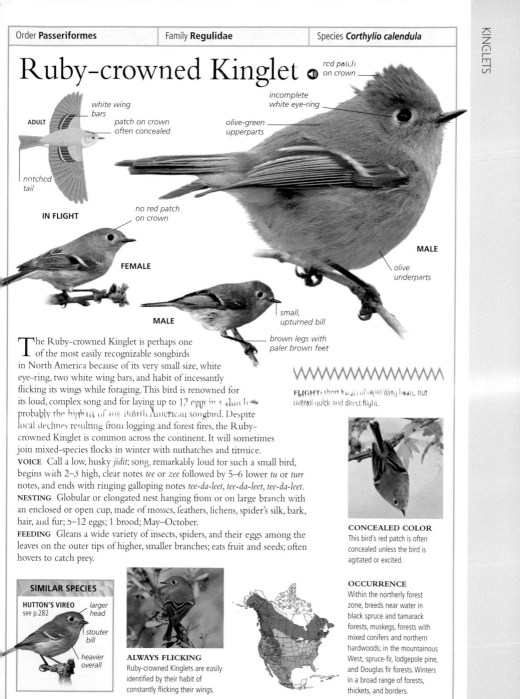

red patch on crown

white wing bars

ADULT

patch on crown often concealed

incomplete white eye-ring

olive-green upperparts

notched tail

IN FLIGHT

no red patch on crown

FEMALE

MALE

olive underparts

MALE

small, upturned bill

brown legs with paler brown feet

The Ruby-crowned Kinglet is perhaps one of the most easily recognizable songbirds in North America because of its very small size, white eye-ring, two white wing bars, and habit of incessantly flicking its wings while foraging. This bird is renowned for its loud, complex song and for laying up to 12 eggs in a clutch, probably the highest of any North American songbird. Despite local declines resulting from logging and forest fires, the Ruby-crowned Kinglet is common across the continent. It will sometimes join mixed-species flocks in winter with nuthatches and titmice.

VOICE Call a low, husky *jidit*; song, remarkably loud for such a small bird, begins with 2–3 high, clear notes *tee* or *zee* followed by 5–6 lower *tu* or *turr* notes, and ends with ringing galloping notes *tee-da-leet, tee-da-leet, tee-da-leet*.

NESTING Globular or elongated nest hanging from or on large branch with an enclosed or open cup, made of mosses, feathers, lichens, spider's silk, bark, hair, and fur; 5–12 eggs; 1 brood; May–October.

FEEDING Gleans a wide variety of insects, spiders, and their eggs among the leaves on the outer tips of higher, smaller branches; eats fruit and seeds; often hovers to catch prey.

FLIGHT: short bursts of rapid wing beats, but overall quick and direct flight.

CONCEALED COLOR
This bird's red patch is often concealed unless the bird is agitated or excited.

SIMILAR SPECIES

HUTTON'S VIREO see p.282

larger head

stouter bill

heavier overall

ALWAYS FLICKING
Ruby-crowned Kinglets are easily identified by their habit of constantly flicking their wings.

OCCURRENCE
Within the northerly forest zone, breeds near water in black spruce and tamarack forests, muskegs, forests with mixed conifers and northern hardwoods; in the mountainous West, spruce-fir, lodgepole pine, and Douglas fir forests. Winters in a broad range of forests, thickets, and borders.

| Length **3½–4¼in (9–11cm)** | Wingspan **6–7in (15–18cm)** | Weight **³⁄₁₆–³⁄₈oz (5–10g)** |
| Social **Winter flocks** | Lifespan **Up to 5 years** | Status **Secure** |

DATE: _____ TIME: _____ LOCATION: _____

Order **Passeriformes**	Family **Regulidae**	Species **Regulus satrapa**

Golden-crowned Kinglet 🔊

whitish wing bars

MALE

IN FLIGHT

yellow crown patch, with black border

FEMALE

orange-and-yellow patch on crown, with black border

broad whitish stripe above eye

olive-green upperparts

short, straight bill

MALE

white wing bar

notched tail

pale-buff to whitish underparts

FLIGHT: quick and erratic, but not direct; high in the air; can hover while foraging.

This hardy little bird, barely more than a ball of feathers, breeds in northern and mountainous coniferous forests in North America. Other unconnected populations are residents of high-elevation forests in Mexico and Guatemala. Planting of spruce trees has been quite beneficial to the Golden-crowned Kinglet, allowing it to expand its range southward into the US Midwest.
VOICE Call a thin, high-pitched and thread-like *tsee* or *see see*; song a series of high-pitched ascending notes for two seconds; complex song *tsee-tsee-tsee-tsee-teet-leetle*, followed by brief trill.
NESTING Deep, cup-shaped nest with rims arching inward, made of moss, lichen, and bark, and lined with finer strips of the same; 8–9 eggs; 1–2 broods; May–August.
FEEDING Gleans flies, beetles, mites, spiders, and their eggs from tips of branches, under bark, tufts of conifer needles; eats seeds and persimmon fruit.

CONIFER CONNOISEUR
This bird particularly favors coniferous forests for foraging for insects and seeds.

SIMILAR SPECIES

RUBY-CROWNED KINGLET
see p.311

white eye-ring

no eye-stripe

olive underparts

HIGHER VOICE
The Golden-crowned has a higher-pitched and less musical song than the Ruby-crowned.

OCCURRENCE
Breeds in remote northern and subalpine spruce or fir forests, mixed coniferous–deciduous forests, single-species stands, and pine plantations; winters in a wide variety of habitats—coniferous and deciduous forests, pine groves, low-lying hardwood forests, swamps, and urban and suburban habitats.

Length 3¼–4¼in (8–11cm)	Wingspan 5½–7in (14–18cm)	Weight ⁵⁄₃₂–⁹⁄₃₂oz (4–8g)
Social **Solitary/Pairs**	Lifespan **Up to 5 years**	Status **Secure**

DATE: _____ TIME:_____ LOCATION:_____

Order **Passeriformes**	Family **Bombycillidae**	Species *Bombycilla garrulus*

Bohemian Waxwing

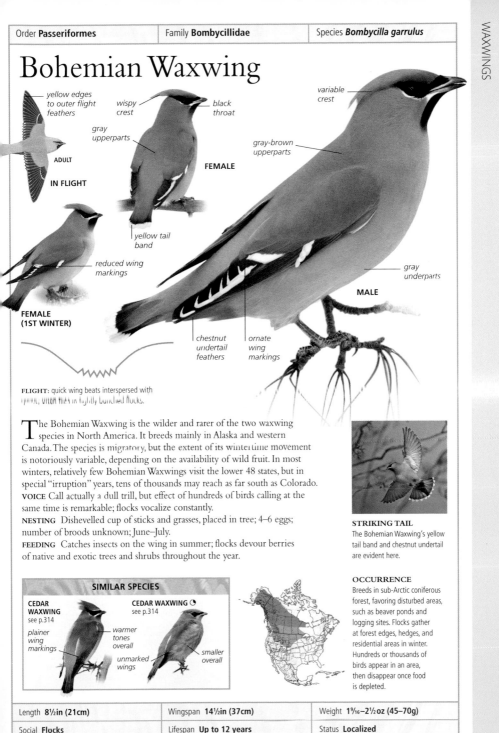

yellow edges to outer flight feathers

wispy crest

black throat

gray upperparts

ADULT

IN FLIGHT

variable crest

gray-brown upperparts

FEMALE

yellow tail band

reduced wing markings

FEMALE (1ST WINTER)

chestnut undertail feathers

ornate wing markings

gray underparts

MALE

FLIGHT: quick wing beats interspersed with pauses; often flies in tightly bunched flocks.

The Bohemian Waxwing is the wilder and rarer of the two waxwing species in North America. It breeds mainly in Alaska and western Canada. The species is migratory, but the extent of its wintertime movement is notoriously variable, depending on the availability of wild fruit. In most winters, relatively few Bohemian Waxwings visit the lower 48 states, but in special "irruption" years, tens of thousands may reach as far south as Colorado.
VOICE Call actually a dull trill, but effect of hundreds of birds calling at the same time is remarkable; flocks vocalize constantly.
NESTING Dishevelled cup of sticks and grasses, placed in tree; 4–6 eggs; number of broods unknown; June–July.
FEEDING Catches insects on the wing in summer; flocks devour berries of native and exotic trees and shrubs throughout the year.

STRIKING TAIL
The Bohemian Waxwing's yellow tail band and chestnut undertail are evident here.

OCCURRENCE
Breeds in sub-Arctic coniferous forest, favoring disturbed areas, such as beaver ponds and logging sites. Flocks gather at forest edges, hedges, and residential areas in winter. Hundreds or thousands of birds appear in an area, then disappear once food is depleted.

SIMILAR SPECIES

CEDAR WAXWING
see p.314

plainer wing markings

CEDAR WAXWING ◑
see p.314

warmer tones overall

unmarked wings

smaller overall

Length **8½in (21cm)**	Wingspan **14½in (37cm)**	Weight **1⁹⁄₁₆–2½oz (45–70g)**
Social **Flocks**	Lifespan **Up to 12 years**	Status **Localized**

DATE: _____ TIME: _____ LOCATION: _____

| Order **Passeriformes** | Family **Bombycillidae** | Species ***Bombycilla cedrorum*** |

Cedar Waxwing 🔊

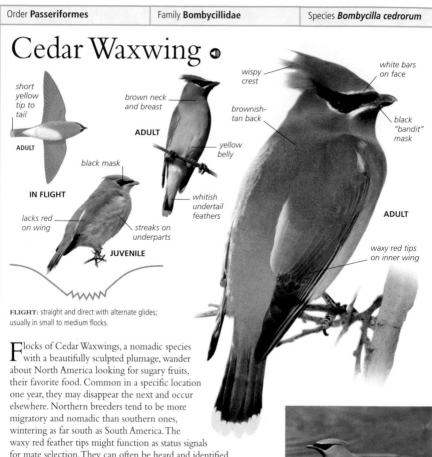

short yellow tip to tail

ADULT

IN FLIGHT

brown neck and breast

ADULT

yellow belly

black mask

lacks red on wing

streaks on underparts

JUVENILE

whitish undertail feathers

wispy crest

brownish-tan back

white bars on face

black "bandit" mask

ADULT

waxy red tips on inner wing

FLIGHT: straight and direct with alternate glides; usually in small to medium flocks.

Flocks of Cedar Waxwings, a nomadic species with a beautifully sculpted plumage, wander about North America looking for sugary fruits, their favorite food. Common in a specific location one year, they may disappear the next and occur elsewhere. Northern breeders tend to be more migratory and nomadic than southern ones, wintering as far south as South America. The waxy red feather tips might function as status signals for mate selection. They can often be heard and identified by their high-pitched calls, long before the flock settles to feed.
VOICE Basic vocalization a shrill trill: *shr-r-r-r-r-r* or *tre-e-e-e-e-e*, which appears to serve the function of both call note and song.
NESTING Open cup placed in fork of tree, often lined with grasses, plant fibers; 3–5 eggs; 1–2 broods; June–August.
FEEDING Eats in flocks at trees and shrubs with ripe berries throughout the year; also catches flying insects in summer.

BATHING ADULT
Cedar Waxwings love to take baths, and use birdbaths in suburban gardens.

SIMILAR SPECIES

BOHEMIAN WAXWING ♂
see p.313

larger overall

more ornate wing pattern

rufous undertail

BOHEMIAN WAXWING ♀♪
see p.313

pale-gray breast

OCCURRENCE
Breeds in woodlands across the northern US and southern Canada, especially near streams and clearings. Winters where trees and shrubs have ripe fruits, especially in Mexico and South America. Spends a lot of time in treetops, but sometimes comes down to shrub level.

Length **7½in (19cm)**	Wingspan **12in (30cm)**	Weight **1¹⁄₁₆–1¼oz (30–35g)**
Social **Flocks**	Lifespan **Up to 7 years**	Status **Secure**

DATE: _____ TIME: _____ LOCATION: _____

| Order **Passeriformes** | Family **Sittidae** | Species *Sitta canadensis* |

Red-breasted Nuthatch 🔊

rounded wings

MALE

white bands on tail

IN FLIGHT

slightly muted head pattern

FEMALE

pale-orange underparts

dark blue-gray crown and eyestripe

black eyestripe

blue-gray upperparts

bold black-and-white head pattern

pointed, chisel-like bill

white cheeks

short blue-gray tail, with black side feathers

rusty underparts

compact body shape

MALE

FLIGHT: short, swift dashes across forest clearings; irregular, undulating motion.

This impulsive nuthatch, with its distinctive black eyestripe, breeds in conifer forests across North America. The bird inhabits mountains in the West; in the East, it is found in lowlands and hills. However, sometimes it breeds in conifer groves away from its core range. Each fall, birds move from their main breeding grounds, but the extent of this exodus varies from year to year, depending on population cycles and food availability.

VOICE Call a one-note tooting sound, often repeated, with strong nasal yet musical quality: *aaank, enk, ink,* rather like a horn.

NESTING Excavates cavity in pine tree; nest of grass lined with feathers, with sticky pine resin applied to entrance; 5–7 eggs, 1 brood; May–July.

FEEDING Probes bark for beetle grubs; also eats insect larvae found on conifer needles; seeds in winter.

TASTY GRUB
This nuthatch has just extracted its dinner from the bark of a tree, a favorite foraging habitat.

SIMILAR SPECIES

PYGMY NUTHATCH
see p.317

grayish-brown cap

dusky underparts

WHITE-BREASTED NUTHATCH
see p.316

larger overall

lacks black eye-stripe

white belly

chestnut undertail

OCCURRENCE
Found year-round in coniferous and mixed hardwood forests. During breeding season, absent from southeastern pine forests, except in the Appalachians. In the West, shares its habitat with the Pygmy Nuthatch, but ranges to higher elevations.

| Length **4¼in (11cm)** | Wingspan **8½in (22cm)** | Weight **⅜–⁷⁄₁₆oz (10–13g)** |
| Social **Solitary/Pairs** | Lifespan **Up to 7 years** | Status **Secure** |

DATE: _____ TIME: _____ LOCATION: _____

| Order **Passeriformes** | Family **Sittidae** | Species *Sitta carolinensis* |

White-breasted Nuthatch 🔊

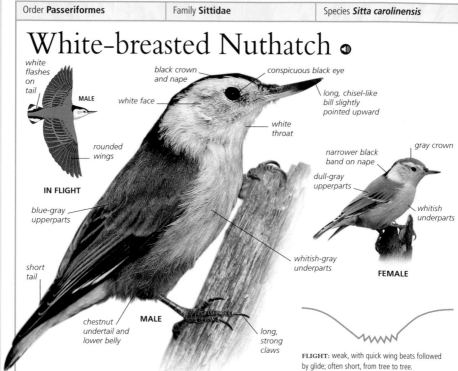

white flashes on tail

MALE

black crown and nape

conspicuous black eye

white face

long, chisel-like bill slightly pointed upward

white throat

gray crown

narrower black band on nape

dull-gray upperparts

whitish underparts

rounded wings

IN FLIGHT

blue-gray upperparts

whitish-gray underparts

short tail

FEMALE

chestnut undertail and lower belly

MALE

long, strong claws

FLIGHT: weak, with quick wing beats followed by glide; often short, from tree to tree.

The amiable White-breasted Nuthatch inhabits woodlands across the US and southern Canada, but often visits bird feeders in winter. The largest of our nuthatches, it spends more time probing furrows and crevices on trunks and boughs than other nuthatches do. It walks irregularly on trees: forward, backward, upside-down, or horizontally. Of the 11 subspecies in its Canada-to-Mexico range, five occur in Canada and in the US. They differ in call notes and, to a lesser extent, in plumage.

VOICE Calls vary geographically: eastern birds nasal *yank yank*; interior birds stuttering *st't't't't*; Pacific-slope birds tremulous *yiiiirk*; song of all populations a mellow *tu tu tu tu tu*, like a flicker, but softer.

NESTING Tree cavity, once used by woodpeckers, lined with grass and hair, adds mud to cavity opening; 5–9 eggs, 1 brood; April–June.

FEEDING Scours bark methodically for insects, such as beetle larvae.

UNUSUAL DESCENT
Nuthatches are unusual in that they routinely descend branches and trunks headfirst.

SIMILAR SPECIES

PYGMY NUTHATCH
see p.317
grayish-brown cap
dusky underparts

RED-BREASTED NUTHATCH
see p.315
reddish underparts

black eye-stripe

smaller overall

OCCURRENCE
More liberal than other nuthatches in the use of forest types; overlaps with the smaller species in coniferous forest ranges, but also common in broadleaf deciduous or mixed forests; weakly migratory: little movement in most falls, but moderate departures from breeding grounds in some years.

| Length **5¾ in (14.5cm)** | Wingspan **11in (28cm)** | Weight **¹¹⁄₁₆–⁷⁄₈ oz (19–25g)** |
| Social **Solitary/Pairs** | Lifespan **Up to 9 years** | Status **Secure** |

DATE: _____ TIME: _____ LOCATION: _____

| Order **Passeriformes** | Family **Sittidae** | Species *Sitta pygmaea* |

Pygmy Nuthatch

rounded wings

ADULT

IN FLIGHT

grayish-brown cap

pointed, chisel-like bill

blue-gray upperparts

black eyestripe

dusky underparts

very short tail

grayish flanks

ADULT

sharp claws

Pygmy Nuthatches are found in noisy and busy flocks throughout the year in their pine forest home of western North America. They are cooperative breeders, with young birds from the previous year's brood often helping adult birds raise the next year's young. They have a particular preference for ponderosa and Jeffery pines and are often absent from mountain ranges that lack their favorite trees. Pygmy Nuthatches are heard more often than they are seen, probably because they like to stick to the treetops.

VOICE Highly vocal species; calls piercing *peep* and *pip* notes, given singly or in frenzied series; in series, call resembles vocalizations of some Red Crossbills; calls of birds in flocks are somewhat bell-like.

NESTING Excavates cavity in pine tree; nest is a mass of plant material and feathers; 5–9 eggs; 1–2 broods; April–July.

FEEDING Forages on pine trees; mainly eats insects, caterpillars, moths, and grubs.

FLIGHT: jerky, undulating motion; appears bobtailed and rotund in flight.

SQUEEZING OUT OF A NEST
All nuthatches nest in tree cavities, which they wholly or partially excavate themselves.

SIMILAR SPECIES

WHITE-BREASTED NUTHATCH
see p.316

black crown

white face

PINE FORAGER
A Pygmy Nuthatch hangs upside down, carrying a tiny piece of food.

OCCURRENCE
Patchily distributed in pine forests of western North America, from British Columbia south to California, Arizona, New Mexico, and Texas; also in Mexico. Most numerous in dry mountain forests up to 650ft (2,000m), but ranges down to sea level in California.

| Length **4¼in (11cm)** | Wingspan **8in (20cm)** | Weight **⅜oz (11g)** |
| Social **Small flocks** | Lifespan **Up to 6 years** | Status **Secure** |

DATE: _____ TIME:_____ LOCATION:_____

| Order **Passeriformes** | Family **Certhiidae** | Species **Certhia americana** |

Brown Creeper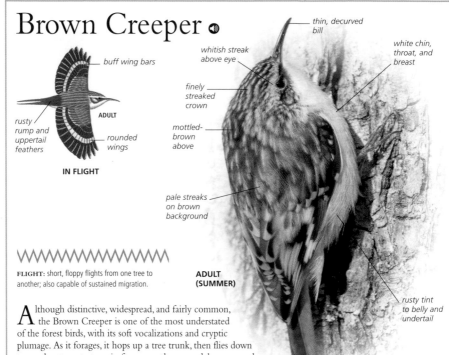

IN FLIGHT

- buff wing bars
- rusty rump and uppertail feathers
- rounded wings
- **ADULT**

- thin, decurved bill
- whitish streak above eye
- finely streaked crown
- mottled-brown above
- white chin, throat, and breast
- pale streaks on brown background

FLIGHT: short, floppy flights from one tree to another; also capable of sustained migration.

ADULT (SUMMER)

- rusty tint to belly and undertail
- long, forked tail

Although distinctive, widespread, and fairly common, the Brown Creeper is one of the most understated of the forest birds, with its soft vocalizations and cryptic plumage. As it forages, it hops up a tree trunk, then flies down to another tree, starts again from near the ground, hops up, and so on. These birds have adapted to habitat changes in the northeast and their numbers have increased in regenerating forests. Mid- and southwestern populations, by contrast, have declined because forest cutting has reduced their breeding habitat. The Brown Creeper is a partial migrant—some individuals move south in the fall, and head north in the spring; others remain close to their breeding grounds.
VOICE High-pitched and easily overlooked call a buzzy *zwiss*, flight call an abrupt *tswit*; song a wheezy jumble of thin whistles and short buzzes.
NESTING Unique hammock-shaped nest, behind piece of peeling bark; 5–6 eggs, 1 brood; May–July.
FEEDING Probes bark for insects, especially larvae, eggs, pupae, and aphids.

SIMILAR SPECIES

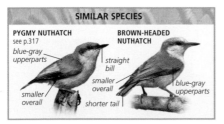

PYGMY NUTHATCH
see p.317
- blue-gray upperparts
- smaller overall

BROWN-HEADED NUTHATCH
- straight bill
- smaller overall
- blue-gray upperparts
- shorter tail

STRONG TAIL
The Brown Creeper uses its stiff forked tail to prop itself against the trunk of this tree.

OCCURRENCE
The only North American creeper, it breeds in a variety of forests, particularly fairly moist coniferous or mixed hardwood forests, also large stands with snags and standing dead trees. In winter, it is seen in small groves without coniferous trees; also in residential districts or suburbs.

| Length **5¼in (13.5cm)** | Wingspan **8in (20cm)** | Weight **¼–⅜oz (7–10g)** |
| Social **Solitary** | Lifespan **At least 5 years** | Status **Secure** |

DATE: _____ TIME: _____ LOCATION: _____

| Order **Passeriformes** | Family **Troglodytidae** | Species *Salpinctes obsoletus* |

Rock Wren

faint eyestripe

rusty rump

ADULT

bright-buff feather tips

IN FLIGHT

grayish-brown upperparts

thin brown streaks

buff-yellow belly

black-and-white barring on undertail

buff-yellow lower flanks

ADULT

FLIGHT: straight, with fast wing beats; sometimes glides from high perch.

An inhabitant of various rocky landscapes—it often sings from the edge of a high precipice—the Rock Wren's voice, while not particularly loud, carries surprisingly far through the dry air of the West. It is perpetually busy running, fluttering, and darting in and out of crevices in search of food. A well-known behavioral quirk of the Rock Wren is to bob and sway conspicuously when a human approaches. However, its oddest habit is to "pave" the area in front of its nest entrance with a walkway of pebbles—the purpose of this is unknown.

VOICE Call a sharp *ch'keer;* varied series of warbles, trills, chatters, and repeated musical phrases such as *chuwee chuwee, teedee teedee,* reminiscent of a mockingbird or a thrasher.

NESTING Cup of various grasses lined with soft materials, in rock crevice or under overhang; 4–8 eggs; 1–2 broods; April–August.

FEEDING Probes in rock crevices on ground and in dirt banks for a variety of insects and spiders.

A CHANGE OF SCENERY
Rock Wrens occasionally venture out into open grasslands and perch on artificial structures, well away from their usual surroundings.

SIMILAR SPECIES

HOUSE WREN (WESTERN) see p.321
smaller overall
black barring
pale gray-brown underparts
bright-rufous rump and tail

CANYON WREN see p.320
rufous breast and sides

OCCURRENCE
Inhabits arid country with rocky cliffs and canyons, as well as rock quarries and gravel piles; a wide variety of elevations from hot, low deserts to windswept mountain tops as high as 10,000ft (3,000m). Northern birds migrate to southern states for winter.

| Length **6in (15cm)** | Wingspan **9in (23cm)** | Weight **⅝oz (17g)** |
| Social **Solitary/Pairs** | Lifespan **Unknown** | Status **Secure** |

| Order **Passeriformes** | Family **Troglodytidae** | Species *Catherpes mexicanus* |

Canyon Wren

grayish cap and cheeks

thinly barred rufous tail

small black-and-white spots on back and wings

long, decurved bill

white throat

bright-rufous rump

long, decurved bill

ADULT

round wings

IN FLIGHT

rufous underparts barred with black and brown

ADULT

The Canyon Wren's loud, clear whistles echo across canyons in the West, but the singer usually stays out of sight, remaining high among the crevices of its cliffside home. When it can be observed, the most striking aspect of its behavior is its extraordinary ability to walk up, down, and sideways on vertical rock walls. This remarkable agility is achieved through its strong toes and long claws; these features enable Canyon Wrens to find a grip in the tiniest of depressions and fissures in the rock.

VOICE Series of 10–15 loud, ringing whistles, descending in pitch, gradually slowing, and ending with several thin buzzes.
NESTING Cup of sticks lined with soft material, like plant down, in crevice or hole; 4–6 eggs; 1–2 broods; April–August.
FEEDING Uses extremely long bill to probe crevices for insects and spiders; can flatten itself by spreading legs to enter low overhangs.

FLIGHT: steady, straight, and fluttery; broad, rounded wings let it glide to a lower perch.

BLENDING IN
Except for the white throat, the Canyon Wren's plumage matches its rocky habitat.

CLIFF-HOPPER
This bird can half-fly and half-hop up steep cliffs by flapping its broad wings for extra lift.

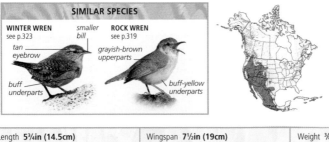

SIMILAR SPECIES

WINTER WREN see p.323
smaller bill
tan eyebrow
buff underparts

ROCK WREN see p.319
grayish-brown upperparts
buff-yellow underparts

OCCURRENCE
Maintains year-round territory on rocky hillsides, outcroppings, and vertical rock-walled canyons through much of the west of the continent and southward to Mexico. Sometimes nests in holes in stone buildings, old sheds, and other structures, apparently unconcerned by nearby human activity.

| Length **5¾in (14.5cm)** | Wingspan **7½in (19cm)** | Weight **⅜oz (11g)** |
| Social **Solitary/Pairs** | Lifespan **Unknown** | Status **Secure** |

DATE: _____ TIME: _____ LOCATION: _____

| Order **Passeriformes** | Family **Troglodytidae** | Species ***Troglodytes aedon*** |

House Wren

plain brown crown

faintly barred wings

ADULT (EASTERN)

IN FLIGHT

browner upperparts

ADULT
T. a. aedon
(EASTERN)

pale-buffy throat

narrow, pale eye-ring

grayish-brown back

thin, indistinct eyebrow

thin, slightly decurved bill

narrow black barring on tail

ADULT
T. a. parkmanii
(WESTERN)

pale gray-brown underparts

FLIGHT: straight, with fast wing beats; typically over short distances.

Of all the North American wrens, the House Wren is the plainest, yet one of the most familiar and endearing, especially when making its home in a backyard nest box. However, it can be a fairly aggressive species, driving away nearby nesting birds of its own species and others by destroying nests, puncturing eggs, and even killing young. In the 1920s, distraught bird-lovers mounted a campaign calling for the eradication of House Wrens, though the campaign did not last long as most were in favor of letting nature take its course.

VOICE Call a sharp *chep* or *cherr*; song opens with several short notes, followed by a bubbly explosion of extending spluttering notes.

NESTING Cup lined with soft material on stick platform in natural or constructed cavities, such as nest boxes; 5–8 eggs; 2–3 broods; April–July.

FEEDING Forages for insects and spiders in trees and shrubs, gardens, and yards.

SIMILAR SPECIES

WINTER WREN *dark-brown overall*
see p.323
shorter tail

heavily barred flanks

NESTING MATERIAL
This small bird has brought an unusually large twig to its nest inside an old woodpecker hole.

OCCURRENCE
Breeds in cities, towns, parks, farms, yards, gardens, and woodland edges. Rarely seen during migration period (late July to early October). Winters south of its breeding range, from the southern US to Mexico, in woodlands, shrubby areas, and weedy fields. Nests, or is resident, as far south as Tierra del Fuego.

| Length **4½in (11.5cm)** | Wingspan **6in (15cm)** | Weight **⅜oz (11g)** |
| Social **Solitary** | Lifespan **Up to 9 years** | Status **Secure** |

| Order **Passeriformes** | Family **Troglodytidae** | Species ***Troglodytes pacificus*** |

Pacific Wren 🔊

short, barred tail often raised

warm-brown back

larger than continental birds

sings with bill wide open

short, round tail

ADULT (T. p. alascensis)

dumpy, rounded body

Bering Sea race paler than birds on continent

rounded, whirring wings

barred primaries

IN FLIGHT

ADULT (T. p. alascensis)

Wrens are a diverse family found almost exclusively in the New World, with 80 species occurring from Alaska to the tip of South America and just a single species in the Old World. They are fairly varied for a passerine family. The Pacific Wren, Winter Wren, and Eurasian Wren were, until recently considered a single variable species. A typical small wren, the Pacific Wren looks practically identical to the Winter Wren and Eurasian Wren, but DNA studies indicate separation from a common ancestor more than 4 million years ago. They are easily overlooked but draw attention to themselves by singing loudly and popping out of dense cover to look around, call, and dive down again out of sight.

VOICE Call shorter, slightly higher-pitched than the Winter Wren; ringing, tinkling song.

NESTING Nests in cavity in stump, roots, or rocks almost at ground level; 5–6 eggs; 1–2 broods.

FEEDING Insects, especially beetles, also bugs, spiders, millipedes, small snails, and caterpillars.

FLIGHT: short, low, fast flights on whirring wings.

ON THE ALERT
Wrens appear highly alert, aware of danger, and always ready to dive out of sight.

OCCURRENCE
Extensive tracts of mature spruce and fir forest, often close to water. Prefer to explore patches of thick, tangled undergrowth and fallen branches under the trees. In winter, populations from higher areas migrate south and east to find milder conditions.

SIMILAR SPECIES

WINTER WREN see p.323 — clearly barred back and wings — similar cocked tail — pale underside

HOUSE WREN see p.321 — grayer body plumage — longer tail — longer, paler foreparts

| Length **4in (10cm)** | Wingspan **5½in (14cm)** | Weight **⁵⁄₁₆oz (9g)** |
| Social **Solitary/Family groups** | Lifespan **At least 4 years** | Status **Secure** |

DATE: _____ TIME: _____ LOCATION: _____

| Order **Passeriformes** | Family **Troglodytidae** | Species *Troglodytes hiemalis* |

Winter Wren

distinct tan eyebrow

stubby tail, usually cocked straight up

dark-brown, barred back

small, thin bill

ADULT

short, barred tail

ADULT

IN FLIGHT

barred, rounded wings

flanks strongly barred

The Winter Wren has one of the loudest songs of any small North American species. Once considered more widespread, it has recently been split from the Pacific Wren, which occupies much of the western fringe of the continent. It is a bird of low undergrowth and tangled roots, often foraging in the upturned roots and broken branches of fall... ...appearing mouse-like as it creeps amid the shadows. It frequently appears in full view, gives a few harsh, scolding calls, then dives back out of sight into the low cover. It can survive periods of intense cold and even snow cover by finding insects and spiders in bark crevices and soil-encrusted roots. Several Winter Wrens may roost together in small cavities for warmth.
VOICE Call a double *chek-chek* or *chimp-chimp*; song a loud, extremely long, complex series of warbles, trills, and single notes.
NESTING Well-hidden in a cavity near ground with dead wood and crevices; nest a messy mound lined with feathers; 4–7 eggs; 1–2 broods; April–July.
FEEDING Forages for insects in low, dense undergrowth, often in wet areas along streams; sometimes thrusts its head into water to capture prey.

...fligh... ...and differ..., with rapid beats of its short, broad wings.

VOCAL VIRTUOSO
The Winter Wren is a skulker, but in the breeding season singing males show up on lower perches.

SIMILAR SPECIES

HOUSE WREN
see p.321
grayish-brown back

long tail

plain, unbarred flanks

NERVOUS REACTION
When alarmed, this wren cocks its tail almost vertically before escaping into a mossy thicket.

OCCURRENCE
Breeds in northerly and mountain forests dominated by evergreen trees with a dense understory, fallen trees, and banks of streams. In the Appalachians, breeds in treeless areas with grass near cliffs. Northernmost birds migrate south to winter in woodlands, brush piles, tangles, and secluded spots.

| Length **4in (10cm)** | Wingspan **5½in (14cm)** | Weight **⁵⁄₁₆oz (9g)** |
| Social **Solitary/Family groups** | Lifespan **At least 4 years** | Status **Secure** |

DATE: _____ TIME: _____ LOCATION: _____

| Order **Passeriformes** | Family **Troglodytidae** | Species **Cistothorus stellaris** |

Sedge Wren

ADULT

reddish-tan rump

streaked back

short, round wings

IN FLIGHT

streaked cap

short bill

buffy eyebrow

streaked back and inner wing feathers

barred wings and tail

faint white barring on chest

buffy underparts

ADULT

FLIGHT: short bursts, from cover to cover, with fast wing beats.

The Sedge Wren, formerly named the Short-billed Marsh Wren, is an extremely shy bird. It stays out of sight in dense cover except when singing atop a sedge stalk or a shrub. If discovered, it flies a short distance, drops down, and runs out of sight through the vegetation. The Sedge Wren has two geographically distinct breeding seasons—May–June in the north central region of its range, and July–September in the southern and eastern regions. A feature of its breeding behavior, also found in other species of wrens, is the male's habit of building up to 8–10 unlined "dummy" nests before the female builds the better-concealed, real nest.

VOICE Call a loud *chap*; song a dry, staccato two-part chatter: *cha cha cha cha ch'ch'ch ch'ch'ch'*.

NESTING Globular, woven structure of sedges with side entrance; lined with plant matter, down, and hair; 4–8 eggs; 1–2 broods; May–August.

FEEDING Forages for spiders and insects, such as grasshoppers, flies, mosquitoes, and bugs, close to or on ground in cover of sedges and grass.

LOOK CLOSELY
Close study is necessary to appreciate the Sedge Wren's subtle patterning, which is plainer than the Marsh Wren's.

OCCURRENCE
In North America, breeds in wet meadows and sedge marshes with low water levels. Widely distributed in the Americas from the Canadian prairies east to Quebec, sand from the northern US to the south central states. Winters from Texas to Florida in drier habitats including grassy fields and coastal-plain prairies.

SIMILAR SPECIES

MARSH WREN
see p.325

heavily striped back

plain cap

white eyebrow

HOUSE WREN
see p.321

plain back

faint eyebrow

grayish-brown underparts

| Length **4in (10cm)** | Wingspan **5½–6in (14–15.5cm)** | Weight **⁵⁄₁₆oz (9g)** |
| Social **Loose colonies** | Lifespan **Unknown** | Status **Secure** |

DATE: _____ TIME:_____ LOCATION:_____

Order **Passeriformes**	Family **Troglodytidae**	Species *Cistothorus palustris*

Marsh Wren

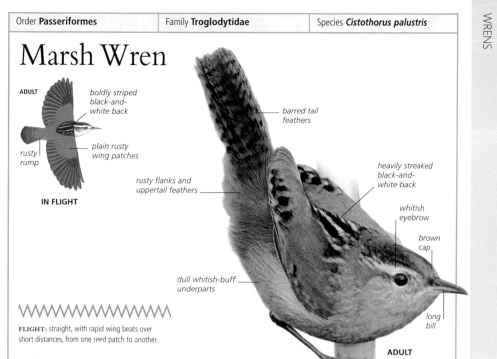

ADULT

boldly striped black-and-white back

barred tail feathers

rusty rump

plain rusty wing patches

heavily streaked black-and-white back

rusty flanks and uppertail feathers

whitish eyebrow

brown cap

IN FLIGHT

dull whitish-buff underparts

long bill

ADULT

FLIGHT: straight, with rapid wing beats over short distances, from one reed patch to another.

The Marsh Wren, a common resident of saltwater and freshwater marshes, is known for singing loudly through both day and night. The males perform fluttery, aerial courtship flights while singing, and are polygamous, mating with two or more females. Like the Sedge Wren, the male builds several "dummy" nests before his mate constructs one herself. The Marsh Wren nests in taller vegetation than the Sedge Wren and over deeper water. Eastern and Western Marsh Wrens differ in voice and behavior, and some ornithologists classify them as separate species.

VOICE Calls a low *chek* and a raspy *churr*; song a loud *chuk chuk chuk*, then fast *tih-tih-tih-rih-tih-tih*, an enthusiastic singer.

NESTING Oblong structure with side entrance, woven of reeds and lined with soft materials; 4–5 eggs; 2 broods; March–July.

FEEDING Forages acrobatically for insects, such as mosquitoes, dragonflies, and beetles, within dense clusters of cattails and reeds.

DELICATELY PERCHED
This wren perches on vertical reeds and often holds itself up by spreading its legs across two stalks.

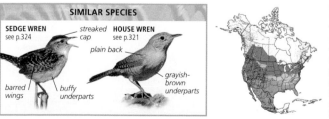

SIMILAR SPECIES

SEDGE WREN see p.324

streaked cap

HOUSE WREN see p.321

plain back

barred wings

buffy underparts

grayish-brown underparts

OCCURRENCE
Breeds from Canada down to the mountains of the western US as well as the central and the northeastern US states. Inhabits freshwater and saltwater marshes with tall vegetation, above water, sometimes more than 3ft (1m) deep. It is irregularly distributed in its range. Winters in grassy marshes.

Length **5in (13cm)**	Wingspan **6in (15cm)**	Weight **⅜oz (11g)**
Social **Loose colonies**	Lifespan **Unknown**	Status **Localized**

DATE: _____ TIME: _____ LOCATION: _____

Order **Passeriformes**	Family **Troglodytidae**	Species ***Thryomanes bewickii***

Bewick's Wren 🔊

black-and-white outer tail tips

brown cheeks

white eyebrow

long, slightly decurved bill

long, rounded tail

largely unmarked, dull-brown upperparts

whitish throat and breast

ADULT

ADULT
T. b. drymoecus
(PACIFIC COAST)

dark-brown flight feathers

IN FLIGHT

plain gray upperparts

pale-gray underparts

ADULT
T. b. eremophilus
(SOUTHWESTERN)

FLIGHT: fast and straight; over short distances.

Like the House Wren, but less common and occupying a smaller range, Bewick's Wren is also familiar around human habitations. It is known to nest in any sort of hole or crevice in barns, houses, abandoned machinery, woodpiles, and even trash heaps in farms and towns. Bewick's Wren has undergone large-scale changes in geographic distribution: in the 19th century its range expanded northward to the eastern and the midwestern US, but it gradually disappeared from those regions in the 20th century. It has been suggested that the more aggressive House Wren slowly replaced Bewick's Wren in these areas.

VOICE Loud, complex, and varied mixture of cheeps, buzzes, and clear notes; vocalizations differ according to geographic location; also mimics other birds.

NESTING Cup of sticks lined with leaves, and other soft materials, in natural or human-made cavity, including nest boxes; 5–10 eggs; 2 broods; March–June.

FEEDING Forages for insects in brush, shrubs, crannies of buildings, and leaf litter on ground.

TALENTED MIMIC
Bewick's is sometimes known as the "Mocking Wren," due to its imitations of other species' songs.

OCCURRENCE
Year-round resident in brushy areas, open woodlands, and around human structures; from southern British Columbia southward to Baja California, east to Arkansas, and as far south as Oaxaca in Mexico. May withdraw slightly southward from northernmost portions of range in winter.

SIMILAR SPECIES

HOUSE WREN (WESTERN)
see p.321
grayish-brown back; barring on wings

shorter tail

TYPICAL POSTURE
Bewick's Wren may often be spotted with its distinctive tail cocked vertically.

Length **5in (13cm)**	Wingspan **7in (18cm)**	Weight **⅜oz (11g)**
Social **Solitary/Pairs**	Lifespan **At least 8 years**	Status **Secure**

DATE: _____ TIME: _____ LOCATION: _____

Families **Mimidae, Sturnidae**

THRASHERS

The family name for thrashers, mockingbirds, and catbirds, Mimidae, is derived from the Latin word for "to imitate" or mimic. Perhaps no other word better describes the dozen or so thrashers of North America. They are well known for their ability to mimic the songs of other species and incorporate phrases into their own complex song sequences. In appearance, they are superficially thrush-like, but thrashers are more elongated and have longer, somewhat more decurved bills, and generally longer legs and tails. While mockingbirds may be bold, brash, and conspicuous—they are often found on open perches—thrashers are more reclusive, tending to forage deep within thickets or low vegetation, hopping on their strong feet, and digging into the leaf layer to find food with their bills.

DISTINCTIVE BILL
This Brown Thrasher is characterized by its slender, decurved bill, long, thin legs, and long, rounded tail.

Families **Muscicapidae, Turdidae**

THRUSHES AND CHATS

Thrushes, chats (wheatears and bluethroats), and their relatives are small- to medium-sized birds. Many are forest species but feed mostly on the ground, while others, such as the Northern Wheatear, are birds of the open countryside. Many thrushes have a plain brown upperside and a spotted underside, but make up for their lack of color with their beautiful flute-like songs. Some, however, are brightly colored and strongly patterned: the American Robin is one of the most familiar birds. The smaller bluebirds are renowned for their bright blues while the North American solitaire is a much grayer species.

GROUND BIRDS
Though they perch to sing, thrushes, including this Varied Thrush, spend a lot of their time on or near the ground.

327

Order **Passeriformes**	Family **Mimidae**	Species *Dumetella carolinensis*

Gray Catbird 🔊

dark-gray to black head

straight blackish bill

gray overall

ADULT

IN FLIGHT

long black tail

gray upperparts

large black eye

gray underparts

ADULT

bright brick-red undertail feathers

In addition to the feline-like, mewing calls that earned it its common name, the Gray Catbird not only has an extraordinarily varied vocal repertoire, but it can also sing two notes simultaneously. It has been reported to imitate the vocalizations of over 40 bird species, at least one frog species, and several sounds produced by machines and electronic devices. Despite their shy, retiring nature, Gray Catbirds tolerate human presence and will rest in shrubs in suburban and urban lots. Another fascinating skill is the Gray Catbird's ability to recognize and remove eggs of the brood parasite, the Brown-headed Cowbird.

VOICE *Mew* call, like a young kitten; song a long, complex series of unhurried, often grouped notes, sometimes interspersed with whistles and squeaks.

NESTING Large, untidy cup of woven twigs, grass, and hair lined with finer material; 3–4 eggs; 1–2 broods; May–August.

FEEDING Feeds on a wide variety of berries and insects, usually whatever is most abundant in season.

FLIGHT: short flights between habitat patches with constant, medium-speed wing beats.

ANGLED ATTITUDE
Between bouts of feeding, a Gray Catbird often rests with its body and tail at a 50-degree angle.

LARGE BLACK EYES
Peering from the foliage, but often hidden, a Gray Catbird investigates its surroundings.

OCCURRENCE
Breeds in mixed young to mid-aged forests with abundant undergrowth, from British Columbia east to the Maritimes and Newfoundland, and in the US diagonally west-east from Washington State to New Mexico, east to the Gulf Coast, north to New England. Northern population migratory.

SIMILAR SPECIES

NORTHERN MOCKINGBIRD
see p.331
white wing patch
longer tail edged in white

TOWNSEND'S SOLITAIRE
see p.337
tan patches
lighter gray
shorter bill
white eye-ring

Length **8–9½in (20–24cm)**	Wingspan **10–12in (25–30cm)**	Weight **1¼–2⅛oz (35–60g)**
Social **Solitary/Pairs**	Lifespan **Up to 11 years**	Status **Secure**

DATE: _____ TIME: _____ LOCATION: _____

| Order **Passeriformes** | Family **Mimidae** | Species *Toxostoma rufum* |

Brown Thrasher 🔊

fairly straight, dark bill

bright-yellow eye

grayish cheeks

indistinct "mustache"

reddish-brown upperparts

dark streaking on pale underparts

rufous wings and upperparts

ADULT

long tail with pale outer tips

IN FLIGHT

two pale wing bars

long tail, paler than back

ADULT

The Brown Thrasher is usually difficult to view clearly because it keeps to dense undergrowth. Like most other thrashers, this species prefers running or hopping to flying. When nesting, it can recognize and remove the eggs of brood parasites like the Brown-headed Cowbird. The current population decline is most likely the result of fragmentation of large, wooded habitats into patches, which lack the forest interior habitat this species needs.

VOICE Calls varied, including rasping sounds; song a long series of musical notes, sometimes imitating other species; repeats phrase twice before moving on to the next one.

NESTING Bulky cup of twigs close to ground, lined with leaves, grass, bark; 3–5 eggs; 1 brood; April–July.

FEEDING Mainly insects (especially beetles) and worms gathered from leaf litter on the forest floor; will peck at cultivated grains, nuts, berries, and fruit.

FLIGHT: slow and heavy with deep wing beats; below treetops, especially in and around ground.

OCCURRENCE
Widespread across central and eastern North America, from Canada to Texas and Florida, in a variety of densely wooded habitats, particularly those with thick undergrowth, but will also use woodland edges, hedges, and riverside trees. A partial migrant, it winters in the southern part of its range.

STREAKED BREAST
Displaying its heavily streaked underparts, this Brown Thrasher is perched and ready to sing.

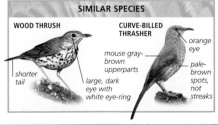

SIMILAR SPECIES

WOOD THRUSH

shorter tail

CURVE-BILLED THRASHER

mouse gray-brown upperparts

large, dark eye with white eye-ring

orange eye

pale-brown spots, not streaks

| Length **10–12in (25–30cm)** | Wingspan **11–14in (28–36cm)** | Weight **2⅛–2⅞oz (60–80g)** |
| Social **Solitary/Flocks** | Lifespan **Up to 13 years** | Status **Declining** |

DATE: _____ TIME:_____ LOCATION:_____

| Order **Passeriformes** | Family **Mimidae** | Species *Oreoscoptes montanus* |

Sage Thrasher 🔊

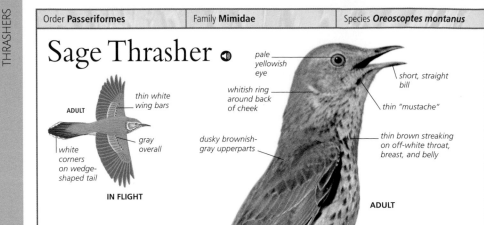

ADULT

thin white
wing bars

gray
overall

white
corners
on wedge-
shaped tail

IN FLIGHT

pale
yellowish
eye

whitish ring
around back
of cheek

dusky brownish-
gray upperparts

short, straight
bill

thin "mustache"

thin brown streaking
on off-white throat,
breast, and belly

ADULT

FLIGHT: prefers to run; may dart low between patches of habitat using short, rapid wing beats.

This plain-colored little bird is the smallest of the North American thrashers. Together with several other members of this group, the Sage Thrasher recognizes and removes the eggs of brood parasites, especially those of the Brown-headed Cowbird. Unfortunately, it may also be the least studied of the thrasher group, perhaps because the dense nature of its habitat makes study difficult. The English name, "Sage Thrasher," truly describes this bird's western habitat.

VOICE Song varies in duration: low, repeated, very musical notes or phrases that may blend together in a melodious song.

NESTING Large cup with stick frame lined with grass, horse hair, sheep's wool, and fur; 3–6 eggs; 1–2 broods; April–July.

FEEDING Eats insects, especially ants and beetles, on the ground; will also consume berries when seasonally available.

JUICY MEAL
This thrasher forages mostly on or near the ground; it feeds on insects and berries.

SHOW-OFF TENDENCIES
Males attract mates and defend their territory with raised wings, in a fluttering display.

SIMILAR SPECIES

NORTHERN MOCKINGBIRD ◑
see p.331

dark eye

white
patch
on wing

CURVE-BILLED THRASHER

orange eye

more gray
on back

pale-
gray
spots

OCCURRENCE
Very closely associated with sagebrush habitat in low-elevation and semi-arid valleys of southwestern Canada and the western US. Winters from the southwestern US to Baja California and continental Mexico, southwards to Sonora and Coahuila.

| Length **8–9in (20–23cm)** | Wingspan **10–13in (25–33cm)** | Weight **1⁷⁄₁₆–1³⁄₄oz (40–50g)** |
| Social **Solitary/Pairs** | Lifespan **Unknown** | Status **Endangered** |

DATE: _____ TIME: _____ LOCATION: _____

Order **Passeriformes**	Family **Mimidae**	Species *Mimus polyglottos*

Northern Mockingbird 🔊

ADULT

white patches on wing

IN FLIGHT

shorter tail

speckled breast and belly

IMMATURE

gray head

pointed, decurved bill

yellow eye

long tail with white outer tail feathers

white undertail feathers

ADULT

white patch on wing feathers

FLIGHT: usually direct and level on constant, somewhat fluttering, quick wing beats.

The ability of the Northern Mockingbird to imitate sounds is truly impressive: some individuals can incorporate more than 100 different phrases of as many different birds in their songs. Phrases are usually repeated, often quite a few times, and somewhat modified at each repetition. This species, once thought to be headed for extinction due to the cagebird trade in the 1700s and 1800s, has largely recovered since then. In fact, the Northern Mockingbird's range has expanded in the last few decades, partly due to its high tolerance for humans and their habitats. A diagnostic field characteristic is its tendency to "wing flash;" that is, display its white outer wing feathers by raising its wings while foraging on the ground, obstensibly to scare insects into the open.

VOICE Long, complex repertoire often imitating other birds, non-bird noises, and the sounds of mechanical devices.

NESTING Bulky cup of twigs, lined, in shrub or tree; 3–5 eggs; 1–3 broods; March–August.

FEEDING Eats a wide variety of fruit, berries, and insects, including ants, beetles, and grasshoppers.

BERRY PICKER
Northern Mockingbirds love berries and make good use of them during the fall.

SIMILAR SPECIES

LOGGERHEAD SHRIKE ◑
see p.280

brown mask

black wings

CLARK'S NUTCRACKER
see p.292

white patch low on wing

darker gray belly

whiter sides to tail

OCCURRENCE
Widespread in the US from coast to coast, primarily along edges of disturbed habitats, including young forests and especially suburban and urban areas with shrubs or hedges. Breeding range has extended into southern Canada.

Length 8½–10in (22–25cm)	Wingspan 13–15in (33–38cm)	Weight 1⁹⁄₁₆–2oz (45–55g)
Social **Pairs**	Lifespan **Up to 20 years**	Status **Secure**

DATE: _____ TIME: _____ LOCATION: _____

| Order **Passeriformes** | Family **Sturnidae** | Species ***Sturnus vulgaris*** |

European Starling 🔊

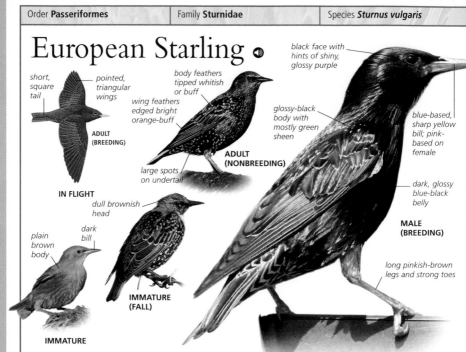

short, square tail

pointed, triangular wings

ADULT (BREEDING)

IN FLIGHT

body feathers tipped whitish or buff

wing feathers edged bright orange-buff

large spots on undertail

ADULT (NONBREEDING)

black face with hints of shiny, glossy purple

glossy-black body with mostly green sheen

blue-based, sharp yellow bill; pink-based on female

dark, glossy blue-black belly

MALE (BREEDING)

long pinkish-brown legs and strong toes

dull brownish head

plain brown body

dark bill

IMMATURE (FALL)

IMMATURE

This distinctive non-native species is perhaps the most successful bird in North America—and probably the most maligned. In the 1890s, 60 to 100 European Starlings were successfully released in New York City's Central Park to become the ancestors of the 200 million birds now living in North America. This adaptable and aggressive bird competes with native species for nest sites, and usually wins—even against larger species such as the Northern Flicker and the American Kestrel.
VOICE Highly varied; gives whooshing *sssssheer*, often in flight; also whistled *wheeeooo*; song an elaborate pulsing series with slurred whistles and clicking notes; imitates other birds and various noises.
NESTING Natural or artificial cavity of any sort; 4–6 eggs; 1–2 broods; March–July.
FEEDING Omnivorous; picks at anything that might be edible; eats insects and berries; raids berry crops and vineyards; visits bird feeders and trashcans; often feeds on grubs in lawns.

FLIGHT: individuals fly in direct, buzzy manner; flocks bunch up tightly in flight.

INSECT EATER
Despite its parents' omnivorous diet, the nestlings are fed almost exclusively on insects and larvae.

OCCURRENCE
In North America from southern Canada to the US-Mexico border; also Puerto Rico and other Caribbean islands. Common to abundant in cities, towns, and farmlands; also occurs in relatively "wild" settings far from human habitation. Forms flocks at all times, huge in winter.

SIMILAR SPECIES

BRONZED COWBIRD ♂
red eye
no spots

BROWN-HEADED COWBIRD
see p.400
no spots
longer tail

| Length **8½in (21cm)** | Wingspan **16in (41cm)** | Weight **2⅝ – 3³⁄₁₀oz (75–95g)** |
| Social **Colonies** | Lifespan **Up to 17 years** | Status **Secure** |

DATE: _____ TIME: _____ LOCATION: _____

Order **Passeriformes**	Family **Cinclidae**	Species *Cinclus mexicanus*

American Dipper

white eyelid

broad, rounded wings

short tail

short wings

straight black bill

ADULT

IN FLIGHT

pinkish bill

frosty scalloping on wings

sturdy pink legs

paler than adult

dark gray overall

ADULT

IMMATURE

The most aquatic North American songbird, the American Dipper is at home in the cold, rushing streams of western North America. It is known for its feeding technique of plunging into streams for aquatic insects and their larvae from under stones or in the streambed. It can also be seen walking with only its head submerged as it looks for prey. When it is not foraging, it watches from a rock or log, bobbing up and down, constantly flashing its nictitating membrane (the transparent third eyelid that protects the eye when the bird is underwater). The American Dipper's slow metabolic rate and its thick coat of waterproof feathers enable it to survive in the cold waters of its preferred habitat during the winter months. Susceptible to changes in water chemistry and turbulence, which alter the abundance of its main food, caddisfly larvae, this bird has been proposed as indicator for the water quality of fast-flowing trout streams.

VOICE Call a harsh *bzzt*, given singly or in rapid series; song a loud, disorganized series of pleasing warbles, whistles, and trills.

NESTING Domed nest with side entrance, placed underneath bridges, behind waterfalls, or in stream embankments always close to moving water; 4–5 eggs; 1–2 broods; March–August.

FEEDING Forages for insects and insect larvae, especially caddisflies; sometimes eats small fish and fish eggs.

FLIGHT: low over water, twisting and turning with the stream with rapid, buzzy wing beats.

BOBBING MOTION
The American Dipper often pauses on rocks in streams, where it bobs up and down.

OCCURRENCE
Found from Alaska, the Yukon, and British Columbia, south to California, Arizona, New Mexico, Mexico, and Panama. On the Pacific slope, breeds down to sea level; in Interior West, breeds mainly in mountains and foothills; retreats to lower elevations in winter.

Length **7½in (19cm)**	Wingspan **11in (28cm)**	Weight **1¾–2¼oz (50–65g)**
Social **Solitary**	Lifespan **Up to 7 years**	Status **Secure**

| Order **Passeriformes** | Family **Turdidae** | Species *Sialia sialis* |

Eastern Bluebird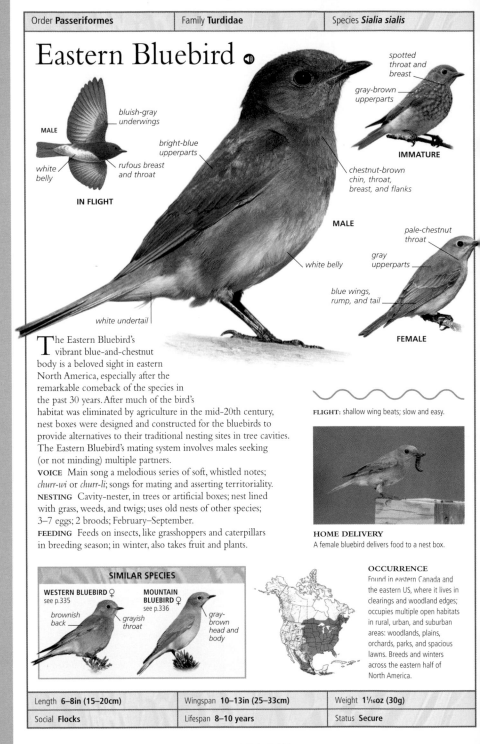

MALE

bluish-gray underwings

bright-blue upperparts

white belly

rufous breast and throat

IN FLIGHT

spotted throat and breast

gray-brown upperparts

IMMATURE

chestnut-brown chin, throat, breast, and flanks

MALE

white belly

pale-chestnut throat

gray upperparts

blue wings, rump, and tail

FEMALE

white undertail

The Eastern Bluebird's vibrant blue-and-chestnut body is a beloved sight in eastern North America, especially after the remarkable comeback of the species in the past 30 years. After much of the bird's habitat was eliminated by agriculture in the mid-20th century, nest boxes were designed and constructed for the bluebirds to provide alternatives to their traditional nesting sites in tree cavities. The Eastern Bluebird's mating system involves males seeking (or not minding) multiple partners.

VOICE Main song a melodious series of soft, whistled notes; *churr-wi* or *churr-li*; songs for mating and asserting territoriality.

NESTING Cavity-nester, in trees or artificial boxes; nest lined with grass, weeds, and twigs; uses old nests of other species; 3–7 eggs; 2 broods; February–September.

FEEDING Feeds on insects, like grasshoppers and caterpillars in breeding season; in winter, also takes fruit and plants.

FLIGHT: shallow wing beats; slow and easy.

HOME DELIVERY
A female bluebird delivers food to a nest box.

SIMILAR SPECIES

WESTERN BLUEBIRD ♀
see p.335

brownish back

grayish throat

MOUNTAIN BLUEBIRD ♀
see p.336

gray-brown head and body

OCCURRENCE
Found in eastern Canada and the eastern US, where it lives in clearings and woodland edges; occupies multiple open habitats in rural, urban, and suburban areas: woodlands, plains, orchards, parks, and spacious lawns. Breeds and winters across the eastern half of North America.

| Length **6–8in (15–20cm)** | Wingspan **10–13in (25–33cm)** | Weight **1¹⁄₁₆oz (30g)** |
| Social **Flocks** | Lifespan **8–10 years** | Status **Secure** |

DATE: _____ TIME: _____ LOCATION: _____

Order **Passeriformes**	Family **Turdidae**	Species *Sialia mexicana*

Western Bluebird 🔊

short wings and tail

MALE

pale-blue belly

IN FLIGHT

brownish back

grayish throat

FEMALE

blue hood

rust patch on back

blue shoulder and wing

chestnut breast and flanks

MALE

pale-blue belly

blue wings and tail

rusty undertail

blue wings

spotted underparts

IMMATURE

Very similar to its close relative, the Eastern Bluebird, but with a distribution restricted to the western part of the continent, the male Western Bluebird is endowed with a spectacular plumage—brilliant-blue upperparts and deep chestnut-orange underparts. Unlike the Eastern Bluebird, the Western Bluebird has a brown back and a complete blue hood. Females and immature birds are harder to distinguish, but their ranges are quite different.

VOICE Vocalizations similar to those of the Eastern Bluebird; calls soft *few, few* or *fewrr-fewrr*; song a pleasant, soft series of churring notes all strung together, often given at dawn.

NESTING Shallow cup of dry grass and feathers in natural tree cavity or old woodpecker cavity; 4–6 eggs; 1–2 broods; March–July.

FEEDING Feeds mainly on insects in breeding season; eats berries, such as juniper, in winter.

FLIGHT: slow and easy-looking, with shallow wing beats.

SIMILAR SPECIES

EASTERN BLUEBIRD ♀
see p.334

MOUNTAIN BLUEBIRD ♀
see p.336

gray-brown head

chestnut throat, breast, and sides

white belly

blue wings and tail

PERCHED MALE
The Western Bluebird hunts from low perches, from which it catches insects from the ground or air.

OCCURRENCE
During breeding season, open woodlands (coniferous and deciduous) and forest edges. In winter, moves to lower elevations and occupies open and semi-open areas, such as pinyon-juniper forests and deserts. Partial migrant; northern birds move south where southern breeders reside.

Length **6–7in (15–18cm)**	Wingspan **11½–13in (29–33cm)**	Weight **⅞–1¹⁄₁₆oz (25–30g)**
Social **Winter flocks**	Lifespan **Up to 7 years**	Status **Secure**

DATE: _____ TIME:_____ LOCATION:_____

Order **Passeriformes**	Family **Turdidae**	Species *Sialia currucoides*

Mountain Bluebird 🔊

long wings
and tail

blue overall

MALE

IN FLIGHT

vibrant-blue
upperparts

light-blue
flanks

whitish
underparts

MALE

lightly
spotted
back

blue wings
and tail

IMMATURE

gray-brown head
and body

gray-brown
flanks and
breast

bright-
blue wings

FEMALE

A bird of the North American West, especially subalpine meadows, the Mountain Bluebird is as striking as the other two *Sialia* species, but, unlike them, lacks any reddish-chestnut in its plumage. It is also more slender-looking, and flies in an almost lazy manner. More often than its two relatives, it feeds by hovering, kestrel-like, over meadows, before pouncing on insects. Males guard their mates from pair bond time to egg-hatching time.

VOICE Calls rolled, soft churring; one song, loud but infrequent, similar to the American Robin's song—*sing-song cheerily cheer-up cheerio*; the other, soft and repetitive whistle.

NESTING Cavity-nest of grass, weeds, and bark; 5–6 eggs; 2 broods; May–July.

FEEDING Insects, including crickets, grasshoppers, bees, and caterpillars, dominate its diet year-round; also berries.

FLIGHT: slow unhurried, almost leisurely, with shallow wing beats.

OCCURRENCE
Breeds in western North America, in grassland or open canyons with scattered trees, or alpine parklands. In winter, prefers open habitats and avoids dry areas. Winter habitat includes juniper and ponderosa pine forests in the south of its territory.

SIMILAR SPECIES

EASTERN BLUEBIRD ♀
see p.334

brownish
back

white
belly

WESTERN BLUEBIRD ♀
see p.335

grayish
throat

pale-orange
on breast
and flanks

BERRY-LOVER
Berries are an important part of the bird's diet, along with insects and caterpillars.

Length **6–8in (15–20cm)**	Wingspan **11–12½in (28–32cm)**	Weight **1¹⁄₁₆oz (30g)**
Social **Flocks**	Lifespan **At least 5 years**	Status **Secure**

DATE: _____ TIME: _____ LOCATION: _____

Order **Passeriformes**	Family **Turdidae**	Species *Myadestes townsendi*

Townsend's Solitaire 🔊

ADULT

dark-gray outer
flight feathers

wide buff
bands on
flight feathers

long
tail

short
head

IN FLIGHT

plain gray

upright
posture

ADULT

spotted
back

heavily
spotted
breast

IMMATURE

long tail

black legs
and feet

large black
eye

white
eye-ring

gray upperparts
and head

short
black
bill

paler
underparts

ADULT

pale
chestnut-tan
patches

long, dark tail
with white
outer feathers

The rather shy
Townsend's Solitaire
inhabits mountainous regions of western
North America, especially
high-elevation coniferous forests of the Sierras and the Rockies. Its
drab-gray plumage, with a chestnut-tan wing pattern, remains the
same throughout the year, and the sexes look alike. From a perch
high on a branch, Townsend's Solitaire darts after flying insects and
snaps its bill shut after catching its prey, unlike other thrushes.
VOICE Calls are single-note, high-pitched whistles; sings all year,
but especially when establishing territories; main song robin-like,
full of rolled or trilled sounds interspersed with squeaky notes.
NESTING Cup of pine needles, dry grass, weed stems, and bark
on ground or under overhang; 4 eggs; 1–2 broods; May–August.
FEEDING Forages for a wide variety of insects and spiders
during breeding season; feeds on fruit and berries after
breeding, particularly junipers.

FLIGHT: unhurried motion, usually over short
distances, with slow, steady wing beats.

JUNIPER-LOVER
Solitaires love the berry-like cones of junipers,
which they eat to supplement their winter diet.

SIMILAR SPECIES

**MOUNTAIN
BLUEBIRD ♀**
see p.336

dull bluish
back

blue in
wings
and
tail

short
tail

GRAY PLUMAGE
Townsend's Solitaire is a
drab gray overall, but has
a conspicuous white eye-ring.

OCCURRENCE
During breeding season,
found in open conifer forests
along steep slopes or areas
with landslides; during winter,
at lower elevations, in open
woodlands where junipers
are abundant. Partial-migrant,
northern populations move
south, as far as central
Mexico, in winter.

Length 8–8½in (20–22cm)	Wingspan 13–14½in (33–37cm)	Weight 1¹⁄₁₆–1¼oz (30–35g)
Social **Solitary**	Lifespan **Up to 5 years**	Status **Secure**

DATE: _____ TIME: _____ LOCATION: _____

| Order **Passeriformes** | Family **Turdidae** | Species *Catharus fuscescens* |

Veery

pale reddish-brown upperparts

inconspicuous, pale eye-ring

black upper bill

less distinct spotting on breast

creamy-pink at base of bill

brownish-tan upperparts

ADULT

IMMATURE
C. f. fuscescens
(EASTERN)

IN FLIGHT

poorly marked brown spots on buff breast and throat

white underparts

tan wash on flanks

ADULT
C. f. salicicola
(WESTERN)

creamy-pink legs and feet

The least spotted of the North American *Catharus* thrushes, the Veery is medium-sized like the others, but browner overall. It has been described as "dusky," but there is a geographical variation in duskiness; four subspecies have been described to reflect this. Eastern birds (*C. f. fuscescens*) are ruddier than their western relatives (*C. f. salicicola*). The Veery is a long-distance migrant, spending the northern winter months in central Brazil, in a variety of tropical habitats.

VOICE A series of descending *da-vee-ur*, *vee-ur*, *veer*, *veer*, somewhat bitonal, sounding like the name Veery; call a rather soft *veer*.

NESTING Cup of dead leaves, bark, weed stems, and moss on or near ground; 4 eggs; 1–2 broods; May–July.

FEEDING Forages on the ground for insects, spiders, snails; eats fruit and berries after breeding.

FLIGHT: rapid and straight, with intermittent hops and glides; makes long hops when on ground.

DAMP DWELLINGS
The Veery breeds in damp habitats, such as moist wooded areas or in trees near or in swamps.

OCCURRENCE
In summer, mainly found in damp deciduous forests, preferring the canopy, but in some places habitat near rivers preferred. In winter, choice of habitat flexible; found in tropical broadleaf evergreen forest, on forest edges, in open woodlands, and in second-growth areas regenerating after fires or clearing.

SIMILAR SPECIES

GRAY-CHEEKED THRUSH
see p.339

gray face

bold black-brown breast spots

BICKNELL'S THRUSH

bold brown breast spots

olive-brown upperparts

SWAINSON'S THRUSH
see p.340

buffy-colored face

bold brown-black breast spots

| Length **7in (18cm)** | Wingspan **11–11½in (28–29cm)** | Weight **1¹⁄₁₆–2oz (28–54g)** |
| Social **Pairs** | Lifespan **Up to 10 years** | Status **Declining** |

DATE: _____ TIME: _____ LOCATION: _____

Order **Passeriformes**	Family **Turdidae**	Species *Catharus minimus*

Gray-cheeked Thrush

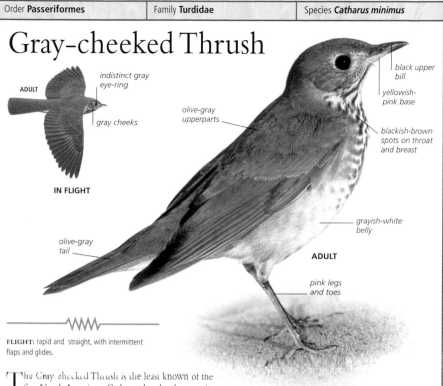

ADULT

indistinct gray eye-ring

gray cheeks

IN FLIGHT

olive-gray upperparts

black upper bill

yellowish-pink base

blackish-brown spots on throat and breast

grayish-white belly

ADULT

olive-gray tail

pink legs and toes

FLIGHT: rapid and straight, with intermittent flaps and glides.

The Gray-cheeked Thrush is the least known of the five North American *Catharus* thrushes because it breeds in remote areas of northern Canada and Alaska. In fact, most of the existing information on this species is a result of research on the Bicknell's Thrush, which was considered to be a subspecies of the Gray-cheeked Thrush until 1993. During migration, the Gray-cheeked Thrush is more likely to be heard in flight at night than seen on the ground by birdwatchers
VOICE Call a thin *kweer*, sometimes two notes; song flute-like, somewhat nasal, several notes ending on a lower pitch.
NESTING Cup of grass, twigs, moss, dead leaves, and mud, placed near ground in shrubbery; 4 eggs; 1 brood; May–July.
FEEDING Forages for insects, including beetles, ants, spiders, earthworms, and fruit.

FEEDING HABITAT
A Gray-cheeked Thrush hops across the forest floor looking for prey.

SIMILAR SPECIES

BICKNELL'S THRUSH olive-brown upperparts

brownish spots

TREETOP SINGER
This bird is most likely to be seen in the evening, singing from treetops on its nesting grounds.

OCCURRENCE
On breeding grounds, occupies densely vegetated areas with small shrubs; preference for spruce forests in northern Canada and Alaska. During migration, favors wooded areas with dense understory. In winter, prefers forested areas and secondary succession woodlands.

Length **6½–7in (16–18cm)**	Wingspan **11½–13½in (29–34cm)**	Weight **⅞–1¹⁄₁₆oz (26–30g)**
Social **Mixed flocks**	Lifespan **Up to 7 years**	Status **Secure**

DATE: _____ TIME: _____ LOCATION: _____

| Order **Passeriformes** | Family **Turdidae** | Species *Catharus ustulatus* |

Swainson's Thrush

ADULT

russet back

more rufous in upperparts

IN FLIGHT

smaller, less distinct, sparser spotting

olive-brown rump and tail

ADULT
C. u. ustulatus
(WESTERN)

buffy eye-ring

olive-brown upperparts

buff breast

distinct blackish spots

ADULT
C. u. swainsoni
(EASTERN)

S wainson's Thrush can be distinguished from other spotted thrushes by its buffy face and the rising pitch of its flute-like, melodious song. This species is also distinctive as it feeds higher up in the understory than most of its close relatives. The western subspecies of Swainson's Thrush is russet-backed and migrates to Central America for the winter, while the other populations are olive-backed and winter in South America.

VOICE Single-note call *whit* or *whooit*; main song delivered by males, several phrases, each one spiraling upward; flute-like song is given during breeding and migration.

NESTING Open cup of twigs, moss, dead leaves, bark, and mud, on branches near trunks of small trees or in shrubs; 3–4 eggs; 1–2 broods; April–July.

FEEDING Forages in the air, using fly-catching methods to capture a wide range of insects during breeding season; berries during migration and in winter.

FLIGHT: rapid and straight, with intermittent flaps and glides.

DISTINCTIVE SONG
This bird's song distinguishes it from other thrushes.

TREE-DWELLER
Shy and retiring, Swainson's Thrush feeds in trees more than other *Catharus* thrushes.

SIMILAR SPECIES

VEERY
see p.338

tawny-brown back

HERMIT THRUSH
see p.341

lightly spotted breast

grayish cheeks

streaks on sides of breast

rust-colored tail

OCCURRENCE
Breeds mainly in coniferous forests, especially spruce and fir, except in California, where it prefers deciduous riverside woodlands and damp meadows with shrubbery. During spring and fall migrations, dense understory is preferred. Winter habitat is mainly old-growth forest.

Length 6½–7½in (16–19cm)	Wingspan 11½–12in (29–31cm)	Weight ⅞–1⁹⁄₁₆oz (25–45g)
Social Pairs/Flocks	Lifespan Up to 11 years	Status Declining

DATE: _____ TIME: _____ LOCATION: _____

Order **Passeriformes**	Family **Turdidae**	Species *Catharus guttatus*

Hermit Thrush 🔊

gray-brown
upperparts

**ADULT
C. q. faxoni
(EASTERN)**

IN FLIGHT

darker brown
upperparts

dark spots on
whitish breast

paler
gray
flanks

**ADULT
C. g. guttatus
(NORTHWESTERN)**

gray-brown
upperparts

more extensive
breast spotting

**ADULT
C. g. audoboni
(ROCKIES)**

reddish
tail

**ADULT
C. g. faxoni
(EASTERN)**

thin white
eye-ring

brownish
back

dark spots
on buff
breast

tawny-buff
flanks

The Hermit Thrush's song is the signature sound of northerly and mountain forests in the West—fluted, almost bitonal, far-carrying, and ending up with almost a question mark. The Hermit Thrush is so named because of its solitary lifestyle, especially in winter, when birds maintain inter-individual territories. Geographical variation within the vast range of the species has led to the recognition of nine subspecies (three are shown here). It winters in the southern US, Mexico, Guatemala, and El Salvador.

VOICE Calls *tchek*, soft, dry; song flute-like, ethereal, falling, repetitive, and varied; several phrases delivered on a different pitch.

NESTING Cup of grasses, mosses, twigs, leaves, mud, hair, on ground or in low tree branches; 4 eggs; 1–2 broods; May–July.

FEEDING Mainly forages on ground for insects, larvae, earthworms, and snails; in winter, also eats fruit.

FLIGHT: rapid and straight, with intermittent flaps and glides.

URBAN VISITOR
This thrush is frequently seen in wooded areas in urban and suburban parks.

OCCURRENCE
Occurs in coniferous forests and mixed conifer-deciduous woodlands; prefers to nest along the edges of a forest interior, like a bog location. Found in forests and other open woodlands during winter. During migration, found in many wooded habitats.

SIMILAR SPECIES		
VEERY
see p.338

tawny-brown
back

lightly
spotted
breast | **BICKNELL'S THRUSH**

olive-brown
back

yellow
base of
bill | **SWAINSON'S THRUSH**
see p.340

olive-brown
upperparts |

Length **6–7in (15–18cm)**	Wingspan **10–11in (25–28cm)**	Weight **⅞–1¹⁄₁₆oz (25–30g)**
Social **Solitary**	Lifespan **Up to 9 years**	Status **Secure**

DATE: _____ TIME: _____ LOCATION: _____

| Order **Passeriformes** | Family **Turdidae** | Species ***Turdus migratorius*** |

American Robin 🔊

MALE

dark head

IN FLIGHT

more complete white eye-ring

gray back

orangish-red breast

white rump

broken white eye-ring

yellow bill

dark streaks on chin

dark-gray back

FEMALE

mottled-gray back

spotted breast

IMMATURE

fairly long, dark tail

brick-red underparts

MALE

〜〜〜〜〜

FLIGHT: strong, swift flights with intermittent flaps and glides.

The American Robin, the largest and most abundant of the North American thrushes, is probably the most familiar bird on the continent. Its presence on suburban lawns is an early sign of spring. Unlike other species, it has adapted and prospered in human-altered habitats. It breeds across all of Canada and the US, and it winters across the US, migrating out of most of Canada in the fall. The decision to migrate is largely governed by changes in the availability of food. As the breeding season approaches, it is the males that sing first, either late in winter or early spring. The bird's brick-red breast—more vivid in males than in females—is its most distinguishing feature.

VOICE Calls a high-pitched *tjip* and a multi-note, throaty *tjuj-tjuk*; primary song a melodious *cheer-up*, *cheer-up*, *cheer-wee*, one of the first birds to be heard during dawn chorus, and one of the last to cease singing in the evening.

NESTING Substantial cup of grass, weeds, twigs, occasional garbage in tree or shrub, in the fork of a tree, or on the branch of a tree; 4 eggs; 2–3 broods; April–July.

FEEDING Forages in leaf litter, mainly for earthworms and small insects; mostly consumes fruit in the winter season.

SEASONAL DIET
Robins are particularly dependent on the availability of fruit during the winter months.

OCCURRENCE
Breeding habitat a mix of forest, woodland, suburban gardens, lawns, municipal parks, and farms. A partial migrant, these robins tend to be found in woodlands where berry-bearing trees are present. Nonmigrating populations' winter habitat is similar to breeding habitat.

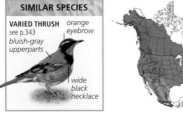

SIMILAR SPECIES

VARIED THRUSH see p.343 — orange eyebrow, bluish-gray upperparts, wide black necklace

| Length **8–11in (20–28cm)** | Wingspan **12–16in (30–41cm)** | Weight **2⅝oz (75g)** |
| Social **Flocks** | Lifespan **Up to 13 years** | Status **Secure** |

DATE: _____ TIME: _____ LOCATION: _____

Order **Passeriformes**	Family **Turdidae**	Species ***Ixoreus naevius***

Varied Thrush 🔊

white double underwing bar

MALE

IN FLIGHT

black breastband

brownish-gray upperparts

orange breast and throat with distinct spotting

FEMALE

bluish-gray upperparts

rusty-orange patches

white undertail feathers

orange eyebrow

black cheeks

MALE

rusty-orange breast, faintly spotted

The voice of the old-growth forests of southern Alaska and British Columbia, the Varied Thrush is also the most beautiful of the thrushes. Its song is so haunting and ethereal that hearing it can give the listener goosebumps. To see the bird is another matter, as it is often rather shy, except when bringing food to its nestlings. The Varied Thrush's orange-and-black head, deep bluish-black back, and its two rusty wing bars are an unmistakable combination of markings.

VOICE Song is a single note that rises or falls in tone; repeats its song after about 10 seconds; sings for long periods of time from one perch, then moves to another to start anew.

NESTING Bulky cup of twigs, dead leaves, pieces of bark, stems of grass and weeds, lined with fine grass stems, mainly in conifer trees, against trunk; 3–4 eggs; 1–2 broods; April–August.

FEEDING Feeds on insects and caterpillars while breeding; fruit and berries in winter.

FLIGHT: rapid wing beats; fast and direct.

SUMMER DIET
During its breeding season, this thrush forages for insects, often outside the forest interior.

SIMILAR SPECIES

AMERICAN ROBIN see p.342

dark back

yellow bill

brick-red breast

FOREST DWELLER
The Varied Thrush is often difficult to find, because it inhabits dark forests.

OCCURRENCE
Breeds from Alaska south to Montana; prefers moist coniferous forests throughout its breeding range; likely to be found in mature forests. Winters south of its breeding range; habitat varies between ravines and thickets to suburban lawns. Habitat in migration much like winter choices.

Length **7–10in (18–25cm)**	Wingspan **13–15in (33–38cm)**	Weight **2¼–3½oz (65–100g)**
Social **Solitary/Flocks**	Lifespan **At least 5 years**	Status **Declining**

DATE: _____ TIME: _____ LOCATION: _____

| Order **Passeriformes** | Family **Muscicapidae** | Species *Oenanthe oenanthe* |

Northern Wheatear 🔊

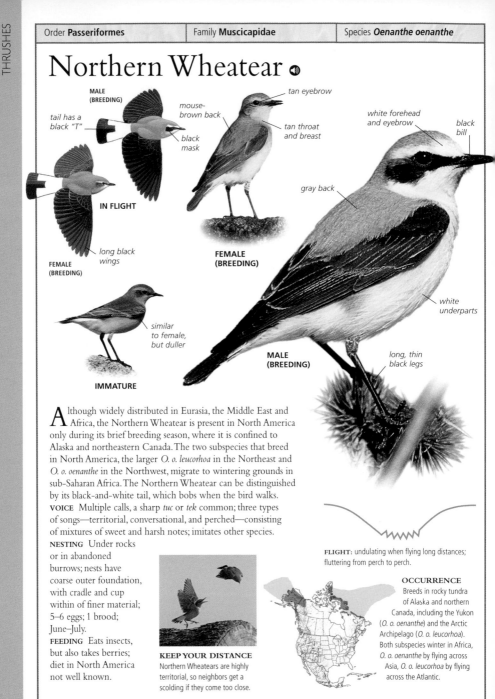

MALE (BREEDING)

tail has a black "T"

mouse-brown back

black mask

tan eyebrow

tan throat and breast

white forehead and eyebrow

black bill

gray back

IN FLIGHT

long black wings

FEMALE (BREEDING)

FEMALE (BREEDING)

white underparts

MALE (BREEDING)

long, thin black legs

similar to female, but duller

IMMATURE

Although widely distributed in Eurasia, the Middle East and Africa, the Northern Wheatear is present in North America only during its brief breeding season, where it is confined to Alaska and northeastern Canada. The two subspecies that breed in North America, the larger *O. o. leucorhoa* in the Northeast and *O. o. oenanthe* in the Northwest, migrate to wintering grounds in sub-Saharan Africa. The Northern Wheatear can be distinguished by its black-and-white tail, which bobs when the bird walks.

VOICE Multiple calls, a sharp *tuc* or *tek* common; three types of songs—territorial, conversational, and perched—consisting of mixtures of sweet and harsh notes; imitates other species.

NESTING Under rocks or in abandoned burrows; nests have coarse outer foundation, with cradle and cup within of finer material; 5–6 eggs; 1 brood; June–July.

FEEDING Eats insects, but also takes berries; diet in North America not well known.

KEEP YOUR DISTANCE
Northern Wheatears are highly territorial, so neighbors get a scolding if they come too close.

FLIGHT: undulating when flying long distances; fluttering from perch to perch.

OCCURRENCE
Breeds in rocky tundra of Alaska and northern Canada, including the Yukon (*O. o. oenanthe*) and the Arctic Archipelago (*O. o. leucorhoa*). Both subspecies winter in Africa, *O. o. oenanthe* by flying across Asia, *O. o. leucorhoa* by flying across the Atlantic.

| Length 5½–6in (14–15cm) | Wingspan 10¾in (27cm) | Weight ½oz (14g) |
| Social **Solitary/Flocks** | Lifespan **Up to 7 years** | Status **Secure** |

DATE: _____ TIME: _____ LOCATION: _____

OLD WORLD SPARROWS

THESE SMALL, SHORT-LEGGED, short-billed, principally seed-eating birds were introduced to North America from Europe and Asia, and their name has carried over to many unrelated New World species. House and Tree Sparrows are small and finch-like, but always unstreaked below. Male and female House Sparrows differ in appearance, while Tree Sparrows of both sexes are more like the male House Sparrow, with pale cheeks and a black bib. House Sparrows are familiar urban and suburban birds, always associated with buildings, parks, or farmsteads.

FEEDING FRENZY
House Sparrows feed their chicks on caterpillars, visiting the nest scores of times each day.

DECLINING POPULATIONS
Due to changing land-use patterns and possible competition from the House Finch, which has expanded its range eastward, House Sparrow numbers are on the decline.

Family **Motacillidae**

PIPITS

THIS GROUP OF ground-dwelling songbirds occurs across most of the world, although only two are found in Canada, and only one—the American Pipit—is Canada-wide. The two species of pipit that breed in North America also winter there. They inhabit open, treeless country, walking rather than hopping on the ground. They are more likely to be seen in their widespread wintering areas than in their remote breeding range.

COUNTRY-LOVERS
Pipits, such as this American Pipit, live in open country, including beaches, dunes, and tundra.

| Order **Passeriformes** | Family **Passeridae** | Species ***Passer domesticus*** |

House Sparrow 🔊

white wing bar

buff eyestripe

yellowish bill

pale rump

MALE (SUMMER)

IN FLIGHT

drab-brown underparts

FEMALE

brown nape

black-and-brown streaks on upperparts

gray crown

black throat

gray breast

white wing bar

MALE (SUMMER)

This is the familiar "sparrow" of towns, cities, suburbs, and farms. The House Sparrow is not one of the American or New World Sparrows—family Passerellidae—more commonly known in North America; rather it is a member of the Eurasian family, Passeridae. It was first introduced in Brooklyn, New York in 1850. From this modest beginning, and with the help of several other introductions up until the late 1860s, this hardy, and aggressive bird eventually spread right through the North American continent. In a little more than 150 years, the House Sparrow has evolved and shows the same sort of geographic variation as some widespread native birds. It is pale in the arid southwest US, and darker in wetter regions.
VOICE Variety of calls, including a cheery chirp, a dull *jurv* and a rough *jigga*; song consists of *chirp* notes repeated endlessly.
NESTING Untidy mass of dried vegetable material in either natural or artificial cavities; 3–5 eggs; 2–3 broods; April–August.
FEEDING Mostly seeds; sometimes gleans insects and fruit.

FLIGHT: fast and bouncing, with rapid wing beats; short wings and tail give it a portly profile.

APTLY NAMED
House Sparrows are often seen near human structures—fences, roofs, curbs, and streetlights.

SIMILAR SPECIES

DICKCISSEL ♀
see p.438

pale bill

pale throat

yellowish highlights

DICKCISSEL ♂ ❊
see p.438

black-and-tan streaks

pale bill

OCCURRENCE
Flourishes in the downtown sections of cities and anywhere near human habitations, including agricultural outbuildings in remote areas of the continent. Also found in Mexico, Central and South America, the West Indies, Eurasia, southern Africa, Australia, and New Zealand.

| Length **6in (15.5cm)** | Wingspan **9½in (24cm)** | Weight **⅝–1¹/₁₆oz (18–30g)** |
| Social **Flocks** | Lifespan **Up to 7 years** | Status **Declining** |

DATE: _____ TIME: _____ LOCATION: _____

Order **Passeriformes**	Family **Motacillidae**	Species *Anthus rubescens*

American Pipit

ADULT

faint streaking on gray upperparts

pale eyebrow

"mustache"

gray cheek with buffy eyestripes

whitish, with heavier streaking on chest and flanks

buffy eyestripe

thin, dark bill

dark "mustache"

no streaking on grayish back

wing bars

IN FLIGHT

white outer tail feathers

ADULT (NONBREEDING)

pale edges to wing feathers

light reddish-buffy chest and flanks

long tail with white outer tail feathers

ADULT (BREEDING)

long hind claw

dark legs and toes

FLIGHT: typically strong with a distinct, undulating, rise and fall pattern.

The American Pipit is divided into four subspecies, three of which breed in North America, and the fourth in Siberia. In its nonbreeding plumage, the American Pipit is a drab-looking, brownish-gray bird that forages for insects along water and shores, or in cultivated fields with short stems. In the breeding season, molting transforms it into a beauty—with gray upperparts and reddish underparts. American Pipits are known for pumping their tails up and down. When breeding, males display by rising into the air, then flying down with wings open and singing. Its migration takes the American Pipit as far south as Guatemala.

VOICE Alarm call a *tzeeep*; song repeated *tzwee-tzooo* from the air.

NESTING Cup in shallow depression on ground, outer frame of grass, lined with fine grass and hair; 4–6 eggs; 1 brood; June–July.

FEEDING Picks insects; also eats seeds during migration.

WINTER DRAB
Foraging in short vegetation, this bird is almost the same color as its surroundings.

SIMILAR SPECIES

HORNED LARK ☾
see p.301

less white on tail edge

SPRAGUE'S PIPIT
see p.348

heavy streaking on back

less streaking on throat and chest

pale cheeks and throat

pale legs

OCCURRENCE
Breeds in the Arctic tundra in the north, and alpine tundra in the Rockies; also breeds on treeless mountaintops in Maine and New Hampshire. Winters in open coastal areas and harvested agricultural fields across the US. Some North American migrants fly to Asia for the winter.

Length **6–8in (15–20cm)**	Wingspan **10–11in (25–28cm)**	Weight **11/16oz (20g)**
Social **Flocks**	Lifespan **Up to 6 years**	Status **Secure**

DATE: _____ TIME:_____ LOCATION:_____

| Order **Passeriformes** | Family **Motacillidae** | Species **Anthus spragueii** |

Sprague's Pipit

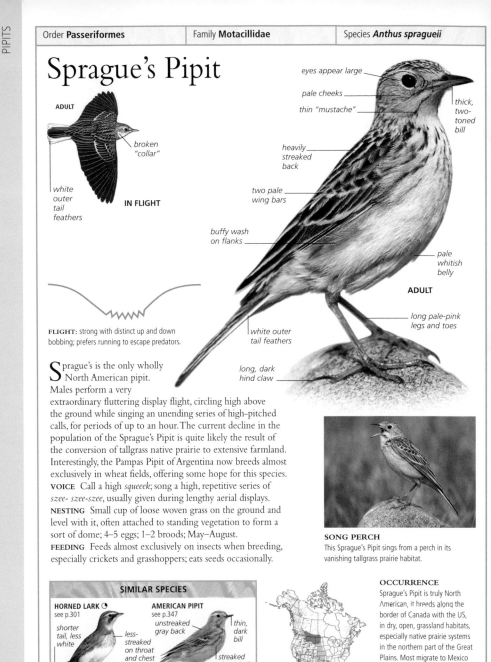

ADULT

broken "collar"

white outer tail feathers

IN FLIGHT

eyes appear large

pale cheeks

thin "mustache"

thick, two-toned bill

heavily streaked back

two pale wing bars

buffy wash on flanks

pale whitish belly

ADULT

long pale-pink legs and toes

FLIGHT: strong with distinct up and down bobbing; prefers running to escape predators.

white outer tail feathers

long, dark hind claw

Sprague's is the only wholly North American pipit. Males perform a very extraordinary fluttering display flight, circling high above the ground while singing an unending series of high-pitched calls, for periods of up to an hour. The current decline in the population of the Sprague's Pipit is quite likely the result of the conversion of tallgrass native prairie to extensive farmland. Interestingly, the Pampas Pipit of Argentina now breeds almost exclusively in wheat fields, offering some hope for this species.

VOICE Call a high *squeeek*; song a high, repetitive series of *szee- szee-szee*, usually given during lengthy aerial displays.

NESTING Small cup of loose woven grass on the ground and level with it, often attached to standing vegetation to form a sort of dome; 4–5 eggs; 1–2 broods; May–August.

FEEDING Feeds almost exclusively on insects when breeding, especially crickets and grasshoppers; eats seeds occasionally.

SONG PERCH
This Sprague's Pipit sings from a perch in its vanishing tallgrass prairie habitat.

SIMILAR SPECIES

HORNED LARK ♂
see p.301

shorter tail, less white

less-streaked on throat and chest

AMERICAN PIPIT
see p.347

unstreaked gray back

thin, dark bill

streaked chest, belly and flanks

dark legs

OCCURRENCE
Sprague's Pipit is truly North American, it breeds along the border of Canada with the US, in dry, open, grassland habitats, especially native prairie systems in the northern part of the Great Plains. Most migrate to Mexico in winter, where habitat is similar to its breeding grounds.

| Length **4–6in (10–15cm)** | Wingspan **6–8in (15–20cm)** | Weight **¹¹/₁₆–⁷/₈oz (20–25g)** |
| Social **Solitary** | Lifespan **Unknown** | Status **Threatened** |

DATE: _____ TIME:_____ LOCATION:_____

FINCHES

Finches in the family Fringillidae comprise a family of seed-eating birds, of which 16 species can be found in North America. They vary in size and shape from the small and fragile-looking redpolls to the robust and chunky Evening Grosbeak. Finch colors range from whitish with some pink (redpolls) to gold (American Goldfinch), bright-red (crossbills), and yellow, white, and black (Evening Grosbeak). However, irrespective of body shape, size, and color, all have conical bills with razor-sharp edges. Finches do not crush seeds. Instead, they cut open the hard hull, then seize the seed inside with their tongue and swallow it. The bills of conifer-loving crossbills are crossed at the tip, a unique arrangement that permits them to open tough-hulled pine cones. Roughly 50 percent of crossbills are "left-billed" and 50 percent "right-billed"— lefties are right-footed, and vice versa. Most finches are social. Although they breed in pairs, post-nesting finches form flocks, some of which are huge. Most finch populations fluctuate in size, synchronized with seed production and abundance, which can lead to periodic irruptions in the south. All finches are vocal, calling constantly while flying, and singing in the spring. Calls are usually sharp, somewhat metallic sounds, although the American Goldfinch's tinkling calls are sweeter. Songs can be quite musical, clear-sounding melodies, like that of the Cassin's Finch. Finches make open cup-shaped nests of grasses and lichens, in trees or shrubs, and are remarkably adept at hiding them.

NOT REALLY PURPLE
The inaccurately named Purple Finch actually has a lovely wine-red coloration.

CROSSBILL
Perched on a pine tree branch, a female Red Crossbill grinds a seed in her bill to break open the hull and reach the fat-rich kernel inside.

LATE NESTERS
American Goldfinches often nest late in the season, perhaps related to the flowering of thistles, an important food plant.

| Order **Passeriformes** | Family **Fringillidae** | Species **Coccothraustes vespertinus** |

Evening Grosbeak

conspicuous yellow eyebrow

very dark gray head and shoulders

black wingtips

yellow rump

MALE

large white wing patches

large white wing patch

huge yellowish-white bill

MALE

IN FLIGHT

black outer wing feathers

large grayish bill

mustard-yellow underparts

grayish wing patch

short, square tail

FEMALE

There is no mistaking a noisy, boisterous winter flock of husky gold-and-black Evening Grosbeaks when they descend upon a feeder. The bird's outsized yellow bill seems to be made as much for threatening would-be rivals as it is designed for efficiently cracking sunflower seeds. In the breeding season, by contrast, the Evening Grosbeak is secretive and seldom seen, neither singing loudly nor displaying ostentatiously and nesting high in a tree. Once a bird of western North America, it has extended its range eastward in the past 200 years, and now nests as far east as Newfoundland. This is partly due to the planting of ornamental box elders, which provides year-round seeds, as well as outbreaks of insects like the spruce budworm.

FLIGHT: undulating, with dips between bouts of wing beats, may hover briefly.

VOICE Call descending *feeew*; also buzzy notes and beeping chatter.

NESTING Loose, grass-lined twig cup, usually on conifer branch; 3–4 eggs; 1–2 broods; May–July.

FEEDING Eats seeds of pines and other conifers, maple, and box elder seeds; also insects and their larvae, particularly spruce budworm.

CAPABLE BILL
This bird's extremely robust bill can deal with all kinds of winter fruits and seeds.

OCCURRENCE
Breeds in mixed conifer and spruce forests from the Rocky Mountain region to eastern Canada, and on mountain ranges south to Mexico. Winters in coniferous or deciduous woodlands, often in suburban locations; may move south from northern range, depending on food supply.

SIMILAR SPECIES

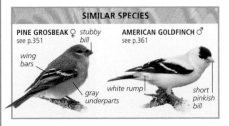

PINE GROSBEAK ♀ *stubby bill* see p.351

wing bars

gray underparts

AMERICAN GOLDFINCH ♂ see p.361

white rump

short pinkish bill

| Length **6½–7in (16–18cm)** | Wingspan **12–14in (30–36cm)** | Weight **2–2½oz (55–70g)** |
| Social **Flocks** | Lifespan **Up to 15 years** | Status **Special Concern** |

DATE: _____ TIME: _____ LOCATION: _____

| Order **Passeriformes** | Family **Fringillida** | Species *Pinicola enucleator* |

Pine Grosbeak

greenish head

two white
wing bars

greenish
rump

MALE

pale patch
under eye

gray belly

FEMALE

pinkish-red head

short neck

stubby,
rounded
blackish bill

IN FLIGHT

pinkish
rump

long
blackish
tail

**IMMATURE
MALE**

pinkish-red
underparts
(but
regionally
variable)

MALE

FLIGHT: undulating, buoyant, calm wing beats
interrupted by glides.

The largest member of the family Fringillidae in
North America, and easily distinguished by the male's
unmistakable thick, stubby bill, the Pine Grosbeak is a resident
of boreal forests across Canada and Alaska and some mountain
ranges in the western US. In winter, northern birds occasionally
move south into the northern US. Due to extensive color
variation of individual plumages, the age and sex of the bird
are not always easily determined.
VOICE Contact calls of eastern birds *tee-tew*, or *tee-tee-tew*;
western forms give more complex *tweedle*; warbling song.
NESTING Well-hidden, open cup nest usually in spruce or
larch trees; 2–5 eggs, 1 brood; June–July.
FEEDING Eats spruce buds, maple seeds, and mountain ash
berries throughout the year; consumes insects in summer.

FRUIT-LOVER
This species can often be seen hanging from
branches, gorging on ripe fruit.

SIMILAR SPECIES

RED CROSSBILL
see p.358

WHITE-WINGED CROSSBILL
see p.359

brownish
wings

mandibles
crossed

white bars
on wing

mandibles
crossed

OCCURRENCE
Found in the boreal zone from
Alaska to Newfoundland in
Canada, and in California, the
Southwest, and the Rockies in
the US. Occurs in open, northerly
coniferous forests in summer,
usually near fresh water. Winters
throughout its breeding range, but
may move southward to southern
Canada and the northeastern US.

| Length **8–10in (20–25cm)** | Wingspan **13in (33cm)** | Weight **2–2¹/₂oz (55–70g)** |
| Social **Flocks** | Lifespan **Up to 10 years** | Status **Secure** |

DATE: _____ TIME:_____ LOCATION:_____

| Order **Passeriformes** | Family **Fringillidae** | Species *Leucosticte tephrocotis* |

Gray-crowned Rosy-Finch

brown upperparts

more extensive gray on head

dark chin

ADULT (WESTERN)

gray behind eye

dark crown

rosy rump

ADULT (WESTERN) IN FLIGHT

pinkish shoulder patch

chocolate-brown overall

ADULT (BERING SEA)

rusty-brown underparts

ADULT (INTERIOR)

notched tail

whitish undertail feathers

The often lifeless and windswept rocks and crags of high western mountains are the domain of these brown-and-pink birds, which are seldom in contact with humanity. The Gray-crowned Rosy-Finch is one of several mountain finch species that extend across the Bering Strait into eastern Asia. Geographically variable in size and coloration, with exceptionally large forms occurring on the Pribilof and Aleutian Islands, the Gray-crowned Rosy-Finch is the most abundant of the North American rosy-finches.

VOICE High-pitched *peew*, given singly or in short series; song repetitive series of *twee* notes.

NESTING Bulky assemblage of grasses, lichens, and twigs in cracks or under rock overhangs; 3–5 eggs; 1–2 broods; May–June.

FEEDING Feeds on the ground on a variety of seeds, with insects and their larvae comprising a larger part of the diet in summer.

FLIGHT: undulating but often irregular with glides.

ROCK-LOVER
This dark rusty-brown species watches its surroundings from a rocky perch near an icy field.

SIMILAR SPECIES

DARK-EYED JUNCO (OREGON) see p.376

dark hood

pale underparts

OCCURRENCE
Most widely distributed of the three North American rosy-finch species, occurring from Alaska south to the Rockies; breeds in alpine habitats like screes above the snow line and the Arctic tundra; in winter also occurs at lower elevations; sometimes at feeders.

| Length **5½–8½in (14–21cm)** | Wingspan **13in (33cm)** | Weight **⅞–2⅛oz (25–60g)** |
| Social **Flocks** | Lifespan **Up to 7 years** | Status **Localized** |

DATE: _____ TIME: _____ LOCATION: _____

Order **Passeriformes**	Family **Fringillidae**	Species *Haemorhous mexicanus*

House Finch 🔊

brown cap

grayish streaks all over

red face

brown upperparts

usually strawberry-red bib and head

FEMALE

MALE
(BREEDING)

IN FLIGHT

pinkish head

pale-brown streaking

streaked belly

**MALE
(NON-
BREEDING)**

brown streaked undertail feathers

long tail feathers

MALE (BREEDING)

FLIGHT: bouncy, undulating flight typical of finches; usually flies above treetop level

H istorically, the House Finch was a western bird, and was first reported in the eastern side of the US on Long Island, New York City in 1941. These birds are said to have originated from the illegal bird trade. The population of the eastern birds started expanding in the 1960s; by the late 1990s, their population had expanded westward to link up with the original western population. The male House Finch is distinguished from the Purple and Cassin's Finches by its brown streaked underparts, while the females have plainer faces and generally blurrier streaking. The former also has a heavier, triangular bill.

VOICE Call note *queet*; varied jumble of notes, often starting with husky notes to whistled and burry notes, and ending with a long *wheeerr*.

NESTING Females build nests from grass stems, thin twigs, and thin weeds in trees and on artificial structures; 1–6 eggs; 2–3 broods; March–August.

FEEDING Eats, almost exclusively, vegetable matter, such as buds, fruit, and seeds; readily comes to feeders.

RED IN THE FACE
The breeding male House Finch can be identified by its stunning strawberry-red plumage.

SIMILAR SPECIES

PURPLE FINCH
see p.354

CASSIN'S FINCH
see p.355

pinkish neck

reddish head

whitish underparts

white underparts

OCCURRENCE
Found in urban, suburban, and settled areas; in the West, also in wilder areas, such as prairies, desert grasslands, and chaparral, particularly near people; in the East, almost exclusively in settled areas, including the centers of large cities. Resident, some birds migrate after breeding.

Length **5–6in (12.5–15cm)**	Wingspan **8–10in (20–25cm)**	Weight **⁹/₁₆–1oz (16–27g)**
Social **Flocks**	Lifespan **Up to 12 years**	Status **Secure**

DATE: _____ TIME:_____ LOCATION:_____

| Order **Passeriformes** | Family **Fringillidae** | Species **Haemorhous purpureus** |

Purple Finch 🔊

IN FLIGHT

pinkish-red body

darker, streaked wings

rounded brownish wings

MALE

pale-brown overall

lightly streaked overall

brownish, conical bill

FEMALE

pink-and-brown streaked upperparts

brown stripe between eye and bill

raspberry-red crown

pink rump and upper tail

MALE

whitish belly with rosy patches

One of three difficult-to-distinguish members of the genus *Haemorhous* in North America, the Purple Finch is best known as a visitor to winter feeding stations. The western subspecies (*californicus*) is slightly darker and duller than the eastern form (*purpureus*). Only moderately common, the raspberry-red males pose less of an identification challenge than the brown-streaked females. Even on their breeding grounds in open and mixed coniferous forest, Purple Finches are more often heard than seen.

VOICE Flight call single, rough *pikh*; songs rich series of notes, up and down in pitch.

NESTING Cup of sticks and grasses on a conifer branch; 4 eggs; 2 broods; May–July.

FEEDING Eats buds, seeds, and flowers of deciduous trees; insects and caterpillars in summer; also seeds and berries.

FLIGHT: rapid wing beats, alternating with downward glides.

RASPBERRY TINTED
On a lichen-covered branch this male's delicate coloring is quite striking.

OCCURRENCE
Breeds in northern mixed conifer and hardwood forests in all Canadian provinces, the Yukon and Northwest Territories, where it is partially migratory. Resident from Baja California north along the Pacific Coast and the Cascade Mountains to Washington and a small part of southern British Columbia.

SIMILAR SPECIES		
HOUSE FINCH ♀ western; see p.353 — thinner streaks	**CASSIN'S FINCH** ♀ see p.355 — more marked facial patterning	**RED-WINGED BLACKBIRD** ♀ see p.399 — larger overall, heavily streaked, darker overall

Length 4³/₄–6in (12–15cm)	Wingspan 8¹/₂–10in (22–26cm)	Weight ¹¹/₁₆–1¹/₁₆oz (20–30g)
Social **Flocks**	Lifespan **Up to 14 years**	Status **Declining**

DATE: _____ TIME: _____ LOCATION: _____

Order **Passeriformes**	Family **Fringillidae**	Species *Haemorhous cassinii*

Cassin's Finch 🔊

notched tail

red face

MALE

IN FLIGHT

streaked all over

streaked upperparts

FEMALE

bright rose-red crown

dark reddish cheeks

grayish bill

rosy-red neck

whitish underparts

reddish rump

streaked undertail feathers

MALE

Named after the 19th-century ornithologist John Cassin, this finch has a rich, melodious song that incorporates phrases from the songs of several different Rocky Mountain species. From below, the male Cassin's Finch resembles a sparrow, but when it alights on a tree stump, its full, raspberry-red plumage is immediately evident. This species closely resembles the other two species in the genus *Haemorhous*, the Purple and House Finches, with whose ranges it overlaps, so it may take time and practice to be certain of this species' identity in the field. The female Cassin's Finch is not distinctive—it resembles a generic fledgling or a sparrow.

VOICE Call *tee-uhh* or *piddlit*; song rich and warbling; may include high-frequency whistles and imitations of other species.

NESTING Open cup on lateral branch of conifers, also in aspen or sagebrush; 4–5 eggs; 1 brood; May–July.

FEEDING Eats berries, pine seeds, aspen buds, insects, larvae; feeds mainly on ground but frequents feeding stations in winter.

FLIGHT: rapid wing beats, then a glide, in a regular sequence.

ARBOREAL FINCH
Cassin's Finch likes to perch on an elevated twig or branch, often in coniferous forests.

SIMILAR SPECIES

PURPLE FINCH
see p.354

HOUSE FINCH
see p.353

shorter, less pointed bill

pinkish neck

reddish-orange bib and head

OCCURRENCE
Found in coniferous forests in mountains of southwestern Canada and the western US; may occur in sagebrush-juniper plains or open areas with ponderosa or lodgepole pine. Migratory both toward lower elevations and southward. Winters throughout its breeding range.

Length 5¹/₂–6¹/₂in (14–16cm)	Wingspan 10–10¹/₂in (25–27cm)	Weight ⁷/₈–1¹/₄oz (25–35g)
Social **Flocks**	Lifespan **Up to 10 years**	Status **Secure**

DATE: _____ TIME:_____ LOCATION:_____

| Order **Passeriformes** | Family **Fringillidae** | Species *Acanthis flammea* |

Common Redpoll

red cap

MALE

wing bars

IN FLIGHT

MALE (BREEDING)

rosy-red breast

reddish cap

streaked underparts

FEMALE

pale wing bars

notched tail

JUVENILE

ruby-red cap

small, pointed yellow bill

black streaks on rosy-red breast

pale wing bar

MALE (NONBREEDING)

Every other year, spruce, birch, and other trees in the northern forest zone fail to produce a good crop of seeds, forcing the Common Redpoll to look for food farther south than usual—as far south as the northern US states. The Common Redpoll is oddly tame around people and is easily attracted to winter feeders. The degree of whiteness in its plumage varies greatly among individuals, based on sex and age. Recent DNA studies suggest that Common, Hoary, and Lesser Redpolls are one and the same species.
VOICE Flight call dry *zit-zit-zit-zit* and rattling *chirr*; also high *too-ee* call while perched; song series of rapid trills.
NESTING Cup of small twigs in spruces, larches, willows, alders; 4–6 eggs; 1–2 broods; May–June.
FEEDING Feeds on small seeds from conifers, sedge, birch, willow, alder; also insects and spiders.

FLIGHT: deeply undulating, with dips between bouts of wing beats.

SIMILAR SPECIES

PINE SISKIN
see p.360

yellow on tail

two wing bars

HOARY REDPOLL
see p.357

brownish upperparts

pale overall

red cap

whitish underparts

FRIENDLY FLOCK
Common Redpolls are only weakly territorial, sometimes even nesting close together.

OCCURRENCE
Mainly in extreme northern North America from Alaska to Quebec and Labrador, in low forest, sub-Arctic, and shrubby tundra habitats. More southerly winter appearances typically occur every other year, rarely south of the northern US, from Dakota east to New York and New England.

| Length **4³/₄–5¹/₂in (12–14cm)** | Wingspan **6¹/₂–6³/₄in (16–17cm)** | Weight **³/₈–¹¹/₁₆oz (11–19g)** |
| Social **Flocks** | Lifespan **Up to 10 years** | Status **Secure** |

DATE: _____ TIME: _____ LOCATION: _____

| Order **Passeriformes** | Family **Fringillidae** | Species *Acanthis hornemanni* |

Hoary Redpoll

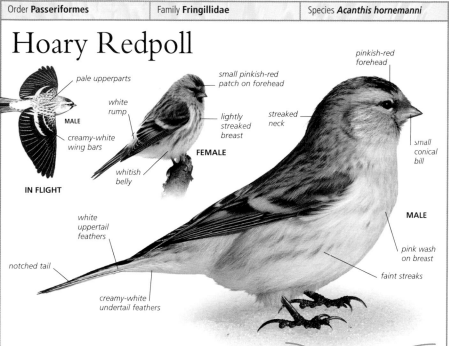

IN FLIGHT

pale upperparts

MALE

white rump

creamy-white wing bars

whitish belly

small pinkish-red patch on forehead

lightly streaked breast

FEMALE

pinkish-red forehead

streaked neck

small conical bill

MALE

pink wash on breast

faint streaks

white uppertail feathers

notched tail

creamy-white undertail feathers

When a flock of redpolls settles at a feeding station, one or more may stand out as exceptionally white, broad, somewhat fluffier, and with a stubbier bill. These may be Hoary Redpolls, a distinct species from the rest of the redpoll group. This bird of the high Arctic has two recognized subspecies—*A. h. exilipes* and *A. h. hornemanni*. These close relatives of the Common Redpoll often breed in the same areas, but do not interbreed. However, recent DNA studies may see the Hoary Redpoll lumped in with the Common Redpoll in the near future. Their chattering flocks buzz rapidly over trees and fields and are tame around humans.
VOICE Flight calls dry *zit-zit-zit-zit* and rattling *chirr*; also high *too-ee* call while perched; song series of rapid trills.
NESTING Lined cup of twigs, grasses in scrubby trees; 4–6 eggs; 1–2 broods; May–July.
FEEDING Eats seeds, insects, and spiders; in winter, prefers niger thistle seed.

FLIGHT: flurries of energetic wing beats alternating with glides.

GROUND FEEDER
Seeds that fall from trees or bird feeders onto the snow provide a good meal for the Hoary Redpoll.

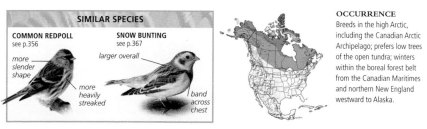

SIMILAR SPECIES

COMMON REDPOLL
see p.356

more slender shape

more heavily streaked

SNOW BUNTING
see p.367

larger overall

band across chest

OCCURRENCE
Breeds in the high Arctic, including the Canadian Arctic Archipelago; prefers low trees of the open tundra; winters within the boreal forest belt from the Canadian Maritimes and northern New England westward to Alaska.

| Length **5–5¹/₂in (12.5–14cm)** | Wingspan **8¹/₂–9¹/₄in (21–23.5cm)** | Weight **⁷/₁₆–¹¹/₁₆oz (12–20g)** |
| Social **Flocks** | Lifespan **Up to 5 years** | Status **Secure** |

DATE: _____ TIME: _____ LOCATION: _____

Order **Passeriformes**	Family **Fringillidae**	Species *Loxia curvirostra*

Red Crossbill

black wings

MALE

red body

IN FLIGHT

dark-brown wings

red rump

black stripe over eye

streaked belly

IMMATURE

crown usually brick-red

crossed mandibles

some males greenish-red overall

MALE

MALE

greenish breast

dark wings

FEMALE

FLIGHT: strong and deeply undulating.

Crossbills have evolved an efficient mechanism to unlock the seeds of conifers. They push the tips of their slightly open, cross-tipped bills between the scales of a conifer cone to pry it apart and lift out the seeds with their tongues. Red Crossbills occur in many forms, varying in size and bill shape. They have slightly different flight calls and rarely interbreed. One, the Cassia Crossbill, is treated as a separate species, *Loxia sinesciuris*. Other forms are nomadic, but this species remains in a tiny part of Idaho all year, feeding on lodgepole pine. It is nearly impossible to identify the different forms of the Red Crossbill other than by voice or DNA.

VOICE Common call *jit* repeated 2–5 times; song complex, continuous warbling of notes, whistles, and buzzes.
NESTING Cup nest on lateral conifer branch; 3–5 eggs; 2 broods; can breed year-round.
FEEDING Feeds on pine seeds; also insects and larvae, particularly aphids; also other seeds.

PROCESSING SEEDS
The Red Crossbill manipulates seeds with its tongue before swallowing them.

SIMILAR SPECIES

WHITE-WINGED CROSSBILL see p.359

conspicuous wing bars

SCARLET TANAGER

vivid-red plumage

no black stripe

pinker plumage

OCCURRENCE
Range covers coniferous or mixed-coniferous and deciduous forests from Newfoundland to British Columbia and southern Alaska; also mountain forests in the Rockies, south to Mexico; irregular movements, depending on the availability of pine cones.

Length 5–6³/₄in (13–17cm)	Wingspan 10–10¹/₂in (25–27cm)	Weight ⁷/₈–1¹/₄oz (25–35g)
Social **Flocks**	Lifespan **Up to 10 years**	Status **Declining**

DATE: ———— TIME: ———— LOCATION: ————

| Order **Passeriformes** | Family **Fringillidae** | Species *Loxia leucoptera* |

White-winged Crossbill

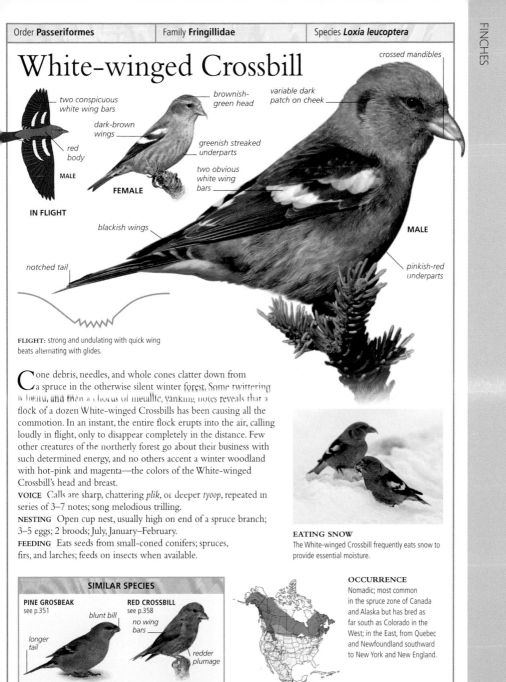

crossed mandibles

two conspicuous white wing bars

brownish-green head

variable dark patch on cheek

dark-brown wings

red body

greenish streaked underparts

MALE

two obvious white wing bars

FEMALE

blackish wings

MALE

IN FLIGHT

notched tail

pinkish-red underparts

FLIGHT: strong and undulating with quick wing beats alternating with glides.

Cone debris, needles, and whole cones clatter down from a spruce in the otherwise silent winter forest. Some twittering is heard, and then a chorus of metallic, yanking notes reveals that a flock of a dozen White-winged Crossbills has been causing all the commotion. In an instant, the entire flock erupts into the air, calling loudly in flight, only to disappear completely in the distance. Few other creatures of the northerly forest go about their business with such determined energy, and no others accent a winter woodland with hot-pink and magenta—the colors of the White-winged Crossbill's head and breast.

VOICE Calls are sharp, chattering *plik*, or deeper *tyoop*, repeated in series of 3–7 notes; song melodious trilling.

NESTING Open cup nest, usually high on end of a spruce branch; 3–5 eggs; 2 broods; July, January–February.

FEEDING Eats seeds from small-coned conifers; spruces, firs, and larches; feeds on insects when available.

EATING SNOW
The White-winged Crossbill frequently eats snow to provide essential moisture.

SIMILAR SPECIES

PINE GROSBEAK
see p.351

blunt bill

longer tail

RED CROSSBILL
see p.358

no wing bars

redder plumage

OCCURRENCE
Nomadic; most common in the spruce zone of Canada and Alaska but has bred as far south as Colorado in the West; in the East, from Quebec and Newfoundland southward to New York and New England.

| Length **5¹/₂–6in (14–15cm)** | Wingspan **10–10¹/₂in (26–27cm)** | Weight **1¹/₁₆–1¹/₁₆oz (20–30g)** |
| Social **Flocks** | Lifespan **Up to 10 years** | Status **Secure** |

DATE: _____ TIME: _____ LOCATION: _____

Order **Passeriformes**	Family **Fringillidae**	Species **Spinus pinus**

Pine Siskin 🔊

pale eyebrow

brownish cheek

slender, pointed bill

notched tail

conspicuous yellow wing bar

MALE

IN FLIGHT

heavily streaked back

yellow in outer wing feathers

yellow base of tail

ADULT

heavily streaked underparts

FLIGHT: undulating, with quick series of wing beats and closed-winged glides.

This unpredictable little bird of the conifer belt runs in gangs and hordes, zipping as a part of one collective mass over the trees with incessant twittering. An expert at disguise, the Pine Siskin can resemble a cluster of pine needles or cones, and even disappear when a Sharp-shinned Hawk appears. Often abundant wherever there are pines, spruces, and other conifers, Pine Siskins may still disappoint birdwatchers by making a mass exodus from a region if the food supply is not to their liking. A vicious fighter at feeding tables, nomadic by nature, with high energy and fearlessness, the Pine Siskin is a fascinating species.

VOICE Rising *toooeeo*, mostly when perched; also raspy *chit-chit-chit* in flight.

NESTING Shallow cup of grass and lichens near the end of a conifer branch; 3–4 eggs; 1–2 broods; February–August.

FEEDING Eats conifer seeds; gleans insects and spiders; also seen feeding on roadsides, lawns, and weed fields.

FOREST DWELLER
The streaked Pine Siskin inhabits northern and western coniferous forests.

QUARRELSOME
A bird warns off a neighbor at a food source, displaying its yellow wing stripe.

OCCURRENCE
Widespread across North America; occurs in coniferous and mixed coniferous forests, but also seen in parkland and suburbs. In some winters, it may appear south of its regular breeding range to Missouri and Tennessee, also Mexico. Prefers open areas to continuous forest.

SIMILAR SPECIES

COMMON REDPOLL
see p.356

tiny, pale bill

heavier streaking

YELLOW-RUMPED WARBLER ♀
see p.425

yellow rump

yellow patches

Length **4¼–5½in (11–14cm)**	Wingspan **7–9in (18–23cm)**	Weight **⁷/₁₆–⁵/₈oz (12–18g)**
Social **Flocks**	Lifespan **Up to 10 years**	Status **Secure**

DATE: _____ TIME: _____ LOCATION: _____

Order **Passeriformes**	Family **Fringillidae**	Species *Spinus tristis*

American Goldfinch 🔊

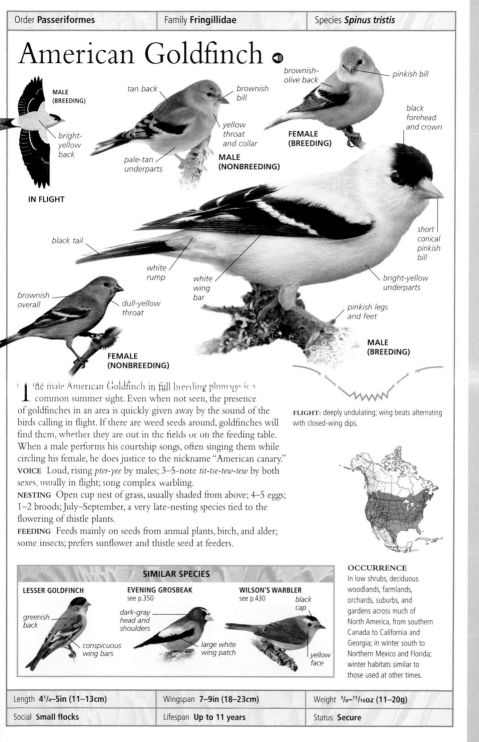

MALE (BREEDING)

tan back

brownish bill

yellow throat and collar

brownish-olive back

pinkish bill

black forehead and crown

bright-yellow back

pale-tan underparts

MALE (NONBREEDING)

FEMALE (BREEDING)

IN FLIGHT

short conical pinkish bill

black tail

white rump

white wing bar

bright-yellow underparts

brownish overall

dull-yellow throat

pinkish legs and feet

FEMALE (NONBREEDING)

MALE (BREEDING)

The male American Goldfinch in full breeding plumage is a common summer sight. Even when not seen, the presence of goldfinches in an area is quickly given away by the sound of the birds calling in flight. If there are weed seeds around, goldfinches will find them, whether they are out in the fields or on the feeding table. When a male performs his courtship songs, often singing them while circling his female, he does justice to the nickname "American canary."
VOICE Loud, rising *pter-yee* by males; 3–5-note *tit-tse-tew-tew* by both sexes, usually in flight; song complex warbling.
NESTING Open cup nest of grass, usually shaded from above; 4–5 eggs; 1–2 broods; July–September, a very late-nesting species tied to the flowering of thistle plants.
FEEDING Feeds mainly on seeds from annual plants, birch, and alder; some insects; prefers sunflower and thistle seed at feeders.

FLIGHT: deeply undulating; wing beats alternating with closed-wing dips.

OCCURRENCE
In low shrubs, deciduous woodlands, farmlands, orchards, suburbs, and gardens across much of North America, from southern Canada to California and Georgia; in winter south to Northern Mexico and Florida; winter habitats similar to those used at other times.

SIMILAR SPECIES

LESSER GOLDFINCH

greenish back

conspicuous wing bars

EVENING GROSBEAK
see p.350

dark-gray head and shoulders

large white wing patch

WILSON'S WARBLER
see p.430

black cap

yellow face

Length **4¼–5in (11–13cm)**	Wingspan **7–9in (18–23cm)**	Weight **⅜–¹¹⁄₁₆oz (11–20g)**
Social **Small flocks**	Lifespan **Up to 11 years**	Status **Secure**

DATE: _____ TIME:_____ LOCATION:_____

Family **Calcariidae**

LONGSPURS AND SNOW BUNTINGS

Four species of longspurs, the Snow Bunting, and McKay's Bunting all generally forage on bare or open ground, from tundra and mountain tops to open prairies, often in flocks. Their short blackish legs help give longspurs a long, low shape on the ground. Their calls provide useful clues for identification as they fly. Snow Buntings have distinctive white bands on their wings.

CHANGING COLORS
Snow Buntings are well camouflaged against exposed rocks and snow throughout the year. Brown edges on the feathers in winter wear off, so they become pristine black and white in spring.

Family **Passerellidae**

NEW WORLD SPARROWS

New world sparrows are more akin to Old World buntings than other sparrows, but, as with robins, familiar names were given to quite different birds by early European settlers and have stayed with us. New World sparrows are rounded but long-tailed, and have small conical or triangular bills that are adapted to feed on grass seeds. While some birds are distinctive, especially the more brightly patterned males, many are small, "streaky-brown" species that present considerable identification difficulties.

Range, habitat, behavior, and voice are all often used together as a suite of characteristics for identification. Not only are the species much alike, but studies conducted in recent years have revealed different relationships between them, with some subspecies being split as separate species and others being grouped together. Nevertheless, their neat, subtle patterns make even the duller species worth studying: the exquisite streaking of a Lincoln's Sparrow, for example, repays close observation.

TYPICAL SPECIES
A White-crowned Sparrow shows the typical stout beak of New World sparrows.

| Order **Passeriformes** | Family **Calcariidae** | Species *Calcarius lapponicus* |

Lapland Longspur

streaked crown

white eye-line

thick yellowish bill

bright-rufous nape

black streak on throat

thin white edge to tail

MALE (BREEDING)

black face

rich buffy hood

IN FLIGHT

FEMALE (BREEDING)

rusty wing panel

thick streaking on flanks

ADULT (NONBREEDING)

white underparts

MALE (BREEDING)

black flanks

FLIGHT: deeply undulating, with birds often calling in troughs as they flap.

One of the most numerous breeding birds of the Arctic tundra, the Lapland Longspur is found in huge flocks over open habitats of Canada's southern prairies and in the US in the winter. They can be seen on gravel roads and in barren countryside immediately following heavy snowfalls. The longspurs and the Snow Bunting were formerly part of the Emberizidae family but are now placed in a distinct family of their own. This species is known as the Lapland Bunting in Great Britain and Ireland.

VOICE Flight call a dry rattle, *tyew*, unlike other longspurs; song a series of thin tinklings and whistles, often in flight.

NESTING Cup of grass and sedges placed in depression on ground next to a clump of vegetation; 4–6 eggs; 1 brood; May–July.

FEEDING Eats insects during breeding season; seeds in winter.

CONSPICUOUS SPECIES
This longspur is one of the most conspicuous breeding birds in the Arctic tundra.

OCCURRENCE
Breeds in tundra right across Arctic North America and Eurasia. Winters in open grasslands and barren fields, and on beaches across the northern and central US and parts of southern Canada.

SIMILAR SPECIES		
SMITH'S LONGSPUR ♀ see p.365 white bars on wing	**CHESTNUT-COLLARED LONGSPUR** ♀ ✳ see p.364 thin bill	dark cheek patch more white in tail

Length **6½in (16cm)**	Wingspan **10½–11½in (27–29cm)**	Weight **⅞–1¹⁄₁₆oz (25–30g)**
Social **Large flocks**	Lifespan **Up to 5 years**	Status **Secure**

DATE: _____ TIME: _____ LOCATION: _____

| Order **Passeriformes** | Family **Calcariidae** | Species *Calcarius ornatus* |

Chestnut-collared Longspur

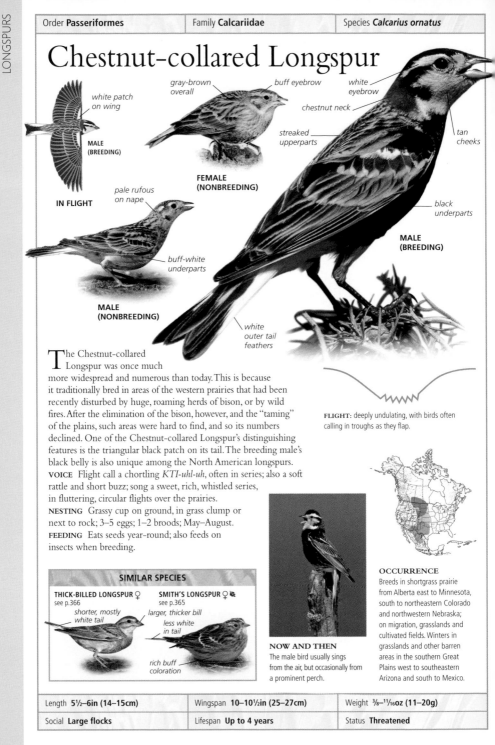

white patch
on wing

**MALE
(BREEDING)**

IN FLIGHT

gray-brown
overall

buff eyebrow

FEMALE
(NONBREEDING)

white
eyebrow

chestnut neck

streaked
upperparts

tan
cheeks

black
underparts

**MALE
(BREEDING)**

pale rufous
on nape

buff-white
underparts

**MALE
(NONBREEDING)**

white
outer tail
feathers

The Chestnut-collared Longspur was once much more widespread and numerous than today. This is because it traditionally bred in areas of the western prairies that had been recently disturbed by huge, roaming herds of bison, or by wild fires. After the elimination of the bison, however, and the "taming" of the plains, such areas were hard to find, and so its numbers declined. One of the Chestnut-collared Longspur's distinguishing features is the triangular black patch on its tail. The breeding male's black belly is also unique among the North American longspurs.
VOICE Flight call a chortling *KTI-uhl-uh*, often in series; also a soft rattle and short buzz; song a sweet, rich, whistled series, in fluttering, circular flights over the prairies.
NESTING Grassy cup on ground, in grass clump or next to rock; 3–5 eggs; 1–2 broods; May–August.
FEEDING Eats seeds year-round; also feeds on insects when breeding.

FLIGHT: deeply undulating, with birds often calling in troughs as they flap.

SIMILAR SPECIES

THICK-BILLED LONGSPUR ♀
see p.366

shorter, mostly
white tail

SMITH'S LONGSPUR ♀
see p.365

larger, thicker bill

less white
in tail

rich buff
coloration

NOW AND THEN
The male bird usually sings from the air, but occasionally from a prominent perch.

OCCURRENCE
Breeds in shortgrass prairie from Alberta east to Minnesota, south to northeastern Colorado and northwestern Nebraska; on migration, grasslands and cultivated fields. Winters in grasslands and other barren areas in the southern Great Plains west to southeastern Arizona and south to Mexico.

| Length **5½–6in (14–15cm)** | Wingspan **10–10½in (25–27cm)** | Weight **⅜–¹¹⁄₁₆oz (11–20g)** |
| Social **Large flocks** | Lifespan **Up to 4 years** | Status **Threatened** |

DATE: _____ TIME: _____ LOCATION: _____

| Order **Passeriformes** | Family **Calcariidae** | Species *Calcarius pictus* |

Smith's Longspur

MALE (BREEDING)
white cheek patch
white outer tail feathers
relatively long wings
IN FLIGHT

rich buff color overall
fine breast streaks
wings extend past tail
FEMALE (FALL)

black-and-white "helmet"
thin bill
orange collar
white shoulder
rich pumpkin-colored underparts

MALE (BREEDING)
white undertail feathers

With its pumpkin-colored breast and black-and-white "helmet," Smith's Longspur in its breeding plumage contrasts strongly with its drab winter plumage. On both its remote breeding grounds in the Arctic, and its restricted range of shortgrass prairie in winter, this bird hides on the ground at all times, making it very hard to spot. Smith's Longspur migrates through the Great Plains to reach its wintering grounds, but on the return journey it swings east, giving it an elliptical migration path. This species breeds communally: males mate with several females who, in turn, mate with other males.
VOICE Flight call a mechanical, dry, sharp rattle; also a nasal *nief* when squabbling; song a series of thin, sweet whistles.
NESTING Concealed cup of sedges, lined with feathers, placed in hummock on ground; 3–5 eggs; 1 brood; June–July.
FEEDING Eats mainly seeds and insects; migrants may rely heavily upon introduced foxtail grass.

FLIGHT: deeply undulating, with birds often calling in troughs as they flap.

LINEBACK LONGSPUR
On his breeding or spring staging grounds, the male sports a striking black-and-white "helmet."

SIMILAR SPECIES

LAPLAND LONGSPUR ♀ ✳
see p.308
thicker bill
broad reddish edges to wings

CHESTNUT-COLLARED LONGSPUR ♀ ✳
see p.364
lacks rich-buff color and streaks
more white in tail

OCCURRENCE
Breeds along the tundra-taiga timberline from northern Alaska southeast to northern Ontario; also mountainous southeastern Alaska and southwestern Yukon. Migrant birds are found in shortgrass prairie. Winters in various open areas with shortgrass in Kansas, Texas, and Arkansas.

| Length **6–6½in (15–16cm)** | Wingspan **10–11½in (25–29cm)** | Weight **⅞–1¹⁄₁₆oz (25–30g)** |
| Social **Large flocks** | Lifespan **Up to 5 years** | Status **Secure** |

DATE: _____ TIME: _____ LOCATION: _____

Order **Passeriformes**	Family **Calcariidae**	Species *Rhynchophanes mccownii*

Thick-billed Longspur

MALE (BREEDING)

black "T" on white tail

IN FLIGHT

pale-gray head

large, pointed bill

conspicuous black breast patch

pale, broad eyebrow

thick pinkish bill

duller face markings

grayish-brown breast

bright-rufous shoulder

FEMALE (BREEDING)

grayish, lightly barred underparts

MALE (BREEDING)

short tail

FLIGHT: deeply undulating, with birds often calling in troughs as they flap.

Like other longspurs, this range-restricted species is often found flocking with Horned Larks in winter. It is a characteristic inhabitant of native shortgrass prairies, and males can often be found performing their spectacular flight displays over this barren, windswept habitat. Flying high, these birds sing as they hover and float downward on wings held in a V position, similar to that of a Monarch butterfly. With their black chest patches and gray underparts, males look surprisingly dark against the pale sky. A dull female could be potentially confused with a female House Sparrow, but the former can be distinguished by the white patches on its tail. Recent genetic (DNA) evidence suggests that the Thick-billed Longspur may actually be more closely related to the Snow Bunting than to the other species of longspurs.

VOICE Flight call a short, liquid *rit-up;* also an abrupt *poink* and metallic *tink;* song melodious; high-pitched tinklings in flight.

NESTING Cup of dried grass placed in depression on the ground, often against a clump of grass; 3–4 eggs; 1–2 broods; April–July.

FEEDING Eats insects while breeding; seeds in winter.

IN THE OPEN
This species favors open habitats, such as heavily grazed fields and other areas with very short grass.

SIMILAR SPECIES

CHESTNUT-COLLARED LONGSPUR ♀ ❀
see p.364

dark cheek patch

longer tail

OCCURRENCE
Breeds in the shortgrass prairie of the High Plains, from Alberta and Saskatchewan, southward to northwest Nebraska and northeast Colorado. Winters in grasslands and barren ground from southeast Colorado southward into Texas and westward into southeast Arizona.

Length **6in (15cm)**	Wingspan **10–11in (25–28cm)**	Weight **⁷⁄₈–1¹⁄₁₆oz (25–30g)**
Social **Large flocks**	Lifespan **Unknown**	Status **Threatened**

DATE: _____ TIME: _____ LOCATION: _____

| Order **Passeriformes** | Family **Calcariidae** | Species ***Plectrophenax nivalis*** |

Snow Bunting

less white in wings

white outer tail feathers

MALE (NONBREEDING)

black back

yellow bill

IN FLIGHT

large white patches on black wings

MALE (BREEDING)

FEMALE (NONBREEDING)

white head and underparts

black bill

FEMALE (BREEDING)

pale-rufous crown

white underparts

dark-brown eyes

rusty-orange cheek patch

black peeks through buffy feather edgings

gray body

white eye-ring

MALE (NONBREEDING)

rusty-orange breast patch

white underparts

IMMATURE

The bold white wing patches of the Snow Bunting make it immediately recognizable in a whirling winter flock of dark-winged longspurs and larks. In winter, heavy snowfall forces flocks onto roadsides, where they can be seen more easily. To secure and defend the best territories, some of the males of this remarkably hardy species arrive as early as April in their barren high-Arctic breeding grounds. The Snow Bunting is very similar in appearance to the rare and localized McKay's Bunting. Although McKay's Bunting generally has less black on the back, in the wings, and on the tail, the two species cannot always be conclusively identified. This is especially true since Snow and McKay's Buntings sometimes interbreed, producing hybrids.

VOICE Flight call a musical, liquid rattle, also *tyew* notes and short buzz; song a pleasant series of squeaky and whistled notes.

NESTING Bulky cup of grass and moss, lined with feathers, and placed in sheltered rock crevice; 3–6 eggs; 1 brood; June–August.

FEEDING Eats seeds (sedge in the Arctic), flies and other insects, and buds on migration.

FLIGHT: deeply undulating; flocks "roll" along as birds at back overtake those in front.

ROCKY GROUND
About the only perches in the Snow Bunting's barren breeding grounds are large boulders.

SIMILAR SPECIES

McKAY'S BUNTING

mostly white tail, back, and wings

OCCURRENCE
Breeds in rocky areas, usually near sparsely vegetated tundra, right across the Arctic. North American birds winter in open country and on shores across the whole of southern Canada and the northern US, and in southern and western coastal areas of Alaska.

| Length **6½–7in (16–18cm)** | Wingspan **12½–14in (32–35cm)** | Weight **1¼–2oz (35–55g)** |
| Social **Large flocks** | Lifespan **At least 4 years** | Status **Declining** |

DATE: _____ TIME: _____ LOCATION: _____

Order **Passeriformes**	Family **Passerellidae**	Species ***Ammodramus savannarum***

Grasshopper Sparrow

large head

fairly long bill

pale eyebrow

white eye-ring

short, spiky tail

buff overall

reddish-and-dark spots on upperparts

buff breast, sides, and flanks

yellow at bend of wing

ADULT

IN FLIGHT

ADULT
A. s. perpallidus
(WESTERN)

darker crown

darker overall

shorter tail

ADULT
A. s. pratensis
(EASTERN)

FLIGHT: low and weak, with spiky tail pointed down; much flapping.

A Grasshopper Sparrow singing briefly atop a weed is usually the first glimpse people get of this secretive bird—it is more often heard than seen. The bird is small, with a large head, spiky tail, and plain breast. It is one of the few North American sparrows that has two completely different songs. While it does eat grasshoppers, its common name derives from its song, which resembles the sounds grasshoppers make. It varies geographically, with about 12 subspecies.

VOICE Sharp *tik* call; flight call a long, high *tseeee*; song an insect-like trill *tik'-tok-TREEEE*, or series of quick buzzes.

NESTING Cup of grass placed in clump of grass; 3–6 eggs; 1–2 broods; April–August.

FEEDING Forages on ground for seeds and insects.

YELLOW PATCH
The pale crown stripe and the small yellow patch at the bend of its wings are visible here.

SIMILAR SPECIES

LeCONTE'S SPARROW
see p.382

brighter overall

orange eyebrow

gray cheek patch

BAIRD'S SPARROW
see p.384

ocher crown

dark lateral throat stripe

OCCURRENCE
Breeds in short grassland, pastures, and even mown areas across much of the US and southern Canada. Locally distributed in the Southwest, also patchily through the central US. Winters in similar habitats from the southern US to Colombia; also found in the West Indies.

Length **5in (13cm)**	Wingspan **8in (20cm)**	Weight **½–¹¹⁄₁₆oz (15–20g)**
Social **Solitary/Flocks**	Lifespan **Up to 7 years**	Status **Declining**

DATE: _____ TIME:_____ LOCATION:_____

| Order **Passeriformes** | Family **Passerellidae** | Species *Chondestes grammacus* |

Lark Sparrow

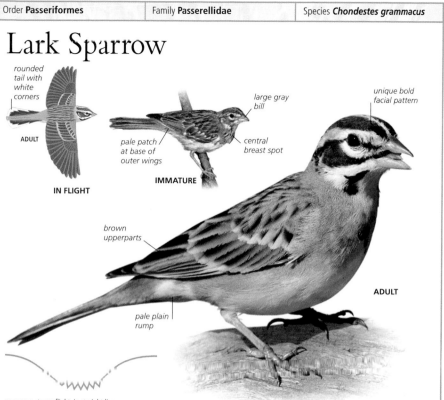

rounded tail with white corners

ADULT

IN FLIGHT

large gray bill

pale patch at base of outer wings

central breast spot

IMMATURE

unique bold facial pattern

brown upperparts

ADULT

pale plain rump

FLIGHT: strong flight, in straight lines; often perches when flushed.

The bold harlequin face pattern, single central breast spot, and long, rounded black tail with white corners make the Lark Sparrow one of the most easily identifiable of all sparrows. It is commonly found singing from the top of a fencepost or small tree in the western US and southern Canadian prairies. Conversely, Lark Sparrow numbers have declined precipitously in the East, where the species is mostly associated with western-like sandy soils. It is likely that its presence in the East was only possible because of the clearing of forests, so the species may, in fact, simply be retreating to its natural range. Male birds are strongly territorial of their nesting sites, though this does not extend as a wider area to other species.

VOICE Thin, upslurred *tseep* call, flight call sharp *tink*; song series of trills, whistles, and rattles on varying pitches.

NESTING Cup usually placed on ground at base of plant, or off-ground in tree or bush; 3–5 eggs; 1–2 broods; April–August.

FEEDING Eats seeds and insects.

ON THE FENCE
The Lark Sparrow is a common roadside bird, often found perching on barbed wire fences.

OCCURRENCE
Breeds in varied open habitats, such as sage flats and grassland from British Columbia and Saskatchewan to Baja California and central Mexico, east to Ohio; localized breeder in the East, associated with well-drained, poor soils. Winters from the southern US to southwest Mexico.

| Length **6–6¾in (15–17cm)** | Wingspan **11in (28cm)** | Weight **¹¹⁄₁₆–1¹⁄₁₆oz (20–30g)** |
| Social **Large flocks** | Lifespan **Up to 8 years** | Status **Secure** |

DATE: _____ TIME: _____ LOCATION: _____

| Order **Passeriformes** | Family **Passerellidae** | Species *Calamospiza melanocorys* |

Lark Bunting

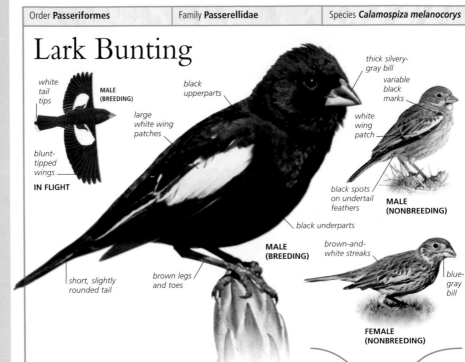

white tail tips

MALE (BREEDING)

black upperparts

thick silvery-gray bill

variable black marks

large white wing patches

white wing patch

blunt-tipped wings

IN FLIGHT

black spots on undertail feathers

MALE (NONBREEDING)

black underparts

MALE (BREEDING)

brown-and-white streaks

blue-gray bill

short, slightly rounded tail

brown legs and toes

FEMALE (NONBREEDING)

Perhaps the most frequently seen bird on the North American High Plains, the stocky Lark Bunting—unlike the Chestnut-collared Longspur, which lives alongside it—has been able to cope with the changes wrought on its habitat by humans, and occurs in extraordinary density throughout its range. Nomadic flocks of thousands scour the high deserts, open grasslands, and sagebrush for seeds. Males in breeding plumage are unmistakable: black with large white wing patches. Females and immature birds are duller, with more subdued wing patches.

VOICE Call a low, soft, whistled *hwoik*; song a partly melodious, partly "scratchy," with repetitions of phrases, then whistles.

NESTING Open cup of grass, lined with fine plant material, in depression in ground; 4–5 eggs; 1 brood; May–August.

FEEDING Mainly seeds in winter, insects in summer.

FLIGHT: low and undulating, short glides alternating with stiff wing beats.

CAUGHT BY ANY MEANS
The Lark Bunting hawks, gleans, and forages insect prey throughout the breeding season.

SIMILAR SPECIES

PURPLE FINCH ♀
see p.354

VESPER SPARROW
see p.381

no white wing patches

pink bill

no white in notched tail

longer, squarer tail

OCCURRENCE
Breeds in grasslands and sage flats on the High Plains from Alberta south to the Texas panhandle. Winters in similar habitats—and also in desert, cultivated plains, and open shrub–steppe—across the interior southwestern US and northern Mexico. Migrants use similar open-country habitats.

| Length **7in (18cm)** | Wingspan **10½–11in (27–28cm)** | Weight **1¹⁄₁₆–1¾oz (30–50g)** |
| Social **Large flocks** | Lifespan **At least 3 years** | Status **Threatened** |

DATE: _____ TIME: _____ LOCATION: _____

Order **Passeriformes**	Family **Passerellidae**	Species *Spizella passerina*

Chipping Sparrow 🔊

pale underparts

ADULT

IN FLIGHT

rusty cast to crown

pinkish bill

ADULT (WINTER)

bright-rufous crown

white eyebrow

black eye-line

blackish bill

ADULT (BREEDING)

gray underparts

heavily streaked, especially on breast

IMMATURE

cleft tail

The Chipping Sparrow is a common, trusting bird, which breeds in backyards across most of North America. While they are easily identifiable in the summer, "Chippers" molt into a drab, nonbreeding plumage during fall, at which point they are easily confused with the Clay-colored and Brewer's Sparrows they flock with. Most reports of this species across the north in winter are actually of the larger American Tree Sparrow. In the winter, Chipping Sparrows can be easily recognized as they lack their bright rusty crown and are restricted to the south.

VOICE Call a sharp *tsip*; flight call a sharp, thin *tsiiit*; song an insect-like trill of *chip* notes, variable in duration and quality.

NESTING Nest cup usually placed well off the ground in tree or shrub; 3–5 eggs; 1–2 broods; April–August.

FEEDING Eats seeds of grasses and annuals, plus some fruit; when breeding, also eats insects and other invertebrates.

FLIGHT: slightly undulating, often to open perch when flushed.

BACKYARD BIRD
Chipping Sparrows are a very common sight in gardens and backyards all across the continent.

SIMILAR SPECIES

CLAY-COLORED SPARROW
see p.372

heavy streaks

partial "necklace"

BREWER'S SPARROW
see p.373

streaked crown

pale underparts

OCCURRENCE
Found in a wide variety of habitats: open forest, woodlands, grassy, park-like areas, shorelines, and backyards. Breeds in North America south of the Arctic timberline and in Mexico, and in Central America, as far south as Nicaragua. Winters from southern states to Nicaragua.

Length **5½in (14cm)**	Wingspan **8½in (21cm)**	Weight **⅜–½oz (10–15g)**
Social **Large flocks**	Lifespan **Up to 9 years**	Status **Secure**

DATE: _____ TIME: _____ LOCATION: _____

| Order **Passeriformes** | Family **Passerellidae** | Species *Spizella pallida* |

Clay-colored Sparrow

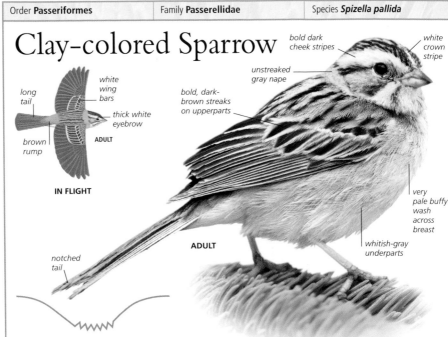

bold dark cheek stripes

white crown stripe

unstreaked gray nape

bold, dark-brown streaks on upperparts

white wing bars

long tail

thick white eyebrow

brown rump

ADULT

IN FLIGHT

very pale buffy wash across breast

whitish-gray underparts

ADULT

notched tail

FLIGHT: slightly undulating, often flies to open perch when flushed.

The little Clay-colored Sparrow is best known for its mechanical, buzzy song. This bird spends much of its foraging time away from the breeding habitat; consequently, males' territories are quite small, allowing for dense breeding populations. Clay-colored Sparrows have shifted their breeding range eastward and northward over the last century, most likely because of changes in land practices. During the nonbreeding season, they form large flocks in open country, associating with other *Spizella* sparrows, especially Chipping and Brewer's.

VOICE Call a sharp *tsip*; flight call a short, rising *sip*; song a series of 2–7 mechanical buzzes on one pitch.

NESTING Cup of grass placed just off the ground in shrub or small tree; 3–5 eggs; 1–2 broods; May–August.

FEEDING Forages on or low to the ground for seeds and insects.

CHRISTMAS PRESENT
The Clay-colored Sparrow is fond of short conifers for breeding, so Christmas tree farms form a perfect habitat.

SIMILAR SPECIES

CHIPPING SPARROW ❄
see p.371

grayish rump

dark stripe through eye

grayer breast

BREWER'S SPARROW
see p.373

streaked nape

lacks bold crown stripe

OCCURRENCE
Breeds in open habitats: prairies, shrubland, forest edges, and Christmas tree farms along the US/Canadian border and northward to the southern Northwest Territories. Winters in a large variety of brushy, weedy areas from south Texas to Mexico. Migration takes it to the Great Plains.

| Length **5½in (14cm)** | Wingspan **7½in (19cm)** | Weight **⅜–½oz (10–15g)** |
| Social **Large flocks** | Lifespan **Up to 5 years** | Status **Secure** |

DATE: _____ TIME: _____ LOCATION: _____

| Order **Passeriformes** | Family **Passerellidae** | Species *Spizella breweri* |

Brewer's Sparrow

dark streaks on crown

streaked nape

conspicuous white eye-ring

small, conical bill

pale grayish rump

buff wing bars

ADULT

notched tail

IN FLIGHT

pale grayish-brown upperparts with marked dark streaks

brown facial markings

long, notched tail

grayish-white underparts

ADULT

Brewer's Sparrow is a small, fairly drab-looking bird, but its conspicuous eye-ring and streaked nape are good identification features. In addition, its varied, loud, trilling and chattering song is a memorable sound of the West. Most Brewer's Sparrows nest on arid sagebrush in the western US, but there is an isolated subspecies, *S. b. taverneri*, the Timberline Sparrow, which breeds in the Canadian Rockies and into Alaska. It is usually darker, more boldly marked, and longer-billed with a lower, slower, more musical song than its relative.

VOICE Call a sharp *tsip*; flight call a short, rising *sip*; song a series of descending trills, rattles, and buzzes on different pitches.

NESTING Compact cup on or near ground in small bush; 3–4 eggs; 1–2 broods; May–August.

FEEDING Forages on ground for insects and seeds.

FLIGHT: slightly undulating; alternates rapidly between glides and active flight.

CONTINUOUS CHORUS
Across its range in spring, the male Brewer's Sparrow sings continuously to attract a mate.

HIGH AND DRY
These sparrows are fond of the arid brushland and deserts of the High Plains and Great Basin.

OCCURRENCE
Timberline subspecies breeds in valleys in eastern Alaska through Yukon to northwestern British Columbia. Brewer's subspecies breed in brushland, shrubland, thickets, and mountain basins of the western US. Winters in desert scrub and weedy fields in the Southwest and northwestern Mexico.

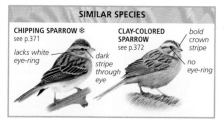

SIMILAR SPECIES

CHIPPING SPARROW ❋
see p.371

lacks white eye-ring

dark stripe through eye

CLAY-COLORED SPARROW
see p.372

bold crown stripe

no eye-ring

| Length **5½in (14cm)** | Wingspan **7½in (19cm)** | Weight **⁵⁄₁₆–½oz (9–14g)** |
| Social **Solitary/Flocks** | Lifespan **Unknown** | Status **Secure** |

DATE: _____ TIME: _____ LOCATION: _____

| Order **Passeriformes** | Family **Passerellidae** | Species **Passerella iliaca** |

Fox Sparrow 🔊

ADULT (RED)

dark-rufous overall

IN FLIGHT

gray head and back

two white wing bars

P. i. altivagans (SLATE-COLORED)

gray nape

rusty streaks on back

darker upper mandible

dark-brown head and upperparts

densely spotted breast

rusty tail

P. i. unalaschensis (SOOTY)

grayish-brown head and upperparts

rusty wings and tail

very large bill

fine streaks on throat

long rusty tail

P. i. stephensi (THICK-BILLED)

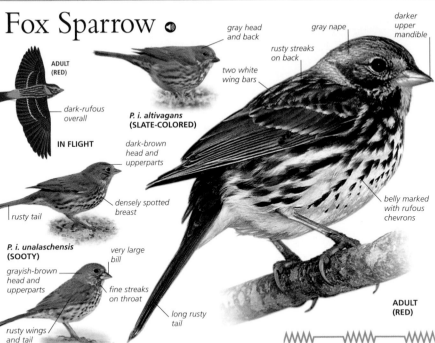

belly marked with rufous chevrons

ADULT (RED)

FLIGHT: alternates wing beats and glides; straight and fluttery, from cover to cover.

Larger, more robust, and more colorful than its close relatives, the Fox Sparrow is a beautiful species. When it appears in backyards, its presence can be detected by its foraging habits; it crouches low in leaf litter, and hops to disturb leaves, under which it finds seeds or insects. It varies considerably over its huge range, from thick-billed birds in the Sierras to dark ones in the Northwest, and distinctive red Fox Sparrows in taiga forest from Newfoundland to Alaska.

VOICE Call is sharp, dry *tshak* or *tshuk*; flight call a high-pitched *tzeep!*; song is complex and musical with trills and whistles.

NESTING Dense cup of grasses or moss lined with fine material; usually placed low in shrub; 2–5 eggs; 1 brood; April–July.

FEEDING Forages for insects, seeds, and fruit.

FOXY RED
The Fox Sparrow gets its name from the rusty coloration of the eastern "red" birds.

SIMILAR SPECIES

HERMIT THRUSH see p.341

unstreaked flanks

different bill shape

SONG SPARROW see p.386

thinner bill

longer tail

breast streaking less marked

OCCURRENCE
Encompasses the entire boreal forest zone, from Alaska in the West to Quebec, Labrador, and Newfoundland in the East. In the West, it occurs in coastal and near-coast thickets within coniferous or mixed woodlands. Winters in the Pacific West, south to Baja California; also from Texas to Massachusetts.

| Length **6–7½in (15–19cm)** | Wingspan **10½–11½in (27–29cm)** | Weight **⅞–1⁹⁄₁₆oz (25–45g)** |
| Social **Solitary/Small flocks** | Lifespan **Up to 9 years** | Status **Secure** |

DATE: _____ TIME: _____ LOCATION: _____

| Order **Passeriformes** | Family **Passerellidae** | Species ***Spizelloides arborea*** |

American Tree Sparrow

IN FLIGHT

rusty tones
on shoulder
and wings

**ADULT
(BREEDING)**

IMMATURE

streaked
underparts

gray head
and nape

rusty stripe
behind eye

rufous
crown

black-and-
yellow bill

rust
patch on
shoulder

dark central
spot

black-and-rust
streaking on
back

**ADULT
(BREEDING)**

striped
back

cleft
tail

**ADULT
(NONBREEDING)**

long,
squarish tail

FLIGHT: slightly undulating, often flies to open
perch when flushed.

T he first heavy snowfalls of
winter often bring large flocks of American Tree Sparrows
to bird feeders. This bird is commonly mistaken for the smaller
Chipping Sparrow, but the two species look quite dissimilar
in the winter. The American Tree Sparrow is larger and has
a central breast spot and a bicolored bill. A highly social, vocal,
and misnamed species, noisy winter flocks numbering in the
hundreds can be found feeding in weedy fields and along
the roadsides of the northern US and southern Canada.
VOICE Call a bell-like *teedle-ee*; flight call a thin, slightly descending
tsiiiu; song *seee seee di-di-di di-di-di dyew dyew*.
NESTING Nest cup on ground concealed within thicket; 4–6 eggs;
1 brood; June–July.
FEEDING Feeds on seeds, berries, and a variety of insects.

WINTER HABITATS
In winter, this species frequents barren habitats,
like old fields and roadsides, as well as feeders.

SIMILAR SPECIES

CHIPPING SPARROW
see p.371

lacks rusty
eye-line

FIELD SPARROW

all-pale
bill

bold white
eye-ring

no central
black breast
spot

smaller
overall

OCCURRENCE
Breeds in scrubby thickets
of birch and willows in the
area between taiga and tundra
across Alaska and north Canada.
Nonbreeders choose open,
grassy, brushy habitats. Winters
across south Canada and the
northern US. Casual to the Pacific
Coast and the southern US.

| Length **6¼in (16cm)** | Wingspan **9½in (24cm)** | Weight **⁷⁄₁₆–⁷⁄₈oz (13–25g)** |
| Social **Flocks** | Lifespan **Up to 11 years** | Status **Secure** |

DATE: _____ TIME: _____ LOCATION: _____

| Order **Passeriformes** | Family **Passerellidae** | Species *Junco hyemalis* |

Dark-eyed Junco 🔊

**MALE
(SLATE-COLORED)**

dark area between
eye and bill

dark-gray
head

bluish-gray
hood

gray body
with brown
wash to back

dull, brownish
back

white
outer tail
feathers

IN FLIGHT

pinkish flanks

**FEMALE
(PINK-SIDED)**

reddish-
brown back

gray
rump

black mask

pale-gray
underparts

white
belly

**MALE
(SLATE-COLORED)**

**MALE
(GRAY-HEADED)**

rust
back

blackish
hood

reddish flanks

**MALE
(OREGON)**

The Dark-eyed Junco's appearance at bird feeders during
snowstorms has earned it the colloquial name of "snowbird."
They generally prefer to feed on the ground, and can be found
hopping about on the forest floor in search of seeds and insects,
or on the ground underneath a bird feeder in backyards across
North America. The name "Dark-eyed Junco" is actually used
to describe a group of birds that vary geographically in an incredibly
diverse way. Sixteen subspecies have been described. "Slate-colored"
populations occur in central Alaska, Canada, and the northeastern
US; the "White-winged" nests in the Black Hills of South Dakota;
"Pink-sided" birds breed in Idaho, Montana, and Wyoming,
and "Oregon" birds breed in the Pacific West, from coastal Alaska
to British Columbia and the mountainous western US in the Sierras
south to Mexico. "Red-backed" populations reside in the mountains
of Arizona and New Mexico, while "Gray-headed" birds range
between the "Red-backed" and "Pink-sided" populations.
Dark-eyed Juncos can form large flocks in the winter;
where ranges overlap, several subspecies may be found
foraging together with sparrows and other birds.
VOICE Loud, smacking *tick* and soft *dyew* calls; flight call a rapid,
twittering, and buzzy *zzeet*; song a simple, liquid, 1-pitch trill.
NESTING Cup placed on ground hidden under vegetation or
next to rocks; 3–5 eggs; 1–2 broods; May–August.
FEEDING Eats insects and seeds; also berries.

FLIGHT: low and direct, staying within cover
whenever possible.

PINK-SIDED MALE
Like most juncos, this male is brighter with greater
contrasts, darker eye areas, and more vivid colors.

OCCURRENCE
Breeds in coniferous
and mixed forests across
Canada, south to the east
Appalachians and Georgia.
In the West, in mountains
from Alaska and British
Columbia to New Mexico
and northern Baja California.
Winters from southern
Canada to northern Mexico.

| Length **6–6¾in (15–17cm)** | Wingspan **8–10in (20–26cm)** | Weight **⅝–1¹⁄₁₆oz (18–30g)** |
| Social **Flocks** | Lifespan **Up to 11 years** | Status **Secure** |

DATE: _____ TIME: _____ LOCATION: _____

| Order **Passeriformes** | Family **Passerellidae** | Species *Zonotrichia leucophrys* |

White-crowned Sparrow 🔊

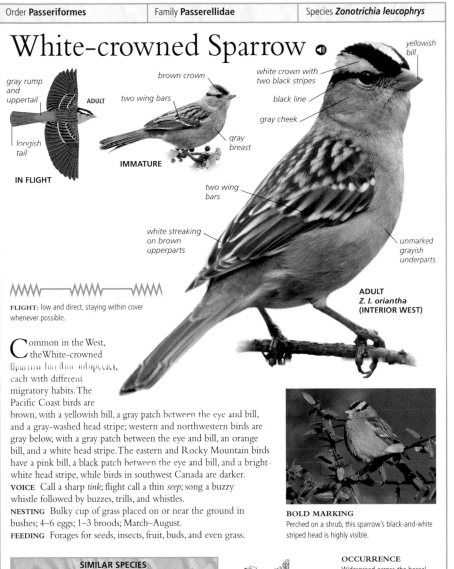

ADULT

gray rump and uppertail

two wing bars

brown crown

yellowish bill

white crown with two black stripes

black line

gray cheek

longish tail

gray breast

IMMATURE

IN FLIGHT

two wing bars

white streaking on brown upperparts

unmarked grayish underparts

FLIGHT: low and direct, staying within cover whenever possible.

ADULT
Z. l. oriantha
(INTERIOR WEST)

C ommon in the West, the White-crowned Sparrow has five subspecies, each with different migratory habits. The Pacific Coast birds are brown, with a yellowish bill, a gray patch between the eye and bill, and a gray-washed head stripe; western and northwestern birds are gray below, with a gray patch between the eye and bill, an orange bill, and a white head stripe. The eastern and Rocky Mountain birds have a pink bill, a black patch between the eye and bill, and a bright-white head stripe, while birds in southwest Canada are darker.

VOICE Call a sharp *tink*; flight call a thin *seep*; song a buzzy whistle followed by buzzes, trills, and whistles.
NESTING Bulky cup of grass placed on or near the ground in bushes; 4–6 eggs; 1–3 broods; March–August.
FEEDING Forages for seeds, insects, fruit, buds, and even grass.

BOLD MARKING
Perched on a shrub, this sparrow's black-and-white striped head is highly visible.

SIMILAR SPECIES

WHITE-THROATED SPARROW
see p.380

yellow patch

gray bill

chunkier overall

more reddish

GOLDEN-CROWNED SPARROW ◑
see p.378

plain face

yellowish forecrown

gray bill

OCCURRENCE
Widespread across the boreal forest and tundra limit, from Alaska eastward to Quebec and Labrador, and southward from British Columbia to coastal California and the interior mountainous West. Preferred nesting habitats include dense brush near open grasslands; in winter, open woods and gardens.

| Length 6½–7in (16–18cm) | Wingspan 9½–10in (24–26cm) | Weight ¹¹⁄₁₆–1¼oz (20–35g) |
| Social **Flocks** | Lifespan **Up to 13 years** | Status **Secure** |

DATE: _____ TIME: _____ LOCATION: _____

Order **Passeriformes**	Family **Passerellidae**	Species **Zonotrichia atricapilla**

Golden-crowned Sparrow

bright-yellow crown

streaks on head

dull-yellow crown

thick black eyebrow

white wing bars

ADULT (BREEDING)

IMMATURE

IN FLIGHT

duller yellow on crown

much less black on face

long tail

ADULT (NONBREEDING)

ADULT (BREEDING)

light grayish-brown underparts

The large Golden-crowned Sparrow is common along the Pacific Coast of North America. It sings in a minor key and, as a result, has a reputation for sounding melancholy. Many late 19th-century Klondike gold prospectors called this bird "Weary Willie"—to them, its song sounded remarkably like *I'm so tired* or *No gold here*. It has been regarded as a pest in the past because of its habit of consuming crops in agricultural fields and gardens. Nonbreeding adults retain their distinctive golden crown in the winter, but it appears duller.

VOICE Call loud *tsik*; flight call soft, short *seeep*; song variable series of melancholy whistles, sometimes slurred or trilled.

NESTING Concealed bulky cup placed on ground at base of bush; 3–5 eggs; 1–2 broods; June–August.

FEEDING Predominantly forages on the ground for seeds, insects, fruit, flowers, and buds.

FLIGHT: low and direct, staying within cover whenever possible.

GROUND FORAGER
This sparrow can be found by listening for the noise it makes as it roots around in the leaf litter.

SIMILAR SPECIES

WHITE-CROWNED SPARROW
see p.377

orange bill

WHITE-THROATED SPARROW (TAN-STRIPED)
see p.380

lacks yellowish fore-crown

white throat

OCCURRENCE
Breeds in shrubby habitat along the tree line and open, boggy forests from Alaska east to southwest Northwest Territories, south to British Columbia and southwest Alberta. Winters in dense thickets from south coastal British Columbia to north Baja California.

Length **7in (18cm)**	Wingspan **9–10in (23–25cm)**	Weight **1¹⁄₁₆–1¹⁄₄oz (20–35g)**
Social **Flocks**	Lifespan **Up to 10 years**	Status **Secure**

DATE: _____ TIME:_____ LOCATION:_____

| Order **Passeriformes** | Family **Passerellidae** | Species *Zonotrichia querula* |

Harris's Sparrow

ADULT (NONBREEDING)

indistinct facial markings

IN FLIGHT

two wing bars

ADULT (NONBREEDING)

pinkish bill

gray rump and undertail feathers

gray cheeks

black cheek patch

black crown

pinkish or yellow bill

black chin and throat

tan cheek

white chin

concentration of streaks on chest

IMMATURE

ADULT (BREEDING)

An unmistakable black-faced, pink-billed bird, Harris's Sparrow is the only breeding bird endemic to Canada. It can be seen in the US during migration or in winter on the Great Plains. This species is occasionally found in large flocks of White-throated and White-crowned Sparrows. Harris's Sparrow is the largest sparrow in Canada, approaching the Northern Cardinal in size. Its scientific name, *querula*, comes from the plaintive quality of its whistled song. The first Harris's Sparrow nest was found in 1907 in the Northwest Territories.

VOICE Call a sharp *week*; song a melancholy series of 2–4 whistles on the same pitch.

NESTING Bulky cup placed on ground among vegetation or near ground in brush; 3–5 eggs; 1 brood; June–August.

FEEDING Eats seeds, insects, buds, and even young conifer needles in summer.

FLIGHT: low and direct, staying within cover whenever possible.

NORTHERN ACROBAT
This nonbreeding Harris's Sparrow grips two different weeds, one in each foot.

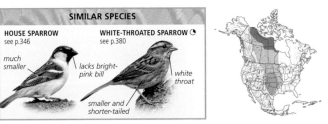

SIMILAR SPECIES

HOUSE SPARROW
see p.346

much smaller

WHITE-THROATED SPARROW ◐
see p.380

lacks bright-pink bill

smaller and shorter-tailed

white throat

OCCURRENCE
Breeds in scrub-tundra along the Canadian taiga–tundra timberline from northern Northwest Territories to north Ontario. Winters in the US Great Plains from South Dakota and Iowa south to northern Texas. Nonbreeders found in thickets and hedges. Casual to rare in the East and West.

| Length 6¾–7½in (17–19cm) | Wingspan 10½–11in (27–28cm) | Weight 1¹⁄₁₆–1⁷⁄₁₆oz (30–40g) |
| Social **Flocks** | Lifespan **Up to 12 years** | Status **Secure** |

DATE: _____ TIME: _____ LOCATION: _____

| Order **Passeriformes** | Family **Passerellidae** | Species *Zonotrichia albicollis* |

White-throated Sparrow 🔊

two white wing bars

ADULT

IN FLIGHT

tan stripe

browner face

ADULT (TAN-STRIPED)

bold white-and-black stripes

bright-rufous back and tail

yellow patch

white throat

gray underparts

gray bill

streaking on breast

IMMATURE (TAN-STRIPED)

fairly long tail

ADULT (WHITE-STRIPED)

Common almost everywhere in eastern North America, White-throated Sparrows sing all year round. Their distinctive, whistled, rhythmic song can be remembered with the popular mnemonic *Oh sweet Canada Canada Canada*, or the less accurate *Old Sam Peabody*. This species has two different color forms, one with a white stripe above its eye, and the other with a tan stripe. In the nonbreeding season, large flocks roam the leaf litter of woodlands in search of food. Often, the only indication of their presence is the occasional moving leaf or thin, lisping flight call.
VOICE Call loud, sharp *jink*; flight call lisping *tssssst!*; song clear whistle comprising 1–2 higher notes, then three triplets.
NESTING Cup placed on or near ground in dense shrubbery; 2–6 eggs; 1 brood; May–August.
FEEDING Mainly forages on the ground for seeds, fruit, insects, buds, and various grasses.

FLIGHT: low and direct, staying within cover whenever possible.

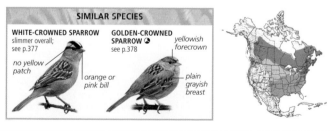

DIFFERENT COLOR FORMS
The presence of white or tan stripes on White-throated Sparrows is not related to their sex.

SIMILAR SPECIES

WHITE-CROWNED SPARROW
slimmer overall; see p.377

no yellow patch

orange or pink bill

GOLDEN-CROWNED SPARROW ♀
see p.378

yellowish forecrown

plain grayish breast

OCCURRENCE
Breeds in forests from eastern Yukon to Newfoundland, south into the Great Lakes and northern Appalachians. Nonbreeders prefer wooded thickets and hedges. Winters across the eastern US and extreme south of the Southwest. Rare but regular along the Pacific Coast.

| Length 6½–7½in (16–17.5cm) | Wingspan 9–10in (23–26cm) | Weight ¹¹⁄₁₆–1¼oz (20–35g) |
| Social **Flocks** | Lifespan **Up to 10 years** | Status **Secure** |

DATE: _____ TIME:_____ LOCATION:_____

Order **Passeriformes**	Family **Passerellidae**	Species **Pooecetes gramineus**

Vesper Sparrow

rusty shoulders

ADULT

IN FLIGHT

dark-bordered ear patches

bold white eye-ring

pale-brown upperparts

streaked breast

bold white-edged long, dark, square tail

ADULT

uniformly colored and streaked overall

white outer tail feathers

ADULT

The Vesper Sparrow got its common name because its pleasant song was considered to sound sweetest in the evening, when prayers known as "Vespers" are sung in the Catholic and Eastern Orthodox churches. When Henry David Thoreau wrote of this species, he called it the "Bay-winged Bunting," because of its (sometimes concealed) rusty shoulder patches and its resemblance to the Old World Emberizidae buntings. The Vesper Sparrow needs areas with bare ground to breed, so it is one of the few species that can successfully nest in areas of intense agriculture; the bird's numbers seem to be declining in spite of this.

VOICE Full *tchup* call, flight call thin *tseent*; song consists of two whistles of same pitch, followed by two higher-pitched ones, then trills, ends lazily.

NESTING Cup placed on patch of bare ground, against grass, bush, or rock; 3–5 eggs; 1 brood; April–August.

FEEDING Eats insects and seeds.

FLIGHT: strong, often perches when flushed; often moves on ground

SIMILAR SPECIES

SAVANNAH SPARROW (EAST) see p.385	SAVANNAH SPARROW (IPSWICH) see p.385
smaller bill	lacks white eye-ring / orange feet

GIFTED SONGSTER
The sweet song of the Vesper Sparrow is a characteristic sound of more northerly open areas.

OCCURRENCE
Breeds in sparse grassland, cultivated fields, recently burned areas, and mountain parks across south Canada and the northern US. Winters in sparsely vegetated, open habitats from the southern US to southwest Mexico. Found in patches of bare earth in all seasons.

Length **6¼in (16cm)**	Wingspan **10in (25cm)**	Weight **¹¹⁄₁₆–1¹⁄₁₆oz (20–30g)**
Social **Flocks**	Lifespan **Up to 7 years**	Status **Declining**

DATE: _____ TIME: _____ LOCATION: _____

| Order **Passeriformes** | Family **Passerellidae** | Species *Ammospiza leconteii* |

LeConte's Sparrow

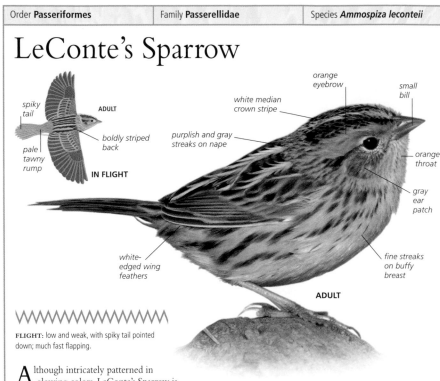

spiky tail

ADULT

pale tawny rump

boldly striped back

IN FLIGHT

orange eyebrow

white median crown stripe

purplish and gray streaks on nape

small bill

orange throat

gray ear patch

white-edged wing feathers

fine streaks on buffy breast

ADULT

VVVVVVVVVVVVVV

FLIGHT: low and weak, with spiky tail pointed down; much fast flapping.

Although intricately patterned in glowing colors, LeConte's Sparrow is usually very difficult to see. Not only is it tiny—one of the smallest of all sparrows—but in the grasslands and marshes of interior North America where it lives, it prefers to dart for cover under grasses instead of flushing when disturbed. Meanwhile, the flight call and song of this elusive little bird are remarkably insect-like. Many people who hear it often pass off the unseen bird as a grasshopper. Its nest is even harder to find, making this bird a real challenge to study or observe.

VOICE Call long, downslurred *zheeep*; flight call similar to grasshopper; song insect-like, buzzy *tik'-uht-tizz-ZHEEEEEE-k*.

NESTING Concealed little cup placed on or near ground; 3–5 eggs; 1 brood; June–August.

FEEDING Forages on the ground and in grasses for insects and their larvae, spiders, and seeds.

HIDEAWAY BIRD
LeConte's Sparrow is usually found skulking in medium-to-tall grass in all seasons.

OCCURRENCE
Breeds in marshes, wet meadows, and bogs from southwest Yukon to Lake Superior and west Quebec. Migrants or wintering birds found in tall grass and marshes from southwest Kansas to south Indiana, and central Texas to the coastal Carolinas.

SIMILAR SPECIES

NELSON'S SPARROW
see p.383

gray nape

less streaked

GRASSHOPPER SPARROW
see p.368

larger bill

duller overall

| Length **4½–5in (11.5–13cm)** | Wingspan **6½–7in (16–18cm)** | Weight **⁷⁄₁₆–⁹⁄₁₆oz (12–16g)** |
| Social **Solitary/Loose flocks** | Lifespan **At least 4 years** | Status **Secure** |

DATE: _____ TIME: _____ LOCATION: _____

| Order **Passeriformes** | Family **Passerellidae** | Species *Ammospiza nelsoni* |

Nelson's Sparrow

dark, rounded, spiky tail

ADULT
A. n. subvirgatus

no bold streaks on underparts

IN FLIGHT

short, pointed tail

FLIGHT: low and weak, with spiky tail pointed down; much flapping.

brighter upperparts

smaller bill

ADULT
A. n. nelsoni

bright-orange triangle on side of face

medium-sized bill

streaked, washed-out pattern on back

dark cheek marks

faint streaking on underparts

ADULT
A. n. subvirgatus

This rather shy species includes three subspecies that differ in plumage, as well as breeding habitat and location. *A. n. nelsoni* is the most brightly colored, and is found from the southern Northwest Territories south to northwest Wisconsin. *A. n. subvirgatus* breeds in coastal Maine and the Maritimes, and along the St. Lawrence River. It is visually duller than *A. n. nelsoni*, with a longer bill and flatter head. The intermediate-looking *A. n. alterus* breeds along the southern and western coasts of the Hudson Bay.

VOICE Sharp *tik* call; song a husky *t-SHHHHEE-uhrr*.
NESTING Cup of grass placed on or just above ground; 4–5 eggs; 1 brood; May–July.
FEEDING Forages on the ground mainly for insects, spiders, and seeds.

SIMILAR SPECIES

SALTMARSH SPARROW

longer bill

darker streaks

LeCONTE'S SPARROW
see p.382

white stripes on back

darker streaking

white crown stripe

IDENTIFYING MARKS
The orange-and-gray facial pattern and streaks on the breast are clearly visible.

OCCURRENCE
Breeds in a variety of marsh habitats across North America. Nonbreeders found in marshes and wet, weedy fields. *A. n. nelsoni* and *A. n. alterus* winter on coast from Texas northeast to New Jersey; *A. n. subvirgatus* from eastern Florida to New Jersey.

| Length **4¾in (12cm)** | Wingspan **7in (17.5cm)** | Weight **⁷⁄₁₆–¹¹⁄₁₆oz (13–20g)** |
| Social **Solitary/Flocks** | Lifespan **Unknown** | Status **Secure** |

DATE: _____ TIME:_____ LOCATION:_____

| Order **Passeriformes** | Family **Passerellidae** | Species *Centronyx bairdii* |

Baird's Sparrow

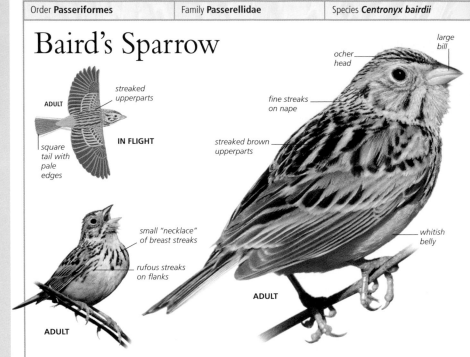

ADULT

streaked upperparts

IN FLIGHT

square tail with pale edges

small "necklace" of breast streaks

rufous streaks on flanks

ADULT

large bill

ocher head

fine streaks on nape

streaked brown upperparts

whitish belly

ADULT

ADULT

The sweet, tinkling song of the Baird's Sparrow is a sure sign of high-quality mixed-grass prairie on the Northern Plains. This sparrow's musical song is quite different to the buzzy songs of the other streaky-brown sparrows. Its square, pale-edged tail is also a useful distinguishing feature. Baird's Sparrow is usually seen only on its breeding grounds, for it is very difficult to find elsewhere, scurrying out of sight if disturbed. Like other birds that depend on native grasslands, it has not coped well with the intensive agriculture that has swept across the Northern Plains in the last century or so.
VOICE Call soft, metallic *tsink*; flight call insect-like *tisk*; song *tsk tsk tsuck tsooweeeeee.*
NESTING Well-concealed grass cup placed on ground in depression or in grass clump or shrub; 4–5 eggs; 1–2 broods; May–August.
FEEDING Forages for seeds and insects.

FLIGHT: low and weak, short in duration, much flapping.

SIMILAR SPECIES

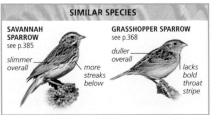

SAVANNAH SPARROW see p.385

slimmer overall

more streaks below

GRASSHOPPER SPARROW see p.368

duller overall

lacks bold throat stripe

HABITAT SPECIALIST
Baird's Sparrow needs the previous year's dead grass as suitable breeding habitat.

OCCURRENCE
Breeds in light mixed-grass prairie, from south Alberta southeast to northern South Dakota and northern Wyoming. Migrates through the High Plains. Winters in diverse, patchy grasslands, in Chihuahua, northern Sonora in Mexico, and in the adjacent US.

| Length 5½ in (14cm) | Wingspan 8½–8¾ in (21–22.5cm) | Weight ½–¹¹⁄₁₆oz (15–20g) |
| Social **Solitary/Loose flocks** | Lifespan **At least 3 years** | Status **Special Concern** |

DATE: _____ TIME:_____ LOCATION:_____

Order **Passeriformes**	Family **Passerellidae**	Species *Passerculus sandwichensis*

Savannah Sparrow 🔊

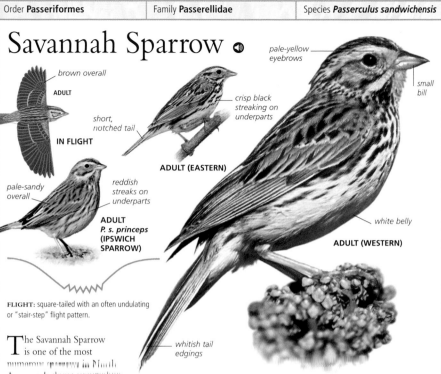

pale-yellow eyebrows

small bill

brown overall

ADULT

short, notched tail

IN FLIGHT

crisp black streaking on underparts

ADULT (EASTERN)

pale-sandy overall

reddish streaks on underparts

**ADULT
P. s. princeps
(IPSWICH
SPARROW)**

white belly

ADULT (WESTERN)

FLIGHT: square-tailed with an often undulating or "stair-step" flight pattern.

whitish tail edgings

The Savannah Sparrow is one of the most numerous sparrows in North America. It shows tremendous variation—21 subspecies—across its vast range, but it is always brown, with dark streaks above and white with dark streaks below. The pale "Ipswich Sparrow" (*P. s. princeps*), originally described as a species, breeds on Sable Island, Nova Scotia, and winters along the East Coast. The "Large-billed Sparrow" (*P. s. rostratus* and *P. s. atratus*) breeds in Baja California and Sonora, Mexico. Their distinct song consists of three buzzy trills, and their flight calls are lower and more metallic than other populations.

VOICE Call a sharp but full *stip*; flight call a thin, weak, downslurred *tseew*; song a *sit sit sit sit suh-EEEEE say*, from perch or in display flight with legs dangling.

NESTING Concealed cup of grass placed in depression on ground, protected by overhanging grass or sedges; 2–6 eggs; 1–2 broods; June–August.

FEEDING Forages on the ground, mostly for insects; in summer also eats seeds in summer; in winter, berries and fruit when available; also small snails and crustaceans.

SWEET LOW DOWN
Savannah Sparrows like to vocalize from low vegetation and fenceposts near farms.

SIMILAR SPECIES

SONG SPARROW
see p.386

larger overall

longer rounded tail

VESPER SPARROW
see p.381

rusty shoulder

dark tail

OCCURRENCE
Breeds in meadows, grasslands, pastures, bushy tundra, and some cultivated land across northern North America. Also along the Pacific Coast and in Mexican interior. Nonbreeders use varied open habitats. Winters across the southern US to Honduras; also Cuba, the Bahamas, and the Cayman Islands.

Length **5½–6in (14–15cm)**	Wingspan **6¾in (17cm)**	Weight **½–1¹⁄₁₆oz (15–30g)**
Social **Solitary/Loose flocks**	Lifespan **Up to 8 years**	Status **Secure**

DATE: _____ TIME: _____ LOCATION: _____

| Order **Passeriformes** | Family **Passerellidae** | Species *Melospiza melodia* |

Song Sparrow 🔊

ADULT (WEST COAST)

IN FLIGHT

streaked underparts

grayish head with brown markings

central breast spot

heavily streaked brownish-gray upperparts

M. m. melodia (EASTERN)

grayish head with dark chestnut-brown crown

dark "mustache" bordering whitish throat

heavily streaked underparts

long, dark, rounded tail

paler neck

whitish lower belly

more rusty overall

M. m. saltonis (SOUTHWEST)

ADULT (WEST COAST)

The familiar song of this species can be heard in backyards across the continent, including in winter, although it varies both individually and geographically. In the southeastern US, where it does not breed, migrant birds start singing in early spring before departing for northern areas. The Song Sparrow may be the North American champion of geographical variation—about 30 subspecies have been described. These vary from the large, dark birds of the Aleutian Islands (*M. m. maxima*) to the smaller, paler birds of southern Arizona (*M. m. saltonis*). Eastern birds, such as *M. m. melodia*, fall between the two in size.

VOICE A dry *tchip* call; flight call a clear *siiiti*; song a jumble of variable whistles and trills, *deeep deeep-deep-deep chrrrr tiiiiiiiiiiiii tyeeur* most common.

NESTING Bulky cup on or near ground, in brush or marsh vegetation; 3–5 eggs; 1–3 broods; March–August.

FEEDING In summer, feeds mainly on insects; in winter, eats mainly seeds, but also fruit.

FLIGHT: low and direct, staying within cover whenever possible.

OCCURRENCE
Widespread in a range of habitats (although not in dense forests) across Canada and the US, from the Atlantic to the Pacific Coasts and north to Alaska. Some populations move south of their breeding range in winter.

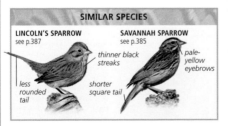

SIMILAR SPECIES

LINCOLN'S SPARROW see p.387

thinner black streaks

less rounded tail

shorter square tail

SAVANNAH SPARROW see p.385

pale-yellow eyebrows

BREAST SPOT
The Song Sparrow often sings from exposed perches, showing off its characteristic breast spot.

| Length **5–7½in (13–19cm)** | Wingspan **8½–12in (21–31cm)** | Weight **7/16–1¾oz (13–50g)** |
| Social **Solitary/Flocks** | Lifespan **Up to 9 years** | Status **Secure** |

DATE: _____ TIME: _____ LOCATION: _____

| Order **Passeriformes** | Family **Passerellidae** | Species *Melospiza lincolnii* |

Lincoln's Sparrow 🔊

crested or peaked rufous crown

broad gray eyebrow

bold eye-ring

small, thin bill

dark-brown streak under cheek

streaks on throat

pencil-thin streaking on buffy breast

rounded tail

ADULT

rufous-edged wings

ADULT

IN FLIGHT

A t first glance, the Lincoln's Sparrow appears plain, but on close inspection it reveals itself to be a bright-eyed little bird with subtly varying, but crisply outlined, markings. In the breeding season, it seeks out predominantly in its willow scrub in the tundra-taiga timberline; outside the breeding season, Lincoln's Sparrow can be found in scrubby habitats right across North America. It will occasionally visit backyard feeders in winter, but it is generally a secretive bird that stays within fairly dense cover wherever it can. However, Lincoln's Sparrow's rich, musical song is unmistakable, and it varies remarkably little from region to region.

VOICE Call a variable, loud *tchip*, flight call a rolling *ziiiit*; song series of rich, musical trills, *ju-ju-ju dodododo didididi whrrrrr*.

NESTING Grass cup, lined with fine grass, and hidden in depression in ground under overhanging sedges or grasses; 3–5 eggs; 1 brood; June–August.

FEEDING Mainly seeds in winter; in summer, mostly insects, such as beetles, mosquitoes, and moths.

FLIGHT: low and direct, staying within cover whenever possible.

RAISE THE ALARM
When disturbed, the Lincoln's Sparrow often raises its central crown feathers, which form a crest.

SIMILAR SPECIES

SONG SPARROW see p.386
larger overall
more coarse streaking

SAVANNAH SPARROW see p.385
short, square, notched tail
pale-yellow eyebrows

OCCURRENCE
Breeds in muskeg and wet thickets across northern North America, also south into the western ranges of California and Arizona. Migrants and wintering birds use a variety of scrubby habitats. Winters in the southern US (and farther south), and on the Pacific Coast north to British Columbia.

| Length 5¼–6in (13.5–15cm) | Wingspan 7½–8½in (19–22cm) | Weight ½–⅞oz (15–25g) |
| Social **Solitary/Small flocks** | Lifespan **Up to 7 years** | Status **Secure** |

DATE: _____ TIME: _____ LOCATION: _____

| Order **Passeriformes** | Family **Passerellidae** | Species *Melospiza georgiana* |

Swamp Sparrow 🔊

rufous crown

gray-and-rufous face

rufous flanks

ADULT (BREEDING)

unstreaked gray nape

tawny flanks

IN FLIGHT

dark, rounded tail

ADULT (NON-BREEDING)

tan upperparts with dark streaks

gray breast with fine streaking

rusty margins to wing feathers

ADULT (BREEDING)

FLIGHT: low and direct, staying within cover whenever possible.

The Swamp Sparrow is a common breeder in wet habitats across eastern North America and Canada west to the Yukon and British Columbia. It is especially abundant in its preferred habitat of tall reed marshes. A somewhat skittish bird, the Swamp Sparrow is often seen darting rapidly into cover, but usually repays the patient observer with a reappearance, giving its characteristic *chimp* call. Though often confused with both the Song Sparrow and the Lincoln's Sparrow, the Swamp Sparrow never shows more than a very faint, blurry streaking on its gray breast, and sports conspicuous rusty-edged wing feathers.

VOICE Call a slightly nasal, forceful *chimp*, flight call a high, buzzy *ziiiiii*; song a slow, monotonous, loose trill of chirps.

NESTING Bulky cup of dry plants placed 1–4ft (30–120cm) above water in marsh vegetation; 3–5 eggs; 1–2 broods; May–July.

FEEDING Mostly insects in the breeding season, especially grasshoppers; seeds in winter; occasionally fruit.

WATCH TOWER
This male Swamp Sparrow is perusing his territory from atop a seeding cattail flower.

OCCURRENCE
Breeds in marshes, cedar bogs, damp meadows, and wet hayfields, from Yukon east to Newfoundland and south to Nebraska and the Delmarva Peninsula; winters in marshes in the eastern US and south through Mexico; rare but regular on the Pacific Coast.

SIMILAR SPECIES

SONG SPARROW
see p.386

brown tail

brown wings

streaked breast

LINCOLN'S SPARROW
see p.387

less red overall

fine breast streaks

| Length **5–6in (12.5–15cm)** | Wingspan **7–7½in (18–19cm)** | Weight **½–⅞oz (15–25g)** |
| Social **Solitary/Small flocks** | Lifespan **Up to 6 years** | Status **Secure** |

DATE: _____ TIME: _____ LOCATION: _____

| Order **Passeriformes** | Family **Passerellidae** | Species *Pipilo maculatus* |

Spotted Towhee 🔊

rounded tail

white wing bars

white tail tips

MALE

IN FLIGHT

long tail with white outer feathers

white spots on dark sepia-brown upperparts

brown tail

FEMALE

blackish-brown head

broad white spots on black upperparts

reddish eye

blackish head

rusty flanks

white underparts

MALE

FLIGHT: low and direct, with much gliding, usually within cover.

This large and colorful sparrow can often be heard rummaging through dry leaves in the undergrowth in search of food, when it may even produce roughly simultaneously in the soil, using its feet like a garden rake. The Spotted Towhee is variable across its range, and has been separated into 20 rather complex subspecies, but they are all distinguished from the Eastern Towhee by the presence of white spots and bars on their upperwings.

VOICE Depending on geographical location, call *zhreee* or a buzzy, nasal, descending *reeeer*; song ends with a trill.

NESTING Large cup in depression on ground, under cover, also low in thicket; 3–5 eggs; 1–2 broods; April–June.

FEEDING Scratches for food, including insects, fruit, seeds, and acorns; sometimes eats small snakes and lizards.

RUFOUS SIDES
The Spotted Towhee was once grouped with the Eastern Towhee under the name "Rufous-sided Towhee."

DIVERGENT DIALECTS
The vocalizations of the Spotted Towhees vary according to geographical location.

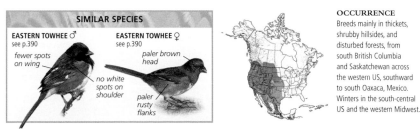

SIMILAR SPECIES

EASTERN TOWHEE ♂
see p.390

fewer spots on wing

no white spots on shoulder

EASTERN TOWHEE ♀
see p.390

paler brown head

paler rusty flanks

OCCURRENCE
Breeds mainly in thickets, shrubby hillsides, and disturbed forests, from south British Columbia and Saskatchewan across the western US, southward to south Oaxaca, Mexico. Winters in the south-central US and the western Midwest.

| Length **8in (20cm)** | Wingspan **10½in (27cm)** | Weight **1¼–1⁹⁄₁₆oz (35–45g)** |
| Social **Solitary/Small flocks** | Lifespan **Up to 11 years** | Status **Secure** |

DATE: _____ TIME: _____ LOCATION: _____

| Order **Passeriformes** | Family **Passerellidae** | Species *Pipilo erythrophthalmus* |

Eastern Towhee 🔊

white corners to tail

single white patch in each wing

ADULT

IN FLIGHT

black hood and upperparts

reddish eye

MALE

white belly

white wing patches

long tail

brown hood and upperparts

small white markings on wings

rusty flanks

FEMALE

The Towhees get their name from the upslurred *chew-eee* (or *to-whee*) call they make. The Eastern Towhee is famous for its vocalizations and has one of the best-known mnemonics for its song: "drink your tea." The Eastern Towhee was once lumped with the Spotted Towhees under the name "Rufous-sided Towhee," because they interbreed in the Great Plains. In the southeastern US, Eastern Towhees have paler eyes the farther south they are located; individuals with nearly white eyes are found in Florida. Like all towhees, the Eastern Towhee feeds noisily by jumping backward with both feet at once to move leaves and reveal the insects and seeds that may be hidden underneath.

VOICE Call a nasal, upslurred *chew-eee*; flight call *zeeeooooweeet*; song sounds like *dweee, dyooo di-i-i-i-i-i-i-i-i-i-i-i*.
NESTING Large cup in depression on ground under cover, also low in thicket; 3–5 eggs; 1–2 broods; May–August.
FEEDING Eats seeds, fruits, insects, and buds.

FLIGHT: low and direct with much gliding, usually within cover.

TERRESTRIAL LIFE
The bird stays close to the ground and is usually found not more than a few yards off it.

OCCURRENCE
Found in dense thickets, woodland, dense shrubbery, forest edges and disturbed forests from southeast Saskatchewan, east Nebraska, west Louisiana, east to south Quebec, south Maine, and south Florida. Retreats from the northern parts of its range to winter in the southeastern US.

SIMILAR SPECIES

SPOTTED TOWHEE ♂
see p.389

SPOTTED TOWHEE ♀
see p.389

two white wing bars

two white wing bars

white spots on shoulder

| Length **7½–8in (19–20cm)** | Wingspan **10½in (27cm)** | Weight **1¹⁄₁₆–1³⁄₄oz (30–50g)** |
| Social **Solitary/Small flocks** | Lifespan **Up to 12 years** | Status **Secure** |

DATE: _____ TIME: _____ LOCATION: _____

Family **Icteridae**

ORIOLES AND BLACKBIRDS

THE ICTERIDS exemplify the wonderful diversity that exists among birds. Its members are common and widespread, occurring from coast to coast in nearly every habitat in North America. The species reveal extremes of color, nesting, and social behavior—from the vibrant, solitary orioles to the vast nesting colonies of comparatively drab blackbirds.

ORIOLES

Generally recognized by their contrasting black-and-orange plumage, although some species tend more toward yellow or chestnut shades, orioles are common tropical to subtropical seasonal migrants to North America. Their intricate hanging nests are an impressive combination of engineering and weaving. Most species boast a melodious song and tolerance for humans, a combination that makes them popular throughout their range.

COWBIRDS

These strictly parasitic birds have been known to lay eggs in the nests of close to 300 different species in North and South America. The species found in Canada is readily identified by its thick bill and dark, iridescent body contrasting with a brown head.

NECTAR LOVER
The magnificently colored Baltimore Oriole inserts its bill into the base of a flower, taking the nectar, but playing no part in pollination.

BLACKBIRDS

As their name suggests, this group of birds is largely covered in dark feathers, and their long, pointed bills and tails add to their streamlined appearance. Not as brilliantly colored as some other Icterids, these are among the most numerous birds on the continent after the breeding season, and form an impressive sight during migration.

SUBTLE BRILLIANCE
Although its plumage is dark, the Common Grackle displays a beautiful iridescence.

MEADOWLARKS

The Eastern and Western Meadowlarks are the only two species in this group in North America, but they are distinctive (although difficult to tell apart). Birds of open country, both species have a characteristic bright-yellow chest with a black bib but differing sweet songs.

BIG VOICE
A meadowlark's melodious voice is a defining feature in many rural landscapes.

Order **Passeriformes**	Family **Icteridae**	Species *Icteria virens*

Yellow-breasted Chat

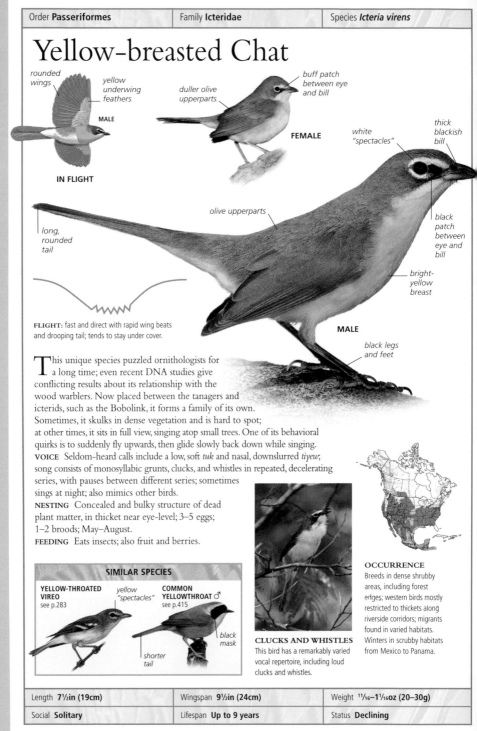

rounded wings

yellow underwing feathers

MALE

duller olive upperparts

buff patch between eye and bill

FEMALE

white "spectacles"

thick blackish bill

IN FLIGHT

olive upperparts

long, rounded tail

black patch between eye and bill

bright-yellow breast

FLIGHT: fast and direct with rapid wing beats and drooping tail; tends to stay under cover.

MALE

black legs and feet

This unique species puzzled ornithologists for a long time; even recent DNA studies give conflicting results about its relationship with the wood warblers. Now placed between the tangers and icterids, such as the Bobolink, it forms a family of its own. Sometimes, it skulks in dense vegetation and is hard to spot; at other times, it sits in full view, singing atop small trees. One of its behavioral quirks is to suddenly fly upwards, then glide slowly back down while singing.
VOICE Seldom-heard calls include a low, soft *tuk* and nasal, downslurred *tiyew*; song consists of monosyllabic grunts, clucks, and whistles in repeated, decelerating series, with pauses between different series; sometimes sings at night; also mimics other birds.
NESTING Concealed and bulky structure of dead plant matter, in thicket near eye-level; 3–5 eggs; 1–2 broods; May–August.
FEEDING Eats insects; also fruit and berries.

CLUCKS AND WHISTLES
This bird has a remarkably varied vocal repertoire, including loud clucks and whistles.

OCCURRENCE
Breeds in dense shrubby areas, including forest edges; western birds mostly restricted to thickets along riverside corridors; migrants found in varied habitats. Winters in scrubby habitats from Mexico to Panama.

SIMILAR SPECIES

YELLOW-THROATED VIREO see p.283

yellow "spectacles"

COMMON YELLOWTHROAT ♂ see p.415

black mask

shorter tail

Length **7½in (19cm)**	Wingspan **9½in (24cm)**	Weight **11⁄16–1 1⁄16oz (20–30g)**
Social **Solitary**	Lifespan **Up to 9 years**	Status **Declining**

DATE: _____ TIME:_____ LOCATION:_____

| Order **Passeriformes** | Family **Icteridae** | Species *Xanthocephalus xanthocephalus* |

Yellow-headed Blackbird 🔊

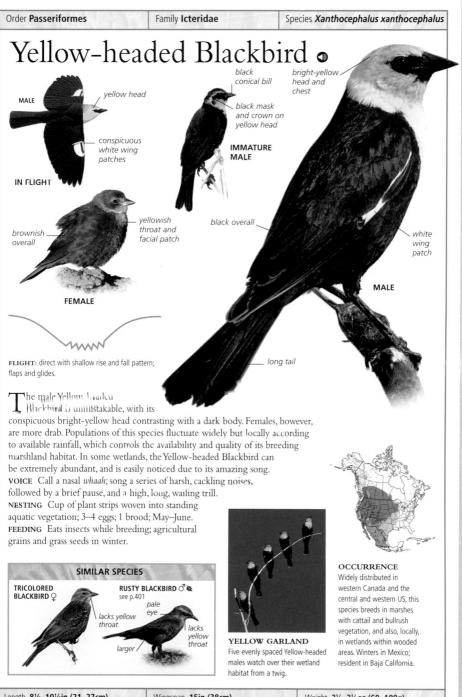

MALE — yellow head

IN FLIGHT — conspicuous white wing patches

black conical bill

bright-yellow head and chest

black mask and crown on yellow head

IMMATURE MALE

FEMALE — brownish overall — yellowish throat and facial patch

black overall

white wing patch

MALE

long tail

FLIGHT: direct with shallow rise and fall pattern; flaps and glides.

The male Yellow-headed Blackbird is unmistakable, with its conspicuous bright-yellow head contrasting with a dark body. Females, however, are more drab. Populations of this species fluctuate widely but locally according to available rainfall, which controls the availability and quality of its breeding marshland habitat. In some wetlands, the Yellow-headed Blackbird can be extremely abundant, and is easily noticed due to its amazing song.

VOICE Call a nasal *whaah*; song a series of harsh, cackling noises, followed by a brief pause, and a high, long, wailing trill.

NESTING Cup of plant strips woven into standing aquatic vegetation; 3–4 eggs; 1 brood; May–June.

FEEDING Eats insects while breeding; agricultural grains and grass seeds in winter.

SIMILAR SPECIES

TRICOLORED BLACKBIRD ♀ — lacks yellow throat

RUSTY BLACKBIRD ♂ 🔊 see p.401 — pale eye — lacks yellow throat — larger

YELLOW GARLAND Five evenly spaced Yellow-headed males watch over their wetland habitat from a twig.

OCCURRENCE Widely distributed in western Canada and the central and western US, this species breeds in marshes with cattail and bullrush vegetation, and also, locally, in wetlands within wooded areas. Winters in Mexico; resident in Baja California.

| Length 8½–10½in (21–27cm) | Wingspan **15in (38cm)** | Weight 2⅛–3½oz (60–100g) |
| Social **Flocks/Colonies** | Lifespan **Up to 9 years** | Status **Localized** |

DATE: _____ TIME: _____ LOCATION: _____

| Order **Passeriformes** | Family **Icteridae** | Species ***Dolichonyx oryzivorus*** |

Bobolink

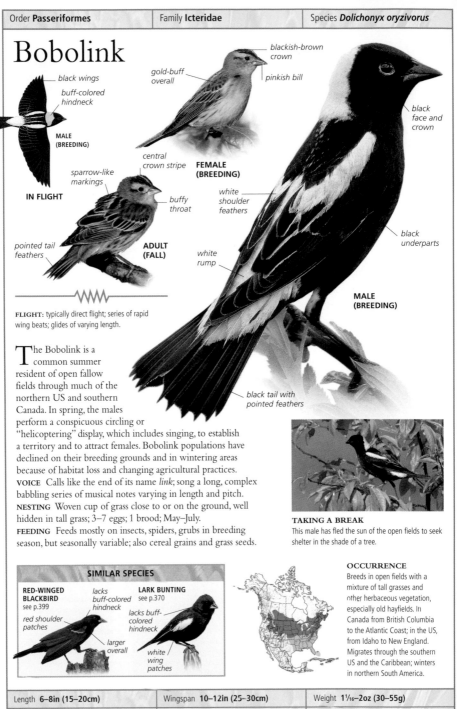

black wings

buff-colored hindneck

MALE (BREEDING)

IN FLIGHT

blackish-brown crown

gold-buff overall

pinkish bill

black face and crown

central crown stripe

FEMALE (BREEDING)

sparrow-like markings

white shoulder feathers

buffy throat

pointed tail feathers

ADULT (FALL)

white rump

black underparts

MALE (BREEDING)

black tail with pointed feathers

FLIGHT: typically direct flight; series of rapid wing beats; glides of varying length.

The Bobolink is a common summer resident of open fallow fields through much of the northern US and southern Canada. In spring, the males perform a conspicuous circling or "helicoptering" display, which includes singing, to establish a territory and to attract females. Bobolink populations have declined on their breeding grounds and in wintering areas because of habitat loss and changing agricultural practices.

VOICE Calls like the end of its name *link*; song a long, complex babbling series of musical notes varying in length and pitch.

NESTING Woven cup of grass close to or on the ground, well hidden in tall grass; 3–7 eggs; 1 brood; May–July.

FEEDING Feeds mostly on insects, spiders, grubs in breeding season, but seasonally variable; also cereal grains and grass seeds.

TAKING A BREAK
This male has fled the sun of the open fields to seek shelter in the shade of a tree.

SIMILAR SPECIES

RED-WINGED BLACKBIRD
see p.399

red shoulder patches

lacks buff-colored hindneck

larger overall

LARK BUNTING
see p.370

lacks buff-colored hindneck

white wing patches

OCCURRENCE
Breeds in open fields with a mixture of tall grasses and other herbaceous vegetation, especially old hayfields. In Canada from British Columbia to the Atlantic Coast; in the US, from Idaho to New England. Migrates through the southern US and the Caribbean; winters in northern South America.

| Length **6–8in (15–20cm)** | Wingspan **10–12in (25–30cm)** | Weight **1¹⁄₁₆–2oz (30–55g)** |
| Social **Winter flocks** | Lifespan **Up to 10 years** | Status **Threatened** |

DATE: _____ TIME:_____ LOCATION:_____

| Order **Passeriformes** | Family **Icteridae** | Species *Sturnella neglecta* |

Western Meadowlark 🔊

short wings

ADULT

IN FLIGHT

yellow throat

white outer tail feathers

yellow patch between bill and eye

blackish-brown stripe behind eye

chunky body

long, pointed bill

black "V" on yellow chest

duller pattern than breeding bird

ADULT (NONBREEDING)

short, wide tail

black spots and streaks on sides and flanks

yellow underparts

ADULT (BREEDING)

long toes

FLIGHT: several rapid wing beats followed by a short glide.

The Western Meadowlark is one of the most abundant and widespread grassland birds in North America. It inhabits open country in the western Great Plains, the Great Basin, and the Central Valley of California. It is frequently encountered along roadsides, singing its melodious song from atop a fencepost or utility pole. Although the range of the Western Meadowlark overlaps widely with that of its eastern counterpart, hybrids between the two species are very rare and usually sterile.

VOICE Series of complex, bubbling whistled notes; lower frequency with no ascending whistles as heard in the Eastern Meadowlark.

NESTING Domed grass cup, well hidden in tall grasses; 3–7 eggs; 1 brood; March–August.

FEEDING Feeds mostly on insects, including beetles, grubs, and grasshoppers; also grains and grass seeds.

SIMILAR SPECIES

AMERICAN PIPIT see p.347

shorter bill

lacks yellow chest and black "necklace"

EASTERN MEADOWLARK

less yellow at corner of beak

slightly darker overall

A SHRUB WILL DO
In spring and summer, male Western Meadowlarks can be seen perching on shrubs to sing.

OCCURRENCE
Common in western North America, across much of southern Canada and the western US, south to Mexico. Breeds primarily in open grassy plains, but also uses agricultural fields with overgrown edges and hayfields. Partial migrant in the US, winters south to Mexico.

| Length **7–10in (18–26cm)** | Wingspan **13–15in (33–38cm)** | Weight **2⅞–4oz (80–125g)** |
| Social **Pairs/Winter flocks** | Lifespan **Up to 10 years** | Status **Secure** |

DATE: _____ TIME: _____ LOCATION: _____

| Order **Passeriformes** | Family **Icteridae** | Species *Icterus spurius* |

Orchard Oriole 🔊

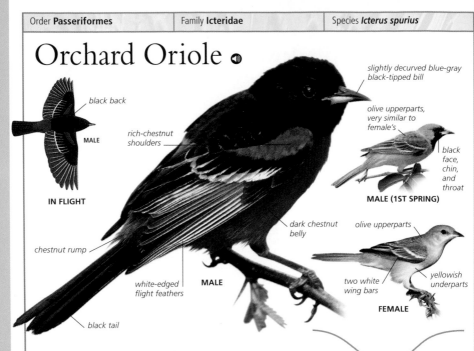

black back

MALE

IN FLIGHT

rich-chestnut shoulders

chestnut rump

white-edged flight feathers

black tail

MALE

dark chestnut belly

slightly decurved blue-gray black-tipped bill

olive upperparts, very similar to female's

black face, chin, and throat

MALE (1ST SPRING)

olive upperparts

two white wing bars

yellowish underparts

FEMALE

A small oriole, the Orchard Oriole resembles a large warbler in size, color, and the way it flits among leaves while foraging for insects. It bobs its tail, unlike other orioles. It spends less time on the breeding grounds than other migrant orioles, often arriving there as late as mid-May and leaving as early as late July. The Orchard Oriole tolerates humans and can be found breeding in suburban parks and gardens. In recent years, its numbers have increased in the eastern part of its range.

VOICE Fast, not very melodious, series of high warbling notes mixed with occasional shorter notes ending in slurred *shheere*.

NESTING Woven nest of grass suspended in fork between branches; 4–5 eggs; 1 brood; April–July.

FEEDING Mainly eats insects during breeding season, but will also feed on seeds, fruit, and occasionally, nectar; in winter, mostly fruit and nectar, and some insects.

FLIGHT: quite bouncy flight due to shallow, quick wing beats; interrupted by glides.

CHESTNUT SPLASH
The male Orchard Oriole has distinctive black upperparts and rich-chestnut underparts.

SIMILAR SPECIES

SCOTT'S ORIOLE

BALTIMORE ORIOLE
see p.398

yellow shoulder

bright-yellow underparts

black breast

orange underparts

larger overall

OCCURRENCE
Breeds in the eastern US and south-central Canada, in open forest and woodland edges with a mixture of evergreen and deciduous trees, especially along river bottoms and in shelter belts surrounding agricultural land. Winters in Mexico, Central America, and South America.

| Length **7–8in (18–20cm)** | Wingspan **9in (23cm)** | Weight **11/16oz (20g)** |
| Social **Pairs** | Lifespan **Up to 9 years** | Status **Secure** |

DATE: _____ TIME:_____ LOCATION:_____

| Order **Passeriformes** | Family **Icteridae** | Species *Icterus bullockii* |

Bullock's Oriole 🔊

black cap and nape

black eyestripe

large white wing patch

orange face

black bib

black back and wings

MALE (on the in-flight bird)

conspicuous white wing patch

pale yellow underparts

MALE (1ST FALL)

IN FLIGHT

yellow face, throat, and breast

olive-brown back and wings

olive tail

orange underparts

MALE

buffy-gray belly and rump

FEMALE

black tail with orange outer feathers

gray legs and toes

The Bullock's Oriole is the western counterpart of the Baltimore Oriole in both behavior and habitat. The two were thought to belong to a single species, the Northern Oriole (*I. galbula*), because they interbreed where they overlap in the Great Plains. Recent studies, however, suggest that they are separate species. Unlike many other orioles, the Bullock's is more resistant to brood parasites—it punctures and removes cowbird eggs from its nest.

VOICE Varied string of one- and two-part notes often mumbled or slurred at the end; similar to, but less melodious than, the Baltimore Oriole's song.

NESTING Hanging basket of woven plant strips located at the tips of branches; 4–5 eggs; 1 brood; March–June.

FEEDING Forages for insects, in particular grasshoppers and caterpillars, but also ants, beetles, and spiders; nectar and fruit when available.

FLIGHT: full, powerful wing beats, resulting in a "heavier" flight aspect than similar species.

SIMILAR SPECIES

HOODED ORIOLE

orange head

long, slender black tail

BALTIMORE ORIOLE
see p.398

black hood

black face

less white in wings

OBLIVIOUS TO THORNS
This male Bullock's Oriole perches on a branch with long thorns, but it is not perturbed.

OCCURRENCE
Found in the western US, especially in riverside woodlands with willows and cottonwoods; also mixed hardwood forests, mesquite woodland, and groves of fruit trees. Breeds in open mixed hardwood forests, especially those surrounding waterways and containing stands of oak, cottonwood, and willow.

| Length **6½–7½in (16–19cm)** | Wingspan **10–12in (25–30cm)** | Weight **1¹⁄₁₆–1⁹⁄₁₆oz (30–45g)** |
| Social **Pairs/Flocks** | Lifespan **Up to 8 years** | Status **Secure** |

DATE: _____ TIME: _____ LOCATION: _____

Order **Passeriformes**	Family **Icteridae**	Species *Icterus galbula*

Baltimore Oriole 🔊

black-and-orange tail

white-edged black wings

orange-yellow shoulder patch

MALE

IN FLIGHT

orange-yellow head

MALE (1ST FALL)

black back

black head

straight blue-gray bill

black upper breast

orange underparts

MALE

black tail with orange outer tail feathers

orange rump

yellow-olive rump

olive upperparts

pale-orange underparts

two wing bars

FEMALE

The Baltimore Oriole's brilliant colors are familiar to many in eastern North America because this bird is so tolerant of humans. This species originally favored the American elm for nesting, but the Dutch elm disease decimated these trees. The oriole has since adapted to using sycamores, cottonwoods, and other tall trees as nesting sites. Its ability to use suburban gardens and parks has helped expand its range to incorporate areas densely occupied by humans.

VOICE Loud, clear, melodious song comprising several short notes in series, often of varying lengths.

NESTING Round-bottomed basket usually woven from grass, hung toward the end of branches; 4–5 eggs; 1 brood; May–July.

FEEDING Hops or flits among leaves and branches picking insects and spiders; fond of caterpillars; also eats fruit and sips nectar.

FLIGHT: strong with rapid wing beats; full downstrokes during flight provide great power.

PERFECT FOR FORAGING
The Baltimore Oriole forages alone in the dense foliage of trees and bushes, or on the ground.

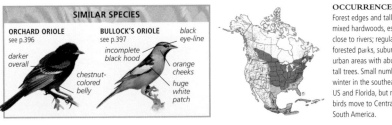

SIMILAR SPECIES

ORCHARD ORIOLE see p.396

darker overall

chestnut-colored belly

BULLOCK'S ORIOLE see p.397

incomplete black hood

black eye-line

orange cheeks

huge white patch

OCCURRENCE
Forest edges and tall, open mixed hardwoods, especially close to rivers; regularly uses forested parks, suburban and urban areas with abundant tall trees. Small numbers winter in the southeastern US and Florida, but most birds move to Central and South America.

Length **8–10in (20–26cm)**	Wingspan **10–12in (26–30cm)**	Weight **1¹⁄₁₆–1¹⁄₄oz (30–35g)**
Social **Solitary/Pairs**	Lifespan **Up to 11 years**	Status **Secure**

DATE: _____ TIME: _____ LOCATION: _____

Order **Passeriformes**	Family **Icteridae**	Species *Agelaius phoeniceus*

Red-winged Blackbird 🔊

MALE

red-and-yellow "flags"

dark grayish-brown body

IMMATURE (BICOLORED)

pale throat

no clear yellow edging on red shoulder patches

dull reddish or yellowish shoulder patches

buff to brown edging on feathers

IMMATURE MALE

black outer wings

IN FLIGHT

light-brown eyebrow

MALE (BICOLORED)

all-black back and tail

black eye

pointed bill

bright-red shoulder patches with yellow edge

off-white underparts with dark streaks

FEMALE

MALE

FLIGHT: swift wing beats interrupted by brief bobbing, flapping, and gliding sequences

One of the most abundant native bird species in North America, the Red-winged Blackbird is also one of the most conspicuous in wetland habitats. The sight and sound of males singing from the tops of cattails is a sure sign that spring is near. This adaptable species migrates and roosts in flocks that may number in the millions. There are numerous subspecies, one of the most distinctive being the "Bicolored" Blackbird (*A. p. gubernator*.)

VOICE Various brusk *chek*, *chit*, or *chet* calls; male song a *kronk-a-rhee* with a characteristic nasal, rolling and metallic "undulating" ending.

NESTING Cup of grasses and mud woven into dense standing reeds or cattails; 3–4 eggs; 1–2 broods; March–June.

FEEDING Forages for seeds and grains; largely insects when breeding.

DENSE FLOCKS
The huge flocks of Red-winged Blackbirds seen in migration are quite an amazing sight.

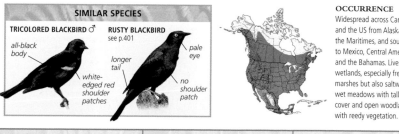

SIMILAR SPECIES

TRICOLORED BLACKBIRD ♂

all-black body

white-edged red shoulder patches

RUSTY BLACKBIRD
see p.401

longer tail

pale eye

no shoulder patch

OCCURRENCE
Widespread across Canada and the US from Alaska to the Maritimes, and south to Mexico, Central America, and the Bahamas. Lives in wetlands, especially freshwater marshes but also saltwater; wet meadows with tallgrass cover and open woodlands with reedy vegetation.

Length **7–10in (18–25cm)**	Wingspan **11–14in (28–35cm)**	Weight **1⁹⁄₁₆–2½oz (45–70g)**
Social **Flocks**	Lifespan **At least 14 years**	Status **Secure**

DATE: _____ TIME: _____ LOCATION: _____

Order **Passeriformes**	Family **Icteridae**	Species **Molothrus ater**

Brown-headed Cowbird 🔊

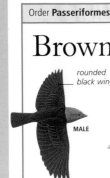

rounded black wings

MALE

IN FLIGHT

thick, short bill

dull sepia-brown head

glossy greenish-black back and wings

dull, unmarked brownish plumage

faintly streaked underparts

FEMALE

brown throat and upper breast

MALE

black feet and legs

fairly long black tail

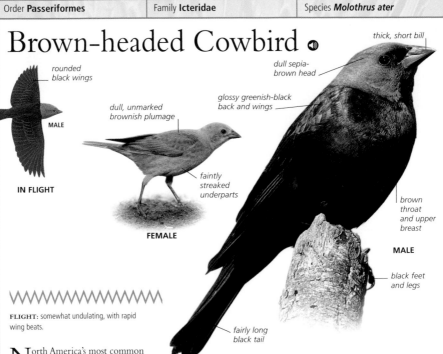

〰〰〰〰〰〰〰〰

FLIGHT: somewhat undulating, with rapid wing beats.

North America's most common and best known brood parasite, the Brown-headed Cowbird was once a bird of the Great Plains, following vast herds of bison to prey on insects kicked up by their hooves. Now, due to forest clearance and suburban development, it is found continent-wide. It has recently become a serious threat to North American songbirds, laying its eggs in the nests of more than 220 different species, and having its young raised to fledglings by more than 140 species, including the highly endangered Kirtland's Warbler.

VOICE High-pitched, squeaky whistles and bubbling notes, *dub-dub-come-tzeee*; also various clucks and *cheks*.

NESTING No nest, lays eggs in nests of other species; a single female may lay 25–55 (or more) eggs per season; April–August.

FEEDING Primarily eats grass seeds and cereal grains; also eats insects when available, especially grasshoppers and beetles.

AT A FEEDER
A female Brown-headed Cowbird enjoys a snack of seeds at a suburban feeder.

SIMILAR SPECIES

RUSTY BLACKBIRD ♂
see p.401

pale eyebrow
pale eye

thinner bill

BREWER'S BLACKBIRD ♀
see p.402

gray-brown overall

thinner bill

OCCURRENCE
Favors habitats modified by human activity, such as open wooded patches, low grass fields, fruit orchards, agricultural pastures with livestock, and gardens and residential areas. Widespread across North America except in Alaska and northern Canada.

Length **6–8in (15–20cm)**	Wingspan **11–13in (28–33cm)**	Weight **1⁷⁄₁₆–1³⁄₄oz (40–50g)**
Social **Large flocks**	Lifespan **Up to 16 years**	Status **Secure**

DATE: _____ TIME: _____ LOCATION: _____

| Order **Passeriformes** | Family **Icteridae** | Species *Euphagus carolinus* |

Rusty Blackbird 🔊

MALE (BREEDING)
long tail
short, narrow bill

IN FLIGHT

pale eyebrow

rusty-brown edging to feathers

MALE (FALL)

rusty-brown crown

black mask between eye and bill

FEMALE (FALL)
gray-brown eyebrow
pale-gray to rusty-brown underparts

green sheen on head
pale whitish or yellow eye

black overall, with blue-green to greenish sheen

MALE (BREEDING)

FLIGHT: strong, direct, with slight undulations between flapping and brief gliding.

The Rusty Blackbird is perhaps the least studied of all North American blackbirds. This is mainly because it breeds in remote, inaccessible swampy areas, and is much less of a pest to agricultural operations than some of the other members of its family. Unlike most other blackbirds, the plumage on the male Rusty Blackbird changes to a dull reddish-brown during the fall—giving the species its common name. It is also during the fall migrations that this species is most easily observed, moving south in long, wide flocks that often take several minutes to pass overhead. Its vocalizations are useful for distinguishing it from Brewer's Blackbird.

VOICE Both sexes use *chuk* call during migration flights; male song a musical *too-ta-lee*.
NESTING Small bowl of branches and sticks, lined with wet plants and dry grass, usually near water; 3–5 eggs; 1 brood; May–July.
FEEDING Eats seasonally available insects, spiders, grains, seeds of trees, and fleshy fruit or berries.

OPEN WIDE
Seldom seen, the male's courtship display includes gaping and tail-spreading.

OCCURRENCE
Breeds in moist to wet forests up to the timberline in the far north (farther north than any other species of North American blackbird); winters in eastern US, in various swampy forests.

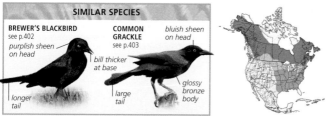

SIMILAR SPECIES

BREWER'S BLACKBIRD see p.402
purplish sheen on head
longer tail

bill thicker at base

COMMON GRACKLE see p.403
large tail

bluish sheen on head
glossy bronze body

| Length **8–10in (20–25cm)** | Wingspan **12–15in (30–38cm)** | Weight **1⁹⁄₁₆–2⁷⁄₈oz (45–80g)** |
| Social **Pairs/Winter flocks** | Lifespan **At least 9 years** | Status **Declining** |

DATE: _____ TIME:_____ LOCATION:_____

Order **Passeriformes**	Family **Icteridae**	Species *Euphagus cyanocephalus*

Brewer's Blackbird 🔊

stout bill

brown eyes

gray-brown overall

MALE

FEMALE

long, dark tail

IN FLIGHT

purplish sheen on head

whitish-yellow eyes

black body with greenish-blue sheen

MALE

black legs and feet

FLIGHT: several wing beats followed by short glides with shallow rise and fall pattern.

The Brewer's Blackbird, unlike the swamp-loving Rusty Blackbird, seems to prefer areas disturbed by humans to natural ones throughout much of its range. It is likely that the relatively recent eastward range expansion of the Brewer's Blackbird has been aided by changes in land practices. Interestingly, when its range overlaps with that of the Common Grackle, it wins out in rural areas, but loses out in urban areas. This species can be found feasting on waste grains left behind after the harvest or even in supermarket parking lots.
VOICE Buzzy *tshrrep* song ascending in tone.
NESTING Bulky cup of dry grass, stem and twig framework lined with soft grasses and animal hair; 3–6 eggs; 1–2 broods; April–July.
FEEDING Forages on the ground for many species of insects during breeding season, also snails; seeds, grain, and occasional fruit in fall and winter.

BROWN-EYED BIRD
Brown eyes distinguish the female Brewer's from the yellow-eyed female Rusty Blackbird.

SIMILAR SPECIES

RUSTY BLACKBIRD
see p.401

shorter tail

bill thinner at base

COMMON GRACKLE
see p.403

glossy bronze body

long, wedge-shaped tail

OCCURRENCE
Breeds and winters in open areas, readily adapting to, and preferring, disturbed areas and human developments, such as parks, gardens, supermarket parking lots, clear-felled forests, and fallow fields edged with dense trees or shrubs.

Length **10–12in (25–30cm)**	Wingspan **13–16in (33–41cm)**	Weight **1³/₄–2¹/₂oz (50–70g)**
Social **Flocks/Colonies**	Lifespan **Up to 13 years**	Status **Secure**

DATE: _____ TIME: _____ LOCATION: _____

| Order **Passeriformes** | Family **Icteridae** | Species *Quiscalus quiscula* |

Common Grackle 🔊

dark wings

ADULT

IN FLIGHT

iridescent brownish-bronze back

iridescent bluish-purple head

pale-yellow eye

long, thick bill

long, V-shaped tail

bluish to purplish head

MALE (BRONZED FORM)

pale eye

iridescent purplish to greenish or bluish back

dull purplish-bronze overall

MALE (PURPLE FORM)

FEMALE

This adaptable species has expanded its range rapidly in the recent past, thanks to human land-clearing practices. The Common Grackle is so well suited to urban and suburban habitats that it successfully excludes other species from them; it is often a nuisance at bird feeders. During migration and winter, Common Grackles form immense flocks, sometimes numbering over 1 million individuals. This tendency, combined with its preference for cultivated areas, has made this species an agricultural pest in some regions.

VOICE Call a low, harsh *chek*; loud song series of odd squeaks and whistles.
NESTING Small bowl in trees, with a frame of sticks filled with mud and grasses; 4–6 eggs; 1–2 broods; April–July.
FEEDING Eats beetles, flies, spiders, and worms, as well as small vertebrates; also seeds and grain, especially in nonbreeding season; an omnivore.

FLIGHT: straight, level, and direct without the up and down undulation of blackbird species.

SIMILAR SPECIES

GREAT-TAILED GRACKLE larger

BOAT-TAILED GRACKLE

purplish gloss to feathers

very long, deeply wedged tail

longer tail

bluish gloss on black feathers

HIGHLY ADAPTABLE
This grackle is comfortable near human developments, resulting in the expansion of its range.

OCCURRENCE
The Common Grackle lives in a wide variety of open woodlands, suburban woodlots, city parks, gardens, and hedgerows. It is absent west of the Great Plains. Wintering range extends south to the Gulf Coast.

| Length **11–13½in (28–34cm)** | Wingspan **15–18in (38–46cm)** | Weight **3⅛–4oz (90–125g)** |
| Social **Flocks** | Lifespan **Up to 20 years** | Status **Secure** |

DATE: _____ TIME: _____ LOCATION: _____

WOOD WARBLERS

THE FAMILY PARULIDAE IS REMARKABLE for its diversity: in plumage, song, feeding, breeding biology, and sexual dimorphism. In general, though, wood warblers share similar shapes: all are smallish birds with longish, thin bills (unlike thick vireo bills) used mostly for snapping up invertebrates. Their varied colors and patterns make the lively, busy, mixed groups seen on migration especially appealing and fascinating to watch. Ground-dwelling warblers tend to be larger and clad in olives, browns, and yellows, while many arboreal species are small and sport bright oranges, cool blues, and even ruby-reds. The color, location, and presence or absence of paler wing bars and tail spots is often a good identification aid. Warblers recently underwent an explosion of speciation in the East, and over 30 species may be seen there in a morning of spring birding. The arrival of beautiful singing males in spring is the birding highlight of the year for many birdwatchers. Eastern-breeding species utilize three different migration strategies to deal with the obstacle of the Gulf of Mexico when coming from and going to their Neotropical wintering grounds. Circum-Gulf migrants fly through Mexico, along the western shore of the Gulf of Mexico.

VARIABLE PLUMAGE
Many male *Setophaga* warblers (like this Blackburnian) are only brightly colored when breeding.

Caribbean migrants travel through Florida and island-hop through the Caribbean. And finally, trans-Gulf migrants fly directly across the Gulf of Mexico between the Yucatan Peninsula and the northern Gulf Coast. Birds flying this last and most deadly route are subject to abrupt weather changes over the Gulf, which sometimes yield spectacular fallout events at famed locations like High Island, Texas. The family is restricted to the Americas.

FEEDING STRATEGIES
Some warblers, such as this Black-and-white, probe the cracks in tree trunks for food.

STATIC PLUMAGE
In other warbler species, such as this Golden-winged, males keep their stunning plumage year-round.

| Order **Passeriformes** | Family **Parulidae** | Species *Seiurus aurocapilla* |

Ovenbird

plain olive overall

ADULT

IN FLIGHT

FLIGHT: fast, slightly undulating, and direct with rapid wing beats.

orange-and-black striped crown

bold white eye-ring

olive upperparts

white throat

black streaked underparts

ADULT

Like members of the unrelated, tropical ovenbird family (Furnariidae), this little bird is so-called for the domed, oven-like nests built on the ground, which are unique structures for North American warblers. The Ovenbird is also noted for its singing. Males flit about boisterously, often at night, incorporating portions of their main song into a jumble of spluttering notes. In the forest, one male singing loudly to declare his territory can set off a whole chain of responses from his neighbors, until the whole forest rings.

VOICE Call variably pitched, sharp *chik* in series; flight call high, rising *siiii*; song loud, ringing crescendo of paired notes *chur-tee' chur-tee' chur-tee' chur-tee' chur-TEE chur-TEE chur-TEE*.

NESTING Domed structure of leaves and grass on ground with side entrance; 3–6 eggs; 1 brood; May–July.

FEEDING Forages mainly on the forest floor for insects and other invertebrates.

STRUTTING ITS STUFF
The Ovenbird is noted for the way it struts across the forest floor like a tiny chicken.

SIMILAR SPECIES

NORTHERN WATERTHRUSH *dark-brown upperparts* much slimmer; see p.406

no eye-ring

LOUISIANA WATERTHRUSH *white eyebrow*

dark-brown upperparts

OCCURRENCE
Ranges from parts of the Yukon and British Columbia to the eastern US; breeds in closed-canopy mixed and deciduous forests with suitable amount of fallen plant material for nest building and foraging; migrants and wintering birds use similar habitats.

Length **6in (15cm)**	Wingspan **9½in (24cm)**	Weight **⁹⁄₁₆–⁷⁄₈oz (16–25g)**
Social **Solitary/Flocks**	Lifespan **Up to 7 years**	Status **Declining**

DATE: _____ TIME: _____ LOCATION: _____

| Order **Passeriformes** | Family **Parulidae** | Species *Parkesia noveboracensis* |

Northern Waterthrush 🔊

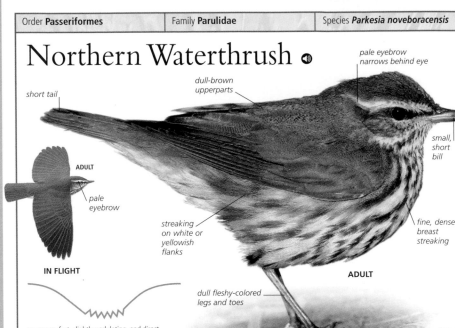

pale eyebrow narrows behind eye

dull-brown upperparts

short tail

ADULT

pale eyebrow

IN FLIGHT

small, short bill

streaking on white or yellowish flanks

fine, dense breast streaking

dull fleshy-colored legs and toes

ADULT

FLIGHT: fast, slightly undulating, and direct with rapid wing beats.

The tail-bobbing Northern Waterthrush is often heard giving a *spink!* call as it swiftly flees from observers. Although this species may be mistaken for the closely related Louisiana Waterthrush, there are clues that can help identify it. While the Northern Waterthrush prefers still water, its relative greatly prefers running water; in addition, its song is quite unlike that of the Louisiana Waterthrush.

VOICE Call a sharp, rising, ringing *spink!*; flight call a rising, buzzy *ziiiit*; song a loud series of rich, accelerating, staccato notes, usually decreasing in pitch *teet, teet, toh-toh toh-toh tyew-tyew!*

NESTING Hair-lined, mossy cup placed on or near ground, hidden in roots of fallen or standing tree or in riverbank; 4–5 eggs; 1 brood; May–August.

FEEDING Mostly eats insects, such as ants, mosquitoes, moths, and beetles, both larvae and adult, plus slugs and snails; when migrating, also eats small crustaceans, and even tiny fish.

YELLOW FORM
Many Northern Waterthrushes have yellow underparts, like this one, while others have white.

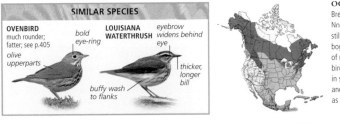

SIMILAR SPECIES

OVENBIRD much rounder; fatter; see p.405

olive upperparts

bold eye-ring

LOUISIANA WATERTHRUSH

eyebrow widens behind eye

thicker, longer bill

buffy wash to flanks

OCCURRENCE
Breeds right across northern North America in dark, still-water swamps and bogs; also in the still edges of rivers and lakes; migrant birds use wet habitats; winters in shrubby marshes, mangroves, and occasionally in crops, such as rice fields and citrus groves.

| Length **6in (15cm)** | Wingspan **9½in (24cm)** | Weight **½–⅞oz (14–23g)** |
| Social **Solitary** | Lifespan **Up to 9 years** | Status **Secure** |

DATE: _____ TIME: _____ LOCATION: _____

Order **Passeriformes**	Family **Parulidae**	Species ***Vermivora chrysoptera***

Golden-winged Warbler

IN FLIGHT

gray back

bright-yellow wing panel

white outer tail feathers

MALE

black mask

gray back suffused with yellow

unstreaked wings

bright-yellow crown

black throat

yellow wing panel

MALE

white undertail

gray mask

greenish-yellow crown

FEMALE

One of the continent's most beautiful warblers, this species is unfortunately being genetically swamped by the more southerly Blue-winged Warbler. This situation is worsening as more habitat is cleared and climate changes intensify. The Golden-winged interbreeds with the Blue-winged, resulting in two more frequently seen hybrid forms: the Brewster's Warbler, which resembles the Blue-winged Warbler, and the Lawrence's Warbler, which looks like a Blue-winged Warbler with the mask and black throat of a Golden-winged.

VOICE Call a sharp *tsip*; flight call high, slightly buzzy *ziiih*; song buzzy *zee zuu zuu zuu*, first note higher; birds that deviate from this song pattern may be hybrids.

NESTING Shallow bulky cup, on or just above ground; 4–6 eggs; 1 brood; May–July.

FEEDING Hangs upside down at clusters of curled-up dead leaves; feeds on moth larvae, other winged insects, and spiders.

FLIGHT: typical warbler flight: fast, slightly undulating, and direct with rapid wing beats.

SMALL TREES REQUIRED
Golden-winged Warblers breed in shrubby habitats created by clearance and re-growth.

SIMILAR SPECIES

BLUE-WINGED WARBLER

blue-gray wings

CHESTNUT-SIDED WARBLER
see p.422

black eye-line

white throat

chestnut flanks

OCCURRENCE
Breeds in the northeastern US and southeastern Canada in short secondary growth habitat with dense patches of deciduous shrubs or tangles, or in marshes with a forest edge; uses any wooded habitat on migration; winters in Central America from Guatemala to north Colombia; mostly on the Caribbean side.

Length **4³/₄in (12cm)**	Wingspan **7¹/₂in (19cm)**	Weight **⁹/₃₂–³/₈oz (8–11g)**
Social **Migrant/Winter flocks**	Lifespan **Unknown**	Status **Threatened**

DATE: _____ TIME: _____ LOCATION: _____

| Order **Passeriformes** | Family **Parulidae** | Species *Mniotilta varia* |

Black-and-white Warbler 🔊

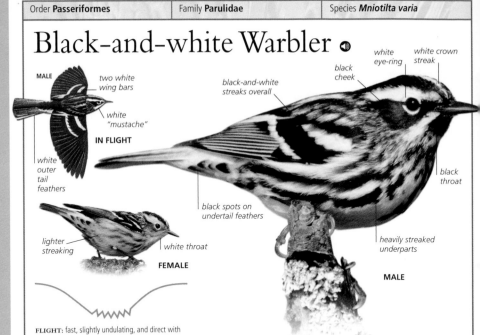

MALE

two white wing bars

white "mustache"

IN FLIGHT

white outer tail feathers

white eye-ring

white crown streak

black cheek

black-and-white streaks overall

black throat

black spots on undertail feathers

heavily streaked underparts

lighter streaking

white throat

FEMALE

MALE

FLIGHT: fast, slightly undulating, and direct with rapid wing beats.

The Black-and-white Warbler is best known for its creeper-like habit of feeding in vertical and upside-down positions as it pries into bark crevices, where its relatively long bill allows it to reach into tiny nooks and crannies. These habits, combined with a streaked plumage, make this bird one of the most distinctive warblers in North America. It is a long-distance migrant, with some birds wintering in parts of northern South America.

VOICE Sharp *stik* call; flight call a very high, thin *ssiit*, often doubled; song a thin, high-pitched, wheezy series *wheesy wheesy wheesy wheesy wheesy wheesy*.

NESTING Cup on ground against stump, fallen logs, or roots; 4–6 eggs; 1 brood; April–August.

FEEDING Creeps along branches and trunks, probing into bark for insects and insect larvae.

SQUEAKY WHEEL
The high-pitched, wheezy song of this warbler is said to be reminiscent of a squeaky wheel.

UPSIDE DOWN
Black-and-white Warblers often creep headfirst along trunks and branches of trees.

SIMILAR SPECIES

BLACKPOLL WARBLER ♂
see p.423
white cheek patch

black cap

BLACK-THROATED GRAY WARBLER ♂
see p.426

yellow patch

bright-orange legs

OCCURRENCE
Breeds in deciduous and mixed mature and second-growth woodlands; migrants occur on a greater variety of habitats; winters in a wide range of wooded habitats in the southern US, Mexico and into Central and South America.

| Length **5in (13cm)** | Wingspan **8in (20cm)** | Weight **5/16–1/2oz (9–14g)** |
| Social **Migrant/Winter flocks** | Lifespan **Up to 11 years** | Status **Secure** |

DATE: _____ TIME:_____ LOCATION:_____

Order **Passeriformes**	Family **Parulidae**	Species *Leiothlypis peregrina*

Tennessee Warbler

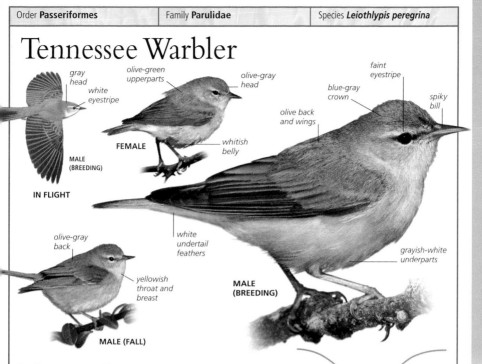

gray head
white eyestripe

olive-green upperparts

olive-gray head

faint eyestripe
blue-gray crown
spiky bill

olive back and wings

FEMALE

whitish belly

MALE (BREEDING)

IN FLIGHT

olive-gray back

white undertail feathers

grayish-white underparts

yellowish throat and breast

MALE (BREEDING)

MALE (FALL)

The Tennessee Warbler was named after its place of discovery, but this bird would have been an apt choice, as it breeds almost entirely in Canada and winters in Central America. These warblers inhabit fairly remote areas, and their nests are difficult to find. It is one of a number of species that takes advantage of outbreaks of spruce budworm; the population of Tennessee Warblers tends to increase in years when budworms are abundant.

VOICE Call a sharp *tzit*; flight call a thin slightly rolling *seet*; song usually three-part staccato series, *chip-chip-chip*, each series increasing in pitch and usually in tempo.

NESTING Nest woven of fine plant matter, in ground depression, concealed from above by shrubbery; 4–7 eggs; 1 brood; June.

FEEDING Searches outer branches of trees for caterpillars, bees, wasps, beetles, and spiders; also eats fruit in winter and drinks nectar by piercing the base of flowers.

FLIGHT: fast, slightly undulating, and direct with rapid wing beats.

UNIQUE UNDERPARTS
The breeding male is the only North American warbler with unmarked grayish-white underparts.

OCCURRENCE
Breeds in a variety of habitats, especially woodlands with dense understory and thickets of willows and alders. Very common in suburban parks and gardens during migration, particularly in the Midwest. Winters from southern Mexico to northern Ecuador and northern Venezuela.

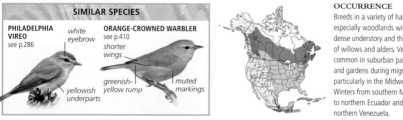

SIMILAR SPECIES

PHILADELPHIA VIREO
see p.286

white eyebrow

yellowish underparts

ORANGE-CROWNED WARBLER
see p.410
shorter wings

greenish-yellow rump

muted markings

Length **4¾in (12cm)**	Wingspan **7¾in (19.5cm)**	Weight **⁹⁄₃₂–⁵⁄₈oz (8–17g)**
Social **Flocks**	Lifespan **Up to 6 years**	Status **Secure**

DATE: _____ TIME:_____ LOCATION:_____

| Order **Passeriformes** | Family **Parulidae** | Species *Leiothlypis celata* |

Orange-crowned Warbler 🔊

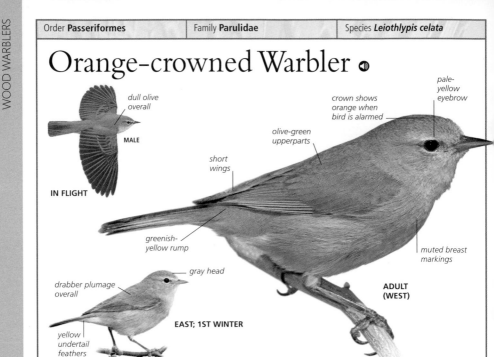

dull olive overall

MALE

IN FLIGHT

crown shows orange when bird is alarmed

olive-green upperparts

short wings

pale-yellow eyebrow

muted breast markings

ADULT (WEST)

greenish-yellow rump

gray head

drabber plumage overall

yellow undertail feathers

EAST; 1ST WINTER

Common and relatively brightly colored in the West but uncommon and duller in the East, the Orange-crowned Warbler has a large breeding range. The 19th-century American naturalist Thomas Say described this species on the basis of specimens collected in Nebraska. He was struck by the tiny orange cap, but because it was so concealed in the plumage of the crown, he named it *celata*, which is Latin for "hidden." The orange cap is not usually visible in the field.

VOICE Call a clean, sharp *tsik*; flight call a high, short *seet*; song a loose, lazy trill; eastern birds lazier, western birds more emphatic.

NESTING Cup of grasses, fibers, and down, usually on the ground under a bush; 4–5 eggs; 1 brood; March–July.

FEEDING Gleans mostly arthropods, such as beetles, ants, spiders, and their larvae; also eats fruit; collects nectar by piercing the base of a flower.

FLIGHT: fast, slightly undulating, and direct with rapid wing beats.

FACE MARKINGS
The eastern populations of this warbler have whitish facial markings during their first winter.

SIMILAR SPECIES

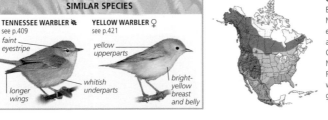

TENNESSEE WARBLER ♂
see p.409
faint eyestripe
longer wings
whitish underparts

YELLOW WARBLER ♀
see p.421
yellow upperparts
bright-yellow breast and belly

OCCURRENCE
Breeds in varied habitats across North America from Alaska eastward to Newfoundland, and in the West from British Columbia southward to California, New Mexico, and western Texas. Prefers streamside thickets. Some winter in the West, while others go to Mexico and Guatemala.

| Length **5in (13cm)** | Wingspan **7¼ in (18.5cm)** | Weight **¼–⅜oz (7–11g)** |
| Social **Winter flocks** | Lifespan **Up to 6 years** | Status **Secure** |

DATE: _____ TIME:_____ LOCATION:_____

| Order **Passeriformes** | Family **Parulidae** | Species *Leiothlypis ruficapilla* |

Nashville Warbler 🔊

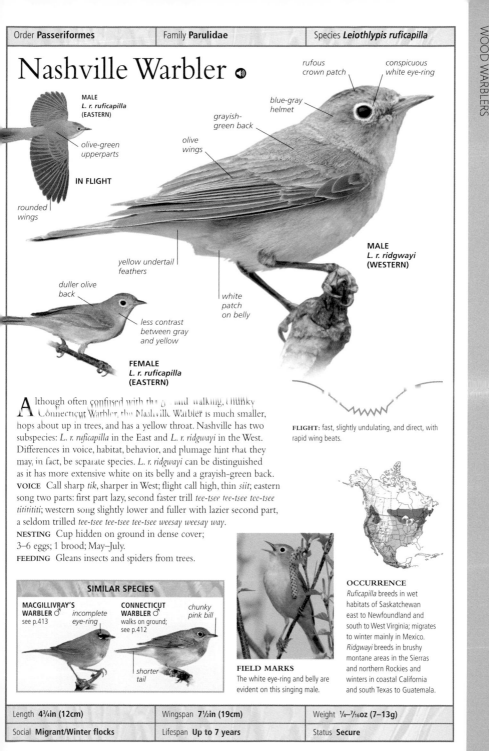

MALE
L. r. ruficapilla
(EASTERN)

olive-green
upperparts

IN FLIGHT

rounded
wings

rufous
crown patch

conspicuous
white eye-ring

blue-gray
helmet

grayish-
green back

olive
wings

yellow undertail
feathers

duller olive
back

less contrast
between gray
and yellow

FEMALE
L. r. ruficapilla
(EASTERN)

white
patch
on belly

MALE
L. r. ridgwayi
(WESTERN)

Although often confused with the ground-walking, chunky
Connecticut Warbler, the Nashville Warbler is much smaller,
hops about up in trees, and has a yellow throat. Nashville has two
subspecies: *L. r. ruficapilla* in the East and *L. r. ridgwayi* in the West.
Differences in voice, habitat, behavior, and plumage hint that they
may, in fact, be separate species. *L. r. ridgwayi* can be distinguished
as it has more extensive white on its belly and a grayish-green back.
VOICE Call sharp *tik*, sharper in West; flight call high, thin *siit*; eastern
song two parts: first part lazy, second faster trill *tee-tsee tee-tsee tee-tsee
titititi*; western song slightly lower and fuller with lazier second part,
a seldom trilled *tee-tsee tee-tsee tee-tsee weesay weesay way*.
NESTING Cup hidden on ground in dense cover;
3–6 eggs; 1 brood; May–July.
FEEDING Gleans insects and spiders from trees.

FLIGHT: fast, slightly undulating, and direct, with
rapid wing beats.

SIMILAR SPECIES

**MACGILLIVRAY'S
WARBLER** ♂
see p.413 · *incomplete
eye-ring*

**CONNECTICUT
WARBLER** ♂
walks on ground;
see p.412 · *chunky
pink bill*

*shorter
tail*

FIELD MARKS
The white eye-ring and belly are
evident on this singing male.

OCCURRENCE
Ruficapilla breeds in wet
habitats of Saskatchewan
east to Newfoundland and
south to West Virginia; migrates
to winter mainly in Mexico.
Ridgwayi breeds in brushy
montane areas in the Sierras
and northern Rockies and
winters in coastal California
and south Texas to Guatemala.

| Length **4¾in (12cm)** | Wingspan **7½in (19cm)** | Weight **¼–⁷⁄₁₆oz (7–13g)** |
| Social **Migrant/Winter flocks** | Lifespan **Up to 7 years** | Status **Secure** |

| Order **Passeriformes** | Family **Parulidae** | Species *Oporornis agilis* |

Connecticut Warbler

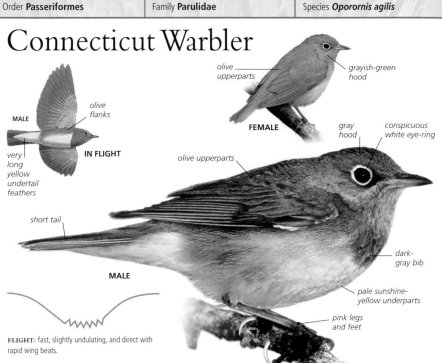

olive upperparts

grayish-green hood

FEMALE

MALE

olive flanks

IN FLIGHT

very long yellow undertail feathers

gray hood

conspicuous white eye-ring

olive upperparts

short tail

MALE

dark-gray bib

pale sunshine-yellow underparts

pink legs and feet

FLIGHT: fast, slightly undulating, and direct with rapid wing beats.

The shy Connecticut Warbler, which incidentally does not breed in Connecticut, breeds in remote, boggy habitats in Canada and is hard to spot during its spring and fall migrations. It arrives in the US in late May and leaves its breeding grounds in August. It is the only warbler that walks along the ground in a bouncy manner, with its tail bobbing up and down.

VOICE Seldom-heard call a nasal *champ*, flight call a buzzy *ziiiit*; song a loud "whippy," accelerating series, often ending with upward inflection *tweet, chuh WHIP-uh chee-uh-WHIP-uh chee-uh-WAY*.

NESTING Concealed cup of grass or leaves, lined with fine plant matter and hair; placed near or on the ground in damp moss or grass clump; 3–5 eggs; 1 brood; June–July.

FEEDING Gleans a variety of adult insects, insect larvae, and spiders from under leaves; also eats small fruit.

EXCEPTIONAL UNDERTAIL
The yellow undertail feathers nearly reach the tip of the Connecticut Warbler's tail.

SIMILAR SPECIES

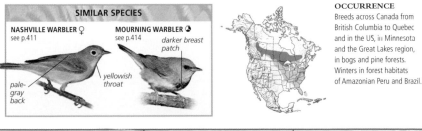

NASHVILLE WARBLER ♀
see p.411

pale-gray back

MOURNING WARBLER ♂
see p.414

darker breast patch

yellowish throat

OCCURRENCE
Breeds across Canada from British Columbia to Quebec and in the US, in Minnesota and the Great Lakes region, in bogs and pine forests. Winters in forest habitats of Amazonian Peru and Brazil.

| Length **6in (15cm)** | Wingspan **9in (23cm)** | Weight ⁷⁄₁₆–¹¹⁄₁₆oz (13–20g) |
| Social **Solitary** | Lifespan **Up to 4 years** | Status **Secure (p)** |

DATE: _____ TIME:_____ LOCATION:_____

MacGillivray's Warbler

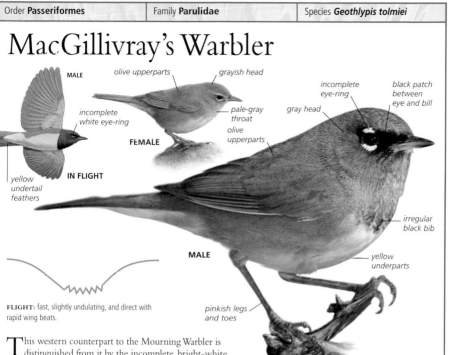

MALE

olive upperparts

grayish head

FEMALE

incomplete white eye-ring

pale-gray throat

olive upperparts

incomplete eye-ring

black patch between eye and bil

gray head

IN FLIGHT

yellow undertail feathers

MALE

irregular black bib

yellow underparts

pinkish legs and toes

FLIGHT: fast, slightly undulating, and direct with rapid wing beats.

This western counterpart to the Mourning Warbler is distinguished from it by the incomplete, bright-white eye-ring. Ornithologists have suggested that the English name of this species should be "Tolmie's Warbler," as this species was described and given its Latin species name, *tolmiei*, in April 1839, to honor the Scottish-born physician W. F. Tolmie. But a month later, John James Audubon, apparently unaware of the name *tolmiei*, named the same species *macgillivrayi*, to honor the naturalist William MacGillivray. This problem was easily solved, as the rule of priority establishes the earliest scientific name as the valid one, so the name *tolmiei* was retained. However, the English name, MacGillivray, has also stuck.

VOICE Call a sharp *tssik*; flight call a high, thin, clear *svit*; song a loud, staccato, rolling series; ends lower or higher than rest of song.

NESTING Cup of plant material just off the ground in deciduous shrubs and thickets; 3–5 eggs; 1 brood; May–August.

FEEDING Gleans beetles, flies, bees, caterpillars from low foliage.

FAIRLY EASY TO FIND
This species is easy to spot, often popping up onto a branch in response to some disturbance.

SIMILAR SPECIES

MOURNING WARBLER ♀
see p.414

shorter tail

NASHVILLE WARBLER ♂
see p.411

no bold eye markings

white belly patch

rufous crown patch

OCCURRENCE
Breeds in thickets within mixed and coniferous forests, often along streams from southeast Alaska and British Columbia south to California and Baja California, and across the western states. Winters in varied habitats with sufficient thickets in Mexico and in Central America.

| Length **5in (13cm)** | Wingspan **7½in (19cm)** | Weight ⁵⁄₁₆–⁷⁄₁₆oz **(9–12g)** |
| Social **Solitary** | Lifespan **Up to 4 years** | Status **Secure** |

DATE: _____ TIME: _____ LOCATION: _____

| Order **Passeriformes** | Family **Parulidae** | Species *Geothlypis philadelphia* |

Mourning Warbler

MALE (BREEDING)

pattern like male's (breeding), but more subdued

gray head

black mask

olive upperparts

yellow undertail feathers

"hooded" look

IN FLIGHT

IMMATURE MALE

black bib and speckled throat

yellow underparts

pink toes and legs

pale-gray hood

lacks speckled markings on throat

FEMALE

MALE (BREEDING)

The pleasant song of the Mourning Warbler is often used in commercials and movies as a background sound of idyllic suburban settings. It is doubtful, however, that you would find this gray-headed, gray-throated warbler in a backyard, as it prefers dense, herbaceous tangles—both for breeding and during migration. These birds are late spring migrants and the leaves are fully out when they arrive in the eastern US, making it difficult to see them. The easiest way to see a Mourning Warbler is to track a male by its song.

VOICE Call a flat *tchik*; flight call a high, thin, clear *svit*; song a very burry series of paired notes with low-pitched ending: *churrr-ee churrr-ee churrr-ee churr-ee churrr-ee-oh.*

NESTING Well-concealed cup of leaves, lined with grass, on or near ground in dense tangle; 2–5 eggs; 1 brood; June–August.

FEEDING Mainly gleans insects and spiders in low foliage; eats some plant material in winter.

FLIGHT: fast, slightly undulating, and direct with rapid wing beats.

FOLLOW THAT BIRD
Tracking down a singing male is the easiest way to find this skulking species.

SIMILAR SPECIES

MACGILLIVRAY'S WARBLER ♀ see p.413

incomplete eye-ring

longer tail

CONNECTICUT WARBLER ♂ see p.412

conspicuous white eye-ring

dark-gray bib

OCCURRENCE
Breeds in dense thickets of disturbed woodlands from the Yukon and British Columbia, east to Quebec and Newfoundland, south to the Great Lakes, New England, New York, and the Appalachians. Winters in dense thickets in Central and South America.

| Length **5in (13cm)** | Wingspan **7½in (19cm)** | Weight **⅜–⁷⁄₁₆oz (10–13g)** |
| Social **Solitary** | Lifespan **Up to 8 years** | Status **Secure** |

DATE: _____ TIME:_____ LOCATION:_____

| Order **Passeriformes** | Family **Parulidae** | Species *Geothlypis trichas* |

Common Yellowthroat 🔊

plain olive-green overall

black mask

MALE

IN FLIGHT

olive upperparts

yellow throat

FEMALE

pale eye-ring

olive-green upperparts

pale stripe over mask, varies from gray to white or yellowish

black mask including forehead

olive-green tail

yellow throat

greenish-gray underparts

MALE

FLIGHT: fast, slightly undulating, and direct with rapid wing beats.

This common and easy-to-see warbler is noticeable partly because of its loud, simple song. This species varies in voice and plumage across its range and 14 subspecies have been described. In the western US, the birds have yellower underparts, brighter white head stripes, and louder, simpler songs than the eastern birds. The male often flies upward rapidly, delivering a more complex version of its song.

VOICE Call a harsh, buzzy *tchak*, repeated into chatter when agitated; flight call a low, flat, buzzy *dzzzit*; song a variable but distinctive series of rich (often three-note) phrases: *WITCH-uh-tee WITCH-uh-tee WITCH-uh-tee WHICH*; more complex flight song.

NESTING Concealed bulky cup of grasses just above ground or water; 3–5 eggs; 1 brood; May–August.

FEEDING Eats insects and spiders in low vegetation; also seeds.

UNFORGETTABLE CALL
The song of the male Common Yellowthroat is an extremely helpful aid in its identification.

OCCURRENCE
Found south of the tundra, from Alaska and the Yukon to Quebec and Newfoundland, and south to California, Texas, and to the southeastern US. Inhabits dense herbaceous understory, from marshes and grasslands to pine forest and hedgerows. Winters from Mexico to Panama and the Antilles.

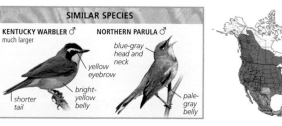

SIMILAR SPECIES

KENTUCKY WARBLER ♂
much larger

yellow eyebrow

shorter tail

bright-yellow belly

NORTHERN PARULA ♂

blue-gray head and neck

pale-gray belly

| Length **5in (13cm)** | Wingspan **6¾in (17cm)** | Weight **⁵⁄₁₆–³⁄₈oz (9–10g)** |
| Social **Migrant/Winter flocks** | Lifespan **Up to 11 years** | Status **Secure** |

DATE: _____ TIME: _____ LOCATION: _____

| Order **Passeriformes** | Family **Parulidae** | Species *Setophaga ruticilla* |

American Redstart 🔊

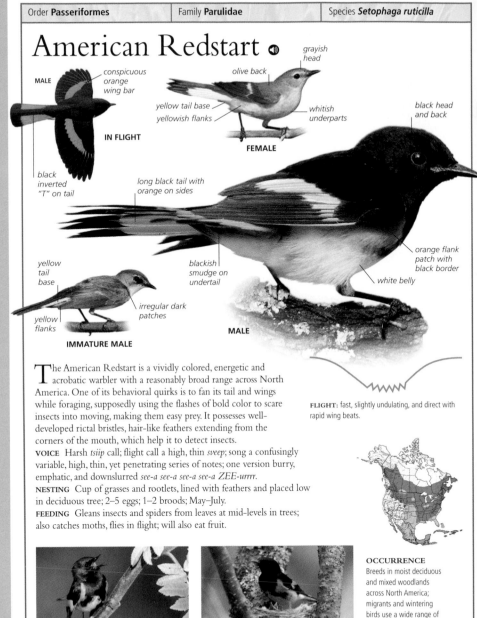

MALE — conspicuous orange wing bar

IN FLIGHT

black inverted "T" on tail

grayish head

olive back

yellow tail base

yellowish flanks

whitish underparts

FEMALE

black head and back

long black tail with orange on sides

orange flank patch with black border

white belly

MALE

yellow tail base

blackish smudge on undertail

irregular dark patches

yellow flanks

IMMATURE MALE

The American Redstart is a vividly colored, energetic and acrobatic warbler with a reasonably broad range across North America. One of its behavioral quirks is to fan its tail and wings while foraging, supposedly using the flashes of bold color to scare insects into moving, making them easy prey. It possesses well-developed rictal bristles, hair-like feathers extending from the corners of the mouth, which help it to detect insects.

VOICE Harsh *tsiip* call; flight call a high, thin *sweep*; song a confusingly variable, high, thin, yet penetrating series of notes; one version burry, emphatic, and downslurred *see-a see-a see-a see-a ZEE-urrrr*.

NESTING Cup of grasses and rootlets, lined with feathers and placed low in deciduous tree; 2–5 eggs; 1–2 broods; May–July.

FEEDING Gleans insects and spiders from leaves at mid-levels in trees; also catches moths, flies in flight; will also eat fruit.

FLIGHT: fast, slightly undulating, and direct with rapid wing beats.

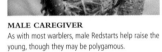

TRANSVESTITE BEHAVIOR
Immature males sneakily sport female plumage to gain access to mates and food.

MALE CAREGIVER
As with most warblers, male Redstarts help raise the young, though they may be polygamous.

OCCURRENCE
Breeds in moist deciduous and mixed woodlands across North America; migrants and wintering birds use a wide range of habitats. Winters from Baja California and south Florida through Middle America and the Caribbean to northern South America.

| Length **5in (13cm)** | Wingspan **8in (20cm)** | Weight $7/32$–$3/8$oz (6–11g) |
| Social **Flocks** | Lifespan **Up to 10 years** | Status **Secure** |

DATE: _____ TIME:_____ LOCATION:_____

Order **Passeriformes**	Family **Parulidae**	Species **Setophaga tigrina**

Cape May Warbler

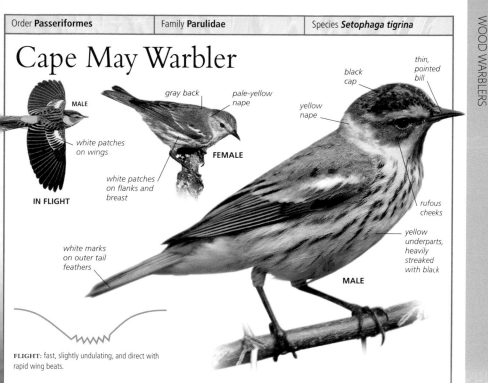

MALE

white patches on wings

IN FLIGHT

gray back

pale-yellow nape

FEMALE

white patches on flanks and breast

white marks on outer tail feathers

black cap

thin, pointed bill

yellow nape

rufous cheeks

yellow underparts, heavily streaked with black

MALE

FLIGHT: fast, slightly undulating, and direct with rapid wing beats.

The Cape May Warbler is a spruce budworm specialist, and so the populations of this bird increase during outbreaks of that insect. These birds often chase away other birds aggressively from flowering trees, where they use their especially thin and pointed bills and semitubular tongues to suck the nectar from blossoms. In its summer forest habitat, the Cape May Warbler uses its bill to feed on insects by plucking them from clumps of conifer needles.

VOICE Song a high, even-pitched series of whistles *see see see see.*
NESTING Cup placed near trunk, high in spruce or fir near top; 4–9 eggs; 1 brood; June–July.
FEEDING Gleans arthropods, especially spruce budworms, but also flies, moths, and beetles from mid-high levels in canopy; also takes fruit and nectar during the nonbreeding season.

SPRING FLASH
Magnificently colored, a male warbler displays its chestnut cheek, yellow "necklace," and yellow rump.

SIMILAR SPECIES

YELLOW-RUMPED WARBLER (MYRTLE) ♀
see p.425

yellow rump

thicker, heavier bill

yellow flank patches

PALM WARBLER (WESTERN) ◄
see p.424

browner overall

yellow undertail feathers

OCCURRENCE
Breeds from the Yukon and British Columbia to the Great Lakes, the Maritimes, and New England in mature spruce-fir forests. Migrants found in varied habitats. Winters in varied habitats in Central America, as far south as the Honduras.

Length **5in (13cm)**	Wingspan **8in (20cm)**	Weight **⁵⁄₁₆–⁷⁄₁₆oz (9–13g)**
Social **Migrant flocks**	Lifespan **Up to 4 years**	Status **Secure**

| Order **Passeriformes** | Family **Parulidae** | Species **Setophaga magnolia** |

Magnolia Warbler 🔊

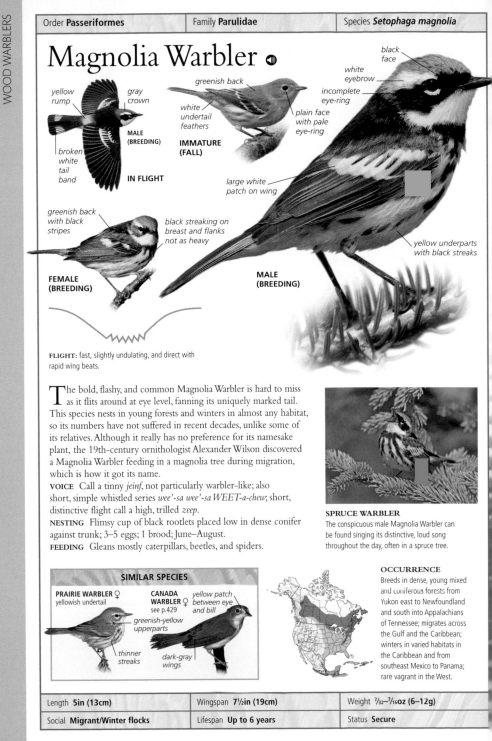

yellow rump

gray crown

MALE (BREEDING)

broken white tail band

IN FLIGHT

greenish back

white undertail feathers

plain face with pale eye-ring

IMMATURE (FALL)

black face

white eyebrow

incomplete eye-ring

large white patch on wing

yellow underparts with black streaks

greenish back with black stripes

black streaking on breast and flanks not as heavy

FEMALE (BREEDING)

MALE (BREEDING)

FLIGHT: fast, slightly undulating, and direct with rapid wing beats.

The bold, flashy, and common Magnolia Warbler is hard to miss as it flits around at eye level, fanning its uniquely marked tail. This species nests in young forests and winters in almost any habitat, so its numbers have not suffered in recent decades, unlike some of its relatives. Although it really has no preference for its namesake plant, the 19th-century ornithologist Alexander Wilson discovered a Magnolia Warbler feeding in a magnolia tree during migration, which is how it got its name.

VOICE Call a tinny *jeinf*, not particularly warbler-like; also short, simple whistled series *wee'-sa wee'-sa WEET-a-chew*; short, distinctive flight call a high, trilled *zeep*.

NESTING Flimsy cup of black rootlets placed low in dense conifer against trunk; 3–5 eggs; 1 brood; June–August.

FEEDING Gleans mostly caterpillars, beetles, and spiders.

SPRUCE WARBLER
The conspicuous male Magnolia Warbler can be found singing its distinctive, loud song throughout the day, often in a spruce tree.

SIMILAR SPECIES

PRAIRIE WARBLER ♀
yellowish undertail

thinner streaks

CANADA WARBLER ♀
see p.429

greenish-yellow upperparts

yellow patch between eye and bill

dark-gray wings

OCCURRENCE
Breeds in dense, young mixed and coniferous forests from Yukon east to Newfoundland and south into Appalachians of Tennessee; migrates across the Gulf and the Caribbean; winters in varied habitats in the Caribbean and from southeast Mexico to Panama; rare vagrant in the West.

| Length **5in (13cm)** | Wingspan **7½in (19cm)** | Weight **⁷/₃₂–⁷/₁₆oz (6–12g)** |
| Social **Migrant/Winter flocks** | Lifespan **Up to 6 years** | Status **Secure** |

DATE: _____ TIME: _____ LOCATION: _____

Order **Passeriformes**	Family **Parulidae**	Species **Setophaga castanea**

Bay-breasted Warbler

MALE (BREEDING)
two white wing bars
bold buffy neck patch
white tips on outer tail feathers
IN FLIGHT

FEMALE (BREEDING)
buffy wash on flanks and under tail
two white wing bars

chestnut crown, streaked black
dusky ear patch

olive crown and back
two wing bars
greenish cheeks
IMMATURE FEMALE (FALL)
unstreaked breast

gray upperparts with black streaks
chestnut brown crown
black face
chestnut-brown chin and flanks

buff undertail
yellowish-buff belly

MALE (BREEDING)

FLIGHT: fast, slightly undulating, and direct, with rapid wing beats.

Splashed with deep chestnut, crisp white, warm buff, and jet-black, a male Bay-breasted Warbler in breeding plumage is a particularly striking bird, but dull females are very different with their dull greenish plumage. Like the Tennessee Warbler, this species depends largely on outbreaks of spruce budworm (a major food source), so its numbers rise and fall according to those outbreaks. Overall, the Bay-breasted Warbler population has decreased because of the increased use of pesticide sprays.

VOICE Call a somewhat upslurred *tsip;* flight call a high, buzzy, short, and sharp *tzzzt;* song of very high, thin notes, often ending on lower pitch: *wee-si wee si wee-si wee.*
NESTING Fragile-looking cup of grass and lichens on horizontal branch at mid-level in forest; 4–5 eggs; 1 brood; May–July.
FEEDING Mostly eats moths, smaller insects, worms, spiders, and caterpillars during migration and on breeding grounds; eats mainly fruit in winter.

SINGING IN THE FOREST
A brilliantly colored breeding male sings its high-pitched song on a spruce branch.

SIMILAR SPECIES

CHESTNUT-SIDED WARBLER ♂
see p.422
yellow crown
yellow and black streaks on upperparts

PINE WARBLER ♀
yellow around eye
white sides to tail

OCCURRENCE
Breeds in mature spruce-fir boreal forest across the forest belt from Yukon to the Maritimes, and south to the Great Lakes area and northern New England. Migrants occur in varied habitat, but especially woodland edges. Winters in wet forest in Central America.

Length **5½in (14cm)**	Wingspan **9in (23cm)**	Weight **⅜–½oz (11–15g)**
Social **Migratory/Winter flocks**	Lifespan **Up to 4 years**	Status **Vulnerable**

DATE: _____ TIME: _____ LOCATION: _____

Order **Passeriformes**	Family **Parulidae**	Species **Setophaga fusca**

Blackburnian Warbler

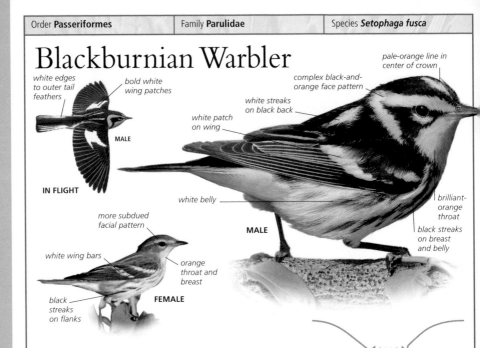

white edges to outer tail feathers

bold white wing patches

MALE

IN FLIGHT

white patch on wing

white streaks on black back

pale-orange line in center of crown

complex black-and-orange face pattern

brilliant-orange throat

black streaks on breast and belly

white belly

MALE

more subdued facial pattern

white wing bars

orange throat and breast

black streaks on flanks

FEMALE

This fiery beacon of the treetops is considered one of the most beautiful members of its family; its orange throat is unique among the North American warblers. The Blackburnian Warbler coexists with many other *Setophaga* warblers in the coniferous and mixed woods of the North and East, but is able to do so by exploiting a slightly different niche for foraging—in this case the treetops. It also seeks the highest trees for nesting.

VOICE Call a slightly husky *chik*; flight-call a high, thin *zzee*; song variable, but always high-pitched; swirling series of lisps, spiraling upward to end in an almost inaudible *trill*.

NESTING Fine cup in conifer on horizontal branch away from trunk, usually high in tree; 4–5 eggs; 1 brood; May–July.

FEEDING Gleans arthropods, such as spiders, worms, and beetles; also fruit.

FLIGHT: fast, slightly undulating, and direct with rapid wing beats.

DISTINGUISHING FEATURES
The female is like a dull adult male, but with two wing bars and no black on the face.

AVIAN FIREFLY
This male in breeding plumage glows when seen against a dark forest background.

SIMILAR SPECIES

BAY-BREASTED WARBLER (FALL) ♀ ⚲
see p.419

greenish back

unstreaked underparts

BLACK-THROATED GREEN WARBLER ♂
see p.428

greenish cap

heavily streaked underparts

OCCURRENCE
Breeds in coniferous and mixed forests from Alberta east through the North Great Lakes to Newfoundland and south into the Appalachians of Georgia; migrants found in wooded, shrubby, or forest edge habitats. Winters in wet forests in Costa Rica and Panama, and southward as far as Peru.

Length **5in (13cm)**	Wingspan **8½in (21cm)**	Weight **5/16–7/16oz (9–12g)**
Social **Winter flocks**	Lifespan **Up to 8 years**	Status **Vulnerable**

DATE: _____ TIME: _____ LOCATION: _____

| Order **Passeriformes** | Family **Parulidae** | Species *Setophaga petechia* |

Yellow Warbler 🔊

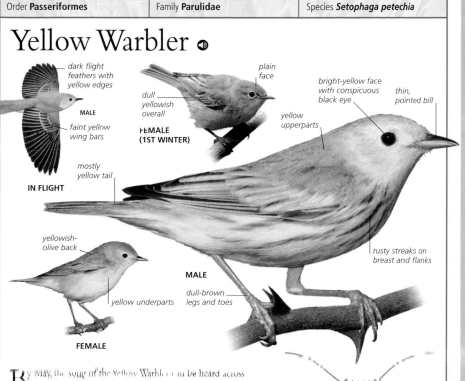

IN FLIGHT

dark flight feathers with yellow edges

MALE

faint yellow wing bars

mostly yellow tail

dull yellowish overall

plain face

FEMALE (1ST WINTER)

bright-yellow face with conspicuous black eye

thin, pointed bill

yellow upperparts

rusty streaks on breast and flanks

MALE

dull-brown legs and toes

yellowish-olive back

yellow underparts

FEMALE

By May, the song of the Yellow Warbler can be heard across North America as the birds arrive for the summer. This warbler is treated as a single species with about 35 subspecies, mostly in its tropical range (West Indies and South America). The Yellow Warbler is known to build a new nest on top of an old one when cowbird eggs appear in it, which can result in up to six different tiers. The Yellow Warbler does not walk, but rather hops from branch to branch.

VOICE Call a variable *chip*, sometimes given in series; flight call buzzy *zeep*; song variable series of fast, sweet notes; western birds often add an emphatic ending.

NESTING Deep cup of plant material, grasses in vertical fork of deciduous tree or shrub; 4–5 eggs; 1 brood; May–July.

FEEDING Eats mostly insects and insect larvae, plus some fruit.

FLIGHT: fast, slightly undulating, and direct, with rapid wing beats.

ONE OF A KIND
This species has more yellow in its plumage than any other North American wood warbler.

SIMILAR SPECIES

ORANGE-CROWNED WARBLER
see p.410

olive-green overall

WILSON'S WARBLER ♀
see p.430

dark crown

longer tail

OCCURRENCE
Widespread in most shrubby and second-growth habitats of North America. Migrates to the southern US and southward to Mexico, Central America, and South America. Resident populations live in Florida and the West Indies.

| Length **5in (13cm)** | Wingspan **8in (20cm)** | Weight **⁹⁄₃₂–¹⁄₂oz (8–14g)** |
| Social **Flocks** | Lifespan **Up to 9 years** | Status **Secure** |

DATE: _____ TIME: _____ LOCATION: _____

Order **Passeriformes**	Family **Parulidae**	Species *Setophaga pensylvanica*

Chestnut-sided Warbler 🔊

MALE (BREEDING)
two yellow wing bars
IN FLIGHT
white outer tail feathers

yellow cap
black "mustache"
chestnut band along flanks
FEMALE (BREEDING)
white tail spots

yellow-and-black streaks on upperparts

conspicuous white cheeks
yellow crown
white throat
two wing bars
rich-chestnut flanks
MALE (BREEDING)

olive crown
bright lime-green above
plain face with white eye-ring
FEMALE (1ST FALL)
plain gray underside

The Chestnut-sided Warbler is one of the few wood warbler species that has benefited from deforestation, because it depends on deciduous second-growth trees and forest edges for breeding. Once a rare bird, it is more common now than it was in the early 19th century. These birds vary in appearance, immature females looking quite unlike adult males in breeding. In all plumages, yellowish wing bars and whitish belly are the most distinguishing characteristics. Its pleasant song has long been transcribed as *pleased pleased pleased to MEET'cha.*
VOICE Call a sweet *chip*; flight call a low, burry *brrrt*; song a series of fast, sweet notes, usually ending with emphatic *WEET-chew.*
NESTING Open, easy-to-find cup just off ground in small deciduous tree or shrub; 3–5 eggs; 1 brood; May–August.
FEEDING Eats insects, especially larvae; also berries and seeds.

FLIGHT: fast, slightly undulating, and direct with rapid wing beats.

MALE TERRITORY
This singing, territorial male prefers second-growth thickets as its habitat.

OCCURRENCE
Breeds in successive stages of regrowth in deciduous forests, from Alberta to the Great Lakes, Nova Scotia, and the Appalachians; isolated populations in the Midwest. Winters in the Caribbean, Mexico, and Central America, south to Venezuela and northern Colombia.

SIMILAR SPECIES

PALM WARBLER ♂
see p.424
chestnut crown
dark upperparts

BAY-BREASTED WARBLER ♟
see p.419
olive upperparts
white wing bars
buffy undertail
greenish underside

Length **5in (13cm)**	Wingspan **8in (20cm)**	Weight $^9/_{32}$–$^7/_{16}$**oz (8–13g)**
Social **Winter flocks**	Lifespan **Up to 7 years**	Status **Secure**

DATE: _____ TIME: _____ LOCATION: _____

| Order **Passeriformes** | Family **Parulidae** | Species *Setophaga striata* |

Blackpoll Warbler 🔊

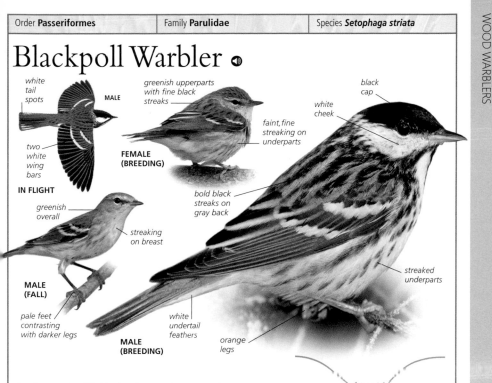

white tail spots

MALE

greenish upperparts with fine black streaks

black cap

white cheek

faint, fine streaking on underparts

two white wing bars

FEMALE (BREEDING)

IN FLIGHT

greenish overall

bold black streaks on gray back

streaking on breast

streaked underparts

MALE (FALL)

pale feet contrasting with darker legs

white undertail feathers

orange legs

MALE (BREEDING)

The Blackpoll Warbler is well known for undergoing a remarkable fall migration that takes it over the Atlantic Ocean from southern Canada and the northeastern US to northern Venezuela. Before departing, it almost doubles its body weight with fat to serve as fuel for the nonstop journey. In spring, most of these birds travel the shorter Caribbean route back north.
VOICE Call piercing *chip*; flight call high, buzzy yet sharp *tzzzt*; common song crescendo of fast, extremely high-pitched ticks, ending with a decrescendo *tsst tsst TSST TSST TSST tsst tsst*; less commonly, ticks run into even faster trill.
NESTING Well-hidden cup placed low against conifer trunk; 3–5 eggs; 1–2 broods; May–July.
FEEDING Gleans arthropods, such as worms and beetles, but will take small fruit in fall and winter.

FLIGHT: fast, slightly undulating, and direct, with rapid wing beats.

HITTING THE HIGH NOTES
The song of the male Blackpoll is so high-pitched that it is inaudible to many people.

SIMILAR SPECIES

CERULEAN WARBLER ♂
blue upperparts

white belly

BLACK-AND-WHITE WARBLER ♂
see p.408

black cheek

distinct black-and-white stripes

OCCURRENCE
Breeds in spruce-fir forests across the northern boreal forest zone from Alaska eastward to Newfoundland, southward to coastal coniferous forests in the Maritimes and northern New England. Migrants fly over the Atlantic Ocean to landfall in the Caribbean and northern South America.

| Length **5½in (14cm)** | Wingspan **9in (23cm)** | Weight **⅜–⅝oz (10–18g)** |
| Social **Flocks** | Lifespan **Up to 8 years** | Status **Secure** |

Order **Passeriformes**	Family **Parulidae**	Species *Setophaga palmarum*

Palm Warbler 🔊

ADULT (EASTERN)

chestnut crown

IN FLIGHT

white-edged tail

dark upperparts

yellow undertail feathers

dull-gray upperparts

ADULT S. p. hypochrysea (EASTERN; BREEDING)

chestnut streaks on breast

rich-yellow underparts

yellow eyestripe

grayish-green "mustache"

ring below eye

yellow throat

dark-gray upperparts

dusky streaks on breast and belly

ADULT S. p. palmarum (WESTERN MALE; BREEDING)

dull grayish-brown overall

whitish below with brown streaks

yellowish rump

yellow under tail

ADULT S. p. palmarum (WESTERN; NONBREEDING)

The Palm Warbler is one of North America's most abundant warblers. Its constant tail-pumping habit makes it easy to identify in any plumage. It was named *palmarum* (meaning "palm") in 1789 because it was first recorded among palm thickets on the Caribbean island of Hispaniola. The western subspecies (*S. p. palmarum*) is found in Western and Central Canada. It is grayish-brown above and lacks the chestnut streaks of the eastern sub-species (*S. p. hypochrysea*), which has a yellower face, and breeds in southeastern Canada and northeastern US.

VOICE Call a husky *chik* or *tsip*; flight call a light *ziint*; slow, loose, buzzy trill: *zwi zwi zwi zwi zwi zwi zwi zwi*.

NESTING Cup of grasses on or near ground, often in peat moss, at base of small coniferous tree or shrub; 4–5 eggs; 1 brood; May–July.

FEEDING Eats insects, sometimes caught in flight; also takes seeds and berries.

FLIGHT: fast, slightly undulating, and direct with rapid wing beats.

SIMILAR SPECIES

BAY-BREASTED WARBLER ♀ see p.419

dusky ear patch

YELLOW-RUMPED WARBLER (MYRTLE) ♀ see p.425

streaking on back

white throat

FAR FROM THE PALMS
This male Palm Warbler is far north of the coastal palms where its kin spend the winter.

OCCURRENCE
In North America, breeds in spruce bogs within the northerly forest zone, across Canada from Yukon to the Maritimes and Labrador, and in the US, from Minnesota to Maine. Often migrates through central portions of the eastern US; winters in the southeastern US, Florida, and Central America.

Length **5½in (14cm)**	Wingspan **8in (20cm)**	Weight **¼–⁷/₁₆oz (7–13g)**
Social **Flocks**	Lifespan **Up to 6 years**	Status **Secure**

DATE: _____ TIME: _____ LOCATION: _____

| Order **Passeriformes** | Family **Parulidae** | Species *Setophaga coronata* |

Yellow-rumped Warbler 🔊

white wing bars

MALE (MYRTLE)

dark cheeks

black streaks on gray back

IN FLIGHT

bright-yellow rump

white throat

black streaks across breast

MALE
S. c. coronata
(MYRTLE)

large white wing patch

whitish eyebrow

same pattern as male's, but duller

whitish throat

white lower and upper eye crescents

yellow flanks

FEMALE
S. c. coronata
(MYRTLE)

solid black breast

unmarked undertail

white corners on outer tail feathers

FEMALE
S. c. auduboni
(AUDUBON'S)

yellowish throat

grayish overall

MALE
S. c. auduboni
(AUDUBON'S)

The abundant and widespread Yellow-rumped Warbler is not choosy about its wintering habitats. It was often considered to consist of two species "Myrtle" (*S. coronata*) in the North, and "Audubon's" (*S. auduboni*) in the West. Since they interbreed freely in a narrow zone of contact in British Columbia and Alberta, the American Ornithological Society merged them. Recent evidence, however, suggests that they are indeed separate species so the designations may change again.
VOICE Myrtle's call a flat, husky *tchik*; Audubon's a higher-pitched, relatively musical, rising *jip*; flight call of both a clear, upslurred *sviiit*; song loose, warbled trill with an inflected ending; Myrtle's song higher and faster, Audubon's lower and slower.
NESTING Bulky cup of plant matter in conifer; 4–5 eggs; 1 brood; March–August.
FEEDING Feeds mostly on flies, beetles, wasps, and spiders during breeding; takes fruit and berries at other times of the year; often sallies to catch prey.

FLIGHT: fast, slightly undulating, and direct with rapid wing beats.

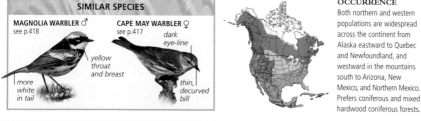

WIDESPREAD WARBLER
Yellow-rumped Warblers are widespread and are likely to be spotted often.

SIMILAR SPECIES

MAGNOLIA WARBLER ♂
see p.418

yellow throat and breast

more white in tail

CAPE MAY WARBLER ♀
see p.417

dark eye-line

thin, decurved bill

OCCURRENCE
Both northern and western populations are widespread across the continent from Alaska eastward to Quebec and Newfoundland, and westward in the mountains south to Arizona, New Mexico, and Northern Mexico. Prefers coniferous and mixed hardwood coniferous forests.

| Length **5in (13cm)** | Wingspan **9in (23cm)** | Weight **⅜–⅝oz (10–17g)** |
| Social **Flocks** | Lifespan **Up to 7 years** | Status **Secure** |

DATE: _____ TIME: _____ LOCATION: _____

| Order **Passeriformes** | Family **Parulidae** | Species **Setophaga nigrescens** |

Black-throated Gray Warbler

MALE
white wing bars
gray overall

IN FLIGHT

pattern more subdued than male

white throat
black band across breast

FEMALE

white outer tail feathers
MALE

bold white cheeks
no eye-ring
yellow spot between eye and bill
plain gray back
one or two white wing bars
heavy black streaks on underparts

white undertail feathers

FLIGHT: fast, slightly undulating, and direct with rapid wing beats.

The Black-throated Gray Warbler, a somewhat chickadee-like bird, inhabits the understory of forests and oak and mixed woodlands in dry to arid western North America. Remarkably, considering that it is fairly common, not much is known about its life history, except that it has a rather leisurely foraging style, that its nest is built by both males and females, placed only a feet few away from the ground, and that it lingers in its range until late fall, sometimes even wintering in California and Arizona.

VOICE Call a hard, flat *chep*; flight call a rising *siiit*; song a series of mid-range, paired, buzzy notes, slightly rising then dropping in pitch with the last note, *buzz-zu buzz-zu buzz-zu buzz-zo buzz-zo buzz-zee BEE-chu!*

NESTING Deep and compact cup of grass, lined with feathers, in brush; 3–5 eggs; 2 broods; May–July.

FEEDING A rather deliberate forager, gleans insects, especially caterpillars, from foliage at mid-levels.

LIVELY SONG
The buzzy song of this species is typical of the "black-throated" warbler group.

SIMILAR SPECIES

BLACK-AND-WHITE WARBLER ♂
see p.408
white eyebrow
streaked undertail feathers

BLACK-CAPPED CHICKADEE ♂
see p.297
black cap and bib
faded buff flanks

OCCURRENCE
Ranges from British Columbia south to California. Breeds in open coniferous and mixed woodlands with dense scrubby understory of pinyon, juniper, and/or oak; migrants use a greater variety of habitats; winters in dry scrub and woodlands southward away from its breeding range.

| Length **5in (13cm)** | Wingspan **7½in (19cm)** | Weight **¼–⅜oz (7–10g)** |
| Social **Flocks** | Lifespan **Unknown** | Status **Secure** |

DATE: _____ TIME: _____ LOCATION: _____

Order **Passeriformes**	Family **Parulidae**	Species *Setophaga townsendi*

Townsend's Warbler 🔊

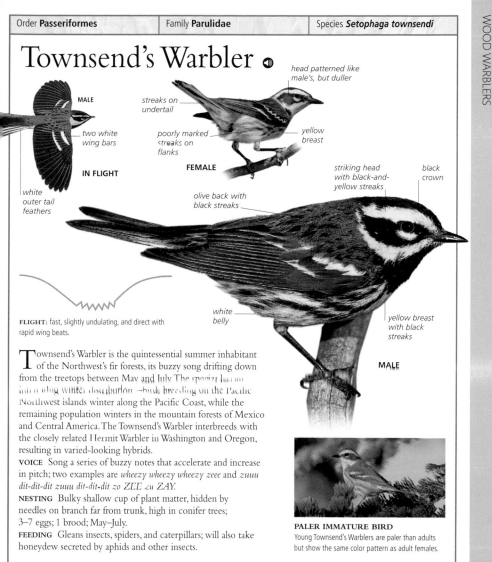

MALE

two white wing bars

IN FLIGHT

white outer tail feathers

streaks on undertail

poorly marked streaks on flanks

FEMALE

head patterned like male's, but duller

yellow breast

striking head with black-and-yellow streaks

black crown

olive back with black streaks

white belly

yellow breast with black streaks

MALE

FLIGHT: fast, slightly undulating, and direct with rapid wing beats.

Townsend's Warbler is the quintessential summer inhabitant of the Northwest's fir forests, its buzzy song drifting down from the treetops between May and July. The species has an interesting winter distribution—birds breeding on the Pacific Northwest islands winter along the Pacific Coast, while the remaining population winters in the mountain forests of Mexico and Central America. The Townsend's Warbler interbreeds with the closely related Hermit Warbler in Washington and Oregon, resulting in varied-looking hybrids.

VOICE Song a series of buzzy notes that accelerate and increase in pitch; two examples are *wheezy wheezy wheezy zeee* and *zuuu dit-dit-dit zuuu dit-dit-dit zo ZEE zu ZAY*.

NESTING Bulky shallow cup of plant matter, hidden by needles on branch far from trunk, high in conifer trees; 3–7 eggs; 1 brood; May–July.

FEEDING Gleans insects, spiders, and caterpillars; will also take honeydew secreted by aphids and other insects.

PALER IMMATURE BIRD
Young Townsend's Warblers are paler than adults but show the same color pattern as adult females.

SIMILAR SPECIES

BLACK-THROATED GREEN WARBLER ♂ see p.428

larger bib

no yellow on breast

BLACK-THROATED GREEN WARBLER ♀ see p.428

paler cheek patch

lacks bright-yellow breast

OCCURRENCE
Breeds from southern Alaska to Wyoming in mature fir, coniferous, and mixed coniferous-deciduous forests; elevations range from sea level to subalpine. Populations winter either in Mexico and Central America or in California and Oregon, in different habitats including coastal, woodland, and suburban parks and gardens.

Length **5in (13cm)**	Wingspan **8in (20cm)**	Weight **¼–⅜oz (7–11g)**
Social **Flocks**	Lifespan **Up to 4 years**	Status **Secure**

DATE: _____ TIME: _____ LOCATION: _____

| Order **Passeriformes** | Family **Parulidae** | Species *Setophaga virens* |

Black-throated Green Warbler 🔊

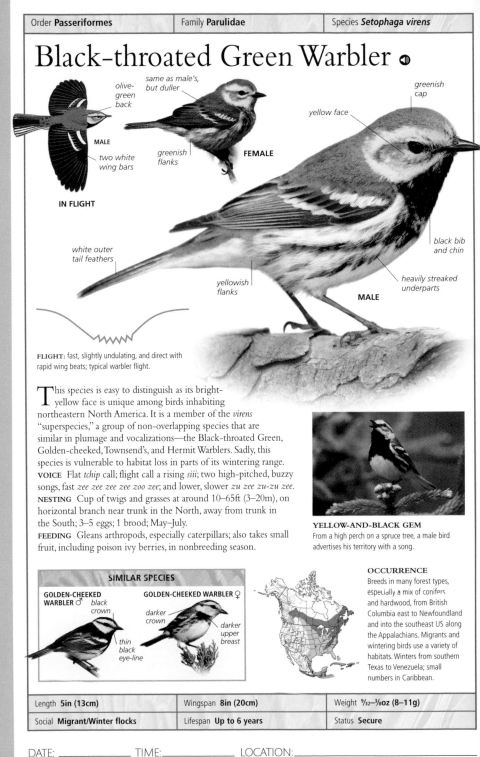

olive-green back

same as male's, but duller

greenish cap

yellow face

MALE

two white wing bars

greenish flanks

FEMALE

IN FLIGHT

white outer tail feathers

yellowish flanks

MALE

black bib and chin

heavily streaked underparts

FLIGHT: fast, slightly undulating, and direct with rapid wing beats; typical warbler flight.

This species is easy to distinguish as its bright-yellow face is unique among birds inhabiting northeastern North America. It is a member of the *virens* "superspecies," a group of non-overlapping species that are similar in plumage and vocalizations—the Black-throated Green, Golden-cheeked, Townsend's, and Hermit Warblers. Sadly, this species is vulnerable to habitat loss in parts of its wintering range.

VOICE Flat *tchip* call; flight call a rising *siii*; two high-pitched, buzzy songs, fast *zee zee zee zee zoo zee*; and lower, slower *zu zee zu-zu zee*.

NESTING Cup of twigs and grasses at around 10–65ft (3–20m), on horizontal branch near trunk in the North, away from trunk in the South; 3–5 eggs; 1 brood; May–July.

FEEDING Gleans arthropods, especially caterpillars; also takes small fruit, including poison ivy berries, in nonbreeding season.

YELLOW-AND-BLACK GEM
From a high perch on a spruce tree, a male bird advertises his territory with a song.

SIMILAR SPECIES

GOLDEN-CHEEKED WARBLER ♂
black crown
thin black eye-line

GOLDEN-CHEEKED WARBLER ♀
darker crown
darker upper breast

OCCURRENCE
Breeds in many forest types, especially a mix of conifers and hardwood, from British Columbia east to Newfoundland and into the southeast US along the Appalachians. Migrants and wintering birds use a variety of habitats. Winters from southern Texas to Venezuela; small numbers in Caribbean.

| Length **5in (13cm)** | Wingspan **8in (20cm)** | Weight **⁹⁄₃₂–³⁄₈oz (8–11g)** |
| Social **Migrant/Winter flocks** | Lifespan **Up to 6 years** | Status **Secure** |

DATE: _____ TIME:_____ LOCATION:_____

Order **Passeriformes**	Family **Parulidae**	Species ***Cardellina canadensis***

Canada Warbler

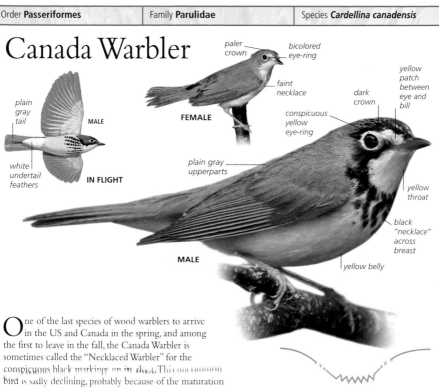

paler crown

bicolored eye-ring

faint necklace

FEMALE

plain gray tail

MALE

white undertail feathers

IN FLIGHT

yellow patch between eye and bill

dark crown

conspicuous yellow eye-ring

plain gray upperparts

yellow throat

black "necklace" across breast

MALE

yellow belly

One of the last species of wood warblers to arrive in the US and Canada in the spring, and among the first to leave in the fall, the Canada Warbler is sometimes called the "Necklaced Warbler" for the conspicuous black marking on its chest. This uncommon bird is sadly declining, probably because of the maturation and draining of its preferred breeding habitat, consisting of old mixed hardwood forests with moist undergrowth.

VOICE Call a thick *tchip;* flight call a variable, clear *plip;* song a haphazard jumble of sweet notes, often beginning with or interspersed with *tchip,* followed by a pause.

NESTING Concealed cup of leaves, in moss or grass, on or near ground; 4–5 eggs; 1 brood; May–June.

FEEDING Gleans at mid-levels for many species of insects; also catches flies and forages on ground.

FLIGHT: fast, slightly undulating, and direct with rapid wing beats.

TAKING FLIGHT
This species often waits for prey to fly by, before launching into flight to pursue it.

FAMILIAR MEAL
Flying insects, including crane flies, make up the bulk of the Canada Warbler's diet.

SIMILAR SPECIES

MAGNOLIA WARBLER ♀
see p.418

white eyebrow

streaked flanks

KIRTLAND'S WARBLER ♂

streaked mantle and flanks

OCCURRENCE
Breeds in moist deciduous, mixed, and coniferous forests with well-developed understory, especially swampy woods; migrants use well-vegetated habitats; winters in dense, wet thickets and a variety of tropical woodlands in South America.

Length **5in (13cm)**	Wingspan **8in (20cm)**	Weight **⁹/₃₂–¹/₂oz (8–15g)**
Social **Flocks**	Lifespan **Up to 8 years**	Status **Threatened**

DATE: _____ TIME: _____ LOCATION: _____

| Order **Passeriformes** | Family **Parulidae** | Species **Cardellina pusilla** |

Wilson's Warbler

MALE

IN FLIGHT

long, narrow tail

olive or blackish crown

yellow eyebrow and chin

FEMALE

olive upperparts

black cap

large black eye

yellow brightest on face

MALE

FLIGHT: fast, slightly undulating, and direct with rapid wing beats.

The tiny Wilson's Warbler is perhaps the most common spring migrant of all the wood warblers across many areas of the western US and Canada. In the East, however, it is much scarcer in spring. Wilson's Warblers have a wide range of habitats, yet their numbers are declining, especially in the West, as its riverside breeding habitats are gradually being destroyed by development. This species is named after the renowned early 19th-century ornithologist, Alexander Wilson.

VOICE Call a rich *chimp* or *champ;* flight call a sharp, liquid *tsik;* song a variable, chattering trill, often increases in speed *che che che che chi-chi-chi-chit.*

NESTING Cup of leaves and grass placed on or near ground in mosses or grass, higher along the Pacific Coast; 4–6 eggs; 1 brood; April–June.

FEEDING Captures insects in foliage, leaf litter, or during flight; also takes berries and honeydew.

BRIGHT WESTERN BIRD
In its western range, male Wilson's Warblers have a glowing yellow-orange face; eastern birds are duller.

EASY IDENTIFICATION
The black cap and yellow face of the otherwise olive-colored Wilson's Warbler are good field markers.

SIMILAR SPECIES

YELLOW WARBLER ♀ see p.421
yellow edges to wing feathers
shorter tail
yellow overall

HOODED WARBLER ♀
larger body
larger bill

OCCURRENCE
Breeds in wet shrubby thickets with no canopy, often along streams and lakes; Pacific slope birds use more varied habitats, including moist forests. Widespread in forests south of tundra, from Newfoundland to northern New England, west to Alaska and south through the western US to California and New Mexico down into Mexico.

| Length **4¾in (12cm)** | Wingspan **7in (17.5cm)** | Weight **⁷⁄₃₂–⁵⁄₁₆oz (6–9g)** |
| Social **Flocks** | Lifespan **Up to 6 years** | Status **Declining** |

DATE: _____ TIME: _____ LOCATION: _____

CARDINALS AND RELATIVES

BIRDS BELONGING to the Cardinalidae family are visually stunning, noisy birds. Some tanagers (those in the genus *Piranga*) and grosbeaks and buntings (those in the genus *Passerina*) are grouped together with the Northern Cardinal and Pyrrhuloxia in this family. Tanagers are slender-bodied, cone-billed, finch-like birds that feed on insects, such as wasps and bees, and fruits in high foliage. Males are brightly colored, while the females are duller and greener. They have similar songs but more distinctive calls.

CARDINALS
Cardinals are striking birds: the Northern Cardinal is almost entirely red, while the Pyrrhuloxia of the southwestern states is gray with vivid-red patches. Both species have pointed, upstanding crests. Females are grayer, but still have the crest. Their bills are stout but short, adapted to feed on small fruits, berries, and seeds.

MALE COLORS
Male Western Tanagers are among North America's most colorful birds.

GROSBEAKS AND BUNTINGS
Grosbeaks in the genus *Pheucticus* are stocky, heavily built, sluggish species, with characteristically heavy, deeply triangular bills for splitting and peeling seeds. Again, males are bright and boldly colored, while females are duller but distinctively patterned. The colorful buntings in this family (with a preponderance of blues in their plumage) are similar to the grosbeaks, but more lightly built and with more delicate, triangular bills.

| Order **Passeriformes** | Family **Cardinalidae** | Species *Piranga ludoviciana* |

Western Tanager 🔊

MALE (BREEDING) IN FLIGHT
- two wing bars
- orange head
- black tail
- bright-yellow rump

FEMALE (NONBREEDING)
- more olive-and-grayish overall

MALE (BREEDING)
- orange head and hood blending into yellow
- yellow collar
- yellow upperwing bar
- jet-black back
- white lower wing bar
- bright-yellow underparts
- bluish-gray feet and legs
- black tail
- bright-yellow rump

MALE (NONBREEDING)
- red wash on face

FEMALE (BREEDING)
- olive-green upperparts

FLIGHT: strong and direct; deliberate.

The hoarse song of the exquisitely plumaged male Western Tanager is a characteristic sound of coniferous forests in western North America. All *Piranga* tanagers have songs and whistled flight calls that closely resemble those of the *Pheucticus* grosbeaks. Recent studies indicate that this is not a coincidence and that *Piranga* tanagers are actually part of the family Cardinalidae, not Thraupidae tanagers.

VOICE Distinctive call, a rolled *pruh-DHIT!* or *pur-duh-RIT!*; flight call a *hweee*; song similar to Scarlet Tanager, but less burry.
NESTING Loosely woven cup of grasses, lined with rootlets, high in tree; 3–5 eggs; 1 brood; May–August.
FEEDING Forages for insects, such as termites, flies, moths, and bees in breeding season; eats berries in nonbreeding season.

ORANGE AND YELLOW
Two Western Tanagers proudly display their bright fall-colored plumage.

SIMILAR SPECIES

SCARLET TANAGER ♀
- greener overall
- lacks bold wing bars

BRIGHT BLEND
This colorful bird blends into its surroundings surprisingly well.

OCCURRENCE
Breeds farther north than any other tanager, in open coniferous and mixed forests of the West, from southeastern Alaska and southwestern Northwest Territories to Baja California and western Texas. Winters in the southern half of Mexico.

| Length **7½in (19cm)** | Wingspan **11½in (29cm)** | Weight **⅞–1¼oz (25–35g)** |
| Social **Solitary** | Lifespan **Up to 8 years** | Status **Secure** |

DATE: _____ TIME: _____ LOCATION: _____

| Order **Passeriformes** | Family **Cardinalidae** | Species **_Cardinalis cardinalis_** |

Northern Cardinal 🔊

MALE

warm-red overall

IN FLIGHT

smaller, duller crest

brownish wings

darker bill

IMMATURE

reddish crest

buff-olive upperparts

red on outer tail feathers

dark patch not as extensive as male's

grayish-brown underparts

FEMALE

long red tail

prominent crest

thick orange-red bill

bright-red back and wings

black patch on face, extends onto throat

MALE

brownish toes and legs

The Northern Cardinal, or "redbird," is a familiar sight across the eastern US and southeastern Canada. Females are less showy, but have a prominent reddish crest and red accents on their tan-colored outer tail and wing feathers. The male aggressively repels intruders and will occasionally attack his own reflection in windows and various shiny surfaces.
VOICE Sharp, metallic _tik_ call, also bubbly chatters; song a loud, variable, sweet, slurred whistle, _tsee-ew-tsee-ew-whoit-whoit-whoit-whoit-whoit._
NESTING Loose, flimsy cup of grass, bark, and leaves, in deciduous thicket; 2–4 eggs; 1–3 broods; April–September.
FEEDING Eats seeds and insects, such as beetles and caterpillars; also buds and fruit.

FLIGHT: weak, flapping with downward-angled tail; interrupted by short glides; low within cover.

CONSPICUOUS COLOR
This Northern Cardinal's vivid plumage means that it is often easy to spot on snowy winter days.

SIMILAR SPECIES

SUMMER TANAGER ♂

rosy-red plumage

no black patch

PYRRHULOXIA ♀

red on outer wing feathers

pointed crest

stubby yellow bill

OCCURRENCE
Resident in thickets of various relatively moist habitats, such as deciduous woodland, scrub, desert washes, and backyards. Range spans across the eastern US, southernmost Canada, the extreme Southwest, and south into Mexico, northern Guatemala, and northern Belize.

| Length **8½in (22cm)** | Wingspan **12in (30cm)** | Weight **1⁷⁄₁₆–1³⁄₄oz (40–50g)** |
| Social **Solitary** | Lifespan **Up to 16 years** | Status **Secure** |

DATE: _____ TIME: _____ LOCATION: _____

Order **Passeriformes**	Family **Cardinalidae**	Species *Pheucticus ludovicianus*

Rose-breasted Grosbeak 🔊

- **MALE (BREEDING)**
- white rump
- short tail with white corners
- **IN FLIGHT**
- white wing bars
- rosy or orange breast
- **MALE (1ST FALL)**
- white marks on head
- large pinkish bill
- thick streaks on underparts
- **FEMALE**
- brown patches on back
- streaked underparts
- **MALE (NONBREEDING)**
- black head and back
- bold white wing patches
- massive bill
- rose-red breast
- white belly
- **MALE (BREEDING)**

For many birdwatchers in the East, the appearance of a flock of dazzling male Rose-breasted Grosbeaks in early May signals the peak of spring songbird migration. Adult males in their tuxedo attire, with rose-red ties, are unmistakable, but females and immature males are more somber. In the fall, immature male Rose-breasted Grosbeaks often have orange breasts, and are commonly mistaken for female Black-headed Grosbeaks. The difference is in the pink wing lining usually visible on perched birds, pink bill, and streaking across the center of the breast.

VOICE Call a high, sharp, explosive *sink* or *eeuk*, reminiscent of the squeak of sneakers on floor tiles, flight call an airy *vreee*; song a liquid, flute-like warble, rather slow in delivery, almost relaxed.

NESTING Loose, open cup or platform, usually in deciduous saplings, at mid to high level; 2–5 eggs; 1–2 broods; May–July.

FEEDING Eats arthropods, fruit, seeds, and buds.

FLIGHT: undulating but powerful flight with bursts of wing beats.

SIMILAR SPECIES

PURPLE FINCH ♀
see p.354
much smaller

BLACK-HEADED GROSBEAK ♀
see p.435
smaller, dark bill
thick lateral throat stripe
tawny breast
pencil-thin streaks on underparts

STUNNING MALE
A striking male Rose-breasted Grosbeak in springtime is quite unmistakable on a tree.

OCCURRENCE
Breeds in deciduous and mixed woods, parks, and orchards across the northeastern quarter of the US, and across Canada westward from Newfoundland through Ontario to southeast Yukon. Winters from Mexico and the Caribbean, south to Guyana and Peru. Rare in the West.

Length **8in (20cm)**	Wingspan **12½in (32cm)**	Weight **1¼–2oz (35–55g)**
Social **Solitary/Small flocks**	Lifespan **Up to 13 years**	Status **Secure**

DATE: _____ TIME: _____ LOCATION: _____

Black-headed Grosbeak 🔊

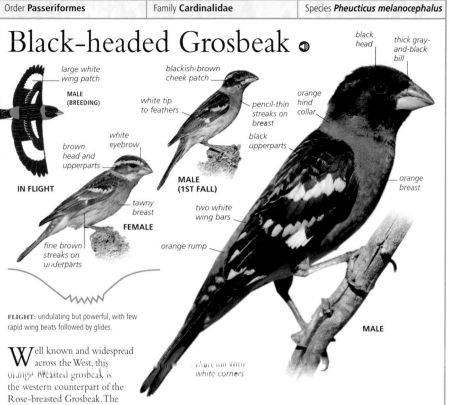

large white wing patch

MALE (BREEDING)

blackish-brown cheek patch

white tip to feathers

pencil-thin streaks on breast

black upperparts

orange hind collar

black head

thick gray-and-black bill

orange breast

brown head and upperparts

white eyebrow

MALE (1ST FALL)

IN FLIGHT

tawny breast

two white wing bars

orange rump

FEMALE

fine brown streaks on underparts

MALE

short tail with white corners

FLIGHT: undulating but powerful, with few rapid wing beats followed by glides.

W ell known and widespread across the West, this orange-breasted grosbeak is the western counterpart of the Rose-breasted Grosbeak. The two species are closely related, despite their color differences, and interbreed where their ranges meet in the Great Plains. The Black-headed Grosbeak is aggressive on its breeding grounds, with both sexes fighting off intruders.

VOICE Call a *hwik*, similar to Rose-breasted Grosbeak, but flatter, "hollow," and less squeaky; song generally higher, faster, less fluid, and harsher.

NESTING Loose, open cup or platform, usually in deciduous sapling, not far above eye level; 3–5 eggs; 1–2 broods; May–September.

FEEDING Gleans insects and spiders; also eats seeds and fruit.

STREAMSIDE SONGSTER
Through much of its range, this species is common along riverside corridors containing a variety of trees.

SIMILAR SPECIES

CASSIN'S FINCH ♀ smaller, see p.355 dark bill

much smaller overall

lacks bold wing markings

ROSE-BREASTED GROSBEAK ♀ see p.434

pink bill

dense, thick streaking below

white belly

OCCURRENCE
Breeds in dense deciduous growth—old fields, hedgerows, next to waterways, disturbed forests, and hillside thickets—from British Columbia and Saskatchewan, south to Baja California and central Mexico. Winters in interior, highlands, and the Pacific slope of Mexico.

Length 8½in (21cm)	Wingspan 12½in (32cm)	Weight 1⁷⁄₁₆–2oz (40–55g)
Social **Solitary/Small flocks**	Lifespan **Up to 9 years**	Status **Secure**

| Order **Passeriformes** | Family **Cardinalidae** | Species *Passerina amoena* |

Lazuli Bunting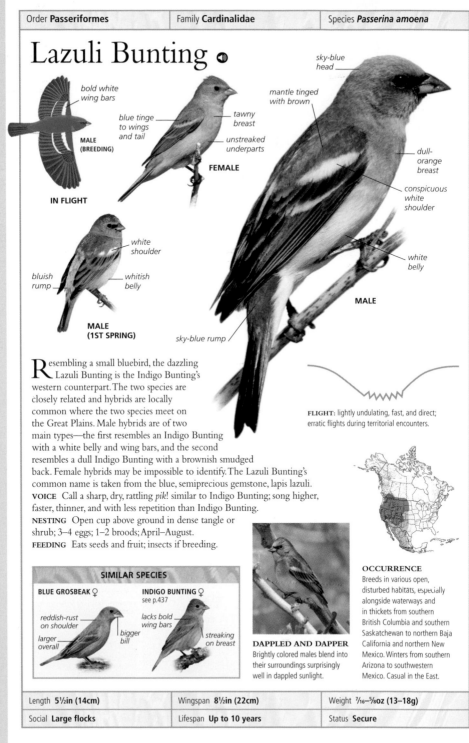

bold white wing bars

MALE (BREEDING)

IN FLIGHT

blue tinge to wings and tail

tawny breast

unstreaked underparts

FEMALE

sky-blue head

mantle tinged with brown

dull-orange breast

conspicuous white shoulder

white belly

MALE

white shoulder

bluish rump

whitish belly

MALE (1ST SPRING)

sky-blue rump

Resembling a small bluebird, the dazzling Lazuli Bunting is the Indigo Bunting's western counterpart. The two species are closely related and hybrids are locally common where the two species meet on the Great Plains. Male hybrids are of two main types—the first resembles an Indigo Bunting with a white belly and wing bars, and the second resembles a dull Indigo Bunting with a brownish smudged back. Female hybrids may be impossible to identify. The Lazuli Bunting's common name is taken from the blue, semiprecious gemstone, lapis lazuli.

VOICE Call a sharp, dry, rattling *pik!* similar to Indigo Bunting; song higher, faster, thinner, and with less repetition than Indigo Bunting.

NESTING Open cup above ground in dense tangle or shrub; 3–4 eggs; 1–2 broods; April–August.

FEEDING Eats seeds and fruit; insects if breeding.

FLIGHT: lightly undulating, fast, and direct; erratic flights during territorial encounters.

SIMILAR SPECIES

BLUE GROSBEAK ♀

reddish-rust on shoulder

larger overall

bigger bill

INDIGO BUNTING ♀
see p.437

lacks bold wing bars

streaking on breast

DAPPLED AND DAPPER
Brightly colored males blend into their surroundings surprisingly well in dappled sunlight.

OCCURRENCE
Breeds in various open, disturbed habitats, especially alongside waterways and in thickets from southern British Columbia and southern Saskatchewan to northern Baja California and northern New Mexico. Winters from southern Arizona to southwestern Mexico. Casual in the East.

| Length 5½in (14cm) | Wingspan 8½in (22cm) | Weight ⁷⁄₁₆–⅝oz (13–18g) |
| Social **Large flocks** | Lifespan **Up to 10 years** | Status **Secure** |

DATE: _____ TIME: _____ LOCATION: _____

Order **Passeriformes**	Family **Cardinalidae**	Species *Passerina cyanea*

Indigo Bunting 🔊

blue overall; often appears black in flight

MALE (BREEDING)

IN FLIGHT

intermediate between male and female plumage

MALE (1ST SPRING)

darker head

indigo face

bright cyan-blue body

dull brown overall

small bill

whitish throat

blurry streaks on breast

bluish cast to wings and tail

FEMALE

MALE (BREEDING)

Few North American birds are more brilliantly colored than the Indigo Bunting. However, it is not particularly well named, because the bird is really not indigo but rather a vibrant, almost cyan-blue. The color only turns to indigo on the male's head before finally becoming a rich violet on the face. Indigo Buntings are specialists of disturbed habitats, originally depending on tree-fall within forests and the grassland-forest edge. Human activity, however, has radically increased suitable breeding habitats. As a result, Indigo Buntings are much more common and widespread than they were a hundred years ago. This adaptable species has even learned to nest in cornfields.

VOICE Call a sharp, dry, rattling *pik*!; flight call a long buzz; song a series of simple, high-pitched, paired whistles, often described as "*fire!-fire!, where?-where?, there!-there!, put-it-out!, put-it-out!*"

NESTING Open cup above ground in dense tangle or shrub; 3–4 eggs; 1–3 broods; May–September.

FEEDING Eats seeds, insects, fruit, and buds.

FLIGHT: slightly undulating, fast, and direct; gliding and fluttering in territorial encounters.

SIMILAR SPECIES

BLUE GROSBEAK ♂

deep indigo-violet overall

much larger bill

rich reddish-rust shoulder

VARIED BUNTING ♀

unstreaked underparts

SOUND OF SUMMER
This is one of the most common and cheerful songbirds found in eastern North America.

OCCURRENCE
Breeds in moist disturbed habitats—weedy fields, forest edges, and areas of heavy cultivation across the eastern US, southeastern Canada, and also locally in the Southwest. Winters from Mexico and the Caribbean south to Panama, and in small numbers along the Gulf Coast and in Florida.

Length **5½in (14cm)**	Wingspan **8in (20cm)**	Weight ⁷⁄₁₆–¹¹⁄₁₆oz (12–19g)
Social **Large flocks**	Lifespan **Up to 11 years**	Status **Secure**

DATE: _____ TIME: _____ LOCATION: _____

| Order **Passeriformes** | Family **Cardinalidae** | Species *Spiza americana* |

Dickcissel

MALE (BREEDING)

streaked back

IN FLIGHT

yellow eyebrow

gray nape

rufous shoulder

large, pointed bill

yellow-tinged, long eye-line

bold braces on back

black "V" on yellow breast

FEMALE

finely streaked underparts

MALE (BREEDING)

paler gray on face

no rufous shoulder

MALE (NONBREEDING)

The Dickcissel is a tallgrass prairie specialist and seldom breeds outside this core range. Known for its dramatic seasonal movements, the Dickcissel winters in Venezuela, with flocks in tens of thousands ravaging rice fields and damaging seed crops. Immature birds, without yellow-and-rusty plumage, are very similar to female House Sparrows—vagrant and wintering Dickcissels in North America are often mistaken for sparrows.

VOICE Call a flat *chik*; flight call a distinctive, low, electric buzz *frrrrrrt*; song a short series of sharp, insect-like stutters followed by few longer chirps or trill *dick-dick-dick-SISS-SISS-suhl*.
NESTING Bulky cup placed near ground in dense vegetation; 3–6 eggs; 1–2 broods; May–August.
FEEDING Forages on ground for insects, spiders, and seeds.

FLIGHT: strong, direct, and slightly undulating; flocks in tight balls.

UNIQUE SONG
The Dickcissel's onomatopoetic song is the classic sound of a healthy tallgrass prairie.

SIMILAR SPECIES

HOUSE SPARROW ♀
see p.346

shorter bill

shorter tail

no streaking on underparts

EASTERN MEADOWLARK

bright yellow underparts

OCCURRENCE
Breeds in tallgrass prairie, grassland, hayfields, unmown roadsides, and untilled cropfields across the east-central US. Barely reaches southernmost Canada and northeast Mexico. Winters in huge flocks in Venezuela, in open areas with tallgrass-like vegetation, including rice fields.

| Length 6¼in (16cm) | Wingspan 9½in (24cm) | Weight ⅞–1¼oz (25–35g) |
| Social **Large flocks** | Lifespan **Up to 5 years** | Status **Secure** |

DATE: _____ TIME: _____ LOCATION: _____

RARE SPECIES

Family **Anatidae**	Species **Spatula querquedula**

Garganey

The Garganey is a small dabbling duck, the same size and shape as the Blue-winged Teal. A male in breeding plumage is unmistakable, its bold white eyebrow contrasting sharply with its dark brown head. In flight, it has a silver-gray forewing with a broad white trailing edge.

OCCURRENCE Native to Eurasia, records span North America; prefers wetland habitats with emergent vegetation.

VOICE Male a low, dry rattling *knerek* or *kerrek* call; female a high-pitched quack.

bold white eyebrow extends to nape

gray sides contrast with brown breast

MALE

Length **14½–16in (37–41cm)**	Wingspan **23½–25in (60–64cm)**

Family **Anatidae**	Species **Polysticta stelleri**

Steller's Eider

The smallest of the four species of eiders, Steller's Eider resembles a dabbling duck, with its steeper forehead, flatter crown, and the way that it floats higher on the water. In late winter, large groups dive in unison to feed, creating a spray.

OCCURRENCE The Pacific population breeds mainly in Russia's far northeast; small numbers breed in Alaska. Can winter as far south as the Queen Charlotte Islands.

VOICE Female a rapid, harsh growling call; also loud *qua-haaa* or *cooay*; males growl but are mostly silent.

flat crown

rufous-cream belly and breast

ADULT

Length **17–18in (43–46cm)**	Wingspan **28–30in (70–76cm)**

Family **Columbidae**	Species **Zenaida asiatica**

White-winged Dove

This large gray-colored dove is best identified in flight by the conspicuous white bands on its wings. Perched birds display bright-blue skin around orange eyes and longish square tails with white tips. This species has been expanding its population northwards into Canada in recent decades.

OCCURRENCE Breeds and winters in dense, thorny woodlands, deserts, orchards, and residential areas. It is now expanding north into Canada.

VOICE Distinctive, drawn-out cooing: *who-cooks-for-you*; also makes five-note variation from the nest: *la-coo-kla-coo-kla.*

black mark below ear feathers

ADULT

longish, square, gray tail

Length **11½in (29cm)**	Wingspan **19in (48cm)**

Family **Charadriidae**	Species **Charadrius nivosus**

Snowy Plover

The smallest and palest of all North American plovers, the Snowy Plover's cryptic coloration blends in well with its beach and dune habitat. The species is designated as endangered, due to habitat destruction.

OCCURRENCE Breeds on open beach and dune habitats on the Pacific and Gulf Coasts; occasionally shows up in western Canada.

VOICE Repeated *tow-heet*; *purrt* and single *churr* during breeding, tinkling *ti* at roosts or before flight.

short, stubby bill

grayish to pinkish legs

MALE (BREEDING)

Length **6–6½in (15–17cm)**	Wingspan **16–18in (41–46cm)**

| Family **Scolopacidae** | Species *Calidris pugnax* |

Ruff

The Ruff is well known for the elaborately colored head ruffs and tufts of breeding male birds. Males are 20 percent larger than the females (known as Reeves), which are more muted in appearance.

OCCURRENCE Rare migrant along the Pacific Coast, occasional in St. Lawrence River and the Great Lakes.

VOICE Mostly silent; occasionally gives a soft *krruk*.

short, slightly drooped bill

JUVENILE (FALL)

| Length 8–12in (20–30cm) | Wingspan 19–23in (48–58cm) |

| Family **Scolopacidae** | Species *Calidris acuminata* |

Sharp-tailed Sandpiper

This intermediate-sized sandpiper is similar to the Pectoral Sandpiper, but breeds only in Siberia. It is slightly rounder in body shape than the Pectoral Sandpiper, with longer legs and a shorter, slimmer bill. Breeding birds have rufous caps, a buff wash on the face and breast, and V-shaped breast markings.

OCCURRENCE Accidental in spring but common in fall in western Alaska; rare fall migrant along the Pacific Coast; accidental in fall elsewhere in North America.

VOICE Call a rolled, soft *prrrt*.

small head

JUVENILE

| Length 6¾–8in (17–20cm) | Wingspan 16½–19in (42–48cm) |

| Family **Scolopacidae** | Species *Calidris ferruginea* |

Curlew Sandpiper

The Curlew Sandpiper is a medium-sized sandpiper that breeds in northern Siberia. It resembles the Dunlin and Stilt Sandpiper in nonbreeding plumage. It is slimmer than the Dunlin, with longer wings, neck, legs, and bill, and differs from the nonbreeding Stilt Sandpiper by its shorter legs and faint white eyebrow.

OCCURRENCE Rare, but regular migrant on the Pacific Coast; accidental elsewhere.

VOICE Flight call musical, trilled, or rolled *chrreep*, dropping in the middle.

JUVENILE

black legs

long decurved bill

| Length 7–7½in (18–19cm) | Wingspan 16½–18in (42–46cm) |

| Family **Scolopacidae** | Species *Calidris ruficollis* |

Red-necked Stint

This small Siberian stint or peep is very similar to nonbreeding and juvenile Semipalmated Sandpipers. However, it has a slimmer and more tapered body, slimmer, finer-tipped bill, and unwebbed toes. Breeding birds have a rich rufous-orange face, throat, and upper breast, with spotted breast sides.

OCCURRENCE Uncommon migrant and rare breeder in western Alaska; rare but annual migrant along the Pacific coast.

VOICE Flight call rough *kiirp*, similar to Semipalmated Sandpiper but usually higher pitched.

MALE

white underparts

short, dark legs

| Length 5–6½in (13–16cm) | Wingspan 14–15in (35–38cm) |

| Family **Stercorariidae** | Species *Stercorarius maccormicki* |

South Polar Skua

The South Polar Skua is a large, aggressive relative of the jaegers. Away from its breeding areas in the South Shetland Islands and along the coast and islands of the Antarctic, it is a daunting presence on the ocean. It lurks menacingly on the water when not badgering other seabirds for food, or battling for scraps behind fishing boats.

OCCURRENCE
A scarce visitor to seas on the East and West Coasts; most numerous in spring and fall in the Pacific, and in spring in the Atlantic far offshore.
VOICE Deep gull-like burbling; generally silent at sea in North America.

hooked bill

cold brown-toned body and head

ADULT

| Length **21in (53cm)** | Wingspan **4¼ft (1.3m)** |

| Family **Laridae** | Species *Pagophila eburnea* |

Ivory Gull

The Ivory Gull, all-white with black legs, is unlikely to be confused with any other gull. Adults are pure white in summer and winter. Juveniles are patterned to varying degrees, with black spots on the tips of their flight feathers, including the tail and wing outer feathers; they also have a smudgy black face.
OCCURRENCE High-Arctic breeder; rarely strays far south of the pack ice, even in winter; casual in winter to British Columbia and the Maritime Provinces; accidental elsewhere.
VOICE Tern-like, harsh *keeuur*; rarely heard away from breeding grounds.

pure-white plumage

yellow-tipped slate-blue bill

ADULT

black legs

| Length **15½–17in (40–43cm)** | Wingspan **3½–4ft (1.1–1.2m)** |

| Family **Laridae** | Species *Rhodostethia rosea* |

Ross's Gull

In adult breeding plumage, this small, delicate gull is unmistakable. Dove-gray upperparts, pale-pink underparts, red legs, and a black collar make it an elegant and beautiful-looking bird.
OCCURRENCE Siberian breeder found only along the Alaskan north coast in fall; expanded as a breeding bird into Arctic Canada; winter strays found across Canada and to the northeast and northwest US.
VOICE Rarely heard in winter; tern-like *kik-kik-kik*.

black "necklace" collar

wedge-shaped tail

ADULT (BREEDING)

| Length **11½–12in (29–31cm)** | Wingspan **35–39in (90–100cm)** |

| Family **Laridae** | Species *Larus schistisagus* |

Slaty-backed Gull

This rare visitor from eastern Russia and Japan is most likely to be confused with the Western Gull. Adults have a series of white spots on the outer wing feather tips, referred to as "a string of pearls." Winter adults have heavily streaked heads with white linings to their underwings that contrast with the gray outer and inner wing feathers.
OCCURRENCE Occurs occasionally in northern and southwestern British Columbia; accidental in winter across Canada and the US.
VOICE Slow *aah-aah-aah*.

ADULT (BREEDING)

| Length **24–26in (61–66cm)** | Wingspan **4½–5ft (1.4–1.5m)** |

Family **Laridae**	Species *Sternula antillarum*

Least Tern

The Least Tern is the smallest of the North American terns. In summer, its distinctive black cap and white forehead distinguish it from other members of its family. In the 19th century their numbers declined. They have rebounded but are now threatened by ongoing habitat loss.

OCCURRENCE Breeds along both coasts, major rivers, lakes, and reservoirs; favors sandy areas, such as beaches and sandbars. Scattered sightings across Canada.

VOICE Extremely vocal during breeding; a high-pitched *ki-deek, ki-deek*; also a rapid, almost non-stop chatter.

ADULT
(BREEDING)

two dark outer
wing feathers

yellow
bill

Length **8½–9in (21–23cm)**	Wingspan **19–21in (48–53cm)**

Family **Diomedeidae**	Species *Phoebastria immutabilis*

Laysan Albatross

The Laysan Albatross generally stays far offshore, and is usually only ever seen from boats on the Pacific Ocean. It breeds mainly in the Hawaiian Islands and then travels thousands of miles to find food over the northern Pacific Ocean.

OCCURRENCE Seen with increasing frequency off of Canada's west coast; when feeding, found throughout the north ocean, offshore from the western coast of Canada and the US.

VOICE A variety of calls given in colonies, including a range of squeaks, whinnies, whines, and moans.

white
head

dark tail

dark
back and
upperwings

ADULT

Length **31–32in (79–81cm)**	Wingspan **6¼– 6½ft (1.9–2m)**

Family **Procellariidae**	Species *Ardenna bulleri*

Buller's Shearwater

Like other species of tubenoses that occur occasionally off the West Coast of North America, this migrant breeds on islands off New Zealand. Abundant, yet threatened by long-line fishing operations, Buller's Shearwater is the only silvery-gray *Ardenna* species to show a black zigzag wing pattern that is found in North American waters.

OCCURRENCE Breeds at Poor Knights Island, New Zealand. Uncommon but regular in open ocean off British Columbia during late summer and fall.

VOICE Silent at sea; strange wailing calls at colonies.

dark
zigzag
pattern

dark-gray
cap

long,
dark,
wedge-
shaped
tail

ADULT

Length **18–18½in (46–47cm)**	Wingspan **38–39in (97–99cm)**

Family **Procellariidae**	Species *Ardenna tenuirostris*

Short-tailed Shearwater

Short-tailed Shearwaters are abundant off the Alaskan coast in the summer, where they form groups numbering, perhaps, in the millions. They spend most of their life at sea, and field identification is difficult as they look very similar to Sooty Shearwaters. Distinguishing features include being more compact overall, with a dark head contrasting with a paler throat and breast.

OCCURRENCE Spends the summer off the coast of Alaska; migrates in fall along the West Coast.

VOICE Silent at sea; varied, agitated vocalizations when feeding.

dark cap contrasts
with paler cheeks
and white throat

"bulb"
at tip

dark sooty-
brown overall

ADULT

Length **17in (43cm)**	Wingspan **3ft 3in (1m)**

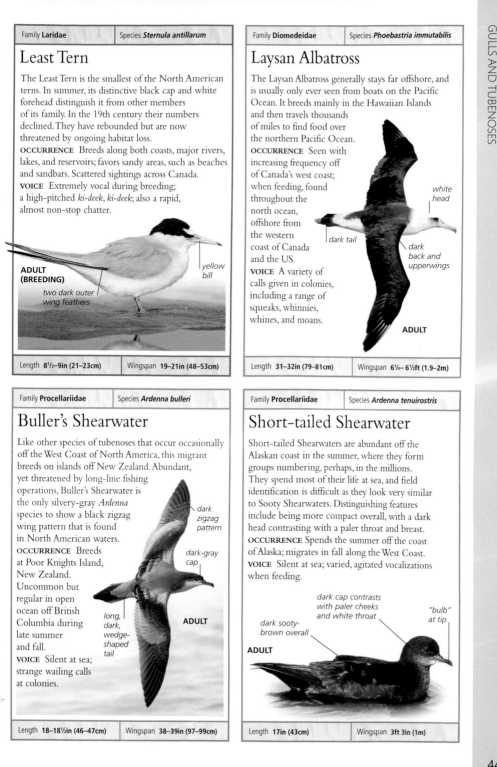

| Family **Procellariidae** | Species *Ardenna carneipes* |

Flesh-footed Shearwater

The Flesh-footed Shearwater, an uncommon visitor to the nutrient-rich marine waters off the Pacific Coast of North America, can be found mingling with with other tubenoses. It is distinguished from the Sooty and Short-tailed Shearwaters by its dark color and pink bill and legs.

OCCURRENCE Two breeding populations: one in the southwest Pacific Ocean, the other in the Indian Ocean; occasional summer visitor to open ocean off British Columbia northward to Alaska.

VOICE Silent at sea; mewing calls at the breeding sites at night.

ADULT

dark body and wings

pale feet

pink bill with dusky tip

| Length **18in (46cm)** | Wingspan **4½ft (1.4m)** |

| Family **Ardeidae** | Species *Egretta caerulea* |

Little Blue Heron

The shy and retreating Little Blue Heron is often overlooked because of its blue-gray color and secretive eating habits. First-year birds, which may be mistaken for Snowy Egrets, are white. They gradually acquire blue-gray, mottled feathers before eventually molting into their all-dark adult plumage.

OCCURRENCE Breeds in various wetlands, such as swamps, marshes, lakes, streams, rivers, and flooded fields. Range has expanded north, particularly into eastern Canada.

VOICE Vocal during courtship; generally silent.

purplish-maroon neck

gray bill with black tip

ADULT

yellowish to greenish legs

| Length **24in (61cm)** | Wingspan **3ft 3in (100cm)** |

| Family **Tyrannidae** | Species *Tyrannus forficatus* |

Scissor-tailed Flycatcher

Often perched on a wire or fence, the Scissor-tailed Flycatcher also has a spectacular aerial courtship display, with its long tail streaming behind it. Its nest incorporates many human products, such as string, cloth, and paper. Pre-migratory roosting flocks during late summer consist of 100 to 1,000 birds.

OCCURRENCE Breeds in the southern states and in Mexico; prairie, open grasslands, pastures, and golf courses. Sporadically appears from coast to coast in Canada.

VOICE Male song variable number of *pups* followed by *perleep* or *peroo* in breeding territories and communal roots.

pale-gray head

black rump and inner wing feathers

ADULT

| Length **11–12in (27–31cm)** | Wingspan **15in (38cm)** |

| Family **Corvidae** | Species *Aphelocoma californica* |

California Scrub-Jay

California Scrub-Jays are active and vocal, often moving in groups of up to 30 birds, most of which are immatures that have not found a nesting territory yet. Established pairs defend their territories year-round, and within each group there are one or two dominant birds. They are easily attracted to suburban backyards with feeders and may nest if conditions are right.

OCCURRENCE From British Columbia to southern California, typically in quite dry, open woodland.

VOICE Short, harsh, rising shriek and quicker, repeated *chirr chirr chirr chirr chirr.*

ADULT

long blue tail

pale underparts

| Length **11–12in (27–31cm)** | Wingspan **15in (39cm)** |

Family **Alaudidae**	Species *Alauda arvensis*

Eurasian Skylark

The Eurasian Skylark's streaked brown plumage resembles pipits' and sparrows', but its slightly raised crest is distinctive. It stays close to the ground and is hard to see unless flushed, displaying its fluttery flight.
OCCURRENCE Introduced to North America in the Seattle and Vancouver areas; also occurs as a vagrant in the Bering Sea region of Alaska from Eurasia, where it breeds. Likes windswept, hilly, and grassy areas near the ocean.
VOICE Flight call a sudden *jeerup;* famous aerial song consists of endless trills and buzzes.

prominent crest

ADULT

short tail with white outer feathers

Length 7¼in (18.5cm)	Wingspan 12–14in (30–36cm)

Family **Fringillidae**	Species *Fringilla montifringilla*

Brambling

Widespread in northern Eurasia, from Scandinavia to the far east of Russia, the Brambling is unlike any native North American finch. In all seasons, males and females have a conspicuous white rump and orange outer wing feathers.
OCCURRENCE Regular migrant to the Aleutian and Pribilof Islands, and mainland western Alaska. Occasionally seen elsewhere in Canada and the US.
VOICE Call a characteristic, mewing *jee-eek;* song a trilled *zhreeeee.*

blackish head, with white spots

MALE

yellow bill with black tip

white rump and uppertail feathers

orange chin and breast

Length 5¾in (14.5cm)	Wingspan 10–11in (25–28cm)

GLOSSARY

Many terms defined here are illustrated in the general introduction (pp.10–21).

adult A fully developed, sexually mature bird. It is in its final plumage, which no longer changes pattern with age and remains the same after yearly molt, although it may change with season. *See also* **immature, juvenile**.

aerie The nest of birds of prey, like eagles or peregrine falcons, usually on a cliff, and often used by the same pair of adult birds in successive years.

alarm call A call made by a bird to signal danger. Alarm calls are often short and urgent in tone, and a few species use different calls to signify the precise nature of the threat. *See also* **call**.

allopreening Mutual preening between two birds, the main purpose of which is to reduce the instinctive aggression when birds come into close contact. In the breeding season, allopreening helps to strengthen the pair bond between the male and female. *See also* **preening**.

altitudinal migrant *see* **vertical migrant**

alula A small group of two to six feathers projecting from a bird's "thumb," at the bend of its wing that reduces turbulence when raised.

Audubon, John James (1785–1851) American naturalist and wildlife illustrator, whose best known work was his remarkable collection of prints, *Birds of North America*.

axillary A term describing feathers at the base of the underwing. Axillary feathers often form small patches, with coloration differing from the rest of the underwing.

barred With marks crossing the body, wing, or tail; the opposite of streaked. *See also* **streaks**.

bastard wing *see* **alula**

beak *see* **bill**

bill A bird's jaws. A bill is made of bone, with a hornlike outer covering of keratin.

bird of prey Any of the predatory birds in the orders Accipitriformes (eagles, hawks, kites, and osprey), Falconiformes (falcons), and Strigiformes (owls). They are characterized by their acute eyesight, powerful legs, strongly hooked bill,

and sharp talons. These birds are also known as raptors. *See also* **talon, raptor**.

body feather *see* **contour feather**

booming A sound produced by bitterns and some species of grouse. The booming of male bitterns is a deep, resonant, hollow sound that can carry for several miles. The booming of male grouse is produced by wind from air pouches in the sides of the bird's neck.

brackish Containing a mixture of saltwater and freshwater.

breeding plumage A general term for the plumage worn by adult birds when they display and form breeding pairs. It is usually (but not always) worn in the spring and summer. *See also* **nonbreeding plumage**.

brood (noun) The young birds produced from a single clutch of eggs and incubated together. *See also* **clutch**. **(verb)** In birds, to sit on nestlings to keep them warm. Brooding is usually carried out by the adult female. *See also* **incubate**.

brood parasite A bird that lays its eggs in the nest of other birds. Some brood parasites always breed this way, while others do so only occasionally.

brood patch An area of bare skin on the belly of a parent bird, usually the female, that is richly supplied with blood vessels and thus helps keep the eggs warm during incubation. This area loses its feathers in readiness for the breeding season and is fully feathered at other times.

cagebird A species of bird commonly kept in captivity.

call A sound produced by the vocal apparatus of a bird to communicate a variety of messages to other birds. Calls are often highly characteristic of individual species and can help to locate and identify birds in the field. Most bird calls are shorter and simpler than songs. *See also* **alarm call, booming, contact call, song**.

casque A bony extension on a bird's head—seen in hornbills, for example.

cere A leathery patch of skin that covers the base of a bird's bill. It is found only in a few groups, including birds of prey, pigeons, and parrots.

claw In birds, the nail that prolongs their toes. *See also* **talon**.

cloaca An anal-like opening on the rear of a bird under its tail. It is

present in both sexes and is used in reproduction—for example, to release sperm and eggs—and excretion.

clutch The group of eggs in a single nest, usually laid by one female and incubated together.

cock A term sometimes used to describe the adult male in Galliformes and songbirds. *See also* **hen**.

collar The area around a bird's neck, which in some species is a prominent feature of its plumage pattern and can be used for identification.

color form One of two or more clearly defined plumage variations found in the same species. Also known as a color morph or phase, a color form may be restricted to part of a species's range or occur side by side with other color forms over the entire range. Adults of different color forms are able to interbreed, and these mixed pairings can produce young of either form.

comb A fleshy growth of bare skin usually above the eyes.

contact call A call made by a bird to give its location as a means of staying in touch with others of the same species. Contact calls are used by birds in flocks and by breeding pairs. Contact calls are crucial for nocturnal migrants. *See also* **call**.

contour feather A general term for any feather that covers the outer surface of a bird, including its wings and tail. Also known as body feathers, contour feathers help streamline the bird in flight, and provide warmth and waterproofing.

cooperative breeding A breeding system in which a pair of parent birds are helped in raising their young by several other birds, which are often related to them and may be young birds from previous broods.

courtship display Ritualized, showy behavior used in courtship by the male, and sometimes by the female, involving plumage, sound (vocal and non-vocal), and movements.

covert A small feather covering the base of a bird's flight feather. Together, coverts form a well-defined feather tract on the wing or at the base of the tail. *See also* **feather tract**.

creche A group of young birds of about the same age, produced by different parents but tightly herded together. One or more adults guards the entire creche.

crepuscular Relating to the period just before dusk, when many birds are active, especially during courtship. In reference to birds, the term is sometimes used to mean both twilight and dawn.

crest A group of elongated feathers on top of a bird's head, which may be raised during courtship or to indicate alarm.

crissum *see* **vent**

crown The area on top of a bird's head. It is often a prominent plumage feature, with a different color from the feathers on the rest of the head.

dabble To feed in shallow water by sieving water and obtain food through comblike filters in the bill; used mostly for ducks (dabbling ducks or dabblers).

decurved A term describing a bird's bill that curves downward from the forehead toward the tip.

dimorphism *see* **sexual dimorphism**

display *see* **courtship display**, **distraction display**, **threat display**

distraction display A display in which a bird deliberately attempts to attract a predator's attention in order to lure it away from its nest or nestlings.

diurnal Active during the day.

down feather A soft, fluffy feather, lacking the system of barbs of contour or flight feathers, that provides good insulation. Young birds are covered by down feathers until they molt into their first juvenile plumage. Adult birds have a layer of down feathers under their contour feathers. *See also* **contour feather**, **juvenile**.

drake An adult male duck. The adult female is known as the duck.

drift The diversion of migrating birds from their normal migration route by strong winds.

dynamic soaring *see* **soaring**

ear tuft A distinct tuft of feathers on each side of a bird's forehead, with no connection to the true ears, which can be raised as a visual signal. Many owls have ear tufts.

echolocation A method of sensing nearby objects using pulses of high-frequency sound. Echoes bounce back from obstacles, enabling the sender to build up a "picture" of its surroundings.

eclipse plumage A female-like plumage worn in some birds, especially waterfowl, by adult males for a short period after the breeding season is over. The eclipse plumage helps camouflage them during their molt, when they are flightless.

elevational migrant *see* **vertical migrant**

endemic A species (or subspecies) native to a particular geographic area—such as an island, a forest patch, a mountain, or province, or country—and found nowhere else.

escape An individual bird that has escaped from a zoo or other collection to live in the wild. *See also* **exotic**

eye-ring A ring of color, usually narrow and well defined, around the eye of a bird.

eyestripe A stripe of color running as a line through the eye of a bird.

eyrie *see* **aerie**

exotic A bird found in a region from which it is not native. Some of these are escapes, or were originally, but now live as wild birds.

feather tract A well-defined area on a bird's skin where feathers grow, leaving patches of bare skin in between. *See also* **pterylae**.

fledge In young birds, to leave the nest or acquire the first complete set of flight feathers. Known as fledglings, these birds may still remain dependent on their parents for some time. *See also* **flight feather**.

fledgling *see* **fledge**

fledging period The average time taken by the young of a species to fledge, timed from the moment they hatch. Fledging periods in birds range from 11 days in some small songbirds to as long as 280 days in the Wandering Albatross.

flight feather A collective term for a bird's wing and tail feathers, used in flight. More specifically, it refers to the largest feathers on the outer part of the wing, the primaries and secondaries.

forewing The front section of a bird's wing, including the primary coverts and secondary coverts. *See also* **hindwing**.

gamebird Generally, any bird that is legally hunted, including some doves and waterfowl. This name is generally used for members of the order Galliformes.

gular sac Also known as a gular pouch, it is a large, fleshy, extendable sac just below the bill of some birds, especially fish-eaters such as pelicans. It forms part of the throat.

habitat The geographical and ecological area where a particular organism usually lives.

hen A term sometimes used to describe the adult female in Galliformes, especially grouse and songbirds. *See also* **cock**.

hindwing The rear section of a bird's spread wing, including the secondary feathers, especially when it has a distinctive color or pattern. *See also* **forewing**.

hybrid The offspring produced when two species, sometimes from different genera, interbreed. Hybrids are usually rare in the wild. Among birds, they are most frequent in Galliformes and waterfowl, especially ducks. Hybrid progeny may or may not be fertile.

immature In birds, an individual that is not yet sexually mature or able to breed. Some birds pass through a series of immature plumages over several years before adopting their first adult plumage and sexual maturity. *See also* **adult**, **juvenile**.

incubate In birds, to sit on eggs to keep them warm, allowing the embryo inside to grow. Incubation is often carried out by the female. *See also* **brood**.

incubation period In birds, the period when a parent incubates its eggs. It may not start until the clutch is completed.

injury feigning *see* **distraction display**.

inner wing The inner part of the wing, comprising the secondaries and rows of coverts (typically marginal, lesser, median, and greater coverts).

introduced species A species that humans have accidentally or deliberately brought into an area where it does not normally occur.

iridescent plumage Plumage that shows brilliant, luminous colors, which seem to sparkle and change color when seen from different angles.

irruption A sporadic mass movement of animals outside their normal range. Irruptions are usually short-lived and occur in response to food shortage. Also called irruptive migration.

juvenile A term referring to the plumage worn by a young bird at the time it makes its first flight and until it begins its first molt. *See also* **adult**, **immature**.

keratin A tough but lightweight protein. In birds, keratin is found in the claws, feathers, and outer part of the bill.

kleptoparasite A bird that gets much of its food by stealing it from other birds, usually by following them in flight and forcing them to disgorge their food.

lamellae Delicate, comblike structures on the sides of the bill of some birds used for filtering tiny food particles out of water.

leap-frog migration A pattern of migration in which some populations of a species travel much further than the other populations, by "leap-frogging" over the area where these sedentary (nonmigratory) birds are found. *See also* **migration**.

lek An area, often small, used by males as a communal display arena, where they show off special plumage features accompanied by vocal and non-vocal sounds, to attract females. Females wait along the lek and select the male or males that they will mate with.

lobed feet Feet with loose, fleshy lobes on the toes, adapted for swimming.

lore A small area between a bird's eye and the base of its upper bill.

mandible The upper or lower part of a bird's bill, known as the upper or lower mandible, respectively.

mantle The loose term used to define the back of a bird between its neck and rump.

migrant A species that regularly moves between geographical areas. Most migrants move on an annual basis between a breeding area and a wintering area. *See also* **partial migrant**, **sedentary**.

migration A journey to a different region, following a well-defined route. *See also* **leap-frog migration**, **partial migrant**, **reverse migration**, **sedentary**, **vertical migrant**.

mobbing A type of defensive behavior in which a group of birds flock together to harass a predator, such as a bird of prey or an owl, swooping repeatedly to drive it away.

molt In birds, to shed old feathers so that they can be replaced. Molting enables birds to keep their plumage in good condition, change their level of insulation, and change their coloration or markings so that they are ready to breed or display.

monogamous Mating with a single partner, either in a single breeding season or for life. *See also* **polygamous**.

morph *see* **color form**

nape The back of the neck.

nares Paired nasal openings located in different places on the bill, depending on the species.

nestling A young bird still in the nest.

New World The Americas, from Alaska to Cape Horn, including the Caribbean and offshore islands in the Pacific and Atlantic oceans. *See also* **Old World**.

nictitating membrane A transparent or semitransparent "third eyelid," which moves sideways across the eye for protection and moistening. Diving waterbirds often use them to aid in their vision underwater.

nocturnal Active at night.

nomadic Being almost constantly on the move. Birds of deserts, grasslands, and the coniferous forests of the far north are commonly nomadic.

nonbreeding plumage The plumage worn by adult birds outside the breeding season. In many species, particularly in temperate regions, it is also known as winter plumage. *See also* **breeding plumage**.

nonmigrant *see* **sedentary**

nonpasserine Any bird that is not a member of the order Passeriformes (or passerines). *See also* **passerine**.

oil gland Also called the preen gland or the uropygial gland, a gland at the base of a bird's tail that secretes oils that are spread over the feathers for waterproofing them during preening.

Old World Europe, Asia, Africa, and Australasia. *See also* **New World**.

orbital ring A thin, bare, fleshy ring around the eye, sometimes with a distinctive color. *See also* **eye-ring**.

outer wing The outer half of the wing, comprising the primaries, their coverts, and the alula (the "thumb").

partial migrant A species in which some populations migrate while others are sedentary. This situation is common in broadly distributed species that experience a wide range of climatic conditions. *See also* **migration**, **sedentary**.

passerine A bird belonging to the vast order Passeriformes (the passerines). This group contains more species than all other orders of birds combined. Passerines are also called songbirds or perching birds. *See also* **nonpasserine**.

pelagic Relating to the open ocean. Pelagic birds spend most of their life at sea and only come to land to nest.

phase *see* **color form**

polygamous Mating with two or more partners during the course of a single breeding season. *See also* **monogamous**.

population A group of individual birds of the same species living in a geographically and ecologically circumscribed area.

preening Routine behavior by which birds keep their feathers in good condition. Each individual feather is pulled through the bill, sometimes with oil added from the preen gland, to help smooth and clean the plumage. *See also* **allopreening**.

primary feather One of the large outer wing feathers, growing from the digits of a bird's "hand." *See also* **secondary feather**.

pterylae Bare patches of skin lying between the feather tracts. *See also* **feather tracts**.

race *see* **subspecies**

range A term to indicate the geographical distribution of a species or population.

raptor A general name for birds belonging to the orders Accipitriformes, Falconiformes, and Strigiformes. Often used interchangeably with bird of prey. *See also* **bird of prey**.

ratite A member of an ancient group of flightless birds that includes the ostrich, cassowaries, emus, rheas, and kiwis. In the past, the group was larger and more diverse.

resident *see* **sedentary**

reverse migration A phenomenon that occurs when birds from a migratory species mistakenly travel in the opposite direction from normal, causing birds to turn up in places far outside their normal range. *See also* **migration**.

roost A place where birds sleep, either at night or by day.

rump The area between a bird's back and the base of its upper tail coverts. In many species, the rump is a different color from the rest of the plumage and can be a useful diagnostic character for identification.

sally A feeding technique (sallying), used especially by tyrant flycatchers, in which a bird makes a short flight from a perch to catch an insect, often in midair, followed by a return to a perch, often the same one.

salt gland A gland located in a depression of the skull, just above the eye of some birds, particularly seabirds. This enables them to extract the fluids they need from saltwater and then expel the excess salts through the nostrils.

scapular Any one of a group of feathers on the "shoulder," forming a more or less oval patch on each side of the back, at the base of the wing.

scrape A simple nest that consists of a shallow depression in the ground, which may be unlined or lined with material such as feathers, bits of grass, or pebbles.

secondary feather One of the row of long, stiff feathers along the rear edge of a bird's wing, between the body and the primary feathers at the wingtip. *See also* **primary feather**.

sedentary Having a settled lifestyle that involves little or no geographic movement. Sedentary birds are also said to be resident or nonmigratory. *See also* **migration**.

semipalmated The condition in which two or more of the toes are partially joined by an incomplete membrane at their base.

sexual dimorphism The occurrence of physical differences between males and females. In birds, the most common differences are in size and plumage.

shield In birds, a hard structure on the forehead that joins the bill and often appears to be an extension of it.

shorebird Also known as a wader, any member of several families in the order Charadriiformes, including plovers, sandpipers, godwits, snipe, avocets, stilts, oystercatchers, and curlews. Not all species actually wade in water and some live in dry habitats.

soaring In birds, flight without flapping of the wings to preserve or gain altitude and save energy. Updraft soaring usually results from rising air hitting cliffs and mountain ridges or rising thermals of warm air. Some seabirds, flying for days at a time, use dynamic soaring by repeatedly catching rising air deflected off the waves.

song A vocal performance by a bird, usually the adult male, to attract and impress a potential mate, advertise ownership of a territory, or drive away rival birds. Songs are often highly characteristic of individual species and can be a major aid in locating and identifying birds in the field. *See also* **call**.

songbird A general term used to describe a member of the suborder Passeri (or oscines), a subdivision of the largest order of birds, the Passeriformes (passerines).

species A group of similar organisms that are capable of breeding among themselves in the wild and producing fertile offspring that resemble themselves, but that do not interbreed in the wild with individuals of another similar group, are called a species. *See also* **subspecies**.

speculum A colorful patch on the wing of a duck, formed by the secondary feathers. *See also* **secondary feather**.

spur A sharply pointed, clawlike structure at the back of the leg of some birds, like the Wild Turkey.

staging ground A stopover area where migrant birds regularly pause while on migration, to rest and feed.

stoop A near-vertical and often very fast dive made by falcons and some other birds of prey when chasing prey in the air or on the ground.

streaks Marks that run lengthwise on feathers; opposite of bars.

subspecies When species show geographical variation in color, voice, or other characters, these differentiated populations are recognized by ornithologists as subspecies (formerly also called races). *See also* **species**.

supercillium Also called supercillial stripe, a stripe running from the base of a bird's beak above its eye.

syrinx A modified section of a bird's trachea (windpipe), equivalent to the voicebox in humans, that enables birds to call and sing.

talon One of the sharp, hooked claws of a bird of prey.

territory An area that is defended by an animal, or a group of animals, against other members of the same species. Territories often include useful resources, such as good breeding sites or feeding areas, which help a male attract a mate.

tertial Any one of a small group of feathers, sometimes long and obvious, at the base of the wing adjacent to the inner secondaries.

thermal A rising bubble or column of warm air over land that soaring birds can use to gain height with little effort. *See also* **soaring**.

threat display A form of defense in which a bird adopts certain postures, sometimes accompanied by loud calls, to drive away a rival or a potential predator.

tiercel A term referring to a male falcon.

trachea The breathing tube in animals, also known as the windpipe.

tubenose A general term used to describe members of the order Procellariiformes, including albatrosses, petrels, and shearwaters; their nostrils form two tubes on the upper mandible and are used to expel salt.

underwing The underside of a bird's wing, usually visible only in flight or when a bird is preening, displaying, or swimming.

upperwing The upper surface of a bird's wing clearly exposed in flight

but often mostly hidden when the bird is perched with its wings closed.

vagrant A bird that has strayed far from its normal range. Usually, vagrants are long-distance migrants that have been blown off course by storms, have overshot their intended destination due to strong winds, or have become disoriented.

vent Also called the crissum, the undertail feathers between the lower belly feathers and tail feathers, which in some species are differently colored from either belly or tail feathers. Can be helpful in identification.

vertical migrant Also called altitudinal migrant, a species that migrates up and down mountains, usually in response to changes in the weather or food supply. *See also* **migration**.

wader *see* **shorebird**.

waterfowl A collective term for members of the family Anatidae, including ducks, geese, and swans.

wattle A bare, fleshy growth that hangs loosely below the bill in some birds. It is often brightly colored, and may play a part in courtship.

wildfowl *see* **waterfowl**

Wilson, Alexander (1766–1813) A contemporary of J.J. Audubon, Wilson's seminal *American Ornithology* marks the start of scientific ornithology in the US.

wing bar A line or bar of color, sometimes more than one, across the upper surface of the wing, often used in identification. Most obvious when a bird is on the ground or perched with its wings closed. Sometimes obvious in flight in some birds.

wingbar A line or bar of color across the upper surface of a bird's wing. Wingbars can often be seen when a bird is on the ground or perched and its wings are in the closed position, but they are normally much more obvious in flight. Wingbars may be single or in groups of two or more.

wingspan The distance across a bird's outstretched wings and back, from one wingtip to the other.

zygodactyl Having two toes pointed forward and two backward, often seen in tree climbers like woodpeckers.

INDEX

Acknowledgments

From the Editor of the Third Edition
The Editor's task benefited immensely from the invaluable assistance of three equally important resources for ornithologists and birders in North America. Official taxonomic names and orders are based upon the American Ornithological Society's *Checklist of North and Middle American Birds* and the annual Supplements produced by its North American Classification and Nomenclature Committee. The online version of *Birds of the World* managed by the Cornell Laboratory of Ornithology is simply unparalleled for providing up-to-date range maps, lifespan data, population status, and many other interesting facts on the biology of Canadian birds. Assigning full species, rare birds, and vagrants to the Canadian list is greatly facilitated by *eBird*, an online database of bird observations supplied by volunteers all over the world and offering real-time data on bird distribution and abundance. The Committee on the Status of Endangered Wildlife in Canada is the ultimate resource for determining the official status of Canadian wildlife, including birds, as being endangered and threatened wildlife or of special concern. Finally, the Editor offers his gratitude to the ornithology staff at the American Museum of Natural History, the editorial staff of DK's *Birds of North America* for their contributions to *Birds of Western Canada*, Barbara Campbell, formerly of DK Canada, Angeles Gavira Guerrero and Christine Stroyan at DK London, and especially Dharini Ganesh, Senior Editor at DK India, whose sharp eyes easily matched my own.

For the Second Edition, Dorling Kindersley would like to thank Kshitij Anand, Barbara Campbell, Dharini Ganesh, Ishita Jha, Sonali Jindal, Aishvarya Misra, Priyanjali Narain, and Rohan Sinha for editorial assistance; Sudakshina Basu, Nobina Chakravorty, and Anjali Sachar for design assistance; Harish Aggarwal and Sachin Gupta for DTP assistance; Jaypal Singh Chauhan and Anita Yadav for CTS assistance; Priyanka Bansal, Sophia MTT, Priyanka Sharma Saddi, and Saloni Singh for jackets assistance.

Dorling Kindersley would like to thank the following people for their help in compiling this book: Lucy Baker, Rachel Booth, Kim Bryan, Arti Finn, Peter Frances, Lynn Hassett, Riccie Janus, Maxine Lea, Megan Jones, Ruth O'Rourke, Yen-Mai Tsang.

Producing such a comprehensive book would be impossible without the research and observations of hundreds of field and museum ornithologists and birdwatchers. The Editor-in-Chief of the first edition of *Birds of North America* would like to name four who have been especially inspirational and supportive over the years: the late Paul Géroudet, the late Ernst Mayr, Patricia Stryker Joseph, and Helen Hays. In addition, we acknowledge *Birds of North America Online*, edited by Alan Poole, a joint project of the American Ornithologists' Union and Cornell's Laboratory of Ornithology, and The Howard Moore *Complete Checklist of the Birds of the World*, 3rd edition.

The publisher would like to thank the following for their kind permission to reproduce their photographs:

Almost without exception, the birds featured in the profiles in this book were photographed in the wild.

(Key: a-above; b-below/bottom; c-center; f-far; l-left; r-right; t-top)

Alamy Images: AfriPics.com 11cra; Derrick Alderman 18cl; Arterra Picture Library / Arndt Sven-Erik 39tr, Steve Taylor ARPS 39crb; All Canada Photos 161bc, 162tr; Blickwinkel 19cr; Rick & Nora Bowers, 97t; Bruce Coleman Inc. 14tr, 19crb; Gay Bumgarner 18cb; Nancy Camel 19clb; Redmond Durrell 15cb; Elvele Images Ltd 18-19c; David Hosking 13fcrb; Juniors Bildachiv 13tr; Don Kates 16cla; Charles Melton 29fbl; Renee Morris 361; Rolf Nussbaumer 16clb; Peter Arnold, Inc. 16cl; Stock Connection Blue 13clb.
Ardea: Ian Beames 11cr.
Doug Backlund: 12-13ca, 27cb, 28crb, 108tr, 215crb, 221cra, 260cra, 260tc, 337cla, 337cra, 337crb, 330cr, 384bc.
The Barn Owl Centre, UK: 224cla.
Giff Beaton: 419tr.
Corbis: Joe McDonald 14cla, 210cra; Neil Bowman/ Glenn Bartley / BIA / Minden Pictures 131cr; Jacob S. Spendelow / BIA / Minden Pictures 322t; Nick Saunders / All Canada Photos 362tr.
Mike Danzenbaker: 94ca, 94tl, 98ca, 98crb, 98tc, 99cra, 99crb, 99tc, 111bc, 159cla, 161ca, 161crb, 161tc, 162crb, 162bc, 164ca, 164crb, 164tc, 166tc, 187tc, 192cra, 191crb, 267cb, 365tc, 401tc, 443clb, 443br, 444cla.
DK Images: Robin Chittenden 59tr; Chris Gomersall Photography 36crb, 40ca, 40crb, 40tr, 56crb, 71crb, 71tr, 127crb, 129crb, 135bc, 158cla, 158cra, 176cra, 183cb, 204crb, 212cra, 212tc, 85cra, 259ca, 259crb, 295cla, 332tc, 440cla, 440tl; David Cottridge 344cla; David Tipling Photo Library 34ca, 46cr, 46cra, 59tc, 61tc, 80tc, 85cla, 117cla, 133cla, 176cla, 212crb, 301tc; Mark Hamblin 41ca, 46cla, 186c, 225cra, 238cra, 344tc; Chris Knights 60crb; Mike Lane 46tr, 54cla, 61tr, 66tc, 71cla, 71cra, 71ca, 79ca, 132cla, 135tr, 140tc, 157cra, 157crb, 172tc, 182ca, 295ca, 444bl; Gordon Langsbury 120cra, 122tc, 131tr, 146cla, 206cla; Tim Loseby 41crb, 154crb, 356cla; George McCarthy 66tr, 70crb, 127cla, 156ca, 183tc, 206cra, 208ca; Natural History Museum, London 10cla, 12cl; Kim Taylor 281tr; Roger Tidman 30ca, 30tc, 33ca, 42tr, 50ca, 56ca, 61ca, 87ca, 186tr, 127tr, 135tc, 141tc, 153ca, 154ca, 154tr, 155cra, 182crb, 344cra, 332cla, 367cla, 367tc, 441tl; Ray Tipper 118tr; Steve Young, 42cr, 46crb, 46tc, 54cra, 54tr, 56tc, 56tr, 60ca, 60tc, 71tc, 100cla, 102cra, 133tc, 155tc, 157cla, 172cla, 182tc, 182tr, 192crb, 192tc, 323ca, 367cra.
Dreamstime.com: Feng Yu 39ca.
Dudley Edmondson: 24b, 24cra, 24tl, 27tc, 32tr, 62cra, 70cla, 81ca, 81tc, 92crb, 108crb, 110crb, 112tc, 113ca, 114crb, 115crb, 150crb, 130cra, 136tc, 170crb, 171cr, 173tr, 174cla, 174cr, 181crb, 201cla, 202cb, 218ca, 218cb, 218cla, 218tc, 215cla, 215cra, 215tc, 217crb, 220cla, 220cra, 221crb, 231cb, 236tl, 239cla, 239cra, 253bc, 262ca, 266crb, 291ca, 324crb, 334crb, 335bc, 371cra, 370ca, 374cra, 399crb.
Tom Ennis: 139ca.
Hanne & Jens Eriksen: 118cla, 123crb, 180tc.
Neil Fletcher: 24cla, 26bc, 26cla, 29tc, 32ca, 32cra, 41tr, 43tc, 44crb, 44tr, 71tr, 87crb, 332cra, 345b.
FLPA: Tui De Roy/Minden Pictures 17ca; Goetz Eichhorn/Foto Natura 79fbl, 189ca; John Hawkins 17cla; S Jonasson 185cra; Daphne Kinzler 17tr; S & D & K Maslowski 18clb; Geoff Moon; Roger Tidman 185tr; Winfried Wisniewski/Foto Natura 17cr.
Joe Fuhrman: 198cra, 123ca, 276crb, 343bc.
Getty Images: Marc Moritsch 14-15c; Brad Sharp 18c.
Melvin Grey: 34crb, 88ca, 109cra, 116tr, 129ca, 132cra, 200bc, 203cla, 206crb, 207crb, 260cla, 440tl; Tom Grey: 83crb, 109crb, 160ca, 160crb, 172cl, 180crb, 194cr, 202cra, 211crb, 216crb, 221cla, 227bc, 247bc, 259cra, 294cra, 299tc, 314tc, 319crb, 378crb, 395cla, 395cra, 399fcla, 399fcra, 440br.
Martin Hale: 191ca.
Josef Hlasek: 153crb.
Barry Hughes: 111cr, 158crb.
Arto Juvonen: 65tc, 222cra.
Kevin T. Karlson: 27cla, 53ca, 53crb, 69tc, 125ca, 125cra, 143cr, 143cra, 143crb, 143fcla, 155tc, 187ca, 219cla, 219tc, 257tr, 260crb, 385cla, 439.
Garth McElroy: 1c, 15cl, 27cla, 48tr, 52tc, 53tc, 54ca, 55tc, 57cla, 58crb, 69tc, 89cra, 90crb, 100cla, 100tc, 104cra, 188tc, 79tc, 81cla, 105tr, 107cra, 107crb, 115ca, 116cra, 120cla, 120crb, 121cla, 121crb, 119ca, 140crb, 125crb, 125tc, 128ca, 128crb, 130crb, 132crb, 132tr, 136ca, 137tc, 138crb, 138tc, 141cb, 143ca, 144tr, 145cr, 145tc, 146cra, 147crb, 149cra, 150ca, 150cra, 151ca, 151cra, 151crb, 154tc, 169cra, 171crb, 173ca, 177ca, 177cla, 177cra, 177crb, 179crb, 179tc, 179tl, 196bc, 196tr, 198crb, 198tc, 198tl, 203tc, 204ca, 205cra, 205tc, 207cla, 208tr, 233crb, 235cr, 237cla, 238bc, 238tc, 240crb, 251cb, 251cla, 251cra, 268crb, 273cla, 273crb, 277crb, 277tc, 266ca, 279cra, 282crb, 288bc, 289cla, 289cra, 289crb, 297crb, 300bc, 300ca, 301cr, 303ca, 303crb, 305cra, 308bc, 308ca, 308crb, 300crb, 310ra, 310br, 313cla, 313cra, 313tc, 314cla, 316cra, 316crb, 317crb, 318bc, 318cra, 320tr, 323bc, 328cb, 328crb, 329bc, 333crb, 312crb, 327b, 334ca, 334cra, 338cb, 338tc, 340cb, 340crb, 341cb, 341cra, 342crb, 342tc, 347cra, 349tr, 350bc, 350ca, 351cra, 351crb, 354cb, 354cra, 354tc, 356bc, 357crb, 358cr, 359cra, 359crb, 359tc, 360crb, 361cra, 361tc, 368cra, 371crb, 371tc, 372ca, 374crb, 375cra, 376cra, 379cra, 379crb, 380cla, 380crb, 380tc, 381ca, 383bc, 383tc, 386bc, 386tc, 387ca, 388tc, 389cb, 389tc, 390ca, 390crb, 394crb, 394tc, 398crb, 401crb, 401tr, 403bc, 405ca, 405crb, 406crb, 408cb, 408cra, 411bc, 414crb, 416bl, 418cla, 418crb, 418tc, 419crb, 420cla, 422cra, 422crb, 422tc, 423cra, 423tc, 428cra, 429cb, 432cra, 433crb, 434cra, 436tr, 437bc, 441br.
Bob Moul: 79cla, 119crb, 379tc, 403cla.
Alan Murphy: 62cl, 78ca, 84b, 89cl, 95b, 95cl, 240bl, 240br, 242ca, 242cb, 243l, 247cla, 283cb, 283crb, 282crb, 296b, 297ca, 391b 404b, 421cla.
Tomi Muukonen: 37crb, 80tr, 167cla, 167crb, 176fcla, 177bc, 183ca, 185cl, 214tr, 222cla, 363crb, 367crb.
naturepl.com: Vincent Munier 10-11c; Barry Mansell 23c; Nigel Marven 162ca; Tom Vezo 17crb; Markus Varesvuo 362b.
NHPA/Photoshot: Bill Coster 77bc, 112bc; Dhritiman Mukherjee; Kevin Schafer 185cb.
Photoshot: Picture Alliance 257b.
Wayne Nicholas: 111c, 111tr.
Judd Patterson: 22, 74cra, 74tc,219bc, 219cra, 226cla, 397ca.
E. J. Peiker: 2-3, 25cra, 30fcra, 30tr, 33tc, 38cb, 34tc, 35ca, 35tr, 42cla, 42cra, 43ca, 43crb, 43tr, 44ca, 44cb, 44tc, 45cb, 45crb, 47ca, 47crb, 57crb, 58tc, 76cra, 82crb, 88bc, 100crb, 101tr, 102tr, 112cr, 113crb, 114ca, 114cra, 117cra, 117crb, 121cra, 124ca, 127cr, 144tc, 146crb, 148cla, 148crb, 159cb, 166cra, 166crb, 167cra, 171ca, 178crb, 184tr, 185tr, 187crb, 188crb, 198fcra, 200tr, 203cra, 204cra, 223cla, 223crb, 225cla, 225tc, 229cra, 243br, 248cb, 258ca, 258cla, 263cl, 265cb, 290tc, 291cb, 293crb, 298crb, 298tc, 299bc, 304cla, 311c, 311crb, 314cra, 321bc, 353crb, 353tr, 361tr, 369ca, 373crb, 391tr, 392bc, 393bc, 396crb, 397bc, 400tr, 410cla, 421crb, 425tr, 431tr, 434bc, 436cla, 444bl.
Jari Peltomäki: 26ca, 48crb, 54crb, 65cra, 70tc, 85crb, 123ca, 123cra, 123crb, 183crb, 185bc, 210bc, 224b, 236cb, 281crb, 302cra, 302crb, 349cla 363cra.
Mike Read: 64bc, 193crb, 261crb.
George Reszeter: 442tr.
Robert Royse: 29crb, 30cla, 52ca, 69cla, 70cra, 82ca, 118cra, 151cla, 149ca, 123cra, 129tr, 138ca, 179cra, 180ca, 180tr, 89bc, 90cra, 103ca, 273cra, 321tc, 326cra, 330crb, 365cra, 365crb, 366crb, 367tr, 412crb, 412tr, 414cla, 424cra, 372crb, 370crb, 384cla, 384cra, 382ca, 382crb, 442bl.
Chris Schenk: 54fcla.
Bill Schmoker: 27cra, 28ca, 30crb, 32tc, 81crb, 86crb, 96ca, 96crb, 139crb, 189cla, 189tc, 193cr, 195ca, 195crb, 195tr, 194ca, 194crb, 194tr, 202ca, 221tc, 223cr, 223cra, 262crb, 280ca.
Brian E. Small: 11fcra, 26tc, 26tr, 24tc, 24tr, 29ca, 30tr, 31ca, 31tc, 32crb, 38ca, 38tc, 41tc, 45ca, 45tc, 47tc, 51tc, 52tr, 55ca, 58ca, 69cra, 72cla, 72cra, 72crb, 76cr, 77tr, 86ca, 88tc, 91cl, 93ca, 94crb, 97crb, 101cla, 101crb, 102cra, 103bc, 104cla, 106ca, 106crb, 110c, 110cla, 116tc, 117tc, 121tc, 124cra, 126ca, 126tc, 129tc, 130ca, 130tr, 134tc, 137tr, 141ca, 142ca, 142cra, 146ca, 147ca, 149cla, 153fcla, 168ca, 170tr, 173cra, 174ca, 174tr, 175cra, 181ca, 184ca, 186ca, 187cla, 190cla, 190cra, 197cla, 197crb, 201cra, 205cla, 211ca, 211tc, 218cra, 214ca, 216cra, 226cra, 226crb, 227ca, 228cra, 229cla, 231cla, 231cra, 232cb, 233cra, 235ca, 235cra, 236cra, 242cra, 242tr, 243cra, 244cla, 245bc, 245cra, 246bc, 246tc, 248cla, 248cra, 249cb, 249cla, 249cra, 250tc, 254cb, 254cla, 254cra, 252cb, 255ca, 255cb, 255cra, 255fcla, 256cla, 256cra, 263tr, 264bc, 264ca, 266cra, 267ca, 268cra, 268tc, 269cb, 269cra, 271ca, 271crb, 272cra, 274ca, 274crb, 275crb, 276cra, 277cb, 278ca, 279cla, 280crb, 282tr, 282cra, 283ca, 284ca, 284crb, 285ca, 285crb, 286ca, 286crb, 288ca, 289tc, 290cra, 292ca, 292cra, 301tr, 302ca, 305crb, 306cra, 307ca, 309ca, 311cla, 312bc, 312cra, 314crb, 315cra, 315tc, 316cla, 317bc, 317ca, 324cra, 325crb, 326crb, 328ca, 331ca, 331crb, 331tc, 334tr, 335tc, 336ca, 336cra, 336tr, 338ca, 339bc, 339ca, 340cra, 340tc, 341cla, 341tc, 343cra, 343tc, 347tc, 348cra, 348crb, 351cla, 351tc, 352tc, 355ca, 355crb, 356cra, 358ca, 358cra, 358tl, 360ca, 361cla, 364bc, 364cla, 364cra, 366cla, 366cra, 368ca, 369tc, 370tr, 371cla, 374cl, 376cl, 376crb, 376fcla, 376tc, 377cra, 377crb, 377tc, 378cla, 379cra, 380cra, 381cra, 383cra, 386cra, 387crb, 388cra, 388crb, 385tr, 389ca, 390cra, 392ca, 392tc, 393cra, 393tc, 394cla, 394cra, 395bc, 396cla, 396cra, 396tr, 398cla, 398cra, 398tc, 399cra, 400tc, 402crb, 403ca, 403cra, 404tr, 406ca, 407cla, 407cra, 407crb, 408cla, 409cra, 409tc, 410crb, 411tr, 412ca, 413cra, 413crb, 414tc, 414tr, 415ca, 416cra, 416tc, 417cra, 417crb, 417tc, 418tr, 419ca, 419tc, 420tr, 421cra, 423crb, 424bc, 424cla, 424tc, 425cla, 426cra, 426crb, 426tc, 427cra, 427tc, 428tc, 429tc, 430ca, 430tc, 432cr, 432tc, 433cla, 433cra, 433tc, 434cl, 434cla, 434tc, 435cla, 435cra, 435crb, 435tc, 436bc, 436tc, 437cla, 437tc, 437tr, 438cla, 438cr, 438crb, 438tr, 440bl, 441bl, 443tr.
Bob Steele: 1, 4-5, 13cb, 24tc, 26cla, 26crb, 26cra, 27ca, 28tc, 28tr, 29ca, 29crb, 29tc, 32crb, 33tr, 34tr, 35crb, 38crb, 40tc, 42cla, 42crb, 45crb, 47tr, 51crb, 51tr, 55crb, 57tc, 58tr, 62cla, 64ca, 72tc, 74cla, 74crb, 76tr, 78crb, 78tc, 82tc, 83ca, 83cb, 91tr, 91b, 92ca, 93crb, 95t, 100cra, 101tc, 102ca, 102crb, 103cla, 103cr, 104cb, 104crb, 105b, 107cla, 108ca, 108tc, 109cla, 110cra, 113bl, 113cra, 113tc, 114cla, 115cra, 116ca, 118tc, 120tc, 122ca, 124crb, 126crb, 128cra, 131bc, 131ca, 133cra, 134cla, 134cra, 134crb, 134tr, 136crb, 137ca, 137crb, 140ca, 140bc, 142crb, 142tr, 144ca, 144crb, 147tc, 148ca, 149crb, 150tc, 152ca, 152crb, 152tc, 152tr, 153fcra, 155bc, 155fcla, 157tc, 159cra, 160tc, 165bc, 165cra, 168cla, 168crb, 169cla, 169tc, 170ca, 171tr, 172cra, 172crb, 173cla, 173crb, 173tc, 174cra, 174crb, 175cla, 175cr, 175crb, 175tr, 176crb, 176tc, 178cla, 178cra, 178tc, 178tr, 181tc, 184crb, 184tc, 186crb, 188tr, 190cb, 190tr, 193ca, 197cra, 199cra, 199tc, 201tc, 206tc, 208crb, 214cra, 216ca, 220bc, 220ca, 220tr, 222crb, 223tr, 224tr, 229cb, 230cra, 230tc, 232cra, 232tc, 233cla, 234cla, 234cra, 234crb, 237crb, 240cra, 240tc, 244cra, 244fclb, 244fcrb, 246cra, 247ca, 247cra, 250cla, 250cra, 250crb, 252cla, 252cra, 253ca, 253tr, 258crb, 258tr, 263b, 265ca, 265cra, 265crb, 267crb, 269cr, 270cra, 270crb, 270tc, 272crb, 275cla, 275cra, 277cra, 278crb, 279b, 280cra, 281tc, 282tc, 288crb, 290cb, 291crb, 292crb, 293ca, 294ca, 294crb, 294ca, 294crb, 295crb, 296a, 298cb, 298cra, 299cra, 299crb, 301bc, 301cla, 303cra, 303tr, 304cra, 304crb, 305tc, 306crb, 306tc, 308tc, 307crb, 307tc, 309crb, 309tc, 309tr, 311bc, 311tr, 312tc, 315crb, 316ca, 319cra, 320crb, 321cra, 325cra, 326bc, 326ca, 327ra, 329ca, 330ca, 332fcla, 333cla, 333tr, 335cla, 335cra, 336cb, 337tc, 339crb, 342cla, 342cra, 343crb, 349b, 350cra, 352cla, 352cra, 352crb, 353cla, 353cra, 355tc, 356cl, 356tc, 360cb 364tc, 368crb, 369bc, 370cra, 373cb, 374cla, 374tc, 375cla, 375crb, 375tc, 373ca, 378cra, 378tc, 379cla, 379crb, 379tc, 381bc, 385crb, 385tc, 386cl, 389crb, 391cr, 393cla, 397ca, 397cra, 397tr, 399cla, 399tr, 400crb, 401cla, 402cra, 402tc, 404cl, 408crb, 409cla, 409crb, 410cra, 411cla, 413tc, 415crb, 415tc, 416bc, 416cla, 420cb, 420crb, 421tc, 422cla, 423cla, 425c, 425cra, 425crb, 427crb, 428crb, 429ca, 429crb, 430cb, 430crb, 431br, 432bc, 432ca, 432crb.
Andy & Gill Swash: 193tr, 201crb, 207cra, 320cb.
Glen Tepke: 163tc.
Markus Varesvuo: 12-13bc, 16-17c, 23cra, 26crb, 30crb, 36ca, 36cb, 36tr, 48ca, 48tc, 50cb, 50crb, 50tc, 52crb, 57ca, 59ca, 59crb, 62cb, 65crb, 66cra, 66fbr, 71ca, 77cl, 79crb, 80ca, 80crb, 133crb, 135ca, 154cb, 156crb, 156tc, 158tc, 186crb, 188ca, 188cb, 214crb, 217cra, 217tr, 222ca, 222tr, 230crb, 237cra, 261cla, 281cra, 313crb, 323crb, 332crb, 357cra, 357tc, 358crb, 363cla, 363tc, 440cr, Vireo: Dr. Yuri Artukhin, Rick and Nora Bowers 308fbl; Herbert Clarke, 191bc; Robert L. Pitman 163ca; Glen Tepke 162fbl, 163crb.
Peter S Weber: 25tc, 51ca, 63crb, 74crb, 76crb, 84cla, 86cr, 92tr, 203ca, 205crb, 207tr, 228crb, 239crb, 245cla, 248fcla, 253tc, 256clb, 315crb.
Roger Wilmshurst: 261cra.

BIRDS OF CANADA

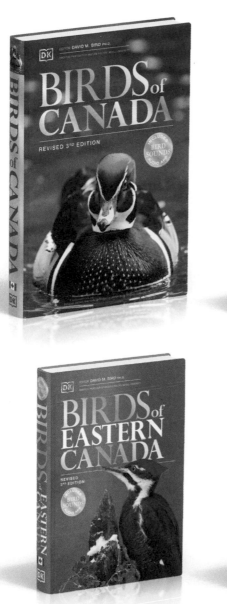

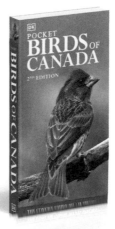

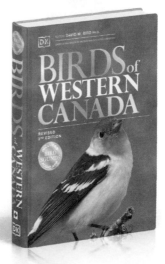

 For the curious